The Complete Instant Pot Cookbook 1000 Recipes

by Rebecca White

Contents

INTRODUCTION

Do you want to make the leap from good to great in your kitchen? Are you dreaming of making complete meals before you can say Jack Robinson? The Instant Pot come to fulfill your needs!

The Instant Pot is a modern-day invention that performs various cooking tasks such as steaming, sautéing, boiling, slow cooking, baking, and so forth. The Instant Pot utilizes a super-heated steam and high pressure to cook the best one-pot meals ever. This revolutionary kitchen gadget can significantly cut cooking time, save electricity, and help you eat healthier.

Whether you're a newbie or a skilled cook, you'll soon find yourself whipping up grandma's recipes in your Instant Pot. In reality, an electric pressure cooker is a "fusion" of an old-fashioned cookware and advanced technology. You will be pleasantly suppressed what your Instant Pot can do for you. If you want a new, well-balanced and improved life, you should adopt healthy eating habits and embrace a new, super-sophisticated technology. Food is, actually, an integral part of our lives; thus, we should care about where our food comes from. The Instant Pot and this recipe collection will improve your cooking, your health, and your entire life!

Getting to Know Your Instant Pot

Nowadays, we don't have hours to spend in the kitchen; on the other hand, we agree that a well-balanced diet and healthy, homemade meals are the key factors that contribute to a productive lifestyle. Therefore, people, especially busy moms and older people, want kitchen devices that make everyday cooking enjoyable, funny and easy. Inspired by a grandma's way of cooking and the cooking style of the world's greatest chefs, manufacturers develop the third generation cookware where technology and sophisticated design go hand in hand.

The Instant Pot is a programmable multicooker that utilizes high pressure and high temperatures to cook your food as much as 60 to 70 percent faster than regular cooking methods. The Instant Pot is an electric device for automated cooking using a timer. Your time is priceless, isn't it?

Should I Buy an Instant Pot Electric Pressure Cooker?
The short answer is: Yes. If you are passionate about cooking, you deserve an outstanding electric pressure cooker with high performance. The Instant Pot is the seven-in-one cooker, capable of multiple cooking methods, all in one device. Sautéing, steaming, baking, boiling, and slow cooking are just a few of the cooking techniques that your Instant Pot is capable to perform.

In addition to significantly reducing cooking time, the Instant Pot will help you cook amazing one-pot meals. Simply toss your ingredients into the Instant Pot and turn it on. As simple as that! You will be able to cook the whole bird for Thanksgiving dinner, old-fashioned soups, the best meatloaf ever, breads, snacks, and even desserts. The perfect kitchen tool for holidays, potlucks, and family gatherings.

Furthermore, your food retains its nutrients and natural aromas because it is cooked in a sealed environment. This is an easy way to meet your nutritional requirements. For those who are not convinced yet, here is one more argument – the Instant Pot saves your hard-earned money by cooking cheap cuts, beans, and grains in bulk.

This multifunctional cooker offers a number of cooking functions. It does the job of a pressure cooker, slow cooker, rice maker, steamer, sauté pan, and yogurt maker. Here are eight pressure cooking rules to achieve the best results with your Instant Pot:

Carefully and thoroughly read the manual that comes with the appliance. Make sure to consult it periodically. Just like when you learned any other new skill, it takes time and patience to get to know your new device.

Keep in mind that the Instant Pot takes about 15 to 20 minutes to release the pressure completely; then and only then, you can remove the lid.

This is an intelligent kitchen gadget; you can set up your Instant Pot to 24 hours in advance and go about your business; it allows you to plan every meal.

Although your Instant Pot has many buttons that may confuse you, they are incredibly simple to use. They all work using the same principles but they utilize different cooking times that are designed for different types of food. In addition, you can always use the "Manual" button and "+" and "-" buttons to adjust the cooking time.

When it comes to the minimum liquid requirement, it is about 1 cup of water (broth, milk, tomato sauce) for the Instant Pot. However, if you cook food that absorbs water, you should follow the recipe directions.

Most recipes can be adapted to the Instant pot as long as you keep some general rules in mind. The Instant Pot operates at 11.5 PSI so always consult the chart for the proper cooking times. Since the Instant Pot doesn't allow evaporation, you will need less liquid. Further, if you want to thicken the cooking liquid, do it at the end, using the "Sauté" function. And last but not least, do not overfill your cooker; it requires enough room to create the steam.

High pressure is default setting on the Instant Pot and it is used in most recipes. Delicate foods such as seafood, eggs and some vegetables should be cooked under a Low pressure.

You cannot fry your food in the Instant Pot.

With all of that in mind, pressure cooking may sound complicated. Nevertheless, once you understand the basics, it will open up new possibilities! Thus, with a good cooker and willingness to learn, anyone can become a great cook!

How You'll Benefit from Your Instant Pot

For so long home cooks have been searching for a cooking method to make healthy tasty foods. Pressure cooking became one of the hottest new culinary trends nowadays while the Instant Pot has come to offer new ideas by providing better and healthier food options. The Instant Pot electric pressure cooker is a multifunctional programmable kitchen appliance that can do the job of a slow cooker, rice maker, a steamer, a sautéing pan, a warming pot, and yogurt maker.

Now, we can pose the question: Which Instant Pot button to use? Listed below are the Instant Pot smart cooking programs:

Sauté function is the perfect flavor-enhancing technique. You will be able to sauté your veggies before pressure cooking as well as sear and brown the meat without an additional pan.

Manual is an all-purpose button. You can actually adjust the time and temperature and cook almost every meal using this function.

Meat/Stew is the perfect program for cooking red meats and old-fashioned stews.

Poultry is an excellent choice for chicken, turkey, and duck.

Porridge is a function designed for cooking grains.

Rice, as the name indicates, is designed to cook all types of rice.

Soup is the fully automated function for cooking the best homemade soups and chowders quickly and effortlessly.

Bean/Chili is the program for making your favorite chilies.

Slow cook is the perfect option if you want to have a warm meal ready when you arrive home.

Multigrain is designed for cooking grains.

Yogurt is a two-step program for making a homemade yogurt.

Keep Warm/Cancel is a very practical feature. Once cooking is complete, you need to push the "Cancel" button; otherwise, the warming function is automatically activated.

If you are a fan of one-pot meals, keep in mind these obvious benefits of using an Instant Pot.

1. **Cook fast and eat well.** Do you think that cooking at home is time-consuming? Do all these cookware and appliances make you feel uncomfortable in the kitchen? We've got news for you – you probably don't have the right kitchen tools. The Instant Pot is an intelligent, third-generation cooker so you don't need to stand by the stove, watching and stirring your food. In addition to speed, you will save your time by cooking an entire meal in the Instant Pot.

Instant Pot cooks your food as much as 70 percent quicker than other conventional cookware. You will love its hands-off functionality! Simply choose your favorite ketogenic recipe, set up the Instant Pot, sit back, relax and try to spend quality time out of the kitchen!

The Instant Pot has proven to be the efficient home appliance of everyone who does not want to spend all day slaving over a hot stove but eager to start cooking for his/her families. The Instant Pot cooks our food way faster than conventional cookers and pots, which makes it the perfect choice for busy households.

2. **Palatability and succulence are the main goals.** Obviously, a high-temperature cooking produces more flavor in your meals. This cooking method requires very little fat and other flavor enhancers so that your food retains most of their natural flavors and nutrients. It provides a good balance of flavors because it is practically impossible to overdo food in the Instant Pot and end up with a wishy-washy food.

3. **Health is the greatest wealth.** It may sound like a cliché, but everything begins with you. Your own health and your values. This is a logical reason why you need to cook your food properly.

As a modern-day pressure cooker, the Instant Pot utilizes short cooking time, high temperature and pressure to cook food efficiently without nutrient loss. Since liquids do not evaporate in your Instant Pot, you can cook very lean meats because they remain succulent, juicy and buttery tender. Moreover, the Instant Pot is an eco-friendly gadget because it uses two to three times less energy than much other cookware.

What is so Fascinating about Home-Cooked Meals?

In today's fast-paced life, it's difficult to fit cooking into our busy schedules. However, looking at the bigger picture helps you find and understand your core values. What do you think is the most important to you? Health? Family? Happiness?

Let's explore the benefits of home-cooked meals in the Instant Pot.

- First, and most practical, cooking at home is cheaper than going out.

- Then, cooking at home can help you lose weight. Being happy with your body is an essential component of a good life. An ideal body weight goes hand in glove with a good physical health.

- Further, love and food both have something in common, they are important to achieving an overall well-being, physical and mental balance. A good food can help you build a deep relationship with your partner. It is worth investing a little time in the kitchen!

- And last but not least, studies have shown that there are many psychological and emotional benefits of cooking for others. It improves your creativity, which makes you feel good; it can feel like a meditation practice for many people. Cooking can improve your relationships and social life, too. Cooking at home has a strong part in many cultures worldwide.

POULTRY

1. Saucy Duck with Wild Mushrooms

(Ready in about 30 minutes | Servings 4)

Ingredients

1 pound duck breast, sliced
1/2 teaspoon red chili pepper
1 teaspoon cayenne pepper
1/2 teaspoon sea salt
1/2 teaspoon mustard powder
1/2 teaspoon freshly ground black pepper
1 tablespoon tallow, melted
1/4 cup Port wine
2 medium-sized shallots, sliced
2 garlic cloves, minced
1 (1-inch) piece fresh ginger, peeled and grated
1 pound wild mushrooms, sliced
1 cup water
1 mushroom soup cube

Directions

Season the duck breast with chili pepper, cayenne pepper, salt, mustard powder, and black pepper.

Press the "Sauté" button to heat up your Instant Pot. Then, melt the tallow. Sear the seasoned duck for 4 to 6 minutes, turning periodically; set it aside.

Pour in wine to scrape up any brown bits from the bottom of the Instant Pot. Stir in the remaining ingredients.

Secure the lid. Choose the "Poultry" mode and High pressure; cook for 20 minutes. Once cooking is complete, use a quick pressure release; carefully remove the lid. Serve immediately.

Per serving: 203 Calories; 8.5g Fat; 5.5g Carbs; 26.5g Protein; 2.7g Sugars

2. Classic Coq au Vin

(Ready in about 25 minutes | Servings 4)

Ingredients

2 teaspoons peanut oil
2 chicken drumettes
1 chicken breast
2 shallots, chopped
2 cloves garlic, crushed
1/2 pound chestnut mushrooms, halved
1 cup vegetable stock
1/3 cup red wine
Sea salt and ground black pepper, to your liking
1/2 teaspoon red pepper flakes
1/4 teaspoon curry powder
1/4 cup tomato puree
2 teaspoons all-purpose flour
2 sprigs fresh thyme, leaves picked

Directions

Press the "Sauté" button and heat the peanut oil. Add the chicken, skin-side down, and cook for 7 minutes or until browned; reserve.

Now, add the shallots and sauté until they're tender and fragrant. Now, stir in the garlic and mushrooms, and cook until aromatic.

Add 1/2 cup of the vegetable stock and red wine, and scrape the bottom of your Instant Pot to loosen any stuck-on bits.

Add the salt, black pepper, red pepper flakes, and curry powder; continue to cook, stirring constantly.

Now, add the reserved chicken, tomato puree and the remaining 1/2 cup of vegetable stock. Sprinkle with all-purpose flour and fresh thyme leaves.

Secure the lid. Choose the "Manual" and cook at High pressure for 11 minutes. Once cooking is complete, use a quick pressure release; carefully remove the lid. Bon appétit!

Per serving: 255 Calories; 12.1g Fat; 6.9g Carbs; 29.2g Protein; 2.7g Sugars

3. Christmas Chicken Cutlets

(Ready in about 20 minutes | Servings 4)

Ingredients

1 pound chicken cutlets, pounded to 1/4-inch thickness
2 garlic cloves, peeled and halved
1/3 teaspoon salt
Ground black pepper and cayenne pepper, to taste
2 teaspoons sesame oil
3/4 cup water
1 ½ tablespoons dry sherry
1 chicken bouillon cube
2 tablespoons fresh lime juice
1 teaspoon dried thyme
1 teaspoon dried marjoram
1 teaspoon mustard powder
3 teaspoons butter, softened

Directions

Rub the chicken with garlic halves; then, season with salt, black pepper, and cayenne pepper. Press the "Sauté" button.

Once hot, heat the sesame oil and sauté the chicken cutlets for 5 minutes, turning once during cooking. Add water and dry sherry and stir; scrape the bottom of the pan to deglaze.

Secure the lid. Choose the "Manual" mode and High pressure; cook for 4 minutes. Once cooking is complete, use a quick pressure release; carefully remove the lid. Reserve the chicken cutlets, keeping them warm.

Stir the bouillon cube, lime juice, thyme, marjoram, and mustard powder into the cooking liquid.

Press the "Sauté" button and simmer for 6 minutes or until the cooking liquid has reduced and concentrated.

Add the butter to the sauce, stir to combine, and adjust the seasonings. Pour the prepared sauce over the reserved chicken cutlets and serve warm. Bon appétit!

Per serving: 190 Calories; 8.4g Fat; 4.3g Carbs; 23.6g Protein; 2g Sugars

4. Turkey and Green Bean Soup

(Ready in about 25 minutes | Servings 4)

Ingredients

1 pound turkey breasts, boneless, skinless and diced
2 cups water
2 cups chicken stock
2 tablespoons apple cider vinegar
1 (28-ounce) can diced tomatoes
1 yellow onion, chopped
2 cloves garlic, minced
2 carrots, diced
1 teaspoon dried oregano
1/2 teaspoon dried marjoram
1/2 teaspoon dried thyme
1/2 teaspoon ground cumin
Salt and ground black pepper, to taste
12 ounces green beans, cut into halves

Directions

Place all of the above ingredients, except for the green beans, into the Instant Pot.

Secure the lid. Choose the "Poultry" mode and High pressure; cook for 15 minutes. Once cooking is complete, use a quick pressure release; carefully remove the lid.

Then, stir in the green beans. Seal the lid again; let it sit for 5 minutes to blanch the green beans. Bon appétit!

Per serving: 295 Calories; 12.2g Fat; 16.4g Carbs; 30.6g Protein; 8.4g Sugars

5. Grandma's Chicken Stew with Beans

(Ready in about 20 minutes | Servings 4)

Ingredients

1 tablespoon olive oil
1/2 cup shallots, chopped
2 carrots, trimmed and chopped
1 celery stalk, chopped
2 garlic cloves, minced
1/2 pound potatoes, peeled and quartered
2 ripe tomatoes, chopped
1 (15-ounce) can red kidney beans, rinsed and drained
1 cup chicken broth
1/2 cup dry white wine
1/2 cup water
4 chicken drumsticks
1/2 teaspoon salt
1/4 teaspoon ground black pepper
1 teaspoon cayenne pepper

Directions

Press the "Sauté" button to preheat your Instant Pot.

Then, heat the oil and cook the shallots, carrots, and celery until they are tender.

Stir in the garlic; cook for another minute. Add the remaining ingredients.

Secure the lid. Choose the "Poultry" mode and High pressure; cook for 15 minutes. Once cooking is complete, use a natural pressure release; carefully remove the lid.

Then, pull the meat off the bones; return the chicken to the Instant Pot. Serve warm and enjoy!

Per serving: 463 Calories; 23.6g Fat; 19.8g Carbs; 41.1g Protein; 3.6g Sugars

6. Easy Autumn Chicken Soup

(Ready in about 40 minutes | Servings 6)

Ingredients

1 pound chicken thighs
2 carrots, trimmed and chopped
2 parsnips, chopped
1 celery with leaves, chopped
1 leek, chopped
2 garlic cloves, minced
1 teaspoon dried basil

6 cups chicken stock, preferably homemade
1/2 teaspoon sea salt
Freshly ground black pepper, to taste
1 tablespoon fresh coriander leaves, chopped

Directions

Simply throw all of the above ingredients into your Instant Pot.

Secure the lid. Choose the "Meat/Stew" mode and High pressure; cook for 35 minutes. Once cooking is complete, use a quick pressure release; carefully remove the lid.

Serve in individual bowls garnished with garlic croutons. Enjoy!

Per serving: 245 Calories; 14.6g Fat; 9.8g Carbs; 18.5g Protein; 2.7g Sugars

7. Hot Chicken Drumsticks with Parsley Dip

(Ready in about 1 hour 15 minutes | Servings 6)

Ingredients

2 garlic cloves, minced
1 cup dry white wine
1 red chili pepper
Sea salt and ground black pepper, to taste
1/4 cup sesame oil
6 chicken drumsticks

Parsley Dip:
1/2 cup fresh parsley leaves, chopped
1/3 cup cream cheese
1/3 cup mayonnaise
1 garlic clove, minced
1/2 teaspoon cayenne pepper
1 tablespoon fresh lime juice

Directions

Place the garlic, whine, chili pepper, salt, black pepper, and sesame oil in a ceramic container. Add chicken drumsticks; let them marinate for 1 hour in your refrigerator.

Add the chicken drumsticks, along with the marinade, to the Instant Pot.

Secure the lid. Choose the "Poultry" setting and cook for 10 minutes. Once cooking is complete, use a quick pressure release; carefully remove the lid.

In a mixing bowl, thoroughly combine the parsley, cream cheese mayonnaise, garlic, cayenne pepper, and lime juice.

Serve the chicken drumsticks with the parsley sauce on the side. Bon appétit!

Per serving: 468 Calories; 37.8g Fat; 2.1g Carbs; 28.7g Protein; 0.7g Sugars

8. Chicken Breasts with Gruyère Sauce

(Ready in about 15 minutes | Servings 4)

Ingredients

1 tablespoon olive oil
4 chicken breasts halves
1/4 teaspoon ground black pepper, or more to taste
1/4 teaspoon ground bay leaf
1/2 teaspoon dried basil
Salt, to taste
1 teaspoon dried marjoram

1 cup water
Cheese Sauce:
2 tablespoons mayonnaise
1/2 cup Gruyère cheese, grated
1/2 cup Cottage cheese, at room temperature
1 teaspoon garlic powder
1/2 teaspoon porcini powder

Directions

Press the "Sauté" button to heat up your Instant Pot; heat the oil. Once hot, sear the chicken breasts for 2 minutes per side.

Add the black pepper, ground bay leaf, dried basil, salt, and marjoram; pour in the water.

Secure the lid. Choose the "Poultry" setting and cook for 5 minutes at High pressure. Once cooking is complete, use a natural pressure release; carefully remove the lid.

Clean the Instant Pot and press the "Sauté" button again. Add the sauce ingredients and stir until everything is heated through.

Top the chicken with the sauce and serve immediately. Bon appétit!

Per serving: 268 Calories; 14.9g Fat; 1.5g Carbs; 30.5g Protein; 0.8g Sugars

9. Festive Turkey and Cheese Meatloaf

(Ready in about 35 minutes | Servings 8)

Ingredients

1 ½ pounds ground turkey
1 pound ground pork
1 cup breadcrumbs
1 cup Romano cheese, grated
1 tablespoon Worcestershire sauce
1 egg, chopped
Salt and ground black pepper, to taste

1/2 cup scallions, chopped
2 garlic cloves, minced
6 ounces tomatoes, puréed
2 tablespoons tomato ketchup
1/2 cup water
1 teaspoon Old Sub Sailor seasoning

Directions

Prepare your Instant Pot by adding a metal rack and 1 ½ cups of water to the bottom.

In a large mixing bowl, thoroughly combine the ground turkey, pork, breadcrumbs, Romano cheese, Worcestershire sauce, egg, salt, black pepper, scallions, and garlic.

Shape this mixture into a meatloaf; place the meatloaf in a baking dish and lower the dish onto the rack.

Then, in a mixing bowl, thoroughly combine the puréed tomatoes, ketchup, water, and Old Sub Sailor seasoning. Spread this mixture over the top of your meatloaf.

Secure the lid. Choose the "Meat/Stew" setting and cook for 20 minutes at High pressure. Once cooking is complete, use a natural pressure release; carefully remove the lid.

You can place the meatloaf under the preheated broiler for 4 to 6 minutes if desired. Bon appétit!

Per serving: 387 Calories; 24g Fat; 5g Carbs; 36.9g Protein; 1.7g Sugars

10. Holiday Chicken Salad

(Ready in about 15 minutes + chilling time | Servings 6)

Ingredients

1 ½ pounds chicken breasts
1 cup water
1 fresh or dried rosemary sprig
1 fresh or dried thyme sprig
2 garlic cloves
1/2 teaspoon seasoned salt
1/3 teaspoon black pepper, ground

2 bay leaves
1 teaspoon yellow mustard
1 cup mayonnaise
2 tablespoons sour cream
1 yellow onion, thinly sliced
1 carrot, grated
2 stalks celery, chopped

Directions

Place the chicken, water, rosemary, thyme, garlic, salt, black pepper, and bay leaves in the Instant Pot.

Secure the lid. Choose the "Poultry" setting and cook for 10 minutes under High pressure. Once cooking is complete, use a natural pressure release; carefully remove the lid.

Remove the chicken breasts from the Instant Pot and allow them to cool.

Slice the chicken breasts into strips; place the chicken in a salad bowl. Add the remaining ingredients; stir to combine well. Serve well-chilled.

Per serving: 337 Calories; 23.7g Fat; 3.1g Carbs; 26.4g Protein; 0.9g Sugars

11. Hungarian Turkey Paprikash

(Ready in about 20 minutes | Servings 4)

Ingredients

2 tablespoons butter, at room temperature
1 pound turkey legs
Sea salt and ground black pepper, to taste
2 cups turkey stock
1/2 cup leeks, chopped
2 garlic cloves, minced
1 red bell pepper, chopped
1 green bell pepper, chopped
1 Serrano pepper, chopped
1 parsnip, chopped
1 cup turnip, chopped
1/2 pound carrots, chopped
2 tablespoons fresh cilantro leaves, chopped
1/2 teaspoon Hungarian paprika

Directions

Press the "Sauté" button to preheat your Instant Pot and melt the butter. Now, sear the turkey, skin side down, 3 minutes on each side.

Sprinkle the turkey legs with salt and black pepper as you cook them.

Stir the remaining ingredients into the Instant Pot. Secure the lid and select the "Manual" mode. Cook for 15 minutes at High pressure.

Once cooking is complete, use a natural pressure release. Transfer the turkey legs to a bowl and let them cool. Then, strip the meat off the bones, cut it into small pieces and return to the Instant Pot.

Serve hot and enjoy!

Per serving: 403 Calories; 18.5g Fat; 17.1g Carbs; 40.9g Protein; 6g Sugars

12. Chèvre Stuffed Turkey Tenderloins

(Ready in about 35 minutes | Servings 4)

Ingredients

3 tablespoons olive oil
2 shallots, chopped
2 garlic cloves, smashed
1 carrot, chopped
1 parsnip, chopped
2 tablespoons fresh coriander, chopped
Sea salt and freshly ground black pepper, to your liking
1 teaspoon paprika
1 cup dried bread flakes
1/2 teaspoon garlic powder
1/2 teaspoon cumin powder
1/3 teaspoon turmeric powder
2 ½ cups turkey stock, preferably homemade
4 ounces chèvre cheese
2 pounds turkey breast tenderloins

Directions

Press the "Sauté" button to preheat your Instant Pot. Now, heat 1 tablespoon of olive oil and sauté the shallots, garlic, carrot, and parsnip until they have softened.

Add the coriander, salt, black pepper, paprika, dried bread flakes, garlic powder, cumin, and turmeric powder; stir to combine well. Now, slowly and gradually pour in 1/2 cup of turkey stock. Add the chèvre and mix to combine well.

Place the turkey breast on a work surface and spread the stuffing mixture over it. Tie a cotton kitchen string around each tenderloin.

Press the "Sauté' button on High heat.

Once hot, add the remaining 2 tablespoons of olive oil. Sear the turkey for about 4 minutes on each side. Add the remaining turkey stock and secure the lid.

Choose "Manual", High pressure and 25 minutes cooking time. Use a natural pressure release; carefully remove the lid. Transfer the stuffed turkey tenderloins to a serving platter.

Press the "Sauté" button again and thicken the cooking liquid. Serve with the stuffed turkey tenderloins and enjoy!

Per serving: 475 Calories; 25.4g Fat; 8.2g Carbs; 50g Protein; 2.9g Sugars

13. Thai-Style Chicken with Mushrooms

(Ready in about 20 minutes | Servings 6)

Ingredients

1 tablespoon peanut oil
1 ½ pounds chicken breast, cubed
1 stalk lemongrass
1/2 teaspoon cayenne pepper
Salt and freshly ground black pepper, to taste
1 tablespoon red Thai curry paste
1 ½ cups button mushrooms, sliced
2 garlic cloves, minced
1 cup vegetable broth
1 tablespoon fish sauce
1 cup coconut cream
1 tablespoon fresh coriander

Directions

Press the "Sauté" button to heat up the Instant Pot; heat the oil. Once hot, cook the chicken for 5 minutes, stirring periodically.

Add the lemongrass, cayenne pepper, salt, black pepper, and Thai curry paste, mushrooms, and garlic. Continue to sauté for 3 minutes more or until the mushrooms are fragrant.

Now, stir in the vegetable broth and fish sauce.

Secure the lid. Choose the "Manual" setting and cook for 10 minutes at High pressure. Once cooking is complete, use a quick pressure release; carefully remove the lid.

Afterwards, fold in the coconut cream; press the "Sauté" button and stir until the sauce is reduced and thickened. Serve garnished with fresh coriander. Bon appétit!

Per serving: 296 Calories; 19.6g Fat; 4.9g Carbs; 26.3g Protein; 0.2g Sugars

14. Chicken-and-Bacon Meatballs

(Ready in about 15 minutes | Servings 6)

Ingredients

1 ¼ pounds ground chicken
4 slices bacon, chopped
1 cup seasoned breadcrumbs
1 onion, finely chopped
3 garlic cloves, minced
1/2 tablespoon fresh rosemary, finely chopped
2 eggs, beaten
Salt and ground black pepper, to taste
1/2 teaspoon paprika
2 tablespoons olive oil
2 cups tomato purée
2 tablespoons Dijon mustard
1 tablespoon Worcestershire sauce
2 tablespoons ruby port
1/4 cup chicken broth

Directions

Thoroughly combine the ground chicken, bacon, breadcrumbs, onion, garlic, rosemary, eggs, salt, black pepper, and paprika.

Shape the mixture into meatballs and reserve.

Press the "Sauté" button on High heat to preheat your Instant Pot. Heat the olive oil and sear the meatballs until they are browned on all sides; work in batches.

Add the other ingredients. Choose the "Manual" setting and cook at High pressure for 7 minutes. Use a quick pressure release and carefully remove the lid. Bon appétit!

Per serving: 412 Calories; 23.1g Fat; 21.2g Carbs; 26g Protein; 7.2g Sugars

15. Cheddar and Chicken Bake

(Ready in about 30 minutes | Servings 6)

Ingredients

2 tablespoons butter
1 ½ pounds chicken breasts
2 garlic cloves, halved
1 teaspoon cayenne pepper
1/2 teaspoon mustard powder
Sea salt, to taste
1/2 teaspoon ground black pepper
8 ounces Cheddar cheese, sliced
1/2 cup mayonnaise
1 cup Parmesan cheese, grated

Directions

Press the "Sauté" button to heat up the Instant Pot. Melt the butter; sear the chicken for 2 to 3 minutes per side.

Add the garlic and continue to sauté for 30 seconds more. Season with cayenne pepper, mustard powder, salt, and black pepper.

Add the cheddar cheese and mayonnaise; top with grated Parmesan cheese.

Secure the lid. Choose the "Meat/Stew" mode and High pressure; cook for 20 minutes. Once cooking is complete, use a quick pressure release; carefully remove the lid. Bon appétit!

Per serving: 424 Calories; 28.7g Fat; 7.2g Carbs; 33.2g Protein; 2.8g Sugars

16. Chicken Sandwiches with Mayo and Cheese

(Ready in about 20 minutes | Servings 4)

Ingredients

1 pound chicken breasts	4 hamburger buns
Sea salt and ground black pepper, to taste	1 tablespoon Dijon mustard
2 bay leaves	4 tablespoons mayonnaise
1 cup vegetable stock	4 ounces goat cheese, crumbled
	1/2 cup tomatoes, sliced

Directions

Add the chicken, salt, black pepper, bay leaves, and stock to the Instant Pot.

Secure the lid. Choose the "Poultry" setting and cook for 15 minutes under High pressure. Once cooking is complete, use a quick pressure release; carefully remove the lid.

Assemble your sandwiches with the chicken, hamburger buns, mustard, mayo, goat cheese, and tomatoes. Serve and enjoy!

Per serving: 439 Calories; 20.1g Fat; 24.1g Carbs; 38.6g Protein; 4.5g Sugars

17. Sloppy Joe with a Twist

(Ready in about 15 minutes | Servings 6)

Ingredients

1 tablespoon olive oil	Sea salt and ground black pepper, to taste
1 pound ground chicken	
1/2 pound ground pork	1/2 teaspoon paprika
2 garlic cloves, minced	1/2 teaspoon porcini powder
1 yellow onion, chopped	1/2 teaspoon fennel seeds
2 tomatoes, chopped	2 bay leaves
1 cup chicken broth	

Directions

Press the "Sauté" button to heat up your Instant Pot; heat the oil. Now, cook the ground meat until it is delicately browned; reserve.

Sauté the garlic and onion in the pan drippings for 2 to 3 minutes. Stir in the remaining ingredients.

Now, secure the lid. Choose the "Poultry" setting and cook for 5 minutes under High pressure.

Once cooking is complete, use a natural pressure release; carefully remove the lid.

Spoon the mixture on toasted slider buns and serve.

Per serving: 329 Calories; 23.3g Fat; 3.2g Carbs; 25.1g Protein; 1.7g Sugars

18. Crispy Chicken Carnitas

(Ready in about 25 minutes | Servings 6)

Ingredients

2 pounds chicken stew meat, cut into pieces	Sea salt and ground black pepper, to taste
2 cloves garlic, pressed	1/2 teaspoon paprika
1 teaspoon chili powder	1/3 cup apple juice
1 teaspoon dried Mexican oregano	2 tablespoons fresh coriander, chopped
2 tablespoons olive oil	
2/3 cup vegetable stock	

Directions

Simply throw all of the above ingredients, except for the coriander, in the Instant Pot.

Secure the lid. Choose the "Poultry" setting and cook for 15 minutes. Once cooking is complete, use a quick pressure release; carefully remove the lid.

Shred the chicken with two forks. Spread the chicken on a sheet pan and broil for 7 minutes until crispy.

Add fresh coriander leaves. Serve in taco shells and enjoy!

Per serving: 227 Calories; 9g Fat; 3.1g Carbs; 31.9g Protein; 1.7g Sugars

19. Old-Fashioned Chicken Soup

(Ready in about 25 minutes | Servings 4)

Ingredients

1 ½ tablespoons butter, softened	2 garlic cloves, finely minced
1 cup leeks, thinly sliced	3 cups water
Sea salt and freshly ground black pepper, to taste	1 tablespoon chicken granulated bouillon
1 pound chicken wings, halved	1 tablespoon flaxseed meal
2 carrots, chopped	1 tablespoon champagne vinegar
1 celery with leaves, chopped	1/2 cup garlic croutons, to garnish

Directions

Press the "Sauté" button to preheat your Instant Pot. Now, melt the butter; sauté the leeks until just tender and fragrant.

Now, add the salt, pepper, chicken, carrots, celery, and garlic. Continue to sauté until the chicken is no longer pink and the vegetables are softened.

Add a splash of water to prevent burning and sticking. Press the "Cancel" button. Add the water and chicken granulated bouillon. Secure the lid.

Choose the "Poultry" setting, High pressure. Cook for 20 minutes. Once cooking is complete, use a natural release.

Then, press the "Sauté" button again. Make the slurry by whisking the flaxseed meal with a few tablespoons of the cooking liquid. Return the slurry to the Instant Pot and stir to combine.

Add the champagne vinegar and cook for 1 to 2 minutes more. Serve in individual bowls with garlic croutons. Bon appétit!

Per serving: 263 Calories; 9.9g Fat; 15.2g Carbs; 27.7g Protein; 3.3g Sugars

20. Turkey and Cheese Meatballs

(Ready in about 15 minutes | Servings 6)

Ingredients

1 ½ pounds ground turkey	1/2 teaspoon dried basil
2 eggs	1/2 teaspoon dried oregano
1 yellow onion, chopped	8 ounces Swiss cheese, cubed
2 garlic cloves, minced	1 tablespoon olive oil
1 cup tortilla chips, crumbled	1/2 cup tomato, pureed
1/2 teaspoon paprika	1/2 cup water
Kosher salt, to taste	1 tablespoon sugar
1/4 teaspoon freshly ground black pepper	1/2 teaspoon chili powder

Directions

Thoroughly combine the ground turkey, eggs, onion, garlic, crumbled tortilla chips, paprika, salt, pepper, basil, and oregano.

Roll the mixture into meatballs. Press 1 cheese cube into the center of each meatball, sealing it inside.

Press the "Sauté" button to heat up your Instant Pot; now, heat the olive oil. Brown the meatballs for a couple of minutes, turning them periodically. Add the tomato sauce, water, sugar, and chili powder.

Secure the lid. Choose the "Manual" setting and cook for 9 minutes under High pressure. Once cooking is complete, use a quick pressure release; carefully remove the lid. Bon appétit!

Per serving: 404 Calories; 24.9g Fat; 9.6g Carbs; 35.3g Protein; 3.1g Sugars

21. Stuffed Peppers with Yogurt

(Ready in about 20 minutes | Servings 6)

Ingredients

2 teaspoons olive oil
1 ½ pounds ground chicken
1 red onion, chopped
1 teaspoon garlic, minced
Sea salt and ground black pepper, to taste

1 teaspoon cayenne pepper
1/4 teaspoon ground cumin
5 ounces Colby cheese, grated
6 bell peppers, tops, membrane and seeds removed
1 cup Greek-Style yogurt

Directions

Press the "Sauté" button to heat up the Instant Pot. Then, heat the oil until sizzling.

Cook the chicken with onion and garlic for 3 minutes, stirring periodically. Add the salt, black pepper, cayenne pepper, and cumin; stir to combine.

Fold in the Colby cheese, stir, and reserve.

Wipe down the Instant Pot with a damp cloth. Add 1 ½ cups of water and a metal rack to the Instant Pot.

Fill the peppers with the meat/cheese mixture; don't pack the peppers too tightly.

Place the peppers on the rack and secure the lid. Choose the "Poultry" mode and High pressure; cook for 15 minutes.

Once cooking is complete, use a natural pressure release; carefully remove the lid. Serve with Greek-style yogurt and enjoy!

Per serving: 321 Calories; 19.7g Fat; 8.8g Carbs; 27.9g Protein; 5.1g Sugars

22. Spicy Mexican-Style Chicken Drumettes

(Ready in about 15 minutes | Servings 3)

Ingredients

6 chicken drumettes, skinless and boneless
Seasoned salt and ground black pepper, to taste
1/2 teaspoon red pepper flakes, crushed
1/2 teaspoon Mexican oregano
2 ripe tomatoes, chopped

2 garlic cloves, minced
1 teaspoon fresh ginger, grated
1 Cascabel chili pepper, minced
1/2 cup scallions, chopped
1 tablespoon fresh coriander, minced
1 tablespoon fresh lime juice

Directions

Press the "Sauté" button to heat up your Instant Pot. Sear the chicken drumettes for 3 minutes on each side or until they are browned.

In a bowl, mix the remaining ingredients. Spoon the mixture over the browned chicken.

Secure the lid. Choose the "Manual" mode and High pressure; cook for 10 minutes. Once cooking is complete, use a natural pressure release; carefully remove the lid. Bon appétit!

Per serving: 199 Calories; 4.3g Fat; 7.1g Carbs; 32.2g Protein; 3.4g Sugars

23. Asian Honey-Glazed Chicken with Peanuts

(Ready in about 25 minutes | Servings 4)

Ingredients

1 pound chicken, cubed
1 teaspoon paprika
Salt and black pepper, to taste
1/2 teaspoon cassia
1 tablespoon butter, melted
1/2 cup honey
4 garlic cloves, minced

1 ¼ cups water
1/2 cup Worcestershire sauce
1/2 pound mushrooms, sliced
1 teaspoon Sriracha
1 ½ tablespoons lemongrass
1 ½ tablespoons arrowroot powder
1/4 cup peanuts, chopped

Directions

Press the "Sauté" button to preheat your Instant Pot. Toss the chicken cubes with the paprika, salt, black pepper, and cassia.

Heat the butter and sauté the chicken for 4 minutes, stirring periodically. After that, stir in the honey, garlic, water, Worcestershire sauce, mushrooms, Sriracha, and lemongrass; stir well to combine.

Secure the lid and choose the "Poultry" mode. Cook for 12 minutes. Afterwards, use a natural release and carefully remove the lid.

Press the "Sauté" button.

To make a thickener, add the arrowroot powder to a small bowl; add a cup or so of the hot cooking liquid and whisk until they're combined.

Add the thickener to the Instant Pot and cook for 4 to 5 minutes more or until the sauce has thickened. Garnish with chopped peanuts. Bon appétit!

Per serving: 435 Calories; 12.3g Fat; 55.2g Carbs; 30g Protein; 41.9g Sugars

24. Bacon Wrapped Chicken with Bourbon Sauce

(Ready in about 35 minutes | Servings 3)

Ingredients

3 chicken breast halves, butterflied
2 garlic cloves, halved
Sea salt and ground black pepper, to taste
1 teaspoon cayenne pepper
1 teaspoon dried parsley flakes

1 teaspoon mustard powder
1/4 teaspoon ground allspice
6 slices bacon
1/2 cup BBQ sauce
2 tablespoons bourbon whiskey

Directions

Add 1 ½ cups of water and metal trivet to the Instant Pot.

Then, rub the chicken breasts with garlic. Sprinkle the chicken with the seasonings.

Then, wrap each chicken breast into 2 bacon slices; secure with toothpicks. Lower the wrapped chicken onto the metal trivet.

Secure the lid. Choose the "Poultry" setting and cook for 15 minutes under High pressure. Once cooking is complete, use a natural pressure release; carefully remove the lid.

Then, baste the chicken with BBQ Sauce and bourbon whiskey; bake in your oven for 15 minutes. Bon appétit!

Per serving: 414 Calories; 24.8g Fat; 8.3g Carbs; 38.5g Protein; 5.3g Sugars

25. Rainbow Veggie Chicken Soup

(Ready in about 25 minutes | Servings 5)

Ingredients

2 tablespoons olive oil
1 pound chicken drumettes
1 yellow onion, chopped
2 cloves garlic, minced
1 red bell peppers, seeded and sliced
1 green bell pepper, seeded and sliced
1 orange bell pepper, seeded and sliced

1 carrot, thinly sliced
1 parsnip, thinly sliced
1/4 cup Rose wine
Sea salt and ground black pepper, to your liking
1/2 teaspoon dried dill
1/2 teaspoon dried oregano
1 tablespoon granulated chicken bouillon
4 cups water

Directions

Press the "Sauté" button to heat up your Instant Pot; now, heat the oil until sizzling. Then, sauté the onion and garlic until tender and fragrant.

Add the peppers, carrots and parsnip; cook an additional 3 minutes or until the vegetables are softened. Add a splash of rose wine to deglaze the bottom of your Instant Pot.

Then, stir in the remaining ingredients; stir to combine well.

Secure the lid. Choose the "Soup" mode and High pressure; cook for 20 minutes. Once cooking is complete, use a quick pressure release. Carefully remove the lid.

Remove the chicken wings from the cooking liquid; discard the bones and chop the meat.

Add the chicken meat back to the Instant Pot, stir, and serve hot. Bon appétit!

Per serving: 238 Calories; 17g Fat; 5.4g Carbs; 16.4g Protein; 2.6g Sugars

26. Cavatappi and Meatball Soup

(Ready in about 20 minutes | Servings 6)

Ingredients

1 pound ground turkey	1 teaspoon cayenne pepper
1/2 pound ground pork	1 whole egg
2 tablespoons fresh coriander, chopped	2 teaspoons sesame oil
1/2 white onion, finely chopped	1 pound cavatappi pasta
2 garlic cloves, minced	1 teaspoon dill weed
1 tablespoon oyster sauce	1 cup tomato puree
Sea salt and ground black pepper, to your liking	1 carrot, thinly sliced
	1 celery with leaves, chopped
	6 cups chicken stock

Directions

Thoroughly combine the ground meat, coriander, onion, garlic, oyster sauce, salt, black pepper, and cayenne pepper. Shape the mixture into meatballs; set aside.

Press the "Sauté" button to heat up the Instant Pot. Heat the oil and sear the meatballs until they are browned on all sides.

Now, stir in the remaining ingredients.

Secure the lid. Choose the "Manual" setting and cook for 12 minutes under High pressure. Once cooking is complete, use a quick pressure release; carefully remove the lid. Bon appétit!

Per serving: 408 Calories; 18.4g Fat; 27.4g Carbs; 33.8g Protein; 2.8g Sugars

27. Sunday Turkey and Sausage Meatloaf

(Ready in about 25 minutes | Servings 6)

Ingredients

3/4 pound ground turkey	1 onion, chopped
1/2 pound cooked beef sausage, crumbled	2 garlic cloves, chopped
1/2 cup tortilla chips, crushed	Salt and ground black pepper, to taste
1/2 cup dried bread flakes	1 teaspoon cayenne pepper
1 tablespoon oyster sauce	1 cup tomato puree
2 eggs	3 teaspoons brown sugar

Directions

In a mixing bowl, thoroughly combine the ground turkey, beef sausage, tortilla chips, dried bread flakes, oyster sauce, eggs, onion, and garlic.

Season with salt, black pepper, and cayenne pepper; stir until everything is well incorporated.

Add 1 ½ cups of water to the bottom of your Instant Pot. Shape the meat mixture into a log that will fit into the steamer rack.

Place the aluminum foil sling on the rack and carefully lower the meatloaf onto the foil. Mix the tomato puree with 3 teaspoons of brown sugar. Spread this mixture over the top of your meatloaf.

Secure the lid and choose the "Manual" mode. Cook at High pressure for 20 minutes or to an internal temperature of 160 degrees F.

Once cooking is complete, use a natural release and carefully remove the lid. Bon appétit!

Per serving: 273 Calories; 14.8g Fat; 14.5g Carbs; 22.6g Protein; 4.5g Sugars

28. Chicken Sausage Chowder with Spinach

(Ready in about 15 minutes | Servings 8)

Ingredients

1 tablespoon lard, melted	4 cups vegetable broth
8 ounces chicken sausage, cooked and thinly sliced	1 pinch red pepper flakes
1/2 cup scallions, chopped	Kosher salt, to taste
1 teaspoon ginger garlic paste	1/2 teaspoon freshly ground black pepper, to taste
1 pound cauliflower, chopped into florets	1 cup spinach, torn into pieces

Directions

Add all ingredients, except for the spinach, to your Instant Pot.

Secure the lid. Choose the "Manual" setting and cook for 9 minutes under High pressure. Once cooking is complete, use a quick pressure release; carefully remove the lid.

Puree the mixture in your food processor.

Afterwards, add the spinach and seal the lid. Let it stand until the spinach is wilted. Serve in individual bowls. Enjoy!

Per serving: 360 Calories; 28.1g Fat; 7.8g Carbs; 19.1g Protein; 2.7g Sugars

29. Turkey, Pepper and Zucchini Bake

(Ready in about 15 minutes | Servings 4)

Ingredients

1 tablespoon sesame oil	1 teaspoon dried basil
1 pound ground turkey	2 zucchini, thinly sliced
1/2 cup Romano cheese, grated	2 red bell pepper, sliced lengthwise into strips
1/4 cup breadcrumbs	1 cup tomato paste
Salt and ground black pepper, to taste	1 teaspoon brown sugar
1 teaspoon serrano pepper, minced	5 ounces Swiss cheese, freshly grated
1 teaspoon garlic, smashed	
1/2 teaspoon dried thyme	

Directions

Press the "Sauté" button to heat up the Instant Pot. Now, heat the oil until sizzling.

Then, sauté the ground turkey until it is delicately browned, crumbling it with a spoon. Now, stir in the cheese, crumbs, salt, black pepper, serrano pepper, garlic, thyme, and basil.

Cook for 1 to 2 minutes more; reserve.

Wipe down the Instant Pot with a damp cloth; brush the inner pot with a nonstick cooking spray. Arrange 1/2 of the zucchini slices on the bottom.

Spread 1/3 of the meat mixture over zucchini. Place a layer of bell peppers; add the ground meat mixture. Repeat the layering until you run out of ingredients.

Next, thoroughly combine the tomato paste and sugar. Pour this tomato mixture over the layers.

Secure the lid. Choose the "Manual" mode and High pressure; cook for 10 minutes. Once cooking is complete, use a quick pressure release; carefully remove the lid.

Afterwards, top your casserole with the grated Swiss cheese; allow the Swiss cheese to melt in the residual heat. Bon appétit!

Per serving: 464 Calories; 24.4g Fat; 11.2g Carbs; 43.2g Protein; 1.8g Sugars

30. Chicken Soup with Green Beans

(Ready in about 20 minutes | Servings 6)

Ingredients

4 chicken thighs	1 teaspoon cayenne pepper
Kosher salt and ground black pepper, to taste	1/2 teaspoon dried rosemary
2 tablespoons ghee	2 cups tomato puree
2 shallots, chopped	1 cup green beans
4 cloves garlic minced	6 cups water
1 (1-inch) piece ginger root, finely chopped	1 ½ tablespoons chicken bouillon granules
2 carrots, thinly sliced	2 bay leaves
1 turnip, chopped	1/3 cup crumbled crackers, for garnish
1/2 teaspoon dried oregano	

Directions

Season the chicken thighs with salt and black pepper to your liking. Press the "Sauté" button to preheat your Instant Pot.

Once hot, melt the ghee and sear the chicken thighs for 3 minutes per side.

Add the shallots, garlic, chopped ginger, carrot, and turnip; continue to sauté until just tender, about 4 minutes.

Now, add the oregano, cayenne pepper, and rosemary. Stir for 30 seconds more.

Add the tomato puree, green beans, water, chicken bouillon granules, and bay leaves. Secure the lid.

Choose the "Manual", High pressure and 10 minutes. Once cooking is complete, use a natural release and carefully remove the lid. Discard the bay leaves.

Ladle into individual bowls and serve garnished with crumbled crackers.

Per serving: 354 Calories; 10.8g Fat; 11.4g Carbs; 51.3g Protein; 5.3g Sugars

31. Classic Buffalo Wings

(Ready in about 40 minutes | Servings 4)

Ingredients

2 pounds chicken wings
2 garlic cloves, halved
1 teaspoon sea salt
1/2 teaspoon ground black pepper
1/2 teaspoon cayenne pepper flakes
4 tablespoons butter, melted
1/2 cup roasted vegetable broth
1/2 cup Cholula hot sauce
1 tablespoon brown sugar
1 teaspoon barbecue sauce
1 teaspoon corn starch, dissolved in 1 tablespoon of water

Directions

Rub the chicken legs with the garlic halves; then, season with salt, black pepper, and cayenne pepper. Press the "Sauté" button.

Once hot, melt 2 tablespoons of the melted butter and sear the chicken wings approximately 4 minutes, turning them once during the cooking time. Add a splash of vegetable broth to deglaze the bottom of the pan.

Now, add the remaining broth and secure the lid. Choose the "Manual" mode and High pressure; cook for 12 minutes. Once the cooking is complete, use a quick pressure release; carefully remove the lid.

Remove the chicken wings from the Instant Pot, reserving the cooking liquid. Place the chicken wings on a lightly greased baking sheet.

Turn your oven on to High Broil. Broil the chicken wings approximately 15 minutes until it is crisp and golden brown; make sure to turn them over halfway through the cooking time.

Press the "Sauté" button and add the remaining 2 tablespoons of butter. Once hot, add the hot sauce, sugar, and barbecue sauce; pour in the reserved cooking liquid.

Let it simmer for 4 minutes; add the corn starch slurry and continue to simmer until the cooking liquid has reduced and concentrated.

Pour the prepared sauce over the reserved chicken and serve warm. Bon appétit!

Per serving: 408 Calories; 22.1g Fat; 8.8g Carbs; 41.6g Protein; 2.8g Sugars

32. Cheesy Chicken Tenders with Potatoes

(Ready in about 25 minutes | Servings 6)

Ingredients

2 tablespoons olive oil
2 pounds chicken tenders
2 pounds Yukon Gold potatoes, peeled and diced
2 cloves garlic, smashed
1/4 teaspoon ground black pepper
1 teaspoon red pepper flakes
Pink Himalayan salt, to taste
1 teaspoon shallot powder
1 teaspoon dried basil
1 teaspoon dried rosemary
1 ½ cups chicken stock
6 tablespoons Romano cheese, grated

Directions

Press the "Sauté" button to preheat your Instant Pot. Now, heat the olive oil and sear the chicken tenders for 3 to 4 minutes.

Add the potatoes and garlic; sprinkle with black pepper, red pepper, salt, shallot powder, basil, and rosemary.

Pour in the chicken stock and secure the lid. Choose the "Poultry" mode and High pressure; cook for 15 minutes. Once cooking is complete, use a quick pressure release; carefully remove the lid.

Top with the grated Romano cheese and serve warm. Enjoy!

Per serving: 377 Calories; 12.3g Fat; 28.3g Carbs; 37.3g Protein; 2.3g Sugars

33. 20-minute Ground Chicken Tacos

(Ready in about 20 minutes | Servings 6)

Ingredients

1 tablespoon olive oil
1 pound ground chicken
1 pound ground turkey
2 cloves garlic, minced
1 onion, chopped
2 sweet peppers, deseeded and chopped
1 serrano pepper, deseeded and chopped
1/3 cup hoisin sauce
1 cup water
1 tablespoon tamari sauce
Salt, to taste
1/2 teaspoon freshly ground black pepper
1 teaspoon Mexican oregano
6 (approx. 6-inch diameter) tortillas
1 cup sweet corn kernels, cooked
1 cup canned black beans, drained
1 tablespoon Dijon mustard
1 teaspoon jalapeno pepper, minced
2 tomatoes, sliced
1 head butter lettuce

Directions

Press the "Sauté" button. Once hot, heat the olive oil until sizzling. Now, brown the ground meat for 2 to 3 minutes, stirring continuously.

Add the garlic, onion, peppers, hoisin sauce, water, tamari sauce, salt, black pepper, and Mexican oregano.

Secure the lid. Choose the "Manual" mode and High pressure; cook for 6 minutes. Once cooking is complete, use a quick pressure release; carefully remove the lid.

Assemble the tortillas with the ground chicken filling, corn, beans, mustard, jalapeno pepper, tomatoes, and lettuce. Enjoy!

Per serving: 502 Calories; 22.5g Fat; 39.4g Carbs; 36.3g Protein; 6.9g Sugars

34. Sticky Asian Glazed Chicken

(Ready in about 25 minutes | Servings 4)

Ingredients

2 tablespoons sesame seed oil
4 chicken drumsticks
1/4 teaspoon fresh ground pepper, or more to taste
Sea salt, to taste
1 tablespoon Chinese rice vinegar
6 tablespoons honey
2 tablespoons sweet chili sauce
3 cloves garlic, minced
1/3 cup low-sodium soy sauce
1/3 cup no salt ketchup
1/2 cup water
1 tablespoon fresh cilantro, chopped
Small bunch scallions, chopped

Directions

Press the "Sauté" button to preheat your Instant Pot.

Heat the sesame seed oil and sear the chicken for 5 minutes, stirring periodically. Season with black pepper and salt.

After that, stir in the vinegar, honey, chili sauce, garlic, soy sauce, ketchup, water, and cilantro; stir well to combine.

Secure the lid and choose the "Poultry" mode. Cook for 15 minutes. Afterwards, use a natural release and carefully remove the lid.

Garnish with chopped scallions. Bon appétit!

35. Creamed Chicken Cutlets with Herbs

(Ready in about 25 minutes | Servings 6)

Per serving: 422 Calories; 8.5g Fat; 41.5g Carbs; 45.6g Protein; 2g Sugars

Ingredients

2 pounds chicken cutlets
Kosher salt and ground black pepper, to taste
1 teaspoon dried oregano
1 teaspoon dried basil
1 teaspoon dried rosemary
1 teaspoon dried parsley flakes
1/4 cup dry white wine
2 cups vegetable broth
2 garlic cloves, minced
1/2 cup double cream
2 tablespoons cornstarch
6 cups pasta, cooked

Directions

Season the chicken cutlets with salt, black pepper, oregano, basil, rosemary, and parsley. Press the "Sauté" button to preheat your Instant Pot.

Once hot, cook the seasoned chicken cutlets for 5 minutes, turning once during cooking. Add the white wine and scrape the bottom of the pan to deglaze.

Pour in the vegetable broth. Add the garlic and secure the lid.

Choose the "Manual" mode and High pressure; cook for 8 minutes. Once cooking is complete, use a quick release and remove the lid. Reserve the chicken cutlets, keeping them warm.

Stir the double cream and cornstarch into the cooking liquid.

Press the "Sauté" button and simmer for 6 minutes or until the cooking liquid has reduced by half. Serve with warm pasta. Bon appétit!

Per serving: 394 Calories; 18.9g Fat; 30.6g Carbs; 26g Protein; 27.2g Sugars

36. Greek-Style Chicken Fillets

(Ready in about 20 minutes | Servings 6)

Ingredients

2 pounds chicken fillets
2 garlic cloves, halved
1 ½ tablespoons olive oil
1/2 cup tamari sauce
1/2 cup tomato puree
1/2 cup chicken broth
1 tablespoon molasses

Sea salt and freshly ground black pepper, to taste
1/2 teaspoon red pepper flakes
1 bay leaf
1 rosemary sprig
1/2 cup Kalamata olives, pitted and halved

Directions

Rub the chicken fillets with the garlic halves on all sides. Press the "Sauté" button to preheat your Instant Pot.

Heat the olive oil and sear the chicken fillets for 2 minutes per side.

Add the tamari sauce, tomato puree, broth, molasses, salt, black pepper, red pepper, bay leaf and rosemary sprig.

Secure the lid. Choose the "Manual" mode and High pressure; cook for 9 minutes. Once cooking is complete, use a quick release; remove the lid.

Serve garnished with Kalamata olives. Enjoy!

Per serving: 268 Calories; 10.1g Fat; 7g Carbs; 35.9g Protein; 4.4g Sugars

37. Sunday Chicken Salad

(Ready in about 10 minutes + chilling time | Servings 4)

Ingredients

1 pound chicken breasts, skinless and boneless
1 cup chicken stock
2 garlic cloves, crushed
2 tablespoons fresh basil leaves, roughly chopped
4 tablespoons sour cream

1/2 cup mayonnaise
1 tablespoon yellow mustard
1 tablespoon fresh lime juice
1 Lebanese cucumber, sliced
1/2 cup scallions, chopped
Coarse sea salt and ground black pepper, to taste

Directions

Place the chicken breasts, stock, and garlic in the Instant Pot.

Secure the lid. Choose the "Manual" mode and High pressure; cook for 8 minutes. Once cooking is complete, use a quick release.

Shred the chicken breasts with 1/2 cup of cooking liquid and transfer to a salad bowl; add the remaining ingredients and gently stir to combine.

Place in your refrigerator until ready to serve. Bon appétit!

Per serving: 386 Calories; 26.5g Fat; 3.1g Carbs; 34.3g Protein; 0.6g Sugars

38. Authentic Chicken Taco Meat

(Ready in about 35 minutes | Servings 6)

Ingredients

2 pounds whole chicken, meat and skin
1 Old El Paso Taco spice mix
1 tablespoon canola oil
1 fresh jalapeño chili, seeded and finely chopped

Kosher salt and ground black pepper, to taste
Fresh juice of 1 orange
1 cup chicken broth
A small handful of coriander, roughly chopped

Directions

Toss the chicken in the Taco spice mix to coat. Press the "Sauté" button to preheat your Instant Pot.

Heat the canola oil and sear the chicken, stirring periodically, for 3 to 4 minutes or until golden brown.

Add the jalapeño chili, salt, black pepper, fresh orange juice, and chicken broth; stir to combine. Secure the lid.

Choose the "Poultry" mode and High pressure; cook for 30 minutes. Once cooking is complete, use a quick release.

Shred the chicken and garnish with fresh coriander leaves. Enjoy!

Per serving: 412 Calories; 27.8g Fat; 1.1g Carbs; 36.9g Protein; 0.4g Sugars

39. Cheesy Chicken and Pasta Casserole

(Ready in about 20 minutes | Servings 5)

Ingredients

2 tablespoons olive oil
2 garlic cloves, minced
2 strips bacon, diced
1 ½ pounds chicken legs, boneless skinless, cubed
2 ounces vermouth
7 ounces Ricotta cheese, crumbled, at room temperature

1 cup water
4 cups elbow pasta
1 onion, sliced
2 sweet peppers, seeded and thinly sliced
1 cup chicken broth

Directions

Press the "Sauté" button to preheat your Instant Pot.

Once hot, heat the olive oil. Now, cook the garlic and bacon until they are fragrant.

Stir in the cubed chicken and cook for 3 minutes more or until it is no longer pink. Use vermouth to scrape the remaining bits of meat off the bottom of the inner pot.

Add the softened Ricotta cheese and water. Secure the lid. Choose the "Poultry" mode and High pressure; cook for 5 minutes. Once cooking is complete, use a quick release.

Add the elbow pasta, onion, and peppers. Pour in the chicken broth; gently stir to combine.

Secure the lid and choose the "Manual" mode. Cook for 4 minutes longer. Afterwards, use a quick release and carefully remove the lid. Bon appétit!

Per serving: 544 Calories; 21.8g Fat; 39.7g Carbs; 44.9g Protein; 1.1g Sugars

40. Saucy Chicken with Root Vegetables

(Ready in about 20 minutes | Servings 5)

Ingredients

2 pounds whole chicken, boneless, skinless, and cubed
1 celery stalk, trimmed and sliced
2 carrots, trimmed and sliced
2 parsnips, trimmed and sliced
1 bell pepper, seeded and thinly sliced
1 habanero pepper, seeded and thinly sliced

1 cup vegetable broth
2 garlic cloves, smashed
1/2 teaspoon ginger, grated
1 teaspoon smoked paprika
1 tablespoon sesame seed oil
1 tablespoon arrowroot powder
2 tablespoons toasted sesame seeds

Directions

Place the chicken pieces in the inner pot. Place the vegetables on the top. Pour in the vegetable broth.

Add the remaining ingredients, except for the toasted sesame seeds.

Secure the lid. Choose the "Poultry" mode and High pressure; cook for 15 minutes. Once cooking is complete, use a quick release.

Transfer the chicken and veggies to serving plates using a slotted spoon. Press the "Sauté" button to preheat the Instant Pot. Stir the arrowroot powder into the cooking liquid to thicken the sauce.

Spoon the sauce over the warm chicken and vegetables. Garnish with the toasted sesame seeds. Bon appétit!

Per serving: 300 Calories; 8g Fat; 16.1g Carbs; 40.1g Protein; 4.3g Sugars

41. Ranch Chicken Thighs

(Ready in about 25 minutes | Servings 5)

Ingredients

1 tablespoon butter, melted
2 pounds chicken thighs, bone-in, skin-on
2 garlic cloves, minced
1 yellow onion, sliced
1 packet dry ranch salad dressing mix

1 teaspoon paprika
1/2 teaspoon ground bay leaf
1/2 teaspoon ground black pepper
Sea salt, to taste
2 tablespoons champagne vinegar
1 cup chicken bone broth

Directions

Press the "Sauté" button and melt the butter.

Now, sear the chicken thighs for 4 to 5 minutes or until browned on all sides.

Add the remaining ingredients in the order listed above.

Secure the lid. Choose the "Poultry" setting and cook for 15 minutes at High pressure. Once cooking is complete, use a natural release and carefully remove the lid.

You can thicken the sauce on the "Sauté" mode. Serve over hot cooked rice if desired. Enjoy!

Per serving: 435 Calories; 33.1g Fat; 1.4g Carbs; 30.1g Protein; 0.1g Sugars

42. Spanish Arroz con Pollo

(Ready in about 20 minutes | Servings 5)

Ingredients

1 tablespoon olive oil
1/2 cup brown onion, chopped
1 pound chicken breasts, trimmed and cut into bite-sized pieces
2 tablespoons Rueda
1 cup short-grain white rice
1 ½ cups chicken broth
1 cup tomato puree
1 teaspoon dried oregano

Sea salt and ground black pepper, to taste
1/2 teaspoon saffron threads
5 ounces seafood mix
5 ounces chorizo sausage, casings removed and crumbled
1 lemon, juiced and zested
2 tablespoons fresh parsley, roughly chopped

Directions

Press the "Sauté" button and heat the olive oil.

Now, cook the brown onion and chicken until the onion is translucent and the chicken is no longer pink or about 4 minutes. Deglaze the pot with the Rueda wine.

Stir in the rice, broth, tomato puree, oregano, salt, black pepper, and saffron.

Secure the lid and choose the "Manual" mode. Cook for 5 minutes at High pressure. Afterwards, use a quick release and carefully remove the lid.

Add the seafood mix and sausage. Secure the lid and choose the "Manual" mode. Cook for 4 to 5 minutes at High pressure; use a quick release and carefully remove the lid.

Add the lemon and parsley and serve immediately. Bon appétit!

Per serving: 537 Calories; 23.1g Fat; 44.4g Carbs; 36.9g Protein; 6.1g Sugars

43. Easy Millet and Chicken Bowl

(Ready in about 25 minutes | Servings 4)

Ingredients

4 chicken drumsticks, skinless and boneless
Sea salt and ground black pepper, to taste
1/2 teaspoon red pepper flakes, crushed
1/2 teaspoon dried basil
1/2 teaspoon dried oregano
1/2 teaspoon ground cumin
1 ½ tablespoons olive oil

1/2 cup shallots, chopped
2 garlic cloves, finely chopped
1 bell pepper, deseeded and chopped
1 cup millet
1 cup vegetable broth
1 cup tomato puree
1 bay leaf
1 cup green beans

Directions

Season the chicken drumsticks with salt, black pepper, red pepper, basil, oregano, and cumin.

Press the "Sauté" button and heat the olive oil. Sear the chicken drumsticks for 5 minutes, turning them to ensure even cooking.

Add the shallots, garlic, pepper, millet, broth, tomato puree, and bay leaf to the Instant Pot.

Secure the lid and choose the "Poultry" mode. Cook for 15 minutes at High pressure. Once cooking is complete, use a quick pressure release; carefully remove the lid.

Add the green beans and secure the lid again; let it sit in the residual heat until wilts. Enjoy!

Per serving: 440 Calories; 12.8g Fat; 47.1g Carbs; 34g Protein; 4.6g Sugars

44. Chicken and Kidney Bean Casserole

(Ready in about 25 minutes | Servings 4)

Ingredients

2 tablespoons olive oil
1 pound chicken drumettes, cut into bite-sized pieces
1 onion, chopped
1 cup chicken bone broth
1 teaspoon granulated garlic
1 teaspoon cayenne pepper

Salt and ground black pepper, to taste
1 teaspoon Sriracha sauce
16 ounces canned kidney beans, drained
1 tablespoon fresh cilantro, chopped

Directions

Press the "Sauté" button and heat the olive oil.

Now, cook the chicken drumettes until no longer pink or about 4 minutes.

Add the onion, chicken broth, garlic, cayenne pepper, salt, black pepper, and Sriracha sauce to the inner pot; gently stir to combine.

Secure the lid and choose the "Poultry" mode. Cook for 15 minutes at High pressure. Once cooking is complete, use a quick pressure release; carefully remove the lid.

Stir in the kidney beans; secure the lid and let it sit in the residual heat until thoroughly heated. Serve garnished with fresh cilantro. Enjoy!

Per serving: 352 Calories; 17.7g Fat; 7.8g Carbs; 38.7g Protein; 1.8g Sugars

45. Tender Chicken with Garden Vegetables

(Ready in about 20 minutes | Servings 4)

Ingredients

2 tablespoons lard, at room temperature
1 pound chicken breasts, sliced into serving-size pieces
1 teaspoon dried marjoram
1/2 teaspoon dried sage
1/2 teaspoon ground black pepper
Sea salt, to taste

1/2 cup leeks, sliced
2 garlic cloves, sliced
1 cup chicken bone broth
2 cups butternut squash, diced
1 eggplant, diced
1/2 head cabbage, diced
1/4 cup fresh chives, chopped

Directions

Press the "Sauté" button and melt the lard until sizzling.

Then, sear the chicken breasts until it is lightly browned or about 5 minutes. Add the spices and stir to combine.

Add the leeks and garlic. Pour in the chicken bone broth. Afterwards, add the vegetables and secure the lid.

Choose the "Manual" mode. Cook for 8 minutes at High pressure. Once cooking is complete, use a quick pressure release; carefully remove the lid.

Using a slotted spoon, remove the chicken and vegetables to a serving platter.

Press the "Sauté" button and simmer the cooking liquid for about 3 minutes until slightly thickened. Serve garnished with fresh chives. Bon appétit!

Per serving: 447 Calories; 21.5g Fat; 24.5g Carbs; 40.1g Protein; 9.5g Sugars

46. Famous New Orleans Gumbo

(Ready in about 25 minutes | Servings 4)

Ingredients

4 tablespoons olive oil
1 onion, chopped
2 sweet peppers, deseeded and chopped
1 ½ pounds chicken breasts, boneless, skinless, and cubed
8 ounces Andouille sausage, sliced
1 red chili pepper, deseeded and chopped
2 celery stalks, trimmed and diced
2 carrots, trimmed and diced
2 cloves garlic, sliced
2 large ripe tomatoes, pureed

1 teaspoon basil, dried
1 teaspoon paprika
Kosher salt and ground black pepper, to taste
2 bay leaves, dried
1 tablespoon gumbo file
1 tablespoon chicken bouillon granules
6 cups water
1/3 cup all-purpose flour
1/2 pound okra, cut into bite-sized pieces

Directions

Press the "Sauté" button and heat 2 tablespoons of oil until sizzling. Now, sweat the onion and peppers until tender and aromatic or about 3 minutes; reserve.

Then, heat the remaining 2 tablespoons of olive oil and cook the chicken and sausage until no longer pink, about 4 minutes. Make sure to stir periodically to ensure even cooking.

Stir the chili pepper, celery, carrot, garlic, tomatoes, basil, paprika, salt, black pepper, bay leaves, gumbo file, and chicken bouillon granules into the inner pot. Add the reserved onion/pepper mixture. Pour in 6 cups of water.

Secure the lid. Choose the "Manual" mode. Cook for 7 minutes at High pressure. Once cooking is complete, use a quick pressure release; carefully remove the lid.

Mix the flour with 1 cup of cooking liquid and reserve. Afterwards, stir in the okra and flour mixture into the inner pot.

Secure the lid. Choose "Manual" mode. Cook for 3 minutes at High pressure. Once cooking is complete, use a natural pressure release; carefully remove the lid.

Serve in individual bowls, garnished with garlic croutons if desired. Bon appétit!

Per serving: 592 Calories; 29.2g Fat; 30.2g Carbs; 52.1g Protein; 6.2g Sugars

47. Creamy Lemon Chicken

(Ready in about 25 minutes | Servings 4)

Ingredients

2 tablespoons sesame oil
4 chicken drumsticks, boneless and skinless
2/3 cup chicken broth
1 teaspoon garlic powder
1/2 teaspoon cayenne pepper
1/4 teaspoon ground black pepper, or more to taste

1 teaspoon oregano
1 teaspoon basil
1/2 teaspoon thyme
1 onion, chopped
1 lemon, juiced and zested
1/3 heavy cream

Directions

Press the "Sauté" button and heat the oil until sizzling. Sear the chicken drumsticks, stirring occasionally, for about 4 minutes.

Add a few tablespoons of broth to deglaze the bottom of the pan. Stir in the spices, onion, and chicken broth; stir to combine well.

Secure the lid. Choose the "Poultry" mode. Cook for 15 minutes at High pressure. Once cooking is complete, use a quick pressure release; carefully remove the lid.

Remove the chicken from the Instant Pot using a slotted spoon.

Add the lemon and heavy cream to the cooking liquid; stir to combine. Press the "Sauté" button and let it simmer until the sauce has thickened slightly.

Spoon the sauce over the reserved chicken and serve warm. Enjoy!

Per serving: 388 Calories; 25.2g Fat; 5.4g Carbs; 33.1g Protein; 2g Sugars

48. Christmas Roast Chicken

(Ready in about 35 minutes | Servings 4)

Ingredients

4 tablespoons butter, softened
1 head of garlic, crushed
Salt and ground black pepper, to taste
1 tablespoon paprika

2 rosemary sprigs, crushed
2 thyme sprigs, crushed
2 quarts water
1 (3 ½ pounds) whole chicken

Directions

In a small mixing dish, thoroughly combine the butter, garlic, salt, black pepper, paprika, rosemary, and thyme.

Pour the water into the inner pot.

Pat the chicken dry. Then, rub the butter mixture all over the chicken to season well. Place the chicken in the inner pot.

Secure the lid. Choose "Manual" mode. Cook for 20 minutes at High pressure. Once cooking is complete, use a natural pressure release; carefully remove the lid.

Afterwards, place the chicken under the broiler for 10 minutes until the skin is lightly crisped. Bon appétit!

Per serving: 376 Calories; 18.2g Fat; 2g Carbs; 49.1g Protein; 0.7g Sugars

49. Mom's Orange Chicken

(Ready in about 15 minutes | Servings 4)

Ingredients

1 tablespoon olive oil
2/3 pound ground chicken
1/3 pound bacon, chopped
2 tablespoons sherry wine
1 medium red onion, chopped
2 garlic cloves, minced

1 jalapeno pepper, chopped
Sea salt and ground black pepper, to taste
1 teaspoon paprika
Fresh juice and zest of 1/2 orange
1 tablespoon arrowroot powder

Directions

Press the "Sauté" button and heat the oil until sizzling. Sear the chicken and bacon until they are slightly brown.

Add the sherry wine and stir with a wooden spoon, scraping up the browned bits on the bottom of the pan. Add the red onion, garlic, and jalapeno pepper; stir to combine.

Season with salt, black pepper, and paprika. Pour in 1 cup of water.

Secure the lid. Choose "Poultry" mode. Cook for 5 minutes at High pressure. Once cooking is complete, use a quick pressure release; carefully remove the lid.

Add the orange juice and zest; stir in the arrowroot powder. Press the "Sauté" button and simmer, stirring occasionally, until it thickens. Bon appétit!

Per serving: 337 Calories; 26g Fat; 8.8g Carbs; 18.9g Protein; 2g Sugars

50. Chinese-Style Chicken Congee

(Ready in about 20 minutes | Servings 6)

Ingredients

3 tablespoons sesame oil
6 chicken drumsticks
4 garlic cloves, minced
2 tablespoons Worcestershire sauce
2 tablespoons champagne vinegar
2 cups vegetable broth

2 cups water
1/4 cup honey
Salt and ground black pepper, to taste
1 teaspoon Wuxiang powder
1 cup rice
2 tablespoons flaxseed meal

Directions

Press the "Sauté" button and heat 2 tablespoons of the sesame oil. Sear the chicken drumsticks until slightly brown on all sides. Add the garlic and cook for 1 minute or so, until aromatic.

Add the remaining ingredients, except for the flaxseed meal.

Secure the lid. Choose "Poultry" mode. Cook for 15 minutes at High pressure. Once cooking is complete, use a quick pressure release; carefully remove the lid.

Afterwards, stir in the flaxseed meal; stir until everything is well combined. Press the "Sauté" button and cook until the cooking liquid is reduced by about half. Bon appétit!

Per serving: 471 Calories; 20.8g Fat; 41.1g Carbs; 28.2g Protein; 12.7g Sugars

51. French-Style Creamy Mustard Chicken

(Ready in about 20 minutes | Servings 4)

Ingredients

2 tablespoons olive oil, divided
1 pound chicken breasts, boneless
1 teaspoon dried basil
1/2 teaspoon dried oregano
1/2 teaspoon dried sage
1 teaspoon paprika

1 teaspoon garlic powder
Sea salt and ground black pepper, to taste
1 tablespoon Dijon mustard
1 cup chicken bone broth
1/2 cup heavy cream

Directions

Press the "Sauté" button and heat the olive oil. Sear the chicken breasts until they are no longer pink.

Add the seasonings, mustard, and chicken bone broth.

Secure the lid. Choose "Manual" mode and cook for 8 minutes at High pressure. Once cooking is complete, use a natural pressure release; carefully remove the lid.

Lastly, add the heavy cream, cover with the lid, and let it sit in the residual heat for 6 to 8 minutes. Serve in individual bowls. Enjoy!

Per serving: 413 Calories; 27.2g Fat; 3.3g Carbs; 37.5g Protein; 1.2g Sugars

52. Fiesta Chicken Bake

(Ready in about 20 minutes | Servings 4)

Ingredients

2 tablespoons olive oil
1 pound chicken breast, boneless, cut into chunks
2 cups cream of celery soup
2 cups spiral pasta

1 cup Cotija cheese, crumbled
1 cup queso fresco, crumbled
1 ½ cups spiral pasta
1 cup salsa
1 cup fresh breadcrumbs

Directions

Press the "Sauté" button and heat the olive oil. Now, brown the chicken breasts for 3 to 4 minutes.

Add the remaining ingredients in the order listed above.

Secure the lid. Choose "Manual" mode and cook for 6 minutes at High pressure. Once cooking is complete, use a natural pressure release; carefully remove the lid.

Serve warm.

Per serving: 756 Calories; 34.9g Fat; 66g Carbs; 45.2g Protein; 4.7g Sugars

53. Chicken Tenders with Cottage Cheese

(Ready in about 25 minutes | Servings 4)

Ingredients

2 tablespoons butter, softened
1 ½ pounds chicken tenders
1 cup vegetable broth
1 teaspoon shallot powder
1 teaspoon garlic powder
1/2 teaspoon smoked paprika

Sea salt and freshly ground black pepper, to taste
1 cup Cottage cheese, crumbled
2 heaping tablespoons fresh chives, roughly chopped

Directions

Press the "Sauté" button and melt the butter. Sear the chicken tenders for 2 to 3 minutes.

Add the vegetable broth, shallot powder, garlic powder, paprika, salt, and black pepper.

Secure the lid. Choose "Manual" mode and cook for 8 minutes at High pressure. Once cooking is complete, use a natural pressure release; carefully remove the lid.

Stir in the cheese; cover with the lid and let it sit in the residual heat for 5 minutes. Garnish with fresh chives and serve immediately.

Per serving: 305 Calories; 13.1g Fat; 2.8g Carbs; 41.9g Protein; 1.7g Sugars

54. Sicilian-Style Chicken Wings

(Ready in about 25 minutes | Servings 4)

Ingredients

2 tablespoons butter, room temperature
4 chicken drumsticks, boneless
1/4 cup all-purpose flour
1 teaspoon Italian seasoning mix
Sea salt and ground black pepper, to taste

2 bell peppers, deseeded and sliced
1 cup scallions, chopped
4 cloves garlic, smashed
1/4 cup Marsala wine
1 cup chicken broth
1/4 cup cream cheese

Directions

Press the "Sauté" button to preheat your Instant Pot. Melt 1 tablespoon of the butter.

Dredge your chicken in the flour; season with spices and cook until slightly brown; reserve.

Melt the remaining tablespoon of butter and sauté the peppers, scallions, and garlic. Pour in the wine, scraping up any browned bits from the bottom of the pan. Add the chicken broth and secure the lid.

Choose the "Manual" mode and cook for 10 minutes at High pressure. Once cooking is complete, use a natural pressure release; carefully remove the lid.

Press the "Sauté" button to preheat your Instant Pot one more time. Add the cream cheese and cook for a further 4 to 5 minutes or until everything is thoroughly heated.

To serve, spoon the sauce over the chicken drumsticks. Bon appétit!

Per serving: 457 Calories; 26.3g Fat; 13.7g Carbs; 39.8g Protein; 3.1g Sugars

55. Chicken with Couscous and Haloumi Cheese

(Ready in about 20 minutes | Servings 4)

Ingredients

2 teaspoons butter, at room temperature
1 pound chicken fillets, diced
1 onion, diced
1 sweet pepper, deseeded and sliced
1 red chili pepper, deseeded and sliced
3 cloves garlic, minced

1 teaspoon dried rosemary
1 teaspoon dried oregano
Kosher salt and ground black pepper, to taste
2 cups vegetable broth
1 cup dry couscous
4 ounces halloumi cheese, crumbled

Directions

Press the "Sauté" button to preheat your Instant Pot. Melt 1 teaspoon of the butter. Cook the chicken fillets until golden brown. Set aside.

Then, melt the remaining 1 teaspoon of butter. Now, sauté the onion, peppers, and garlic until tender and aromatic.

Add the rosemary, oregano, salt, pepper, and vegetable broth.

Secure the lid. Choose the "Poultry" mode and cook for 5 minutes at High pressure. Once cooking is complete, use a quick pressure release; carefully remove the lid.

Add the couscous and stir to combine. Secure the lid. Choose the "Manual" mode and cook for 2 minutes at High pressure. Once cooking is complete, use a quick pressure release; carefully remove the lid.

Divide between four serving plates; garnish each serving with halloumi cheese and enjoy!

Per serving: 444 Calories; 12.2g Fat; 45.1g Carbs; 37g Protein; 4.5g Sugars

56. Easy Teriyaki Chicken

(Ready in about 30 minutes | Servings 4)

Ingredients

2 tablespoons sesame oil
1 pound chicken drumettes, skinless, boneless, cut into bite-sized chunks
2 garlic cloves, minced
1/4 cup soy sauce
1/2 cup water
1/2 cup rice vinegar
1/4 cup brown sugar
1 teaspoon ground ginger
2 tablespoons rice wine
3 tablespoons Mirin
1 pound broccoli florets
1 teaspoon arrowroot powder

Directions

Press the "Sauté" button to preheat your Instant Pot. Heat the sesame oil and cook the chicken drumettes for 3 to 4 minutes.

Then, add the garlic and cook for 30 seconds more or until fragrant. Add the soy sauce, water, vinegar, sugar, ginger, rice wine, and Mirin. Secure the lid.

Choose the "Manual" mode and cook for 10 minutes at High pressure. Once cooking is complete, use a quick pressure release; carefully remove the lid.

Add the broccoli florets and secure the lid. Choose the "Manual" mode and cook for 2 minutes at High pressure. Once cooking is complete, use a quick pressure release; carefully remove the lid.

Transfer the chicken and broccoli to a nice serving platter.

Press the "Sauté" button to preheat your Instant Pot again. Add the arrowroot powder and stir until it is completely dissolved. Cook for 5 to 6 minutes or until the sauce thickens slightly. Spoon over the chicken and serve.

Per serving: 294 Calories; 13.3g Fat; 15.1g Carbs; 27g Protein; 9.8g Sugars

57. Chicken Enchilada Sliders

(Ready in about 25 minutes | Servings 4)

Ingredients

1 pound chicken breasts, boneless and skinless
Kosher salt and freshly ground black pepper, to taste
1 cup chicken broth
8 ounces canner red enchilada sauce
1 cup spring onions, sliced
8 slider buns

Directions

Place the chicken breasts in the inner pot. Season with salt and pepper; pour in the chicken broth and enchilada sauce.
Secure the lid. Choose the "Manual" mode and cook for 9 minutes at High pressure. Once cooking is complete, use a quick pressure release; carefully remove the lid.

Place the bottom half of the slider buns on a baking sheet. Top with layers of the chicken mixture and spring onions. Put on the top buns and spritz with cooking spray. Bake about 10 minutes in the preheated oven until buns are golden. Enjoy!

Per serving: 504 Calories; 17.2g Fat; 49.1g Carbs; 36.3g Protein; 6.7g Sugars

58. Favorite Chicken Sandwiches

(Ready in about 25 minutes | Servings 4)

Ingredients

2 tablespoons butter, at room temperature
1 pound whole chicken, skinless and boneless
2 garlic cloves, crushed
1 yellow onion, chopped
Sea salt and ground black pepper, to your liking
1 teaspoon cayenne pepper
4 hamburger buns
1 tablespoons mustard
1 large tomato, sliced
1 Lebanese cucumber, sliced
1 tablespoon fresh cilantro, chopped
2 tablespoons fresh green onions, chopped

Directions

Press the "Sauté" button to preheat your Instant Pot. Melt the butter and cook the chicken for 3 to 4 minutes or until slightly brown.

Add the garlic, onion, salt, black pepper, and cayenne pepper.

Secure the lid. Choose the "Poultry" mode and cook for 15 minutes at High pressure. Once cooking is complete, use a quick pressure release; carefully remove the lid.

Shred the chicken with two forks.

Spread the mustard on the bottom half of each hamburger bun. Top with the tomato, cumber, chicken, cilantro, and green onions; top with the remaining bun halves. Serve immediately.

Per serving: 452 Calories; 27.1g Fat; 25.2g Carbs; 26.1g Protein; 4.5g Sugars

59. Cholula Chicken Meatballs

(Ready in about 15 minutes | Servings 4)

Ingredients

4 tablespoons olive oil
1 carrot, finely chopped
1 celery stalk, finely chopped
1 shallot, minced
2 garlic cloves, minced
1 ½ pounds ground chicken
1 egg, beaten
1/2 cup buttermilk
1 teaspoon celery seeds
1/2 teaspoon mustard seeds
Sea salt and ground black pepper, to taste
1 cup fine panko crumbs
1 cup chicken broth
1/2 cup Cholula's hot sauce
1 tablespoon arrowroot powder

Directions

Press the "Sauté" button and heat 1 tablespoon of olive oil. Cook the carrot, celery, shallot, and garlic until tender and fragrant.

Stir in the ground chicken, egg, buttermilk, celery seeds, mustard seeds, salt, pepper, and panko crumbs. Mix to combine well and shape the chicken/vegetable mixture into 1-inch balls.

Heat 1 tablespoon of olive oil and sear the meatballs until golden brown on all sides.

Add 2 tablespoons of olive oil, chicken broth, Cholula's hot sauce, and arrowroot to the inner pot; stir to combine. Fold in the prepared meatballs.

Secure the lid. Choose the "Poultry" mode and cook for 5 minutes at High pressure. Once cooking is complete, use a quick pressure release; carefully remove the lid. Serve warm.

Per serving: 532 Calories; 30.7g Fat; 26.5g Carbs; 37.6g Protein; 4.6g Sugars

60. Favorite BBQ Meatloaf

(Ready in about 45 minutes | Servings 5)

Ingredients

2 tablespoons olive oil
1 tablespoon Worcestershire sauce
1 pound ground chicken
1/2 pound ground beef
1/2 cup crackers, crushed
1/4 cup Parmesan cheese, grated
1 medium carrot, grated
2 sweet peppers, deseeded and chopped
1 chili pepper, deseeded and finely chopped
1 onion, finely chopped
2 garlic cloves, minced
1 egg, beaten
1/2 cup BBQ sauce
Smoked salt flakes and freshly ground black pepper, to taste

Directions

Place a steamer rack inside the inner pot; add 1/2 cup water. Cut 1 sheet of heavy-duty foil and brush with cooking spray.

In large mixing dish, thoroughly combine all ingredients until mixed well.

Shape the meat mixture into a loaf; place the meatloaf in the center of the foil. Wrap your meatloaf in the foil and lower onto the steamer rack.

Secure the lid. Choose the "Poultry" mode and cook for 30 minutes at High pressure. Once cooking is complete, use a quick pressure release; carefully remove the lid.

Then, transfer your meatloaf to a cutting board. Let it stand for 10 minutes before cutting and serving. To serve, brush with some extra BBQ sauce, if desired. Bon appétit!

Per serving: 450 Calories; 27.8g Fat; 15.6g Carbs; 34.2g Protein; 5.9g Sugars

61. The Best Thanksgiving Turkey Ever

(Ready in about 45 minutes | Servings 5)

Ingredients

3 tablespoons olive oil
1 teaspoon sage, chopped
1 teaspoon basil, chopped
1 teaspoon rosemary, chopped
Sea salt and freshly cracked black pepper, to taste
1 teaspoon paprika

2 pounds turkey breasts, boneless
1 splash dry white wine
1 cup chicken bone broth
1 tablespoon mustard
2 tablespoons half-and-half
1 tablespoon cornstarch, dissolved in 1 tablespoon of water

Directions

Mix the olive oil with the spices; brush the mixture all over the turkey breasts. Press the "Sauté" button to preheat your Instant Pot.

Add the turkey breasts, skin side down and cook until slightly brown on all sides. Add a splash of wine to deglaze the pot.

Pour the chicken bone broth into the inner pot. Add the mustard and half-and-half.

Secure the lid. Choose the "Poultry" mode and cook for 30 minutes at High pressure. Once cooking is complete, use a natural pressure release; carefully remove the lid.

Afterwards, place the turkey breast under the broiler until the outside is crisp.

Meanwhile, press the "Sauté" button to preheat your Instant Pot again; add the cornstarch slurry and whisk to combine well. Let it cook until the sauce is slightly thickened. Slice the turkey breasts and serve with the pan juices. Enjoy!

Per serving: 449 Calories; 24.4g Fat; 3.7g Carbs; 50.6g Protein; 0.8g Sugars

62. Herbed Turkey Meatloaf

(Ready in about 40 minutes | Servings 5)

Ingredients

1 tablespoon olive oil
1 shallot, minced
1 ½ pounds ground turkey
1/2 cup Romano cheese, grated
1/3 cup fine breadcrumbs
1 egg, whisked
Sea salt and ground black pepper, to taste

1 tablespoon garlic and herb seasoning blend
1/2 cup ketchup
1 teaspoon molasses
1 teaspoon Dijon mustard
1 tablespoon soy sauce

Directions

Press the "Sauté" button to preheat your Instant Pot. Heat the oil and sauté the shallot until tender and aromatic.

Add the ground turkey, cheese, breadcrumbs, egg, salt, pepper, and herb seasoning blend. Shape the mixture into a meatloaf and wrap it into a piece of foil.

Mix the ketchup, molasses, mustard and soy sauce in a small bowl. Pour the mixture on top of the meatloaf, spreading it into an even layer.

Place a steamer rack and 1/2 cup of water inside the inner pot. Lower your meatloaf onto the steamer rack.

Secure the lid. Choose the "Poultry" mode and cook for 30 minutes at High pressure. Once cooking is complete, use a quick pressure release; carefully remove the lid.

Let your meatloaf stand for 10 minutes before cutting and serving. Bon appétit!

Per serving: 365 Calories; 19.8g Fat; 14.6g Carbs; 33.3g Protein; 9.1g Sugars

63. Turkey Breasts with Bacon and Gravy

(Ready in about 35 minutes | Servings 4)

Ingredients

1 tablespoon butter, melted
1 ½ pounds turkey breasts, boneless and skinless
4 rashers smoked bacon
2 garlic cloves, minced
1 teaspoon onion powder
Salt, to taste

1/2 teaspoon mixed peppercorns, crushed
2 sweet peppers, sliced
1 cup cherry wine
1 cup chicken stock
1 tablespoon arrowroot powder

Directions

Press the "Sauté" button to preheat your Instant Pot. Melt the butter and cook the turkey breasts for 4 to 6 minutes until golden brown on both sides.

Top with the bacon; add the garlic, onion powder, salt, and crushed peppercorns. Add the sweet peppers.

Pour in the wine and chicken stock and secure the lid.

Choose the "Manual" mode and cook for 25 minutes at High pressure. Once cooking is complete, use a quick pressure release; carefully remove the lid.

Press the "Sauté" button again and thicken the pan juices with the arrowroot powder. Spoon the gravy over the turkey breasts and serve immediately. Bon appétit!

Per serving: 392 Calories; 16.3g Fat; 14.4g Carbs; 45.9g Protein; 4.9g Sugars

64. Turkey and Barley Tabbouleh

(Ready in about 20 minutes | Servings 4)

Ingredients

1 pound turkey breast fillet, slice into bite-sized pieces
1 cup pearl barley
1 bay leaf
2 carrots, trimmed and thinly sliced
2 ½ cups vegetable broth
1 bunch spring onions, thinly sliced
1 medium cucumber, sliced

2 medium vine-ripened tomatoes, sliced
1 garlic clove, crushed
1 tablespoon harissa paste
2 limes, freshly squeezed
4 tablespoons extra-virgin olive oil
1/4 teaspoon freshly ground black pepper
Pink salt, to taste

Directions

Add the turkey breast fillets, barley, bay leaf, carrots, and vegetable broth to the inner pot.

Secure the lid. Choose the "Manual" mode and cook for 9 minutes at High pressure. Once cooking is complete, use a quick pressure release; carefully remove the lid.

Drain, chill and transfer to a serving bowl. Add the spring onions, cucumber, tomatoes, and garlic to the bowl.

In a small mixing dish, thoroughly combine the remaining ingredients. Drizzle this dressing over your salad and serve immediately. Bon appétit!

Per serving: 426 Calories; 14.5g Fat; 43.6g Carbs; 30.1g Protein; 2.4g Sugars

65. Greek-Style Turkey Salad

(Ready in about 25 minutes + chilling time | Servings 4)

Ingredients

1 pound turkey breast, skinless and boneless, slice into bite-sized pieces
1 cup chicken bone broth
1 red onion
2 sweet peppers, deseeded and thinly sliced
1 serrano pepper, deseeded and thinly sliced
1 tablespoon mustard

1 tablespoon fresh lime juice
1 tablespoon champagne vinegar
1/4 cup extra-virgin olive oil
1/2 teaspoon dried dill
1/2 teaspoon dried oregano
Sea salt and ground black pepper, to taste
1 cup feta cheese, cubed
1/2 cup Kalamata olives, pitted and sliced

Directions

Place the turkey breasts in the inner pot; pour in the chicken bone broth.

Secure the lid. Choose the "Manual" mode and cook for 12 minutes at High pressure. Once cooking is complete, use a quick pressure release; carefully remove the lid. Transfer to a big tray and allow it to cool.

Place the chilled turkey breast in a serving bowl. Add the red onion and peppers. In a small dish, whisk the mustard, lime juice, vinegar, olive oil, dill, oregano, salt, and black pepper.

Dress the salad and serve topped with feta cheese and Kalamata olives. Serve well chilled and enjoy!

Per serving: 473 Calories; 32.2g Fat; 13.2g Carbs; 33.1g Protein; 3.5g Sugars

66. Copycat Panera Turkey Sandwich

(Ready in about 35 minutes | Servings 4)

Ingredients

1 ½ pounds turkey breast
1 clove garlic
Salt and ground black pepper, to taste
1 teaspoon thyme
1 teaspoon marjoram
1 teaspoon basil

2 tablespoons butter, at room temperature
1 cup vegetable broth
8 slices walnut bread
2 tablespoons Dijon mustard
8 lettuce leaves
4 (1-ounce) slices white cheddar cheese

Directions

Place the turkey breasts, garlic, salt, black pepper, thyme, marjoram, basil, and butter in the inner pot; pour in the vegetable broth.

Secure the lid. Choose the "Manual" mode and cook for 25 minutes at High pressure. Once cooking is complete, use a natural pressure release; carefully remove the lid.

Spread the mustard on 4 slices of bread. Layer the slices of bread with the turkey, lettuce, and cheese.

Place remaining 4 slices of bread on top of the sandwiches and serve immediately.

Per serving: 560 Calories; 29.1g Fat; 22.5g Carbs; 49g Protein; 3.1g Sugars

67. Turkey with Peppers and Gravy

(Ready in about 35 minutes | Servings 6)

Ingredients

2 ½ pounds turkey breasts
2 bell peppers, deseeded and chopped
1 serrano pepper, deseeded and chopped
2 garlic cloves, minced
1 cup turkey stock
3 tablespoons olive oil
2 thyme sprigs

1 teaspoon dried sage
1/2 teaspoon dried dill
Sea salt and ground black pepper, to taste
2 tablespoons butter
1 tablespoon flour
1/4 cup dry white wine
Sea salt and ground black pepper, to taste

Directions

Add the turkey, peppers, garlic, turkey stock, olive oil, thyme, sage, dried dill, salt, and black pepper to the inner pot.

Secure the lid. Choose the "Manual" mode and cook for 25 minutes at High pressure. Once cooking is complete, use a natural pressure release; carefully remove the lid.

Press the "Sauté" button again and melt the butter. Now, add the flour, wine, salt, and pepper; let it cook until the sauce has thickened.

Spoon the gravy over the turkey breasts and serve warm. Bon appétit!

Per serving: 458 Calories; 26.1g Fat; 4.1g Carbs; 49g Protein; 1.3g Sugars

68. Cheese Stuffed Turkey Meatballs in Sauce

(Ready in about 15 minutes | Servings 4)

Ingredients

2 slices bacon, chopped
1 pound ground turkey
1/2 pound ground beef
1 shallot, finely minced
1 bell pepper, deseeded and finely minced
2 garlic cloves, minced
1 cup crushed saltines
Sea salt and freshly cracked black pepper, to taste

1 teaspoon dried basil
1 teaspoon dried rosemary
1 teaspoon dried parsley flakes
1/2 cup buttermilk
4 ounces Fontina cheese, cut into 16 pieces
1 teaspoon mustard
1 cup marinara sauce

Directions

Press the "Sauté" button to preheat your Instant Pot. Cook the chopped bacon until crisp; reserve. Cook the ground turkey, beef, shallot, pepper, and garlic until the meat is no longer pink.

Add the crushed saltines, salt, black pepper, basil, rosemary, parsley, and buttermilk. Stir in the reserved bacon. Shape the meat mixture into 16 meatballs. Insert 1 cube of Fontina cheese into the center of each meatball.

Add the mustard and marinara sauce to the inner pot; stir to combine and fold in the meatballs.

Secure the lid. Choose the "Poultry" mode and cook for 5 minutes at High pressure. Once cooking is complete, use a quick pressure release; carefully remove the lid. Serve warm.

Per serving: 485 Calories; 23.3g Fat; 14.7g Carbs; 54.1g Protein; 6.4g Sugars

69. Caribbean-Style Saucy Turkey Drumsticks

(Ready in about 30 minutes | Servings 5)

Ingredients

2 pounds turkey drumsticks, boneless
1 (12-ounce) bottle beer
2 carrots, sliced
1 medium-sized leek, sliced
2 garlic cloves, sliced

1/2 teaspoon ground allspice
2 sprigs rosemary, chopped
2 bay leaves
Sea salt and freshly ground black pepper, to taste

Directions

Add all ingredients to the inner pot.

Secure the lid. Choose the "Manual" mode and cook for 20 minutes at High pressure. Once cooking is complete, use a natural pressure release; carefully remove the lid.

You can thicken the pan juices if desired. Enjoy!

Per serving: 394 Calories; 17.3g Fat; 3.7g Carbs; 50.1g Protein; 0.7g Sugars

70. Turkey with Harvest Vegetable Bowl

(Ready in about 30 minutes | Servings 6)

Ingredients

3 pounds whole turkey breasts
1 cup cream of celery soup
1 celery stalk, cut into bite-sized chunks
2 medium carrots, cut into bite-sized chunks

2 bell pepper, cut into bite-sized chunks
1 onion, quartered
4 cloves garlic, halved
1/4 cup tomato paste
1 tablespoon Italian spice blend
1 tablespoon arrowroot powder

Directions

Place the turkey breasts and cream of celery soup in the inner pot.

Secure the lid. Choose the "Manual" mode and cook for 20 minutes at High pressure. Once cooking is complete, use a natural pressure release; carefully remove the lid.

Add the vegetables and tomato paste; sprinkle with the Italian spice blend.

Secure the lid. Choose the "Manual" mode and cook for 3 minutes at High pressure. Once cooking is complete, use a quick pressure release; carefully remove the lid.

Transfer the turkey and vegetables to a serving bowl.

Press the "Sauté" button; add the arrowroot powder and cook until the cooking liquid is reduced by about half. Bon appétit!

Per serving: 391 Calories; 5.9g Fat; 11.2g Carbs; 69.9g Protein; 3.9g Sugars

71. Spring Turkey Salad with Apples

(Ready in about 20 minutes + chilling time | Servings 4)

Ingredients

1 ½ pounds turkey breasts, boneless and skinless
1 cup water
2 celery stalks, diced
1 apple, cored and diced
1/2 cup spring onions, chopped
1 head butterhead lettuce, shredded

1/2 cup cream cheese
1 cup mayonnaise
1 tablespoon fresh lemon juice
1 teaspoon sage
Kosher salt and white pepper, to taste

Directions

Place the turkey breasts and water in the inner pot.

Secure the lid. Choose the "Manual" mode and cook for 9 minutes at High pressure. Once cooking is complete, use a natural pressure release; carefully remove the lid.

Add the remaining ingredients; gently stir to combine. Serve well chilled and enjoy!

Per serving: 391 Calories; 5.9g Fat; 11.2g Carbs; 69.9g Protein; 3.9g Sugars

72. Honey-Glazed Turkey Thighs

(Ready in about 25 minutes | Servings 4)

Ingredients

2 pounds turkey thighs
Sea salt and freshly ground black pepper, to taste
1 teaspoon red pepper flakes
1 teaspoon dried parsley flakes
4 tablespoons olive oil

1 orange, sliced
1/2 cup water
1/2 cup turkey stock
4 tablespoons honey
2 tablespoons all-purpose flour

Directions

Rub the salt, black pepper, red pepper, and parsley flakes all over the turkey thighs.

Press the "Sauté" button and heat the olive oil. Sear the turkey thighs for 3 minutes per side. Then, add the orange, water, stock, and honey.

Secure the lid. Choose the "Manual" mode and cook for 15 minutes at High pressure. Once cooking is complete, use a quick pressure release; carefully remove the lid.

Then, add the flour to thicken the cooking liquid. Spoon the sauce over the turkey thighs and serve warm. Bon appétit!

Per serving: 479 Calories; 25g Fat; 20.5g Carbs; 41.7g Protein; 17.2g Sugars

73. Herbed Mayonnaise Roast Turkey

(Ready in about 35 minutes | Servings 8)

Ingredients

3 pounds turkey breasts
4 garlic cloves, smashed
2 thyme sprigs
2 rosemary sprigs
1 cup mayonnaise

2 teaspoons coarse salt
1 teaspoon mixed peppercorns, crushed
2 tablespoons ghee, softened
1 lemon, sliced

Directions

Pat the turkey dry. In a mixing dish, thoroughly combine the garlic, thyme, rosemary, mayonnaise, salt, peppercorns, and ghee.

Rub the mayonnaise mixture all over the turkey breasts.

Add a steamer rack and 1/2 cup of water to the bottom of your Instant Pot. Throw in the lemon slices.

Secure the lid. Choose the "Manual" mode and cook for 20 minutes at High pressure. Once cooking is complete, use a natural pressure release; carefully remove the lid.

Let your turkey stand for 5 to 10 minutes before slicing and serving. Bon appétit!

Per serving: 393 Calories; 25g Fat; 1.9g Carbs; 39.2g Protein; 0.4g Sugars

74. Ground Turkey and Cabbage Casserole

(Ready in about 20 minutes | Servings 4)

Ingredients

1 tablespoon lard
1 ½ pounds ground turkey
1 (1 ½-pound) head of cabbage, shredded
2 ripe tomatoes, pureed
1 sweet pepper, sliced
1 red chili pepper, minced

1 yellow onion, chopped
3 garlic cloves, smashed
2 tablespoons fresh parsley, roughly chopped
1 bay leaf
Salt and ground black pepper, to taste

Directions

Press the "Sauté" button and melt the lard. Now, brown the ground turkey until no longer pink, about 3 minutes.

Add the remaining ingredients and secure the lid.

Secure the lid. Choose the "Manual" mode and cook for 10 minutes at High pressure. Once cooking is complete, use a natural pressure release; carefully remove the lid.

Divide between individual bowls and serve warm. Enjoy!

Per serving: 385 Calories; 19.1g Fat; 19g Carbs; 37.1g Protein; 8.6g Sugars

75. Turkey Meatball Sliders

(Ready in about 15 minutes | Servings 4)

Ingredients

Meatballs:
1 pound ground turkey
1/2 cup seasoned breadcrumbs
2 tablespoons fresh cilantro, chopped
1 egg, whisked
2 cloves garlic, minced
Sea salt, to taste
1/2 teaspoon freshly cracked black pepper

Sauce:
1 tablespoon butter, at room temperature
2 cloves garlic, minced
1 cup tomatoes puree
1 onion, minced
1/4 cup fresh basil, chopped
Salt, to taste
1 teaspoon hot sauce
Meatball Sliders:
1/2 cup mozzarella, shredded
8 honey wheat slider buns, toasted

Directions

Mix all ingredients for the meatballs until everything is well incorporated; form the mixture into small balls.

Spritz the sides and bottom of the inner pot with cooking spray. Press the "Sauté" button and cook your meatball until they are golden brown on all sides.

Add all ingredients for the sauce to the inner pot. Fold in the meatballs.

Secure the lid. Choose the "Poultry" mode and cook for 5 minutes at High pressure. Once cooking is complete, use a quick pressure release; carefully remove the lid. Serve warm.

Preheat your oven to broil.

To assemble the slider, place 1 meatball and a spoonful of sauce on the bottom of each bun. Top with mozzarella. Place under the broiler and bake until the cheese has melted about 2 minutes.

Top with another bun half and serve immediately. Bon appétit!

Per serving: 502 Calories; 15.8g Fat; 52.9g Carbs; 37.3g Protein; 5.5g Sugars

76. Thai Red Duck

(Ready in about 50 minutes | Servings 4)

Ingredients

1 tablespoon Thai red curry paste
Zest and juice of 1 fresh lime
2 pounds duck breast
1 tablespoon olive oil
1/2 teaspoon black peppercorns, crushed
1 teaspoon cayenne pepper
1 teaspoon sea salt

4 garlic cloves, minced
2 thyme sprigs, chopped
2 rosemary sprigs, chopped
1 cup light coconut milk
1/2 cup chicken broth, preferably homemade
1/4 small pack coriander, roughly chopped

Directions

Combine the red curry paste with the lime zest and juice; rub the mixture all over the duck breast and leave it to marinate for 30 minutes.

Press the "Sauté" button and heat the oil until sizzling. Cook the duck breast until slightly brown on both sides.

Then, season the duck breasts with the peppercorns, cayenne pepper, and salt. Add the garlic, thyme, rosemary, coconut milk, and chicken broth.

Secure the lid. Choose the "Poultry" mode and cook for 15 minutes at High pressure. Once cooking is complete, use a quick pressure release; carefully remove the lid.

Garnish with chopped coriander and serve warm. Bon appétit!

Per serving: 467 Calories; 27.8g Fat; 6.8g Carbs; 47.6g Protein; 2.5g Sugars

77. Duck with Sticky Cranberry Sauce

(Ready in about 35 minutes | Servings 6)

Ingredients

3 pounds whole duck	2 cloves garlic, minced
Kosher salt, to taste	1 cup chicken stock
1/2 teaspoon freshly ground black pepper	1 tablespoon butter
1/2 teaspoon red pepper flakes	1/2 cup cranberries, halved
1/2 teaspoon smoked paprika	1 tablespoon brown sugar
1 teaspoon onion powder	1/4 cup raspberry vinegar
	1 teaspoon wholegrain mustard

Directions

Press the "Sauté" button and melt the butter; place the duck skin-side down in the inner pot and sear until the skin is crisp and brown. Turn and cook the other side for about 4 minutes.

Pour away all but a tablespoon of the fat. Add the salt, black pepper, red pepper, paprika, onion powder, garlic, and chicken stock to the inner pot.

Secure the lid. Choose the "Manual" mode and cook for 25 minutes at High pressure. Once cooking is complete, use a natural pressure release; carefully remove the lid.

Now, remove the duck from the inner pot.

Press the "Sauté" button and add the remaining ingredients to the cooking liquid.

Continue to cook for 5 to 6 minutes, until the cranberries start to slightly break down and soften. Spoon over the reserved duck and serve immediately. Bon appétit!

Per serving: 517 Calories; 36.7g Fat; 3.3g Carbs; 40.6g Protein; 1.7g Sugars

78. Asian Ginger-Glazed Duck Breast

(Ready in about 25 minutes | Servings 4)

Ingredients

1 teaspoon sesame oil	Kosher salt and ground black pepper, to taste
2 pounds duck breasts	Ginger Glaze:
1 teaspoon red pepper flakes	1 tablespoon peanut oil
Sea salt and freshly ground black pepper, to taste	1-inch piece ginger, finely chopped
1 teaspoon dry mustard	3 cloves garlic, finely chopped
1 tablespoon paprika	1 tablespoon Sriracha sauce
1 teaspoon ground star anise	1/4 cup low-sodium soy sauce
1 teaspoon ground ginger	1/4 cup honey
1 cup chicken broth	

Directions

Press the "Sauté" button to preheat your Instant Pot.

Heat the sesame seed oil and sear the duck breasts for 5 minutes, stirring periodically. Sprinkle your spices all over the duck breasts. Add the chicken broth.

Secure the lid and choose the "Poultry" mode. Cook for 15 minutes. Afterwards, use a quick release and carefully remove the lid. Remove the duck breasts from the inner pot.

After that, stir in the other ingredients for the ginger glaze; stir well to combine.

Press the "Sauté" button to preheat your Instant Pot. Cook until thoroughly heated. Place the duck breasts in the serving plates and brush with the ginger glaze. Serve warm and enjoy!

Per serving: 411 Calories; 14.5g Fat; 22.1g Carbs; 47.6g Protein; 18.5g Sugars

79. Xiang Su Ya (Szechuan Duck)

(Ready in about 35 minutes | Servings 6)

Ingredients

2 tablespoons Szechuan peppercorns	2 star anise
1 teaspoon Chinese 5-spice powder	1/4 cup soy sauce
2 tablespoons salt	1/4 cup Shaoxing rice wine
3 pounds whole duck	1 red chili pepper, chopped
4 cloves garlic, sliced	1 tablespoon dark brown sugar
	1 cup water

Directions

Press the "Sauté" button to preheat your Instant Pot. Then, add the Szechuan peppercorn to the inner pot and roast until really fragrant. Remove it to a spice grinder and ground into a powder.

Add the Chinese 5-spice powder and salt. Rub the duck with the spice mixture. Leave it to marinate overnight.

Press the "Sauté" button to preheat your Instant Pot. Now, place the duck skin-side down in the inner pot and sear until the skin is crisp and brown. Turn and cook the other side for 4 to 5 minutes.

Stir in the other ingredients.

Secure the lid and choose the "Manual" mode. Cook for 25 minutes at High pressure. Afterwards, use a quick release and carefully remove the lid. Serve warm.

Per serving: 525 Calories; 37.2g Fat; 4.5g Carbs; 40.5g Protein; 2.9g Sugars

80. Braised Duck with Mixed Vegetables

(Ready in about 30 minutes | Servings 4)

Ingredients

2 pounds whole duck	1 green bell pepper, deseeded and sliced
1 cup chicken stock	2 carrots, sliced
Kosher salt and ground black pepper, to taste	1 celery stalk, sliced
1 teaspoon smoked paprika	4 cloves garlic, sliced
1 bay leaf	2 rosemary sprigs
1 tablespoon butter, melted	1 thyme sprig
1 onion, quartered	2 tablespoons balsamic vinegar
1 red bell pepper, deseeded and sliced	2 tablespoons Worcestershire sauce

Directions

Press the "Sauté" button to preheat your Instant Pot. Now, place the duck skin-side down in the inner pot and sear until the skin is crisp and brown. Turn and cook the other side for 4 to 5 minutes.

Add the chicken stock, salt, black pepper, smoked paprika, and bay leaf to the inner pot.

Secure the lid and choose the "Manual" mode. Cook for 20 minutes at High pressure. Afterwards, use a quick release and carefully remove the lid.

Add the remaining ingredients in the order listed above.

Secure the lid. Choose the "Manual" mode and cook for 3 minutes at High pressure. Once cooking is complete, use a quick pressure release; carefully remove the lid. Serve immediately.

Per serving: 554 Calories; 38g Fat; 9.3g Carbs; 41.9g Protein; 5.2g Sugars

81. Aromatic Duck Salad

(Ready in about 25 minutes | Servings 6)

Ingredients

3 pounds duck breasts
1 cup water
Salt and black pepper, to taste
2 heads romaine lettuce, torn into small pieces
2 tomatoes, diced

2 red onions, sliced diagonally
2 tablespoons balsamic vinegar
1 garlic clove, minced
1 teaspoon fresh ginger, grated
2 tablespoons tamari sauce
2 tablespoons peanut butter

Directions

Put the duck breasts and water into the inner pot.

Secure the lid and choose the "Poultry" mode. Cook for 15 minutes at High pressure. Afterwards, use a quick release and carefully remove the lid.

Now, slice the meat into strips and place in a salad bowl. Season with salt and pepper. Add the romaine lettuce, tomatoes, and onion.

In a small mixing dish, whisk the balsamic vinegar, garlic, ginger, tamari sauce, and peanut butter. Dress the salad and serve well chilled. Bon appétit!

Per serving: 349 Calories; 11.3g Fat; 12.3g Carbs; 48.6g Protein; 6.3g Sugars

82. Duck with Hoisin Sauce

(Ready in about 40 minutes | Servings 6)

Ingredients

3 pounds whole duck
Salt and ground black pepper, to your liking
1 cup roasted vegetable broth
2 carrots, chopped
1 head broccoli, chopped into florets

1 leek, white part only, chopped
1 small bunch of fresh coriander stalks, roughly chopped
2 cloves garlic, sliced
1 bay leaf
1/2 cup Hoisin sauce
1 lemon, cut into wedges

Directions

Press the "Sauté" button to preheat your Instant Pot.

Now, cook the duck for 4 to 5 minutes or until the skin turns golden brown. Pour in the roasted vegetable broth.

Secure the lid and choose the "Manual" mode. Cook for 25 minutes at High pressure. Afterwards, use a quick release and carefully remove the lid.

Add the vegetables, coriander, garlic, and bay leaf.

Secure the lid. Choose the "Manual" mode and cook for 3 minutes at High pressure. Once cooking is complete, use a quick pressure release; carefully remove the lid.

Remove the duck to a chopping board and rest for 5 minutes before cutting and serving.

Lastly, slice the duck and serve with the braised vegetables, Hoisin sauce, and lemon wedges. Bon appétit!

Per serving: 385 Calories; 14.6g Fat; 17.5g Carbs; 43.8g Protein; 8.1g Sugars

83. Japanese Duck and Rice Bowl

(Ready in about 20 minutes + marinating time | Servings 4)

Ingredients

2 pounds duck breasts, skinless and boneless
2 tablespoons orange juice
2 tablespoons Mirin
2 tablespoons tamari
1 tablespoon sesame oil
1 cup vegetable broth
2 garlic cloves, grated
1 teaspoon honey
Sea salt and freshly ground pepper, to taste
1 shallot, chopped

1/4 cup loosely packed fresh parsley leaves, roughly chopped
1 fresh lemon, juiced
2 tablespoons extra-virgin oil
1 cup Chinese cabbage, shredded
2 tablespoons sesame seeds, toasted
1 red chili, finely chopped
2 cups cooked rice
1 tablespoon olive oil
4 eggs

Directions

Place the duck breasts, orange juice, Mirin, and tamari sauce in a ceramic dish. Let it marinate for 1 hour in your refrigerator.

Press the "Sauté" button and heat the oil until sizzling. Cook the duck for about 5 minutes or until it is no longer pink.

Add the vegetable broth and secure the lid.

Choose the "Manual" mode and cook for 10 minutes at High pressure. Once cooking is complete, use a quick pressure release; carefully remove the lid.

Slice the duck and transfer to a nice serving bowl. Add the garlic, honey, salt, black pepper, shallot, fresh parsley, lemon, oil, cabbage, sesame seeds, chili pepper, and cooked rice.

Heat the olive oil in a skillet over medium-high flame. Fry the eggs until the whites are completely set. Place the fried eggs on the top and serve immediately.

Per serving: 631 Calories; 31.2g Fat; 28.8g Carbs; 56.6g Protein; 3.6g Sugars

84. Duck with Balsamic Cherry Sauce

(Ready in about 30 minutes | Servings 5)

Ingredients

2 pounds whole duck
1/2 teaspoon curry paste
Salt and ground black pepper, to taste
1 onion, finely chopped
2 garlic cloves, minced

6 ounces canned red tart cherries
1 tablespoon lemon rind, grated
2 tablespoons dry white wine
2 tablespoons balsamic vinegar
1 cup vegetable broth

Directions

Place all ingredients in the inner pot.

Secure the lid. Choose the "Manual" mode and cook for 20 minutes at High pressure. Once cooking is complete, use a quick pressure release; carefully remove the lid.

Remove the duck from the inner pot.

Press the "Sauté" button and cook the cooking liquid until it is reduced by about half. Bon appétit!

Per serving: 454 Calories; 28.2g Fat; 14.6g Carbs; 34.1g Protein; 7.5g Sugars

85. Father's Day Duck Ragù

(Ready in about 30 minutes | Servings 4)

Ingredients

1 pound fettuccine
1 pound duck legs
2 cloves garlic, crushed
1 onion, chopped
1 red chili pepper, minced
2 sweet peppers, deseeded and finely chopped

Sea salt and freshly ground black pepper, to taste
1/2 cup tomato purée
1/2 cup chicken bone broth
2 tablespoons dry cooking wine

Directions

Bring a pot of salted water to a boil. Cook the fettuccine, stirring occasionally, until al dente. Drain, reserving 1 cup of the pasta water; set aside.

Add the reserved pasta water along with the duck legs to the Instant Pot.

Secure the lid. Choose the "Manual" mode and cook for 20 minutes at High pressure. Once cooking is complete, use a quick pressure release; carefully remove the lid.

Shred the meat with two forks. Add the meat back to the Instant Pot. Add the remaining ingredients and press the "Sauté" button.

Let it cook for 5 to 7 minutes more or until everything is heated through. Serve with the reserved pasta and enjoy!

Per serving: 496 Calories; 23.2g Fat; 26.1g Carbs; 45.5g Protein; 7.8g Sugars

86. Exotic Duck Masala

(Ready in about 35 minutes | Servings 6)

Ingredients

2 tablespoons butter, melted at room temperature
3 pounds duck thighs
Sea salt, to taste
1/4 teaspoon crushed black peppercorns, or more to taste
1 teaspoon ginger powder
1/2 teaspoon chili powder
1 tablespoon rosemary
1 tablespoon sage
1/2 teaspoon allspice berries, lightly crushed
2 garlic cloves, sliced
1/2 cup tomato paste
1/2 cup bone broth
1 tablespoon Garam masala
1 small bunch of fresh coriander, roughly chopped

Directions

Press the "Sauté" button and melt the butter. Now, cook the duck thighs until golden brown on both sides. Add all seasonings.

Next, stir in the garlic, tomato paste, broth, and Garam masala.

Secure the lid. Choose the "Manual" mode and cook for 25 minutes at High pressure. Once cooking is complete, use a quick pressure release; carefully remove the lid.

Serve with fresh coriander. Enjoy!

Per serving: 539 Calories; 38.2g Fat; 5.2g Carbs; 45.1g Protein; 2.7g Sugars

87. Duck Breasts in Blood Orange Sauce

(Ready in about 35 minutes | Servings 4)

Ingredients

1 tablespoon olive oil
1 ½ pounds duck breast
2 blood oranges, juiced
Sea salt and ground black pepper, to taste
1/2 teaspoon cayenne pepper
1 teaspoon dried dill weed
1 cup chicken bone broth
1/2 cup dry white wine
2 tablespoons apricot jam
2 tablespoons potato starch

Directions

Press the "Sauté" button and heat the oil until sizzling. Then, cook the duck breasts for 4 minutes per side.

Add the oranges, salt, black pepper, cayenne pepper, dill, and broth.

Secure the lid. Choose the "Poultry" mode and cook for 15 minutes at High pressure. Once cooking is complete, use a quick pressure release; carefully remove the lid.

Remove the duck from the cooking liquid using a slotted spoon. Add the remaining ingredients to the cooking liquid and press the "Sauté" button again.

Let it simmer for 5 to 7 minutes or until slightly thickened. Spoon the sauce onto the duck and serve immediately. Bon appétit!

Per serving: 472 Calories; 14.2g Fat; 42.8g Carbs; 42.4g Protein; 9.7g Sugars

88. Chicken Wings with Sesame Coleslaw

(Ready in about 25 minutes | Servings 4)

Ingredients

2 teaspoons sesame oil
1 ½ pounds chicken wings, bone-in, skin-on
2 garlic cloves, minced
Sea salt and ground black pepper, to taste
1 teaspoon paprika
1 cup chicken bone broth
Sesame Cole Slaw:
1 cup white cabbage
1 red onion, thinly sliced
1 garlic clove, minced
1 ½ tablespoons sesame oil
1 tablespoon soy sauce
1 teaspoon honey
1 teaspoon mustard
1 tablespoon lemon juice, freshly squeezed
1 tablespoon toasted sesame seeds

Directions

Press the "Sauté" button to heat up your Instant Pot. Then, heat the 2 teaspoons of sesame oil and sear the chicken wings for 2 to 3 minutes per side.

Add a splash of chicken broth to scrape off any brown bits from the bottom of your Instant Pot.

Secure the lid. Choose the "Poultry" mode and High pressure; cook for 15 minutes. Once cooking is complete, use a natural pressure release; carefully remove the lid.

Meanwhile, mix all ingredients for the sesame coleslaw; place in your refrigerator until ready to serve. Serve with warm chicken wings. Bon appétit!

Per serving: 424 Calories; 28.3g Fat; 7.7g Carbs; 34.3g Protein; 3.9g Sugars

89. The Best Turkey Beer Chili

(Ready in about 25 minutes | Servings 4)

Ingredients

1 tablespoon olive oil
2 garlic cloves, finely minced
1/2 cup shallots, finely chopped
1 carrot, sliced
1 bell pepper, chopped
1 jalapeño pepper, chopped
1 pound ground turkey
1 cup chicken bone broth
6 ounces beer
1 tablespoon cacao powder
1 tablespoon apple butter
1 teaspoon dried basil
1 (14-ounce) can tomatoes
1 (14-ounce) can kidney beans, drained and rinsed

Directions

Press the "Sauté" button to heat up your Instant Pot. Then, heat the oil; cook the garlic, shallot, carrot, and bell peppers for about 5 minutes.

Stir in the ground turkey and cook for 3 minutes more, crumbling with a fork.

Secure the lid. Choose the "Poultry" setting and cook for 5 minutes under High pressure. Once cooking is complete, use a quick pressure release; carefully remove the lid. Serve hot and enjoy!

Per serving: 484 Calories; 29.3g Fat; 14.1g Carbs; 41.5g Protein; 4.4g Sugars

90. Spicy Chicken Lasagna

(Ready in about 20 minutes | Servings 6)

Ingredients

1 tablespoon olive oil
1 onion, chopped
1 serrano pepper, seeded and chopped
1 bell pepper, seeded and chopped
2 garlic cloves, minced
1 pound ground chicken
2 slices bacon, chopped
Sea salt and ground black pepper, to taste
1 (28-ounce) can tomatoes, crushed
1 cup chicken stock
8 ounces lasagna noodles
1 cup Pepper-Jack cheese, grated

Directions

Press the "Sauté" button to heat up your Instant Pot. Heat the oil until sizzling. Then, sauté the onion, peppers, and garlic about 5 minutes or until they are fragrant and tender.

Stir in the ground chicken; continue to cook an additional 3 minutes.

Stir in the bacon, salt, pepper, tomatoes, stock, and noodles.

Secure the lid. Choose the "Poultry" setting and cook for 10 minutes under High pressure. Once cooking is complete, use a quick pressure release; carefully remove the lid.

Top with the Pepper-Jack cheese and seal the lid. Let it sit in the residual heat until it is melted. Bon appétit!

Per serving: 335 Calories; 19.4g Fat; 17.6g Carbs; 23.8g Protein; 5.1g Sugars

91. Juicy Turkey Breasts with Apricot Sauce

(Ready in about 20 minutes | Servings 8)

Ingredients

2 teaspoons sesame oil
2 pounds turkey breasts, cubed
Sea salt and freshly ground black pepper, to taste
1 teaspoon red pepper flakes, crushed
1 teaspoon dried rosemary
1/2 teaspoon dried sage
1/3 cup Port wine

1/3 cup chicken stock, preferably homemade
For the Sauce:
1/3 cup all-natural apricot jam
1 ½ tablespoons rice vinegar
1 teaspoon fresh ginger root, minced
1/2 teaspoon chili powder
1/2 teaspoon soy sauce
3 teaspoons honey

Directions

Press the "Sauté" button and preheat your Instant Pot. Now, heat the oil; sear the turkey breasts, stirring occasionally, for 3 to 4 minutes.

Season the turkey breasts with salt, black pepper, red pepper flakes, rosemary, and sage.

Add Port wine and chicken stock to the Instant Pot and deglaze the bottom.

Return the turkey to the Instant Pot and secure the lid. Choose the "Manual" setting and High pressure. Cook for 10 minutes.

Once cooking is complete, use a natural release and carefully remove the lid. Transfer the turkey breasts to a platter.

Add the sauce ingredients to the Instant Pot. Cook until the sauce reaches the preferred consistency. Pour over the turkey and serve immediately. Bon appétit!

Per serving: 256 Calories; 10.2g Fat; 5.9g Carbs; 33.1g Protein; 5.2g Sugars

92. Mediterranean Chicken Drumsticks

(Ready in about 20 minutes | Servings 4)

Ingredients

1 pound chicken drumsticks
1 cup chicken stock
1 cup tomato puree
1 rosemary sprig, chopped
2 thyme sprigs, chopped
2 garlic cloves, minced

Sea salt and ground black pepper, to taste
1/2 teaspoon smoked paprika
1 bay leaf
1/2 cup Kalamata olives, pitted and sliced

Directions

Add all ingredients to the Instant Pot; gently stir to combine well.

Secure the lid. Choose the "Poultry" setting and cook for 15 minutes under High pressure. Once cooking is complete, use a quick pressure release; carefully remove the lid.

You can thicken the sauce on the "Sauté" setting for a couple of minutes if desired.

Divide the chicken drumsticks among serving plates. Top with the sauce and enjoy!

Per serving: 273 Calories; 14.4g Fat; 8.5g Carbs; 27.6g Protein; 3.6g Sugars

93. Turkey Fillets with Coconut-Mushroom Sauce

(Ready in about 30 minutes | Servings 6)

Ingredients

1 tablespoon olive oil
1 ½ pounds turkey fillets
A bunch of scallions, chopped
2 cups Crimini mushrooms, halved or quartered
2 cloves garlic, peeled and crushed
Sea salt and freshly ground black pepper, to taste

1/2 teaspoon brown yellow mustard
1/2 teaspoon turmeric powder
1 cup water
1 cup coconut cream
1 teaspoon fresh coriander, minced

Directions

Press the "Sauté" button to preheat your Instant Pot. Heat the oil and sear the turkey fillets for 2 to 3 minutes per side.

Stir in the scallion, mushrooms and garlic; sauté them for 2 minutes more or until they are tender and fragrant.

Next, add the salt, black pepper, mustard, turmeric powder, and water to the Instant Pot.

Secure the lid. Choose the "Meat/Stew" setting and cook for 20 minutes under High pressure. Once cooking is complete, use a quick pressure release; carefully remove the lid.

Then, fold in the coconut cream and seal the lid. Let it sit in the residual heat until everything is thoroughly warmed. Garnish with coriander. Bon appétit!

Per serving: 289 Calories; 18.3g Fat; 4.7g Carbs; 28g Protein; 0.6g Sugars

94. Easy Chicken Française

(Ready in about 15 minutes | Servings 6)

Ingredients

1 tablespoon butter, melted
2 pounds chicken wings, skin-on
2 garlic cloves, sliced
1 teaspoon mustard powder
1 teaspoon smoked paprika
Sea salt and ground black pepper, to taste

1/2 cup Pinot Grigio
1 cup tomato puree
1/2 cup water
1 cup cream cheese
1/2 lemon, cut into slices

Directions

Press the "Sauté" button to preheat the Instant Pot. Melt the butter and brown the chicken wings for 1 to 2 minutes on each side.

Stir in the garlic, mustard powder, paprika, salt, black pepper, Pinot Grigio, tomato puree, and water.

Secure the lid. Choose the "Manual" mode and High pressure; cook for 10 minutes. Once cooking is complete, use a natural pressure release; carefully remove the lid.

Serve with cream cheese and lemon slices. Bon appétit!

Per serving: 273 Calories; 14.1g Fat; 5.3g Carbs; 27.8g Protein; 2.9g Sugars

95. Classic Chicken Chasseur

(Ready in about 25 minutes | Servings 4)

Ingredients

1 tablespoon olive oil
4 chicken drumsticks, skinless and boneless
1 red onion, chopped
1 celery with leaves, chopped
1 carrot, trimmed and chopped
3 garlic cloves, minced
1 teaspoon dried thyme
1/2 pound brown mushrooms, sliced

2 cups water
2 chicken bouillon cubes
Salt and ground black pepper, to taste
1 teaspoon paprika
2 bay leaves
1 tablespoon flour
4 tablespoons dry vermouth

Directions

Press the "Sauté" button to preheat the Instant Pot. Now, heat the oil; cook the chicken until delicately browned on all sides; reserve.

Then, sauté the onion, celery and carrot in the pan drippings; sauté until tender or about 4 minutes.

Now, stir in the garlic, thyme, mushrooms, water, bouillon cubes, salt, black pepper, paprika, and bay leaves; stir to combine well. Add the reserved chicken.

Secure the lid. Choose the "Poultry" setting and cook for 15 minutes at High pressure. Once cooking is complete, use a natural pressure release; carefully remove the lid.

Add the flour and dry vermouth. Press the "Sauté" button again and let it simmer until the cooking liquid has reduced. Enjoy!

Per serving: 343 Calories; 21.1g Fat; 14.4g Carbs; 24.4g Protein; 7g Sugars

96. Dilled Turkey Thighs

(Ready in about 30 minutes | Servings 6)

Ingredients

2 tablespoons lard, melted
1 ½ pounds turkey thighs
Sea salt, to taste
1/2 teaspoon ground black pepper
1/2 teaspoon paprika
1 teaspoon dried dill weed
1 shallot, chopped
1 cup turkey bone broth
1 tablespoon maple syrup
1/2 cup dry white wine

Directions

Press the "Sauté" button to preheat the Instant Pot; melt the lard. Now, brown the turkey thighs for 4 to 5 minutes on each side.

Add the remaining ingredients.

Secure the lid. Choose the "Meat/Stew" setting and cook for 20 minutes. Once cooking is complete, use a natural pressure release; carefully remove the lid.

Press the "Sauté" button again to thicken the cooking liquid. Spoon the sauce over the turkey thighs and serve warm.

Per serving: 257 Calories; 13.3g Fat; 5.6g Carbs; 27.2g Protein; 3.8g Sugars

97. Saucy Chicken Legs with Crimini Mushrooms

(Ready in about 20 minutes | Servings 4)

Ingredients

2 teaspoons sesame oil
4 chicken legs, skinless, bone-in
Salt, to your liking
2 garlic cloves, crushed
2 tablespoons spring onion, chopped
1 cup brown mushrooms, chopped
2 tablespoons dry sherry
1 teaspoon dried rosemary
1 cup water
1 tablespoon chicken bouillon granules
1 teaspoon brown sugar
2 tablespoons Worcestershire sauce
2 tablespoons arrowroot powder
4 tablespoons cold water

Per serving: 384 Calories; 13.7g Fat; 10.5g Carbs; 51.8g Protein; 3.7g Sugars

Directions

Press the "Sauté" button to heat up your Instant Pot. Heat the oil; season the chicken with salt.

Brown the chicken in the hot oil on all sides; reserve. Cook the garlic, onion, and mushrooms in the pan drippings until they are tender and aromatic.

Add the dry sherry and deglaze the bottom of your Instant Pot with a wooden spoon.

Add the rosemary, water, chicken bouillon granules, brown sugar, and Worcestershire sauce. Return the reserved chicken to the Instant Pot.

Secure the lid. Choose the "Manual" setting and cook at High Pressure for 6 minutes. Once cooking is complete, use a natural release and carefully remove the lid.

Meanwhile, whisk the arrowroot powder with cold water. Add the slurry to the Instant Pot to thicken the cooking liquid. Press the "Sauté" button and cook until the sauce has thickened.

Spoon the sauce over the chicken and mushrooms and serve on individual plates. Enjoy!

98. Chicken Drumsticks with Aioli

(Ready in about 1 hour 15 minutes | Servings 4)

Ingredients

4 chicken drumsticks, bone-in, skin-on
2 teaspoons olive oil
1 tablespoon oyster sauce
1 cup water
1 tablespoon chicken bouillon granules
1/2 teaspoon freshly ground black pepper
1/2 cup dry white wine
3/4 cup mayonnaise
3 cloves garlic, minced
2 tablespoons lemon juice

Directions

Place the chicken, olive oil, oyster sauce, water, chicken bouillon granules, black pepper and wine in a ceramic bowl.

Allow it to marinate for 1 hour in your refrigerator. Add the chicken and marinade to the Instant Pot.

Secure the lid. Now, press the "Manual" button. Cook for 12 minutes under High pressure.

Once cooking is complete, use a natural pressure release; carefully remove the lid.

In the meantime, mix the mayonnaise with garlic and lemon juice until well combined. Serve the chicken drumsticks with the aioli on the side. Bon appétit!

Per serving: 441 Calories; 34.8g Fat; 3.4g Carbs; 27.1g Protein; 0.5g Sugars

99. Turkey Tacos with Pico de Gallo

(Ready in about 15 minutes | Servings 6)

Ingredients

2 pounds turkey breasts
1/2 cup turkey stock
2 garlic cloves, smashed
1/2 teaspoon seasoned salt
1/4 teaspoon ground black pepper
1/2 teaspoon crushed red pepper flakes
1/4 cup fresh cilantro leaves, chopped
6 corn tortillas, warmed
1 cup Pico de Gallo

Directions

Put the turkey breast into your Instant Pot. Now, pour in the stock.

Add the garlic, salt, black pepper, red pepper flakes, and cilantro leaves. Secure the lid. Choose the "Manual" setting and cook for 10 minutes at High pressure.

Once cooking is complete, use a natural release and carefully remove the lid. Shred the turkey breasts.

Serve the shredded turkey breasts over corn tortillas garnished with Pico de Gallo. Bon appétit!

Per serving: 323 Calories; 12g Fat; 15.2g Carbs; 37.1g Protein; 2.8g Sugars

100. Elegant Chicken Fillets with Apples

(Ready in about 20 minutes | Servings 4)

Ingredients

1 pound chicken fillets
Sea salt and ground black pepper, to taste
1/2 teaspoon smoked paprika
1/2 teaspoon ground bay leaf
1 teaspoon garlic powder
1 teaspoon shallot powder
1 tablespoon butter
1 tablespoon honey
1 tablespoon tamari sauce
2 cooking apples, cored, peeled and diced

Directions

Place the chicken fillets on the bottom of the Instant Pot. Sprinkle the seasonings over the chicken fillets.

Add the remaining ingredients.

Secure the lid. Choose the "Manual" setting and cook for 7 minutes under High pressure. Once cooking is complete, use a quick pressure release; carefully remove the lid.

Transfer to a serving platter and serve warm. Bon appétit!

Per serving: 341 Calories; 16.6g Fat; 19.1g Carbs; 28.9g Protein; 14.6g Sugars

101. Turkey and Arborio Rice Delight

(Ready in about 25 minutes | Servings 4)

Ingredients

1 tablespoon butter, melted
2 chicken breasts, cut into slices
2 slices bacon, chopped
1 onion, chopped
1 serrano pepper, chopped
2 cloves garlic, finely minced
1/2 cup dry white wine
1 (28-ounce) can diced tomatoes
1 ½ cups water
1 cup Arborio rice
Sea salt and ground black pepper, to taste
1/2 teaspoon dried rosemary
1 teaspoon dried oregano

Directions

Press the "Sauté" button to preheat your Instant Pot. Melt the butter. Then, sear the chicken breasts for 5 minutes. Set them aside.

Stir in the bacon, onion, serrano pepper, and garlic; cook until the vegetables are tender.

Stir in the remaining ingredients. Return the reserved chicken to the Instant Pot.

Secure the lid. Choose the "Poultry" setting and cook for 15 minutes under High pressure. Once cooking is complete, use a quick pressure release; carefully remove the lid. Bon appétit!

Per serving: 498 Calories; 21.2g Fat; 25.4g Carbs; 59g Protein; 7.1g Sugars

102. Ranch Chicken Drumettes

(Ready in about 25 minutes | Servings 6)

Ingredients

1 ½ pounds chicken drumettes
1 teaspoon celery salt
1/4 teaspoon freshly ground black pepper, or more to taste
1 ½ tablespoons butter, melted
1/4 cup tamari sauce
3 tablespoons brown sugar
2 tablespoons champagne vinegar
1 packet dry ranch salad dressing mix
1/2 cup onion, sliced
4 cloves garlic, smashed

Directions

Season the chicken drumettes with celery salt and black pepper. Press the "Sauté" button and warm the butter.

Now, sear the chicken pieces for 6 minutes or until browned on all sides.

Add the remaining ingredients in the order listed above. Secure the lid.

Choose the "Manual" setting and cook for 10 minutes at High pressure. Once cooking is complete, use a natural release and carefully remove the lid.

You can thicken the sauce on the "Sauté" mode. Serve over hot cooked pasta and enjoy!

Per serving: 189 Calories; 7.2g Fat; 6.3g Carbs; 23.5g Protein; 4.8g Sugars

103. Chicken Legs with Shallots and Port Wine

(Ready in about 25 minutes | Servings 4)

Ingredients

1 pound chicken legs, bone-in
1 cup tomato puree
1 cup vegetable broth
1/4 cup Port wine
2 shallots, cut into wedges
1 teaspoon fresh ginger, grated
2 cloves garlic, chopped
Salt and freshly ground black pepper, to taste
1 teaspoon dried oregano
1 teaspoon dried rosemary

Directions

Place the chicken legs in the Instant Pot. Pour in the tomato puree, vegetable broth, and Port wine.

Secure the lid. Choose the "Poultry" setting and cook for 15 minutes under High pressure. Once cooking is complete, use a quick pressure release; carefully remove the lid.

Stir in the remaining ingredients. Secure the lid. Choose the "Manual" setting and cook for 3 minutes under High pressure.

Once cooking is complete, use a quick pressure release; carefully remove the lid. Serve warm and enjoy!

Per serving: 308 Calories; 17.6g Fat; 12.9g Carbs; 24.4g Protein; 6.2g Sugars

104. Cheesy and Peppery Chicken Pottage

(Ready in about 15 minutes | Servings 4)

Ingredients

1 tablespoon olive oil
1 pound chicken fillets
2 cloves garlic, smashed
1 jalapeño pepper, seeded and chopped
1 white onion, chopped
1 red bell pepper, seeded and sliced
1 green bell pepper, seeded and sliced
1 orange bell pepper, seeded and sliced
1/2 teaspoon dried basil
1/2 teaspoon dried oregano
1 teaspoon dried sage
Kosher salt and ground black pepper, to taste
1 teaspoon cayenne pepper
1 cup roasted vegetable broth
1 cup heavy cream
1/2 cup cream cheese
1/2 cup Cheddar cheese, grated

Directions

Press the "Sauté" button to preheat your Instant Pot. Now, heat the oil and cook the chicken for 2 to 3 minutes per side.

Stir in the garlic, jalapeño pepper, onion, and peppers.

Add the seasonings and gently stir to combine. Pour in the roasted vegetable broth.

Secure the lid. Choose the "Poultry" setting and cook for 5 minutes at High pressure. Once cooking is complete, use a natural pressure release; carefully remove the lid.

Now, add the heavy cream, cream cheese and Cheddar cheese; press the "Sauté" button again and cook until the cheese is melted and everything is thoroughly heated. Serve immediately and enjoy!

Per serving: 463 Calories; 32.3g Fat; 11.1g Carbs; 32.6g Protein; 6.1g Sugars

105. Peasant Turkey Thigh Soup

(Ready in about 25 minutes | Servings 5)

Ingredients

1 tablespoon peanut oil
1 medium-sized leek, chopped
1/2 teaspoon ginger-garlic paste
1 (28-ounce) can diced tomatoes
1 celery stalk, chopped
1 carrot, chopped
1/2 teaspoon dried rosemary
2 bay leaves
Sea salt and ground black pepper
1/2 teaspoon cayenne pepper
1 pound turkey thighs
5 cups turkey bone broth
2 tablespoons fresh coriander, roughly chopped

Directions

Press the "Sauté" button to preheat your Instant Pot. Heat the peanut oil until sizzling. Cook the leek until tender.

Add the ginger-garlic paste, tomatoes, celery, carrot, rosemary, bay leaves, salt, black pepper, cayenne pepper, turkey thighs, and broth.

Secure the lid. Choose the "Soup" setting and cook for 20 minutes at High pressure. Once cooking is complete, use a quick pressure release; carefully remove the lid.

Remove the turkey thighs from the soup, shred the meat and discard the bones. After that, return the meat to the Instant Pot.

Divide among five soup bowls. Top each bowl with fresh coriander and serve immediately.

Per serving: 194 Calories; 7.9g Fat; 12.7g Carbs; 18.8g Protein; 7.4g Sugars

106. Southwestern Chicken Salad

(Ready in about 15 minutes | Servings 5)

Ingredients

2 chicken breasts, boneless and skinless
Seasoned salt and ground black pepper, to taste
1/2 teaspoon taco seasoning
1 sprig thyme
1 sprig rosemary
1 sprig sage
2 garlic cloves, pressed
1 cup green onions, sliced
1/2 cup sour cream
1/2 cup mayonnaise
1 teaspoon Dijon mustard
1 cup frozen corn, thawed
1 carrot, shredded
1 bell pepper, sliced
1/2 cup radishes, sliced
1 cucumber, chopped
2 tablespoons cilantro, chopped

Directions

Add 1 ½ cups of water and a metal trivet to your Instant Pot.

Then, season the chicken breast with salt, black pepper and taco seasoning. Place the seasoned chicken breast onto the trivet. Top with thyme, rosemary, sage, and garlic.

Now, secure the lid. Choose the "Poultry" setting and cook for 5 minutes under High pressure. Once cooking is complete, use a natural pressure release; carefully remove the lid.

Allow the chicken to cool and cut it into strips. Stir in the remaining ingredients; gently stir to combine well. Serve well-chilled.

Per serving: 441 Calories; 30.2g Fat; 14.1g Carbs; 27.1g Protein; 3.7g Sugars

107. Four-Cheese Italian Butter Chicken

(Ready in about 15 minutes | Servings 4)

Ingredients

2 tablespoons butter, softened
3 garlic cloves, minced
2 rosemary sprigs, leaves picked
2 ripe tomatoes, chopped
1/2 teaspoon cumin, ground
1 teaspoon paprika
1/2 teaspoon curry powder
Salt and ground black pepper, to taste
4 chicken fillets, boneless and skinless
Water
1/2 cup 4-Cheese Italian, shredded
1/4 cup fresh chives, chopped

Directions

Press the "Sauté" button to heat up your Instant Pot. Now, melt the butter.

Add the garlic and rosemary, and sauté until they are fragrant.

Now, stir in the chopped tomatoes, ground cumin, paprika, curry powder, salt, and black pepper. Top with the chicken fillets and pour in water to cover the chicken.

Secure the lid and select the "Poultry" mode. Cook for 6 minutes. Once cooking is complete, use a natural release and carefully remove the lid.

Press the "Sauté" button. Add the shredded cheese and cook 2 to 3 minutes more or until the cheese is melted. Serve right away garnished with fresh chopped chives. Bon appétit!

Per serving: 193 Calories; 12.5g Fat; 5g Carbs; 15.8g Protein; 2.3g Sugars

PORK

108. Boston Butt with Home-Style Sauce

(Ready in about 1 hour 5 minutes | Servings 8)

Ingredients

3 pounds Boston butt
1 teaspoon salt
1/2 teaspoon whole black peppercorns
1 bay leaf
1 teaspoon celery seeds
1 teaspoon fennel seeds
For the Sauce:

1 cup water
1 ½ cups ketchup
1/4 cup balsamic vinegar
4 tablespoons brown sugar
1 teaspoon shallot powder
1 teaspoon chipotle powder
1 tablespoon Worcestershire sauce

Directions

Season the Boston butt with salt and add it to your Instant Pot that is previously greased with a nonstick cooking spray.

Add enough water to cover the meat. Stir in the black peppercorns, bay leaf, celery seeds, and fennel seeds.

Secure the lid and select the "Manual" mode. Cook for 55 minutes at High pressure.

In the meantime, in a saucepan, place the remaining ingredients for the sauce. Bring this mixture to a boil, and then, immediately, reduce heat to medium-low.

Cook until it is thickened and heated through, stirring continuously.

Once cooking is complete, use a quick pressure release; remove the lid; reserve about 1 cup of cooking liquid. Shred the pork with two forks, add cooking liquid and stir to combine well.

Serve with the prepared sauce.

Per serving: 333 Calories; 8.6g Fat; 55.5g Carbs; 10.8g Protein; 27.1g Sugars

109. Vermouth Pork Shanks with Vegetables

(Ready in about 40 minutes | Servings 4)

Ingredients

2 teaspoons olive oil
1 pound pork shanks, trimmed of skin
1 teaspoon turmeric powder
2 tablespoons vermouth
1 carrot, sliced
1 celery stalk, chopped
1 parsnip, sliced
1 bell pepper, deveined and sliced

1 serrano pepper, deveined and sliced
Sea salt and ground black pepper, to taste
1 teaspoon red pepper flakes, crushed
1 teaspoon garlic powder
1 cup beef bone broth
2 bay leaves

Directions

Press the "Sauté" button to preheat your Instant Pot; heat the olive oil. Once hot, cook the pork shanks until they are delicately browned.

Stir in the remaining ingredients.

Secure the lid. Choose the "Meat/Stew" setting and cook at High pressure for 35 minutes. Once cooking is complete, use a natural pressure release; carefully remove the lid.

Serve warm over mashed potatoes and enjoy!

Per serving: 348 Calories; 25.1g Fat; 12.1g Carbs; 17.3g Protein; 4.5g Sugars

110. Herbed Pork Steaks

(Ready in about 15 minutes | Servings 6)

Ingredients

2 teaspoons lard
1 ½ pounds pork steaks
1 cup roasted vegetable broth
2 sprigs rosemary

1 sprig thyme
1 tablespoon fresh parsley
Salt, to taste
1/2 teaspoon mixed peppercorns

Directions

Press the "Sauté" button to preheat your Instant Pot; melt the lard. Once hot, sear the pork until delicately browned.

Stir in the remaining ingredients.

Secure the lid. Choose the "Manual" setting and cook at High pressure for 8 minutes. Once cooking is complete, use a quick pressure release; carefully remove the lid.

Press the "Sauté" button to thicken the sauce. Serve warm and enjoy!

Per serving: 476 Calories; 44.2g Fat; 0.1g Carbs; 21.2g Protein; 0.1g Sugars

111. Sticky Pork Ribs

(Ready in about 30 minutes | Servings 8)

Ingredients

2 pounds pork ribs
1/2 teaspoon ground black pepper
Sea salt, to taste
1 teaspoon garlic powder
1/2 teaspoon shallot powder
1 teaspoon paprika

1 cup tomato paste
1 (12-ounce) bottle light beer
1 tablespoon honey
1/2 cup beef bone broth
1 tablespoon ground cumin

Directions

Add all ingredients to your Instant Pot.

Secure the lid. Choose the "Meat/Stew" setting and cook at High pressure for 20 minutes. Once cooking is complete, use a natural pressure release; carefully remove the lid.

Serve over roasted potatoes and enjoy!

Per serving: 268 Calories; 8.9g Fat; 19.7g Carbs; 26.7g Protein; 15.1g Sugars

112. Family Pork Stew

(Ready in about 15 minutes | Servings 5)

Ingredients

2 teaspoons olive oil
1 pound pork stew meat, cubed
1 cup tomato paste
2 tablespoons fresh cilantro, chopped
2 tablespoons fresh parsley, chopped
1 leek, chopped

1 habanero pepper, deveined and minced
1 teaspoon ginger-garlic paste
1 teaspoon ground cumin
1 teaspoon paprika
Kosher salt and black pepper, to taste
5 cups beef bone broth
1 cup sour cream, for garnish

Directions

Press the "Sauté" button to preheat your Instant Pot; heat the oil. Now, sear the meat until it is delicately browned.

Add the tomato paste, cilantro, parsley, leek, habanero pepper, ginger-garlic paste, cumin, paprika, salt, black pepper, and broth.

Secure the lid. Choose the "Manual" setting and cook at High pressure for 8 minutes. Once cooking is complete, use a quick pressure release; carefully remove the lid.

Divide your stew among serving bowls; top each serving with sour cream. Enjoy!

Per serving: 279 Calories; 10.1g Fat; 18.1g Carbs; 30g Protein; 8.2g Sugars

113. Country-Style Spare Ribs

(Ready in about 30 minutes + marinating time | Servings 6)

Ingredients

1/4 cup honey
1/4 cup soy sauce
2 tablespoons hoisin sauce
1/4 cup tomato sauce
2 garlic cloves, smashed
1 teaspoon fresh ginger, finely grated
2 teaspoons sesame oil

6 country-style spare rib rashes
1 teaspoon chili powder
Salt and black pepper, to your liking
1/2 teaspoon ground allspice
1 teaspoon whole grain mustard
1 teaspoon smoked paprika

Directions

Thoroughly combine the honey, soy sauce, hoisin sauce, tomato sauce, garlic, ginger, and sesame oil in a bowl.

Place the spare rib rashes in a large ceramic dish and pour over the honey/sauce. Cover with a plastic wrap and transfer to your refrigerator; let it sit at least 4 hours to develop the flavors.

Add the spare rib rashes to the Instant Pot; add the remaining ingredients, along with the reserved marinade.

Secure the lid. Select the "Manual" button and cook for 23 minutes at High pressure.

Once cooking is complete, use a natural release; remove the lid carefully. Now, press the "Sauté" button and continue to cook, uncovered, until the liquid is concentrated. Serve warm and enjoy!

Per serving: 388 Calories; 14.7g Fat; 19.2g Carbs; 42.2g Protein; 16.3g Sugars

114. Summer Barbeque Pork Loin

(Ready in about 30 minutes | Servings 6)

Ingredients

3 pounds pork butt roast	1/2 teaspoon sea salt
1/2 cup water	1/2 tablespoon fresh ground black
1 cup ketchup	pepper.
1/4 cup champagne vinegar	1 teaspoon ground mustard
3 tablespoons brown sugar	1 teaspoon garlic powder

Directions

Add all of the above ingredients to your Instant Pot.

Secure the lid and select the "Meat/Stew" mode. Cook for 20 minutes under High pressure. Once cooking is complete, use a natural pressure release; carefully remove the lid.

Shred the meat and return it back to the Instant Pot. Serve the pork loin with the sauce and enjoy!

Per serving: 435 Calories; 18.9g Fat; 15.1g Carbs; 48.8g Protein; 12.4g Sugars

115. Pork Shoulder with Gravy

(Ready in about 45 minutes | Servings 4)

Ingredients

1 pound pork shoulder, cut into 4 pieces	1 onion, thinly sliced
Salt and ground black pepper, to taste	1 ½ teaspoons garlic paste
	3/4 cup plain milk
1/2 teaspoon cayenne pepper	1/2 teaspoon agar agar
1 ½ tablespoons lard, at room temperature	2 tablespoons fresh cilantro leaves, chopped

Directions

Add the pork shoulder, salt, black pepper, cayenne pepper to a resealable plastic bag. Shake until the meat is coated on all sides.

Press the "Sauté" button and heat the lard; once hot, sear the pork for 4 minutes on each side; reserve.

Then, cook the onion in the pan drippings until translucent. Now, add the garlic paste and top with reserved pork.

Secure the lid. Choose the "Manual" setting and cook at High pressure for 35 minutes. Once cooking is complete, use a natural release; carefully remove the lid.

Remove the pork to a serving plate. Press the "Sauté" button again; add plain milk to the cooking liquid. Now, stir in the agar-agar and whisk until it is dissolved.

Allow it to simmer for 4 minutes or until the sauce has thickened. Serve the pork shoulder, carrots, and broccoli garnished with the gravy and cilantro leaves. Bon appétit!

Per serving: 379 Calories; 26.4g Fat; 3.2g Carbs; 30.3g Protein; 2.5g Sugars

116. Creamy Smothered Pork Cutlets

(Ready in about 15 minutes | Servings 4)

Ingredients

1 cup water	2/3 teaspoon cayenne pepper
2 chicken bouillon cubes	1 pound pork cutlets
2 cloves garlic, finely chopped	1 ½ tablespoons cornstarch, plus 2 tablespoons water
Sea salt and freshly ground black pepper, to taste	6 ounces Ricotta cheese

Directions

Add the water, bouillon cubes, garlic, salt, black pepper, cayenne pepper, and pork cutlets to the Instant Pot.

Secure the lid. Choose the "Manual" setting and cook at High pressure for 8 minutes. Once cooking is complete, use a quick pressure release; carefully remove the lid.

Then, whisk the cornstarch and water in a mixing bowl; add the slurry to the cooking liquid. Press the "Sauté" button and let it cook until thickened.

Afterwards, fold in the Ricotta cheese and serve immediately. Bon appétit!

Per serving: 334 Calories; 18.3g Fat; 5.8g Carbs; 34.2g Protein; 0.4g Sugars

117. Maple Mustard Pork Belly

(Ready in about 50 minutes | Servings 8)

Ingredients

1 ½ pounds pork belly, scored and patted dry	1/2 teaspoon red pepper flakes, crushed
1 teaspoon garlic paste	1/2 cup water
Sea salt and ground black pepper, to taste	1/2 dry white wine
	3 tablespoons maple syrup
1/2 teaspoon dried marjoram	1 teaspoon stone-ground mustard
	1/2 teaspoon ground allspice

Directions

Spread the garlic paste over the pork belly; sprinkle with salt, black pepper, dried marjoram and red pepper flakes.

Press the "Sauté" button to preheat your Instant Pot. Then, sear the pork belly for 3 minutes per side.

In a mixing bowl, thoroughly combine water, wine, maple syrup, mustard, and allspice. Pour this mixture over the pork belly in the Instant Pot.

Secure the lid. Choose the "Meat/Stew" setting and cook at High pressure for 40 minutes. Once cooking is complete, use a natural pressure release; carefully remove the lid.

Cut the prepared pork belly into pieces; serve with some extra mustard, if desired. Bon appétit!

Per serving: 475 Calories; 45.1g Fat; 6.1g Carbs; 8.1g Protein; 4.9g Sugars

118. Garden Vegetable Soup with Pork

(Ready in about 40 minutes | Servings 4)

Ingredients

1 tablespoon olive oil	1 celery, sliced
1 pound pork stew meat, cubed	1 turnip, peeled and sliced
4 cups beef bone broth	Sea salt and ground black pepper, to taste
1 cup scallion, chopped	
1 carrot, sliced	2 cups spinach

Directions

Press the "Sauté" button to preheat your Instant Pot; heat the oil. Now, sear the meat until it is delicately browned.

Add the remaining ingredients, except for the spinach.

Secure the lid. Choose the "Soup" setting and cook at High pressure for 30 minutes. Once cooking is complete, use a quick pressure release; carefully remove the lid.

Add the spinach to the Instant Pot; seal the lid and allow it to sit in the residual heat until wilted.

Ladle the soup into individual bowls and serve right away. Bon appétit!

Per serving: 264 Calories; 8.6g Fat; 6.6g Carbs; 38.2g Protein; 2.5g Sugars

119. Pork in Sweet Wine Sauce

(Ready in about 30 minutes | Servings 6)

Ingredients

2 tablespoons lard, melted
2 pounds pork shoulder, cut into four pieces
2 garlic cloves, chopped
2 tablespoons honey
1/2 cup Riesling

1/2 cup water
1 tablespoon Worcestershire sauce
2 sprigs rosemary
1 sprig thyme
Kosher salt and ground black pepper, to taste

Directions

Press the "Sauté" button to preheat your Instant Pot. Melt the lard. Then, sear the meat for 2 to 3 minutes, stirring frequently.

Add the remaining ingredients and gently stir to combine.

Secure the lid. Choose the "Meat/Stew" setting and cook at High pressure for 20 minutes. Once cooking is complete, use a quick pressure release; carefully remove the lid. Bon appétit!

Per serving: 483 Calories; 31g Fat; 7.3g Carbs; 38g Protein; 6.1g Sugars

120. Texas-Style Pulled Pork Sandwiches

(Ready in about 1 hour 5 minutes + marinating time | Servings 6)

Ingredients

2 pounds Boston butt, cut into 4 pieces
1 teaspoon chipotle powder
Seasoned salt and ground black pepper, to your liking
1 teaspoon shallot powder
1/2 teaspoon granulated garlic
1 teaspoon mustard powder

1 teaspoon paprika
2 tablespoons lard, at room temperature
1 (16-ounce) bottle BBQ sauce
2 cloves garlic, peeled and pressed
6 burger buns, split
2 tablespoons butter, softened

Directions

Place the Boston butt, chipotle powder, salt, ground black pepper, shallot powder, granulated garlic, mustard powder, and paprika in a resealable plastic bag; shake to coat on all sides.

Place the seasoned Boston butt in your refrigerator for 3 hours.

Now, press the "Sauté" button and add lard; once hot, sear the pork on all sides until it is just browned.

Add the BBQ sauce and garlic; secure the lid. Select the "Manual" button and cook for 55 minutes at High pressure.

Once cooking is complete, use a natural release; remove the lid carefully.

Remove the pork from the Instant Pot, and shred the meat with Bear Paws or two forks. Return the shredded pork to the Instant Pot, and stir it into the hot cooking juices.

Spread the halves of burger buns with butter; then, toast the buns. Spoon the pork into the toasted burger buns and eat warm. Bon appétit!

Per serving: 518 Calories; 17.5g Fat; 72.5g Carbs; 15.6g Protein; 23.1g Sugars

121. Saucy Pork Sausage with Macaroni

(Ready in about 15 minutes | Servings 6)

Ingredients

1 tablespoon olive oil
1 yellow onion, finely chopped
2 cloves garlic, minced
1 pound pork sausage, casing removed, coarsely chopped
Salt, to taste
1/2 teaspoon ground black pepper
1/2 teaspoon red pepper flakes, crushed

1 teaspoon dried basil
1 teaspoon dried oregano
1 teaspoon stone-ground mustard
1 cup water
1 cup tomato purée
1 pound macaroni
4 ounces Colby cheese, shredded

Directions

Press the "Sauté" button to preheat your Instant Pot. Then, heat the oil; now, cook the onion until translucent.

Now, add the garlic and sausage; continue to cook for 4 minutes more. Stir in the seasonings, mustard, water, tomato purée, and macaroni

Secure the lid. Choose the "Manual" setting and cook at High pressure for 6 minutes. Once cooking is complete, use a quick pressure release; carefully remove the lid.

Top with the Colby cheese; seal the lid and let it sit in the residual heat until the cheese is melted. Bon appétit!

Per serving: 495 Calories; 15.2g Fat; 60g Carbs; 27.8g Protein; 4.5g Sugars

122. Apple Maple Pulled Pork

(Ready in about 35 minutes | Servings 8)

Per serving: 434 Calories; 25.2g Fat; 13.6g Carbs; 36.1g Protein; 10.5g Sugars

Ingredients

2 ½ pounds pork butt, cut into bite-sized cubes
1/2 cup vegetable broth
1/2 cup barbecue sauce
Sea salt and ground black pepper
1 teaspoon dried oregano

1/2 teaspoon dried basil
1 tablespoon maple syrup
1 red chili pepper, minced
1 cooking apple, cored and diced
1 lemon, sliced

Directions

Add the pork, broth, barbecue sauce, salt, black pepper, oregano, basil, maple syrup, chili pepper, and apple to your Instant Pot. Secure the lid. Choose the "Soup" setting and cook at High pressure for 30 minutes. Once cooking is complete, use a natural pressure release; carefully remove the lid.

Shred the pork with two forks. Return it back to the Instant Pot. Serve with lemon slices. Bon appétit!

123. Holiday Pork Ham Hock

(Ready in about 55 minutes | Servings 6)

Ingredients

1 cup water
1/2 cup ale beer
Sea salt and ground black pepper, to taste
1/2 teaspoon cayenne pepper, or more to taste

1/2 teaspoon marjoram
1/2 teaspoon dried sage, crushed
A bunch of scallions, chopped
2 pounds pork ham hocks
2 bay leaves
2 garlic cloves, minced

Directions

Place all of the above ingredients in the Instant Pot.

Secure the lid. Choose the "Meat/Stew" setting and cook at High pressure for 45 minutes. Once cooking is complete, use a natural pressure release; carefully remove the lid.

Remove the ham hocks from the Instant Pot; allow them to cool enough to be handled. Remove the meat from the ham hocks and return it to the cooking liquid.

Serve on individual plates and enjoy!

Per serving: 304 Calories; 19.1g Fat; 2.6g Carbs; 30.5g Protein; 0.6g Sugars

124. Old-Fashioned Pork Stew

(Ready in about 50 minutes | Servings 6)

Ingredients

1 ½ tablespoons lard, at room temperature
1 ½ pounds pork stew meat, cubed
Hickory smoked salt and ground black pepper, to taste
1 cup leeks, chopped
2 garlic cloves, minced
1 (1-inch) piece fresh ginger root, grated

1 teaspoon mustard seeds
1 teaspoon fennel seeds
2 tablespoons soy sauce
1/4 cup dry red wine
5 cups beef bone broth
1/4 cup fresh parsley leaves, roughly chopped

Directions

Press the "Sauté" button and melt the lard. Now, brown the pork stew meat for 4 to 6 minutes, stirring occasionally.

Season the pork with salt and black pepper to taste and set it aside. In the pan drippings, cook the leeks along with the garlic and ginger until tender and aromatic.

Add the pork back to the Instant Pot; add the remaining ingredients and gently stir to combine. Secure the lid.

Choose "Meat/Stew" mode and cook at High pressure for 40 minutes. Once cooking is complete, use a quick release; remove the lid carefully.

Ladle into individual bowls and serve garnished with fresh parsley leaves. Bon appétit!

125. Mexican-Style Meatballs

(Ready in about 15 minutes | Servings 6)

Per serving: 476 Calories; 24.5g Fat; 33.2g Carbs; 27.9g Protein; 19.5g Sugars

Ingredients

1 pound ground pork	Sea salt and ground black pepper,
2 slices bacon, chopped	to taste
1 white onion, minced	1 teaspoon dried marjoram
1 teaspoon garlic, minced	1 cup ketchup
1/3 cup tortilla chips, crushed	2 cups tomato sauce
1/2 cup Romano cheese, freshly grated	2 chipotle chile in adobo
1 egg	2 tablespoons fresh cilantro

Directions

Thoroughly combine the ground pork, bacon, onion, garlic, tortilla chips, Romano cheese, egg, salt, black pepper, and marjoram. Shape the mixture into balls.

Now, add the ketchup, tomato sauce, and chipotle chile in adobo to the Instant Pot. Place the meatballs in your Instant Pot.

Secure the lid. Choose the "Manual" setting and cook at High pressure for 6 minutes. Once cooking is complete, use a quick pressure release; carefully remove the lid.

Serve warm garnished with fresh cilantro. Enjoy!

Per serving: 307 Calories; 17.2g Fat; 4.8g Carbs; 31.1g Protein; 2.5g Sugars

126. Easy Pork Soup with Corn

(Ready in about 15 minutes | Servings 4)

Ingredients

1 tablespoon olive oil	1/4 teaspoon bay leaf, ground
1/2 cup onion, chopped	1/2 teaspoon dried basil
1 pound pork stew meat, cubed	1 teaspoon celery seeds
4 cups water	1 cup corn, torn into pieces

Directions

Press the "Sauté" button to preheat your Instant Pot. Heat the olive oil; cook the onion until tender and translucent.

Add the pork and continue to cook until it is delicately browned. Add the water, ground bay leaf, basil, and celery seeds to the Instant Pot.

Secure the lid. Choose the "Manual" setting and cook at High pressure for 8 minutes. Once cooking is complete, use a quick pressure release; carefully remove the lid.

Stir in the corn kernels; seal the lid and allow it to sit in the residual heat until the corn is warmed through. Serve in individual bowls and enjoy!

Per serving: 358 Calories; 9.1g Fat; 32.4g Carbs; 36.1g Protein; 0.8g Sugars

127. Quick Pork Goulash

(Ready in about 25 minutes | Servings 4)

Ingredients

1 tablespoon olive oil	Sea salt and ground black pepper,
1 pound ground pork	to taste
1/2 pound ground turkey	1 cup beef bone broth
1 onion, chopped	1/2 cup rice wine
2 cloves garlic, minced	2 ripe tomatoes, pureed
1 bay leaf	1 cup sweet corn kernels
1 thyme sprig	1 cup green peas
1 rosemary sprig	1/2 cup Colby cheese, shredded
1 teaspoon paprika	

Directions

Press the "Sauté" button to preheat your Instant Pot. Heat the oil and sear the meat until no longer pink, stirring continuously with a spatula.

Use a splash of wine to deglaze the pan.

Add the onion and garlic to the meat mixture and cook an additional 3 minutes or until tender and fragrant.

Next, stir in the spices, broth, wine, and tomatoes.

Secure the lid. Choose the "Manual" mode and cook for 10 minutes at High pressure. Once cooking is complete, use a quick pressure release; carefully remove the lid.

Press the "Sauté" button and add the corn and green peas. Cook an additional 3 minutes or until everything is heated through.

Top with cheese and allow it to stand until the cheese has melted. Bon appétit!

Per serving: 570 Calories; 37.4g Fat; 22.2g Carbs; 38.2g Protein; 5.1g Sugars

128. Old-Fashioned Roast Pork

(Ready in about 1 hour 10 minutes | Servings 6)

Ingredients

2 garlic cloves, minced	1 tablespoon lard, at room
2 teaspoons stone-ground mustard	temperature
Sea salt and ground black pepper,	1/2 cup red wine
to taste	1 large leek, sliced into long
1 teaspoon freshly grated lemon	pieces
zest	1 carrot, halved lengthwise
2 ½ pounds pork butt	

Directions

Combine the garlic, mustard, salt, pepper and lemon zest in a mixing bowl. Using your hands, spread the rub evenly onto the pork butt.

Press the "Sauté" button to preheat your Instant Pot. Melt the lard and sear the meat for 3 minutes per side.

Pour a splash of wine into the inner pot, scraping any bits from the bottom with a wooden spoon.

Place a trivet and 1 cup of water in the bottom of the inner pot. Lower the pork butt onto the trivet; scatter the leeks and carrots around.

Secure the lid. Choose the "Manual" mode and cook for 50 minutes at High pressure. Once cooking is complete, use a natural pressure release for 10 minutes; carefully remove the lid.

Transfer the pork butt to a cutting board and let it sit for 5 minutes before carving and serving. Enjoy!

Per serving: 545 Calories; 35.4g Fat; 4.2g Carbs; 48.2g Protein; 1.5g Sugars

129. Milk-Braised Pork Loin Roast

(Ready in about 45 minutes | Servings 6)

Ingredients

2 tablespoons sesame oil
2 ½ pounds pork loin roast, boneless
Sea salt and freshly ground black pepper, to taste
1 teaspoon dried basil
1 teaspoon dried oregano
1/2 teaspoon paprika
1/2 lemon, juiced and zested
1 cup vegetable broth
1 cup milk

Directions

Press the "Sauté" button and heat the oil until sizzling; once hot, sear the pork for 4 to 5 minutes or until browned on all sides. Work in batches.

Add the remaining ingredients.

Secure the lid. Choose the "Meat/Stew" mode and cook for 35 minutes at High pressure. Once cooking is complete, use a quick pressure release; carefully remove the lid.

Turn on your broiler. Roast the pork under the broiler for about 3 minutes or until the skin is crisp.

To carve the pork, remove the cracklings and cut the crisp pork skin into strips. Carve the pork roast across the grain into thin slices and serve.

Per serving: 436 Calories; 22.8g Fat; 2.6g Carbs; 52.2g Protein; 2.2g Sugars

130. Spicy Paprika and Pork Omelet

(Ready in about 25 minutes | Servings 2)

Ingredients

1 tablespoon canola oil
1/2 pound ground pork
1 yellow onion, thinly sliced
1 red chili pepper, minced
4 eggs, whisked
1/2 teaspoon garlic powder
1/3 teaspoon cumin powder
1 teaspoon oyster sauce
Kosher salt and ground black pepper, to taste
1/2 teaspoon paprika

Directions

Press the "Sauté" button and heat the oil until sizzling; once hot, cook the ground pork until no longer pink, crumbling with a spatula.

Add the onion and pepper; cook an additional 2 minutes. Whisk the eggs with the remaining ingredients. Pour the egg mixture over the meat mixture in the inner pot.

Secure the lid. Choose the "Manual" mode and cook for 8 minutes at High pressure. Once cooking is complete, use a natural pressure release for 10 minutes; carefully remove the lid. Bon appétit!

Per serving: 449 Calories; 33.6g Fat; 4.3g Carbs; 32.2g Protein; 1.6g Sugars

131. Barbecued Pork Spare Ribs

(Ready in about 45 minutes | Servings 4)

Ingredients

2 pounds pork spare ribs, cut into 4 equal portions
1 tablespoon sea salt
1/2 teaspoon black pepper
1/2 teaspoon chili flakes
1 teaspoon cayenne pepper
1 teaspoon shallot powder
1 teaspoon garlic powder
1 teaspoon fennel seeds
1 tablespoon sugar
1 cup chicken stock
1 cup tomato ketchup
1/4 cup dark soy sauce

Directions

Generously sprinkle the pork spare ribs with all spices and sugar. Add the chicken stock and secure the lid.

Choose the "Meat/Stew" mode and cook for 35 minutes at High pressure. Once cooking is complete, use a quick pressure release; carefully remove the lid.

Transfer the pork ribs to a baking pan. Mix the tomato ketchup and soy sauce; pour the mixture over the pork ribs and roast in the preheated oven at 425 degrees F for 6 to 8 minutes. Bon appétit!

Per serving: 500 Calories; 28.6g Fat; 8.9g Carbs; 49.2g Protein; 6.1g Sugars

132. Pork Medallions with Asian Flair

(Ready in about 30 minutes | Servings 3)

Ingredients

1 tablespoon sesame oil
1 ½ pounds pork medallions
1/2 cup tamari sauce
1/2 cup chicken stock
1/4 cup rice vinegar
1/2 teaspoon cayenne pepper
1/2 teaspoon salt
1 tablespoon maple syrup
1 tablespoon Sriracha sauce
2 cloves garlic, minced
6 ounces mushrooms, chopped
1 tablespoon arrowroot powder, dissolved in 2 tablespoons of water

Directions

Press the "Sauté" button and heat the oil; once hot, cook the pork medallions for 3 minutes per side.

Add the tamari sauce, chicken stock, vinegar, cayenne pepper, salt, maple syrup, Sriracha, garlic, and mushrooms to the inner pot.

Secure the lid. Choose the "Meat/Stew" mode and cook for 20 minutes at High pressure. Once cooking is complete, use a quick pressure release; carefully remove the lid. Remove the pork from the inner pot.

Add the thickener to the cooking liquid. Press the "Sauté" button again and let it boil until the sauce has reduced slightly and the flavors have concentrated.

Serve over hot steamed rice if desired. Enjoy!

Per serving: 355 Calories; 10.1g Fat; 13g Carbs; 51g Protein; 7.2g Sugars

133. Cholula Pork Sandwiches

(Ready in about 40 minutes | Servings 4)

Ingredients

1 tablespoon olive oil
2 pounds pork shoulder roast
1/2 cup tomato paste
1/2 cup beef bone broth
1/4 cup balsamic vinegar
1/4 cup brown sugar
1 tablespoon mustard
1 teaspoon Cholula hot sauce
2 cloves garlic, minced
1 teaspoon dried marjoram
4 hamburger buns

Directions

Add all ingredients, except for the hamburger buns, to the inner pot.

Secure the lid. Choose the "Meat/Stew" mode and cook for 35 minutes at High pressure. Once cooking is complete, use a quick pressure release; carefully remove the lid.

Remove the pork from the inner pot and shred with two forks. Spoon the pulled pork into the hamburger buns and serve with your favorite toppings. Bon appétit!

Per serving: 516 Calories; 14.4g Fat; 37.1g Carbs; 56.7g Protein; 15.2g Sugars

134. Pork Chops in White Mushroom Sauce

(Ready in about 30 minutes | Servings 6)

Ingredients

2 tablespoons butter
6 pork chops
1 tablespoon Italian seasoning blend
1/2 teaspoon coarse sea salt
1/2 teaspoon cracked black pepper
1 pound white mushrooms, sliced
1 tablespoon fresh coriander, chopped
1 teaspoon dill weed, minced
2 cloves garlic crushed
1/2 cup double cream
1/2 cup cream of onion soup

Directions

Press the "Sauté" button and melt the butter. Once hot, sear the pork chops until golden browned, about 4 minutes per side.

Add the remaining ingredients and gently stir to combine.

Secure the lid. Choose the "Meat/Stew" mode and cook for 20 minutes at High pressure. Once cooking is complete, use a quick pressure release; carefully remove the lid.

Serve over mashed potatoes. Bon appétit!

Per serving: 438 Calories; 25.8g Fat; 7.2g Carbs; 42.8g Protein; 2.7g Sugars

135. Aunt's Pork and Pepper Casserole

(Ready in about 40 minutes | Servings 4)

Ingredients

1 tablespoon lard, melted
2 pounds pork steaks, cut into large pieces
1 onion, thinly
2 cloves garlic, sliced
4 mixed colored peppers, deveined and chopped
1 serrano pepper, deveined and chopped
Sea salt and ground black pepper, to taste
1 tablespoon Cajun seasonings
4 sage leaves
1 teaspoon mustard
2 tablespoons red wine
1 cup chicken broth
1 cup goat cheese, crumbled

Directions

Press the "Sauté" button and melt the lard; once hot, sear the pork in batches until golden brown all over.

Add the onions, garlic, and peppers. Season with salt, black pepper, and Cajun seasonings. Add the sage leaves, mustard, wine, and broth.

Secure the lid. Choose the "Manual" mode and cook for 30 minutes at High pressure. Once cooking is complete, use a quick pressure release; carefully remove the lid.

Add the goat cheese on top, seal the lid again, and let it sit in the residual heat until the cheese melts.

Let it rest for 5 to 10 minutes before slicing and serving. Bon appétit!

Per serving: 501 Calories; 26.8g Fat; 10g Carbs; 53.5g Protein; 4.7g Sugars

136. Lemon Rosemary Pork Medallions

(Ready in about 30 minutes | Servings 4)

Ingredients

1 tablespoon butter, melted
2 pounds pork medallions
Kosher salt and freshly ground black pepper, to taste
1 teaspoon garlic powder
1 teaspoon shallot powder
1 cup vegetable broth
2 sprigs fresh rosemary
1 lemon, juice and zest

Directions

Press the "Sauté" button and melt the butter. Sear the pork medallions until no longer pink.

Add the salt, black pepper, garlic powder, shallot powder, and vegetable broth.

Secure the lid. Choose the "Manual" mode and cook for 20 minutes at High pressure. Once cooking is complete, use a quick pressure release; carefully remove the lid.

Remove the pork medallions to a serving platter. Now, add the fresh rosemary, lemon juice and zest to the cooking liquid. Let it simmer for 2 to 3 minutes.

Spoon the sauce over the pork medallions and serve immediately. Enjoy!

Per serving: 340 Calories; 12.5g Fat; 1.7g Carbs; 52.2g Protein; 0.4g Sugars

137. Mexican Pork Carnitas

(Ready in about 50 minutes | Servings 4)

Ingredients

2 pounds pork butt roast
1 cup Mexican coke
1 cup beef bone broth
1/2 cup tomato ketchup
1/4 cup honey
1 teaspoon liquid smoke
2 tablespoons balsamic vinegar
1 jalapeno, deveined and chopped
1/2 teaspoon cumin powder
1 teaspoon shallot powder
1 teaspoon garlic powder
1/2 teaspoon Mexican oregano
Sea salt and ground black pepper, to taste
4 warm tortillas

Directions

Place all ingredients, except for the tortillas, in the inner pot.

Secure the lid. Choose the "Meat/Stew" mode and cook for 35 minutes at High pressure. Once cooking is complete, use a quick pressure release; carefully remove the lid.

Remove the pork from the inner pot and shred with two forks.

Transfer the pork to a baking sheet lightly greased with cooking spray. Pour 1 ladle of the cooking liquid over the pork. Broil for 7 to 10 minutes until the meat becomes crispy on the edges.

Spoon the pulled pork into the warm tortillas and serve with your favorite toppings. Bon appétit!

Per serving: 555 Calories; 12.4g Fat; 54.3g Carbs; 55.2g Protein; 29.5g Sugars

138. Bavarian-Style Pork and Sauerkraut

(Ready in about 40 minutes | Servings 4)

Ingredients

1 tablespoon oil
1 ½ pounds pork shoulder, cubed
4 ounces pork sausage, sliced
Sea salt and, to taste
1/2 teaspoon black peppercorns
14 ounces sauerkraut, drained
1 cup beef broth
1 onion, sliced
2 garlic cloves, minced
2 bay leaves
1/2 teaspoon smoked paprika
1 dried chili pepper, minced

Directions

Press the "Sauté" button and heat the oil. Once hot, cook the pork and sausage until they are no longer pink.

Add the remaining ingredients; gently stir to combine.

Secure the lid. Choose the "Meat/Stew" mode and cook for 35 minutes at High pressure. Once cooking is complete, use a quick pressure release; carefully remove the lid. Enjoy!

Per serving: 435 Calories; 27.7g Fat; 6.5g Carbs; 38.2g Protein; 2.5g Sugars

139. Parmesan Pork Chops

(Ready in about 20 minutes | Servings 4)

Ingredients

1 tablespoon lard, at room temperature
4 pork chops, bone-in
Sea salt and freshly ground black pepper, to taste
1/4 cup tomato puree
1 cup chicken bone broth
4 ounces parmesan cheese, preferably freshly grated

Directions

Press the "Sauté" button and melt the lard. Sear the pork chops for 3 to 4 minutes per side. Season with salt and pepper.

Place the tomato puree and chicken broth in the inner pot.

Secure the lid. Choose the "Manual" mode and cook for 10 minutes at High pressure. Once cooking is complete, use a natural pressure release; carefully remove the lid.

Top with parmesan cheese and serve warm. Bon appétit!

Per serving: 475 Calories; 21.7g Fat; 5.8g Carbs; 60.4g Protein; 0.7g Sugars

140. Festive Pork Roast with Gravy

(Ready in about 20 minutes | Servings 4)

Ingredients

2 tablespoons olive oil
1 pound Boston-style butt, sliced into four pieces
Coarse sea salt and freshly ground black pepper, to taste
1 shallot, sliced
2 cloves garlic, sliced
1 stalk celery, chopped
1 bell pepper, deveined and sliced
1/2 cup apple juice
1/2 cup chicken broth
1 tablespoon stone ground mustard
1 teaspoon basil
1 teaspoon thyme
2 tablespoons plain flour, mixed with 2 tablespoons of cold water

Directions

Press the "Sauté" button and heat the oil. Then, sear the Boston butt until it is golden brown on all sides.

Add the salt, pepper, shallot, garlic, celery, bell pepper, apple juice, chicken broth, mustard, basil, and thyme to the inner pot.

Secure the lid. Choose the "Manual" mode and cook for 15 minutes at High pressure. Once cooking is complete, use a quick pressure release; carefully remove the lid. Remove the meat from the cooking liquid.

Add the slurry and press the "Sauté" button one more time. Let it simmer until your sauce has thickened. Spoon the gravy over the pork and serve. Bon appétit!

Per serving: 388 Calories; 22.1g Fat; 6.8g Carbs; 36.7g Protein; 3.7g Sugars

141. Venezuelan-Style Arepas with Pork

(Ready in about 40 minutes | Servings 6)

Ingredients

1 tablespoon butter
2 pounds boneless pork butt roast
1 cup cream of mushroom soup
2 tablespoons Worcestershire sauce
4 cloves garlic, finely chopped
Sea salt and ground black pepper, to taste

1 teaspoon cayenne pepper
1 teaspoon garlic powder
1 teaspoon onion powder
1/4 teaspoon ground cumin
6 Venezuelan-style arepas (corn cakes)

Directions

Place all ingredients, except for the arepas, in the inner pot.

Secure the lid. Choose the "Meat/Stew" mode and cook for 35 minutes at High pressure. Once cooking is complete, use a quick pressure release; carefully remove the lid.

Remove the pork from the inner pot and shred with two forks.

Fill each arepa with the pork mixture and serve with your favorite toppings. Enjoy!

Per serving: 386 Calories; 17.2g Fat; 21.2g Carbs; 34.7g Protein; 5.4g Sugars

142. Loin Chops with Garlic Mayo

(Ready in about 25 minutes | Servings 4)

Ingredients

1 ½ pounds center-cut loin chops
Kosher salt and ground black pepper, to taste
1 teaspoon paprika
1/2 teaspoon mustard powder

1/2 teaspoon celery seeds
1 tablespoon canola oil
1 cup beef bone broth
1/2 cup mayonnaise
2 cloves garlic, crushed

Directions

Press the "Sauté" button and heat the oil. Sear the pork until it is golden brown on both sides.

Add the salt, black pepper, mustard powder, celery seeds oil, and broth.

Secure the lid. Choose the "Manual" mode and cook for 10 minutes at High pressure. Once cooking is complete, use a natural pressure release for 10 minutes; carefully remove the lid.

Meanwhile, whisk the mayonnaise with the garlic; serve the warm loin chops with the garlic mayo on the side. Bon appétit!

Per serving: 444 Calories; 30.5g Fat; 2.1g Carbs; 38.1g Protein; 0.8g Sugars

143. Spicy Peppery Pork Burgers

(Ready in about 20 minutes | Servings 3)

Ingredients

1 pound ground pork
1 large sweet pepper, minced
1 chipotle pepper, minced
2 cloves garlic, minced
Sea salt and ground black pepper, to taste

1/2 teaspoon red pepper flakes, crushed
3 burger buns
3 (1-ounce) slices Swiss cheese, sliced

Directions

Mix the ground pork, peppers, garlic, salt, black pepper, and red pepper flakes until well combined.

Form the meat mixture into 3 patties. Place your patties on squares of aluminum foil and wrap them loosely.

Add 1 cup water and a metal trivet to the Instant Pot; lower the foil packs onto the top of the metal trivet.

Secure the lid. Choose the "Meat/Stew" mode and cook for 10 minutes at High pressure. Once cooking is complete, use a natural pressure release; carefully remove the lid.

Place your patties on a baking sheet and broil for 5 to 6 minutes. Serve on buns topped with Swiss cheese. Enjoy!

Per serving: 428 Calories; 15.4g Fat; 28.4g Carbs; 44.2g Protein; 6.5g Sugars

144. Country-Style Pork Meatballs

(Ready in about 20 minutes | Servings 4)

Ingredients

2 tablespoons vegetable oil
Meatballs:
1 ½ pounds ground pork
Kosher salt and ground black pepper, to your liking
1 teaspoon chili flakes
1 teaspoon mustard powder
1 egg
1/2 cup Parmesan, grated
2 bread slices, soaked in 4 tablespoons of milk

Marinara Sauce:
2 tablespoons olive oil
1 onion, chopped
3 cloves garlic, minced
1 tablespoon cayenne pepper
1 teaspoon maple syrup
2 large ripe tomatoes, crushed
1 teaspoon dried parsley flakes
1 cup water

Directions

Mix all ingredients for the meatballs until everything is well incorporated. Shape the mixture into small meatballs.

Press the "Sauté" button and heat 2 tablespoons of vegetable oil. Sear your meatballs until golden brown on all sides. Work in batches as needed. Reserve.

Press the "Sauté" button one more time; heat 2 tablespoons of olive oil. Cook the onion and garlic until tender and fragrant.

Now, add the remaining ingredients for the marinara sauce. Gently fold in the meatballs and secure the lid.

Choose the "Poultry" mode and cook for 5 minutes at High pressure. Once cooking is complete, use a quick pressure release; carefully remove the lid. Serve warm.

Per serving: 468 Calories; 24g Fat; 19.7g Carbs; 44.8g Protein; 6.2g Sugars

145. Loin Roast in Cheesy Garlic Sauce

(Ready in about 30 minutes | Servings 4)

Ingredients

1 tablespoon lard, at room temperature
1 pound pork loin roast, cut into three pieces
Sauce:
2 garlic cloves, chopped
2 tablespoons maple syrup

1/4 cup rice vinegar
1/2 cup water
1/4 cup dry white wine
2 tablespoons tamari sauce
1 tablespoons flaxseed meal
1 cup cream cheese

Directions

Press the "Sauté" button and melt the lard. Once hot, cook the pork loin until no longer pink.

Add the garlic, maple syrup, vinegar, water, wine and tamari sauce.

Secure the lid. Choose the "Manual" mode and cook for 10 minutes at High pressure. Once cooking is complete, use a natural pressure release for 10 minutes; carefully remove the lid. Reserve the meat.

Meanwhile, make the slurry by whisking the flaxseed meal with 2 tablespoons of cold water.

Stir in the slurry and press the "Sauté" button again. Cook the sauce until it has thickened; fold in the cheese and stir until heated through. Bon appétit!

Per serving: 491 Calories; 32.9g Fat; 10.9g Carbs; 36.4g Protein; 8.6g Sugars

146. Marinated Roasted Pork Picnic Ham

(Ready in about 30 minutes + marinating time | Servings 5)

Ingredients

2 tablespoons olive oil
1/2 teaspoon cayenne pepper
1/3 cup red wine
2/3 cup fresh orange juice
2 cloves garlic, minced

1 tablespoon mustard
2 pounds picnic ham
2 tablespoons parsley, chopped
1 shallot, sliced
2 sweet peppers, julienned

Directions

Mix the olive oil, cayenne pepper, red wine, orange juice, garlic, and mustard in a glass bowl. Add the pork and let it marinate for 2 hours.

Transfer the pork along with its marinade to the inner pot. Add the parsley, shallot, and peppers.

Secure the lid. Choose the "Meat/Stew" mode and cook for 20 minutes at High pressure. Once cooking is complete, use a quick pressure release; carefully remove the lid.

Spoon over hot steamed rice. Bon appétit!

Per serving: 427 Calories; 28.1g Fat; 9.5g Carbs; 32.9g Protein; 3.1g Sugars

147. Pork Masala Curry

(Ready in about 30 minutes | Servings 3)

Ingredients

1 pound pork stew meat, cubed	1 tablespoon garam masala
1/3 cup all-purpose flour	1 tablespoon cider vinegar
1 tablespoon ghee	Salt and black pepper, to taste
2 onions, sliced	1 teaspoon curry powder
1 (1-inch) piece ginger	1 teaspoon coriander seeds
2 cloves garlic, sliced	1/2 teaspoon Fenugreek seeds
2 green cardamoms	2 dried chiles de árbol, chopped
1/2 teaspoon ground allspice	1 cup yogurt

Directions

Toss the pork stew meat with the flour until well coated.

Press the "Sauté" button and melt the ghee. Once hot, cook the pork for 3 to 4 minutes, stirring frequently to ensure even cooking.

Add the remaining ingredients, except for the yogurt.

Secure the lid. Choose the "Manual" mode and cook for 15 minutes at High pressure. Once cooking is complete, use a natural pressure release for 10 minutes; carefully remove the lid.

Add the yogurt and press the "Sauté" button; let it cook for a few minutes more or until everything is thoroughly heated. Bon appétit!

Per serving: 436 Calories; 19.8g Fat; 18.3g Carbs; 43.7g Protein; 5.2g Sugars

148. Tender Pork in Ricotta Sauce

(Ready in about 30 minutes | Servings 3)

Ingredients

2 tablespoons olive oil	1 onion, thinly sliced
3 pork cutlets	2 chicken bouillon cubes
Sea salt and freshly ground black pepper, to taste	1 cup water
	6 ounces Ricotta cheese

Directions

Press the "Sauté" button and heat the oil until sizzling. Sear the pork cutlets for 3 minutes per side.

Add the salt, black pepper, onion, chicken bouillon cubes, water to the Instant Pot.

Secure the lid. Choose the "Manual" mode and cook for 10 minutes at High pressure. Once cooking is complete, use a natural pressure release for 10 minutes; carefully remove the lid.

Top with Ricotta cheese; seal the lid and let it stand for 5 to 10 minutes or until thoroughly heated. Bon appétit!

Per serving: 447 Calories; 30.3g Fat; 3.6g Carbs; 38.1g Protein; 0.6g Sugars

149. Pork Chops with Pineapple Glaze

(Ready in about 35 minutes | Servings 4)

Ingredients

1 tablespoon canola oil	1 teaspoon ground ginger
1 pound pork tenderloin, slice into 4 pieces	1 thyme sprig
	1 rosemary sprig
Kosher salt and freshly ground black pepper, to taste	1/2 cup unsweetened pineapple juice
1 shallot, chopped	1/2 cup vegetable broth
2 garlic cloves, chopped	4 pineapple rings

Directions

Press the "Sauté" button to preheat your Instant Pot. Heat the canola oil.

Season the pork tenderloin on both sides with salt and black pepper. Cook the pork chops with shallot and garlic for 3 minutes or until the pork chops are no longer pink.

Add the ginger, thyme, rosemary, pineapple juice, and vegetable broth.

Secure the lid. Choose the "Manual" mode and cook for 10 minutes at High pressure. Once cooking is complete, use a natural pressure release for 10 minutes; carefully remove the lid.

Preheat the broiler. Place the pork chops on a broil pan. Brush with the pan juices and place one pineapple ring on top of each pork piece. Broil for 5 minutes. Serve warm.

Per serving: 480 Calories; 34.3g Fat; 13.6g Carbs; 30.1g Protein; 11.5g Sugars

150. Pork and Romano Cheese Meatloaf

(Ready in about 35 minutes | Servings 4)

Ingredients

4 ounces bacon, chopped	1/4 cup Romano cheese, grated
1 onion, chopped	1/2 cup tomato sauce
4 cloves garlic, minced	1 tablespoon mustard
1 pound ground pork	1 teaspoon dried basil
1 egg, beaten	1 teaspoon dried sage
1 tablespoon fish sauce	1 teaspoon dried oregano
1/2 cup breadcrumbs	1/2 teaspoon chili flakes

Directions

Place a steamer rack inside the inner pot; add 1/2 cup of water. Cut 1 sheet of heavy-duty foil and brush with cooking spray.

In mixing dish, thoroughly combine all ingredients.

Shape the meat mixture into a loaf; place the meatloaf in the center of the foil. Wrap your meatloaf in foil and lower onto the steamer rack.

Secure the lid. Choose the "Meat/Stew" mode and cook for 20 minutes at High pressure. Once cooking is complete, use a quick pressure release; carefully remove the lid. Let it stand for 10 minutes before cutting and serving. Bon appétit!

Per serving: 520 Calories; 36.6g Fat; 18.7g Carbs; 28.4g Protein; 5.7g Sugars

151. Marsala Pork Ribs

(Ready in about 45 minutes | Servings 4)

Ingredients

1 rack country style pork ribs	1/2 cup Marsala wine
Coarse sea salt and freshly ground black pepper, to taste	1/2 cup chicken broth
	1 cup BBQ sauce
1 teaspoon red pepper flakes	

Directions

Place the pork ribs, salt, black pepper, red pepper, wine, and chicken broth in the inner pot.

Choose the "Meat/Stew" mode and cook for 35 minutes at High pressure. Once cooking is complete, use a quick pressure release; carefully remove the lid.

Transfer the pork ribs to a baking pan. Pour the BBQ sauce over the pork ribs and roast in the preheated oven at 425 degrees F for 6 to 8 minutes. Bon appétit!

Per serving: 386 Calories; 14.9g Fat; 4.9g Carbs; 54.7g Protein; 2.9g Sugars

152. Tender St. Louis-Style Ribs

(Ready in about 45 minutes | Servings 6)

Ingredients

1 (3-pounds) rack St. Louis-style pork ribs
1 cup tomato sauce
1/2 cup water
1 tablespoon brown sugar
2 cloves garlic, minced
1 tablespoon oyster sauce
1 tablespoon soy sauce
1 tablespoon paprika
Pink salt and ground black pepper, to taste

Directions

Place all ingredients in the inner pot.

Choose the "Meat/Stew" mode and cook for 35 minutes at High pressure. Once cooking is complete, use a quick pressure release; carefully remove the lid.

Turn your broiler to low. Coat the ribs with the pan juices and cook under the broiler for about 2 minutes.

Turn them over, coat with another layer of sauce and cook for 2 to 3 minutes more. Taste, adjust the seasonings and serve. Enjoy!

Per serving: 381 Calories; 13.4g Fat; 11.6g Carbs; 48.5g Protein; 6.6g Sugars

153. Pork Tenderloin Fajitas

(Ready in about 50 minutes | Servings 4)

Ingredients

1 teaspoon paprika
1 tablespoon brown sugar
1 teaspoon dried sage
1/2 teaspoon ground cumin
Coarse sea salt and freshly ground pepper, to taste
2 pounds pork tenderloins, halved crosswise
1 tablespoon grapeseed oil
1/4 cup balsamic vinegar
1/4 cup tomato puree
1/2 cup beef broth
16 small flour tortillas
A bunch of scallions, chopped
1 cup sour cream
1 cup Pico de Gallo

Directions

Mix the paprika, sugar, sage, cumin, salt, and black pepper. Rub the spice mixture all over the pork tenderloins.

Press the "Sauté" button to preheat your Instant Pot. Heat the oil and sear the pork until browned, about 4 minutes per side.

Add the balsamic vinegar, tomato puree, and beef broth.

Secure the lid. Choose the "Manual" mode and cook for 40 minutes at High pressure. Once cooking is complete, use a quick pressure release; carefully remove the lid.

Warm the tortillas until soft; serve with the pork mixture, scallions, sour cream, and Pico de Gallo. Enjoy!

Per serving: 618 Calories; 18.8g Fat; 53.8g Carbs; 55.7g Protein; 11.7g Sugars

154. Smothered Pork Chop

(Ready in about 30 minutes | Servings 3)

Ingredients

1 tablespoon ghee, at room temperature
3 pork chops
1 cup beef broth
1 teaspoon garlic powder
1/2 teaspoon onion powder
1 tablespoon paprika
Sea salt and ground black pepper, to taste
1/2 cup double cream
1/2 teaspoon xanthan gum

Directions

Press the "Sauté" button and melt the ghee. Once hot, sear the pork chops until golden browned, about 4 minutes per side.

Add the beef broth, garlic powder, onion powder, paprika, salt, and black pepper to the inner pot.

Secure the lid. Choose the "Manual" mode and cook for 10 minutes at High pressure. Once cooking is complete, use a natural pressure release; carefully remove the lid.

Transfer just the pork chops to a serving plate and cover to keep them warm. Press the "Sauté" button again.

Whisk in the cream and xanthan gum. Let it simmer approximately 4 minutes or until the sauce has thickened. Spoon the sauce over the pork chops and enjoy!

Per serving: 472 Calories; 28.8g Fat; 11.1g Carbs; 42.7g Protein; 6.6g Sugars

155. Pork Liver Pâté

(Ready in about 20 minutes | Servings 6)

Ingredients

2 tablespoons butter
1 onion, chopped
2 cloves garlic, minced
1 pound pork livers
1 cup water
2 sprigs thyme
2 sprigs rosemary
Himalayan pink salt and ground black pepper, to taste
1/4 cup brandy
1/2 cup heavy cream

Directions

Press the "Sauté" button and melt the butter. Then, sauté the onion and garlic until just tender and aromatic.

Add the pork livers and cook for 3 minutes on both sides or until the juices run clear. Deglaze the pan with a splash of brandy.

Add the water, thyme, rosemary, salt, and ground black pepper.

Secure the lid. Choose the "Manual" mode and cook for 5 minutes at High pressure. Once cooking is complete, use a quick pressure release; carefully remove the lid.

Add the brandy and heavy cream. Press the "Sauté" button and cook for 2 to 3 minutes more.

Transfer to your food processor and blend the mixture to a fine mousse. Bon appétit!

Per serving: 177 Calories; 11.7g Fat; 3.1g Carbs; 14.4g Protein; 1.5g Sugars

156. Boston Butt with Root Vegetables

(Ready in about 30 minutes | Servings 5)

Ingredients

1 ½ pounds Boston butt, cut into small chunks
1 teaspoon garlic powder
1 teaspoon shallot powder
Sea salt and ground black pepper
1 teaspoon dried marjoram
1 teaspoon mustard powder
1 teaspoon smoked paprika
2 tablespoons olive oil
1/2 cup port
1/2 cup roasted vegetable broth
2 large carrots, cut into 1.5-inch chunks
2 large celery stalks, cut into 1.5-inch chunks
1 parsnip, cut into 1.5-inch chunks
2 mild green chilies, roasted, seeded and diced
1 tablespoon arrowroot powder

Directions

In a resealable bag, mix the garlic powder, shallot powder, salt, black pepper, marjoram, mustard powder, and paprika.

Add the pork cubes and shake to coat well. Press the "Sauté" button and heat the oil until sizzling.

Cook the Boston butt for 2 to 4 minutes, stirring periodically to ensure even cooking. Add the remaining ingredients, except for the arrowroot powder.

Secure the lid. Choose the "Meat/Stew" mode and cook for 20 minutes at High pressure. Once cooking is complete, use a quick pressure release; carefully remove the lid.

Stir in the arrowroot powder and let it simmer until the sauce thickens. Serve in individual bowls and enjoy!

Per serving: 511 Calories; 38.9g Fat; 11.6g Carbs; 29.7g Protein; 3.6g Sugars

157. Pork Chile Verde

(Ready in about 40 minutes | Servings 4)

Ingredients

2 pounds pork shoulder, cut into bite-sized pieces
1/4 cup all-purpose flour
Kosher salt and ground black pepper, to your liking
1 tablespoon canola oil
1 onion, chopped
2 cloves garlic, sliced
1 teaspoon Mexican oregano
1/2 teaspoon coriander seeds
1 teaspoon ground cumin
1/2 teaspoon turmeric powder
1 cup beef broth
1 sweet pepper, seeded and sliced
3 fresh chili pepper, seeded and sliced
1 pound fresh tomatillos, husked and sliced into 1/2-inch wedges
1/4 cup fresh cilantro leaves, roughly chopped

Directions

Toss the pork pieces with the flour until everything is well coated. Generously season the pork with salt and pepper.

Press the "Sauté" button and heat the oil. Once hot, sear the pork, stirring periodically to ensure even cooking.

Now, add the remaining ingredients, except for the cilantro leaves.

Secure the lid. Choose the "Meat/Stew" mode and cook for 35 minutes at High pressure. Once cooking is complete, use a quick pressure release; carefully remove the lid.

Serve in individual bowls, garnished with fresh cilantro. Enjoy!

Per serving: 444 Calories; 18.1g Fat; 23.6g Carbs; 46.4g Protein; 8g Sugars

158. Spicy Sausage Bake

(Ready in about 20 minutes | Servings 4)

Ingredients

2 tablespoons canola oil
1 pound pork sausages, sliced
4 ounces streaky bacon
1 onion, sliced
4 garlic cloves, minced
1 bell pepper, sliced
1 red chili pepper, sliced
1 teaspoon brown sugar
1 teaspoon dried rosemary
1 teaspoon dried basil
Sea salt and freshly ground black pepper, to taste
2 tomatoes, pureed 1 cup chicken stock
1 cup white wine

Directions

Press the "Sauté" button and heat the oil. Sear the pork sausage until no longer pink. Add the bacon and cook until it is crisp.

Add a layer of onions and garlic; then, add the peppers. Sprinkle with sugar, rosemary, basil, salt and black pepper.

Add the tomatoes, chicken stock, and wine to the inner pot.

Secure the lid. Choose the "Manual" mode and cook for 10 minutes at High pressure. Once cooking is complete, use a natural pressure release; carefully remove the lid. Bon appétit!

Per serving: 484 Calories; 41.8g Fat; 6.3g Carbs; 21.6g Protein; 4.1g Sugars

159. Pork and Mushroom Stuffed Peppers

(Ready in about 30 minutes | Servings 4)

Ingredients

1 tablespoon olive oil
1 onion, chopped
2 cloves garlic, minced
3/4 pound ground pork
1/2 pound brown mushrooms, sliced
1 1/2 cups cooked rice
Sea salt and white pepper, to taste
1 teaspoon cayenne pepper
1/2 teaspoon celery seeds
1/2 teaspoon ground cumin
4 bell peppers, deveined and halved
1 (15-ounce) can tomatoes, crushed
2 ounces Colby cheese, shredded

Directions

Press the "Sauté" button and heat the oil. Cook the onion, garlic, and pork until the onion is translucent and the pork is no longer pink. Add the mushrooms and sauté until fragrant or about 2 minutes.

Add the rice, salt, white pepper, cayenne pepper, celery seeds, and ground cumin.

Add 1 cup of water and a metal trivet to the bottom. Fill the pepper halves with the meat/mushroom mixture. Place the peppers in a casserole dish; stir in the canned tomatoes.

Lower the casserole dish onto the trivet in the Instant Pot.

Secure the lid. Choose the "Manual" mode and cook for 9 minutes at High pressure. Once cooking is complete, use a natural pressure release for 5 minutes; carefully remove the lid.

Top with the cheese and secure the lid again; let it sit in the residual heat until the cheese melts approximately 10 minutes. Serve and enjoy!

Per serving: 499 Calories; 26.4g Fat; 35.6g Carbs; 30.8g Protein; 8.1g Sugars

160. Pulled Pork and Cream Cheese Frittata

(Ready in about 50 minutes | Servings 3)

Ingredients

2 tablespoons butter, at room temperature
1 pound pork shoulder
1 cup chicken broth
Sea salt and ground black pepper, to taste
2 cloves garlic, minced
1 shallot, thinly sliced
6 eggs, beaten
1/2 cup cream cheese
1/2 teaspoon paprika
1/2 teaspoon hot sauce

Directions

Press the "Sauté" button to preheat your Instant Pot. Melt the butter and brown the pork for 4 minutes per side.

Add the chicken broth, salt, and black pepper.

Secure the lid. Choose the "Manual" mode and cook for 15 minutes at High pressure. Once cooking is complete, use a natural pressure release for 5 minutes; carefully remove the lid.

Shred the meat with two forks.; add the remaining ingredients and stir to combine well.

Lightly spritz a baking pan with cooking oil. Spoon the meat/egg mixture into the baking pan.

Cover with foil. Add 1 cup of water and a metal trivet to the Instant Pot. Lower the baking pan onto the trivet.

Secure the lid. Choose the "Manual" mode and cook for 15 minutes at High pressure. Once cooking is complete, use a natural pressure release for 10 minutes; carefully remove the lid. Bon appétit!

Per serving: 533 Calories; 36.6g Fat; 4.4g Carbs; 44.3g Protein; 2.6g Sugars

161. Pork Huevos Rancheros

(Ready in about 35 minutes | Servings 4)

Ingredients

1 tablespoon coarse sea salt
1/2 teaspoon ground black pepper
1 teaspoon paprika
1 teaspoon onion powder
1 teaspoon garlic powder
1 teaspoon ancho chili powder
1 tablespoon dark brown sugar
2 pounds Boston butt, cut into bite-sized pieces
1 tablespoon olive oil
1 cup tomato paste
1/2 cup roasted vegetable broth
1 tablespoon fish sauce
4 eggs
2 tablespoons corn salsa
4 warm corn tortillas

Directions

In a resealable bag, mix the all spices and sugar. Add the pork chunks and shake to coat well.

Press the "Sauté" button and heat the oil until sizzling. Now, sear and brown the Boston butt on all sides until you have a crispy crust.

Add the tomato paste, broth, and fish sauce.

Secure the lid. Choose the "Manual" mode and cook for 30 minutes at High pressure. Once cooking is complete, use a quick pressure release; carefully remove the lid.

Meanwhile, crack the eggs into a lightly greased pan; fry your eggs until the whites are set.

Stack the tortilla, pork mixture, and corn salsa on a plate. Place the fried egg onto the stack using a spatula. Make four servings and enjoy!

Per serving: 533 Calories; 18.3g Fat; 29.5g Carbs; 62.2g Protein; 8.8g Sugars

162. Classic Pork Chops and Potatoes

(Ready in about 20 minutes | Servings 4)

Ingredients

2 tablespoons lard, at room temperature
4 pork chops
1 cup chicken broth
1 onion, sliced
1 pound potatoes, quartered
Sea salt and ground black pepper, to taste

Directions

Press the "Sauté" button and melt the lard. Once hot, brown the pork chops for 3 minutes per side.

Add the remaining ingredients.

Secure the lid. Choose the "Manual" mode and cook for 10 minutes at High pressure. Once cooking is complete, use a natural pressure release; carefully remove the lid.

Serve warm.

Per serving: 484 Calories; 24.3g Fat; 20.2g Carbs; 43.7g Protein; 1.1g Sugars

163. Easy Pork Mélange with Polenta

(Ready in about 30 minutes | Servings 4)

Ingredients

1 tablespoon olive oil
1 pound boneless pork top loin roast, cut into cubes
2 spicy pork sausages, sliced
1 bell pepper, sliced
1 jalapeno pepper, sliced
2 garlic cloves, chopped
1 cup chicken bone broth
Salt and ground black pepper, to taste
1 cup polenta
4 cups water
1 teaspoon salt
1/2 teaspoon paprika

Directions

Press the "Sauté" button and heat the oil. Once hot, cook the pork until no longer pink; add the sausage and cook for 2 to 3 minutes more.

Add the peppers, garlic, broth, salt, and black pepper.

Secure the lid. Choose the "Manual" mode and cook for 15 minutes at High pressure. Once cooking is complete, use a quick pressure release; carefully remove the lid.

Clean the inner pot. Add the polenta, water and 1 teaspoon of salt and mix to combine.

Secure the lid. Choose the "Manual" mode and cook for 9 minutes at High pressure. Once cooking is complete, use a quick pressure release; carefully remove the lid.

Divide your polenta between serving bowls; top with the pork mélange and paprika. Serve warm.

Per serving: 474 Calories; 22.4g Fat; 16.8g Carbs; 45.9g Protein; 1.5g Sugars

164. Japanese Ground Pork (Buta Niku No Mushimono)

(Ready in about 15 minutes | Servings 4)

Ingredients

1 teaspoon sesame oil
1 pound ground pork
4 fresh shiitake, sliced
1 cup chicken broth
2 tablespoons tamari sauce
2 cloves garlic, minced
2 tablespoons sake
1 teaspoon fresh ginger, grated
Sea salt and ground black pepper, to taste

Directions

Press the "Sauté" button and heat the oil. Once hot, cook the ground pork until no longer pink.

Add the fresh shiitake, chicken broth, tamari sauce, garlic, sake, ginger, salt, and black pepper.

Secure the lid. Choose the "Poultry" mode and High pressure; cook for 5 minutes. Once cooking is complete, use a quick release.

Spoon into individual bowls. Enjoy!

Per serving: 460 Calories; 28.9g Fat; 2.7g Carbs; 42.7g Protein; 0.8g Sugars

165. Ground Pork and Vegetable Casserole

(Ready in about 25 minutes | Servings 4)

Ingredients

1 teaspoon olive oil
1 ½ pounds ground pork
2 carrots, sliced
1 parsnip, sliced
1 stalk celery, sliced
2 sweet peppers, sliced
1 onion, sliced
4 cloves garlic, sliced
1 cup whole kernel corn, frozen
1/4 cup Marsala wine
2 fresh tomatoes, pureed
1/2 cup water
Kosher salt and ground black pepper, to taste

Directions

Press the "Sauté" button and heat the oil. Once hot, cook the ground pork for 2 to 3 minutes, stirring frequently.

Add a splash of wine to deglaze the pot. Add the remaining ingredients.

Secure the lid. Choose the "Manual" mode and cook for 18 minutes at High pressure. Once cooking is complete, use a quick pressure release; carefully remove the lid.

Taste and adjust the seasonings. Bon appétit!

Per serving: 462 Calories; 29.9g Fat; 19.1g Carbs; 33.2g Protein; 5.7g Sugars

166. Holiday Orange Glazed Ham

(Ready in about 20 minutes | Servings 6)

Ingredients

3 pounds spiral sliced ham
1/2 cup orange juice
2 tablespoons bourbon
4 tablespoons maple syrup
Sea salt and ground black pepper, to taste

Directions

Place 1 cup of water and a metal trivet in the inner pot.

Then, thoroughly combine the orange juice, bourbon, maple syrup, salt and pepper.

Place the ham on foil. Fold up the sides of the foil to make a bowl-like shape. Pour the orange glaze all over the ham; wrap the foil around the ham. Lower the ham onto the trivet.

Secure the lid. Choose the "Manual" mode and cook for 10 minutes at High pressure. Once cooking is complete, use a quick pressure release; carefully remove the lid.

Transfer to a cooling rack before serving. Bon appétit!

Per serving: 415 Calories; 19.5g Fat; 20g Carbs; 37.8g Protein; 9.7g Sugars

167. Saucy Pork Sausage with Macaroni

(Ready in about 15 minutes | Servings 6)

Ingredients

1 tablespoon olive oil
1 yellow onion, finely chopped
2 cloves garlic, minced
1 pound pork sausage, casing removed, coarsely chopped
Salt, to taste
1/2 teaspoon ground black pepper
1/2 teaspoon red pepper flakes, crushed
1 teaspoon dried basil
1 teaspoon dried oregano
1 teaspoon stone-ground mustard
1 cup water
1 cup tomato purée
1 pound macaroni
4 ounces Colby cheese, shredded

Directions

Press the "Sauté" button to preheat your Instant Pot. Then, heat the oil; now, cook the onion until translucent.

Now, add the garlic and sausage; continue to cook for 4 minutes more. Stir in the seasonings, mustard, water, tomato purée, and macaroni

Secure the lid. Choose the "Manual" setting and cook at High pressure for 6 minutes. Once cooking is complete, use a quick pressure release; carefully remove the lid.

Top with the Colby cheese; seal the lid and let it sit in the residual heat until the cheese is melted. Bon appétit!

Per serving: 495 Calories; 15.2g Fat; 60g Carbs; 27.8g Protein; 4.5g Sugars

168. Apple Maple Pulled Pork

(Ready in about 35 minutes | Servings 8)

Ingredients

2 ½ pounds pork butt, cut into
bite-sized cubes
1/2 cup vegetable broth
1/2 cup barbecue sauce
Sea salt and ground black pepper
1 teaspoon dried oregano
1/2 teaspoon dried basil
1 tablespoon maple syrup
1 red chili pepper, minced
1 cooking apple, cored and diced
1 lemon, sliced

Directions

Add the pork, broth, barbecue sauce, salt, black pepper, oregano, basil,
maple syrup, chili pepper, and apple to your Instant Pot.

Secure the lid. Choose the "Soup" setting and cook at High pressure for
30 minutes. Once cooking is complete, use a natural pressure release;
carefully remove the lid.

Shred the pork with two forks. Return it back to the Instant Pot. Serve
with lemon slices. Bon appétit!

Per serving: 434 Calories; 25.2g Fat; 13.6g Carbs; 36.1g Protein;
10.5g Sugars

169. Pork with Raisin and Port Sauce

(Ready in about 35 minutes | Servings 6)

Ingredients

1 tablespoon canola oil
2 pounds pork loin roast, boneless
Kosher salt, to taste
1/2 teaspoon ground black pepper
1 teaspoon paprika
1/2 teaspoon mustard powder
1 teaspoon dried marjoram
2 cloves garlic, crushed
4 ounces raisins
1/2 cup port wine
1 cup pomegranate juice
1/2 teaspoon fresh ginger, grated

Directions

Press the "Sauté" button to preheat your Instant Pot. Now, heat the oil;
sear the pork loin for 3 minutes on each side.

Then, add the remaining ingredients to your Instant Pot.

Secure the lid. Choose the "Poultry" setting and cook at High pressure
for 15 minutes. Once cooking is complete, use a natural pressure release;
carefully remove the lid.

Serve the pork topped with the raisin-port sauce. Bon appétit!

Per serving: 395 Calories; 15.9g Fat; 21.4g Carbs; 40.9g Protein;
16.7g Sugars

170. Chipotle Pork with Salsa

(Ready in about 35 minutes | Servings 6)

Ingredients

1 ½ pounds pork loin, boneless
and well-trimmed
Kosher salt and ground black
pepper, to your liking
1 teaspoon grainy mustard
1 (1-inch) piece fresh ginger root,
grated
1/3 teaspoon ground allspice
1/2 teaspoon ground bay leaf
2 tablespoons brown sugar
1 tablespoon chipotle paste
1 cup broth
For the Salsa Sauce:
2 ripe tomatoes, peeled, seeds
removed, chopped
2 tablespoons onion, finely
chopped
1 clove garlic, minced
1 mild chile pepper
2 tablespoons cilantro, chopped
1 ½ tablespoons lime juice
Salt, to your liking

Directions

Sprinkle the pork loin with all seasonings. Spritz the Instant Pot with a
nonstick cooking spray.

Press the "Sauté" button to heat up your Instant Pot. Sear pork loin on
both sides until just browned.

Add the brown sugar, chipotle paste, and broth. Secure the lid. Choose the
"Manual" setting and cook for 25 minutes at High Pressure.

Once cooking is complete, use a natural release; remove the lid carefully.

Meanwhile, make the salsa by mixing all ingredients. Serve the pork loin
with fresh salsa on the side. Bon appétit!

Per serving: 398 Calories; 19.4g Fat; 8.1g Carbs; 45.5g Protein;
5.9g Sugars

171. Pork Carnitas Taquitos

(Ready in about 1 hour | Servings 8)

Ingredients

1 tablespoon lard, melted
2 pounds pork shoulder
1 tablespoon granulated sugar
1 teaspoon shallot powder
1 teaspoon granulated garlic
Salt and black pepper, to taste
1 teaspoon ground cumin
1 cup ketchup
1 cup tomato paste
1/2 cup dry red wine
1 teaspoon mixed peppercorns
2 bay leaves
1 teaspoon chipotle powder
1/2 cup Manchego cheese,
shredded
16 corn tortillas, warmed

Directions

Press the "Sauté" button to preheat your Instant Pot. Then, melt the lard.
Sear the pork shoulder until it is delicately browned on all sides.

Add the sugar, shallot powder, garlic, salt, black pepper, cumin, ketchup,
tomato paste, wine, peppercorns, bay leaves, and chipotle powder.

Secure the lid. Choose the "Meat/Stew" setting and cook at High pressure
for 45 minutes. Once cooking is complete, use a natural pressure release;
carefully remove the lid.

Shred the meat with two forks. Divide the shredded pork among tortillas.
Top with the cheese. Roll each tortilla and brush it lightly with oil.

Arrange the tortillas on a cookie sheet. Bake approximately 13 minutes
and serve. Enjoy!

Per serving: 417 Calories; 24.4g Fat; 16.6g Carbs; 32.3g Protein; 11.8g Sugars

172. Pork Chops with Creamed Mustard Sauce

(Ready in about 15 minutes | Servings 4)

Ingredients

2 tablespoons canola oil
4 pork loin chops
Salt and ground black pepper, to
taste
1 teaspoon smoked paprika
1/2 cup cream of celery soup
1/2 cup chicken broth
1 cup sour cream
1 tablespoon Dijon mustard

Directions

Press the "Sauté" button to preheat your Instant Pot. Then, heat the oil and
sear the pork chops for 2 minutes per side.

Then, stir in the salt, black pepper, paprika, cream of celery soup, and
chicken broth.

Secure the lid. Choose the "Manual" setting and cook at High pressure
for 9 minutes. Once cooking is complete, use a quick pressure release;
carefully remove the lid.

Remove the pork chops from the Instant Pot.

Fold in the sour cream and Dijon mustard. Press the "Sauté" button again
and let it simmer until the sauce is reduced and heated through. Bon appétit!

Per serving: 433 Calories; 22.7g Fat; 7g Carbs; 48.3g Protein; 0.8g Sugars

173. French-Style Pork and Bean Casserole

(Ready in about 40 minutes | Servings 6)

Ingredients

1 tablespoon olive oil
1 pound pork shoulder, cut into
cubes
1/2 pound pork sausage, sliced
1 cup water
1 tablespoon beef bouillon
granules
1 pound dry cannellini beans
1 cloves garlic, finely minced
1 yellow onion, sliced
1 parsnip, sliced
1 carrots, sliced
1 teaspoon celery seeds
1/2 teaspoon mustard seeds
1/2 teaspoon cumin powder
Sea salt and ground black pepper,
to taste
1 ½ cups sour cream

Directions

Press the "Sauté" button to preheat your Instant Pot. Heat the olive oil
until sizzling.

Then, brown the meat and sausage for 3 to 4 minutes, stirring periodically.

Add the water, beef bouillon granules, cannellini beans, garlic, onion,
parsnip, carrot, and seasonings.

Secure the lid. Choose the "Bean/Chili" setting and cook at High pressure
for 30 minutes. Once cooking is complete, use a natural pressure release;
carefully remove the lid.

Serve topped with sour cream. Enjoy!

Per serving: 491 Calories; 27g Fat; 25.5g Carbs; 36.1g Protein; 7.1g Sugars

174. Easy Louisiana Ribs

(Ready in about 30 minutes | Servings 6)

Ingredients

2 pounds baby back ribs
2 slices fresh ginger
1/2 cup dry wine
1 tablespoon brown sugar
2 cloves garlic, sliced
2 tablespoons soy sauce
1 cup beef bone broth
1 teaspoon Cajun seasoning
Sat, to taste

Directions

Add all of the above ingredients to your Instant Pot.

Secure the lid. Choose the "Meat/Stew" setting and cook at High pressure for 20 minutes. Once cooking is complete, use a natural pressure release; carefully remove the lid.

Serve warm and enjoy!

Per serving: 365 Calories; 25g Fat; 3.7g Carbs; 3.1g Protein; 2.6g Sugars

175. Pork Steaks Marchand de Vin

(Ready in about 15 minutes | Servings 6)

Ingredients

1 tablespoon lard, melted
1 ½ pounds pork steaks
1 cup demi-glace
1/2 cup red wine
2 bay leaves
Sea salt and ground black pepper, to taste
1 teaspoon dried oregano

Directions

Press the "Sauté" button to preheat your Instant Pot. Melt the lard. Now, sear the pork steaks approximately 3 minutes per side.

Add the remaining ingredients to the Instant Pot.

Secure the lid. Choose the "Manual" setting and cook at High pressure for 8 minutes. Once cooking is complete, use a quick pressure release; carefully remove the lid.

Press the "Sauté" button one more time and continue simmering until the cooking liquid has reduced by three-fourths. Bon appétit!

Per serving: 330 Calories; 22.2g Fat; 1.7g Carbs; 28.7g Protein; 0.6g Sugars

176. Filipino Pork Soup

(Ready in about 40 minutes | Servings 4)

Ingredients

2 tablespoons vegetable oil
3/4 pound bone-in pork chops
1/2 cup sweet onion, chopped
1 teaspoon fresh garlic, crushed
2 sweet peppers, deveined and chopped
4 potatoes, peeled and diced
2 carrots, trimmed and thinly sliced
1 parsnip, trimmed and thinly sliced
4 cups vegetable broth, preferably homemade
Salt and freshly ground black pepper, to taste
1/2 teaspoon paprika
1 teaspoon dried thyme
1 (1/2-inch) piece fresh ginger, grated
1 (1.41-ounce) package tamarind soup base

Directions

Preheat your Instant Pot on "Sauté" setting. Then, heat the vegetable oil and brown the pork chops for 4 minutes on each side.

Add the remaining ingredients and secure the lid. Choose the "Soup" mode and cook for 30 minutes at High pressure.

Once cooking is complete, use a natural pressure release; remove the lid carefully. Serve hot with toasted bread. Bon appétit!

Per serving: 444 Calories; 16.9g Fat; 42.2g Carbs; 31.6g Protein; 5.1g Sugars

177. Kid-Friendly Pork Sandwiches

(Ready in about 50 minutes | Servings 6)

Ingredients

2 teaspoons lard, at room temperature
2 pounds pork shoulder roast, rind removed, boneless
2 garlic cloves, chopped
1 (1-inch) piece fresh ginger, peeled and grated
1 tablespoon maple syrup
1/4 cup dry red wine
1 cup water
1/2 tablespoon Worcestershire sauce
Sea salt, to taste
1/3 teaspoon ground black pepper
2 sprig thyme
2 whole star anise
1 tablespoon arrowroot powder
12 soft lunch rolls, warmed
1 cup pickles, sliced

Directions

Press the "Sauté" button to preheat your Instant Pot. Now, melt the lard. Once hot, sear the pork shoulder roast for 3 minutes per side.

Add the garlic, ginger, maple syrup, wine, water, Worcestershire sauce, and seasonings to the Instant Pot.

Secure the lid. Choose the "Meat/Stew" setting and cook at High pressure for 45 minutes. Once cooking is complete, use a natural pressure release; carefully remove the lid.

Transfer the pork shoulder to a chopping board. Shred the meat and return it back to the Instant Pot.

Whisk the arrowroot powder with 2 tablespoons of water; press the "Sauté" button again and add the slurry. Let it simmer until thickened.

Assemble the sandwiches with the pork and pickles. Bon appétit!

Per serving: 480 Calories; 18.4g Fat; 30.1g Carbs; 45.1g Protein; 3.3g Sugars

178. Tender Aji Panca Pork

(Ready in about 55 minutes | Servings 6)

Ingredients

1 tablespoon lard
2 pounds pork shoulder
3/4 cup broth, preferably homemade
1/3 cup honey
2 tablespoons champagne vinegar
1 teaspoon garlic, minced
2 tablespoons soy sauce
1 teaspoon aji panca powder
Kosher salt and ground black pepper, to your liking
1 tablespoon flaxseed, ground

Directions

Press the "Sauté" button, and melt the lard. Once hot, sear the pork shoulder on all sides until just browned.

Add the broth, honey, vinegar, garlic, soy sauce, aji panca powder, salt, and pepper. Secure the lid. Select the "Manual" mode, High pressure and 50 minutes.

Once cooking is complete, use a natural release; remove the lid carefully. Set the pork shoulder aside keeping it warm.

Now, press the "Sauté" button again and add ground flaxseed to the cooking liquid. Let it simmer until the sauce has thickened.

Taste, adjust the seasoning and pour the sauce over the reserved pork shoulder. Bon appétit!

Per serving: 511 Calories; 30.7g Fat; 17.5g Carbs; 39.2g Protein; 16.4g Sugars

179. Southwestern-Style Cheese Meatloaf

(Ready in about 35 minutes | Servings 6)

Ingredients

1 pound ground pork
1 egg
1/2 cup scallions, minced
2 garlic cloves, minced
1/2 cup whole grain tortilla chips, finely crushed
1/2 cup Cotija cheese, crumbled
Sea salt and ground black pepper, to taste
1 teaspoon smoked paprika
1 cup bottled chipotle salsa
2 tablespoons ketchup
1 teaspoon fresh lime juice

Directions

Prepare your Instant Pot by adding 1 cup of water and a metal rack to its bottom.

Thoroughly combine the ground pork, egg, scallions, garlic, crushed tortilla chips, Cotija cheese, salt, black pepper, paprika, and 1/2 cup of salsa in a mixing bowl.

Now, shape the mixture into a meatloaf. Transfer the meatloaf to a lightly greased baking pan. Lower the baking pan onto the rack.

In a bowl, mix the remaining 1/2 cup of salsa with ketchup and lime juice. Brush the salsa mixture over top of the meatloaf.

Secure the lid. Choose the "Bean/Chili" setting and cook at High pressure for 30 minutes. Once cooking is complete, use a quick pressure release; carefully remove the lid. Bon appétit!

Per serving: 352 Calories; 22.1g Fat; 13.2g Carbs; 24.8g Protein; 3.7g Sugars

180. Pork Roast with Fresh Avocado Sauce

(Ready in about 35 minutes | Servings 6)

Ingredients

2 pounds pork roast, cut into cubes	2 teaspoons olive oil
1 cup water	Freshly ground black pepper, to taste
1 tablespoon beef bouillon granules	Avocado Sauce:
1 tablespoon fish sauce	1 avocado, pitted and peeled
1 habanero pepper, minced	2 tablespoons mayonnaise
1/2 cup scallions, chopped	2 garlic cloves, pressed
1 teaspoon ginger-garlic paste	1 tablespoon fresh lime juice

Directions

Add the pork roast, water, beef bouillon granules, fish sauce, habanero pepper, scallions, ginger-garlic paste, olive oil, and ground black pepper to the Instant Pot.

Secure the lid. Choose the "Meat/Stew" setting and cook at High pressure for 30 minutes. Once cooking is complete, use a natural pressure release; carefully remove the lid.

Meanwhile, whisk all of the sauce ingredients in a mixing bowl. Serve with the pork roast and enjoy!

Per serving: 442 Calories; 26.4g Fat; 8.7g Carbs; 42.3g Protein; 1.4g Sugars

181. Thai Pork Medallion Curry

(Ready in about 15 minutes | Servings 4)

Ingredients

2 teaspoons coconut oil	2 cloves garlic, minced
1 pound pork medallions	2 tablespoons Thai green curry paste
1/2 teaspoon cumin seeds	1 tablespoon apple cider vinegar
1 jalapeño pepper, seeded and minced	Salt and ground black pepper, to taste
1 bay leaf	1/2 teaspoon cayenne pepper
1 ½ tablespoons fish sauce	Zest and juice of 1 lime
1 cup beef bone broth	

Directions

Press the "Sauté" button to preheat the Instant Pot. Heat the coconut oil. Once hot, sear the pork medallions for 2 to 3 minutes.

Add the remaining ingredients, including roasted seasonings.

Secure the lid. Choose the "Manual" setting and cook at High pressure for 8 minutes. Once cooking is complete, use a quick pressure release; carefully remove the lid.

Serve with basmati rice and enjoy!

Per serving: 286 Calories; 15.3g Fat; 5.8g Carbs; 30.5g Protein; 1.7g Sugars

182. Five-Star Picnic Shoulder

(Ready in about 50 minutes | Servings 4)

Ingredients

1 ½ pounds pork picnic shoulder	1 teaspoon oregano, dried
1 teaspoon garlic powder	Sea salt and ground black pepper, to taste
1/2 teaspoon cumin powder	1/2 cup fresh orange juice
1/4 teaspoon cinnamon, ground	1 cup beef bone broth
1 teaspoon celery seeds	

Directions

Place all of the above ingredients in the Instant Pot.

Secure the lid. Choose the "Meat/Stew" setting and cook at High pressure for 45 minutes. Once cooking is complete, use a natural pressure release; carefully remove the lid.

Test for doneness and thinly slice the pork; transfer to a serving platter. Serve warm and enjoy!

Per serving: 288 Calories; 12.7g Fat; 6.1g Carbs; 35.2g Protein; 3.2g Sugars

183. Goan Pork Vindaloo

(Ready in about 15 minutes + marinating time | Servings 6)

Ingredients

1 cup water	1 bay leaf
1/4 cup dry red wine	1 tablespoon lard, melted
2 tablespoons white vinegar	2 pounds pork rib chops
Salt and ground black pepper, to taste	4 dried Kashmiri chili peppers, stemmed and chopped
1 teaspoon garlic, minced	1 cinnamon stick
2 tablespoons honey	

Directions

Place the water, wine, vinegar, salt, black pepper, garlic, honey and bay leaf in a ceramic dish. Add the rib chops and let them marinate for 2 hours in the refrigerator.

Press the "Sauté" button to preheat your Instant Pot. Melt the lard and sear the pork until it is delicately browned.

Then, transfer the pork along with the marinade to the Instant Pot. Add the Kashmiri chili peppers and cinnamon stick.

Secure the lid. Now, select the "Manual" mode, High pressure and 8 minutes. Once cooking is complete, use a quick release; carefully remove the lid. Serve warm.

Per serving: 340 Calories; 14.8g Fat; 9.5g Carbs; 39.8g Protein; 7.7g Sugars

184. Pork Soup with Queso Fresco Cheese

(Ready in about 25 minutes | Servings 6)

Ingredients

2 pounds pork stew meat, cubed	1 teaspoon dried oregano
2 garlic cloves, smashed	1 teaspoon dried basil
1 teaspoon fresh ginger, grated	Sea salt, to taste
1/2 cup yellow onion, chopped	1/4 teaspoon freshly ground pepper, or more to taste
1 fresh poblano chile, minced	1 cup Queso fresco cheese, crumbled
5 cups water	
1 cup tomato paste	
2 bouillon cubes	

Directions

Place all of the above ingredients, except for the Queso fresco cheese, in your Instant Pot.

Secure the lid. Choose the "Soup" setting and cook at High pressure for 20 minutes. Once cooking is complete, use a quick pressure release; carefully remove the lid.

Divide the warm soup among serving bowls; top each serving with crumbled cheese and serve immediately.

Per serving: 334 Calories; 10.6g Fat; 10g Carbs; 48.4g Protein; 6.1g Sugars

185. Pork Tacos with Tomatillo Sauce

(Ready in about 45 minutes | Servings 6)

Ingredients

2 pounds meaty pork belly, skin-on
4 cloves garlic, halved
Seasoned salt and freshly ground black pepper, to taste
1 teaspoon mustard powder
1/2 teaspoon dried sage, crushed
1 teaspoon dried marjoram
1 cup stock
1 bay leaf
6 large tortillas, warmed
For the Sauce:
1 cup tomatillos, finely chopped
2 morita chiles, finely chopped
1 red onion, finely chopped
1/4 cup fresh lime juice
Salt, to your liking

Directions

Rub the pork belly with garlic halves. Sprinkle the pork belly with salt, black pepper, mustard powder, sage, and marjoram.

Brush the bottom of the Instant Pot with a nonstick cooking oil.

Press the "Sauté" button; add the pork belly, skin side down. Cook until it is browned on all sides.

Add the stock and bay leaf; secure the lid. Now, select the "Manual" mode, High pressure and 35 minutes.

Once cooking is complete, use a quick release; remove the lid carefully.

Meanwhile, make the sauce by mixing all the sauce ingredients.

Allow the pork belly to cool slightly. Place the pork belly, skin side up, on a cutting board. Slice across the grain.

Divide the sliced pork among warm tortillas, add the sauce and serve warm.

Per serving: 477 Calories; 20g Fat; 27.7g Carbs; 43.8g Protein; 3.2g Sugars

186. Hungarian Pork Paprikash

(Ready in about 30 minutes | Servings 8)

Ingredients

2 tablespoons olive oil
1 cup red onions, chopped
2 garlic cloves, minced
1 cup button mushrooms, sliced
2 pounds pork stew meat, cubed
2 bell pepper, deveined and thinly sliced
1 chili pepper, deveined and minced
2 carrots, peeled and cut into large pieces
1 can tomatoes, crushed
6 cups chicken broth
Salt and ground black pepper, to taste
1 teaspoon Hungarian paprika
1 bay leaf
1 cup sour cream

Directions

Press the "Sauté" button to preheat your Instant Pot. Now, heat the oil until sizzling. Then, sauté the onion until tender and translucent.

Stir in the garlic and mushrooms; continue to sauté an additional 2 minute or until they are fragrant. Reserve.

Cook the meat for 2 to 3 minutes, stirring frequently; add the reserved onion/mushroom mixture to your Instant Pot.

Add the pepper, carrots, tomatoes, chicken broth, salt, pepper, paprika, and bay leaf.

Secure the lid. Choose the "Soup" setting and cook at High pressure for 20 minutes. Once cooking is complete, use a quick pressure release; carefully remove the lid.

Garnish each serving with a dollop of sour cream and serve.

Per serving: 549 Calories; 22.6g Fat; 9.6g Carbs; 72.9g Protein; 3.1g Sugars

187. Mexican Posole Rojo

(Ready in about 35 minutes | Servings 8)

Ingredients

1 heaping tablespoon lard, melted
1 cup shallots, chopped
2 cloves garlic, sliced
2 pounds pork butt, cut into 2-inch pieces
2 sprigs thyme, leaves chopped
1/2 teaspoon cumin
1 teaspoon Mexican oregano
Sea salt and ground black pepper, to taste
4 cups chicken bone broth
1/2 cup fresh ripe tomato, puréed
2 bay leaves
1 celery with leaves, chopped
2 dried ancho chiles, chopped
1 red bell pepper, thinly sliced
1 (15-ounce) can white hominy, drained and rinsed

Directions

Press the "Sauté" button to preheat your Instant Pot. Now, melt the lard. Once hot, sauté the shallots and garlic until they are tender and fragrant.

Add the pork and cook an additional 3 minutes or until it is delicately browned. Add the remaining ingredients and gently stir to combine.

Secure the lid. Choose the "Poultry" setting and cook at High pressure for 30 minutes. Once cooking is complete, use a natural pressure release; carefully remove the lid.

Divide between individual bowls and serve warm. Enjoy!

Per serving: 503 Calories; 30.4g Fat; 11.6g Carbs; 42.6g Protein; 2.9g Sugars

188. Easy Pork Sliders

(Ready in about 1 hour 10 minutes + marinating time | Servings 6)

Ingredients

2 pounds pork loin roast, cut into cubes
4 cloves garlic, smashed
2 tablespoons fresh scallions, chopped
1/2 cup pineapple juice
Salt and black pepper, to taste
1 teaspoon cayenne pepper
1/4 teaspoon mustard seeds
1/4 teaspoon cumin
1 ½ tablespoons olive oil
1 head fresh Iceberg lettuce, leaves separated
2 tablespoons Dijon mustard
6 dinner rolls

Directions

Place the pork, garlic, scallions, pineapple, juice, salt, black pepper, cayenne pepper, mustard seeds, and cumin in a mixing bowl; wrap with a foil and transfer to your refrigerator for 2 hours.

Press the "Sauté" button and heat the olive oil. Now, cook the pork, working in batches, until it is well browned.

Secure the lid. Now, select the "Manual" mode, High pressure and 60 minutes. Once cooking is complete, use a natural release; carefully remove the lid.

Serve over dinner rolls, garnished with fresh lettuce and Dijon mustard. Bon appétit!

Per serving: 433 Calories; 18.8g Fat; 20.9g Carbs; 43.9g Protein; 6g Sugars

189. Traditional Pork Ragù

(Ready in about 30 minutes | Servings 6)

Ingredients

2 tablespoons olive oil
1 ½ pounds pork stew meat, cubed
1 onion, chopped
2 garlic cloves, chopped
2 cups roasted vegetable stock
1/4 cup red wine
1/2 (15-ounce) can tomato sauce
2 carrots, sliced
1 celery with leaves, chopped
1 teaspoon Italian seasoning
Salt and ground black pepper, to taste

Directions

Press the "Sauté" button to preheat your Instant Pot. Heat the oil and sauté the pork and onions until the meat is delicately browned.

Add the remaining ingredients.

Secure the lid. Choose the "Soup" setting and cook at High pressure for 20 minutes. Once cooking is complete, use a quick pressure release; carefully remove the lid.

Serve topped with shredded cheese if desired. Bon appétit!

Per serving: 385 Calories; 25.4g Fat; 6.7g Carbs; 31.2g Protein; 3.7g Sugars

190. Pork Medallions with Root Vegetables

(Ready in about 25 minutes | Servings 4)

Ingredients

4 pork medallions
1 teaspoon cayenne pepper
1 teaspoon cumin, ground
Salt and black pepper, to taste
1 ½ tablespoons olive oil
2 shallots, chopped
1 garlic cloves, minced

1 cup vegetable stock
2 sprigs rosemary
2 parsnips, thinly sliced
1 turnip, thinly sliced
2 carrots, thinly sliced
1 tablespoon cornstarch

Directions

Season the pork medallions with cayenne pepper, cumin, salt, and black pepper. Press the "Sauté" button and heat the olive oil.

Sear the pork medallions for 4 minutes on each side; reserve. Cook the shallots in the pan drippings until just tender and fragrant.

Return the pork medallions to the Instant Pot along with garlic, stock, and rosemary. Secure the lid. Choose the "Manual" setting and cook for 10 minutes at High pressure.

Once cooking is complete, use a quick release; remove the lid carefully.

Select the "Manual" mode again and cook root vegetables for 4 minutes; use a quick release again. Remove the vegetables from the Instant Pot.

Add the cornstarch and 1 tablespoons of cold water to a small bowl; stir until smooth paste forms.

Add the slurry to your Instant Pot, press the "Sauté" button and cook until the sauce is concentrated. Serve the sauce over the reserved pork and root vegetables.

Per serving: 438 Calories; 22.3g Fat; 16.9g Carbs; 41g Protein; 4.4g Sugars

191. Braised Pork Leg with Green Onions

(Ready in about 2 hours 50 minutes | Servings 8)

Ingredients

2 garlic cloves, minced
1 ½ tablespoons honey
1 teaspoon Aleppo red pepper
Sea salt and ground black pepper, to taste
2 star anise
3 pounds pork leg

2 tablespoons tamari sauce
1/4 cup tomato paste
1/4 cup shaoxing rice wine
1/2 cup water
2 tablespoons olive oil
A bunch of green onions, chopped

Directions

Add all ingredients, except for the olive oil and green onions, to a ceramic dish. Cover the dish and place in your refrigerator for 2 hours.

Then, press the "Sauté" button to preheat your Instant Pot. Heat the oil until sizzling. Now, cook the pork until delicately browned on all sides, about 10 minutes. Then, add the marinade.

Secure the lid. Choose the "Meat/Stew" setting and cook at High pressure for 35 minutes. Once cooking is complete, use a natural pressure release; carefully remove the lid.

Add the green onions to the Instant Pot; seal the lid and let it sit approximately 5 minutes. Serve warm.

Per serving: 287 Calories; 10g Fat; 10.8g Carbs; 38.2g Protein; 6.8g Sugars

192. Momofuku Bo Ssam (Korean-Style Pork)

(Ready in about 1 hour 5 minutes | Servings 10)

Ingredients

1 heaping tablespoon lard, at room temperature
3 pounds pork shoulder
1/2 cup yellow onions, chopped
2 garlic cloves, minced
1/2 cup chicken bone broth
1/2 cup orange juice
1 tablespoon tamari sauce

Sea salt and ground black pepper, to taste
1/2 teaspoon Gochugaru
1 tablespoon castor sugar
1 stick butter
2 bay leaves
1/4 cup doenjang (korean soybean paste)
2 tablespoons walnuts, ground

Directions

Press the "Sauté" button to preheat your Instant Pot. Melt the lard and brown the pork shoulder for 5 minutes, turning once or twice.

Add the onions, garlic, broth, orange juice, tamari sauce, salt, black pepper, teaspoon Gochugaru, and sugar.

Secure the lid. Choose the "Manual" setting and cook at High pressure for 50 minutes. Once cooking is complete, use a natural pressure release; carefully remove the lid.

Transfer the pork shoulder to a cutting board; allow it to cool; then, cut into slices.

Then, press the "Sauté" button again. Add the remaining ingredients and let it simmer for 5 to 6 minutes or until the sauce is thoroughly heated and reduced by half.

Spoon the sauce over the pork and serve. Bon appétit!

Per serving: 512 Calories; 37.2g Fat; 4.2g Carbs; 38.2g Protein; 2.3g Sugars

193. Provençal Sausage Casserole

(Ready in about 15 minutes | Servings 4)

Ingredients

2 tablespoons olive oil
1 pound pork sausages, sliced
1 leek, thinly sliced
2 garlic cloves, crushed
2 ripe tomatoes, chopped
1 cup vegetable broth
2 tablespoons white wine
1 tablespoon oyster sauce

1 tablespoon Herbs de Provence
1 (15-ounce) can black beans
Sea salt, to taste
1/4 teaspoon freshly ground black pepper
1 teaspoon cayenne pepper
1/2 teaspoon ground bay leaf

Directions

Press the "Sauté" button to preheat your Instant Pot. Then, heat the oil until sizzling. Brown the sausage for 2 to 3 minutes.

Add the remaining ingredients and gently stir to combine.

Secure the lid. Choose the "Manual" setting and cook at High pressure for 8 minutes. Once cooking is complete, use a quick pressure release; carefully remove the lid.

Divide among individual bowls and serve warm. Bon appétit!

Per serving: 376 Calories; 29.6g Fat; 12.9g Carbs; 15g Protein; 3.1g Sugars

194. Sunday Beer-Braised Ribs

(Ready in about 40 minutes | Servings 8)

Ingredients

1/2 cup chicken stock
1 (12-ounce) bottle dark beer
2 ripe tomatillos, chopped
2 garlic cloves, minced
1 bell pepper, deveined and chopped
1 jalapeno pepper, deveined and chopped

2 ½ pounds baby back ribs
Salt and ground black pepper, to taste
1/2 teaspoon ground allspice
1 teaspoon fennel seeds
Lime wedges, for serving

Directions

Simply throw all of the above ingredients, except for the lime wedges, into your Instant Pot. Secure the lid.

Choose the "Manual" setting and cook for 35 minutes at High pressure.

Once cooking is complete, use a natural release; remove the lid carefully. Serve garnished with lime wedges. Bon appétit!

Per serving: 405 Calories; 24.1g Fat; 3.2g Carbs; 40.5g Protein; 0.7g Sugars

195. Fancy Pork Pâté

(Ready in about 55 minutes + chilling time | Servings 10)

Ingredients

1 tablespoon olive oil
1 ½ pounds boneless pork shoulder, cubed
4 ounces pork liver
1 red onion, chopped
2 cloves garlic, minced
1 teaspoon dried basil
1 teaspoon mustard powder

Sea salt and ground black pepper, to taste
1 teaspoon ground nutmeg
1/2 teaspoon ground ginger
1 teaspoon ground coriander
2 tablespoons brandy
1/2 cup heavy cream

Directions

Press the "Sauté" button to preheat your Instant Pot. Heat the olive oil; once hot, sear the pork shoulder and pork liver until they are delicately browned; reserve.

Add the onion and garlic and continue to sauté them in pan drippings. Return the meat and pork liver back to the Instant Pot.

Add the remaining ingredients, except for the heavy cream.

Secure the lid. Choose the "Manual" setting and cook at High pressure for 50 minutes. Once cooking is complete, use a natural pressure release; carefully remove the lid.

Fold in the heavy cream. Give it a good stir and seal the lid. Let it sit in the residual heat until thoroughly warmed. Refrigerate until it is completely chilled.

Per serving: 147 Calories; 6.4g Fat; 2.5g Carbs; 18.2g Protein; 0.9g Sugars

196. Two-Cheese and Bacon Bread Pudding

(Ready in about 40 minutes | Servings 6)

Ingredients

1 loaf of sourdough bread, cut into chunks
2 tablespoons butter, melted
6 slices Canadian bacon, chopped
6 ounces Monterey-Jack cheese, grated
3 eggs, beaten

1/2 cup milk
1/2 cup cream cheese
1/4 teaspoon marjoram
1 teaspoon onion powder
Garlic salt and ground black pepper, to taste

Directions

Prepare your Instant Pot by adding 1 ½ cups of water and a metal rack to its bottom.

Spritz the bottom and sides of a soufflé dish with a nonstick cooking spray. Add 1/2 of the bread cubes to the bottom of the dish; drizzle the melted butter over them.

Add the bacon and grated Monterey-Jack cheese. Add the remaining 1/2 of bread cubes.

In a mixing bowl, thoroughly combine the eggs, milk, cheese marjoram, onion powder, garlic salt, and black pepper. Pour this mixture over the top.

Lower the soufflé dish onto the prepared metal rack. Cover with a piece of foil.

Secure the lid. Choose the "Bean/Chili" setting and cook at High pressure for 25 minutes. Once cooking is complete, use a quick pressure release; carefully remove the lid.

Allow it to stand on a cooling rack for 10 to 15 minutes before cutting and serving. Bon appétit!

Per serving: 385 Calories; 25.3g Fat; 17.1g Carbs; 21.8g Protein; 4.1g Sugars

197. Classic Pasta Bolognese

(Ready in about 30 minutes | Servings 4)

Ingredients

1 ½ tablespoons olive oil
1 cup leeks, chopped
2 garlic cloves, minced
1 pound ground pork
1/2 pound ground beef
1 celery stick, diced small
1 sweet pepper, finely chopped

1 jalapeno, finely chopped
1 ½ cups broth, preferably homemade
1 (28-ounce) can Italian tomatoes, finely chopped
2 pounds penne rigate
1/4 cup heavy cream

Directions

Press the "Sauté" button. Preheat your Instant Pot and add the oil. Once hot, sweat the leeks for 3 to 4 minutes, stirring frequently.

Add the garlic and cook for 30 seconds more. Add the ground meat and cook for 3 minutes more or until it is just browned.

Add the celery, peppers, broth, tomatoes, and penne rigate. Secure the lid. Choose the "Manual" setting and cook for 15 minutes at High pressure.

Once cooking is complete, use a quick release; remove the lid carefully. Press the "Sauté" button and fold in the heavy cream; stir until heated through.

Divide among individual bowls and eat warm. Bon appétit!

Per serving: 677 Calories; 39.5g Fat; 37.9g Carbs; 43.3g Protein; 2.5g Sugars

198. Spicy Sausages with Beans and Cubanelle Peppers

(Ready in about 15 minutes | Servings 4)

Ingredients

1/2 tablespoon shortening
4 pork spicy sausages, without casing
2 shallots, chopped
2 garlic cloves, minced
1/2 cup Cubanelle peppers, chopped

25 ounces canned black beans, rinsed and drained
1/3 cup water
1/2 teaspoon paprika
Sat, to taste
1 bay leaf

Directions

Press the "Sauté" button to preheat your Instant Pot. Once hot, warm the shortening. Now, cook the sausage, crumbling them with a spatula; reserve.

Next, cook the shallots and garlic in pan drippings until tender and fragrant. Add the other ingredients, along with reserved pork sausages.

Secure the lid. Choose the "Manual" mode, High heat, and 6 minutes.

Once cooking is complete, use a natural release; remove the lid carefully. Discard bay leaf and serve over the hot cooked rice. Bon appétit!

Per serving: 322 Calories; 24.4g Fat; 12.4g Carbs; 14.2g Protein; 2g Sugars

199. Pork Chops in Creamy Herbed Sauce

(Ready in about 15 minutes + marinating time | Servings 6)

Ingredients

2 tablespoons fresh lemon juice
2 garlic cloves, smashed
1 teaspoon mustard powder
1/2 teaspoon ground cumin
1 teaspoon rosemary, minced
1 teaspoon thyme, minced
Sea salt and ground black pepper, to taste

2 tablespoons olive oil
6 pork chops
1/2 cup dry white wine
1/2 cup beef bone broth
2 tablespoons fresh parsley, chopped

Directions

Place the lemon juice, garlic, mustard powder, ground cumin, rosemary, thyme, salt, black pepper, 1 tablespoon of olive oil, and pork chops in a ceramic dish. Allow the pork to marinate at least 2 hours.

Press the "Sauté" button to preheat the Instant Pot. Heat the remaining tablespoon of olive oil. Then, brown the pork for 3 minutes per side.

Deglaze the bottom of the inner pot with the white wine. Pour in the broth.

Secure the lid. Choose the "Manual" setting and cook at High pressure for 8 minutes. Once cooking is complete, use a quick pressure release; carefully remove the lid. Serve garnished with fresh parsley. Bon appétit!

Per serving: 405 Calories; 24g Fat; 1.9g Carbs; 42.9g Protein; 0.6g Sugars

BEEF

200. Lavash Beef Wraps

(Ready in about 20 minutes | Servings 4)

Ingredients

1 ½ tablespoons olive oil
1 ¼ pounds ground beef
2 garlic cloves, chopped
1/2 cup scallions, chopped
1 small Habanero pepper, deveined and minced
1 cup tomato puree
Salt and pepper, to taste

1 teaspoon coriander
1/2 teaspoon caraway seeds
1/4 teaspoon chipotle powder
1/4 teaspoon cloves, ground
1/3 cup chicken stock
4 lavash, warmed
1/2 cup baba ghanoush

Directions

Press the "Sauté" button to heat up your Instant Pot; heat the oil.

Once hot, sauté the ground beef along with the garlic, scallions, and Habanero pepper; cook until the ground beef is no longer pink.

Add the tomato puree and continue to cook 3 minutes longer. Add the seasonings and chicken stock.

Secure the lid. Choose the "Manual" mode; cook for 6 minutes at High pressure. Once cooking is complete, use a natural release and carefully remove the lid.

Spread the meat mixture evenly across the lavash. Top with the baba ghanoush. Now, gently wrap the lavash and serve. Bon appétit!

Per serving: 521 Calories; 22.6g Fat; 35.4g Carbs; 44.8g Protein; 6.2g Sugars

201. Beef with Sweet Apricot-Riesling Sauce

(Ready in about 1 hour 5 minutes | Servings 6)

Ingredients

2 tablespoons olive oil
1 ½ pounds beef brisket
3 cloves garlic, minced or pressed
1 tablespoon Worcestershire sauce
1 celery, diced
1 carrot, diced

1 onion, cut into wedges
1 cup vegetable broth
1 tablespoon honey
1/4 cup late-harvest Riesling
1/3 cup dried apricots, chopped

Directions

Press the "Sauté" button to preheat your Instant Pot. Heat the olive oil. Once hot, cook the beef brisket until it is delicately browned on all sides.

Add the remaining ingredients, except for the dried apricots, to the Instant Pot.

Secure the lid. Choose the "Manual" setting and cook at High pressure for 60 minutes. Once cooking is complete, use a natural pressure release; carefully remove the lid.

Garnish with dried apricots and serve immediately. Bon appétit!

Per serving: 338 Calories; 21.7g Fat; 15.5g Carbs; 18.4g Protein; 10.4g Sugars

202. Roast Beef in Sage-Merlot Sauce

(Ready in about 50 minutes | Servings 6)

Ingredients

2 teaspoons lard, at room temperature
1 ½ pounds beef roast
1 red onion, chopped
2 garlic cloves, smashed
1 carrot, chopped
1 celery stalk, diced
1 cup water
1/2 cups Merlot

Sea salt, to taste
1/2 teaspoon ground black pepper
1 teaspoon paprika
2 bay leaves
1 tablespoon fresh sage
1 tablespoon soy sauce
1 teaspoon butter
1/4 cup fresh chives, chopped

Directions

Press the "Sauté" button to preheat the Instant Pot. Melt the lard and sear the beef until it is browned on all sides.

Add the onion, garlic, carrot, celery, water, merlot, salt, black pepper, paprika, bay leaves, sage, and soy sauce.

Secure the lid. Choose the "Meat/Stew" mode and High pressure; cook for 40 minutes. Once cooking is complete, use a natural pressure release; carefully remove the lid.

Transfer the roast to a cutting board; allow it to cool slightly before slicing.

Press the "Sauté" button and let it simmer until the sauce is reduced. Stir in the butter and press the "Cancel" button.

Spoon the sauce over the sliced beef. Serve garnished with fresh chives and enjoy!

Per serving: 283 Calories; 12.2g Fat; 5.4g Carbs; 30.9g Protein; 2.1g Sugars

203. Spicy Beef in White Rum Sauce

(Ready in about 25 minutes | Servings 6)

Ingredients

2 tablespoons olive oil
1 ½ pounds beef flank steak
Sea salt and freshly ground black pepper, to taste
1 teaspoon cayenne pepper
1 teaspoon dried marjoram
1/2 teaspoon dried thyme
1/2 teaspoon dried basil

1/4 cup white rum
1 cup water
2 bell peppers, deveined and chopped
1 Chile de Arbol, deveined and minced
1 shallot, halved and sliced
1 cup sour cream

Directions

Press the "Sauté" button to preheat your Instant Pot. Then, heat the oil until sizzling. Once hot, cook the beef until browned on all sides.

Add the seasonings. Deglaze the inner pot with white rum and add the water, peppers, and shallot.

Secure the lid. Choose the "Poultry" setting and cook at High pressure for 15 minutes. Once cooking is complete, use a quick pressure release; carefully remove the lid.

Transfer the meat to a cutting board; slice the beef against the grain.

Now, fold in the sour cream and press the "Sauté" button; let it simmer until the cooking liquid is thoroughly warmed and reduced. Serve warm.

Per serving: 293 Calories; 15.6g Fat; 4.3g Carbs; 27.3g Protein; 0.9g Sugars

204. Traditional Beef Biryani

(Ready in about 25 minutes | Servings 6)

Ingredients

1 ½ pounds braising steak, cut into bite-sized cubes
1 (28-ounce) can tomatoes, crushed
1 cup shallot, chopped
2 garlic cloves, peeled and chopped
1 teaspoon coriander seeds
1/2 teaspoon ground cumin

1 tablespoon Garam Masala
1 teaspoon saffron strands
Kosher salt and ground black pepper, to taste
1 heaping teaspoon caster sugar
8 ounces natural yoghurt
4 hard-boiled eggs, peeled and sliced
2 ounces almonds, flaked

Directions

Add the beef steak, canned tomatoes, shallot, garlic, coriander seeds, cumin, Garam Masala, saffron strands, salt, black pepper, and sugar to the Instant Pot.

Secure the lid. Choose the "Meat/Stew" setting and cook at High pressure for 20 minutes. Once cooking is complete, use a natural pressure release; carefully remove the lid.

Add the yogurt and seal the lid. Let it sit in the residual heat until everything is heated through. Serve garnished with eggs and flaked almonds. Enjoy!

Per serving: 370 Calories; 16g Fat; 9.4g Carbs; 49g Protein; 5.5g Sugars

205. Classic Mississippi Roast

(Ready in about 45 minutes | Servings 8)

Ingredients

1 tablespoon tallow, at room temperature
3 pounds shoulder roast
1 teaspoon ginger garlic paste
Sea salt and ground black pepper, to taste

1 packet ranch dressing mix
1 ½ cups vegetable broth
4 pepperoncini peppers
2 pounds russet potatoes, peeled and quartered

Directions

Press the "Sauté" button to preheat your Instant Pot. Now, melt the tallow. Sear the roast until it is delicately browned on all sides.

Then, add the ginger garlic paste, salt, black pepper, ranch dressing mix, and vegetable broth. Top with pepperoncini peppers.

Secure the lid. Choose the "Meat/Stew" mode and High pressure; cook for 35 minutes. Once cooking is complete, use a natural pressure release; carefully remove the lid. Shred the meat with two forks.

Add the potatoes and secure the lid. Choose "Manual" mode and High pressure; cook for 5 minutes. Once cooking is complete, use a quick pressure release; carefully remove the lid.

Serve the pulled beef with the potatoes and enjoy!

Per serving: 313 Calories; 8.1g Fat; 24.8g Carbs; 34.6g Protein; 3.1g Sugars

206. Ground Beef Sirloin Soup

(Ready in about 45 minutes | Servings 4)

Ingredients

1 tablespoon olive oil
1/2 pound beef sirloin, ground
1/2 teaspoon salt
1/2 teaspoon ground black pepper
4 cups bone broth
2 teaspoons dark soy sauce
1/2 cup shallots, chopped
1 teaspoon garlic, minced

2 carrots, chopped
2 Yukon Gold potatoes, chopped
1/2 cup tomato puree
2 bay leaves
1/2 teaspoon dried basil
1 teaspoon dried marjoram
1 teaspoon celery seeds

Directions

Press the "Sauté" button to heat up your Instant Pot. Heat the olive oil and brown the ground beef sirloin, crumbling with a fork. Season with salt and black pepper.

Add the bone broth to deglaze the pot. Stir in the remaining ingredients.

Secure the lid and choose the "Soup" button.

Cook for 30 minutes at High pressure. Once cooking is complete, use a natural release for 10 minutes; carefully remove the lid. Bon appétit!

Per serving: 276 Calories; 11.8g Fat; 22.6g Carbs; 19.3g Protein; 4.4g Sugars

207. Delicious Keema Curry

(Ready in about 10 minutes | Servings 6)

Ingredients

1 tablespoon olive oil
2 pounds beef, ground
1/2 cup onion, chopped
2 cloves garlic, smashed
1 ripe tomato, diced
1 red chili pepper
Salt and ground black pepper, to taste

1/2 teaspoon ground cumin
1/2 teaspoon mustard seeds
1 teaspoon chili paste
1 teaspoon curry powder
1 cup water
1/2 cup light plain yogurt
2 tablespoons fresh green onions, chopped

Directions

Press the "Sauté" button to preheat your Instant Pot. Heat the olive oil and cook the ground beef for 2 to 3 minutes.

Then, process the onion, garlic, tomato and chili pepper in your blender. Add this mixture to the Instant Pot.

Next, add the salt, black pepper, cumin, mustard seeds, chili paste, curry powder, and water.

Secure the lid. Choose the "Manual" mode and High pressure; cook for 5 minutes. Once cooking is complete, use a natural pressure release; carefully remove the lid.

After that, fold in the yogurt and seal the lid. Let it sit in the residual heat until thoroughly heated. Serve garnished with fresh green onions. Bon appétit!

Per serving: 265 Calories; 12.5g Fat; 6g Carbs; 3.7g Protein; 4.4g Sugars

208. Mexican-Style Beef Carnitas

(Ready in about 50 minutes | Servings 8)

Ingredients

1 tablespoon corn oil
2 pounds chuck roast, cut into pieces
1 red onion, chopped
2 garlic cloves, minced
1 teaspoon ancho chili powder
Sea salt and ground black pepper, to taste

1 teaspoon Mexican oregano
1/2 teaspoon coriander seeds
1/2 teaspoon fennel seeds
1 teaspoon mustard powder
2 cups tomato purée
1 cup water
2 beef bouillon cubes
1 cup salsa, to serve

Directions

Press the "Sauté" button to preheat your Instant Pot. Then, heat the oil. Brown the chuck roast for 3 minutes.

Add the onion and garlic and cook an additional 2 minutes, stirring continuously. Stir in the remaining ingredients, except for the salsa.

Secure the lid. Choose the "Soup" mode and High pressure; cook for 40 minutes. Once cooking is complete, use a natural pressure release; carefully remove the lid.

Remove the beef from the Instant Pot and let it cool slightly. After that, shred the meat using two forks.

Meanwhile, press the "Sauté" button again and simmer the cooking liquid until the sauce has reduced and thickened. Adjust the seasonings and return the shredded meat back to the Instant Pot.

Serve with the salsa. Enjoy!

Per serving: 250 Calories; 11.6g Fat; 6.1g Carbs; 31.4g Protein; 3.1g Sugars

209. Quinoa Meatball Biscuit Sliders

(Ready in about 20 minutes | Servings 5)

Ingredients

1 pound lean beef, ground
1/2 pound ground pork
1 cup quinoa, cooked
2 garlic cloves, chopped
4 tablespoons scallions, chopped
1 tablespoon fresh cilantro, chopped
1 cup breadcrumbs
1 egg, beaten
1/4 cup milk
Salt and black pepper, to taste

1/2 teaspoon crushed red pepper flakes
1/2 teaspoon dried rosemary, chopped
2 tablespoons olive oil
2 ½ cups tomato sauce
1/4 cup brown sugar
2 tablespoons vinegar
1 dash allspice
1/2 teaspoon chili powder
16 dinner rolls

Directions

In a mixing bowl, combine the ground beef, pork, quinoa, garlic, scallions, cilantro, breadcrumbs egg, and milk; now, season with salt, black pepper, red pepper, and rosemary.

Shape the meat mixture into 16 meatballs. Press the "Sauté" button to preheat your Instant Pot. Now, heat the oil until sizzling. Once hot, brown your meatballs on all sides.

Add the tomato sauce, sugar, vinegar, allspice and chili powder.

Select the "Manual" mode and cook for 12 minutes. Once cooking is complete, use a quick release.

Place one meatball on top of the bottom half of a dinner roll. Spoon the sauce on top of your meatball. Top with the other half of the dinner roll.

Repeat until you run out of ingredients. Bon appétit!

Per serving: 577 Calories; 26.2g Fat; 44.9g Carbs; 40g Protein; 8.4g Sugars

210. Cheesy Meatballs in Mushroom Sauce

(Ready in about 10 minutes | Servings 6)

Ingredients

1 pound ground beef
2 slices bacon, chopped
1/2 cup Romano cheese, grated
1 cup seasoned breadcrumbs
1/2 cup scallions, chopped
2 garlic cloves, crushed
2 large eggs, beaten
1/3 cup milk
1 tablespoon canola oil
1 (10 ¼-ounce) can condensed mushroom soup
1 cup tomato paste

Directions

Thoroughly combine the ground beef, bacon, cheese, breadcrumbs, scallions, garlic, eggs, and milk. Roll the mixture into meatballs.

Press the "Sauté" button to preheat the Instant Pot. Heat the oil and sear the meatballs until they are browned on all sides.

Add the canned mushroom soup and tomato paste to the Instant Pot.

Secure the lid. Choose the "Manual" mode and High pressure; cook for 6 minutes. Once cooking is complete, use a quick pressure release; carefully remove the lid.

Serve warm, garnished with mashed potatoes. Bon appétit!

Per serving: 450 Calories; 24g Fat; 26.7g Carbs; 27.8g Protein; 9.9g Sugars

211. Chili-Beef Tacos

(Ready in about 25 minutes | Servings 6)

Ingredients

2 teaspoons lard
1 pound ground chuck
2 onions, diced
3 garlic cloves, smashed
2 ripe tomatoes, pureed
1 cup beef bone broth
1 envelope (1-ounce) taco seasoning mix
2 cans (16-ounce) pinto beans, drained
1 tablespoon chipotle powder
1 teaspoon cumin, ground
1/2 teaspoon mustard seeds
1 teaspoon dried marjoram
1/2 teaspoon dried basil
Salt and pepper, to taste
2 tablespoons tamari sauce
3/4 teaspoon cocoa powder, unsweetened
6 medium store-bought taco shells
1/2 cup sour cream
2 tablespoons fresh cilantro leaves, chopped

Directions

Press the "Sauté" button to heat up your Instant Pot and melt the lard. Once hot, cook the ground chuck, crumbling with a fork. Set aside.

Cook the onions and garlic in the pan drippings, stirring occasionally; add a splash of bone broth, if necessary, to prevent sticking.

Now, stir in the tomatoes, beef bone broth, and taco seasoning mix; cook, stirring continuously, an additional minute or until warmed through.

Next, stir in the canned beans, chipotle powder, cumin, mustard seeds, marjoram, basil, salt, pepper, tamari sauce, and cocoa powder. Secure the lid.

Select the "Manual" mode and cook at High Pressure for 12 minutes. Once cooking is complete, use a natural release and carefully remove the lid.

To assemble, divide the beef/bean mixture among taco shells; top each with sour cream and fresh chopped cilantro. Bon appétit!

Per serving: 361 Calories; 14.6g Fat; 34.5g Carbs; 24.1g Protein; 3.8g Sugars

212. Muffin-Topped Beef Stew

(Ready in about 45 minutes | Servings 6)

Ingredients

1 heaping tablespoon lard, at room temperature
1 ½ pounds beef steak, thinly sliced
1 large-sized leek, chopped
2 garlic cloves, crushed
1 cup celery with leaves
1 cup carrots, chopped
1 cup parsnip, chopped
2 bell peppers, chopped
1 (14-ounce) can tomatoes, diced
4 cups water
4 bouillon cubes
1 bay leaf
Topping:
1 cup plain flour
1 teaspoon baking powder
1 cup Swiss cheese, grated
1/2 cup full-fat milk

Directions

Press the "Sauté" button to preheat your Instant Pot. Melt the lard and brown the beef for 3 to 4 minutes, stirring occasionally.

Then, add the leeks and cook an additional 2 minutes or until it has softened. Add the garlic, celery, carrot, parsnip, peppers, tomatoes, water, bouillon cubes, and bay leaf.

Secure the lid. Choose the "Meat/Stew" mode and High pressure; cook for 20 minutes. Once cooking is complete, use a quick pressure release; carefully remove the lid.

In a mixing bowl, thoroughly combine all of the topping ingredients. Spread the topping over the top of your stew. Seal the lid and press the "Sauté" button.

Let it simmer for 15 minutes longer or until golden. Serve immediately.

Per serving: 404 Calories; 15.5g Fat; 31.1g Carbs; 34.4g Protein; 7g Sugars

213. Sloppy Joe Soup

(Ready in about 25 minutes | Servings 4)

Ingredients

1 tablespoon olive oil
1 pound ground beef
1 onion, peeled and finely chopped
Sea salt and ground black pepper, to taste
1 teaspoon cayenne pepper
1 parsnip, thinly sliced
2 carrots, thinly sliced
4 cups beef bone broth
2 garlic cloves, minced
1/2 cup tomato purée

Directions

Press the "Sauté" button to preheat your Instant Pot. Heat the olive oil and brown the ground beef and onions until the meat is no longer pink.

Add the remaining ingredients to your Instant Pot

Secure the lid. Choose the "Soup" mode and High pressure; cook for 20 minutes. Once cooking is complete, use a quick pressure release; carefully remove the lid.

Ladle into individual bowls and serve hot. Bon appétit!

Per serving: 340 Calories; 16.3g Fat; 15.7g Carbs; 31.9g Protein; 7.2g Sugars

214. Sticky Beef with Brown Sauce

(Ready in about 40 minutes | Servings 4)

Ingredients

2 tablespoons olive oil
2 pounds beef stew meat, cubed
1/4 cup Syrah wine
1/2 cup dark brown sugar
6 cloves garlic, sliced
1 cup beef bone broth
1/4 cup soy sauce
1 teaspoon red pepper flakes
1 bay leaf
2 tablespoons arrowroot powder
1/4 cup scallions, roughly chopped

Directions

Press the "Sauté" button and heat the oil until sizzling. Then, brown the beef in batches.

Add a splash of red wine to deglaze the pot. Add the remaining wine, sugar, garlic, broth, soy sauce, red pepper, and bay leaf.

Secure the lid. Choose the "Meat/Stew" mode and cook for 35 minutes at High pressure. Once cooking is complete, use a quick pressure release; carefully remove the lid.

Press the "Sauté" button again and add the arrowroot powder. Let it cook until the sauce has reduced slightly and the flavors have concentrated. Serve garnished with fresh scallions and enjoy!

Per serving: 460 Calories; 18.7g Fat; 22.5g Carbs; 51.3g Protein; 15.7g Sugars

215. Creamy Beef and Mushroom Stroganoff

(Ready in about 50 minutes | Servings 5)

Ingredients

2 tablespoons cornstarch
Coarse sea salt, to taste
1/2 teaspoon ground black pepper
1/2 teaspoon cayenne pepper
1 teaspoon smoked paprika
2 pounds beef sirloin, cut into bite-sized chunks
1 tablespoon lard, melted
1 teaspoon dried basil
1/2 teaspoon dried marjoram
2 cloves garlic, peeled and halved
2 cups beef broth
1 ½ pounds button mushrooms, quartered
1 red onion, quartered
2 tablespoons tomato paste
1/2 cup double cream

Directions

In a shallow dish, combine the cornstarch with the salt, black pepper, cayenne pepper, and smoked paprika.

Dredge the beef pieces in the seasoned mixture to coat on all sides.

Press the "Sauté" button to preheat your Instant Pot. Melt the lard and brown the beef until no longer pink.

Add the basil, marjoram, garlic, and beef broth.

Secure the lid. Choose the "Meat/Stew" mode and cook for 35 minutes at High pressure. Once cooking is complete, use a quick pressure release; carefully remove the lid.

Add the button mushrooms, onions and tomato paste.

Secure the lid. Choose the "Manual" mode and cook for 3 minutes at High pressure. Once cooking is complete, use a quick pressure release; carefully remove the lid.

Stir in the double cream; seal the lid and let it sit in the residual heat for 5 to 7 minutes. Serve warm.

Per serving: 474 Calories; 28.1g Fat; 12.5g Carbs; 43.1g Protein; 5.4g Sugars

216. One Pot Beef Enchilada Pasta

(Ready in about 15 minutes | Servings 4)

Ingredients

1 tablespoon olive oil
1 pound ground chuck
1 pound elbow macaroni
8 ounces canned enchilada sauce
1 cup beef bone broth
1 cup water
Sea salt and ground black pepper, to taste
1 bay leaf
1 teaspoon paprika
1/2 cup Cotija cheese, crumbled

Directions

Press the "Sauté" button to preheat your Instant Pot. Heat the oil and brown the ground chuck for 2 to 3 minutes.

Add the other ingredients, except for the cheese, to the Instant Pot.

Secure the lid. Choose the "Manual" mode and cook for 5 minutes at High pressure. Once cooking is complete, use a natural pressure release; carefully remove the lid.

Serve in individual bowls topped with the crumbled cheese. Enjoy!

Per serving: 693 Calories; 18.1g Fat; 90.1g Carbs; 40.1g Protein; 6.1g Sugars

217. Classic Ground Beef Tacos

(Ready in about 30 minutes | Servings 4)

Ingredients

1 tablespoon canola oil
1 ½ pounds ground beef
1 onion, chopped
2 sweet peppers, deseeded and sliced
1 chili pepper, minced
4 garlic cloves, minced
1 teaspoon marjoram
1 teaspoon Mexican oregano
Kosher salt and ground black pepper, to taste
1 teaspoon cumin powder
1/2 teaspoon red pepper flakes
1 teaspoon mustard seeds
12 small taco shells
1 head lettuce
1/2 cup chunky salsa
1/2 cup sour cream

Direction

Press the "Sauté" button to preheat your Instant Pot. Heat the oil and sear the ground chuck for 2 to 3 minutes or until mostly brown.

Add the onion, peppers, garlic, and spices to the inner pot.

Secure the lid. Choose the "Manual" mode and cook for 10 minutes at High pressure. Once cooking is complete, use a natural pressure release; carefully remove the lid.

Press the "Sauté" button and cook, stirring continuously, until the liquid has almost evaporated or about 10 minutes.

To assemble your tacos, layer the beef mixture and lettuce in each taco shell. Serve with the salsa and sour cream. Enjoy!

Per serving: 618 Calories; 37.8g Fat; 21g Carbs; 47.1g Protein; 4.4g Sugars

218. Easy Ground Beef Bowl

(Ready in about 20 minutes | Servings 4)

Ingredients

1 teaspoon olive oil
1 ½ pounds lean ground chuck
1 (1-ounce) packet taco seasoning mix
1 cup vegetable broth
1 onion, chopped
2 garlic cloves, minced
1 red bell pepper, deseeded and sliced
1 green bell pepper, deseeded and sliced
1 cup tomato puree
1 tablespoon chipotle paste
1 (15-ounce) can black beans, drained and rinsed
1 ½ cups Monterey-Jack cheese, shredded
2 tablespoons fresh cilantro leaves, chopped

Directions

Press the "Sauté" button to preheat your Instant Pot. Heat the oil and cook the ground chuck for 2 to 3 minutes or until mostly brown.

Next, add the taco seasoning mix, broth, onion, garlic, and peppers.

Secure the lid. Choose the "Manual" mode and cook for 10 minutes at High pressure. Once cooking is complete, use a natural pressure release; carefully remove the lid.

Divide the meat mixture between four serving bowls. Add the tomato puree, chipotle paste, and black beans; gently stir to combine.

Top with the cheese and serve garnished with fresh cilantro leaves. Enjoy!

Per serving: 535 Calories; 31.2g Fat; 16.9g Carbs; 48.1g Protein; 6.7g Sugars

219. Country-Style Rump Steak

(Ready in about 1 hour | Servings 6)

Ingredients

Sea salt, to taste
1 teaspoon mixed peppercorns, crushed
1/2 teaspoon marjoram
1/2 teaspoon ginger powder
1/4 cup flour
2 tablespoons olive oil
3 pounds rump steak, trimmed and sliced into small pieces
3 garlic cloves, halved
2 carrots, sliced
1 cup vegetable broth
2 ripe tomatoes, pureed
1/2 teaspoon hot sauce

Directions

In a shallow dish, combine the salt, black peppercorns, marjoram, ginger powder, and flour. Dredge the beef pieces in the seasoned mixture to coat on all sides.

Press the "Sauté" button to preheat your Instant Pot. Heat the oil and brown beef until no longer pink.

Add the remaining ingredients.

Secure the lid. Choose the "Manual" mode and cook for 60 minutes at High pressure. Once cooking is complete, use a quick pressure release; carefully remove the lid. Bon appétit!

Per serving: 355 Calories; 14.2g Fat; 6.5g Carbs; 50.9g Protein; 1.3g Sugars

220. Italian-Style Beef Peperonata

(Ready in about 30 minutes + marinating time | Servings 4)

Ingredients

2 tablespoons soy sauce
2 tablespoons tomato paste
1/4 cup rice vinegar
1 tablespoon brown sugar
3 cloves garlic, minced
1 pound blade roast, sliced into
1/2-inch pieces
1 tablespoon canola oil

Salt and ground black pepper, to
taste
1 teaspoon cayenne pepper
1 ½ cups broth
1 onion, thinly sliced
4 sweet peppers, cut Julienne
1 serrano pepper, minced
2 tablespoons capers with juices

Directions

In a ceramic or glass dish, mix the soy sauce, tomato paste, vinegar, sugar, and garlic. Place the blade roast in the dish, cover with plastic wrap and let it marinate at least 3 hours in the refrigerator.

Press the "Sauté" button to preheat your Instant Pot. Heat the oil and brown the beef for 4 to 5 minutes, brushing occasionally with the marinade.

Add the other ingredients. Secure the lid. Choose the "Meat/Stew" mode and cook for 20 minutes at High pressure. Once cooking is complete, use a quick pressure release; carefully remove the lid.

Serve warm.

Per serving: 432 Calories; 28g Fat; 21.1g Carbs; 24.5g Protein; 6.3g Sugars

221. Braised Beef Brisket and Broccoli

(Ready in about 30 minutes | Servings 4)

Ingredients

2 tablespoons sesame oil
1 pound beef brisket, thinly sliced
against the grain
1/4 cup rice wine
1 cup beef bone broth
1/4 cup tamari sauce
1 tablespoon yellow mustard
1 teaspoon fresh ginger, grated

2 cloves garlic, minced
Pink salt and ground black pepper,
to taste
1/2 teaspoon paprika
1 head broccoli, broken into
florets
1 tablespoon arrowroot flour
1/2 cup spring onions, sliced

Directions

Press the "Sauté" button to preheat your Instant Pot. Heat the sesame oil and brown the beef in batches; cook for about 3 minutes per batch.

Add the wine to deglaze the pot. Once your beef is browned, add the beef broth, tamari sauce, mustard, ginger, garlic, salt, pepper, and paprika.

Secure the lid. Choose the "Manual" mode and cook for 15 minutes at High pressure. Once cooking is complete, use a quick pressure release; carefully remove the lid.

Add the broccoli and arrowroot flour and press the "Sauté" button again. Cook until the broccoli florets are tender, but still slightly crisp and not mushy, about 4 minutes.

Garnish with spring onions and serve immediately. Bon appétit!

Per serving: 350 Calories; 24.2g Fat; 13.5g Carbs; 20.9g Protein; 3.6g Sugars

222. Sunday Sesame Beef

(Ready in about 45 minutes | Servings 5)

Ingredients

2 tablespoons sesame oil
2 pounds chuck roast, slice into
pieces
1/2 cup beef bone broth
1/2 (12-ounce) bottle beer
1 tablespoon mustard
1 tablespoon granulated sugar

Kosher salt and freshly ground
black pepper, to taste
1 teaspoon onion powder
1 teaspoon garlic powder
1 teaspoon ginger powder
1/4 teaspoon ground allspice
2 tablespoons sesame seeds,
toasted

Directions

Press the "Sauté" button to preheat your Instant Pot. Heat the oil and brown the beef in batches; cook for about 3 minutes per batch.

Add the broth, beer, mustard, sugar, salt, black pepper, onion powder, garlic powder, ginger, and ground allspice.

Secure the lid. Choose the "Manual" mode and cook for 40 minutes at High pressure. Once cooking is complete, use a quick pressure release; carefully remove the lid.

Serve garnished with toasted sesame seeds. Enjoy!

Per serving: 322 Calories; 17.8g Fat; 3.1g Carbs; 38.1g Protein; 1.6g Sugars

223. Tender Pot Roast with Garden Vegetables

(Ready in about 50 minutes | Servings 5)

Ingredients

1 tablespoon lard, melted
2 pounds pot roast
Pink salt and ground black pepper,
to taste
1/2 teaspoon ground cumin
1 teaspoon onion powder
1 teaspoon garlic powder

2 cups cream of celery soup
2 celery stalks
4 carrots
1 onion, halved
2 tablespoons fresh parsley leaves,
roughly chopped

Directions

Press the "Sauté" button to preheat your Instant Pot. Melt the lard and cook your pot roast until slightly brown on all sides.

Season with salt, black pepper, cumin, onion powder, and garlic powder. Pour in the cream of celery soup.

Secure the lid. Choose the "Meat/Stew" mode and cook for 35 minutes at High pressure. Once cooking is complete, use a natural pressure release; carefully remove the lid.

After that, stir in the celery, carrots, and onion.

Secure the lid. Choose the "Manual" mode and cook for 8 minutes at High pressure. Once cooking is complete, use a quick pressure release; carefully remove the lid.

Garnish with fresh parsley and serve immediately. Bon appétit!

Per serving: 425 Calories; 19.2g Fat; 15.5g Carbs; 48.8g Protein; 4.8g Sugars

224. Hearty Ground Beef Frittata

(Ready in about 25 minutes | Servings 2)

Ingredients

1 tablespoon olive oil
1/2 pound ground chuck
4 eggs, whisked
A small bunch of green onions,
chopped

1 small tomato, chopped
Sea salt and freshly ground black
pepper, to your liking
1/2 teaspoon paprika
1/2 teaspoon garlic powder

Directions

Press the "Sauté" button to preheat your Instant Pot. Heat the oil and brown the beef for 2 to 3 minutes, stirring continuously.

Lightly spritz a baking pan with cooking oil. Add all ingredients, including the browned beef to the baking pan.

Cover with foil. Add 1 cup of water and a metal trivet to the Instant Pot. Lower the baking pan onto the trivet.

Secure the lid. Choose the "Manual" mode and cook for 6 minutes at High pressure. Once cooking is complete, use a natural pressure release for 10 minutes; carefully remove the lid.

Slice in half and serve. Bon appétit!

Per serving: 368 Calories; 24.1g Fat; 3.7g Carbs; 33.9g Protein; 2.4g Sugars

225. Corned Beef Brisket with Root Vegetables

(Ready in about 1 hour 25 minutes | Servings 6)

Ingredients

2 ½ pounds corned beef brisket
2 cloves peeled garlic
2 sprigs thyme
1 sprig rosemary
2 tablespoons olive oil
1 cup chicken broth
1/4 cup tomato puree

1 medium leek, sliced
1/2 pound rutabaga, peeled and cut into 1-inch chunks
1/2 pound turnips, peeled and cut into 1-inch chunks
2 parsnips, cut into 1-inch chunks
2 bell peppers, halved

Directions

Place the beef brisket, garlic, thyme, rosemary, olive oil, chicken broth, and tomato puree in the inner pot.

Secure the lid. Choose the "Manual" mode and cook for 80 minutes at High pressure. Once cooking is complete, use a quick pressure release; carefully remove the lid.

Add the other ingredients. Gently stir to combine.

Secure the lid. Choose the "Manual" mode and cook for 4 minutes at High pressure. Once cooking is complete, use a quick pressure release; carefully remove the lid. Bon appétit!

Per serving: 563 Calories; 35.8g Fat; 19.5g Carbs; 39.3g Protein; 6.5g Sugars

226. Old-Fashioned Short Ribs

(Ready in about 1 hour 45 minutes | Servings 6)

Ingredients

4 pounds beef short ribs, bone-in
Sea salt and ground black pepper, to taste
2 tablespoons olive oil
1 medium leek, sliced
2 cloves garlic, sliced

1 cup water
1 packet of onion soup mix
1 sprig thyme
1 sprig rosemary
1/2 teaspoon celery seeds

Directions

Place all ingredients in the inner pot.

Secure the lid. Choose the "Manual" mode and cook for 90 minutes at High pressure. Once cooking is complete, use a natural pressure release; carefully remove the lid.

Afterwards, place the short ribs under the broiler until the outside is crisp or about 10 minutes.

Transfer the ribs to a serving platter and enjoy!

Per serving: 655 Calories; 50.8g Fat; 3.3g Carbs; 43.7g Protein; 0.6g Sugars

227. Tequila Boom-Boom Ribs

(Ready in about 40 minutes + marinating time | Servings 8)

Ingredients

2 racks chuck short ribs
2 shots tequila
Kosher salt and cracked black pepper, to taste
2 tablespoons honey
1 teaspoon garlic powder
1 teaspoon shallot powder
1 teaspoon marjoram

1 tablespoon Sriracha sauce
1/2 teaspoon paprika
1 cup apple cider
2 tablespoons tomato paste
1 tablespoon stone ground mustard
1 cup beef bone broth

Directions

Place all ingredients, except for beef broth, in a ceramic dish. Cover with a foil and let it marinate for 3 hours in your refrigerator.

Place the beef along with its marinade in the inner pot. Pour in the beef bone broth.

Secure the lid. Choose the "Meat/Stew" mode and cook for 35 minutes at High pressure. Once cooking is complete, use a natural pressure release; carefully remove the lid. Bon appétit!

Per serving: 399 Calories; 29.2g Fat; 13.3g Carbs; 20.7g Protein; 5g Sugars

228. Margarita Glazed Chuck Roast

(Ready in about 1 hour | Servings 6)

Ingredients

2 pounds chuck roast
1 cup beef broth
1/4 cup soy sauce
1/4 cup champagne vinegar
Sea salt and ground black pepper, to taste
1/2 teaspoon red pepper flakes

2 cloves garlic, sliced
Margarita Glaze:
1/2 cup tequila
1/4 cup orange juice
1/4 lime juice
2 tablespoons dark brown sugar

Directions

Add the chuck roast, beef broth, soy sauce, champagne vinegar, salt, black pepper, red pepper flakes, and garlic to the inner pot.

Secure the lid. Choose the "Manual" mode and cook for 40 minutes at High pressure. Once cooking is complete, use a natural pressure release for 10 minutes; carefully remove the lid.

Meanwhile, whisk all ingredients for the margarita glaze. Now, glaze the ribs and place under the broiler for 5 minutes; then, turn them over and glaze on the other side. Broil an additional 5 minutes.

Cut the chuck roast into slices and serve the remaining glaze on the side as a sauce. Bon appétit!

Per serving: 348 Calories; 14.9g Fat; 10.3g Carbs; 42.7g Protein; 7.7g Sugars

229. Juicy Beef Round Roast with Potatoes

(Ready in about 50 minutes | Servings 6)

Ingredients

2 tablespoons olive oil, divided
2 pounds beef round roast, cut into bite-sized pieces
1 white onion, chopped
1 garlic clove, sliced

1 bell pepper, sliced
1/4 cup tomato puree
1/4 cup dry red wine
1 cup beef broth
2 pounds whole small potatoes

Directions '

Press the "Sauté" button to preheat your Instant Pot. Heat the oil and brown the beef round roast for 3 to 4 minutes, working in batches.

Add the white onion, garlic, pepper, tomato puree, red wine, and broth.

Secure the lid. Choose the "Meat/Stew" mode and cook for 35 minutes at High pressure. Once cooking is complete, use a quick pressure release; carefully remove the lid.

Add the potatoes. Secure the lid. Choose the "Manual" mode and cook for 10 minutes at High pressure. Once cooking is complete, use a quick pressure release; carefully remove the lid.

Serve in individual bowls and enjoy!

Per serving: 426 Calories; 11.4g Fat; 29.9g Carbs; 48.7g Protein; 2.8g Sugars

230. Traditional Spaghetti Bolognese

(Ready in about 15 minutes | Servings 4)

Ingredients

2 tablespoons olive oil
1 onion, chopped
2 cloves garlic, chopped
1 pound ground beef
1/4 cup rose wine
2 carrots, thinly sliced
1 (28-ounce) can crushed tomatoes
1/2 cup beef bone broth

1 teaspoon dried basil
1 teaspoon dried oregano
1/2 teaspoon dried rosemary
Sea salt and ground black pepper, to taste
19 ounces spaghetti
1/2 cup Romano cheese, preferably freshly grated

Directions

Press the "Sauté" button to preheat your Instant Pot.

Once hot, heat the olive oil and cook the onion, garlic and beef until the beef is no longer pink.

Use rose wine to scrape the remaining bits of meat off the bottom of the inner pot.

Add the carrots, tomatoes, beef bone broth, basil, oregano, rosemary, salt, and black pepper. Secure the lid. Choose the "Poultry" mode and High pressure; cook for 5 minutes. Once cooking is complete, use a quick release.

Add the spaghetti and gently stir to combine.

Secure the lid and choose the "Manual" mode. Cook for 4 minutes longer. Afterwards, use a quick release and carefully remove the lid. Bon appétit!

Per serving: 585 Calories; 25.6g Fat; 47.8g Carbs; 43.8g Protein; 8.5g Sugars

231. Asian-Style Back Ribs

(Ready in about 1 hour | Servings 8)

Ingredients

2 racks back ribs	2-inch piece fresh ginger, minced
10 ounces beers	4 tablespoons tamari sauce
1 cup Asian BBQ sauce	2 tablespoons agave nectar
1 onion, chopped	Sea salt and ground black pepper,
2 garlic cloves, minced	to taste
1 red Fresno chili, sliced	2 teaspoons toasted sesame seeds

Directions

Place the back ribs, beers, BBQ sauce, onion, garlic, Fresno chili, and ginger in the inner pot.

Secure the lid. Choose the "Manual" mode and cook for 40 minutes at High pressure. Once cooking is complete, use a natural pressure release for 10 minutes; carefully remove the lid.

Add the tamari sauce, agave, salt and pepper and place the beef ribs under the broiler. Broil ribs for 10 minutes or until they are evenly browned. Serve garnished with sesame seeds. Bon appétit!

Per serving: 480 Calories; 14.5g Fat; 10.3g Carbs; 70g Protein; 4.1g Sugars

232. Classic Beef Bourguignon

(Ready in about 55 minutes | Servings 6)

Ingredients

2 pounds boneless beef steak, cut into bite-sized pieces	2 tablespoons olive oil
2 tablespoons cornstarch	1 shallot, chopped
Coarse sea salt and ground black pepper, to taste	2 cloves garlic, sliced
1 teaspoon red pepper flakes	8 ounces mushrooms, sliced
	1/2 cup Burgundy wine
	1 cup beef bone broth

Directions

Toss the beef steak with the cornstarch, salt, black pepper, and red pepper flakes.

Press the "Sauté" button to preheat your Instant Pot. Heat the oil until sizzling. Now, cook the beef until well browned.

Add the remaining ingredients; gently stir to combine.

Secure the lid. Choose the "Manual" mode and cook for 40 minutes at High pressure. Once cooking is complete, use a natural pressure release for 10 minutes; carefully remove the lid.

Divide between individual bowls and serve warm with garlic croutons if desired. Enjoy!

Per serving: 418 Calories; 23.5g Fat; 5.3g Carbs; 44.1g Protein; 1.5g Sugars

233. Easiest Cheeseburgers Ever

(Ready in about 45 minutes | Servings 6)

Ingredients

2 pounds ground chuck	1/2 onion, finely chopped
1 tablespoon tomato puree	2 garlic cloves, minced
Sea salt and freshly ground black pepper, to taste	6 ounces Monterey-Jack cheese, sliced
1/2 teaspoon cayenne pepper	

Directions

Mix the ground chuck, tomato puree, salt, black pepper, cayenne pepper, onion, and garlic until well combined.

Form the meat mixture into patties. Place your patties on squares of aluminum foil and wrap them loosely.

Add 1 cup water and a metal trivet to the Instant Pot; lower the foil packs onto the top of the metal trivet.

Secure the lid. Choose the "Meat/Stew" mode and cook for 35 minutes at High pressure. Once cooking is complete, use a natural pressure release; carefully remove the lid.

Place your patties on a baking sheet and broil for 5 to 6 minutes. Serve on buns topped with cheese. Enjoy!

Per serving: 441 Calories; 25.4g Fat; 2.9g Carbs; 47.5g Protein; 1.7g Sugars

234. Puerto Rican Pot Roast

(Ready in about 55 minutes | Servings 4)

Ingredients

2 pounds pot roast, cut into bite-sized chunks	1 tablespoon bouillon granules
1/4 cup all-purpose flour	1 ½ cups water
1 tablespoon butter, melted	1/2 cup shallots, chopped
1 habanero pepper, minced	2 carrots, cut into bite-sized chunks
2 garlic cloves, chopped	2 celery ribs, cut into bite-sized chunks
1 teaspoon smoked Spanish paprika	Sea salt and ground black pepper, to taste
1 teaspoon achiote seasoning	

Directions

Toss the beef with flour.

Press the "Sauté" button to preheat your Instant Pot. Melt the butter and cook the beef chunks for 4 to 5 minutes, stirring frequently.

Add the habanero pepper, garlic, Spanish paprika, achiote seasoning, bouillon granules, and water.

Secure the lid. Choose the "Meat/Stew" mode and cook for 35 minutes at High pressure. Once cooking is complete, use a natural pressure release; carefully remove the lid.

Add the vegetables, salt, and black pepper.

Secure the lid. Choose the "Manual" mode and cook for 7 minutes at High pressure. Once cooking is complete, use a quick pressure release; carefully remove the lid. Serve the beef and vegetables in individual bowls and enjoy!

Per serving: 393 Calories; 17g Fat; 11.6g Carbs; 48.5g Protein; 1.9g Sugars

235. Balkan-Style Moussaka with Potatoes

(Ready in about 40 minutes | Servings 4)

Ingredients

1 tablespoon olive oil	1 cup cream of celery soup
1 ½ pounds ground beef	1 egg
1 pound Russet potatoes, peeled and thinly sliced	1/2 cup half-and-half
1 shallot, thinly sliced	Kosher salt and ground pepper, to taste
2 garlic cloves, sliced	1/2 cup Colby cheese, shredded

Directions

Press the "Sauté" button to preheat your Instant Pot. Heat the olive oil and cook the ground beef until no longer pink.

Now, add the layer of potatoes; top with the layer of shallots and garlic. Pour in the soup.

Whisk the egg with half-and-half until well combined; season with salt and pepper. Pour the egg mixture over the top of the meat and vegetable layers.

Smooth the sauce on top with a spatula.

Secure the lid. Choose the "Meat/Stew" mode and cook for 35 minutes at High pressure. Once cooking is complete, use a quick pressure release; carefully remove the lid.

Add the shredded cheese and seal the lid again. Let it sit in the residual heat until the cheese melts. Bon appétit!

Per serving: 592 Calories; 33.3g Fat; 31.6g Carbs; 42.8g Protein; 4.9g Sugars

236. Mediterranean Steak Salad

(Ready in about 40 minutes | Servings 4)

Ingredients

1 ½ pounds steak	1 red onion, thinly sliced
1/2 cup red wine	2 sweet peppers, cut into strips
Sea salt and ground black pepper, to taste	1 butterhead lettuce, separate into leaves
1/2 teaspoon red pepper flakes	1/2 cup feta cheese, crumbled
1 cup water	1/2 cup black olives, pitted and sliced
1/4 cup extra-virgin olive oil	
2 tablespoons wine vinegar	

Directions

Add the steak, red wine, salt, black pepper, red pepper, and water to the inner pot.

Secure the lid. Choose the "Manual" mode and cook for 25 minutes at High pressure. Once cooking is complete, use a natural pressure release for 10 minutes; carefully remove the lid.

Thinly slice the steak against the grain and transfer to a salad bowl. Toss with the olive oil and vinegar.

Add the red onion, peppers, and lettuce; toss to combine well. Top with cheese and olives and serve. Bon appétit!

Per serving: 474 Calories; 28.8g Fat; 3.6g Carbs; 50.6g Protein; 1.7g Sugars

237. Granny's Classic Beef and Gravy

(Ready in about 1 hour 15 minutes | Servings 6)

Ingredients

3 pounds top round roast	1 ½ pounds fingerling potatoes
Sea salt and ground black pepper, to taste	1 onion, thinly sliced
1 teaspoon paprika	2 cloves garlic, smashed
1 teaspoon dried rosemary	1 bell pepper, deseeded and sliced
1 tablespoon lard, melted	3 cups beef bone broth
	1 ½ tablespoons potato starch

Directions

Toss the beef with the salt, black pepper, paprika, and rosemary until well coated on all sides.

Press the "Sauté" button to preheat your Instant Pot and melt the lard. Sear the beef for about 4 minutes per side until it is browned.

Scatter the potatoes, onion, garlic, peppers around the top round roast. Add the beef bone broth.

Secure the lid. Choose the "Manual" mode and cook for 60 minutes at High pressure. Once cooking is complete, use a natural pressure release for 10 minutes; carefully remove the lid.

Transfer the roast and vegetables to a serving platter; shred the roast with 2 forks.

Mix the potato starch with 4 tablespoons of water. Press the "Sauté" button to preheat your Instant Pot again. Once the liquid is boiling, add the slurry and let it cook until the gravy thickens.

Taste and adjust the seasonings. Serve warm.

Per serving: 470 Calories; 8.8g Fat; 38.5g Carbs; 60.5g Protein; 2.6g Sugars

238. Yoshinoya Beef Bowl

(Ready in about 40 minutes + marinating time | Servings 4)

Ingredients

2 pounds beef stew meat, cut into 1-inch cubes	2 tablespoons cornstarch
1/4 cup Shoyu sauce	1 tablespoon olive oil
1/4 cup brown sugar	1 teaspoon onion powder
2 cloves garlic, minced	2 bay leaves
1 tablespoon cider vinegar	1 rosemary sprig
2 tablespoons sake	Salt and black pepper, to taste
2 tablespoons pickled red ginger	1 cup beef broth
1 teaspoon hot sauce	2 eggs, whisked
	1 cup steamed rice

Directions

In a ceramic bowl, place the meat, Shoyu sauce, brown sugar, garlic, cider vinegar, sake, ginger, and hot sauce. Let it marinate for 2 hours.

Discard the marinade and toss the beef cubes with the cornstarch.

Press the "Sauté" button and heat the oil until sizzling. Brown the beef cubes for 3 to 4 minutes, stirring periodically.

Add the onion powder, bay leaves, rosemary sprig, salt, black pepper, and beef broth.

Secure the lid. Choose the "Meat/Stew" mode and cook for 35 minutes at High pressure. Once cooking is complete, use a quick pressure release; carefully remove the lid.

Slowly stir in the whisked eggs and press the "Sauté" button. Continue to cook until the eggs are done.

Serve over steamed rice.

Per serving: 598 Calories; 15.2g Fat; 54.5g Carbs; 57.6g Protein; 7.9g Sugars

239. Chunky Beef Chili

(Ready in about 25 minutes | Servings 4)

Ingredients

1 tablespoon olive oil	Kosher salt and ground black pepper, to taste
1 pound ground chuck	1 cup beef stock
1/2 cup leeks, chopped	1 red chili pepper, minced
2 cloves garlic, minced	2 (15-ounces) cans black beans, drained and rinsed
1 teaspoon dried oregano	1 (14-ounce) can tomatoes, diced
1 teaspoon dried basil	4 tablespoon tomato ketchup
1/2 teaspoon cumin powder	
1 teaspoon ancho chili powder	

Directions

Press the "Sauté" button and heat the oil. Once hot, cook the ground chuck, leeks, and garlic until the meat is no longer pink.

Add the remaining ingredients; gently stir to combine.

Secure the lid. Choose the "Manual" mode and cook for 15 minutes at High pressure. Once cooking is complete, use a quick pressure release; carefully remove the lid.

Serve in individual bowls garnished with green onions if desired. Bon appétit!

Per serving: 393 Calories; 17.4g Fat; 23.6g Carbs; 37.4g Protein; 6.9g Sugars

240. Homestyle Sloppy Joes

(Ready in about 20 minutes | Servings 4)

Ingredients

1 teaspoon lard	1 tablespoon stone ground
1 pound ground beef	mustard
1 onion, chopped	1 teaspoon celery seeds
1 teaspoon fresh garlic, minced	1/2 teaspoon dried rosemary
1 sweet pepper, chopped	1 cup beef stock
1 serrano pepper, chopped	1/2 cup tomato puree
Salt and ground black pepper, to	2 tablespoons ketchup
taste	1 teaspoon brown sugar
1/2 teaspoon red pepper flakes	4 soft hamburger buns

Directions

Press the "Sauté" button and melt the lard. Once hot, cook the ground beef until it is brown.

Add the onion, garlic, and peppers; continue to cook for 1 to 2 minutes more.

Add the salt, black pepper, red pepper flakes, mustard, celery seeds, rosemary, stock, tomato puree, ketchup, and brown sugar. Mix to combine.

Secure the lid. Choose the "Manual" mode and cook for 5 minutes at High pressure. Once cooking is complete, use a natural pressure release for 10 minutes; carefully remove the lid.

Serve on hamburger buns and enjoy!

Per serving: 475 Calories; 16.6g Fat; 43g Carbs; 37.6g Protein; 9.2g Sugars

241. Beef and Rice Stuffed Peppers

(Ready in about 25 minutes | Servings 3)

Ingredients

1/2 cup parboiled rice	1/2 teaspoon celery seeds
1 pound ground beef	1/2 teaspoon mustard seeds
1 onion, chopped	1 teaspoon basil
2 garlic cloves, minced	3 large bell peppers, deseeded,
1 carrot, grated	cored and halved
Sea salt and ground black pepper,	1 cup tomato puree
to taste	2 tablespoons ketchup
1 teaspoon cayenne pepper	1 cup cheddar cheese, grated

Directions

In a mixing bowl, thoroughly combine the rice, ground beef, onion, garlic, carrot, salt, black pepper, cayenne pepper, celery seeds, mustard seeds, and basil.

Add 1 cup of water and a metal trivet to the bottom. Fill the pepper halves with the rice/meat mixture. Place the peppers in a casserole dish; add the tomato puree and ketchup.

Lower the casserole dish onto the trivet in the Instant Pot.

Secure the lid. Choose the "Manual" mode and cook for 9 minutes at High pressure. Once cooking is complete, use a natural pressure release for 5 minutes; carefully remove the lid.

Afterwards, broil your peppers until the cheese melts approximately 5 minutes. Serve and enjoy!

Per serving: 331 Calories; 13.5g Fat; 36.9g Carbs; 24.1g Protein; 15.2g Sugars

242. Simple Traditional Bulgogi

(Ready in about 50 minutes + marinating time | Servings 4)

Ingredients

1/4 cup tamari sauce	2 tablespoons sesame oil
2 tablespoons Korean rice wine	1 onion, sliced
2 tablespoons agave syrup	2 cloves garlic, minced
Salt and black pepper, to taste	1 tablespoon pickled red ginger
2 pounds rib-eye steak, cut into	1/2 Asian pear, cored and sliced
strips	2 tablespoons sesame seeds, toasted

Directions

Mix the tamari sauce, rice, wine, agave syrup, salt, and black pepper in a ceramic bowl; add the beef, cover, and let it marinate for 1 hour.

Press the "Sauté" button and heat the sesame oil. Once hot, brown the beef strips in batches. Add the onion, garlic, pickled ginger, and Asian pear.

Secure the lid. Choose the "Meat/Stew" mode and cook for 35 minutes at High pressure. Once cooking is complete, use a natural pressure release for 10 minutes; carefully remove the lid.

Serve garnished with toasted sesame seeds. Enjoy!

Per serving: 530 Calories; 29.5g Fat; 19g Carbs; 50.6g Protein; 13.6g Sugars

243. Delicious Parmesan Meatballs

Ready in about 40 minutes | Servings 4)

Ingredients

2/3 pound ground beef	Kosher salt and ground black
1/3 pound beef sausage, crumbled	pepper, to taste
1 shallot, minced	1/2 teaspoon cayenne pepper
2 cloves garlic, smashed	1 tablespoon canola oil
1 egg, beaten	1 cup tomato puree
2 slices bread (soaked in 4	1 cup chicken bone broth
tablespoons of milk)	1 teaspoon Dijon mustard
1/4 cup parmesan cheese	

Directions

In a mixing dish, thoroughly combine the beef, sausage, shallot, garlic, egg, soaked bread, parmesan, salt, black pepper, and cayenne pepper

Mix to combine well and shape the mixture into 12 meatballs. Set aside.

Press the "Sauté" button and heat the oil. Once hot, brown the meatballs for 7 to 8 minutes, rolling them around so that they will brown evenly all around.

Mix the tomato puree, broth and mustard in the inner pot. Gently fold in the meatballs.

Secure the lid. Choose the "Meat/Stew" mode and cook for 20 minutes at High pressure. Once cooking is complete, use a natural pressure release for 10 minutes; carefully remove the lid. Bon appétit!

Per serving: 509 Calories; 30.2g Fat; 14.6g Carbs; 43.1g Protein; 4.3g Sugars

244. Filet Mignon with Wild Mushrooms

Ready in about 30 minutes | Servings 4)

Ingredients

1 ½ pounds filet mignon, about 1	1/4 cup all-purpose flour
½-inch thick	2 tablespoons butter
1/2 teaspoon sea salt	2 cups wild mushrooms, sliced
1/2 teaspoon red pepper flakes,	1 onion, thinly sliced
crushed	2 garlic cloves, sliced
1/2 teaspoon ground black pepper	1 cup chicken broth

Directions

Toss the filet mignon with salt, red pepper, black pepper, and flour.

Press the "Sauté" button and melt the butter. Once hot, sear the filet mignon for 2 minutes. Turn it over and cook for 2 minutes more on the other side.

Add the remaining ingredients and secure the lid.

Choose the "Meat/Stew" mode and cook for 20 minutes at High pressure. Once cooking is complete, use a quick pressure release; carefully remove the lid.

You can thicken the sauce on the "Sauté" mode if desired. Serve warm.

Per serving: 332 Calories; 14.6g Fat; 8.8g Carbs; 41.8g Protein; 1.3g Sugars

245. Saturday Afternoon Meatloaf

(Ready in about 35 minutes | Servings 4)

Ingredients

1 egg, beaten
1/2 cup milk
1 cup tortilla chips, crushed
1 small-sized onion, finely chopped
1 sweet pepper, finely chopped
2 cloves garlic, minced
Sea salt and ground black pepper, to taste
1/2 teaspoon rosemary
1 pound ground beef
1/2 pound ground pork
1 cup tomato puree
1 teaspoon mustard
2 tablespoons brown sugar
1 tablespoon tamari sauce

Directions

Place a steamer rack inside the inner pot; add 1/2 cup of water. Cut 1 sheet of heavy-duty foil and brush with cooking spray.

In mixing dish, combine the egg, milk, tortilla chips, onion, sweet pepper, garlic, salt, black pepper, rosemary, and ground meat.

Shape the meat mixture into a loaf; place the meatloaf in the center of foil. Wrap your meatloaf in foil and lower onto the steamer rack.

Secure the lid. Choose the "Meat/Stew" mode and cook for 20 minutes at High pressure. Once cooking is complete, use a quick pressure release; carefully remove the lid.

Then, transfer your meatloaf to a cutting board. Let it stand for 10 minutes before cutting and serving. Bon appétit!

Per serving: 564 Calories; 28.7g Fat; 23.8g Carbs; 51.1g Protein; 10.5g Sugars

246. Keto-Friendly Cheeseburger Cups

(Ready in about 30 minutes | Servings 6)

Ingredients

1 ½ pounds ground beef
Sea salt and ground black pepper, to taste
1 teaspoon onion powder
1/2 teaspoon garlic powder
1 tablespoon Italian seasoning blend
1/2 cup tomato paste
1 tablespoon maple syrup
1 teaspoon Dijon mustard
1 cup Cheddar cheese, shredded

Directions

Spritz a silicone muffin pan with non-stick cooking oil.

In a large bowl, thoroughly combine the ground beef, salt, black pepper, onion powder, garlic powder, Italian seasoning blend, tomato paste, and Dijon mustard with your hands.

Scrape the beef mixture into the silicone muffin pan.

Place a steamer rack inside the inner pot; add 1/2 cup of water. Lower the muffin pan onto the rack.

Secure the lid. Choose the "Manual" mode and cook for 20 minutes at High pressure. Once cooking is complete, use a quick pressure release; carefully remove the lid.

Top with cheese; allow the cheese to melt and serve warm.

Per serving: 390 Calories; 24.8g Fat; 6g Carbs; 33.8g Protein; 3.9g Sugars

247. Delicious Cheeseburger Quiche

(Ready in about 45 minutes | Servings 4)

Ingredients

1 tablespoon olive oil
1 pound ground beef
1 onion, chopped
2 cloves garlic, minced
Sea salt and ground black pepper, to taste
1/2 teaspoon basil
1/2 teaspoon thyme
1/2 teaspoon oregano
4 eggs
1/2 cup milk
2 ounces cream cheese, at room temperature
1 cup cheddar cheese, shredded
1 tomato, sliced

Directions

Press the "Sauté" button and heat the olive oil until sizzling. Now, cook the ground beef until no longer pink.

Transfer the browned beef to a lightly greased soufflé dish. Add the onion, garlic, and seasonings.

In a mixing dish, whisk the eggs, milk, and cream cheese. Top with the cheddar cheese. Cover with a foil.

Place the rack and 1 ½ cups of water inside the Instant Pot. Lower the soufflé dish onto the rack.

Secure the lid. Choose the "Manual" mode and cook for 30 minutes at High pressure. Once cooking is complete, use a quick pressure release; carefully remove the lid.

Let it rest for 10 minutes before slicing and serving. Garnish with tomatoes and serve. Enjoy!

Per serving: 465 Calories; 28.2g Fat; 9.4g Carbs; 41.5g Protein; 5.7g Sugars

248. The Classic French Châteaubriand

(Ready in about 25 minutes | Servings 2)

Ingredients

1 pound center-cut beef tenderloin
1 cup cream of onion soup
1 tablespoon butter
1 shallot, sliced
2 cloves garlic, finely minced
1/2 cup red wine
Kosher salt and ground black pepper, to taste
1 tablespoon fresh tarragon

Directions

Add the beef and cream of onion soup to a lightly greased inner pot.

Secure the lid. Choose the "Manual" mode and cook for 13 minutes at High pressure. Once cooking is complete, use a quick pressure release; carefully remove the lid.

Press the "Sauté" button to preheat your Instant Pot. Melt the butter and cook the shallots until tender or about 3 minutes.

Then, stir in the garlic; cook an additional 30 seconds or so.

Pour the wine into the inner pot, scraping up all the browned bits on the bottom of the pan. Add the salt, pepper, and tarragon.

Continue boiling the sauce until it reduces by half. Serve the sliced chateaubriand with the wine sauce and enjoy!

Per serving: 559 Calories; 33.3g Fat; 19.6g Carbs; 47.1g Protein; 5.3g Sugars

249. Double Cheese Burger Dip

(Ready in about 25 minutes | Servings 10)

Ingredients

3 pounds ground chuck roast
2 cloves garlic, minced
1 teaspoon shallot powder
1 teaspoon mustard powder
1 teaspoon dried rosemary
3 bay leaves
2 tablespoons Worcestershire sauce
4 cups water
4 ounces cream cheese, room temperature
1/2 cup mozzarella, shredded

Directions

Add all ingredients, except for the cheese, to your Instant Pot.

Secure the lid. Choose the "Manual" mode and cook for 20 minutes at High pressure. Once cooking is complete, use a quick pressure release; carefully remove the lid.

Top with the cheese and allow it to stand until the cheese has melted

Serve with assorted vegetables or breadsticks if desired. Bon appétit!

Per serving: 294 Calories; 14.7g Fat; 1.6g Carbs; 38.9g Protein; 0.8g Sugars

250. Famous Philly Cheesesteaks

(Ready in about 35 minutes | Servings 8)

Ingredients

1 tablespoon lard, melted
2 ½ pounds top sirloin steak, sliced into thin strips
2 onions, sliced
2 sweet peppers, deseeded and sliced
1 red chili pepper, minced
Kosher salt and freshly ground pepper, to taste
1 teaspoon paprika
1/2 cup dry red wine
1 cup beef broth
8 Hoagie rolls
1 tablespoon Dijon mustard
8 ounces yellow American cheese, sliced
8 ounces mild Provolone cheese, sliced

Directions

Press the "Sauté" button to preheat your Instant Pot. Melt the lard and cook your steak for about 4 minutes.

Add the onions, peppers, salt, black pepper, paprika, wine, and broth.

Secure the lid. Choose the "Manual" mode and cook for 25 minutes at High pressure. Once cooking is complete, use a quick pressure release; carefully remove the lid.

Serve the meat mixture in rolls topped with mustard and cheese. Bon appétit!

Per serving: 579 Calories; 30.6g Fat; 27.1g Carbs; 45.9g Protein; 6.1g Sugars

251. Perfect New York Strip with Cream Sauce

(Ready in about 30 minutes | Servings 4)

Ingredients

2 tablespoons sesame oil
2 pounds New York strip, sliced into thin strips
Kosher salt and ground black pepper, to taste
1/2 cup dry red wine
1 cup cream of mushroom soup
1 small leek, sliced
2 cloves garlic, sliced
2 carrots, sliced
1 tablespoon tamari sauce
1/2 cup heavy cream

Directions

Press the "Sauté" button to preheat your Instant Pot. Heat the sesame oil until sizzling. Once hot, brown the beef strips in batches.

Add wine to deglaze the pan. Stir in the remaining ingredients, except for the heavy cream.

Secure the lid. Choose the "Manual" mode and cook for 20 minutes at High pressure. Once cooking is complete, use a quick pressure release; carefully remove the lid.

Remove the beef from the cooking liquid. Mash the vegetables using a potato masher.

Press the "Sauté" button one more time. Now, bring the liquid to a boil. Heat off and stir in the heavy cream.

Spoon the sauce over the New York strip and serve immediately. Enjoy!

Per serving: 439 Calories; 21.9g Fat; 9.8g Carbs; 50g Protein; 2.3g Sugars

252. Creamed Delmonico Steak

(Ready in about 20 minutes | Servings 4)

Ingredients

2 tablespoons butter
1 ½ pounds Delmonico steak, cubed
2 cloves garlic, minced
1 cup beef broth
1 cup double cream
1/4 cup sour cream
1 teaspoon cayenne pepper
Sea salt and ground black pepper, to taste
1/2 cup gorgonzola cheese, shredded

Directions

Press the "Sauté" button to preheat your Instant Pot. Melt the butter and brown the beef cubes in batches for about 4 minutes per batch.

Add the garlic, broth, double cream, and sour cream to the inner pot; season with cayenne pepper, salt, and black pepper.

Secure the lid. Choose the "Manual" mode and cook for 10 minutes at High pressure. Once cooking is complete, use a quick pressure release; carefully remove the lid.

Top with gorgonzola cheese and serve. Bon appétit!

Per serving: 572 Calories; 36.9g Fat; 5.8g Carbs; 55.3g Protein; 3.4g Sugars

253. Asian Braised Beef Shanks

(Ready in about 45 minutes | Servings 4)

Ingredients

1 ½ pounds beef shank
1 teaspoon garlic, minced
1 tablespoon sesame oil
1/2 cup rice wine
2 tablespoons soy sauce
1 teaspoon Chinese five spice powder
1 dried red chili, sliced
2 cloves star anise
1 cup instant dashi granules
1 cup water

Directions

Add all ingredients to the inner pot.

Secure the lid. Choose the "Manual" mode and cook for 30 minutes at High pressure. Once cooking is complete, use a natural pressure release for 10 minutes; carefully remove the lid.

Slice across the grain and serve over hot cooked rice if desired. Enjoy!

Per serving: 316 Calories; 11.4g Fat; 11.6g Carbs; 39.2g Protein; 1.8g Sugars

254. Chipolata Sausage and Cheese Casserole

(Ready in about 25 minutes | Servings 6)

Ingredients

1 tablespoon olive oil
1 ½ pounds lean beef chipolata sausages
1 leek, thinly sliced
2 garlic cloves, minced
1 cup tomato purée
1/2 cup beef bone broth
2 tablespoons ketchup
1 tablespoon tamari sauce
1 teaspoon cocoa powder
2 bay leaves
1 (20-ounce) can red kidney beans
1 teaspoon red pepper flakes
Salt, to taste
1/3 teaspoon freshly ground black pepper
1 teaspoon dried saffron
3/4 cup Colby cheese, grated

Directions

Press the "Sauté" button to preheat your Instant Pot. Now, heat the oil until sizzling. Brown the sausage for 2 minutes; reserve.

Then, sauté the leeks and garlic in the pan drippings for 2 more minutes; return the sausage back to the Instant Pot.

Add the tomato purée, broth, ketchup, tamari sauce, cocoa powder, bay leaves, beans, red pepper flakes, salt, black pepper, and saffron to the Instant Pot.

Secure the lid. Choose the "Poultry" mode and High pressure; cook for 15 minutes. Once cooking is complete, use a quick pressure release; carefully remove the lid.

Top with the grated cheese and seal the lid again. Let it sit until the cheese is melted. Serve warm.

Per serving: 498 Calories; 40.5g Fat; 11.2g Carbs; 21.8g Protein; 2.6g Sugars

255. Country-Style Ribs with Green Beans

(Ready in about 1 hour 5 minutes | Servings 10)

Ingredients

3 pounds Country-style ribs
2 tablespoons sesame oil
1 shallot, diced
4 garlic cloves, minced
1 (1-inch) piece fresh ginger, grated
1 cup vegetable broth
1/4 cup hoisin sauce
2 tablespoons tamari sauce
1 tablespoon honey
1 tablespoon five-spice powder
Salt, to taste
1/2 teaspoon ground black pepper
1 pound green beans

Directions

Add all of the above ingredients, except for the green beans, to the Instant Pot.

Secure the lid. Choose the "Manual" mode and High pressure; cook for 55 minutes. Once cooking is complete, use a natural pressure release; carefully remove the lid.

Then, add the green beans. Secure the lid. Choose the "Steam" mode and High pressure; cook for 3 minutes. Once cooking is complete, use a quick pressure release; carefully remove the lid.

Transfer the ribs along with the green beans to a nice serving platter and serve immediately.

Per serving: 520 Calories; 43g Fat; 7.8g Carbs; 24.2g Protein; 4g Sugars

256. New York Strip with Sweet Peppers

(Ready in about 25 minutes | Servings 4)

Ingredients

1 pound New York strip, cut into pieces
Salt and ground black pepper, to taste
1 teaspoon paprika
1 tablespoon lard, melted
2 sweet onions, chopped
2 cloves garlic, smashed
1 sweet red bell pepper, chopped
1 sweet green bell pepper, chopped
1/2 cup beef broth
1/2 cup tomato sauce
2 tablespoons Worcestershire sauce
1 tablespoon oyster sauce
2 tablespoons flaxseed meal
2 tablespoons toasted pine nuts, for garnish

Directions

Toss the beef with salt, black pepper, and paprika. Press the "Sauté" button on your Instant Pot. Once hot, melt the lard.

Brown the beef for 4 to 5 minutes, stirring periodically; add a splash of beef broth, if necessary; reserve.

Then, cook the sweet onions, garlic, and bell peppers until they are softened.

Add the beef broth, tomato sauce, Worcestershire, and oyster sauce to the Instant Pot. Return the browned beef to the Instant Pot.

Choose "Manual" setting, High pressure, and 15 minutes. Once cooking is complete, use a quick release.

Press the "Sauté" button, stir in flaxseed meal, and cook until the sauce is concentrated. Serve garnished with toasted pine nuts. Bon appétit!

Per serving: 322 Calories; 12.7g Fat; 25.5g Carbs; 27g Protein; 14.3g Sugars

257. Saucy and Cheesy Beef Brisket

(Ready in about 1 hour 5 minutes | Servings 6)

Ingredients

2 tablespoons lard, at room temperature
2 pounds beef brisket
Sea salt, to taste
1/2 teaspoon ground black pepper
1/2 teaspoon cayenne pepper
1/2 teaspoon ground bay leaf
1/2 teaspoon celery seeds
1 teaspoon mustard seeds
2 garlic cloves, chopped
1 leek, chopped
1 cup beef bone broth
1 cup Monterey Jack cheese, freshly grated

Directions

Press the "Sauté" button to preheat your Instant Pot. Then, melt the lard.

Once hot, sear the brisket for 2 to 3 minutes on each side. Then, add the seasonings, garlic, leek, and beef bone broth.

Secure the lid. Choose the "Manual" mode and High pressure; cook for 60 minutes. Once cooking is complete, use a natural pressure release; carefully remove the lid.

Slice the beef into strips and top with cheese.

Press the "Sauté" button once again and allow it to simmer until the cheese is melted. Serve warm.

Per serving: 434 Calories; 33.7g Fat; 3.2g Carbs; 28g Protein; 0.7g Sugars

258. Beef Stew with Sweet Corn

(Ready in about 30 minutes | Servings 6)

Ingredients

2 pounds beef stewing meat, cut into cubes
4 cups bone broth
1/2 cup Pinot Noir
1 yellow onion, chopped
2 bell peppers, chopped
1 red chili pepper, chopped
1/2 pound carrots, chopped
Sea salt and ground black pepper, to taste
1/2 teaspoon mustard powder
1 teaspoon celery seeds
1 cup sweet corn kernels, frozen

Directions

Add all ingredients, except for the sweet corn, to the Instant Pot.

Secure the lid. Choose the "Soup" mode and High pressure; cook for 20 minutes. Once cooking is complete, use a quick pressure release; carefully remove the lid.

Stir in the sweet corn kernels and press the "Sauté" button. Let it simmer until thoroughly heated. Taste, adjust the seasonings and serve. Bon appétit!

Per serving: 223 Calories; 5.6g Fat; 14.4g Carbs; 28.1g Protein; 3.4g Sugars

259. Hoisin Sirloin Steak

(Ready in about 1 hour | Servings 8)

Ingredients

1 tablespoon lard, at room temperature
2 pounds boneless sirloin steak, thinly sliced
Sea salt and ground black pepper, to your liking
1 teaspoon chili powder
2 tablespoons fresh parsley, chopped
1/2 cup red onion, sliced
2 garlic cloves, minced
2 sweet peppers, deveined and sliced
1/2 cup beef bone broth
1/2 cup hoisin sauce

Directions

Press the "Sauté" button and preheat the Instant Pot; melt the lard. Once hot, brown the sirloin steak for 6 minutes, flipping halfway through cooking time.

Season with salt and pepper; add the chili powder, parsley, onion, garlic, and peppers. Pour in the beef bone broth and secure the lid.

Select "Manual" setting, High pressure and 50 minutes. Once cooking is complete, use a natural release and carefully remove the lid.

Shred the beef and return it to the Instant Pot; stir to combine. Afterwards, pour the hoisin sauce over the shredded beef and vegetables and serve immediately. Bon appétit!

Per serving: 283 Calories; 14.9g Fat; 10.9g Carbs; 24.8g Protein; 4.6g Sugars

260. Beef Brisket with Quick Cabbage Slaw

(Ready in about 1 hour 10 minutes | Servings 6)

Ingredients

2 teaspoons olive oil
1 ½ pounds beef brisket
4 bacon slices, chopped
2 garlic cloves, pressed
1 carrot, chopped
1/2 cup dry red wine
1/2 cup water
2 sprigs rosemary
1/2 teaspoon mixed peppercorns, whole
1/4 cup tomato purée

1/2 teaspoon sea salt
1/2 teaspoon ground black pepper
1/2 teaspoon cayenne pepper
Cole Slaw:
1 head cabbage
1 yellow onion, thinly sliced
1 carrot, grated
4 tablespoons sour cream
4 tablespoons mayonnaise
Salt, to taste

Directions

Press the "Sauté" button to preheat your Instant Pot. Then, heat the oil until sizzling. Sear the beef for 3 to 4 minutes or until it is delicately browned; reserve.

Add the bacon to the Instant Pot; sear the bacon approximately 3 minutes; reserve. Then, cook the garlic for 1 minute or until fragrant.

Add the carrot, wine, water, rosemary, mixed peppercorns, tomato purée, salt, black pepper, and cayenne pepper. Return the beef brisket and bacon back to the Instant Pot.

Secure the lid. Choose the "Manual" mode and High pressure; cook for 60 minutes. Once cooking is complete, use a quick pressure release; carefully remove the lid.

Meanwhile, make the cabbage slaw by mixing the remaining ingredients. Serve and enjoy!

Per serving: 397 Calories; 29.4g Fat; 10.9g Carbs; 21.4g Protein; 5.1g Sugars

261. Country-Style Steak Soup

(Ready in about 25 minutes | Servings 4)

Ingredients

1 pound beef steak, cut into cubes
1 cup water
2 (8-ounce) cans tomato sauce
1 cup roasted vegetable broth
1 shallot, diced
2 carrots, chopped
1 parsnip, chopped

1 turnip, chopped
2 bell peppers, deveined and chopped
2 cloves garlic, minced
Sea salt and ground black pepper, to taste
1 bay leaf

Directions

Simply throw all of the above ingredients in your Instant Pot that is previously greased with a nonstick cooking spray.

Secure the lid. Choose the "Soup" mode and High pressure; cook for 20 minutes. Once cooking is complete, use a quick pressure release; carefully remove the lid.

Divide the soup among four serving bowls and serve warm.

Per serving: 278 Calories; 7.6g Fat; 22.3g Carbs; 30.4g Protein; 9.7g Sugars

262. Hungarian Marha Pörkölt

(Ready in about 30 minutes | Servings 4)

Ingredients

1 tablespoon sesame oil
1 ½ pounds beef stewing meat, cut into bite-sized chunks
1 cup scallions, chopped
2 cloves garlic, minced
Kosher salt, to taste
1/4 teaspoon freshly ground black pepper, or more to taste
2 carrots, sliced
1 jalapeño pepper, minced

4 cups beef bone broth
1 cup tomato purée
2 sprigs thyme
1 teaspoon dried sage, crushed
2 tablespoons sweet Hungarian paprika
1/2 teaspoon mustard seeds
2 bay leaves
1 cup sour cream

Directions

Press the "Sauté" button to preheat your Instant Pot. Then, heat the sesame oil. Sear the beef for 3 to 4 minutes or until it is delicately browned; reserve.

Cook the scallions and garlic in the pan drippings until tender and fragrant. Now, add the remaining ingredients, except for the sour cream.

Secure the lid. Choose the "Soup" mode and High pressure; cook for 20 minutes. Once cooking is complete, use a quick pressure release; carefully remove the lid.

Divide your stew among four soup bowls; serve with a dollop of sour cream and enjoy!

Per serving: 487 Calories; 19g Fat; 11.3g Carbs; 65g Protein; 2.7g Sugars

263. Creamy and Saucy Beef Delight

(Ready in about 30 minutes | Servings 6)

Ingredients

1 tablespoon lard, at room temperature
1 shallot, diced
1 ½ pounds beef brisket, cut into 2-inch cubes
Sea salt and freshly ground pepper, to taste
1 teaspoon red pepper flakes, crushed
2 garlic cloves, minced

2 sprigs dried rosemary, leaves picked
2 sprigs dried thyme, leaves picked
1 teaspoon caraway seeds
1 ½ tablespoons flaxseed meal
1/2 cup chicken stock
6 ounces wonton noodles
3/4 cup cream cheese
2 tablespoons toasted sesame seeds

Directions

Press the "Sauté" button to preheat your Instant Pot. Now, melt the lard; once hot, sweat the shallot for 2 to 3 minutes.

Toss the beef brisket with salt, ground pepper, and red pepper flakes. Add the beef to the Instant pot; continue cooking for 3 minutes more or until it is no longer pink.

After that, stir in the garlic, rosemary, thyme, and caraway seeds; cook an additional minute, stirring continuously.

Add the flaxseed meal, chicken stock, and wonton noodles. Stir to combine well and seal the lid. Choose the "Meat/Stew" setting and cook at High pressure for 20 minutes.

Once cooking is complete, use a quick release; remove the lid. Divide the beef mixture among 6 serving bowls.

To serve, stir in the cream cheese and garnish with toasted sesame seeds. Bon appétit!

Per serving: 485 Calories; 30.9g Fat; 12.8g Carbs; 37.1g Protein; 2.4g Sugars

264. Thai-Style Beef Salad

(Ready in about 45 minutes | Servings 6)

Ingredients

2 pounds beef rump steak
1/2 cup vegetable broth
1/2 cup water
1 tablespoon black peppercorns
2 bay leaves
1 tablespoon tamari sauce
1/4 cup lemon juice, freshly squeezed
1/4 cup sesame oil
Sea salt flakes, to taste

1 cup red onions, thinly sliced
1 fresh tomato, diced
1 large-sized cucumber, sliced
2 long fresh red chilies, chopped
2 cups arugula
1 tablespoon Dijon mustard
1 bunch fresh Thai basil, leaves picked
3 kaffir lime leaves, shredded

Directions

Add the beef, vegetable broth, water, black peppercorns, and bay leaves to your Instant Pot.

Secure the lid. Choose the "Meat/Stew" mode and High pressure; cook for 35 minutes. Once cooking is complete, use a natural pressure release; carefully remove the lid.

Thinly slice the beef across the grain and add to the salad bowl. In a small mixing bowl, make the dressing by whisking the tamari sauce, lemon juice, sesame oil, and salt.

Add the remaining ingredients to the salad bowl; dress the salad. Serve at room temperature.

Per serving: 318 Calories; 17.7g Fat; 5.1g Carbs; 33.4g Protein; 1.9g Sugars

265. Beef Roast with Vegetables

(Ready in about 55 minutes | Servings 6)

Ingredients

2 tablespoons olive oil
2 pounds beef roast
1 cup vegetable broth
1/2 cup Chianti
Sea salt and ground black pepper, to taste

1 teaspoon red pepper flakes, crushed
1 cup shallots, chopped
2 cloves garlic, pressed
2 bay leaves
2 carrots, sliced
1 parsnip, sliced

Directions

Add the olive oil, beef, broth, Chianti, salt, black pepper, red pepper, shallots, garlic, and bay leaves to the Instant Pot.

Secure the lid. Choose the "Meat/Stew" mode and High pressure; cook for 45 minutes. Once cooking is complete, use a quick pressure release; carefully remove the lid.

Then, add the carrots and parsnip to the Instant Pot.

Secure the lid. Choose the "Manual" mode and High pressure; cook for 5 minutes. Once cooking is complete, use a quick pressure release; carefully remove the lid.

You can thicken the cooking liquid on "Sauté" function if desired. Bon appétit!

Per serving: 363 Calories; 17.6g Fat; 6.1g Carbs; 41.6g Protein; 1.8g Sugars

266. Deluxe Beef Sandwich

(Ready in about 45 minutes | Servings 6)

Ingredients

1 tablespoon olive oil
2 pounds sirloin
1/2 cup vegetable broth
1/2 cup water
1/4 cup dry vermouth
1 tablespoon Dijon mustard

1 tablespoon tamari sauce
Salt and black pepper, to taste
1/2 teaspoon cayenne pepper
2 cloves garlic, minced
1 red chili pepper
6 sandwich buns, split

Directions

Press the "Sauté" button to preheat your Instant Pot. Then, heat the oil until sizzling. Sear the beef until browned on all sides.

Add the broth, water, vermouth, mustard, tamari sauce, salt, black pepper, cayenne pepper, garlic, and red chili pepper.

Secure the lid. Choose the "Soup" mode and High pressure; cook for 40 minutes. Once cooking is complete, use a natural pressure release; carefully remove the lid.

Then, pull the cooked beef apart into chunks. Return it back to the Instant Pot and stir well to combine. Assemble the sandwiches with buns and serve. Enjoy!

Per serving: 503 Calories; 23.7g Fat; 36.2g Carbs; 34.3g Protein; 19.8g Sugars

267. Melt in Your Mouth Beef Rump Roast

(Ready in about 40 minutes | Servings 8)

Ingredients

2 pounds beef rump roast
2 garlic cloves, halved
Salt and pepper, to your liking
1 teaspoon dried rosemary
1 teaspoon dried thyme
1 tablespoon olive oil

1 cup leeks, chopped
4 carrots, peeled
2 parsnips, chopped
1/3 cup Shaoxing wine
1 ½ cups vegetable stock

Directions

Rub the beef rump roast with garlic halves. Now, cut it into cubes. Season with salt, pepper, rosemary, and thyme.

Then, press the "Sauté" button and heat olive oil. Sauté the leeks together with the carrot and parsnips.

Add a splash of Shaoxing wine to deglaze the pan. Place the beef pieces in a single layer on top of the sautéed vegetables.

Pour in the vegetable stock and the remaining Shaoxing wine. Secure the lid. Select the "Manual" mode and cook for 35 minutes.

Once cooking is complete, use a quick release. Serve warm. Bon appétit!

Per serving: 269 Calories; 11.5g Fat; 10g Carbs; 31.7g Protein; 3.7g Sugars

268. Classic Hungarian Goulash

(Ready in about 40 minutes | Servings 4)

Ingredients

1/3 cup all-purpose flour
Sea salt and freshly ground pepper, to taste
1 teaspoon garlic powder
1 ½ pounds boneless beef chuck, cut into cubes
2 tablespoons sesame oil
4 cups water

4 bullion cubes
1/4 cup rose wine
1 bay leaf
2 shallots, chopped
1 celery with leaves, chopped
2 carrots, sliced
1 red bell pepper, sliced
1 teaspoon Hungarian paprika

Directions

In a mixing bowl, thoroughly combine the flour, salt, black pepper, and garlic powder. Now add the beef cubes to the flour mixture; toss to coat well.

Press the "Sauté" button. Heat the oil and sear the meat for 4 to 6 minutes.

Add the remaining ingredients and stir to combine.

Secure the lid. Choose the "Soup" mode and High pressure; cook for 30 minutes. Once cooking is complete, use a natural pressure release; carefully remove the lid.

Serve in individual bowls and enjoy!

Per serving: 336 Calories; 16.6g Fat; 10.5g Carbs; 36.5g Protein; 1.2g Sugars

269. Sunday Hamburger Pilaf

(Ready in about 15 minutes | Servings 4)

Ingredients

1 tablespoon sesame oil
1/2 cup leeks, chopped
1 teaspoon garlic, minced
1 jalapeño pepper, minced
1 (1-inch) piece ginger root, peeled and grated
1 ½ pounds ground chuck

1 cup tomato purée
Sea salt, to taste
1/3 teaspoon ground black pepper, or more to taste
1 teaspoon red pepper flakes
2 cups Arborio rice
1 ½ cups roasted vegetable broth

Directions

Press the "Sauté" button to preheat your Instant Pot. Now, heat the sesame oil and sauté the leeks until tender.

Then, add the garlic, jalapeño and ginger; cook for 1 minute more or until aromatic.

Add the remaining ingredients; stir well to combine.

Secure the lid. Choose the "Manual" mode and High pressure; cook for 7 minutes. Once cooking is complete, use a quick pressure release; carefully remove the lid. Serve immediately.

Per serving: 493 Calories; 28.8g Fat; 34.9g Carbs; 42.1g Protein; 3.3g Sugars

270. Italian-Style Steak Pepperonata

(Ready in about 1 hour 10 minutes | Servings 6)

Ingredients

2 teaspoons lard, at room temperature
2 pounds top round steak, cut into bite-sized chunks
1 red onion, chopped
1 pound mixed bell peppers, deveined and thinly sliced
2 cloves garlic, minced

1 tablespoon Italian seasoning blend
Sea salt and ground black pepper, to taste
1 tablespoon salt-packed capers, rinsed and drained
1/2 cup dry red wine
1 cup water

Directions

Press the "Sauté" button to preheat your Instant Pot. Then, melt the lard. Cook the round steak approximately 5 minutes, stirring periodically; reserve.

Then, sauté the onion for 2 minutes or until translucent.

Stir in the remaining ingredients, including the reserved beef.

Secure the lid. Choose the "Manual" mode and High pressure; cook for 60 minutes. Once cooking is complete, use a natural pressure release; carefully remove the lid. Bon appétit!

Per serving: 309 Calories; 7.4g Fat; 10.8g Carbs; 46.9g Protein; 5.1g Sugars

271. Wine-Braised Beef Shanks

(Ready in about 45 minutes + marinating time | Servings 6)

Ingredients

1 ½ pounds beef shanks, cut into pieces
1/2 cup port
1 cup wine
2 garlic cloves, crushed
1 teaspoon celery seeds
12 teaspoon dried thyme
1 tablespoon olive oil
1/2 cup leeks, chopped
2 potatoes, diced
2 carrots, chopped
1 1/3 cups vegetable stock
Salt and black pepper, to taste

Directions

Add the beef shanks to a bowl; now, add port, red wine, garlic, celery seeds, and dried thyme. Let it marinate overnight.

On an actual day, preheat your Instant Pot on "Sauté" function. Add the olive oil; once hot, brown the marinated shanks on all sides; reserve.

Now, cook the leeks, potatoes and carrots in the pan drippings until they have softened. Add the vegetable stock, salt, and pepper to taste.

Pour in the reserved marinade and secure the lid.

Select the "Meat/Stew" and cook for 35 minutes at High pressure. Once cooking is complete, use a quick release; remove the lid.

Now, press the "Sauté" button to thicken the cooking liquid for 5 to 6 minutes. Taste, adjust the seasonings and serve right away!

Per serving: 329 Calories; 10.5g Fat; 25.8g Carbs; 32g Protein; 2.7g Sugars

272. Home-Style Beef Tikka Kebabs

(Ready in about 30 minutes | Servings 4)

Ingredients

2 tablespoons olive oil
1 ½ pounds lean steak beef, cubed
1/2 cup onion, sliced
2 cloves garlic, minced
2 tablespoons fresh cilantro, chopped
Salt and ground black pepper, to taste
1 teaspoon Aleppo chili flakes
1/2 teaspoon sumac
1/2 teaspoon turmeric powder
1/3 cup chicken stock
1 tablespoon champagne vinegar
1/3 cup mayonnaise
4 tablespoons pickled slaw
4 Bazlama flatbread

Directions

Press the "Sauté" button to heat up the Instant Pot. Now, heat the olive oil and brown the beef cubes, stirring frequently.

Add the onion, garlic, and seasonings to the Instant Pot. Cook an additional 4 minutes or until the onion is translucent.

Pour the chicken stock and champagne vinegar over the meat. Seal the lid.

Choose the "Meat/Stew" setting and cook for 20 minutes at High pressure. Once cooking is complete, use a quick release; remove the lid.

Assemble the sandwiches with mayonnaise, pickled slaw, the meat mixture, and Bazlama bread. Bon appétit!

Per serving: 590 Calories; 29g Fat; 22.5g Carbs; 58g Protein; 1.8g Sugars

273. Favorite Tex-Mex Tacos

(Ready in about 15 minutes | Servings 8)

Ingredients

1 tablespoon olive oil
1/2 cup shallots, chopped
2 cloves garlic, pressed
2 pounds ground sirloin
1/2 teaspoon ground cumin
1/2 cup roasted vegetable broth
1/2 ketchup
Sea salt, to taste
1/2 teaspoon fresh ground pepper
1 teaspoon paprika
1 can (16-ounces) diced tomatoes, undrained
2 canned chipotle chili in adobo sauce, drained
12 whole-wheat flour tortillas, warmed
1 head romaine lettuce
1 cup sour cream

Directions

Press the "Sauté" button and preheat the Instant Pot. Heat the oil and cook the shallots and garlic until aromatic.

Now, add the ground sirloin and cook an additional 2 minutes or until it is no longer pink.

Add the ground cumin, broth, ketchup, salt, black pepper, paprika, tomatoes, and chili in adobo sauce to your Instant Pot.

Secure the lid. Choose the "Poultry" mode and High pressure; cook for 5 minutes. Once cooking is complete, use a natural pressure release; carefully remove the lid.

Divide the beef mixture between tortillas. Garnish with lettuce and sour cream and serve.

Per serving: 566 Calories; 33.4g Fat; 38.6g Carbs; 30.7g Protein; 6.5g Sugars

274. Traditional Beef Pho Noodle Soup

(Ready in about 15 minutes | Servings 4)

Ingredients

1 tablespoon sesame oil
1 pound round steak, sliced paper thin
4 cups roasted vegetable broth
1 tablespoon brown sugar
Kosher salt and ground black pepper, to taste
2 carrots, trimmed and diced
1 celery stalk, trimmed and diced
1 cinnamon stick
3 star of anise
1/2 (14-ounce) package rice noodles
1 bunch of cilantro, roughly chopped
2 stalks scallions, diced

Directions

Press the "Sauté" button and preheat the Instant Pot. Heat the oil and sear the round steak for 1 to 2 minutes.

Add the broth, sugar, salt, black pepper, carrots, celery, cinnamon stick, and star anise. Top with the rice noodles so they should be on top of the other ingredients.

Secure the lid. Choose the "Manual" mode and High pressure; cook for 3 minutes. Once cooking is complete, use a quick pressure release; carefully remove the lid.

Serve in individual bowls, topped with cilantro and scallions. Enjoy!

Per serving: 417 Calories; 14g Fat; 27.5g Carbs; 43.1g Protein; 3.6g Sugars

275. Ground Beef Taco Bowls

(Ready in about 15 minutes | Servings 4)

Ingredients

1 tablespoon peanut oil
1 pound ground chuck
1 cup beef bone broth
1 bell pepper, seeded and chopped
1 red chili pepper, seeded and chopped
1 onion, chopped
1 (1.25-ounce) package taco seasoning
4 tortilla bowls, baked
1 (15-ounce) can beans, drained and rinsed
2 fresh tomatoes, chopped

Directions

Press the "Sauté" button and preheat the Instant Pot. Heat the oil and cook the ground chuck until it is no longer pink.

Add the broth, bell pepper, chili pepper, onion, and taco seasoning.

Secure the lid. Choose the "Manual" mode and High pressure; cook for 5 minutes. Once cooking is complete, use a quick pressure release; carefully remove the lid.

Divide the mixture between the tortilla bowls. Top with beans and tomatoes. Enjoy!

Per serving: 409 Calories; 15.7g Fat; 37.5g Carbs; 29.5g Protein; 6.6g Sugars

276. Holiday Osso Buco

(Ready in about 30 minutes | Servings 8)

Ingredients

2 tablespoons olive oil
1 ½ pounds Osso buco
2 carrots, sliced
1 celery with leaves, diced
1 cup beef bone broth
1/2 cup rose wine
2 garlic cloves, chopped
1 onion, chopped
2 bay leaves
1 sprig dried rosemary
1 teaspoon dried sage, crushed
1/2 teaspoon tarragon
Sea salt and ground black pepper, to taste

Directions

Press the "Sauté" button to preheat your Instant Pot. Now, heat the olive oil. Sear the beef on all sides.

Add the remaining ingredients.

Secure the lid. Choose the "Meat/Stew" mode and High pressure; cook for 25 minutes. Once cooking is complete, use a natural pressure release; carefully remove the lid. Bon appétit!

Per serving: 302 Calories; 7.2g Fat; 21.7g Carbs; 34.3g Protein; 3g Sugars

277. Tagliatelle with Beef Sausage and Cheese

(Ready in about 10 minutes | Servings 6)

Ingredients

2 teaspoons canola oil
1 pound beef sausage, sliced
1 ½ pounds tagliatelle pasta
3 cups water
2 cups tomato paste
Sea salt and ground black pepper, to taste
8 ounces Colby cheese, grated
5 ounces Ricotta cheese, crumbled
2 tablespoons fresh chives, roughly chopped

Directions

Press the "Sauté" button to preheat your Instant Pot. Now, heat the oil. Cook the sausages until they are no longer pink; reserve.

Then, stir in the pasta, water, tomato paste, salt, and black pepper.

Secure the lid. Choose the "Manual" mode and High pressure; cook for 4 minutes. Once cooking is complete, use a quick pressure release; carefully remove the lid.

Next, fold in the cheese; seal the lid and let it sit in the residual heat until heated through. Add the reserved sausage and stir; serve garnished with fresh chives. Bon appétit!

Per serving: 596 Calories; 32.6g Fat; 52.1g Carbs; 26.5g Protein; 11.3g Sugars

278. Pepper Jack Beef and Cauliflower Casserole

(Ready in about 35 minutes | Servings 4)

Ingredients

1 head cauliflower, chopped into small florets
2 tablespoons olive oil
1/2 cup yellow onion, chopped
2 garlic cloves, minced
1/2 pound ground beef
2 spicy sausages, chopped
2 ripe tomatoes, chopped
1 ½ tablespoons brown sugar
2 tablespoons tamari sauce
Salt and freshly ground black pepper, to your liking
1 teaspoon cayenne pepper
1/2 teaspoon celery seeds
1/2 teaspoon fennel seeds
1 teaspoon dried basil
1/2 teaspoon dried oregano
1 cup Pepper Jack cheese, shredded

Directions

Parboil the cauliflower in a lightly salted water for 3 to 5 minutes; remove the cauliflower from the water with a slotted spoon and drain.

Press the "Sauté" button to preheat your Instant Pot. Now, heat the oil and sweat the onions and garlic.

Then, add the ground beef and sausage and continue to cook for 4 minutes more or until they are browned.

Stir in the remaining ingredients, except for the shredded cheese, and cook for 4 minutes more or until heated through. Add the cauliflower florets on top.

Secure the lid and choose the "Manual" mode, High pressure and 6 minutes. Once cooking is complete, use a quick release; remove the lid.

Top with the shredded cheese and let it melt for 5 to 6 minutes. Bon appétit!

Per serving: 523 Calories; 39.6g Fat; 10.9g Carbs; 30.8g Protein; 5.3g Sugars

279. Hayashi Rice Stew

(Ready in about 30 minutes | Servings 6)

Ingredients

1 tablespoon lard, at room temperature
1 ½ pounds ribeye steaks, cut into bite-sized pieces
1/2 cup shallots, chopped
4 cloves garlic, minced
Salt and black pepper, to taste
1/2 teaspoon sweet paprika
1 sprig dried thyme, crushed
1 sprig dried rosemary, crushed
1 carrot, chopped
1 celery stalk, chopped
1/4 cup tomato paste
2 cups beef bone broth
1/3 cup rice wine
1 tablespoon Tonkatsu sauce
1 cup brown rice

Directions

Press the "Sauté" button to preheat your Instant Pot. Now, heat the oil and cook the beef until it is delicately browned.

Add the remaining ingredients; stir to combine.

Secure the lid. Choose the "Bean/Chili" mode and High pressure; cook for 25 minutes. Once cooking is complete, use a natural pressure release; carefully remove the lid. Bon appétit!

Per serving: 368 Calories; 16.1g Fat; 30.9g Carbs; 25.5g Protein; 3g Sugars

280. Balkan-Style Beef Stew

(Ready in about 35 minutes | Servings 6)

Ingredients

1 tablespoon olive oil
2 pounds beef sirloin steak, cut into bite-sized chunks
1 cup red onion, chopped
2 garlic cloves, minced
1 pound bell peppers, seeded and sliced
1 cup vegetable broth
4 Italian plum tomatoes, crushed
Salt and ground black pepper, to taste
1 teaspoon paprika
1 egg, beaten

Directions

Press the "Sauté" button to preheat your Instant Pot. Now, heat the oil. Cook the beef until it is no longer pink.

Add the onion and cook an additional 2 minutes. Stir in the minced garlic, peppers, broth, tomatoes, salt, black pepper, and paprika.

Secure the lid. Choose the "Soup" mode and High pressure; cook for 20 minutes. Once cooking is complete, use a quick pressure release; carefully remove the lid.

Afterwards, fold in the egg and stir well; seal the lid and let it sit in the residual heat for 8 to 10 minutes.

Serve in individual bowls with mashed potatoes. Enjoy!

Per serving: 403 Calories; 21.3g Fat; 16.4g Carbs; 36.8g Protein; 8.7g Sugars

281. Bacon and Blade Roast Sandwiches

(Ready in about 1 hour 30 minutes | Servings 8)

Ingredients

2 center-cut bacon slices, chopped
2 1/2 pounds top blade roast
Salt and ground black pepper, to taste
1 teaspoon dried marjoram
1/2 teaspoon dried rosemary
1 teaspoon Juniper berries
1 (12-ounce) bottle lager
1 ½ cups unsalted beef stock
8 slices Cheddar cheese
2 tablespoons Dijon mustard
8 burger buns

Directions

Press the "Sauté" button and preheat the Instant Pot. Cook the bacon for 4 minutes or until crisp; reserve.

Add the beef and sear 8 minutes, turning to brown on all sides.

In the meantime, mix the salt, pepper, marjoram, rosemary, Juniper berries, lager, and beef stock. Pour the mixture over the seared top blade roast and seal the lid.

Choose the "Manual" setting and cook for 1 hour 10 minutes at High pressure. Once cooking is complete, use a quick release; remove the lid.

Now, shred the meat and return to the cooking liquid; stir to soak well. Return the reserved bacon to the Instant Pot.

Assemble sandwiches with the meat/bacon mixture, cheddar cheese, mustard, and burger buns. Enjoy!

Per serving: 698 Calories; 40.1g Fat; 36.9g Carbs; 46g Protein; 19g Sugars

282. Tuscan-Style Cassoulet

(Ready in about 35 minutes | Servings 6)

Ingredients

1 tablespoon olive oil
1 ½ pounds beef shoulder, cut into bite-sized chunks
1/2 pound beef chipolata sausages, sliced
1 onion, chopped
2 garlic cloves, minced
1 cup beef stock
1/2 cup tomato purée
1/2 tablespoon ancho chili powder
Sea salt and ground black pepper, to taste
1 tablespoon fresh thyme leaves
1 (15-ounce) can white beans, drained and rinsed
1 cup sour cream

Directions

Press the "Sauté" button and preheat the Instant Pot. Heat the oil and sear the meat and sausage until they are delicately browned; reserve.

Then, sauté the onion in the pan drippings for 3 to 4 minutes.

Stir in the garlic, stock, tomato purée, ancho chili powder, salt, black pepper, thyme leaves and beans.

Secure the lid. Choose the "Bean/Chili" mode and High pressure; cook for 25 minutes. Once cooking is complete, use a quick pressure release; carefully remove the lid.

Garnish each serving with sour cream and serve. Bon appétit!

Per serving: 376 Calories; 19.3g Fat; 18.1g Carbs; 36.3g Protein; 1.6g Sugars

283. Barbecued Beef Round with Cheese

(Ready in about 50 minutes | Servings 6)

Ingredients

2 pounds bottom round
1 cup beef stock
1 cup barbecue sauce
2 tablespoons tamari sauce
1 cup scallions, chopped
2 cloves garlic, minced
2 teaspoons olive oil
1 teaspoon chili powder
1 cup Cheddar cheese, grated

Directions

Place all of the above ingredients, except for the Cheddar cheese, in your Instant Pot.

Secure the lid. Choose the "Meat/Stew" mode and High pressure; cook for 45 minutes. Once cooking is complete, use a quick pressure release; carefully remove the lid.

Top with the grated cheese and serve immediately. Enjoy!

Per serving: 336 Calories; 9.5g Fat; 23.4g Carbs; 37.5g Protein; 17.6g Sugars

284. Barbeque Chuck Roast

(Ready in about 45 minutes | Servings 6)

Ingredients

2 tablespoons lard, at room temperature
2 pounds chuck roast
4 carrots, sliced
1/2 cup leek, sliced
1 teaspoon garlic, minced
3 teaspoons fresh ginger root, thinly sliced
Salt and pepper, to taste
1 ½ tablespoons fresh parsley leaves, roughly chopped
1 cup barbeque sauce
1/2 cup teriyaki sauce

Directions

Press the "Sauté" button on your Instant Pot. Now, melt the lard until hot.

Sear the chuck roast until browned, about 6 minutes per side. Add the other ingredients.

Choose "Manual" setting and cook for 35 minutes at High pressure or until the internal temperature of the chuck roast is at least 145 degrees F.

Once cooking is complete, use a quick release; remove the lid.

Serve with crusty bread and fresh salad of choice. Bon appétit!

Per serving: 252 Calories; 9.9g Fat; 9g Carbs; 30.1g Protein; 5.9g Sugars

285. Beef Pad Thai

(Ready in about 20 minutes | Servings 6)

Ingredients

2 tablespoons peanut oil
2 pounds skirt steak, cut into thin 1-inch-long slices
1 small Thai chili, finely chopped
1 cup beef bone broth
1/2 cup shallots, chopped
2 tablespoons oyster sauce
1/4 cup peanuts, finely chopped

Directions

Press the "Sauté" button to preheat your Instant Pot. Heat the oil and sear the beef until it is delicately browned on all sides.

Add the Thai chili, broth, shallots, and oyster sauce.

Secure the lid. Choose the "Poultry" mode and High pressure; cook for 15 minutes. Once cooking is complete, use a quick pressure release; carefully remove the lid.

Garnish with chopped peanuts and serve warm.

Per serving: 418 Calories; 24.1g Fat; 5.2g Carbs; 46.1g Protein; 1.2g Sugars

286. Easy Balsamic Beef

(Ready in about 50 minutes | Servings 6)

Ingredients

2 tablespoons sesame oil
2 pounds beef chuck, cut into bite-sized pieces
1/4 cup balsamic vinegar
1/2 teaspoon dried basil
1 teaspoon dried rosemary, crushed
1/2 teaspoon cayenne pepper
1/2 teaspoon ground black pepper
Sea salt, to taste
1 onion, chopped
2 cloves garlic, minced
1 tablespoon cilantro, finely chopped
1/2 cup water
1/2 cup tomato paste
1 jalapeño pepper, finely minced

Directions

Press the "Sauté" button to preheat your Instant Pot. Heat the sesame oil until sizzling.

Once hot, cook the beef for 2 to 3 minutes. Add the remaining ingredients.

Secure the lid. Choose the "Meat/Stew" mode and High pressure; cook for 45 minutes. Once cooking is complete, use a natural pressure release; carefully remove the lid.

Afterwards, thicken the sauce on the "Sauté" function. Serve over hot macaroni and enjoy!

Per serving: 282 Calories; 13.3g Fat; 9.1g Carbs; 32.5g Protein; 5.4g Sugars

287. Juicy Round Steak

(Ready in about 55 minutes | Servings 8)

Ingredients

2 ½ pounds round steak, cut into 1-inch pieces
Kosher salt and freshly ground black pepper, to taste
1/2 teaspoon ground bay leaf
3 tablespoons chickpea flour
1/4 cup olive oil
2 shallots, chopped
2 cloves garlic, minced
1 cup red wine
1/4 cup marinara sauce
1/3 cup bone broth
1 celery with leaves, chopped

Directions

Press the "Sauté" button to preheat your Instant Pot. Toss the round steak with salt, pepper, ground bay leaf, and chickpea flour.

Once hot, heat the olive oil and cook the beef for 6 minutes, stirring periodically; reserve.

Stir in the shallots and garlic and cook until they are tender and aromatic. Pour in wine to deglaze the bottom of the pan. Continue to cook until the liquid has reduced by half.

Add the other ingredients, stir, and seal the lid. Choose the "Meat/Stew" setting and cook at High pressure for 45 minutes.

Once cooking is complete, use a natural release; remove the lid. Taste, adjust the seasonings and serve warm.

Per serving: 363 Calories; 17.9g Fat; 3.1g Carbs; 44.5g Protein; 1.1g Sugars

288. Ground Beef Bulgogi

(Ready in about 15 minutes | Servings 6)

Ingredients

2 tablespoons canola oil
1/2 cup leeks, chopped
1 (2-inch) knob ginger, grated
2 garlic cloves, finely chopped
1 ½ pounds ground chuck
Sea salt and ground black pepper, to taste
2 cups roasted vegetable broth
1/2 cup sour cream
1 ½ tablespoons flax seed meal
2 tablespoons sesame seeds

Directions

Press the "Sauté" button to preheat your Instant Pot. Heat the oil and sweat the leeks until tender.

Then, add the ginger and garlic; continue to sauté an additional 2 minutes or until fragrant.

Add the ground meat and cook for 2 more minutes or until it is no longer pink. Add the salt, black pepper, and broth to the Instant Pot.

Secure the lid. Choose the "Manual" mode and High pressure; cook for 5 minutes. Once cooking is complete, use a natural pressure release; carefully remove the lid.

Lastly, fold in the sour cream and flax seed meal; seal the lid again; let it sit until thoroughly heated.

Ladle into individual bowls and top with sesame seeds. Bon appétit!

Per serving: 274 Calories; 17.5g Fat; 4.1g Carbs; 25.4g Protein; 0.8g Sugars

289. Classic Beef Stroganoff

(Ready in about 25 minutes | Servings 6)

Ingredients

2 tablespoons sesame oil
1/2 cup shallots, chopped
1 teaspoon minced garlic
1 bell pepper, seeded and chopped
1 ½ pounds stewing meat, cubed
1 celery with leaves, chopped
1 parsnip, chopped
1/2 cup rose wine
1 cup tomato paste
1/2 cup ketchup
1 can (10 ¾-ounce) condensed golden mushroom soup
9 ounces fresh button mushrooms, sliced
6 ounces cream cheese
1/4 cup fresh chives, coarsely chopped

Directions

Press the "Sauté" button to preheat your Instant Pot. Heat the oil and sauté the shallots until they have softened.

Stir in the garlic and pepper; continue to sauté until tender and fragrant.

Add the meat, celery, parsnip, wine, tomato paste, ketchup, mushroom soup, and mushrooms.

Secure the lid. Choose the "Meat/Stew" mode and High pressure; cook for 20 minutes. Once cooking is complete, use a quick pressure release; carefully remove the lid.

Stir the cream cheese into the beef mixture; seal the lid and let it sit until melted. Serve garnished with fresh chives. Enjoy!

Per serving: 536 Calories; 19.6g Fat; 45g Carbs; 50g Protein; 8.5g Sugars

SOUPS

290. Old-Fashioned Ham Bone Soup

(Ready in about 30 minutes | Servings 5)

Ingredients

2 tablespoons olive oil
1/2 cup onion, chopped
2 carrots, diced
1 rib celery, diced
1 parsnip, diced

1 ham bone
5 cups chicken stock
Sea salt and ground black pepper, to taste

Directions

Press the "Sauté" button and heat the olive oil until sizzling. Then, sauté the onion, carrot, celery, and parsnip until tender.

Add the ham bone, chicken stock, salt, and black pepper to the inner pot.

Secure the lid. Choose the "Manual" mode and cook for 15 minutes at High pressure. Once cooking is complete, use a natural pressure release for 10 minutes; carefully remove the lid.

Remove the ham bone from the inner pot. Chop the meat from the bone; add back into the soup.

Serve in individual bowls and enjoy!

Per serving: 197 Calories; 10.2g Fat; 9.3g Carbs; 17.7g Protein; 3.7g Sugars

291. Chicken Tortilla Soup

(Ready in about 25 minutes | Servings 4)

Ingredients

2 tablespoons olive oil
1/2 cup shallots, chopped
1 sweet pepper, chopped
1 Poblano chili pepper, chopped
1/2 pound chicken thighs, boneless and skinless
2 ripe tomatoes, chopped
1 can (10-ounce) red enchilada sauce
2 teaspoons ground cumin
1 teaspoon ground coriander

1 teaspoon chili powder
Seasoned salt and freshly cracked pepper, to taste
4 cups roasted vegetable broth
1 bay leaf
1 can (15-ounce) black beans, drained and rinsed
4 (6-inch) corn tortillas, cut crosswise into 1/4-inch strips
1 avocado, cut into 1/2-inch dice
1 cup cheddar cheese, shredded

Directions

Press the "Sauté" button and heat the olive oil. Once hot, sauté the shallots and peppers until tender and aromatic.

Add the chicken thighs, tomatoes, enchilada sauce, cumin, coriander, chili powder, salt, black pepper, vegetable broth, and bay leaf to the inner pot.

Secure the lid. Choose the "Manual" mode and cook for 8 minutes at High pressure. Once cooking is complete, use a natural pressure release for 10 minutes; carefully remove the lid.

Stir in the canned beans and seal the lid; let it sit in the residual heat until everything is heated through.

Divide your soup between individual bowls and serve garnished with tortilla strips, avocado, and cheddar cheese. **Per serving:** 428 Calories; 27.2g Fat; 30.7g Carbs; 19.8g Protein; 6.4g Sugars

292. Greek-Style Lentil and Tomato Soup

(Ready in about 15 minutes | Servings 4)

Ingredients

2 tablespoons butter
1 red onion, chopped
1/2 cup celery, chopped
1 teaspoon ground cumin
1 teaspoon ground coriander
1 teaspoon garlic powder

1 cup yellow lentils
1 teaspoon dried parsley flakes
2 cups roasted vegetable broth
2 cups tomato puree
2 green onions, sliced

Directions

Press the "Sauté" button and melt the butter. Once hot, cook the onion and celery until just tender.

Stir in the remaining ingredients, except for the green onions.

Secure the lid. Choose the "Manual" mode and cook for 8 minutes at High pressure. Once cooking is complete, use a quick pressure release; carefully remove the lid.

Serve warm garnished with green onions. Enjoy!

Per serving: 305 Calories; 7.4g Fat; 45.9g Carbs; 17g Protein; 8.5g Sugars

293. Root Vegetable and Wild Rice Soup

(Ready in about 45 minutes | Servings 5)

Ingredients

3 carrots, chopped
3 stalks celery, chopped
1 turnip, chopped
1 shallot, chopped
1 ½ cups wild rice

10 ounces button mushrooms, sliced
5 cups vegetable broth
1 teaspoon granulated garlic
Sea salt and red pepper, to taste

Directions

Place the ingredients in the inner pot; stir to combine.

Secure the lid. Choose the "Soup/Broth" mode and cook for 40 minutes at High pressure. Once cooking is complete, use a quick pressure release; carefully remove the lid.

Serve warm garnished with a few drizzles of olive oil if desired. Bon appétit!

Per serving: 240 Calories; 2g Fat; 44.6g Carbs; 12.8g Protein; 5.7g Sugars

294. Grandma's Noodle Soup

(Ready in about 20 minutes | Servings 6)

Ingredients

2 tablespoons olive oil
2 carrots, diced
2 parsnips, diced
1 yellow onion, chopped
2 cloves garlic, minced
6 cups chicken bone broth
1 bay leaf

Salt and freshly ground black pepper
2 pounds chicken thighs drumettes
2 cups wide egg noodles
1/4 cup fresh cilantro, roughly chopped

Directions

Press the "Sauté" button and heat the oil. Once hot, cook the carrots, parsnips, and onions until they are just tender.

Add the minced garlic and continue to cook for a minute more.

Add the chicken bone broth, bay leaf, salt, black pepper, and chicken to the inner pot.

Secure the lid. Choose the "Manual" mode and cook for 9 minutes at High pressure. Once cooking is complete, use a quick pressure release; carefully remove the lid.

Shred the cooked chicken and set aside. Stir in noodles and press the "Sauté" button. Cook approximately 5 minutes or until thoroughly heated.

Afterwards, add the chicken back into the soup. Serve garnished with fresh cilantro. Bon appétit!

Per serving: 362 Calories; 25.4g Fat; 21.6g Carbs; 11.5g Protein; 2.9g Sugars

295. Classic Minestrone Soup

(Ready in about 10 minutes | Servings 4)

Ingredients

2 tablespoons canola oil
1 onion, chopped
2 stalks celery, diced
2 carrots, diced
2 cloves garlic, pressed
2 pounds tomatoes, pureed
2 cups chicken broth
1 cup pasta, uncooked
2 teaspoons Italian seasoning
Sea salt and ground black pepper, to taste
1/2 cup fresh corn kernels
2 cups cannellini beans, canned and rinsed
6 ounces Parmesan cheese, grated

Directions

Press the "Sauté" button and heat oil until sizzling, Then, sauté the onion, celery, and carrots for 3 to 4 minutes or until tender.

Add the garlic, tomatoes, broth, pasta, Italian seasoning, salt, and black pepper.

Secure the lid. Choose the "Manual" mode and cook for 5 minutes at High pressure. Once cooking is complete, use a quick pressure release; carefully remove the lid.

Lastly, stir in the corn kernels and beans. Seal the lid and let it sit in the residual heat for 5 to 8 minutes. Ladle into individual bowls and serve topped with Parmesan cheese. Bon appétit!

Per serving: 413 Calories; 21.1g Fat; 39.5g Carbs; 19.8g Protein; 10.6g Sugars

296. Beef Soup with Garden Vegetables

(Ready in about 40 minutes | Servings 5)

Ingredients

2 tablespoons olive oil
1 ½ pounds beef stew meat, cubed
Sea salt and ground black pepper, to taste
1 onion, chopped
2 celery stalks, chopped
2 carrots, chopped
2 cloves garlic, chopped
2 rosemary sprigs
2 thyme sprigs
1/4 cup tamari sauce
2 bay leaves
5 cups beef bone broth
2 ripe tomatoes, pureed
6 ounces green beans, fresh or thawed

Directions

Press the "Sauté" button and heat the oil until sizzling. Now, brown the beef meat for 3 to 4 minutes, stirring frequently to ensure even cooking.

Add the remaining ingredients, except for the green beans.

Secure the lid. Choose the "Manual" mode and cook for 13 minutes at High pressure. Once cooking is complete, use a natural pressure release for 15; carefully remove the lid.

Add the green beans.

Secure the lid. Choose the "Manual" mode and cook for 2 minutes at High pressure. Once cooking is complete, use a quick pressure release; carefully remove the lid. Bon appétit!

Per serving: 244 Calories; 18.6g Fat; 13.1g Carbs; 7g Protein; 6.2g Sugars

297. Autumn Acorn Squash Soup

(Ready in about 20 minutes | Servings 4)

Ingredients

1 tablespoon butter, softened
2 cloves garlic, sliced
1 medium-sized leek, chopped
1 turnip, chopped
1 carrot, chopped
1 ½ pounds acorn squash, chopped
2 cups vegetable broth
2 cups water
1/2 teaspoon ground allspice
1 sprig fresh thyme
Himalayan salt and black pepper, to taste

Directions

Press the "Sauté" button and melt the butter. Once hot, cook the garlic and leek until just tender and fragrant.

Add the remaining ingredients to the inner pot.

Secure the lid. Choose the "Manual" mode and cook for 10 minutes at High pressure. Once cooking is complete, use a quick pressure release; carefully remove the lid.

Puree the soup in your blender until smooth and uniform. Serve warm and enjoy!

Per serving: 152 Calories; 3.9g Fat; 27.4g Carbs; 5.1g Protein; 6.6g Sugars

298. Seafood and Pinot Grigio Soup

(Ready in about 20 minutes | Servings 4)

Ingredients

2 slices bacon, chopped
1 medium leek, chopped
1 celery stalk, chopped
2 carrots, chopped
2 parsnips, chopped
1/3 cup Pinot Grigio
3 cups chicken broth
1/3 cup whole milk
1/2 pound frozen corn kernels, thawed
1 serrano pepper, minced
1 teaspoon granulated garlic
Seas salt and ground black pepper, to taste
1 pound shrimp, deveined

Directions

Press the "Sauté" button and cook the bacon until it is crisp. Chop the bacon and set aside.

Then, sauté the leeks, celery, carrots, and parsnips in the bacon drippings. Cook for about 4 minutes or until they have softened. Add a splash of wine to deglaze the pot.

Press the "Cancel" button. Stir in the broth, milk, corn, pepper, granulated garlic, salt, and black pepper.

Secure the lid. Choose the "Manual" mode and cook for 2 minutes at High pressure. Once cooking is complete, use a quick pressure release; carefully remove the lid.

Stir in the shrimp and seal the lid again; allow it to stand in the residual heat for 5 to 10 minutes. Garnish with the reserved crumbled bacon. Bon appétit!

Per serving: 320 Calories; 8.4g Fat; 27.1g Carbs; 31.6g Protein; 7.7g Sugars

299. Simple Clam Chowder

(Ready in about 15 minutes | Servings 4)

Ingredients

2 tablespoons butter
1 onion, chopped
1 garlic clove, minced
1 stalk celery, diced
1 carrot, diced
1 cup water
2 cups fish stock
Sea salt and white pepper, to taste
1 pound Russet potatoes, peeled and diced
1 teaspoon cayenne pepper
18 ounces canned clams, chopped with juice
1 cup heavy cream

Directions

Press the "Sauté" button and melt the butter; once hot, cook the onion, garlic, celery, and carrot for 3 minutes or until they have softened.

Add the water, stock, salt, white pepper, potatoes, and cayenne pepper.

Secure the lid. Choose the "Manual" mode and cook for 2 minutes at High pressure. Once cooking is complete, use a quick pressure release; carefully remove the lid.

Press the "Sauté" button and use the lowest setting. Stir in the clams and heavy cream. Let it simmer for about 5 minutes or until everything is thoroughly heated. Bon appétit!

Per serving: 349 Calories; 18.4g Fat; 41.1g Carbs; 7.3g Protein; 8.4g Sugars

300. Cod Fish and Tomato Soup

(Ready in about 12 minutes | Servings 4)

Ingredients

1/2 stick butter, at room temperature
1 onion, chopped
2 garlic cloves, minced
2 ripe tomatoes, pureed
2 tablespoons tomato paste
1 cup shellfish stock
1/4 cup cooking wine

1 pound cod fish, cut into bite-sized pieces
1/2 teaspoon basil
1/2 teaspoon dried dill weed
1/4 teaspoon dried oregano
1/4 teaspoon hot sauce
1/2 teaspoon paprika
Sea salt and freshly ground black pepper, to taste

Directions

Press the "Sauté" button and melt the butter; once hot, cook the onion and garlic for about 2 minutes or until they are just tender.

Add the remaining ingredients.

Secure the lid. Choose the "Manual" mode and cook for 5 minutes at High pressure. Once cooking is complete, use a quick pressure release; carefully remove the lid.

Ladle into serving bowls and serve immediately.

Per serving: 232 Calories; 12.4g Fat; 7.3g Carbs; 20.1g Protein; 3.9g Sugars

301. Rustic Beef Stroganoff Soup

(Ready in about 1 hour | Servings 4)

Ingredients

1 pound beef stew meat, cubed
5 cups beef bone broth
1/2 teaspoon dried basil
1/2 teaspoon dried oregano
1/2 teaspoon dried rosemary
1 teaspoon dried sage
1 teaspoon shallot powder
1/2 teaspoon porcini powder

1 teaspoon garlic powder
Sea salt and ground black pepper, to taste
7 ounces button mushrooms, sliced
1/2 cup sour cream
2 tablespoons potato starch, mixed with 4 tablespoons of cold water

Directions

In the inner pot, place the stew meat, broth, and spices.

Secure the lid. Choose the "Manual" mode and cook for 50 minutes at High pressure. Once cooking is complete, use a quick pressure release; carefully remove the lid.

Add the mushrooms and sour cream to the inner pot.

Choose the "Soup/Broth" mode. Bring to a boil and add the potato starch slurry. Continue to simmer until the soup thickens.

Ladle into serving bowls and serve immediately. Bon appétit!

Per serving: 267 Calories; 9.6g Fat; 11.4g Carbs; 34.2g Protein; 2.2g Sugars

302. Spicy Broccoli and Cheese Soup

(Ready in about 10 minutes | Servings 4)

Ingredients

4 tablespoons butter
2 cloves garlic, pressed
1 teaspoon shallot powder
4 cups cream of celery soup
1 pound small broccoli florets
Sea salt and ground black pepper, to taste

1/2 teaspoon chili powder
2 cups half and half
2 cups sharp cheddar cheese, freshly grated
2 scallions stalks, chopped

Directions

Add the butter, garlic, shallot powder, cream of celery soup, broccoli, salt, black pepper, and chili powder to the inner pot.

Secure the lid. Choose the "Manual" mode and cook for 2 minutes at High pressure. Once cooking is complete, use a quick pressure release; carefully remove the lid.

Stir in the half and half and cheese. Let it simmer until everything is thoroughly heated.

Divide between serving bowls and serve garnished with chopped scallions. Bon appétit!

Per serving: 398 Calories; 24.4g Fat; 32.3g Carbs; 17.1g Protein; 10.9g Sugars

303. Authentic French Onion Soup

(Ready in about 10 minutes | Servings 4)

Ingredients

4 tablespoons butter, melted
1 pound onions, thinly sliced
Kosher salt and ground white pepper, to taste

1/2 teaspoon dried sage
4 cups chicken bone broth
1 loaf French bread, sliced
1 cup mozzarella cheese, shredded

Directions

Press the "Sauté" button and melt the butter. Once hot, cook the onions until golden and caramelized.

Add the salt, pepper, sage, and chicken bone broth.

Secure the lid. Choose the "Manual" mode and cook for 2 minutes at High pressure. Once cooking is complete, use a quick pressure release; carefully remove the lid.

Divide the soup between four oven safe bowls; top with the bread and shredded cheese; now, place the bowls under the broiler for about 4 minutes or until the cheese has melted. Bon appétit!

Per serving: 325 Calories; 13.9g Fat; 31.7g Carbs; 19.2g Protein; 7.6g Sugars

304. Meatball and Noodle Soup

(Ready in about 30 minutes | Servings 4)

Ingredients

Meatballs:
1/2 pound ground beef
1/2 pound ground turkey
1/2 cup panko crumbs
1/4 cup Pecorino Romano cheese, grated
1 egg, beaten
2 cloves garlic, crushed
2 tablespoons cilantro, chopped
Sea salt and ground black pepper, to taste

Soup:
1 tablespoon olive oil
1 onion, chopped
1 celery stalk, chopped
2 cloves garlic, minced
2 tomatoes, crushed
4 cups chicken broth
2 bay leaves
6 ounces noodles

Directions

In a mixing bowl, thoroughly combine all ingredients for the meatballs.

Form the mixture into 20 meatballs. Press the "Sauté" button and heat the oil. Now, brown the meatballs in batches; reserve.

Heat the olive oil; sauté the onion, celery, and garlic for 3 to 4 minutes or until they are fragrant.

Add the tomatoes, broth, and bay leaves to the inner pot.

Secure the lid. Choose the "Manual" mode and cook for 12 minutes at High pressure. Once cooking is complete, use a quick pressure release; carefully remove the lid.

Next, sit in the noodles and secure the lid again.

Choose the "Manual" mode and cook for 5 minutes at High pressure. Once cooking is complete, use a quick pressure release; carefully remove the lid. Bon appétit!

Per serving: 487 Calories; 21.9g Fat; 30.1g Carbs; 40.8g Protein; 4.7g Sugars

305. Chipotle Chili Soup

(Ready in about 45 minutes | Servings 4)

Ingredients

1 tablespoon canola oil
1 pound ground beef
2 cloves garlic, smashed
1 medium leek, chopped
2 chipotle chilis in adobo sauce, roughly chopped

1 (14 ½ -ounce) can tomatoes, diced
2 cups vegetable broth
16 ounces pinto beans, undrained
1/2 teaspoon cumin powder
1 teaspoon stone-ground mustard
1 teaspoon chili powder

Directions

Press the "Sauté" button and heat the oil. Brown the ground beef for 2 to 3 minutes, stirring frequently.

Add the remaining ingredients and stir to combine well.

Secure the lid. Choose the "Bean/Chili" mode and cook for 30 minutes at High pressure. Once cooking is complete, use a natural pressure release for 10 minutes; carefully remove the lid. Bon appétit!

Per serving: 343 Calories; 17.5g Fat; 10.9g Carbs; 34.7g Protein; 3.3g Sugars

306. Creamed Corn and Chicken Soup

(Ready in about 20 minutes | Servings 6)

Ingredients

1 tablespoon olive oil
1 yellow onion, chopped
1 celery stalk, diced
1 carrot, finely diced
1 turnip, diced
6 cups roasted vegetable broth
1 pound chicken breasts, skinless, boneless and diced
1 teaspoon garlic powder
1 teaspoon mustard powder
1 (15-ounce) can creamed corn
4 large eggs, whisked
Kosher salt and ground black pepper, to taste

Directions

Press the "Sauté" button and heat the oil. Now, sauté the onion until just tender and translucent.

Add the celery, carrot, turnip, vegetable broth, chicken, garlic powder, and mustard powder.

Secure the lid. Choose the "Manual" mode and cook for 9 minutes at High pressure. Once cooking is complete, use a quick pressure release; carefully remove the lid.

Press the "Sauté" button and use the lowest setting. Stir in the creamed corn and eggs; let it simmer, stirring continuously for about 5 minutes or until everything is thoroughly heated.

Season with salt and pepper to taste and serve warm. Bon appétit!

Per serving: 313 Calories; 15.5g Fat; 19.4g Carbs; 24.7g Protein; 4.6g Sugars

307. Kidney Bean and Chicken Soup

(Ready in about 20 minutes | Servings 4)

Ingredients

2 tablespoons butter, softened
1 onion, chopped
1 sweet pepper, deseeded and chopped
1 habanero pepper, deseeded and chopped
2 cloves garlic, minced
Sea salt and ground black pepper, to taste
1 teaspoon dried basil
1 teaspoon dried oregano
1 teaspoon cayenne pepper
4 cups vegetable broth
1 pound chicken thighs
2 cans (15-ounce) red kidney beans
1/4 cup fresh cilantro, chopped
1/2 cup tortilla chips

Directions

Press the "Sauté" button and melt the butter. Once hot, cook the onion until tender and translucent.

Stir in the peppers and sauté for a few minutes more. Add the minced garlic and continue to sauté for another minute.

Add the spices, vegetable broth, and chicken thighs to the inner pot.

Secure the lid. Choose the "Manual" mode and cook for 13 minutes at High pressure. Once cooking is complete, use a quick pressure release; carefully remove the lid.

Remove the chicken to a cutting board. Add the kidney beans to the inner pot and seal the lid again. Let it sit in the residual heat until thoroughly heated.

Shred the chicken and discard the bones; put it back into the soup. Serve with fresh cilantro and tortilla chips. Enjoy!

Per serving: 374 Calories; 16.8g Fat; 18.9g Carbs; 36g Protein; 2.8g Sugars

308. Sweet Potato Soup with Swiss Chard

(Ready in about 15 minutes | Servings 4)

Ingredients

2 tablespoons butter, softened at room temperature
1 white onion, chopped
1 sweet pepper, deveined and chopped
2 cloves garlic, pressed
1 pound sweet potatoes, peeled and diced
2 ripe tomatoes, pureed
2 cups chicken bone broth
2 cups water
Kosher salt and freshly ground black pepper, to taste
1/4 cup peanut butter
2 cups Swiss chard, torn into pieces

Directions

Press the "Sauté" button and melt the butter. Once hot, cook the onion, pepper, and garlic until tender and fragrant.

Add the sweet potatoes and continue to sauté for about 3 minutes longer. Now, stir in the tomatoes, broth, water, salt, and black pepper.

Secure the lid. Choose the "Manual" mode and cook for 4 minutes at High pressure. Once cooking is complete, use a quick pressure release; carefully remove the lid.

Stir in the peanut butter and Swiss chard; seal the lid again and let it sit in the residual heat until your greens wilt. Serve warm.

Per serving: 254 Calories; 9.7g Fat; 36.3g Carbs; 7.1g Protein; 10.9g Sugars

309. Indian Turkey and Basmati Rice Soup

(Ready in about 15 minutes | Servings 4)

Ingredients

1 tablespoon sesame oil
1 onion, chopped
1 large thumb-sized pieces fresh ginger, peeled and grated
1 pound turkey breast, boneless and cut into chunks
2 carrots, sliced
1 celery stalk, sliced
5 cups chicken broth
1 teaspoon garlic powder
1 teaspoon cumin seeds
1 teaspoon garam masala
1 teaspoon turmeric powder
1 cup basmati rice, rinsed
1 small handful of fresh coriander, roughly chopped

Directions

Press the "Sauté" button and heat the sesame oil until sizzling. Now, sauté the onion and ginger until tender and aromatic.

Add the turkey, carrot, and celery to the inner pot; continue to cook for 3 to 4 minutes more or until the turkey is no longer pink.

Add the chicken broth and spices to the inner pot. Secure the lid. Choose the "Manual" mode and cook for 5 minutes at High pressure. Once cooking is complete, use a quick pressure release; carefully remove the lid.

After that, stir in the basmati rice.

Secure the lid. Choose the "Manual" mode and cook for 4 minutes at High pressure. Once cooking is complete, use a quick pressure release; carefully remove the lid.

Ladle into four serving bowls and serve with fresh coriander. Enjoy!

Per serving: 254 Calories; 9.7g Fat; 36.3g Carbs; 7.1g Protein; 10.9g Sugars

310. Beef and Barley Soup

(Ready in about 25 minutes | Servings 4)

Ingredients

1 tablespoon canola oil
2 shallots, chopped
2 garlic cloves, minced
2 celery stalks, chopped
1 parsnip, chopped
1 cup tomato puree
4 cups beef broth
1 cup pearl barley
2 sprigs thyme
Sea salt and white pepper, to taste
1 teaspoon red pepper flakes, crushed

Directions

Press the "Sauté" button and heat the canola oil. Once hot, sauté the shallots, garlic, celery, and parsnip until tender and aromatic.

Add the remaining ingredients and stir to combine.

Secure the lid. Choose the "Soup/Broth" mode and cook for 20 minutes at High pressure. Once cooking is complete, use a quick pressure release; carefully remove the lid.

Serve in individual bowls. Bon appétit!

Per serving: 300 Calories; 5.7g Fat; 52.6g Carbs; 11.6g Protein; 5.9g Sugars

311. Peppery Ground Pork Soup

(Ready in about 30 minutes | Servings 4)

Ingredients

1 pound ground pork
1 teaspoon Italian seasoning
1 teaspoon garlic powder
Sea salt and ground black pepper, to taste
2 sweet peppers, seeded and sliced
1 jalapeno pepper, seeded and minced
2 ripe tomatoes, pureed
4 cups chicken stock

Directions

Press the "Sauté" button to preheat your Instant Pot. Then, brown the ground pork until no longer pink or about 3 minutes.

Add the remaining ingredients to the inner pot and stir.

Secure the lid. Choose the "Manual" mode and cook for 10 minutes at High pressure. Once cooking is complete, use a natural pressure release for 10; carefully remove the lid.

Serve warm. Bon appétit!

Per serving: 382 Calories; 26.2g Fat; 10.5g Carbs; 26.3g Protein; 2.4g Sugars

312. Mediterranean-Style Lima Bean Soup

(Ready in about 25 minutes | Servings 5)

Ingredients

2 tablespoons sesame oil
1 pound cremini mushrooms, thinly sliced
1 large-sized eggplant, sliced into rounds
1 red onion, chopped
2 garlic cloves, chopped
2 carrots, sliced
2 sweet potatoes, peeled and diced
1/2 teaspoon red curry paste

1/2 teaspoon cayenne pepper
Sea salt and ground black pepper, to taste
2 sprigs thyme
2 sprigs rosemary
2 medium-sized tomatoes, pureed
5 cups roasted vegetable broth
16 ounces lima beans, soaked overnight
Juice of 1 fresh lemon

Directions

Press the "Sauté" button and heat the oil until sizzling. Now, cook the mushrooms, eggplant, onion, and garlic until just tender and fragrant.

Add the carrots, sweet potatoes, curry paste, spices, tomatoes, broth, and lima beans.

Secure the lid. Choose the "Manual" mode and cook for 13 minutes at High pressure. Once cooking is complete, use a quick pressure release; carefully remove the lid.

Divide your soup between individual bowls; add a few drizzles of lemon juice to each serving and enjoy!

Per serving: 263 Calories; 8.1g Fat; 35.7g Carbs; 15.4g Protein; 10.1g Sugars

313. Rich Lobster Bisque

(Ready in about 15 minutes | Servings 4)

Ingredients

1 pound lump lobster meat
2 tablespoons olive oil
1 yellow onion, chopped
1 celery stalk, diced
1 carrot, diced
2 cloves garlic, minced
1 teaspoon rosemary
1 teaspoon basil
1 teaspoon thyme
1/2 teaspoon turmeric powder

1 tomato, pureed
1/4 cup cooking sherry
3 cups clam juice
1 tablespoon soy sauce
1/2 teaspoon smoked paprika
Sea salt and ground white pepper, to taste
1 teaspoon Tabasco sauce
1 cup heavy cream

Directions

In the inner pot of your Instant Pot, place the lobster meat, olive oil, onion, celery, carrot, garlic, rosemary, basil, thyme, turmeric, tomato puree, cooking sherry, and clam juice.

Secure the lid. Choose the "Manual" mode and cook for 4 minutes at High pressure. Once cooking is complete, use a quick pressure release; carefully remove the lid. Set the lobster meat aside and chop into small chunks.

Now, add in the soy sauce, smoked paprika, salt, white pepper, Tabasco sauce, and heavy cream; continue to stir and simmer until it's all blended together and heated through.

Lastly, put the lobster meat back into your bisque. Serve in individual bowls and enjoy!

Per serving: 345 Calories; 14.6g Fat; 31.2g Carbs; 22g Protein; 10.4g Sugars

314. Seafood Chowder with Bacon and Celery

(Ready in about 15 minutes | Servings 4)

Ingredients

3 strips bacon, chopped
1 onion, chopped
2 carrots, diced
2 stalks celery, diced
2 cloves garlic, minced
1 tablespoon Creole seasoning
Sea salt and ground black pepper, to taste

3 cups seafood stock
2 ripe tomatoes, pureed
2 tablespoons tomato paste
2 bay leaves
1 pound clams, chopped
1 ½ tablespoons flaxseed meal

Directions

Press the "Sauté" button to preheat your Instant Pot. Now, cook the bacon until it is crisp; crumble the bacon and set it aside.

Now, sauté the onion, carrot, celery, and garlic in bacon drippings.

Add the remaining ingredients, except for the chopped clams, to the inner pot.

Secure the lid. Choose the "Manual" mode and cook for 4 minutes at High pressure. Once cooking is complete, use a quick pressure release; carefully remove the lid.

Stir in the chopped clams and flaxseed meal.

Press the "Sauté" button and let it simmer for 2 to 3 minutes longer or until everything is heated through.

Serve in individual bowls topped with the reserved bacon. Bon appétit!

Per serving: 264 Calories; 9.4g Fat; 26.2g Carbs; 20.8g Protein; 9.9g Sugars

315. Corn and Potato Chowder

(Ready in about 25 minutes | Servings 4)

Ingredients

2 tablespoons butter
1 sweet onion, chopped
2 garlic cloves, minced
1 sweet pepper, deveined and sliced
1 jalapeno pepper, deveined and sliced
4 tablespoons all-purpose flour

4 cups vegetable broth
1 pound potatoes, cut into bite-sized pieces
3 cups creamed corn kernels
1 cup double cream
Kosher salt and ground black pepper, to taste
1/2 teaspoon cayenne pepper

Directions

Press the "Sauté" button and melt the butter. Once hot, sauté the sweet onions, garlic, and peppers for about 3 minutes or until they are tender and fragrant.

Sprinkle the flour over the vegetables; continue stirring approximately 4 minutes or until your vegetables are coated.

Add the broth and potatoes and gently stir to combine.

Secure the lid. Choose the "Manual" mode and cook for 5 minutes at High pressure. Once cooking is complete, use a quick pressure release; carefully remove the lid.

Press the "Sauté" button and use the lowest setting. Stir in the creamed corn, double cream, salt, black pepper, and cayenne pepper.

Let it simmer, stirring continuously for about 5 minutes or until everything is thoroughly heated. Taste and adjust the seasonings. Bon appétit!

Per serving: 439 Calories; 20.4g Fat; 56.2g Carbs; 12.8g Protein; 9.3g Sugars

316. Halibut Chowder with Swiss Cheese

(Ready in about 15 minutes | Servings 5)

Ingredients

2 tablespoons butter
1 medium-sized leek, sliced
1 carrot, shredded
1 celery stalk, shredded
2 cloves garlic, minced
5 cups chicken bone broth
2 ripe tomatoes, chopped

1 ½ pounds halibut, cut into small cubes
Kosher salt and cracked black pepper, to taste
1 cup milk
1/2 cup double cream
1 cup Swiss cheese, shredded

Directions

Press the "Sauté" button and melt the butter. Once hot, sauté the leeks, carrot, celery, and garlic until they are just tender and fragrant.

Then, add the chicken bone broth, tomatoes, halibut, salt, and black pepper.

Secure the lid. Choose the "Manual" mode and cook for 5 minutes at High pressure. Once cooking is complete, use a quick pressure release; carefully remove the lid.

Press the "Sauté" button and use the lowest setting. Stir in the milk and double cream. Allow it to simmer for about 3 minutes or until heated through.

Ladle your chowder into five serving bowls; top with the shredded Swiss cheese and serve immediately.

Per serving: 456 Calories; 20.2g Fat; 15.7g Carbs; 50.2g Protein; 7.7g Sugars

317. Red Lentil and Spinach Soup

(Ready in about 10 minutes | Servings 5)

Ingredients

2 cups red lentils, rinsed
1 onion, chopped
2 cloves garlic, minced
1 teaspoon cumin
1 teaspoon smoked paprika
Sea salt and ground black pepper, to taste

2 carrots, sliced
6 cups water
2 bay leaves
2 cups fresh spinach leaves, torn into small pieces

Directions

Place all ingredients, except for the fresh spinach, in the inner pot.

Secure the lid. Choose the "Manual" mode and cook for 3 minutes at High pressure. Once cooking is complete, use a quick pressure release; carefully remove the lid.

Stir in the spinach and seal the lid again; let it sit until the spinach just starts to wilt.

Serve in individual bowls and enjoy!

Per serving: 295 Calories; 1.9g Fat; 52.7g Carbs; 19.2g Protein; 1.6g Sugars

318. Chicken Soup with Garden Vegetable

(Ready in about 20 minutes | Servings 3)

Ingredients

2 tablespoons butter, melted
1/2 pound chicken legs, boneless and skinless
1 onion, diced
1 teaspoon garlic, minced
1 teaspoon ginger, peeled and grated
3 cups chicken stock

1/2 teaspoon dried sage
1/2 teaspoon dried thyme leaves
Sea salt and ground black pepper, to taste
2 tablespoons tamari sauce
2 carrots, diced
2 parsnips, diced
2 cups cauliflower florets

Directions

Press the "Sauté" button and melt the butter. Once hot, sauté the chicken until golden brown; reserve.

Cook the onion, garlic, and ginger in pan drippings until just tender and aromatic.

Add the reserved chicken, stock, and spices.

Secure the lid. Choose the "Manual" mode and cook for 13 minutes at High pressure. Once cooking is complete, use a quick pressure release; carefully remove the lid.

Now, add the tamari sauce and vegetables to the inner pot.

Secure the lid. Choose the "Manual" mode and cook for 5 minutes at High pressure. Once cooking is complete, use a quick pressure release; carefully remove the lid. Serve immediately.

Per serving: 257 Calories; 13.1g Fat; 13.6g Carbs; 22.5g Protein; 6.1g Sugars

319. Farmhouse Vegetable Soup

(Ready in about 15 minutes | Servings 4)

Ingredients

2 tablespoons canola oil
1 shallot, chopped
2 garlic cloves, minced
1/2 teaspoon dried oregano
1/2 teaspoon dried basil
1/2 teaspoon dried rosemary
4 ounces frozen carrots, chopped
4 ounces frozen green peas

8 ounces frozen broccoli, chopped
4 ounces frozen green beans
2 ripe tomatoes, pureed
4 cups vegetable broth
Sea salt and ground black pepper, to taste
1/2 teaspoon red pepper flakes

Directions

Press the "Sauté" button and heat the oil. Sauté the shallot until softened, approximately 4 minutes. Stir in the garlic and cook for 30 seconds more.

Add the dried herbs, frozen vegetables, tomatoes, vegetable broth, salt, and black pepper.

Secure the lid. Choose the "Manual" mode and cook for 4 minutes at High pressure. Once cooking is complete, use a quick pressure release; carefully remove the lid.

Divide between serving bowls and garnish with red pepper flakes. Bon appétit!

Per serving: 176 Calories; 9.2g Fat; 15.9g Carbs; 9.5g Protein; 6.1g Sugars

320. Spring Tomato Soup

(Ready in about 30 minutes | Servings 4)

Ingredients

1 tablespoon olive oil
1 cup green onions, chopped
2 stalks green garlic, chopped
1 celery stalk, diced
2 carrots, diced
2 cups vegetable broth
Sea salt and ground black pepper, to your liking
1/2 teaspoon cayenne pepper

1 teaspoon fresh basil, chopped
1 teaspoon fresh rosemary, chopped
1 (28-ounce) can tomatoes, crushed
1/2 cup double cream
1/2 cup feta cheese, cubed
1 tablespoon olive oil

Directions

Press the "Sauté" button and heat 1 tablespoon of olive oil. Sauté the green onions, garlic, celery, and carrots until softened.

Add the vegetable broth, salt, black pepper, cayenne pepper, basil, rosemary, and tomatoes to the inner pot.

Secure the lid. Choose the "Manual" mode and cook for 6 minutes at High pressure. Once cooking is complete, use a natural pressure release for 10 minutes; carefully remove the lid.

Stir in the double cream and seal the lid again; let it sit for 10 minutes more. Ladle into soup bowls; garnish with feta and 1 tablespoon of olive oil. Bon appétit!

Per serving: 245 Calories; 18g Fat; 15g Carbs; 8.3g Protein; 10.1g Sugars

321. Soup Hang Wuao

(Ready in about 1 hour 10 minutes | Servings 4)

Ingredients

2 pounds oxtails
4 cloves garlic, sliced
2 bay leaves
1 thyme sprig
2 rosemary sprigs
1 tablespoon soy sauce
1 teaspoon cumin powder
1 teaspoon paprika
2 potatoes, peeled and diced

2 carrots, diced
1 parsnip, diced
1 cup vegetable broth
2 bird's eye chilis, pounded in a mortar and pestle
2 star anise
Sea salt and ground black pepper, to taste

Directions

Place the oxtails in the inner pot. Cover the oxtails with water. Stir in the garlic, bay leaves, thyme, rosemary, soy sauce, cumin, and paprika.

Secure the lid. Choose the "Manual" mode and cook for 50 minutes at High pressure. Once cooking is complete, use a natural pressure release for 10 minutes; carefully remove the lid.

After that, add the other ingredients to the inner pot.

Secure the lid. Choose the "Manual" mode and cook for 4 minutes at High pressure. Once cooking is complete, use a quick pressure release; carefully remove the lid.

Serve with crusty bread and enjoy!

Per serving: 335 Calories; 9.5g Fat; 37.9g Carbs; 24.3g Protein; 3.8g Sugars

322. Creamy and Minty Asparagus Soup

(Ready in about 10 minutes | Servings 4)

Ingredients

1 tablespoon butter
1 Asian shallot, chopped
2 garlic cloves, minced
2 pounds asparagus stalks, trimmed and chopped

Kosher salt and ground black pepper, to taste
3 cups chicken broth
1 cup yogurt
2 tablespoons fresh mint leaves, chopped

Directions

Press the "Sauté" button and melt the butter. Once hot, cook the Asian shallots and garlic until just tender and fragrant.

Add the asparagus, salt, pepper, and broth.

Secure the lid. Choose the "Manual" mode and cook for 4 minutes at High pressure. Once cooking is complete, use a quick pressure release; carefully remove the lid.

Add the yogurt and blend the soup until it is completely smooth. Taste and season with more salt if desired.

Ladle into individual bowls; then, top each bowl with fresh mint leaves and serve.

Per serving: 146 Calories; 6.2g Fat; 14.4g Carbs; 11.3g Protein; 8g Sugars

323. Zucchini and Quinoa Soup

(Ready in about 10 minutes | Servings 4)

Ingredients

2 tablespoons olive oil
1 shallot, diced
1 teaspoon fresh garlic, minced
Sea salt and ground black pepper, to your liking

1 pound zucchini, cut into rounds
1 cup quinoa
4 cups vegetable broth
2 tablespoons fresh parsley leaves

Directions

Press the "Sauté" button and heat the oil. Once hot, sweat the shallot for 2 to 3 minutes. Stir in the garlic and continue to cook for another 30 seconds or until aromatic.

Stir in the salt, black pepper, zucchini, quinoa, and vegetable broth.

Secure the lid. Choose the "Manual" mode and cook for 3 minutes at High pressure. Once cooking is complete, use a quick pressure release; carefully remove the lid.

Ladle into soup bowls; serve garnished with fresh parsley leaves. Enjoy!

Per serving: 307 Calories; 11.2g Fat; 38.3g Carbs; 15.3g Protein; 3.8g Sugars

324. Shrimp and Vegetable Bisque

(Ready in about 15 minutes | Servings 4)

Ingredients

2 tablespoons butter
1/2 cup white onion, chopped
1 celery rib, chopped
1 parsnip, chopped
1 carrot, chopped
2 tablespoons all-purpose flour

1/4 cup sherry wine
Sea salt and ground black pepper
1 cup tomato puree
3 cups chicken bone broth
16 ounces shrimp, deveined
1 cup heavy whipping cream

Directions

Press the "Sauté" button and melt the butter. Once hot, cook the onion, celery, parsnip, and carrot until softened.

Add the flour and cook for 3 minutes more or until everything is well coated. Pour in sherry wine to deglaze the pot.

Now, add the salt, pepper, tomato puree, and broth.

Secure the lid. Choose the "Manual" mode and cook for 5 minutes at High pressure. Once cooking is complete, use a quick pressure release; carefully remove the lid.

Now, add the shrimp and heavy cream and cook on the "Sauté" function for a further 2 to 3 minutes or until everything is heated through. Bon appétit!

Per serving: 362 Calories; 18.9g Fat; 20.3g Carbs; 29.6g Protein; 7.8g Sugars

325. Authentic Ukrainian Borscht Soup

(Ready in about 20 minutes | Servings 4)

Ingredients

2 tablespoons safflower oil
1 red onion, chopped
2 cloves garlic, minced
1 pound Yukon potatoes, peeled and diced
2 carrots, chopped
1 small red bell pepper, finely chopped

1/2 pound red bee roots, grated
1 tablespoon cider vinegar
2 tablespoons tomato paste
Sea salt and freshly ground black pepper, to taste
2 bay leaves
1/2 teaspoon ground cumin
4 cups chicken stock

Directions

Press the "Sauté" button and heat the oil. Once hot, cook the onion for about 2 minutes or until softened.

Add the garlic, potatoes, carrots, bell pepper, and beets to the inner pot. Add the remaining ingredients to the inner pot and stir until everything is well combined.

Secure the lid. Choose the "Manual" mode and cook for 10 minutes at High pressure. Once cooking is complete, use a natural pressure release; carefully remove the lid.

To serve, add more salt and vinegar if desired. Bon appétit!

Per serving: 276 Calories; 9g Fat; 20.3g Carbs; 9.6g Protein; 16.6g Sugars

326. Chicken Alfredo Ditalini Soup

(Ready in about 25 minutes | Servings 4)

Ingredients

2 tablespoons coconut oil, melted
1 pound chicken breast, skinless and boneless
1 white onion, chopped
2 cloves garlic, pressed
12 serrano pepper, minced
1/4 cup all-purpose flour
4 cups vegetable broth
2 cups cauliflower florets, frozen
2 cups Ditalini pasta
1 cup heavy cream
Sea salt and ground black pepper, to taste

Directions

Press the "Sauté" button and heat the oil. Once hot, brown the chicken for 3 to 4 minutes per side; set aside.

Then, sauté the onion, garlic, and serrano pepper in pan drippings. Add the flour and continue to stir until your veggies are well coated.

Add the vegetable broth, cauliflower, and pasta to the inner pot; put the chicken back into the inner pot.

Secure the lid. Choose the "Manual" mode and cook for 6 minutes at High pressure. Once cooking is complete, use a quick pressure release; carefully remove the lid.

Stir in the cauliflower and Ditalini pasta. Secure the lid. Choose the "Manual" mode and cook for 5 minutes at High pressure. Once cooking is complete, use a quick pressure release; carefully remove the lid.

Shred the cooked chicken and add it back into the soup. Afterwards, add the heavy cream, salt, and black pepper. Seal the lid and let it sit in the residual heat for 5 minutes. Bon appétit!

Per serving: 476 Calories; 20.4g Fat; 38.6g Carbs; 34.4g Protein; 6.6g Sugars

327. Chunky Hamburger Soup

(Ready in about 30 minutes | Servings 5)

Ingredients

1 tablespoon olive oil
1 pound ground beef
1 leek, diced
2 cloves garlic, sliced
2 tablespoons cooking sherry
4 cups beef broth
1 can condensed tomato soup
1 teaspoon fish sauce
1 teaspoon basil
1/2 teaspoon oregano
2 bay leaves
1/4 teaspoon paprika
Sea salt and ground black pepper, to taste

Directions

Press the "Sauté" button and heat the oil. Once hot, brown the ground beef for 2 to 3 minutes, stirring and crumbling with a wooden spoon.

Stir in the leeks and garlic; continue to sauté an additional 2 minutes, stirring continuously.

Add a splash of cooking sherry to deglaze the pot. Add the other ingredients to the inner pot.

Secure the lid. Choose the "Manual" mode and cook for 10 minutes at High pressure. Once cooking is complete, use a natural pressure release for 10 minutes; carefully remove the lid.

Serve warm with crusty bread, if desired. Bon appétit!

Per serving: 283 Calories; 14.4g Fat; 6g Carbs; 29.4g Protein; 1.9g Sugars

328. Italian Sausage and Cabbage Soup

(Ready in about 20 minutes | Servings 5)

Ingredients

2 tablespoons olive oil
1 pound beef sausage, thinly sliced
1 onion, chopped
3 cloves garlic. minced
1 stalk celery, chopped
1 carrot, peeled and chopped
1/4 cup Italian cooking wine
1 (1-pound) head cabbage, shredded into small pieces
5 cups beef bone broth
1 tablespoon Italia seasoning blend
1 teaspoon cayenne pepper
1 bay leaf
Salt and cracked black pepper, to taste

Directions

Press the "Sauté" button and heat the oil. Once hot, cook the beef sausage until no longer pink. Now, stir in the onion and garlic; continue to sauté until they are fragrant.

Add a splash of cooking wine, scraping up any browned bits from the bottom of the inner pot. Add the remaining ingredients.

Secure the lid. Choose the "Manual" mode and cook for 6 minutes at High pressure. Once cooking is complete, use a quick pressure release; carefully remove the lid.

Divide between soup bowls and serve immediately.

Per serving: 427 Calories; 33.4g Fat; 15.1g Carbs; 17.8g Protein; 5.8g Sugars

329. Old-Fashioned Duck Soup with Millet

(Ready in about 20 minutes | Servings 4)

Ingredients

2 tablespoons olive oil
1 pound duck portions with bones
2 garlic cloves, minced
4 cups water
1 tablespoon chicken bouillon granules
1/2 cup millet, rinsed
Salt and freshly cracked black pepper, to taste
1/4 cup fresh scallions, chopped

Directions

Press the "Sauté" button and heat the oil. Once hot, brown your duck for 4 to 5 minutes; stir in the garlic and cook an additional 30 seconds or until aromatic.

Add the remaining ingredients.

Secure the lid. Choose the "Manual" mode and cook for 12 minutes at High pressure. Once cooking is complete, use a quick pressure release; carefully remove the lid.

Remove the cooked duck to a cutting board. Shred the meat and discard the bones. Put your duck back into the inner pot. Stir and serve immediately. Bon appétit!

Per serving: 411 Calories; 25.3g Fat; 21.5g Carbs; 23.3g Protein; 1.1g Sugars

330. Beef Stew with Green Peas

(Ready in about 35 minutes | Servings 4)

Ingredients

2 tablespoons olive oil	Sea salt and ground black pepper, to taste
1 ½ pounds beef stew meat, cut bite-sized pieces	1 teaspoon cayenne pepper
1 red onion, chopped	4 cups beef bone broth
4 cloves garlic, minced	1/2 cup tomato paste
1 carrot, cut into rounds	1 tablespoon fish sauce
1 parsnip, cut into rounds	2 bay leaves
2 stalks celery, diced	1 cup frozen green peas

Directions

Press the "Sauté" button and heat the oil. Once hot, brown the beef stew meat for 4 to 5 minutes; set aside.

Then, cook the onion in pan drippings until tender and translucent; stir in the garlic and cook an additional 30 seconds or until aromatic.

Add the carrots, parsnip, celery, salt, black pepper, cayenne pepper, beef broth, tomato paste, fish sauce, and bay leaves. Stir in the reserved beef stew meat.

Secure the lid. Choose the "Meat/Stew" mode and cook for 20 minutes at High pressure. Once cooking is complete, use a quick pressure release; carefully remove the lid.

Stir in the green peas, cover, and let it sit in the residual heat until warmed through or 5 to 7 minutes. Serve and enjoy!

Per serving: 540 Calories; 29g Fat; 25.5g Carbs; 44.7g Protein; 10.7g Sugars

331. Northern Italian Beef Stew

(Ready in about 35 minutes | Servings 6)

Ingredients

2 pounds beef top round, cut into bite-sized chunks	1/4 cup tomato paste
1/4 cup all-purpose flour	1 pound sweet potatoes, diced
1 tablespoon Italian seasoning	1/2 pound carrots, sliced into rounds
Sea salt and ground black pepper, to taste	2 bell peppers, deveined and sliced
1 tablespoon lard, at room temperature	1 teaspoon fish sauce
1 onion, chopped	2 bay leaves
4 cloves garlic, pressed	4 cups beef broth
1/4 cup cooking wine	2 tablespoons fresh Italian parsley, roughly chopped

Directions

Toss the beef chunks with the flour, Italian seasoning, salt, and pepper until well coated.

Press the "Sauté" button and melt the lard; brown the beef chunks on all sides, stirring frequently; reserve.

Then, sauté the onion and garlic for a minute or so; add the wine and stir, scraping up any browned bits from the bottom of the inner pot.

Add the beef back into the inner pot. Stir in the tomato paste, sweet potatoes, carrots, bell peppers, fish sauce, bay leaves, and beef broth.

Secure the lid. Choose the "Meat/Stew" mode and cook for 20 minutes at High pressure. Once cooking is complete, use a natural pressure release for 10 minutes; carefully remove the lid. Serve garnished with Italian parsley.

Per serving: 434 Calories; 16.6g Fat; 29.5g Carbs; 40.7g Protein; 6.1g Sugars

332. Bosnian Pot Stew (Bosanski Lonac)

(Ready in about 45 minutes | Servings 5)

Ingredients

2 tablespoons safflower oil	Se salt and ground black pepper, to taste
2 pounds pork loin roast, cut into cubes	1 teaspoon paprika
2 garlic cloves, chopped	2 tomatoes, pureed
1 onion, chopped	2 cups chicken bone broth
2 carrots, cut into chunks	1/2 pound green beans, cut into 1-inch pieces
2 celery ribs, cut into chunks	
1 pound potatoes, cut into chunks	2 tablespoons fresh parsley leaves, roughly chopped

Directions

Press the "Sauté" button and heat the oil until sizzling. Once hot, cook the pork until it is no longer pink on all sides.

Add the garlic and onion and cook for a minute or so, stirring frequently.

Stir in the carrots, celery, potatoes, salt, black pepper, paprika, tomatoes, and chicken bone broth.

Secure the lid. Choose the "Meat/Stew" mode and cook for 35 minutes at High pressure. Once cooking is complete, use a quick pressure release; carefully remove the lid.

Add the green beans to the inner pot. Press the "Sauté" button again and let it simmer for a few minutes more. Serve in individual bowls garnished with fresh parsley.

Per serving: 406 Calories; 13.8g Fat; 23.5g Carbs; 45.7g Protein; 3.3g Sugars

333. Favorite Chickpea Stew

(Ready in about 40 minutes | Servings 4)

Ingredients

2 tablespoons olive oil	1 cup tomato puree
1 large-sized leek, chopped	1/2 teaspoon cumin powder
3 cloves garlic, pressed	1/2 teaspoon turmeric powder
3 potatoes, diced	1 teaspoon mustard seeds
2 carrots, diced	2 cups roasted vegetable broth
1 sweet pepper, seeded and chopped	1 ½ cups chickpeas, soaked overnight
1 jalapeno pepper, seeded and chopped	

Directions

Press the "Sauté" button and heat the oil until sizzling. Once hot, cook the leeks and garlic for 2 to 3 minutes or until they are just tender.

Add the remaining ingredients and stir to combine well.

Secure the lid. Choose the "Meat/Stew" mode and cook for 35 minutes at High pressure. Once cooking is complete, use a quick pressure release; carefully remove the lid.

Serve in individual bowls. Bon appétit!

Per serving: 520 Calories; 12.8g Fat; 83g Carbs; 22.4g Protein; 14.7g Sugars

334. Smoked Sausage and Bean Stew

(Ready in about 40 minutes | Servings 4)

Ingredients

1 tablespoon olive oil	1/2 teaspoon fresh rosemary, chopped
10 ounces smoked beef sausage, sliced	1 teaspoon fresh basil, chopped
2 carrots, chopped	1 cup canned tomatoes, crushed
1 onion, chopped	1 cup chicken broth
2 garlic cloves, minced	20 ounces pinto beans, soaked overnight
Sea salt and ground black pepper, to taste	6 ounces kale, torn into pieces

Directions

Press the "Sauté" button and heat the oil. Once hot, brown the sausage for 3 to 4 minutes.

Add the remaining ingredients, except for the kale, to the inner pot.

Secure the lid. Choose the "Bean/Chili" mode and cook for 25 minutes at High pressure. Once cooking is complete, use a quick pressure release; carefully remove the lid.

Next, stir in the kale and seal the lid. Let it sit for 5 minutes before serving. Bon appétit!

Per serving: 396 Calories; 21.8g Fat; 25.8g Carbs; 6.2g Protein; 14.7g Sugars

335. Winter Squash and Chicken Stew with Apples

(Ready in about 35 minutes | Servings 4)

Ingredients

2 tablespoons olive oil, divided
2 pounds chicken thighs
1 onion, chopped
2 garlic cloves, minced
1 (1-inch) piece fresh ginger, peeled and minced
Kosher salt and freshly ground black pepper, to taste
1 teaspoon paprika
1 tablespoon fresh sage, chopped
1 pound winter squash, peeled and cubed
2 carrots, trimmed and diced
1 cup apple cider
1 cup chicken stock
2 cups chopped peeled Granny Smith apple

Directions

Press the "Sauté" button and heat the oil. Once hot, sear the chicken thighs for about 2 minutes per side; reserve.

Add the onion, garlic, and ginger and sauté them for 2 to 3 minutes or until just tender. Add the salt, pepper, paprika, sage, winter squash, carrots, apple cider, and chicken stock. Add the reserved chicken thighs.

Secure the lid. Choose the "Manual" mode and cook for 10 minutes at High pressure. Once cooking is complete, use a natural pressure release for 10 minutes; carefully remove the lid.

Remove the chicken thighs and shred with two forks; discard the bones. Add the shredded chicken back into the inner pot.

Afterwards, stir in the apples; cover, press the "Sauté" button on Low and let it simmer for 10 to 12 minutes longer or until the apples are tender.

Per serving: 413 Calories; 15.4g Fat; 28.5g Carbs; 40.4g Protein; 10.7g Sugars

336. Chicken, Shrimp and Sausage Gumbo

(Ready in about 25 minutes | Servings 4)

Ingredients

2 tablespoons olive oil
1 onion, diced
1 teaspoon garlic, minced
1/2 pound chicken breasts, boneless, skinless and cubed
1/2 pound smoked chicken sausage, cut into slices
2 sweet peppers, diced
1 jalapeno pepper, minced
1 celery stalk, diced
2 cups chicken bone broth
2 tomatoes, chopped
1 tablespoon Creole seasoning
Sea salt and ground black pepper, to taste
1 teaspoon cayenne pepper
1 tablespoon oyster sauce
1 bay leaf
1 pound shrimp, deveined
1/2 pound okra, frozen
2 stalks green onions, sliced thinly
1 tablespoon fresh lemon juice

Directions

Press the "Sauté" button and heat the oil. Sweat the onion and garlic until tender and aromatic or about 3 minutes; reserve.

Then, heat the remaining tablespoon of olive oil and cook the chicken and sausage until no longer pink, about 4 minutes. Make sure to stir periodically to ensure even cooking.

Stir in the peppers, celery, broth, tomatoes, Creole seasoning, salt, black pepper, cayenne pepper, oyster sauce, and bay leaf. Add the reserved onion mixture.

Secure the lid. Choose the "Manual" mode. Cook for 7 minutes at High pressure. Once cooking is complete, use a quick pressure release; carefully remove the lid.

Afterwards, stir in the shrimp and okra.

Secure the lid. Choose the "Manual" mode. Cook for 3 minutes at High pressure. Once cooking is complete, use a natural pressure release; carefully remove the lid.

Divide between individual bowls and garnish with green onions. Drizzle lemon juice over each serving. Bon appétit!

Per serving: 413 Calories; 15.4g Fat; 28.5g Carbs; 40.4g Protein; 10.7g Sugars

337. Steak and Kidney Bean Chili

(Ready in about 25 minutes | Servings 5)

Ingredients

2 pounds beef steak, cut into bite-sized cubes
4 tablespoons all-purpose flour
2 tablespoons vegetable oil
1 onion, chopped
2 cloves garlic, minced
1 jalapeño pepper, seeded and minced
2 cups beef broth
Sea salt and ground black pepper, to taste
1 teaspoon paprika
1 teaspoon celery seeds
1 teaspoon mustard seeds
2 tablespoons ground cumin
1 tablespoon brown sugar
2 cups red kidney beans, soaked overnight and rinsed
1 cup tomato sauce
2 tablespoons cornstarch, mixed with 4 tablespoons of water

Directions

Toss the beef steak with the the flour. Press the "Sauté" button and heat the oil until sizzling. Now, cook the beef steak in batches until browned on all side. Reserve.

Then, cook the onion, garlic, and jalapeño until they soften. Scrape the bottom of the pot with a splash of beef broth. Add the beef broth, spices, sugar, beans, and tomato sauce to the inner pot; stir to combine well.

Secure the lid. Choose the "Manual" mode. Cook for 18 minutes at High pressure. Once cooking is complete, use a natural pressure release; carefully remove the lid.

Press the "Sauté" button. Stir in the cornstarch slurry; stir for a few minutes to thicken the cooking liquid. Bon appétit!

Per serving: 551 Calories; 12.4g Fat; 58.6g Carbs; 51.4g Protein; 9.2g Sugars

338. Marsala Fish Stew

(Ready in about 15 minutes | Servings 5)

Ingredients

2 tablespoons canola oil
1 onion, sliced
3 garlic cloves, sliced
1/2 cup Marsala wine
1 ½ cups shellfish stock
1 cup water
1 pound Yukon Gold potatoes, diced
2 ripe tomatoes, pureed
Sea salt and ground black pepper, to taste
2 bay leaves
1 teaspoon smoked paprika
1/2 teaspoon hot sauce
2 pounds halibut, cut into bite-sized pieces
2 tablespoons fresh cilantro, chopped

Directions

Press the "Sauté" button and heat the oil. Once hot, cook the onions until softened; stir in the garlic and continue to sauté an additional 30 seconds.

Add the wine to deglaze the bottom of the inner pot, scraping up any browned bits.

Add the shellfish stock, water, potatoes, tomatoes, salt, black pepper, bay leaves, paprika, hot sauce, and halibut to the inner pot.

Secure the lid. Choose the "Manual" mode. Cook for 5 minutes at High pressure. Once cooking is complete, use a quick pressure release; carefully remove the lid. Serve with fresh cilantro and enjoy!

Per serving: 487 Calories; 31.5g Fat; 19.9g Carbs; 30.4g Protein; 2.8g Sugars

339. Bœuf à la Bourguignonne

(Ready in about 30 minutes | Servings 6)

Ingredients

4 thick slices bacon, diced
2 pounds beef round roast, cut into 1-inch cubes
Sea salt and ground black pepper, to taste
1 cup red Burgundy wine
2 onions, thinly sliced
2 carrots, diced
2 celery stalks, diced
4 cloves garlic, minced
2 tablespoons tomato paste
2 thyme sprigs
2 bay leaves
2 cups beef broth
2 tablespoons bouquet garni, chopped

Directions

Press the "Sauté" button to preheat your Instant Pot. Cook the bacon until it is golden-brown; reserve.

Add the beef to the inner pot; sear the beef until browned or about 3 minutes per side.

Stir in the other ingredients; stir to combine well.

Secure the lid. Choose the "Meat/Stew" mode. Cook for 20 minutes at High pressure. Once cooking is complete, use a quick pressure release; carefully remove the lid.

Serve in individual bowls topped with the reserved bacon. Bon appétit!

Per serving: 364 Calories; 14.5g Fat; 5.3g Carbs; 49.4g Protein; 2.4g Sugars

340. Hungarian Beef Goulash

(Ready in about 30 minutes | Servings 5)

Ingredients

2 tablespoons olive oil
2 pounds beef chuck, cut into bite-sized pieces
1/4 cup Hungarian red wine
2 onions, sliced
2 garlic cloves, crushed
1 red chili pepper, minced
Sea salt and freshly ground black pepper, to taste
1 tablespoon Hungarian paprika
1 beef stock cube
2 cups water
2 ripe tomatoes, puréed
2 bay leaves

Directions

Press the "Sauté" button and heat the oil. Once hot, cook the beef until no longer pink. Add the red wine and stir with a wooden spoon, scraping up the browned bits on the bottom of the inner pot.

Stir in the remaining ingredients

Secure the lid. Choose the "Meat/Stew" mode. Cook for 20 minutes at High pressure. Once cooking is complete, use a quick pressure release; carefully remove the lid.

Serve in individual bowls and enjoy!

Per serving: 311 Calories; 16g Fat; 4.3g Carbs; 38.1g Protein; 2.1g Sugars

341. Authentic Mexican Pork Chile Verde

(Ready in about 30 minutes | Servings 6)

Ingredients

1 pound tomatillos, halved
4 garlic cloves, sliced
2 chili peppers, minced
2 heaping tablespoons cilantro, chopped
2 tablespoons olive oil
3 pounds pork stew meat, cut into 2-inch cubes
1 onion, chopped
1 bell pepper, deveined and sliced
Salt and freshly ground black pepper, to taste
2 cups vegetable broth

Directions

Place the tomatillos under a preheated broiler for about 6 minutes. Let cool enough to handle.

Purée the tomatillos with the garlic, chili peppers, and cilantro in your blender; process until everything is finely chopped and mixed.

Press the "Sauté" button and heat the oil. Once hot, cook the pork until no longer pink. Add the onion and cook for a few minutes more or until it is tender and translucent.

Add the remaining ingredients, including tomatillo sauce, to the inner pot.

Secure the lid. Choose the "Meat/Stew" mode. Cook for 20 minutes at High pressure. Once cooking is complete, use a quick pressure release; carefully remove the lid.

Ladle into serving bowls and garnish with tortillas if desired. Bon appétit!

Per serving: 518 Calories; 26.6g Fat; 10.8g Carbs; 55.9g Protein; 5.3g Sugars

342. Italian Beef Ragù

(Ready in about 20 minutes | Servings 5)

Ingredients

2 tablespoons butter, melted
1 medium leek, diced
2 carrots, diced
1 stalk celery, diced
5 ounces bacon, diced
1 pound ground chuck
1/2 cup Italian red wine
1/4 cup tomato puree
2 cups chicken stock
1 tablespoon Italian seasoning blend
1/2 teaspoon kosher salt
1/2 teaspoon black pepper

Directions

Press the "Sauté" button and melt the butter. Sauté the leek, carrot, celery and garlic for 2 to 3 minutes.

Add the bacon and ground beef to the inner pot; continue to cook an additional 3 minutes, stirring frequently. Add the remaining ingredients to the inner pot.

Secure the lid. Choose the "Manual" mode and cook for 5 minutes at High pressure. Once cooking is complete, use a quick pressure release; carefully remove the lid.

Serve with hot pasta if desired. Bon appétit!

Per serving: 475 Calories; 40.6g Fat; 6.1g Carbs; 20.7g Protein; 2.5g Sugars

343. Traditional Brunswick Stew

(Ready in about 20 minutes | Servings 4)

Ingredients

2 tablespoons lard, melted
1 onion, diced
2 cloves garlic, minced
1 pound chicken breast, cut into 1-inch cubes
2 cups lima beans, soaked
1 (14 ½-ounce) can tomatoes, diced
2 cups chicken broth
1 tablespoon Worcestershire sauce
1 teaspoon Creole seasoning
Sea salt and ground black pepper, to taste
1 teaspoon hot sauce
1 cup corn kernels

Directions

Press the "Sauté" button and melt the lard. Once hot, cook the onion and garlic until just tender and aromatic.

Now, add the chicken and cook an additional 3 minutes, stirring frequently.

Add the lima beans, tomatoes, broth, Worcestershire sauce, Creole seasoning, salt, black pepper, and hot sauce to the inner pot.

Secure the lid. Choose the "Manual" mode and cook for 12 minutes at High pressure. Once cooking is complete, use a natural pressure release; carefully remove the lid.

Stir in the corn kernels and seal the lid. Let it sit in the residual heat until heated through. Enjoy!

Per serving: 479 Calories; 25.6g Fat; 31.6g Carbs; 31.3g Protein; 7.3g Sugars

344. Bigos (Traditional Polish Stew)

(Ready in about 20 minutes | Servings 5)

Ingredients

2 slices smoked bacon, diced
1 pound Kielbasa, sliced
1/2 pound pork stew meat, cubed
1 onion, chopped
4 garlic cloves, sliced
2 carrots, trimmed and diced
1 pound sauerkraut, drained
1 pound fresh cabbage, shredded
1 teaspoon dried thyme
1 teaspoon dried basil

2 bay leaves
1 tablespoon cayenne pepper
1 teaspoon mustard seeds
1 teaspoon caraway seeds, crushed
Sea salt, to taste
1/2 teaspoon black peppercorns
1/2 cup dry red wine
2 ½ cups beef stock
1/2 cup tomato puree

Directions

Press the "Sauté" button to preheat your Instant Pot. Now, cook the bacon, Kielbasa, and pork stew meat until the bacon is crisp; reserve.

Add the onion and garlic, and sauté them until they're softened and starting to brown. Add the remaining ingredients to the inner pot, including the reserved meat mixture.

Secure the lid. Choose the "Manual" mode and cook for 15 minutes at High pressure. Once cooking is complete, use a quick pressure release; carefully remove the lid.

Ladle into individual bowls and serve warm.

Per serving: 417 Calories; 22.4g Fat; 23.6g Carbs; 31.8g Protein; 8.7g Sugars

345. Vegan Pottage Stew

(Ready in about 15 minutes | Servings 4)

Ingredients

2 tablespoons olive oil
1 onion, chopped
2 garlic cloves, minced
2 carrots, diced
2 parsnips, diced
1 turnip, diced
4 cups vegetable broth

2 bay leaves
2 thyme sprigs
2 rosemary sprigs
Kosher salt and freshly ground black pepper, to taste
1/4 cup red wine
1 cup porridge oats

Directions

Press the "Sauté" button and heat the olive oil until sizzling. Now, sauté the onion and garlic until just tender and fragrant.

Add the remaining ingredients to the inner pot; stir to combine.

Secure the lid. Choose the "Manual" mode and cook for 10 minutes at High pressure. Once cooking is complete, use a quick pressure release; carefully remove the lid.

Ladle into individual bowls and serve immediately. Bon appétit!

Per serving: 315 Calories; 11.1g Fat; 41.6g Carbs; 12.8g Protein; 5.7g Sugars

346. Burgoo (Mulligan Stew)

(Ready in about 30 minutes | Servings 8)

Ingredients

1 tablespoon lard, melted
2 pounds pork butt roast, cut into 2-inch pieces
2 pounds beef stew meat, cut into 2-inch pieces
2 chicken thighs, boneless
2 bell peppers, chopped
1 red chili pepper, chopped
1 onion, chopped
2 carrots, chopped

4 garlic cloves, chopped
4 cups beef bone broth
1 cup beer
1 (28-ounce) can tomatoes, crushed
Sea salt and ground black pepper, to taste
1 pound frozen corn kernels
3 tablespoons Worcestershire sauce

Directions

Press the "Sauté" button and melt the lard. Once hot, brown the meat in batches. Remove the browned meats to a bowl.

Then, sauté the peppers, onion, carrots for about 3 minutes or until tender and fragrant. Add the garlic and continue to cook for 30 seconds more.

Add the meat back to the Instant Pot. Stir in the remaining ingredients, except for the corn kernels.

Secure the lid. Choose the "Meat/Stew" mode and cook for 20 minutes at High pressure. Once cooking is complete, use a quick pressure release; carefully remove the lid.

Lastly, stir in the corn and continue to cook for a few minutes more on the "Sauté" function. Serve immediately.

Per serving: 522 Calories; 20.4g Fat; 22.2g Carbs; 61.6g Protein; 9.3g Sugars

347. Irish Bean and Cabbage Stew

(Ready in about 35 minutes | Servings 4)

Ingredients

2 cups white beans, soaked and rinsed
1/2 cup pearled barley
4 cups roasted vegetable broth
1 shallot, chopped
2 carrots, chopped
2 ribs celery, chopped
1 sweet pepper, chopped
1 serrano pepper, chopped
4 cloves garlic, minced

1 pound cabbage, chopped
1/2 pound potatoes, diced
2 bay leaves
1/2 teaspoon mustard seeds
1/2 teaspoon caraway seeds
1 teaspoon cayenne pepper
Sea salt and freshly ground black pepper, to taste
1 (14 ½-ounce) can tomatoes, diced

Directions

Place the white beans, barley, and vegetable broth in the inner pot.

Secure the lid. Choose the "Bean/Chili" mode and cook for 25 minutes at High pressure. Once cooking is complete, use a quick pressure release; carefully remove the lid.

Add the remaining ingredients and stir to combine.

Secure the lid. Choose the "Manual" mode and cook for 5 minutes at High pressure. Once cooking is complete, use a quick pressure release; carefully remove the lid.

Serve in individual bowls and enjoy!

Per serving: 577 Calories; 3.7g Fat; 85g Carbs; 32.6g Protein; 12.5g Sugars

348. Rich and Easy Chicken Purloo

(Ready in about 25 minutes | Servings 8)

Ingredients

1 tablespoon olive oil
1 onion, chopped
3 pounds chicken legs, boneless and skinless
2 garlic cloves, minced
5 cups water
2 carrots, diced
2 celery ribs, diced

2 bay leaves
1 teaspoon mustard seeds
1/4 teaspoon marjoram
Seasoned salt and freshly ground black pepper, to taste
1 teaspoon cayenne pepper
2 cups white long-grain rice

Directions

Press the "Sauté" button and heat the olive oil. Now, add the onion and chicken legs; cook until the onion is translucent or about 4 minutes.

Stir in the minced garlic and continue to cook for a minute more. Add the water.

Secure the lid. Choose the "Manual" mode and cook for 10 minutes at High pressure. Once cooking is complete, use a quick pressure release; carefully remove the lid.

Add the remaining ingredients.

Secure the lid. Choose the "Manual" mode and cook for 5 minutes at High pressure. Once cooking is complete, use a quick pressure release; carefully remove the lid. Serve warm.

Per serving: 407 Calories; 9.4g Fat; 40.9g Carbs; 36.5g Protein; 1.7g Sugars

349. Creamy Almond and Lentil Vegetable Stew

(Ready in about 20 minutes | Servings 4)

Ingredients

1 tablespoon olive oil
1 onion, chopped
1 teaspoon fresh garlic, minced
1 dried chili pepper, crushed
1 pound potatoes, cut into 1-inch pieces
1 pound cauliflower, broken into florets
1 cup green lentils
3 cups tomato juice

3 cups vegetable broth
Seasoned salt and ground black pepper, to taste
1 teaspoon cayenne pepper
1/2 cup almond butter
2 heaping tablespoons cilantro, roughly chopped
1 heaping tablespoon parsley, roughly chopped

Directions

Press the "Sauté" button and heat the olive oil. Now, sauté the onion until it is transparent. Add garlic and continue to sauté an additional minute.

Stir in the chili pepper, potatoes, cauliflower, lentils, tomato juice, vegetable broth, salt, black pepper, and cayenne pepper.

Secure the lid. Choose the "Manual" mode and cook for 10 minutes at High pressure. Once cooking is complete, use a quick pressure release; carefully remove the lid.

Stir in the almond butter. Press the "Sauté" button and simmer for about 3 minutes on the lowest setting. Garnish with cilantro and parsley. Bon appétit!

Per serving: 450 Calories; 28.6g Fat; 41.9g Carbs; 12.4g Protein; 10.2g Sugars

350. Zarzuela de Mariscos (Catalan Shellfish Stew)

(Ready in about 30 minutes | Servings 6)

Ingredients

4 tablespoons olive oil
1 onion, chopped
3 cloves garlic, minced
4 ounces prosciutto, diced
1 ½ pounds shrimp
1 ½ pounds clams
1 Chile de Árbol, minced
1/2 cup dry white wine
4 cups clam juice

1 laurel (bay leaf)
Sea salt and ground black pepper, to taste
1 teaspoon guindilla (cayenne pepper)
1 teaspoon rosemary, chopped
1 teaspoon basil, chopped
2 tomatoes, pureed
1 fresh lemon, sliced

Directions

Press the "Sauté" button and heat the olive oil. Now, sauté the onion until it is transparent. Add the garlic and continue to sauté an additional 1 minute.

Add the prosciutto and cook an additional 3 minutes. Add the remaining ingredients, except for the lemon.

Secure the lid. Choose the "Manual" mode and cook for 10 minutes at High pressure. Once cooking is complete, use a natural pressure release for 10 minutes; carefully remove the lid.

Serve in individual bowls garnished with lemon slices. Enjoy!

Per serving: 393 Calories; 14.6g Fat; 34g Carbs; 30.8g Protein; 10.5g Sugars

351. Beef and Potato Stew

(Ready in about 30 minutes | Servings 6)

Ingredients

1 tablespoon lard, melted
2 pounds chuck roast, cut into 2-inch cubes
2 onions, chopped
2 cloves garlic, minced
2 tablespoons Hungarian paprika
4 bell peppers, deveined and chopped

1 chili pepper, chopped
1 cup tomato puree
4 potatoes, diced
4 cups beef broth
2 bay leaves
Seasoned salt and ground black pepper, to taste

Directions

Press the "Sauté" button and melt the lard. Once hot, cook the beef until no longer pink. Add a splash of broth and stir with a wooden spoon, scraping up the browned bits on the bottom of the inner pot.

Add the onion to the inner pot; continue sautéing an additional 3 minutes. Now, stir in the garlic and cook for 30 seconds more.

Stir in the remaining ingredients

Secure the lid. Choose the "Meat/Stew" mode. Cook for 20 minutes at High pressure. Once cooking is complete, use a quick pressure release; carefully remove the lid.

Discard the bay leaves and serve in individual bowls. Bon appétit!

Per serving: 425 Calories; 11.7g Fat; 35.3g Carbs; 44g Protein; 7.5g Sugars

352. Hungarian Chicken Stew (Paprikás Csirke)

(Ready in about 30 minutes | Servings 6)

Ingredients

2 tablespoons lard, at room temperature
2 pounds chicken, cut into pieces
2 onions, chopped
2 cloves garlic, minced
1 cup tomato puree
1 Hungarian pepper, diced

2 tablespoons Hungarian paprika
2 cups chicken stock
Kosher salt and cracked ground black pepper
3 tablespoons all-purpose flour
1 cup full-fat sour cream

Directions

Press the "Sauté" button and melt the lard. Once hot, cook the chicken for about 3 minutes or until no longer pink.

Add the onion to the inner pot; continue sautéing an additional 3 minutes. Now, stir in the garlic and cook for 30 seconds more.

Add the tomato puree, Hungarian pepper, paprika, chicken stock, salt, and black pepper to the inner pot.

Secure the lid. Choose the "Manual" mode. Cook for 15 minutes at High pressure. Once cooking is complete, use a quick pressure release; carefully remove the lid. Remove the chicken from the inner pot; shred the chicken and discard the bones.

In a mixing bowl, stir the flour into the sour cream. Add the flour/cream mixture to the cooking liquid, stirring constantly with a wire whisk.

Let it simmer until the sauce is thickened. Return the chicken to your paprikas, stir and press the "Cancel" button. Enjoy!

Per serving: 304 Calories; 9.4g Fat; 18.6g Carbs; 35.7g Protein; 4.5g Sugars

353. Indian Bean Stew (Rajma)

(Ready in about 30 minutes | Servings 4)

Ingredients

2 tablespoons sesame oil
1 onion, sliced
4 cloves garlic, finely chopped
1 (1-inch) piece fresh ginger root, peeled and grated
2 cups red kidney beans, soaked overnight
2 Bhut jolokia peppers, minced
1 teaspoon red curry paste

5 cups vegetable broth
1 teaspoon coriander seeds
1/2 teaspoon cumin seeds
1/4 teaspoon ground cinnamon
Seasoned salt and ground black pepper, to taste
2 tomatoes, pureed
2 tablespoons fresh coriander, chopped

Directions

Press the "Sauté" button and heat the oil. Now, sauté the onion until it is transparent. Add the garlic and ginger and continue to sauté an additional 1 minute.

Add the beans, peppers, curry paste, vegetable broth spices, and tomatoes.

Secure the lid. Choose the "Bean/Chili" mode. Cook for 25 minutes at High pressure. Once cooking is complete, use a quick pressure release; carefully remove the lid.

Serve in individual bowls garnished with fresh coriander. Enjoy!

Per serving: 432 Calories; 9.5g Fat; 62.3g Carbs; 26.6g Protein; 4.1g Sugars

354. Mediterranean Chicken Stew

(Ready in about 35 minutes | Servings 4)

Ingredients

2 tablespoons olive oil
1 onion, chopped
1 stalk celery, chopped
2 carrots, chopped
1 teaspoon garlic, minced
4 chicken legs, boneless skinless
1/4 cup dry red wine
2 ripe tomatoes, pureed

2 cups chicken bone broth
2 bay leaves
Sea salt and ground black pepper, to taste
1/2 teaspoon dried basil
1 teaspoon dried oregano
1/2 cup Kalamata olives, pitted and sliced

Directions

Press the "Sauté" button and heat the oil. Now, sauté the onion, celery, and carrot for 4 to 5 minutes or until they are tender.

Add the other ingredients, except for the Kalamata olives, and stir to combine.

Secure the lid. Choose the "Manual" mode. Cook for 15 minutes at High pressure. Once cooking is complete, use a natural pressure release for 10 minutes; carefully remove the lid.

Serve warm garnished with Kalamata olives. Bon appétit!

Per serving: 400 Calories; 27.9g Fat; 11.3g Carbs; 24.6g Protein; 5.1g Sugars

355. Seafood and Vegetable Ragout

(Ready in about 20 minutes | Servings 4)

Ingredients

2 tablespoons olive oil
1 shallot, diced
2 carrots, diced
1 parsnip, diced
1 teaspoon fresh garlic, minced
1/2 cup dry white wine
2 cups fish stock
1 tomato, pureed
1 bay leaf

1 pound shrimp, deveined
1/2 pound scallops
Seasoned salt and freshly ground pepper, to taste
1 tablespoon paprika
2 tablespoons fresh parsley, chopped
1 lime, sliced

Directions

Press the "Sauté" button and heat the oil. Now, sauté the shallot, carrot, and parsnip for 4 to 5 minutes or until they are tender.

Stir in the garlic and continue to sauté an additional 30 second or until aromatic.

Stir in the white wine, stock, tomato, bay leaf, shrimp, scallops, salt, black pepper, and paprika.

Secure the lid. Choose the "Manual" mode. Cook for 5 minutes at High pressure. Once cooking is complete, use a natural pressure release for 5 minutes; carefully remove the lid. Serve garnished with fresh parsley and lime slices. Enjoy!

Per serving: 312 Calories; 11.9g Fat; 15.9g Carbs; 36.6g Protein; 5g Sugars

356. Spanish Favorite Olla Podrida

(Ready in about 30 minutes | Servings 6)

Ingredients

2 ½ pounds meaty pork ribs in adobo
1/2 pound Spanish chorizo sausage, sliced
1 tablespoon olive oil
2 onions, chopped

2 carrots, sliced
2 garlic cloves, sliced
Salt and black pepper, to taste
1 pound alubias de Ibeas beans, soaked overnight

Directions

Place the pork and sausage in the inner pot; cover with water.

Add the other ingredients and stir to combine.

Secure the lid. Choose the "Meat/Stew" mode. Cook for 20 minutes at High pressure. Once cooking is complete, use a quick pressure release; carefully remove the lid.

Serve hot with corn tortilla if desired. Enjoy!

Per serving: 418 Calories; 20.1g Fat; 11.6g Carbs; 47.6g Protein; 2.7g Sugars

357. Basque Squid Stew

(Ready in about 15 minutes | Servings 4)

Ingredients

2 tablespoons olive oil
1 onion, finely diced
2 cloves garlic, minced
1 thyme sprig, chopped
1 rosemary sprig, chopped
1 serrano pepper, deseeded and chopped
2 tomatoes, pureed
1/2 cup clam juice
1 cup chicken stock

1/2 cup cooking sherry
1 pound fresh squid, cleaned and sliced into rings
Sea salt and ground black pepper, to taste
1 teaspoon cayenne pepper
1 bay leaf
1/4 teaspoon saffron
1 lemon, cut into wedges

Directions

Press the "Sauté" button and heat the oil. Now, sauté the onion until tender and translucent.

Now, add the garlic and continue to sauté an additional minute. Add the remaining ingredients, except for the lemon.

Secure the lid. Choose the "Manual" mode. Cook for 10 minutes at High pressure. Once cooking is complete, use a quick pressure release; carefully remove the lid. Serve garnished with lemon wedges. Bon appétit!

Per serving: 277 Calories; 9.3g Fat; 26.5g Carbs; 22.3g Protein; 8.7g Sugars

358. Winter Slumgullion Stew

(Ready in about 20 minutes | Servings 4)

Ingredients

1 tablespoon canola oil
1 leek, chopped
2 garlic cloves, minced
2 carrots, chopped
1/2 (16-ounce) package macaroni
1/2 pound ground beef
1/2 pound pork sausage, crumbled

1 ½ cups tomato puree
1 ½ cups chicken broth
Seasoned salt and black pepper, to taste
1 (14.5-ounce) can stewed tomatoes
2 cups green beans, cut into thirds

Directions

Press the "Sauté" button and heat the oil. Now, sauté the leek, garlic and carrot until they have softened.

Then, add the macaroni, ground beef, sausage, tomato puree, chicken broth, salt, and black pepper to the inner pot.

Secure the lid. Choose the "Manual" mode. Cook for 10 minutes at High pressure. Once cooking is complete, use a quick pressure release; carefully remove the lid.

After that, add the canned tomatoes and green beans; let it simmer on the "Sauté" function for 2 to 3 minutes more or until everything is heated through. Bon appétit!

Per serving: 536 Calories; 15.1g Fat; 66.8g Carbs; 39g Protein; 11.9g Sugars

359. Lentil and Root Vegetable Hotpot

(Ready in about 15 minutes | Servings 4)

Ingredients

1 tablespoon olive oil
1 onion, chopped
3 cloves garlic, minced
1 carrot, chopped
1 stalk celery, chopped
1 parsnip, chopped
2 cups brown lentils
2 tomatoes, pureed

1 sprig thyme, chopped
1 sprig rosemary, chopped
1 teaspoon basil
Kosher salt and ground black pepper, to taste
2 cups vegetable broth
3 cups Swiss chard, torn into pieces

Directions

Press the "Sauté" button and heat the oil. Sauté the onion until tender and translucent or about 4 minutes.

Then, stir in the garlic and cook an additional 30 seconds or until fragrant.

Now, stir in the carrot, celery, parsnip, lentils, tomatoes, spices, and broth.

Secure the lid. Choose the "Manual" mode. Cook for 10 minutes at High pressure. Once cooking is complete, use a quick pressure release; carefully remove the lid.

Afterwards, add the Swiss chard to the inner pot. Seal the lid and allow it to wilt completely. Bon appétit!

Per serving: 510 Calories; 7.4g Fat; 84.2g Carbs; 31.5g Protein; 10.3g Sugars

360. Easy Vegetarian Ratatouille

(Ready in about 25 minutes | Servings 4)

Ingredients

1 pound eggplant, cut into rounds
1 tablespoon sea salt
3 tablespoons olive oil
1 red onion, sliced
4 cloves garlic, minced
4 sweet peppers, seeded and chopped
1 red chili pepper, seeded and minced
Sea salt and ground black pepper, to taste
1 teaspoon capers
1/2 teaspoon celery seeds
2 tomatoes, pureed
1 cup roasted vegetable broth
2 tablespoons coriander, chopped

Directions

Toss the eggplant with 1 tablespoon of sea salt; allow it to drain in a colander.

Press the "Sauté" button and heat the olive oil. Sauté the onion until tender and translucent, about 4 minutes.

Add the garlic and continue to sauté for 30 seconds more or until fragrant. Add the remaining ingredients to the inner pot, including the drained eggplant.

Secure the lid. Choose the "Manual" mode. Cook for 7 minutes at High pressure. Once cooking is complete, use a quick pressure release; carefully remove the lid.

Press the "Sauté" button and cook on low setting until the ratatouille has thickened or about 7 minutes. Bon appétit!

Per serving: 231 Calories; 11.1g Fat; 33.1g Carbs; 5.7g Protein; 11.3g Sugars

361. Classic French Pot-Au-Feu

(Ready in about 1 hour 10 minutes | Servings 5)

Ingredients

2 tablespoons olive oil
2 pounds beef pot roast, cut into 2-inch pieces
1 onion, chopped
2 carrots, chopped
3 garlic cloves, pressed
2 tomatoes, pureed
1 cup dry red wine
3 cups beef broth
1/2 teaspoon marjoram
1/2 teaspoon sage
Sea salt and ground black pepper, to taste
1 shallot, sliced
1 pound cremini mushrooms, sliced
1 cup chèvres cheese, crumbled

Directions

Press the "Sauté" button and heat the olive oil. Cook the beef in batches and transfer to a bowl.

Then, cook the onion in pan drippings. Stir in the carrots and garlic and continue to cook an additional 3 minutes.

Add the tomatoes, wine, broth, marjoram, sage, salt, and black pepper. Add the browned beef.

Secure the lid. Choose the "Meat/Stew" mode. Cook for 45 minutes at High pressure. Once cooking is complete, use a quick pressure release; carefully remove the lid.

Now, add the shallot and mushrooms; continue to simmer on the "Sauté" function for about 10 minutes or until everything is thoroughly heated.

Transfer your stew to a lightly greased casserole dish; top with the cheese and place under a preheated broiler for 10 minutes or until the cheese melts. Serve warm.

Per serving: 473 Calories; 25.7g Fat; 12.3g Carbs; 48g Protein; 6.2g Sugars

362. Chicken Fricassee with Sherry Wine

(Ready in about 30 minutes | Servings 4)

Ingredients

2 tablespoons canola oil
6 chicken wings
1 onion, chopped
2 garlic cloves, minced
Kosher salt and ground black pepper, to taste
1 teaspoon cayenne pepper
1 teaspoon celery seeds
1/2 teaspoon mustard powder
2 carrots, chopped
2 celery stalks, chopped
3 cups vegetable broth
1/2 cup cooking sherry
2 tablespoons all-purpose flour
1 cup double cream

Directions

Press the "Sauté" button and heat 1 tablespoon of olive oil. Now, cook the chicken wings for 2 to 3 minutes per side; set aside. Add a splash of cooking sherry to deglaze the pot.

Then, heat the remaining tablespoon of olive oil; sauté the onion until just tender or about 3 minutes. Stir in the garlic and continue to cook an additional minute, stirring frequently.

Next, add the reserved chicken, salt, black pepper, cayenne pepper, celery seeds, mustard powder, carrots, celery, broth, and sherry to the inner pot.

Secure the lid. Choose the "Poultry" mode. Cook for 15 minutes at High pressure. Once cooking is complete, use a quick pressure release; carefully remove the lid.

Meanwhile, mix the flour with the double cream. Add the flour mixture to the hot cooking liquid; seal the lid and let it sit in the residual heat until thoroughly warmed.

Ladle into individual bowls and serve. Bon appétit!

Per serving: 442 Calories; 25.5g Fat; 22.4g Carbs; 29.7g Protein; 6.5g Sugars

363. Barley Vegetable Pottage

(Ready in about 25 minutes | Servings 4)

Ingredients

1 tablespoon olive oil
1 onion, chopped
2 cloves garlic, minced
1 red chili pepper, minced
2 sweet peppers, seeded and chopped
1 ½ cups pearled barley
2 cups water
4 cups vegetable broth
2 stalks celery, chopped
2 carrots, chopped
2 tomatoes, pureed
1 teaspoon red pepper flakes
Sea salt and ground black pepper, to taste

Directions

Press the "Sauté" button and heat the olive oil. Now, sauté the onion until tender and translucent.

Then, stir in the garlic and peppers and cook an additional 3 minutes. Stir in the pearled barley. Pour in water and broth.

Secure the lid. Choose the "Manual" mode. Cook for 15 minutes at High pressure. Once cooking is complete, use a quick pressure release; carefully remove the lid.

Add the remaining ingredients to the inner pot.

Secure the lid. Choose the "Manual" mode. Cook for 5 minutes at High pressure. Once cooking is complete, use a quick pressure release; carefully remove the lid. Bon appétit!

Per serving: 401 Calories; 6.5g Fat; 74.4g Carbs; 14.7g Protein; 5.7g Sugars

364. Hyderabadi-Style Lentil Stew

(Ready in about 20 minutes | Servings 4)

Ingredients

2 tablespoons canola oil
1 teaspoon cumin seeds
1 onion, chopped
1 teaspoon garlic paste
2 cups yellow lentils, soaked for 30 minutes and rinsed
1/2 teaspoon tamarind paste
1/2 teaspoon red chili powder
10 curry leaves
1 cup tomato sauce
Kosher salt and white pepper, to taste

Directions

Press the "Sauté" button and heat the oil. Then, sauté the cumin seeds for 1 to 2 minutes, stirring frequently.

Then, add the onion and cook an additional 2 minutes. Stir in the remaining ingredients.

Secure the lid. Choose the "Manual" mode. Cook for 5 minutes at High pressure. Once cooking is complete, use a natural pressure release for 10 minutes; carefully remove the lid.

Ladle into individual bowls and serve immediately. Bon appétit!

Per serving: 492 Calories; 10.1g Fat; 77.5g Carbs; 24g Protein; 9g Sugars

365. Authentic Kentucky Burgoo

(Ready in about 1 hour | Servings 8)

Ingredients

2 tablespoons lard, melted
2 onions, chopped
1 pound pork shank, cubed
2 pounds beef shank, cubed
1 pound chicken legs
1/2 cup Kentucky bourbon
4 cups chicken broth
2 cups dry lima beans, soaked
2 cups tomato puree
1 pound potatoes, diced

2 carrots, sliced thickly
2 parsnips, sliced thickly
1 celery rib, sliced thickly
2 sweet peppers, seeded and sliced
1 jalapeno pepper, seeded and minced
1 teaspoon dried sage, crushed
1 teaspoon dried basil, crushed
Salt and freshly ground black pepper, to taste

Directions

Press the "Sauté" button and melt 1 tablespoon of lard. Once hot, sauté the onion until tender and translucent; reserve.

Add the remaining tablespoon of lard; brown the meat in batches until no longer pink or about 4 minutes.

Add a splash of Kentucky bourbon to deglaze the pot. Pour chicken broth into the inner pot.

Secure the lid. Choose the "Meat/Stew" mode. Cook for 45 minutes at High pressure. Once cooking is complete, use a quick pressure release; carefully remove the lid.

Shred chicken meat and discard the bones; add the chicken back to the inner pot. Next, stir in lima beans and tomato puree.

Secure the lid. Choose the "Manual" mode. Cook for 5 minutes at High pressure. Once cooking is complete, use a quick pressure release; carefully remove the lid.

Then, stir in the remaining ingredients, including the sautéed onion.

Secure the lid. Choose the "Manual" mode. Cook for 5 minutes at High pressure. Once cooking is complete, use a quick pressure release; carefully remove the lid.

Serve with cornbread if desired.

Per serving: 503 Calories; 17.6g Fat; 33.7g Carbs; 58g Protein; 7.5g Sugars

366. Thai Coconut Curry Stew

(Ready in about 50 minutes | Servings 5)

Ingredients

2 tablespoons sesame oil
2 pounds beef chuck, cubed
2 onions, thinly sliced
2 cloves garlic, pressed
1 (2-inch) galangal piece, peeled and sliced
1 Bird's eye chili pepper, seeded and minced
1/2 cup tomato paste
4 cups chicken bone broth
1/4 cup Thai red curry paste
1 tablespoon soy sauce

1/2 teaspoon ground cloves
1/2 teaspoon cardamom
1/2 teaspoon cumin
1 cinnamon quill
Sea salt and ground white pepper, to taste
1/2 (13.5-ounce) can full-fat coconut milk
2 cups cauliflower florets
2 tablespoons fresh cilantro, roughly chopped

Directions

Press the "Sauté" button and heat the sesame oil. When the oil starts to sizzle, cook the meat until browned on all sides.

Add a splash of broth and use a spoon to scrape the brown bits from the bottom of the pot.

Next, stir in the onion, garlic, galangal, chili pepper, tomato paste, broth, curry paste, soy sauce, and spices.

Secure the lid. Choose the "Soup/Broth" mode and cook for 40 minutes at High pressure. Once cooking is complete, use a quick pressure release; carefully remove the lid.

After that, add the coconut milk and cauliflower to the inner pot.

Secure the lid. Choose the "Manual" mode and cook for 4 minutes at High pressure. Once cooking is complete, use a quick pressure release; carefully remove the lid.

Serve garnished with fresh cilantro. Enjoy!

Per serving: 487 Calories; 28.6g Fat; 16.7g Carbs; 45.5g Protein; 7.4g Sugars

367. Oyster Stew with Spanish Chorizo

(Ready in about 15 minutes | Servings 4)

Ingredients

2 tablespoons olive oil
8 ounces Spanish chorizo sausage, sliced
1 onion, chopped
1 teaspoon ginger-garlic paste
1/2 teaspoon dried rosemary
1/2 teaspoon smoked paprika

1/2 pound fresh oysters, cleaned
Sea salt and freshly ground black pepper, to taste
3 cups chicken broth
2 cups kale leaves, washed
1 cup heavy cream

Directions

Press the "Sauté" button and heat the sesame oil. When the oil starts to sizzle, cook the sausage until no longer pink.

Add the onion to the inner pot and continue to sauté for a further 3 minutes or until tender and translucent.

Now, stir in the ginger-garlic paste, rosemary, paprika, oysters, salt, pepper, and chicken broth.

Secure the lid. Choose the "Manual" mode and cook for 6 minutes at Low pressure. Once cooking is complete, use a quick pressure release; carefully remove the lid.

Add the kale leaves and heavy cream, seal the lid again, and let it sit in the residual heat until thoroughly warmed. Serve warm and enjoy!

Per serving: 393 Calories; 30.8g Fat; 12.9g Carbs; 19.4g Protein; 2.3g Sugars

368. Dal Tadka (Indian Lentil Curry Stew)

(Ready in about 20 minutes | Servings 4)

Ingredients

Dahl:
2 tablespoons butter
1 brown onion, chopped
4 garlic cloves, minced
1 (1-inch) piece ginger, peeled and grated
1 red chili pepper, deseeded and minced
6 fresh curry leaves
2 tomatoes, chopped
1/2 teaspoon ground cumin
1/4 teaspoon ground cardamom
1 ½ cups dried chana dal, soaked

4 cups vegetable broth
1/2 teaspoon turmeric powder
Kosher salt and ground black pepper, to taste
Tadka (Tempering):
1 tablespoon butter
A pinch of asafetida
1/2 teaspoon cumin seeds
1 teaspoon mustard seeds
1/2 onion, sliced
1 bay leaf
2 dried chili peppers, seeded and cut in half

Directions

Press the "Sauté" button and melt 2 tablespoons of butter. Once hot, cook the onion until tender and translucent or about 3 minutes.

Then, stir in the garlic and ginger; continue to cook an additional minute or until they are fragrant.

Add the remaining ingredients for the Dal.

Secure the lid. Choose the "Manual" mode and cook for 10 minutes at High pressure. Once cooking is complete, use a quick pressure release; carefully remove the lid.

Clean the inner pot and press the "Sauté" button again. Melt 1 tablespoon of butter.

Now, add a pinch of asafetida, cumin seeds, mustard seeds, onion and bay leaf; sauté for a minute. Stir in the dried chili peppers and cook for 30 seconds longer.

Pour the hot tadka over the hot dal and serve.

Per serving: 420 Calories; 11.4g Fat; 57.6g Carbs; 24.9g Protein; 6.9g Sugars

STOCKS & SAUCES

369. Chicken and Vegetable Stock

(Ready in about 1 hour 10 minutes | Servings 9)

Ingredients

1 chicken carcass
2 carrots, cut into 2-inch pieces
1 celery rib, cut into 2-inch pieces
1 large onion, quartered
Sea salt, to taste
1 teaspoon mixed peppercorns
1 bay leaf
1 bunch parsley
9 cups cold water

Directions

Place all ingredients in the inner pot.

Secure the lid. Choose the "Soup/Broth" mode and cook for 40 minutes at High pressure. Once cooking is complete, use a natural pressure release for 20 minutes; carefully remove the lid.

Remove the bones and vegetables with a slotted spoon. Use immediately or store for later use.

Bon appétit!

Per serving: 79 Calories; 2.9g Fat; 2.6g Carbs; 21.9g Protein; 1.2g Sugars

370. Chicken and Herb Broth

(Ready in about 2 hours 15 minutes | Servings 10)

Ingredients

Chicken bones from 3 pounds roast chicken
1 parsnip
1 celery
2 tablespoons fresh parsley
1 tablespoon fresh thyme
2 tablespoons fresh coriander
1 teaspoon fresh dill
2 tablespoons cider vinegar
1 teaspoon sea salt
1 teaspoon ground black pepper

Directions

Place all ingredients in the inner pot. Add cold water until the pot is 2/3 full.

Secure the lid. Choose the "Soup/Broth" mode and cook for 120 minutes at Low pressure. Once cooking is complete, use a natural pressure release for 10 minutes; carefully remove the lid.

Remove the bones and vegetables using a metal spoon with holes and discard. Pour the liquid through the sieve into the bowl.

Use immediately or store in your refrigerator. Bon appétit!

Per serving: 69 Calories; 2.3g Fat; 3.6g Carbs; 8.5g Protein; 1g Sugars

371. Classic Fish Stock

(Ready in about 55 minutes | Servings 8)

Ingredients

2 pounds meaty bones and heads of halibut, washed
2 lemongrass stalks, chopped
2 carrots, chopped
1 parsnip, chopped
1 onion, quartered
2 sprigs rosemary
2 sprigs thyme
2 tablespoons olive oil

Directions

Place all ingredients in the inner pot. Add cold water until the pot is 2/3 full.

Secure the lid. Choose the "Soup/Broth" mode and cook for 40 minutes at High pressure. Once cooking is complete, use a natural pressure release for 10 minutes; carefully remove the lid.

Strain the vegetables and fish. Bon appétit!

Per serving: 63 Calories; 3.5g Fat; 2.7g Carbs; 4.9g Protein; 1.3g Sugars

372. Homemade Shrimp Stock

(Ready in about 55 minutes | Servings 8)

Ingredients

Shrimp shells from 3 pounds shrimp
8 cups water
1/2 cup cilantro, chopped
2 celery stalks, diced
4 cloves garlic
1 onion, quartered
1 teaspoon mixed peppercorns
1 tablespoon sea salt
2 bay leaves
4 tablespoons olive oil

Directions

Add all ingredients to the inner pot.

Secure the lid. Choose the "Soup/Broth" mode and cook for 30 minutes at High pressure. Once cooking is complete, use a natural pressure release for 10 minutes; carefully remove the lid.

Strain the shrimp shells and vegetables using a colander. Bon appétit!

Per serving: 69 Calories; 6.7g Fat; 1.9g Carbs; 0.3g Protein; 0.7g Sugars

373. White Chicken Stock

(Ready in about 1 hour | Servings 10)

Ingredients

2 pounds chicken white meat
1 white onion, quartered
1 leek, white parts
2 parsnips, sliced thickly
1 celery rib, sliced thickly
2 bay leaves
2 stalks flat-leaf parsley
1/2 teaspoon dried dill weed
1 teaspoon mixed peppercorns

Directions

Add all ingredients to the inner pot.

Secure the lid. Choose the "Soup/Broth" mode and cook for 40 minutes at High pressure. Once cooking is complete, use a natural pressure release for 20 minutes; carefully remove the lid.

Discard the vegetables and bones; save the chicken meat for later use. Bon appétit!

Per serving: 53 Calories; 1.1g Fat; 5.1g Carbs; 5.7g Protein; 1.5g Sugars

374. French Brown Stock

(Ready in about 2 hours 10 minutes | Servings 10)

Ingredients

3 pounds meaty pork bones
2 carrots, chopped
1 celery stalk, chopped
2 brown onions, quartered
1 tablespoon olive oil

Directions

Add all ingredients to the inner pot of your Instant Pot.

Secure the lid. Choose the "Soup/Broth" mode and cook for 120 minutes at Low pressure. Once cooking is complete, use a natural pressure release for 10 minutes; carefully remove the lid.

Remove the bones and vegetables using a metal spoon with holes and discard. Pour the liquid through the sieve into the bowl.

Use immediately or store in your refrigerator. Bon appétit!

Per serving: 91 Calories; 4.1g Fat; 3.3g Carbs; 9.9g Protein; 1.5g Sugars

375. Simple Court Bouillon

(Ready in about 45 minutes | Servings 8)

Ingredients

1 tablespoon salt
1 teaspoon mixed peppercorns
1 cup white wine
2 onions, sliced
2 celery ribs, sliced
2 carrots, sliced
2 bay leaves
2 sprig fresh rosemary
A bunch of fresh parsley
1 lemon, sliced
2 tablespoons olive oil

Directions

Add all ingredients to the inner pot of your Instant Pot. Add cold water until the inner pot is 2/3 full.

Secure the lid. Choose the "Soup/Broth" mode and cook for 30 minutes at High pressure. Once cooking is complete, use a natural pressure release for 10 minutes; carefully remove the lid.

Discard the vegetables. Bon appétit!

Per serving: 55 Calories; 3.4g Fat; 1.6g Carbs; 0.1g Protein; 0.6g Sugars

376. Beef Bone Broth

(Ready in about 3 hours 5 minutes | Servings 8)

Ingredients

3 pounds frozen beef bones
2 onions, halved
2 stalks celery, chopped
2 carrots, chopped
4 cloves garlic, whole
2 bay leaves
2 tablespoons apple cider vinegar
1 teaspoon sea salt
1 teaspoon black pepper
8 cups water

Directions

Start by preheating your oven to 390 degrees F. Line a baking pan with aluminum foil.

Place the beef bones, onions, celery, carrots, and garlic on the baking pan. Roast for 40 to 45 minutes.

Transfer the roasted beef bones and vegetables to the inner pot of your Instant Pot. Add the bay leaves, apple cider vinegar, sea salt, pepper, and boiling water to the inner pot.

Secure the lid. Choose the "Manual" mode and cook for 120 minutes at High pressure. Once cooking is complete, use a natural pressure release for 20 minutes; carefully remove the lid.

Remove the beef bones and vegetables and discard. Pour the broth through a strainer. Enjoy!

Per serving: 65 Calories; 2.4g Fat; 4.6g Carbs; 6.7g Protein; 1.9g Sugars

377. Roasted Vegetable Stock

(Ready in about 1 hour 15 minutes | Servings 10)

Ingredients

4 carrots, cut into 2-inch pieces
4 medium celery ribs, cut into 2-inch pieces
2 onions, peeled and quartered
2 sprigs fresh rosemary
2 sprigs fresh thyme
3 tablespoons olive oil
Kosher salt and black peppercorns, to taste
1 cup dry white wine
10 cups water

Directions

Start by preheating your oven to 400 degrees F. Grease a large roasting pan with cooking spray

Place the carrots, celery, onions, and herbs in the prepared roasting pan. Roast, tossing halfway through the cooking time, until the vegetables are tender about 35 minutes.

Transfer the vegetables to the inner pot. Add the remaining ingredients.

Secure the lid. Choose the "Soup/Broth" mode and cook for 30 minutes at High pressure. Once cooking is complete, use a natural pressure release for 10 minutes; carefully remove the lid.

Strain the broth through a fine-mesh sieve and discard the solids. Let it cool completely before storing.

Per serving: 56 Calories; 3.4g Fat; 3.2g Carbs; 0.3g Protein; 1.4g Sugars

378. Home-Style Pork Stock

(Ready in about 55 minutes | Servings 10)

Ingredients

2 pounds pork bones
4 celery stalks, cut into large chunks
4 carrots, cut into large chunks
1 onion, quartered
3 garlic cloves, smashed
2 bay leaves
Sea salt and black peppercorns, to taste
10 cups water, divided in half

Directions

Preheat your oven to 400 degrees F. Coat a roasting pan with a piece of aluminum foil; brush with a little oil.

Arrange the pork bones and vegetables on the prepared roasting pan. Roast in the preheated oven for 25 to 30 minutes.

Transfer the roasted pork bones and vegetables to the inner pot of your Instant Pot. Now, stir in the bay leaves, salt, black peppercorns, and water.

Secure the lid. Choose the "Manual" mode and cook for 25 minutes at High pressure. Once cooking is complete, use a quick pressure release; carefully remove the lid.

Strain the stock and discard the solids. Keep in your refrigerator or freezer if desired. Enjoy!

Per serving: 91 Calories; 4.1g Fat; 3.3g Carbs; 9.9g Protein; 1.5g Sugars

379. Vegan Tikka Masala Sauce

(Ready in about 30 minutes | Servings 4)

Ingredients

2 teaspoons olive oil
1 onion, chopped
4 cloves garlic, chopped
1 (1-inch) piece fresh ginger, peeled and grated
1 bird's eye chili, minced
1 bell pepper, seeded and chopped
Sea salt and ground black pepper, to taste
1 teaspoon cayenne pepper
1 teaspoon coriander powder
1/2 teaspoon turmeric powder
1 teaspoon Garam Masala
2 ripe tomatoes, pureed
1 cup vegetable broth
1 cup plain coconut yogurt

Directions

Press the "Sauté" button to preheat your Instant Pot. Add the oil and sauté the onion for about 3 minutes or until tender and fragrant.

Now, add the garlic, ginger and peppers; continue to sauté an additional minute or until they are aromatic.

Add the spices, tomatoes, and broth.

Secure the lid. Choose the "Manual" mode and cook for 11 minutes at High pressure. Once cooking is complete, use a natural pressure release for 10 minutes; carefully remove the lid.

Afterwards, add the coconut yogurt to the inner pot and stir to combine. Serve with chickpeas or roasted vegetables. Enjoy!

Per serving: 206 Calories; 17.2g Fat; 12.2g Carbs; 4.1g Protein; 6.1g Sugars

380. Easy Herby Tomato Sauce

(Ready in about 45 minutes | Servings 6)

Ingredients

2 (28-ounce) cans tomatoes, crushed
3 tablespoons olive oil
3 cloves garlic, minced
1/2 teaspoon dried rosemary
1/2 teaspoon dried basil
1/2 tablespoon dried oregano
1 onion, quartered
Kosher salt and freshly ground black pepper, to taste
1 teaspoon tamari sauce
2 tablespoons fresh parsley leaves, finely chopped

Directions

Reserve 1 cup of the crushed tomatoes.

Press the "Sauté" button and heat olive oil. Once hot, cook the garlic for a minute or so or until it is fragrant but not browned.

Now, stir in the rosemary, basil, and oregano; continue to sauté for 30 seconds more. Stir in the tomatoes, onion, salt, and pepper.

Secure the lid. Choose the "Soup/Broth" mode and cook for 40 minutes at High pressure. Once cooking is complete, use a quick pressure release; carefully remove the lid.

Add the reserved tomatoes, tamari sauce and parsley to your tomato sauce. Bon appétit!

Per serving: 115 Calories; 7.5g Fat; 12.1g Carbs; 2.6g Protein; 7.9g Sugars

381. Sicilian-Style Meat Sauce

(Ready in about 55 minutes | Servings 10)

Ingredients

2 tablespoons olive oil
2 ½ pounds pork butt
1 onion, chopped
4 garlic cloves, pressed
1/4 cup Malvasia wine, or other Sicilian wine
2 fresh tomatoes, pureed
5 ounces tomato paste
2 bay leaves
2 tablespoons fresh cilantro, chopped
1 teaspoon dried basil
1 teaspoon dried rosemary
1/2 teaspoon cayenne pepper
1/2 teaspoon black pepper, freshly cracked
1/2 teaspoon salt
1 cup chicken broth

Directions

Press the "Sauté" button and heat the oil. When the oil starts to sizzle, cook the pork until no longer pink.

Add the onion and garlic and continue to cook for a few minutes more or until they are tender and fragrant. Add a splash of wine to deglaze the pot.

Stir in the other ingredients.

Secure the lid. Choose the "Meat/Stew" mode and cook for 35 minutes at High pressure. Once cooking is complete, use a natural pressure release for 15 minutes; carefully remove the lid.

Next, remove the meat from the inner pot; shred the meat, discarding the bones. Return the meat to your sauce and serve over pasta if desired.

Per serving: 378 Calories; 24.5g Fat; 3.2g Carbs; 34.2g Protein; 1.1g Sugars

382. Homemade Applesauce with Dates

(Ready in about 25 minutes | Servings 8)

Ingredients

6 Honeycrisp apples, peeled, cored and chopped
1 cup water
1 tablespoon fresh lemon juice
1/4 teaspoon ground cloves
1/2 teaspoon cinnamon powder
10 dates, pitted and chopped

Directions

Add all ingredients to the inner pot; stir to combine.

Secure the lid. Choose the "Manual" mode and cook for 10 minutes at High pressure. Once cooking is complete, use a natural pressure release for 10 minutes; carefully remove the lid.

Mash the apple mixture to the desired consistency. Serve warm or cold.

Per serving: 97 Calories; 0.3g Fat; 25.7g Carbs; 0.6g Protein; 19.8g Sugars

383. Mixed Berry Sauce

(Ready in about 25 minutes | Servings 12)

Ingredients

2 cups frozen blueberries, thawed
2 cups frozen raspberries, thawed
2 cups frozen strawberries, thawed
1/2 cup granulated sugar
1 teaspoon cornstarch
1 cup water
2 tablespoons orange juice
1/2 cup cream cheese, at room temperature

Directions

Add the berries, sugar, and cornstarch, and water to the inner pot; stir to combine.

Secure the lid. Choose the "Manual" mode and cook for 10 minutes at High pressure. Once cooking is complete, use a natural pressure release for 10 minutes; carefully remove the lid.

Stir in the orange juice and cream cheese; stir to combine and serve with waffles or pancakes.

Per serving: 117 Calories; 3g Fat; 22.4g Carbs; 1.2g Protein; 17.5g Sugars

384. Easiest Marinara Sauce Ever

(Ready in about 25 minutes | Servings 8)

Ingredients

4 tablespoons olive oil
4 garlic cloves, minced
4 tablespoons tomato paste
1 (28-ounce) can crushed tomatoes with juice
1 cup water
Sea salt to taste
2 tablespoons fresh basil, minced
1 tablespoon fresh parsley, minced

Directions

Press the "Sauté" button and heat olive oil. Once hot, cook the garlic for a minute or so or until it is fragrant but not browned.

Now, stir in the remaining ingredients.

Secure the lid. Choose the "Soup/Broth" mode and cook for 40 minutes at High pressure. Once cooking is complete, use a quick pressure release; carefully remove the lid. Bon appétit!

Per serving: 86 Calories; 7g Fat; 5.4g Carbs; 1.3g Protein; 3.6g Sugars

385. Beef Bolognese Pasta Sauce

(Ready in about 20 minutes | Servings 4)

Ingredients

2 tablespoons olive oil
1 pound ground beef
1 onion, chopped
1 teaspoon fresh garlic, minced
Sea salt and ground black pepper, to taste
1 teaspoon brown sugar
1/2 teaspoon dried sage
1 teaspoon dried oregano
1 teaspoon dried basil
1/2 teaspoon cayenne pepper, or to taste
2 cups beef broth
2 ripe tomatoes, pureed
2 tablespoons tomato ketchup

Directions

Press the "Sauté" button and heat the oil. When the oil starts to sizzle, cook the ground beef until no longer pink; crumble it with a wooden spatula.

Add the onion and garlic and continue to cook for a few minutes more or until they are tender and fragrant. Add a splash of beef broth to deglaze the pot.

Stir in the remaining ingredients; stir to combine well.

Secure the lid. Choose the "Manual" mode and cook for 6 minutes at High pressure. Once cooking is complete, use a natural pressure release for 5 minutes; carefully remove the lid.

Serve over pasta if desired. Bon appétit!

Per serving: 358 Calories; 20.3g Fat; 8.7g Carbs; 34.1g Protein; 4.7g Sugars

386. 20-Minute Chicken Ragù

(Ready in about 20 minutes | Servings 4)

Ingredients

2 tablespoons olive oil
1 pound ground chicken
1 onion, chopped
2 cloves garlic, minced
1/4 cup dry red wine
1 stalk celery, chopped
1 bell pepper, chopped
1 teaspoon fresh basil, chopped
1 teaspoon fresh rosemary, chopped
1 teaspoon cayenne pepper
Salt and fresh ground pepper to taste
2 cups tomato sauce
1 cup chicken bone broth

Directions

Press the "Sauté" button and heat the oil. When the oil starts to sizzle, cook the ground chicken until no longer pink; crumble it with a wooden spatula.

Add the onion and garlic to the browned chicken; let it cook for a minute or so. Add a splash of wine to deglaze the pan.

Stir in the remaining ingredients.

Secure the lid. Choose the "Manual" mode and cook for 6 minutes at High pressure. Once cooking is complete, use a natural pressure release for 10 minutes; carefully remove the lid. Bon appétit!

Per serving: 431 Calories; 18g Fat; 33.7g Carbs; 29.1g Protein; 17.1g Sugars

387. Perfect Cranberry Sauce

(Ready in about 20 minutes | Servings 8)

Ingredients

1 ½ pounds fresh cranberries, rinsed
2 blood oranges, juiced
1 tablespoon blood orange zest
3/4 cup sugar
1/4 cup golden cane syrup
2-3 cloves
1 cinnamon stick
1 teaspoon vanilla extract

Directions

Add the cranberries to the inner pot of your Instant Pot.

Add the remaining ingredients to the inner pot; stir to combine well.

Secure the lid. Choose the "Manual" mode and cook for 3 minutes at High pressure. Once cooking is complete, use a natural pressure release for 10 minutes; carefully remove the lid. Bon appétit!

Let it cool. Serve your sauce chilled or at room temperature. Bon appétit!

Per serving: 431 Calories; 18g Fat; 33.7g Carbs; 29.1g Protein; 17.1g Sugars

388. Spanish Chorizo Sauce

(Ready in about 20 minutes | Servings 4)

Ingredients

1 tablespoon olive oil
1 pound Chorizo sausage, sliced
1 onion, chopped
1 teaspoon garlic, minced
1 sweet pepper, seeded and finely chopped
1 habanero pepper, seeded and minced
2 tablespoons sugar
1 teaspoon dried basil
1 teaspoon dried rosemary
1 teaspoon red pepper flakes
Sea salt and freshly ground black pepper, to taste
1 (28-ounce) can diced tomatoes, with juice
1 cup chicken broth

Directions

Press the "Sauté" button and heat the oil. When the oil starts to sizzle, cook the Chorizo until no longer pink; crumble it with a wooden spatula.

Add the onion, garlic, and peppers and cook for a minute or so. Add a splash of chicken broth to deglaze the pan.

Stir in the remaining ingredients.

Secure the lid. Choose the "Manual" mode and cook for 6 minutes at High pressure. Once cooking is complete, use a natural pressure release for 10 minutes; carefully remove the lid. Bon appétit!

Per serving: 385 Calories; 24.9g Fat; 20.2g Carbs; 21.1g Protein; 11.1g Sugars

389. Carolina-Style Sticky Barbecue Sauce

(Ready in about 20 minutes | Servings 6)

Ingredients

2 tablespoons butter
1 shallot, chopped
2 cloves garlic, minced
2 cups tomato sauce
1/2 cup cider vinegar
2 tablespoons coconut sugar
1/3 cup molasses
2 tablespoons Worcestershire sauce
1 teaspoon yellow mustard
1 teaspoon hot sauce
Kosher salt and ground black pepper
1/2 teaspoon paprika
1 cup vegetable broth

Directions

Press the "Sauté" button and melt the butter. Then, sauté the shallot until tender and translucent, about 4 minutes. Add the garlic and cook for a further 30 seconds.

Stir in the remaining ingredients.

Secure the lid. Choose the "Manual" mode and cook for 5 minutes at High pressure. Once cooking is complete, use a natural pressure release for 5 minutes; carefully remove the lid. Bon appétit!

Per serving: 215 Calories; 4.4g Fat; 37.5g Carbs; 3.4g Protein; 27.3g Sugars

390. Zesty Pear Sauce

(Ready in about 25 minutes | Servings 8)

Ingredients

1 ½ pounds cup pears, cored, peeled and chopped
2 teaspoons freshly squeezed lemon juice
1/2 cup sugar
1 teaspoon ground cinnamon
1/2 teaspoon ground cardamom
1 teaspoon vanilla essence

Directions

Add all ingredients to the inner pot; stir to combine.

Secure the lid. Choose the "Manual" mode and cook for 10 minutes at High pressure. Once cooking is complete, use a natural pressure release for 10 minutes; carefully remove the lid.

Mash the pear mixture to the desired consistency. Serve at room temperature or cold. Bon appétit!

Per serving: 73 Calories; 0.1g Fat; 19.2g Carbs; 0.3g Protein; 14.4g Sugars

391. Spinach and Artichoke Dipping Sauce

(Ready in about 15 minutes | Servings 8)

Ingredients

2 tablespoons butter
1 onion, chopped
2 cloves garlic, minced
10 ounces artichoke hearts
1 cup chicken broth
Sea salt and freshly ground black pepper, to taste
1 teaspoon red pepper flakes
1 pound fresh or frozen spinach leaves
9 ounces cream cheese
1 cup goat cheese, crumbled

Directions

Press the "Sauté" button and melt the butter. Then, sauté the onion and garlic until just tender and fragrant.

Then, add the artichoke hearts, broth, salt, black pepper, and red pepper flakes.

Secure the lid. Choose the "Manual" mode and cook for 5 minutes at High pressure. Once cooking is complete, use a quick pressure release; carefully remove the lid.

Add the spinach and cheese to the inner pot; seal the lid and let it sit in the residual heat until thoroughly warmed. Enjoy!

Per serving: 222 Calories; 17.4g Fat; 8.6g Carbs; 9.9g Protein; 2.4g Sugars

392. Rich Southwest Cheese and Bacon Sauce

(Ready in about 15 minutes | Servings 10)

Ingredients

4 ounces bacon, diced
1 onion, chopped
1 red chili pepper, seeded and minced
2 cloves garlic, pressed
2 ripe tomatoes, chopped
1/2 teaspoon ground cumin
1/2 teaspoon turmeric powder
Kosher salt and ground black pepper, to taste
1 cup vegetable broth
10 ounces Cottage cheese, at room temperature
1 cup Pepper Jack cheese, grated

Directions

Press the "Sauté" button to preheat your Instant Pot. Then, cook the bacon for 2 to 3 minutes. Reserve.

Add the onion and pepper to the inner pot and continue to cook until they are fragrant. Stir in the garlic and continue to sauté for 30 seconds more.

Now, add the tomatoes, spices, and broth.

Secure the lid. Choose the "Manual" mode and cook for 5 minutes at High pressure. Once cooking is complete, use a quick pressure release; carefully remove the lid.

Lastly, stir in the cheese. Seal the lid again and let it sit in the residual heat until the cheese melts.

Ladle into a nice serving bowl, top with the reserved bacon, and serve.

Per serving: 135 Calories; 9.5g Fat; 4.5g Carbs; 8.3g Protein; 2.5g Sugars

393. Mexican-Style Black Bean Sauce

(Ready in about 35 minutes | Servings 8)

Ingredients

2 tablespoons olive oil
1 brown onion, chopped
3 garlic cloves, chopped
1 jalapeño pepper, seeded and minced
1 teaspoon dried Mexican oregano
1/2 teaspoon ground cumin
Sea salt and ground black pepper, to taste
1 ½ cups black beans, rinsed, drained
1 ½ cups chicken broth
1/4 cup fresh cilantro, chopped
1/2 cup Pico de Gallo

Directions

Press the "Sauté" button and heat the olive oil until sizzling. Once hot, cook the onion for 3 to 4 minutes or until tender and fragrant.

After that, stir in the garlic; continue sautéing an additional 30 to 40 seconds.

Add the jalapeño pepper, oregano, cumin, salt, black pepper, beans, and broth to the inner pot.

Secure the lid. Choose the "Bean/Chili" mode and cook for 25 minutes at High pressure. Once cooking is complete, use a quick pressure release; carefully remove the lid.

Then, mash your beans with potato masher or use your blender. Serve garnished with cilantro and Pico de Gallo. Bon appétit!

Per serving: 181 Calories; 4.4g Fat; 27.3g Carbs; 9.5g Protein; 3.1g Sugars

394. Eggplant Light Sauce with Wine

(Ready in about 10 minutes | Servings 6)

Ingredients

2 tablespoons olive oil
1 pound eggplants, sliced
4 garlic cloves, minced
2 tomatoes, chopped
1 cup white wine
1 teaspoon oregano
1/2 teaspoon rosemary

1 teaspoon basil
Sea salt and ground black pepper, to taste
2 tablespoons tahini (sesame butter)
1/2 cup Romano cheese, freshly grated

Directions

Press the "Sauté" button and heat the olive oil. Then, cook the eggplant slices until they are charred at the bottom. Work with batches.

Add the garlic, tomatoes, wine, and spices.

Secure the lid. Choose the "Bean/Chili" mode and cook for 3 minutes at High pressure. Once cooking is complete, use a quick pressure release; carefully remove the lid.

Press the "Sauté" button again to thicken the cooking liquid. Add the tahini paste and stir to combine. Top with Romano cheese and serve.

Per serving: 147 Calories; 10.4g Fat; 9.3g Carbs; 5.2g Protein; 4.6g Sugars

395. Perfect Homemade Salsa

(Ready in about 40 minutes | Servings 8)

Ingredients

2 onions, chopped
2 garlic cloves, pressed
2 ripe tomatoes, crushed
12 ounces canned tomato paste
2 sweet peppers, chopped

2 chili peppers, chopped
1/2 cup rice vinegar
2 tablespoons brown sugar
Sea salt and red pepper, to taste
1 teaspoon dried Mexican oregano

Directions

Put all ingredients into the inner pot of your Instant Pot.

Secure the lid. Choose the "Manual" mode and cook for 25 minutes at High pressure. Once cooking is complete, use a natural pressure release for 10 minutes; carefully remove the lid.

Allow your salsa to cool completely; store in your refrigerator or freezer. Bon appétit!

Per serving: 83 Calories; 0.4g Fat; 18.8g Carbs; 3.2g Protein; 10.1g Sugars

396. Salted Caramel Sauce

(Ready in about 20 minutes | Servings 6)

Ingredients

1/2 cup water
1 1/3 cups granulated sugar
4 tablespoons butter, cut into small pieces

1/2 cup heavy whipping cream
1/2 teaspoon coarse sea salt
1 teaspoon vanilla
A pinch of cardamom

Directions

Press the "Sauté" button to preheat the Instant Pot; now, cook the sugar and water, stirring frequently, until the sugar has dissolved.

Let the mixture boiling until it turns an amber color or about 10 minutes.

Then, whisk in the butter, followed by the remaining ingredients.

Allow your sauce to cool. It will thicken up once it's cooled in your refrigerator. Bon appétit!

Per serving: 191 Calories; 11.4g Fat; 22.4g Carbs; 0.3g Protein; 22.1g Sugars

397. Raspberry Ginger Coulis

(Ready in about 20 minutes | Servings 6)

Ingredients

1 (12-ounce) bag fresh or frozen raspberries
1 cup brown sugar
1 cup water
1/2 cup fresh orange juice

1 tablespoon fresh ginger root, peeled and finely grated
Zest from 1 organic orange, finely grated

Directions

Add all the ingredients to the inner pot of your Instant Pot.

Secure the lid. Choose the "Manual" mode and cook for 3 minutes at High pressure. Once cooking is complete, use a natural pressure release for 10 minutes; carefully remove the lid.

Let it cool. Serve your sauce chilled or at room temperature. Bon appétit!

Per serving: 134 Calories; 0.2g Fat; 34g Carbs; 0.5g Protein; 30.3g Sugars

398. Classic Gravy Sauce

(Ready in about 15 minutes | Servings 6)

Ingredients

3 cups pan juices
1/3 cup cornstarch
1/3 cup cold water

Salt and ground black pepper, to taste
1/2 teaspoon cayenne pepper

Directions

Press the "Sauté" button to preheat the Instant Pot; then, cook the pan juices for about 3 minutes, bringing it to a boil.

Whisk the cornstarch with cold water until the cornstarch has dissolved; then whisk the cornstarch slurry into the pan juices.

Add the salt, black pepper, and cayenne pepper; continue cooking on the lowest setting until your sauce has reduced slightly and the flavors have concentrated.

Use the "Keep Warm" function to keep your sauce warm until ready to serve.

Per serving: 89 Calories; 0.2g Fat; 21.9g Carbs; 0.2g Protein; 13.3g Sugars

399. Perfect Hot Sauce

(Ready in about 40 minutes | Servings 10)

Ingredients

1 tablespoon butter, melted
1 banana shallot, chopped
1 teaspoon garlic, minced
5 jalapeño peppers, seeded and chopped
5 serrano peppers, seeded and chopped

2 tomatoes, chopped
1 cup white vinegar
1 cup water
2 tablespoons white sugar
Sea salt and ground black pepper, to taste

Directions

Press the "Sauté" button and melt the butter. Once hot, cook the shallot for 3 to 4 minute or until it is tender and fragrant.

Now, add the garlic and continue to cook an additional 30 seconds or until aromatic.

Add the remaining ingredients.

Secure the lid. Choose the "Manual" mode and cook for 25 minutes at High pressure. Once cooking is complete, use a natural pressure release for 10 minutes; carefully remove the lid.

Let it cool. Serve your sauce hot or at room temperature. Bon appétit!

Per serving: 39 Calories; 1.2g Fat; 5.8g Carbs; 0.8g Protein; 3.9g Sugars

FISH & SEAFOOD

400. Calamari with Roasted Pimentos

(Ready in about 1 hour | Servings 4)

Ingredients

3 Pimentos, stem and core removed
2 tablespoons olive oil
1/2 cup leeks, chopped
2 cloves garlic chopped
1 ½ cups stock, preferably homemade
2 tablespoons fish sauce
1/3 cup dry sherry
Seas salt and ground black pepper, to taste
1/2 teaspoon red pepper flakes, crushed
1 teaspoon dried rosemary, chopped
1 teaspoon dried thyme, chopped
1 ½ pounds frozen calamari, thawed and drained
2 tablespoons fresh chives, chopped

Directions

Split your Pimentos into halves and place them over the flame. Cook, turning a couple of times, until the skin is blistering and blackened.

Allow them to stand for 30 minutes; peel your Pimentos and coarsely chop them.

Press the "Sauté" button to heat up your Instant Pot; add olive oil. Once hot, cook the leeks until tender and fragrant, about 4 minutes.

Now, stir in the garlic and cook an additional 30 seconds or until just browned and aromatic.

Add the stock, fish sauce, dry sherry, salt, pepper, red pepper flakes, rosemary, and thyme. Add the roasted Pimentos. Lastly, place the calamari on top. Pour in 3 cups of water.

Secure the lid. Select the "Manual" mode. Cook for 20 minutes at High pressure. Once cooking is complete, use a quick release; remove the lid carefully.

Serve warm garnished with fresh chopped chives. Enjoy!

Per serving: 325 Calories; 10.7g Fat; 17.2g Carbs; 38.6g Protein; 6.5g Sugars

401. Curried Halibut Steaks

(Ready in about 15 minutes | Servings 4)

Ingredients

1 tablespoon olive oil
1 cup scallions, chopped
1/2 cup beef bone broth
1 pound halibut steaks, rinsed and cubed
1 cup tomato purée
1 jalapeño pepper, seeded and minced
1 teaspoon ginger garlic paste
1 tablespoon red curry paste
1/2 teaspoon ground cumin
1 cup coconut milk, unsweetened
Salt and ground black pepper, to taste

Directions

Press the "Sauté" button to preheat your Instant Pot. Now, heat the olive oil; cook the scallions until tender and fragrant.

Then, use the broth to deglaze the bottom of the inner pot. Stir in the remaining ingredients.

Secure the lid. Choose the "Manual" mode and Low pressure; cook for 7 minutes. Once cooking is complete, use a quick pressure release; carefully remove the lid.

Taste, adjust the seasonings and serve right now.

Per serving: 325 Calories; 10.7g Fat; 17.2g Carbs; 38.6g Protein; 6.5g Sugars

402. Fisherman's Carp Pilaf

(Ready in about 15 minutes | Servings 4)

Ingredients

1 tablespoon olive oil
1 cup chicken stock
1 cup tomato paste
1 teaspoon dried rosemary, crushed
1 tablespoon dried parsley
1/2 teaspoon dried marjoram leaves
Sea salt and ground black pepper, to taste
1/2 teaspoon dried oregano leaves
1 cup Arborio rice
1 pound carp, chopped

Directions

Simply throw all of the above ingredients into your Instant Pot.

Secure the lid. Choose the "Manual" mode and High pressure; cook for 6 minutes. Once cooking is complete, use a quick pressure release; carefully remove the lid.

Serve in individual serving bowls, garnished with fresh lemon slices.

Per serving: 336 Calories; 16.7g Fat; 28.4g Carbs; 28.6g Protein; 8.8g Sugars

403. Tilapia Fillets with Cremini Mushrooms

(Ready in about 15 minutes | Servings 3)

Ingredients

3 tilapia fillets
1/2 teaspoon sea salt
Freshly ground black pepper, to taste
1 teaspoon cayenne pepper
1 cup Cremini mushrooms, thinly sliced
1/2 cup yellow onions, sliced
2 cloves garlic, peeled and minced
2 sprigs thyme, leaves picked
2 sprigs rosemary, leaves picked
2 tablespoons avocado oil

Directions

Season the tilapia fillets with salt, black pepper, and cayenne pepper on all sides. Place the tilapia fillets in the steaming basket fitted for your Instant Pot.

Place the sliced mushroom and yellow onions on top of the fillets. Add the garlic, thyme, and rosemary; drizzle avocado oil over everything.

Add 1 ½ cups of water to the base of your Instant Pot. Add the steaming basket to the Instant Pot and secure the lid.

Select the "Manual" mode. Cook for 8 minutes at Low pressure.

Once cooking is complete, use a quick release; remove the lid carefully. Serve immediately.

Per serving: 218 Calories; 12.9g Fat; 2.2g Carbs; 23.6g Protein; 0.7g Sugars

404. Shrimp in Herbed Tomato Sauce

(Ready in about 15 minutes | Servings 4)

Ingredients

1 tablespoon butter, at room temperature
1 cup green onion, chopped
1 teaspoon garlic, minced
1 ½ pounds shrimp, peeled and deveined
1 tablespoon tamari sauce
1 sprig thyme
1 sprig rosemary
2 ripe tomatoes, chopped

Directions

Press the "Sauté" button to preheat your Instant Pot. Melt the butter and cook the green onions until they have softened.

Now, stir in the garlic and cook an additional 30 seconds or until it is aromatic. Add the rest of the above ingredients.

Secure the lid. Choose the "Manual" mode and Low pressure; cook for 3 minutes. Once cooking is complete, use a quick pressure release; carefully remove the lid.

Serve over hot jasmine rice and enjoy!

Per serving: 214 Calories; 5.4g Fat; 3.9g Carbs; 35.5g Protein; 2.5g Sugars

405. Elegant Trout Salad

(Ready in about 15 minutes | Servings 4)

Ingredients

2 tablespoons olive oil
1 yellow onion, chopped
2 garlic cloves, minced
1 green chili, seeded and minced
2 pieces ocean trout fillets, deboned and skinless
1 cup water
1/2 cup dry vermouth
Sea salt and ground black pepper, to taste
1/2 teaspoon sweet paprika
2 ripe Roma tomatoes, diced
8 ounces dry egg noodles
2 Lebanese cucumbers, chopped
1/2 bunch coriander, leaves picked, roughly chopped
1/4 cup freshly squeezed lime juice

Directions

Press the "Sauté" button to preheat your Instant Pot. Now, heat the olive oil and sauté the onion until translucent.

Stir in the garlic and chili; continue to sauté until they are fragrant.

Add the fish, water, vermouth, salt, black pepper, sweet paprika, tomatoes, and noodles.

Secure the lid. Choose the "Manual" mode and Low pressure; cook for 10 minutes. Once cooking is complete, use a quick pressure release; carefully remove the lid.

Flake the fish and allow the mixture to cool completely. Add the cucumbers and coriander. Drizzle fresh lime juice over the salad and serve. Bon appétit!

Per serving: 506 Calories; 13.6g Fat; 56g Carbs; 39.1g Protein; 12.1g Sugars

406. Tuna Fillets with Eschalots

(Ready in about 10 minutes | Servings 4)

Ingredients

2 lemons, 1 whole and 1 freshly squeezed
1 pound tuna fillets
Sea salt and ground black pepper, to taste

1 tablespoon dried parsley flakes
2 tablespoons butter, melted
2 eschalots, thinly sliced

Directions

Place 1 cup of water and lemon juice in the Instant Pot. Add a steamer basket too.

Place the tuna fillets in the steamer basket. Sprinkle the salt, pepper, and parsley over the fish; drizzle with butter and top with thinly sliced eschalots.

Secure the lid. Choose the "Steam" mode and Low pressure; cook for 3 minutes. Once cooking is complete, use a quick pressure release; carefully remove the lid.

Serve immediately with lemon. Bon appétit!

Per serving: 249 Calories; 9.1g Fat; 11.7g Carbs; 29.5g Protein; 5.6g Sugars

407. Chunky Tilapia Stew

(Ready in about 15 minutes | Servings 4)

Ingredients

2 tablespoons sesame oil
1 cup scallions, chopped
2 garlic cloves, minced
1/3 cup dry vermouth
1 cup shellfish stock
2 cups water
2 ripe plum tomatoes, crushed
Sea salt, to taste

1/4 teaspoon freshly ground black pepper, or more to taste
1 teaspoon hot paprika
1 pound tilapia fillets, boneless, skinless and diced
1 tablespoon fresh lime juice
1 teaspoon dried rosemary
1/2 teaspoon dried oregano
1/2 teaspoon dried basil

Directions

Press the "Sauté" button to preheat your Instant Pot. Heat the oil and sauté the scallions and garlic until fragrant.

Add a splash of vermouth to deglaze the bottom of the inner pot.

Secure the lid. Choose the "Manual" mode and High pressure; cook for 5 minutes. Once cooking is complete, use a quick pressure release; carefully remove the lid.

Serve with some extra lime slices if desired. Bon appétit!

Per serving: 221 Calories; 9.3g Fat; 4.9g Carbs; 25g Protein; 1.8g Sugars

408. Haddock Fillets with Black Beans

(Ready in about 10 minutes | Servings 2)

Ingredients

1 cup water
2 haddock fillets
2 teaspoons coconut butter, at room temperature
Salt and ground black pepper, to taste
2 sprigs thyme, chopped

1/4 teaspoon caraway seeds
1/2 teaspoon tarragon
1/2 teaspoon paprika
4 tomato slices
2 tablespoons fresh cilantro, roughly chopped
1 can black beans, drained

Directions

Add 1 cup of water to the bottom of your Instant Pot. Add a steamer insert.

Brush the haddock fillets with coconut butter. Now, season the haddock fillets with salt and pepper.

Place the haddock fillets on top of the steamer insert. Add thyme, caraway seeds, tarragon, and paprika. Place 2 tomato slices on top of each fillet.

Secure the lid and choose "Manual" setting. Cook for 3 minutes at Low pressure. Once cooking is complete, use a natural release; remove the lid carefully.

Transfer the haddock fillets to serving plates. Scatter chopped cilantro over each fillet and serve garnished with black beans. Bon appétit!

Per serving: 183 Calories; 4.8g Fat; 1.3g Carbs; 31.8g Protein; 0.8g Sugars

409. Foil-Packet Fish with Aioli

(Ready in about 15 minutes | Servings 2)

Ingredients

2 cod fish fillets
1/2 teaspoon seasoned salt
1/4 teaspoon ground black pepper, or more to taste
1/2 teaspoon mustard powder
1/2 teaspoon ancho chili powder
1 shallot, thinly sliced

1 lemon, cut into slices
For Aioli:
1 egg yolk
A pinch of salt
2 garlic cloves, minced
2 teaspoons fresh lemon juice
1/4 cup olive oil

Directions

Prepare your Instant Pot by adding 1 ½ cups of water and steamer basket to the Instant Pot.

Place a fish fillet in the center of each piece of foil. Season with salt, pepper, mustard powder, and chili powder.

Top with shallots and wrap tightly.

Secure the lid and choose "Manual" setting. Cook for 10 minutes at High pressure. Once cooking is complete, use a natural release; remove the lid carefully.

In your food processor, mix the egg, salt, garlic, and lemon juice. With the machine running, gradually and slowly add the olive oil.

Garnish the warm fish fillets with lemon slices; serve with aioli on the side. Bon appétit!

Per serving: 397 Calories; 30.1g Fat; 12.3g Carbs; 20.7g Protein; 4.8g Sugars

410. Baked Fish with Parmesan

(Ready in about 15 minutes | Servings 4)

Ingredients

2 ripe tomatoes, sliced
1 teaspoon dried rosemary
1 teaspoon dried marjoram
1/2 teaspoon dried thyme
4 mahi-mahi fillets

2 tablespoons butter, at room temperature
Sea salt and ground black pepper, to taste
8 ounces Parmesan cheese, freshly grated

Directions

Add 1 ½ cups of water and a rack to your Instant Pot.

Spritz a casserole dish with a nonstick cooking spray. Arrange the slices of tomatoes on the bottom of the dish. Add the herbs.

Place the mahi-mahi fillets on the top; drizzle the melted butter over the fish. Season it with salt and black pepper. Place the baking dish on the rack.

Secure the lid. Choose the "Manual" mode and Low pressure; cook for 9 minutes. Once cooking is complete, use a quick pressure release; carefully remove the lid.

Top with parmesan and seal the lid again; allow the cheese to melt and serve.

Per serving: 376 Calories; 22.1g Fat; 9.4g Carbs; 34.2g Protein; 0.8g Sugars

411. Salmon Steaks with Kale Pesto Sauce

(Ready in about 15 minutes | Servings 4)

Ingredients

1 pound salmon steaks
1 shallot, peeled and sliced
1/2 cup Kalamata olives
2 sprigs rosemary
2 tablespoons olive oil
1/2 teaspoon whole mixed peppercorns
Sea salt, to taste

Kale Pesto Sauce:
1 avocado
1 teaspoon garlic, crushed
2 tablespoons fresh parsley
1 cup kale
2 tablespoons fresh lemon juice
2 tablespoons extra-virgin olive oil

Directions

Prepare your Instant Pot by adding 1 ½ cups of water and a steamer basket to its bottom.

Place the salmon steaks in the steamer basket; add the shallots, olives, rosemary, olive oil, peppercorns, and salt.

Secure the lid. Choose the "Steam" mode and High pressure; cook for 5 minutes. Once cooking is complete, use a quick pressure release; carefully remove the lid.

Add the avocado, garlic, parsley, kale, and lemon juice to your blender. Then, mix on high until a loose paste forms.

Add the olive oil a little at a time and continue to blend until the desired consistency is reached; add a tablespoon or two of water if needed.

Serve the fish fillets with the pesto on the side. Bon appétit!

Per serving: 366 Calories; 27.1g Fat; 6.6g Carbs; 24.8g Protein; 0.7g Sugars

412. Saucy Parmesan Cod with Basmati Rice

(Ready in about 15 minutes | Servings 4)

Ingredients

2 cups basmati rice
2 cups water
1 ¼ pounds cod, slice into small pieces
Salt and ground black pepper, to taste
1 teaspoon paprika

2 bay leaves
1 teaspoon coriander
1 teaspoon lemon thyme
2 tablespoons lemon juice
1/2 cup heavy cream
1 cup Parmesan cheese, freshly grated

Directions

Choose the "Manual" button and cook the basmati rice with water for 4 minutes. Once cooking is complete, use a natural release; carefully remove the lid. Reserve.

Now, press the "Sauté" button on your Instant Pot. Add the remaining ingredients and cook until the Parmesan has melted.

Serve the fish mixture over the hot basmati rice and enjoy!

Per serving: 443 Calories; 25.4g Fat; 33.7g Carbs; 36.9g Protein; 1.1g Sugars

413. Lemon Butter Grouper

(Ready in about 15 minutes | Servings 4)

Ingredients

4 grouper fillets
4 tablespoons butter
2 tablespoons fresh lemon juice
2 garlic cloves, smashed

1/2 teaspoon sweet paprika
1/2 teaspoon dried basil
Sea salt and ground black pepper, to taste

Directions

Add 1 ½ cups of water and steamer basket to the Instant Pot. Then, place the fish fillets in the steamer basket.

Add the butter; drizzle with lemon juice; add the garlic, paprika, basil, salt, and black pepper.

Secure the lid. Choose the "Manual" mode and Low pressure; cook for 4 minutes. Once cooking is complete, use a quick pressure release; carefully remove the lid.

Serve immediately.

Per serving: 344 Calories; 14.1g Fat; 1.1g Carbs; 50.1g Protein; 0.2g Sugars

414. Tuna, Ham and Green Pea Chowder

(Ready in about 15 minutes | Servings 5)

Ingredients

2 tablespoons olive oil
4 slices ham, chopped
1 cup shallots, chopped
2 cloves garlic, minced
2 carrots, chopped
5 cups seafood stock
1 ¼ pounds tuna steak, diced

Sea salt and ground black pepper, to taste
1 teaspoon cayenne pepper
1/2 teaspoon ground bay leaf
1/2 teaspoon mustard powder
1 ½ cups double cream
1 ½ cups frozen green peas

Directions

Press the "Sauté" button to preheat your Instant Pot. Heat the oil and fry the ham until crispy.

Then, add the shallot and garlic; continue to cook an additional 2 minutes or until tender and fragrant.

Add the carrot, stock, tuna, salt, black pepper, cayenne pepper, ground bay leaf, and mustard powder.

Secure the lid. Choose the "Manual" mode and High pressure; cook for 6 minutes. Once cooking is complete, use a natural pressure release; carefully remove the lid.

Add the double cream and frozen peas. Press the "Sauté" button again and cook for a couple of minutes more or until heated through. Bon appétit!

Per serving: 360 Calories; 11.2g Fat; 25.7g Carbs; 38.5g Protein; 9.6g Sugars

415. Sinfully Delicious Ocean Trout Fillets

(Ready in about 15 minutes | Servings 4)

Ingredients

1 pound ocean trout fillets
Sea salt, to taste
1 teaspoon caraway seeds
1/2 teaspoon mustard seeds
1/2 teaspoon paprika
1/2 cup spring onions, chopped

2 garlic cloves, minced
1 teaspoon mixed peppercorns
2 tablespoons champagne vinegar
1 tablespoon fish sauce
2 ½ cups broth, preferably homemade

Directions

Place the steaming basket in your Instant Pot. Sprinkle the ocean trout fillets with salt, caraway seeds, mustard seeds, and paprika.

Place the ocean trout fillet in the steaming basket. Add the other ingredients.

Secure the lid and choose the "Manual" setting. Cook for 3 minutes at Low pressure. Once cooking is complete, use a quick release; carefully remove the lid.

You can thicken the sauce using the "Sauté" button. Bon appétit!

Per serving: 122 Calories; 2.2g Fat; 1.6g Carbs; 22.7g Protein; 0.5g Sugars

416. Red Snapper in Tomatillo-Mushroom Sauce

(Ready in about 15 minutes | Servings 4)

Ingredients

1/2 stick butter, at room temperature
2 shallots, peeled and chopped
2 garlic cloves, minced
1 cup brown mushrooms, thinly sliced
2 tablespoons coriander
2 tablespoons tomato ketchup

1 (11-ounce) can tomatillo, chopped
1 cup chicken stock, preferably homemade
1 pound red snapper, cut into bite-sized chunks
Salt and freshly ground black pepper, to taste

Directions

Press the "Sauté" button to preheat your Instant Pot. Then, melt the butter. Once hot, cook the shallots with garlic until tender and aromatic.

Stir in the mushrooms; cook an additional 3 minutes or until they have softened.

Stir the remaining ingredients into your Instant Pot.

Secure the lid and choose the "Manual" setting. Cook for 6 minutes at High pressure. Once cooking is complete, use a quick release; carefully remove the lid.

Serve over hot basmati rice if desired. Enjoy!

Per serving: 242 Calories; 13.6g Fat; 3.7g Carbs; 25.7g Protein; 1.7g Sugars

417. Portuguese-Style Fish Medley

(Ready in about 15 minutes | Servings 4)

Ingredients

1 pound fish, mixed pieces for fish soup, cut into bite-sized pieces
1 yellow onion, chopped
1 celery with leaves, chopped
2 carrots, chopped
2 cloves garlic, minced
1 green bell pepper, thinly sliced
2 tablespoons peanut oil
1 ½ cups seafood stock
1/3 cup dry vermouth
2 fresh tomatoes, puréed
1 tablespoon loosely packed saffron threads
Sea salt and ground black pepper, to taste
1 teaspoon Piri Piri
2 bay leaves
1/4 cup fresh cilantro, roughly chopped
1/2 lemon, sliced

Directions

Simply throw all of the above ingredients, except for the cilantro and lemon, into your Instant Pot.

Secure the lid and choose the "Manual" setting. Cook for 8 minutes at Low pressure. Once cooking is complete, use a quick release; carefully remove the lid.

Ladle the medley into individual bowls; serve with fresh cilantro and lemon. Enjoy!

Per serving: 342 Calories; 20.8g Fat; 14.7g Carbs; 24.6g Protein; 9.2g Sugars

418. Aromatic Prawns with Basmati Rice

(Ready in about 15 minutes | Servings 5)

Ingredients

2 tablespoons olive oil
1 cup red onions, thinly sliced
2 cloves garlic, pressed
2 bell peppers, seeded and thinly sliced
1 serrano pepper, seeded and thinly sliced
2 cups basmati rice
1 (14-ounce) can tomatoes, diced
2 ½ cups vegetable stock, preferably homemade
1 tablespoon tamari sauce
1 pound prawns, peeled and deveined
Sea salt and ground black pepper, to taste
1/2 teaspoon sweet paprika
1 teaspoon dried rosemary
1/2 teaspoon dried oregano
2 tablespoons fresh mint, roughly chopped

Directions

Press the "Sauté" button to preheat your Instant Pot. Then, heat the oil and sauté the onions until tender and translucent.

Stir in the garlic; continue to sauté until aromatic. Add the rest of the above ingredients, except for the mint, to the Instant Pot.

Secure the lid and choose the "Manual" setting. Cook for 3 minutes at Low pressure. Once cooking is complete, use a natural release; carefully remove the lid.

Serve garnished with fresh mint leaves. Bon appétit!

Per serving: 331 Calories; 17.6g Fat; 31.9g Carbs; 26.2g Protein; 4.6g Sugars

419. Easy Tuna Fillets with Onions

(Ready in about 10 minutes | Servings 2)

Ingredients

1 cup water
A few sprigs of tarragon
1 lemon, sliced
1 pound tuna filets
1 tablespoon butter, melted
Sea salt and freshly ground black pepper, to taste
1 large onion, sliced into rings

Directions

Put the water, herbs and lemon slices in the inner pot; now, place the steamer rack in the inner pot.

Lower the tuna fillets onto the rack. Add butter, salt, and pepper; top with onion slices.

Secure the lid. Choose the "Steam" mode and cook for 3 minutes at Low pressure. Once cooking is complete, use a quick pressure release; carefully remove the lid. Serve immediately.

Per serving: 333 Calories; 7g Fat; 8.7g Carbs; 56.3g Protein; 3.7g Sugars

420 Haddock Fillets with Steamed Green Beans

(Ready in about 15 minutes | Servings 4)

Ingredients

1 lime, cut into wedges
1/2 cup water
4 haddock fillets
1 rosemary sprig
2 thyme sprigs
1 tablespoon fresh parsley
4 teaspoons ghee
Sea salt and ground black pepper, to taste
2 cloves garlic, minced
4 cups green beans

Directions

Place the lime wedges and water in the inner pot. Add a steamer rack.

Lower the haddock fillets onto the rack; place the rosemary, thyme, parsley, and ghee on the haddock fillets. Season with salt and pepper.

Secure the lid. Choose the "Steam" mode and cook for 3 minutes at Low pressure. Once cooking is complete, use a quick pressure release; carefully remove the lid. Reserve.

Then, add the garlic and green beans to the inner pot.

Secure the lid. Choose the "Steam" mode and cook for 3 minutes at Low pressure. Once cooking is complete, use a quick pressure release; carefully remove the lid.

Serve the haddock fillets with green beans on the side. Bon appétit!

Per serving: 288 Calories; 13.1g Fat; 9.1g Carbs; 33.7g Protein; 1.9g Sugars

421. Greek-Style Shrimp with Feta Cheese

(Ready in about 15 minutes | Servings 4)

Ingredients

1 pound frozen shrimp
1 ½ tablespoons extra-virgin olive oil
2 gloves garlic, minced
1 teaspoon basil
1/2 teaspoon dry dill weed
1 teaspoon oregano
1 (26-ounce) canned diced tomatoes
1/2 cup Kalamata olives
2 ounces feta cheese, crumbled
1/2 lemon, sliced
Chopped fresh mint leaves, for garnish

Directions

Add the shrimp, olive oil, garlic, basil, dill, oregano, and tomatoes to the inner pot.

Secure the lid. Choose the "Manual" mode and cook for 2 minutes at Low pressure. Once cooking is complete, use a quick pressure release; carefully remove the lid.

Top with Kalamata olives and feta cheese. Serve garnished with lemon and mint leaves. Enjoy!

Per serving: 210 Calories; 8.2g Fat; 9.4g Carbs; 27g Protein; 5.7g Sugars

422. Indian Meen Kulambu

(Ready in about 10 minutes | Servings 4)

Ingredients

2 tablespoons butter 6 curry leaves
1 onion, chopped
2 cloves garlic, crushed
1 (1-inch) piece fresh ginger, grated
1 dried Kashmiri chili, minced
1 cup canned tomatoes, crushed
1/2 teaspoon turmeric powder
1 teaspoon ground coriander
1/2 teaspoon ground cumin
Kosher salt and ground black pepper, to taste
1/2 (14-ounce) can coconut milk
1 pound salmon fillets
1 tablespoon lemon juice

Directions

Press the "Sauté" button and melt the butter. Once hot, cook the curry leaves for about 30 seconds.

Stir in the onions, garlic, ginger and Kashmiri chili and cook for 2 minutes more or until they are fragrant.

Add the tomatoes, turmeric, coriander, cumin, salt, and black pepper. Continue to sauté for 30 seconds more.

Add the coconut milk and salmon.

Secure the lid. Choose the "Manual" mode and cook for 2 minutes at Low pressure. Once cooking is complete, use a quick pressure release; carefully remove the lid.

Spoon the fish curry into individual bowls. Drizzle lemon juice over the fish curry and serve. Enjoy!

Per serving: 313 Calories; 20.8g Fat; 7.9g Carbs; 25.1g Protein; 3.1g Sugars

423. Cod Fish with Potatoes and Goat Cheese

(Ready in about 10 minutes | Servings 4)

Ingredients

1 pound baby potatoes
2 tablespoons coconut oil, at room temperature
Sea salt and freshly ground pepper, to taste
1 ½ pounds cod fish fillets
1/2 teaspoon smoked paprika
2 tablespoons fresh Italian parsley, chopped
1/2 teaspoon fresh ginger, grated
2 cloves garlic, minced
1 cup goat cheese, crumbled

Directions

Place the potatoes in the bottom of the inner pot. Add 1 cup of water; then, add coconut oil, salt and pepper. Place the rack over the potatoes.

Place the cod fish fillets on the rack. Season the fillets with paprika and parsley.

Secure the lid. Choose the "Steam" mode and cook for 3 minutes at Low pressure. Once cooking is complete, use a quick pressure release; carefully remove the lid.

Remove the salmon and the rack from the inner pot. Continue to cook the potatoes until fork tender; add the ginger and garlic and cook for 2 minutes more.

Top with goat cheese and serve. Bon appétit!

Per serving: 390 Calories; 17.6g Fat; 20.8g Carbs; 36.5g Protein; 1.1g Sugars

424. Three-Cheese Crab Dip

(Ready in about 10 minutes | Servings 10)

Ingredients

1 pound lump crab meat
6 ounces Cottage cheese, at room temperature
1/2 cup Romano cheese, shredded
1 cup sour cream
Kosher salt and ground black pepper, to taste
1 teaspoon smoked paprika
1 ½ cups Cheddar cheese, shredded
1/4 cup fresh chives, chopped
2 tablespoons fresh lime juice

Directions

Place 1 cup of water and a metal trivet in the inner pot.

Spritz a casserole dish with nonstick cooking spray. Place the crab meat, Cottage cheese, Romano cheese and sour cream in the casserole dish.

Season with salt, black pepper, and smoked paprika. Top with the Cheddar cheese. Lower the dish onto the trivet.

Secure the lid. Choose the "Manual" mode and cook for 3 minutes at Low pressure. Once cooking is complete, use a quick pressure release; carefully remove the lid.

Scatter the chopped chives over the top and add a few drizzles of lime juice. Serve warm or at room temperature. Enjoy!

Per serving: 183 Calories; 11.1g Fat; 3.3g Carbs; 17.6g Protein; 0.9g Sugars

425. Classic Creole Gumbo

(Ready in about 15 minutes | Servings 4)

Ingredients

2 tablespoons butter, melted
1 shallot, diced
1 sweet pepper, sliced
1 jalapeno pepper, sliced
1 pound tuna, cut into 2-inch chunks
1 tablespoon Creole seasoning
2 carrots, sliced
2 celery stalks, diced
2 ripe tomatoes, pureed
1/4 cup ketchup
1 bay leaf
1 cup beef broth
2 tablespoons Worcestershire sauce
1 pound raw shrimp, deveined
1 teaspoon filé powder
Sea salt and freshly ground black pepper, to taste

Directions

Press the "Sauté" button and melt the butter. Once hot, cook the shallot and peppers for about 3 minutes until just tender and fragrant.

Add the remaining ingredients; gently stir to combine.

Secure the lid. Choose the "Manual" mode and cook for 5 minutes at High pressure. Once cooking is complete, use a quick pressure release; carefully remove the lid. Serve in individual bowls and enjoy!

Per serving: 339 Calories; 8.7g Fat; 18g Carbs; 47.3g Protein; 8.5g Sugars

426. Blue Crabs with Wine and Herbs

(Ready in about 15 minutes | Servings 4)

Ingredients

2 pounds frozen blue crab
1/2 cup water
1/2 cup dry white wine
Sea salt and ground black pepper, to taste
2 sprigs rosemary
2 sprigs thyme
1 lemon, cut into wedges

Directions

Add the frozen crab legs, water, wine, salt, black pepper, rosemary, and thyme to the inner pot.

Secure the lid. Choose the "Manual" mode and cook for 3 minutes at High pressure. Once cooking is complete, use a quick pressure release; carefully remove the lid.

Serve warm, garnished with fresh lemon wedges. Bon appétit!

Per serving: 145 Calories; 4.3g Fat; 2.1g Carbs; 23.7g Protein; 0.9g Sugars

427. Sausage and Prawn Boil with Old Bay Sauce

(Ready in about 15 minutes | Servings 4)

Ingredients

1/2 pound beef sausage, sliced
4 baby potatoes
1 cup fume (fish stock)
1/4 cup butter
2 cloves garlic, minced
1 teaspoon Old Bay seasoning
1/4 teaspoon Tabasco sauce
Sea salt and white pepper, to taste
1 pound prawns
1 fresh lemon, juiced

Directions

Place the sausage and potatoes in the inner pot; cover with the fish stock.

Secure the lid. Choose the "Manual" mode and cook for 5 minutes at High pressure. Once cooking is complete, use a quick pressure release; carefully remove the lid. Reserve. Clean the inner pot.

Press the "Sauté" button and melt the butter. Once hot, sauté the minced garlic until aromatic or about 1 minute. Stir in the Old Bay seasoning, Tabasco, salt, and white pepper. Lastly, stir in the prawns.

Continue to simmer for 1 to 2 minutes or until the shrimp turn pink. Press the "Cancel" button. Add the sausages and potatoes, drizzle lemon juice over the top and serve warm.

Per serving: 441 Calories; 28.6g Fat; 14.5g Carbs; 32.4g Protein; 1.6g Sugars

428. Braised Sole Fillets with Vegetables

(Ready in about 20 minutes | Servings 4)

Ingredients

2 tablespoons coconut oil
1 small shallot, quartered
4 cloves garlic, sliced
1 cup beef stock
1 ripe tomato, puréed
Salt and ground black pepper, to taste
1 pound fennel, quartered
1 pound sole fillets
1 lemon, cut into wedges
2 tablespoons fresh Italian parsley

Directions

Press the "Sauté" button and melt the coconut oil. Once hot, sauté the shallot and garlic until tender and aromatic.

Add the beef stock, tomato, salt, pepper, and fennel.

Secure the lid. Choose the "Manual" mode and cook for 10 minutes at High pressure. Once cooking is complete, use a quick pressure release; carefully remove the lid.

Then, remove all the vegetables with a slotted spoon and reserve, keeping them warm.

Add the sole fillets to the inner pot. Secure the lid. Choose the "Steam" mode and cook for 3 minutes at Low pressure. Once cooking is complete, use a quick pressure release; carefully remove the lid.

Garnish the fish fillets with lemon and parsley; serve with the reserved vegetables. Enjoy!

Per serving: 218 Calories; 9.8g Fat; 16.6g Carbs; 18.2g Protein; 8.2g Sugars

429. Louisiana-Style Seafood Boil

(Ready in about 25 minutes | Servings 4)

Ingredients

1 cup jasmine rice	1 cup chicken bone broth
1 tablespoon butter	2 bay leaves
1 tablespoon olive oil	1 teaspoon oregano
1/2 pound chicken breasts, cubed	1 teaspoon sage
1 pound shrimp	1 teaspoon basil
2 sweet peppers, deveined and sliced	1 teaspoon paprika
1 habanero pepper, deveined and sliced	1 tablespoon fish sauce
1 onion, chopped	Sea salt and ground black pepper, to taste
4 cloves garlic, minced	1 tablespoon cornstarch

Directions

Combine the rice, butter and 1 ½ cups of water in a pot and bring to a rapid boil. Cover and let it simmer on low for 15 minutes. Fluff with a fork and reserve.

Press the "Sauté" button and heat the oil. Once hot, cook the chicken breasts for 3 to 4 minutes, stirring periodically.

Add the remaining ingredients, except for the cornstarch.

Secure the lid. Choose the "Manual" mode and cook for 3 minutes at Low pressure. Once cooking is complete, use a quick pressure release; carefully remove the lid.

Mix the cornstarch with 2 tablespoons of cold water. Add the cornstarch slurry to the cooking liquid and stir on the "Sauté" mode until the sauce thickens.

Serve over hot jasmine rice. Bon appétit!

Per serving: 492 Calories; 13.1g Fat; 52.1g Carbs; 41.2g Protein; 2.6g Sugars

430. Southern California Famous Cioppino

(Ready in about 50 minutes | Servings 6)

Ingredients

2 tablespoons coconut oil	1 teaspoon dried basil
1 onion, diced	1 teaspoon paprika
4 garlic cloves, minced	1 bay leaf
2 celery stalks, diced	Sea salt and freshly ground black pepper, to taste
2 carrots, diced	
1 sweet pepper, diced	1 pound halibut steaks, cubed
2 (14-ounce) cans of tomatoes, crushed	1/2 pound sea scallops, rinsed and drained
1 cup clam juice	1 pound shrimp, peeled and deveined
1 teaspoon oyster sauce	
1/2 teaspoon dried parsley flakes	1/2 pound crab legs
1 teaspoon dried rosemary	1/4 cup dry white wine

Directions

Press the "Sauté" button to heat the coconut oil. Once hot, sauté the onion, garlic, celery, carrots, and pepper for about 3 minutes or until they are just tender.

Add the canned tomatoes, clam juice, oyster sauce, parsley, rosemary, basil, paprika, bay leaf, salt, and black pepper to the inner pot.

Secure the lid. Choose the "Soup/Broth" mode and cook for 30 minutes at High pressure. Once cooking is complete, use a natural pressure release for 10 minutes; carefully remove the lid.

Add the seafood and wine.

Secure the lid. Choose the "Steam" mode and cook for 3 minutes at Low pressure. Once cooking is complete, use a quick pressure release; carefully remove the lid. Serve in individual bowls and enjoy!

Per serving: 413 Calories; 19.3g Fat; 16.2g Carbs; 44.8g Protein; 6.8g Sugars

431. Foil-Packet Fish and Vegetables

(Ready in about 15 minutes | Servings 4)

Ingredients

12 ounces halibut steaks, cut into four pieces	Sea salt and ground black pepper, to taste
1 red bell pepper, sliced	1 teaspoon dried rosemary
1 green bell pepper, sliced	1 teaspoon basil
1 onion, sliced	1/2 teaspoon oregano
2 garlic cloves, minced	1/2 teaspoon paprika
1 cup cherry tomatoes, halved	4 teaspoon olive oil

Directions

Place 1 cup of water and a metal trivet in the bottom of the inner pot.

Place 4 large sheets of heavy-duty foil on a flat surface. Divide the ingredients between sheets of foil. Add a splash of water.

Bring the ends of the foil together; fold in the sides to seal. Place the fish packets on the trivet.

Secure the lid. Choose the "Steam" mode and cook for 10 minutes at Low pressure. Once cooking is complete, use a quick pressure release; carefully remove the lid. Bon appétit!

Per serving: 238 Calories; 16.4g Fat; 9.5g Carbs; 13.5g Protein; 6.5g Sugars

432. Japanese Seafood Curry

(Ready in about 15 minutes | Servings 4)

Ingredients

2 tablespoons butter, softened	1/2 pound shrimps, deveined
1 onion, chopped	2 tablespoons sesame oil
2 cloves garlic, minced	1 tablespoon garam masala
1 (1-inch) pieces fresh ginger, ground	1 teaspoon curry paste
1 red chili, deseeded and minced	1 (3-inch) kombu (dried kelp)
1 pound pollack, cut into large chunks	1 package Japanese curry roux
	2 tablespoons Shoyu sauce
	2 ripe tomatoes, pureed

Directions

Press the "Sauté" button and melt the butter; cook the onion, garlic, ginger, and red chili until just tender and fragrant.

Add the pollack and shrimp and continue to sauté for a couple of minutes more. Add the remaining ingredients.

Secure the lid. Choose the "Manual" mode and cook for 5 minutes at Low pressure. Once cooking is complete, use a quick pressure release; carefully remove the lid.

Serve your curry over hot steamed rice. Enjoy!

Per serving: 390 Calories; 25.5g Fat; 7.1g Carbs; 34.4g Protein; 3.2g Sugars

433. Spicy Thai Prawns

(Ready in about 10 minutes | Servings 4)

Ingredients

2 tablespoons coconut oil
1 small white onion, chopped
2 cloves garlic, minced
1 ½ pounds prawns, deveined
1/2 teaspoon red chili flakes
1 bell pepper, seeded and sliced
1 cup coconut milk
2 tablespoons fish sauce

2 tablespoons lime juice
1 tablespoon sugar
Kosher salt and white pepper, to your liking
1/2 teaspoon cayenne pepper
1 teaspoon fresh ginger, ground
2 tablespoons fresh cilantro, roughly chopped

Directions

Press the "Sauté" button and heat the coconut oil; once hot, sauté the onion and garlic until aromatic.

Add the prawns, red chili flakes, bell pepper, coconut milk, fish sauce, lime juice, sugar, salt, white pepper, cayenne pepper, and ginger.

Secure the lid. Choose the "Manual" mode and cook for 3 minutes at Low pressure. Once cooking is complete, use a quick pressure release; carefully remove the lid.

Divide between serving bowls and serve garnished with fresh cilantro. Enjoy!

Per serving: 283 Calories; 11.1g Fat; 12.3g Carbs; 32.7g Protein; 7.4g Sugars

434. East Indian Haddock Curry

(Ready in about 10 minutes | Servings 4)

Ingredients

2 tablespoons peanut oil
1 onion, chopped
2 garlic cloves, minced
1 (1-inch) piece fresh root ginger, peeled and grated
2 long red chilis, deseeded and minced
2 tablespoons tamarind paste

1 teaspoon mustard seeds
1 teaspoon turmeric powder
1 teaspoon ground cumin
Sea salt and freshly ground black pepper
1 can reduced fat coconut milk
1 cup chicken stock
1 pound haddock

Directions

Press the "Sauté" button and heat the peanut oil; once hot, sauté the onion, garlic, ginger, and chilis until aromatic.

Add the remaining ingredients and gently stir to combine.

Secure the lid. Choose the "Manual" mode and cook for 4 minutes at Low pressure. Once cooking is complete, use a quick pressure release; carefully remove the lid.

Divide between serving bowls and serve warm. Enjoy!

Per serving: 315 Calories; 22.4g Fat; 8.4g Carbs; 21.9g Protein; 4.3g Sugars

435. Tuna and Asparagus Casserole

(Ready in about 15 minutes | Servings 4)

Ingredients

1 pound tuna fillets
1 pound asparagus, trimmed
2 ripe tomatoes, pureed
Sea salt and ground black pepper, to taste

1 teaspoon paprika
A pinch of fresh thyme
1 tablespoon dry white wine
1 cup Cheddar cheese, grated

Directions

Place the tuna fillets in a lightly greased baking dish. Add the asparagus, tomatoes, salt, black pepper, paprika, thyme, and wine.

Place a steamer rack inside the inner pot; add 1/2 cup water. Cut 1 sheet of heavy-duty foil and brush with cooking spray.

Top with the cheese. Cover with foil and lower the baking dish onto the rack.

Secure the lid. Choose the "Manual" mode and cook for 9 minutes at Low pressure. Once cooking is complete, use a quick pressure release; carefully remove the lid.

Place the baking dish on a cooling rack for a couple of minutes before slicing and serving. Bon appétit!

Per serving: 494 Calories; 30.3g Fat; 21.1g Carbs; 36.4g Protein; 5.3g Sugars

436. Mozzarella and Spinach-Stuffed Salmon

(Ready in about 10 minutes | Servings 3)

Ingredients

3 (6-ounce) salmon fillets
Kosher salt and freshly ground black pepper, to taste
1/2 teaspoon cayenne pepper
1/2 teaspoon celery seed, crushed
1/2 teaspoon dried basil
1/2 teaspoon dried marjoram

1/2 cup sour cream
1/2 cup mozzarella, shredded
1 cup frozen spinach, defrosted
2 cloves garlic, minced
1 tablespoon olive oil
1 lemon, cut into wedges

Directions

Add 1 cup of water and a steamer rack to the bottom of your Instant Pot.

Sprinkle your salmon with all spices. In a mixing bowl, thoroughly combine sour cream, mozzarella, spinach, and garlic.

Cut a pocket in each fillet to within 1/2-inch of the opposite side. Stuff the pockets with the spinach/cheese mixture. Drizzle with olive oil.

Wrap the salmon fillets in foil and lower onto the rack.

Secure the lid. Choose the "Manual" mode and cook for 4 minutes at Low pressure. Once cooking is complete, use a quick pressure release; carefully remove the lid.

Garnish with lemon wedges and serve warm.

Per serving: 374 Calories; 19.9g Fat; 7.7g Carbs; 40.7g Protein; 1.2g Sugars

437. Steamed Tilapia with Butter and Spinach

(Ready in about 15 minutes | Servings 4)

Ingredients

1 cup chicken broth
2 cloves garlic, sliced
1 pound tilapia, cut into 4 pieces
1 tablespoon Worcestershire sauce

Salt and ground black pepper, to taste
2 tablepsoons butter, melted
2 cups fresh spinach

Directions

Place the chicken broth and garlic in the inner pot. Place the trivet on top.

Place the tilapia fillets on a sheet of foil; add Worcestershire sauce, salt, pepper, and butter. Bring up all sides of the foil to create a packet around your fish.

Secure the lid. Choose the "Steam" mode and cook for 10 minutes at Low pressure. Once cooking is complete, use a quick pressure release; carefully remove the lid.

Add the spinach leaves to the cooking liquid. Press the "Sauté" function and let it simmer for 1 to 2 minutes or until wilted.

Place the fish fillets on top of the wilted spinach, adjust the seasonings, and serve immediately. Bon appétit!

Per serving: 265 Calories; 11.9g Fat; 2.7g Carbs; 36.5g Protein; 0.7g Sugars

438. Smoked Codfish with Scallions

(Ready in about 10 minutes | Servings 3)

Ingredients

1 lemon, sliced
1/2 cup water
3 fillets smoked codfish
3 teaspoons butter

3 tablespoons scallions, chopped
Sea salt and ground black pepper, to taste

Directions

Place the lemon and water in the bottom of the Instant Pot. Place the steamer rack on top.

Place the cod fish fillets on the steamer rack. Add the butter, scallions, salt, and black pepper.

Secure the lid. Choose the "Steam" mode and cook for 3 minutes at Low pressure. Once cooking is complete, use a quick pressure release; carefully remove the lid.

Serve warm and enjoy!

Per serving: 203 Calories; 4.8g Fat; 1.5g Carbs; 36.3g Protein; 0.5g Sugars

439. Teriyaki Fish Steaks

(Ready in about 15 minutes | Servings 4)

Ingredients

2 tablespoons butter, melted
4 (6-ounce) salmon steaks
2 cloves garlic, smashed
1 (1-inch) piece fresh ginger, peeled and grated

1/3 cup soy sauce
1/2 cup water
2 tablespoons brown sugar
2 teaspoons wine vinegar
1 tablespoon cornstarch

Directions

Press the "Sauté" button and melt the butter. Once hot, cook the salmon steaks for 2 minutes per side.

Add the garlic, ginger, soy sauce, water, sugar, and vinegar.

Secure the lid. Choose the "Manual" mode and cook for 5 minutes at Low pressure. Once cooking is complete, use a quick pressure release; carefully remove the lid. Reserve the fish steaks.

Mix the cornstarch with 2 tablespoons of cold water. Add the slurry to the cooking liquid. Let it simmer until the sauce thickens. Spoon the sauce over the fish steaks. Bon appétit!

Per serving: 325 Calories; 16.1g Fat; 11.5g Carbs; 31.8g Protein; 7.9g Sugars

440. Traditional Fish Tacos

(Ready in about 13 minutes | Servings 4)

Ingredients

1 lemon, sliced
2 tablespoons olive oil
1 pound haddock fillets
1/2 teaspoon ground cumin
1/2 teaspoon onion powder
1 teaspoon garlic powder
1/2 teaspoon paprika
Sea salt and freshly ground black pepper, to taste

1 teaspoon dried basil
1 tablespoon ancho chili powder
4 (6-inch) flour tortillas
4 tablespoons mayonnaise
4 tablespoons sour cream
2 tablespoons fresh cilantro, chopped

Directions

Add 1/2 cup of water, 1/2 of lemon slices, and a steamer rack to the bottom of the inner pot.

Press the "Sauté" button and heat the olive oil until sizzling. Now, sauté the haddock fillets for 1 to 2 minutes per side.

Season the fish fillets with all the spices and lower them onto the rack.

Secure the lid. Choose the "Steam" mode and cook for 3 minutes at Low pressure. Once cooking is complete, use a quick pressure release; carefully remove the lid.

Break the fish fillets into large bite-sized pieces and divide them between the tortillas.

Add the mayonnaise, sour cream and cilantro to each tortilla. Garnish with the remaining lemon slices and enjoy!

Per serving: 475 Calories; 23.4g Fat; 40g Carbs; 25.2g Protein; 2.9g Sugars

441. Halibut Steaks with Mayo Sauce and Wild Rice

(Ready in about 1 hour | Servings 6)

Ingredients

1 cup wild rice, rinsed and drained
1 tablespoon butter
1/2 teaspoon salt flakes
1/2 teaspoon red pepper flakes, crushed
1 ½ pounds halibut steaks
2 tablespoons olive oil

Sea salt and ground pepper, to your liking
4 tablespoons cream cheese
4 tablespoons mayonnaise
1 teaspoon stone-ground mustard
2 cloves garlic, minced

Directions

In a saucepan, bring 3 cups of water and rice to a boil. Reduce the heat to simmer; cover and let it simmer for 45 to 55 minutes. Add the butter, salt, and red pepper; fluff with a fork. Cover and reserve, keeping your rice warm.

Cut 4 sheets of aluminum foil. Place the halibut steak in each sheet of foil. Add the olive oil, salt, and black pepper to the top of the fish; close each packet and seal the edges.

Add 1 cup of water and a steamer rack to the bottom of your Instant Pot. Lower the packets onto the rack.

Secure the lid. Choose the "Steam" mode and cook for 3 minutes at Low pressure. Once cooking is complete, use a natural pressure release; carefully remove the lid.

Meanwhile, mix the cream cheese, mayonnaise, stone-ground mustard, and garlic until well combined. Serve the steamed fish with the mayo sauce and wild rice on the side. Bon appétit!

Per serving: 431 Calories; 28.5g Fat; 21.7g Carbs; 21.8g Protein; 1.5g Sugars

442. Shrimp Scampi with Scallions and Carrots

(Ready in about 10 minutes | Servings 4)

Ingredients

1 tablespoon olive oil
2 garlic cloves, sliced
1 bunch scallions, chopped
2 carrots, grated
1 ½ pounds shrimp, deveined and rinsed
1/2 cup dry white wine see

1/2 cup cream of celery soup
Sea salt and freshly cracked black pepper, to taste
1 teaspoon cayenne pepper
1/2 teaspoon dried basil
1 teaspoon dried rosemary
1/2 teaspoon dried oregano

Directions

Press the "Sauté" button and heat the oil. Once hot, cook the garlic, scallions, and carrots for 2 to 3 minutes or until fragrant; add a splash of wine to deglaze the inner pot.

Add the remaining ingredients.

Secure the lid. Choose the "Manual" mode and cook for 3 minutes at Low pressure. Once cooking is complete, use a quick pressure release; carefully remove the lid.

Divide between serving bowls and enjoy!

Per serving: 267 Calories; 9.4g Fat; 5.1g Carbs; 38.3g Protein; 1.6g Sugars

443. Sticky Orange Sea Bass

(Ready in about 15 minutes | Servings 4)

Ingredients

1 tablespoon safflower oil
1 pound sea bass
Sea salt, to taste
1/4 teaspoon white pepper
2 tablespoons tamari sauce

2 cloves garlic, minced
1/2 teaspoon dried dill weed
1 orange, juiced
1 tablespoon honey

Directions

Press the "Sauté" button and heat the oil. Now, cook the sea bass for 1 to 2 minutes per side. Season your fish with salt and pepper.

Add 1 cup of water and a steamer rack to the bottom of your Instant Pot. Lower the fish onto the rack.

Secure the lid. Choose the "Steam" mode and cook for 10 minutes at Low pressure. Once cooking is complete, use a quick pressure release; carefully remove the lid. Reserve.

Add the remaining ingredients to the cooking liquid and stir to combine well. Press the "Sauté" button again and let it simmer until the sauce thickens.

Spoon the sauce over the reserved fish. Bon appétit!

Per serving: 217 Calories; 9.4g Fat; 7.8g Carbs; 26.4g Protein; 6.5g Sugars

444. Almost-Famous Prawn Dipping Sauces

(Ready in about 10 minutes | Servings 8)

Ingredients

2 cups crabmeat, flaked
1 onion, chopped
2 cloves garlic, smashed
1/2 cup cream cheese, softened
1/2 cup mayonnaise
1/2 cup Parmesan cheese, grated
1 ½ tablespoons cornichon, finely chopped
1/4 cup tomato paste
2 or so dashes of Tabasco
1/2 cup fresh breadcrumbs

Directions

Place all ingredients, except for the breadcrumbs, in a baking dish. Stir until everything is well incorporated.

Top with breadcrumbs.

Secure the lid. Choose the "Steam" mode and cook for 3 minutes at Low pressure. Once cooking is complete, use a quick pressure release; carefully remove the lid.

Serve with raw vegetable sticks if desired. Bon appétit!

Per serving: 205 Calories; 16.7g Fat; 4.6g Carbs; 9.2g Protein; 2.2g Sugars

445. Tilapia Fillets with Peppers

(Ready in about 10 minutes | Servings 4)

Ingredients

1 lemon, sliced
4 (6-ounce) tilapia fillets, skin on
4 teaspoons olive oil
Sea salt and white pepper, to taste
1 tablespoon fresh parsley, chopped
1 tablespoon fresh tarragon, chopped
1 red onion, sliced into rings
2 sweet peppers, julienned
4 tablespoons dry white wine

Directions

Place the lemon slices, 1 cup of water, and a metal trivet in the bottom of the inner pot.

Place 4 large sheets of heavy-duty foil on a flat surface. Divide the ingredients between the sheets of foil.

Bring the ends of the foil together; fold in the sides to seal. Place the fish packets on the trivet.

Secure the lid. Choose the "Steam" mode and cook for 3 minutes at Low pressure. Once cooking is complete, use a quick pressure release; carefully remove the lid. Bon appétit!

Per serving: 239 Calories; 7.6g Fat; 8.5g Carbs; 35.6g Protein; 1.3g Sugars

446. Extraordinary Greek-Style Fish

(Ready in about 10 minutes | Servings 4)

Ingredients

2 tablespoons olive oil
1 ½ pounds cod fillets
1 pound tomatoes, chopped
Sea salt and ground black pepper, to taste
2 sprigs rosemary, chopped
2 sprigs thyme, chopped
1 bay leaf
2 cloves garlic, smashed
1/2 cup Greek olives, pitted and sliced

Directions

Place 1 cup of water and a metal trivet in the bottom of the inner pot. Brush the sides and bottom of a casserole dish with olive oil.

Place the cod fillets in the greased casserole dish. Add the tomatoes, salt, pepper, rosemary, thyme, bay leaf, and garlic.

Lower the dish onto the trivet.

Secure the lid. Choose the "Steam" mode and cook for 3 minutes at Low pressure. Once cooking is complete, use a quick pressure release; carefully remove the lid.

Serve garnished with Greek olives and enjoy!

Per serving: 246 Calories; 9.9g Fat; 7.1g Carbs; 31.6g Protein; 2.5g Sugars

447. French Fish en Papillote

(Ready in about 10 minutes | Servings 4)

Ingredients

2 tablespoons olive oil
4 (7-ounces) rainbow trout fillets
1 tablespoon fresh chives, chopped
1 tablespoon fresh parsley, chopped
Sea salt and white pepper, to taste
1/2 pound sugar snap peas, trimmed
2 tomatillos, sliced
2 garlic cloves, minced

Directions

Place 1 cup of water and a metal rack in your Instant Pot.

Place all ingredients in a large sheet of foil. Fold up the sides of the foil to make a bowl-like shape. Lower the fish packet onto the rack.

Secure the lid. Choose the "Steam" mode and cook for 3 minutes at Low pressure. Once cooking is complete, use a quick pressure release; carefully remove the lid. Bon appétit!

Per serving: 285 Calories; 12.5g Fat; 6.9g Carbs; 34.6g Protein; 3.5g Sugars

448. Seafood Quiche with Colby Cheese

(Ready in about 20 minutes | Servings 4)

Ingredients

6 eggs
1/2 cup cream cheese
1/2 cup Greek-style yogurt
Himalayan salt and ground black pepper, to taste
1 teaspoon cayenne pepper
1 teaspoon dried basil
1 teaspoon dried oregano
1 pound crab meat, chopped
1/2 pound raw shrimp, chopped
1 cup Colby cheese, shredded

Directions

In a mixing bowl, whisk the eggs with the cream cheese and yogurt. Season with salt, black pepper, cayenne pepper, basil, and oregano.

Stir in the seafood; stir to combine and spoon the mixture into a lightly greased baking pan. Lastly, top with the shredded cheese.

Cover with a piece of aluminum foil.

Secure the lid. Choose the "Steam" mode and cook for 10 minutes at Low pressure. Once cooking is complete, use a quick pressure release; carefully remove the lid. Bon appétit!

Per serving: 468 Calories; 26.9g Fat; 4.5g Carbs; 50.4g Protein; 2.4g Sugars

449. Traditional Spanish Paella

(Ready in about 15 minutes | Servings 5)

Ingredients

2 tablespoons olive oil
2 links (6-ounce) Spanish chorizo sausage, cut into slices
1 yellow onion, chopped
3 cloves garlic, minced
2 sweet peppers, sliced
1 Chiles de Árbol, minced
1 cup Arborio rice, rinsed
1 ½ pounds shrimp, deveined
1 cup chicken broth
1 cup water
1/3 cup white wine
1/2 teaspoon curry paste
Sea salt and white pepper, to taste
1 cup green peas, fresh or thawed
1/4 cup fresh parsley leaves, roughly chopped

Directions

Press the "Sauté" button and heat the oil until sizzling. Cook the sausage for 2 minutes, stirring continuously to ensure even cooking.

Stir in the onions and garlic; cook for about a minute longer, stirring frequently.

Add the peppers, rice, shrimp, broth, water, wine, curry paste, salt, and white pepper.

Secure the lid. Choose the "Manual" mode and cook for 3 minutes at High pressure. Once cooking is complete, use a quick pressure release; carefully remove the lid.

Add the green peas and seal the lid one more time; let it sit in the residual heat until warmed through.

Serve garnished with fresh parsley and enjoy!

Per serving: 435 Calories; 19.6g Fat; 24.8g Carbs; 46g Protein; 2.6g Sugars

450. Crabs in Butter-Garlic Sauce

(Ready in about 15 minutes | Servings 5)

Ingredients

1 ½ pounds crabs
1 stick butter
2 cloves garlic, minced
1 teaspoon Old Bay seasoning
1 lemon, sliced

Directions

Place 1 cup water and a metal trivet in the bottom of your Instant Pot.

Lower the crabs onto the trivet.

Secure the lid. Choose the "Steam" mode and cook for 3 minutes at Low pressure. Once cooking is complete, use a quick pressure release; carefully remove the lid. Reserve.

Press the "Sauté" button and melt butter. Once hot, sauté the garlic and Old Bay seasoning for 2 to 3 minutes or until fragrant and thoroughly heated.

Add the cooked crabs and gently stir to combine. Serve with lemon slices. Bon appétit!

Per serving: 285 Calories; 19.8g Fat; 1.2g Carbs; 24.8g Protein; 0.6g Sugars

451. Easy Lobster Tails with Butter

(Ready in about 10 minutes | Servings 4)

Ingredients

1 ½ pounds lobster tails, halved
1/2 stick butter, at room temperature
Sea salt and freshly ground black pepper, to taste
1/2 teaspoon red pepper flakes

Directions

Add a metal trivet, steamer basket, and 1 cup of water in your Instant Pot.

Place the lobster tails, shell side down, in the prepared steamer basket.

Secure the lid. Choose the "Steam" mode and cook for 3 minutes at Low pressure. Once cooking is complete, use a quick pressure release; carefully remove the lid.

Drizzle with butter. Season with salt, black pepper, and red pepper and serve immediately. Enjoy!

Per serving: 292 Calories; 14.1g Fat; 4.2g Carbs; 35.1g Protein; 0.1g Sugars

452. Steamed Mussels in Scallion Sauce

(Ready in about 10 minutes | Servings 4)

Ingredients

1 cup water
1/2 cup cooking wine
2 garlic cloves, sliced
1 ½ pounds frozen mussels, cleaned and debearded
2 tablespoons butter
1 bunch scallion, chopped

Directions

Add the water, wine, and garlic to the inner pot. Add a metal rack to the inner pot.

Put the mussels into the steamer basket; lower the steamer basket onto the rack.

Secure the lid. Choose the "Steam" mode and cook for 3 minutes at Low pressure. Once cooking is complete, use a quick pressure release; carefully remove the lid.

Press the "Sauté" button and add butter and scallions; let it cook until the sauce is thoroughly heated and slightly thickened. Press the "Cancel" button and add the mussels. Serve warm. Bon appétit!

Per serving: 225 Calories; 9.6g Fat; 7.8g Carbs; 20.4g Protein; 0.4g Sugars

453. Spicy and Saucy Red Snapper

(Ready in about 10 minutes | Servings 4)

Ingredients

1 tablespoon ghee, at room temperature
1 medium-sized leek, chopped
4 cloves garlic, minced
1 tablespoon capers
2 medium ripe tomatoes, chopped
1 cup chicken broth
1 red chili pepper, seeded and chopped
1 teaspoon basil
1/2 teaspoon oregano
1/2 teaspoon rosemary
3 (6-ounce) red snapper fillets
Coarse sea salt and ground black pepper, to taste
1 teaspoon Fish taco seasoning mix
1 lemon, cut into wedges

Directions

Press the "Sauté" button and melt the ghee. Once hot, sauté the leek and garlic until tender.

Add the remaining ingredients, except for the lemon wedges, to the inner pot.

Secure the lid. Choose the "Manual" mode and cook for 4 minutes at High pressure. Once cooking is complete, use a quick pressure release; carefully remove the lid.

Serve in individual bowls, garnished with lemon wedges. Enjoy!

Per serving: 289 Calories; 15.4g Fat; 13.8g Carbs; 24.5g Protein; 5.5g Sugars

454. Delicious Shrimp Salad

(Ready in about 15 minutes + chilling time | Servings 4)

Ingredients

1 pound shrimp, deveined
Kosher salt and white pepper, to taste
1 onion, thinly sliced
1 sweet pepper, thinly sliced
1 jalapeno pepper, deseeded and minced
2 heaping tablespoons fresh parsley, chopped
1 head romaine lettuce, torn into pieces
4 tablespoons extra-virgin olive oil
1 lime, juiced and zested
1 tablespoon Dijon mustard

Directions

Add a metal trivet and 1 cup of water to your Instant Pot.

Put the shrimp into the steamer basket. Lower the steamer basket onto the trivet.

Secure the lid. Choose the "Steam" mode and cook for 3 minutes at Low pressure. Once cooking is complete, use a quick pressure release; carefully remove the lid.

Transfer steamed shrimp to a salad bowl; toss your shrimp with the remaining ingredients and serve well chilled. Bon appétit!

Per serving: 271 Calories; 15.4g Fat; 10.8g Carbs; 25.7g Protein; 2.9g Sugars

455. Crab Salad Sliders

(Ready in about 10 minutes | Servings 4)

Ingredients

10 ounces crabmeat
4 heaping tablespoons fresh chives, chopped
2 garlic cloves, minced
1/2 cup mayonnaise
1/2 teaspoon hot sauce
1 teaspoon Old Bay seasoning
1/2 cup celery stalk, chopped
1 tablespoon fresh lime juice
8 mini slider rolls
2 cups Iceberg lettuce, torn into pieces

Directions

Add 1 cup of water, metal trivet, and a steamer basket to your Instant Pot.

Place the crabmeat in the prepared steamer basket.

Secure the lid. Choose the "Steam" mode and cook for 3 minutes at Low pressure. Once cooking is complete, use a quick pressure release; carefully remove the lid.

Add the chives, garlic, mayo, hot sauce, Old Bay seasoning, celery, and lime juice; stir to combine well.

Divide the mixture between slider rolls and garnish with lettuce. Serve and enjoy!

Per serving: 413 Calories; 25g Fat; 28.5g Carbs; 18.5g Protein; 2.1g Sugars

456. Vietnamese-Style Caramel Fish

(Ready in about 10 minutes | Servings 4)

Ingredients

2 tablespoons coconut oil, melted
1/4 cup brown sugar
2 tablespoons fish sauce
2 tablespoons soy sauce
1 (1-inch) ginger root, grated
Juice of 1/2 lime

Sea salt and white pepper, to taste
1 cup chicken broth
4 (7-ounce) sea bass fillets
2 tablespoons fresh chives, chopped

Directions

Press the "Sauté" button and heat the coconut oil. Once hot, cook the brown sugar, fish sauce, soy sauce, ginger, lime, salt, white pepper, and broth. Bring to a simmer and press the "Cancel" button.

Add sea bass. Secure the lid. Choose the "Manual" mode and cook for 4 minutes at High pressure. Once cooking is complete, use a quick pressure release; carefully remove the lid.

Remove the sea bass fillets from the cooking liquid. Press the "Sauté" button one more time. Reduce the sauce until it is thick and syrupy.

Spoon the sauce over the reserved sea bass fillets. Garnish with fresh chives. Bon appétit!

Per serving: 335 Calories; 15g Fat; 10.5g Carbs; 38.5g Protein; 8.7g Sugars

457. Traditional Fish and Couscous Biryani

(Ready in about 10 minutes | Servings 4)

Ingredients

2 tablespoons butter
1 yellow onion, chopped
2 cups couscous
2 cups water
1 cup vegetable broth
1 cup coconut milk
Sea salt and ground black pepper, to taste
1 teaspoon cayenne pepper
1 teaspoon dried basil

2 ripe tomatoes, pureed
1 ½ pounds halibut, cut into chunks
1 teaspoon coriander
1 teaspoon curry paste
1 teaspoon ancho chili powder
2 bay leaves
4 cardamom pods
1 teaspoon garam masala
2 tablespoons almonds, slivered

Directions

Press the "Sauté" button and melt the butter. Once hot, cook the onions until tender and translucent.

Add the remaining ingredients, except for the slivered almonds, to the inner pot; stir to combine.

Secure the lid. Choose the "Manual" mode and cook for 4 minutes at High pressure. Once cooking is complete, use a quick pressure release; carefully remove the lid.

Serve garnished with almonds. Bon appétit!

Per serving: 505 Calories; 11.2g Fat; 61.1g Carbs; 37.7g Protein; 5.1g Sugars

458. Salmon Salad Croissants

(Ready in about 10 minutes + chilling time | Servings 6)

Ingredients

1 ½ pounds salmon fillets
1 red onion, thinly sliced
1/4 cup prepared horseradish, drained
1/4 cup mayonnaise
2 tablespoons sour cream
Salt and white pepper, to taste
1/2 teaspoon red pepper flakes, crushed

1/2 teaspoon dried rosemary, only leaves crushed
1/2 teaspoon dried oregano
1 cup cherry tomatoes, halved
2 cups Iceberg lettuce leaves, torn into pieces
6 croissants, split

Directions

Add 1 cup of water and metal trivet to your Instant Pot. Lower the salmon fillets onto the trivet.

Secure the lid. Choose the "Steam" mode and cook for 3 minutes at Low pressure. Once cooking is complete, use a quick pressure release; carefully remove the lid.

Add the remaining ingredients and stir to combine well. Place in your refrigerator until ready to serve.

Serve on croissants and enjoy!

Per serving: 412 Calories; 2.7g Fat; 26.8g Carbs; 28.8g Protein; 9.8g Sugars

459. Tuna Steaks with Lime-Butter Sauce

(Ready in about 15 minutes | Servings 3)

Ingredients

3 tuna steaks
1 ½ tablespoons sesame oil, melted
1/2 teaspoon salt
1/4 teaspoon black pepper, to taste
1/4 teaspoon smoked paprika
1 cup water

1 tablespoon fresh cilantro, chopped
For the Sauce:
1 tablespoon butter, at room temperature
1 tablespoon fresh lime juice
1 teaspoon Worcestershire sauce

Directions

Brush the tuna steaks with sesame oil. Season the tuna steaks with salt, black pepper, and smoked paprika.

Place the fish in the steaming basket; transfer it to the Instant Pot.

Pour 1 cup of water into the base of your Instant Pot. Secure the lid.

Choose "Manual" mode, Low pressure and 4 minutes. Once cooking is complete, use a quick release; carefully remove the lid.

Meanwhile, warm the butter over medium-low heat. Add the lime juice and Worcestershire sauce; remove from the heat and stir until everything is well incorporated.

Spoon the sauce over the tuna steaks, sprinkle with fresh cilantro leaves and serve. Bon appétit!

Per serving: 316 Calories; 18g Fat; 1g Carbs; 35.4g Protein; 0.3g Sugars

460. Spicy Beer-Steamed Mussels

(Ready in about 15 minutes | Servings 4)

Ingredients

1 tablespoon olive oil
1/2 cup scallions, chopped
2 cloves garlic, minced
2 medium-sized ripe tomatoes, puréed
1 (12-ounce) bottles lager beer
1 cup water

1 tablespoon fresh cilantro, chopped
Sea salt and freshly ground black pepper, to taste
2 Thai chili peppers, stemmed and split
1 ½ pounds mussels, cleaned and debearded

Directions

Press the "Sauté" button to preheat your Instant Pot. Heat the oil and cook the scallions until tender and fragrant.

Then, stir in the garlic and cook an additional 30 seconds or until fragrant. Add the remaining ingredients.

Secure the lid and choose the "Manual" setting. Cook for 3 minutes at Low pressure. Once cooking is complete, use a quick release; carefully remove the lid.

Serve with garlic croutons. Bon appétit!

Per serving: 241 Calories; 7.3g Fat; 15.3g Carbs; 21.9g Protein; 3g Sugars

461. Classic Fish Paprikash

(Ready in about 15 minutes | Servings 4)

Ingredients

2 tablespoons butter, at room temperature
1 cup leeks, chopped
2 bell peppers, seeded and sliced
2 garlic cloves, minced
2 sprigs thyme
1 sprig rosemary
1 teaspoon sweet paprika
1 teaspoon hot paprika
Sea salt and ground black pepper, to taste
2 tomatoes, puréed
2 cups vegetable broth
2 cups water
1 ½ pounds cod fish, cut into bite-sized chunks
2 tablespoons fresh cilantro, roughly chopped
1 cup sour cream, well-chilled

Directions

Press the "Sauté" button to preheat your Instant Pot. Melt the butter and sauté the leeks until fragrant.

Then, stir in the peppers and garlic and continue to sauté an additional 40 seconds.

Add the thyme, rosemary, paprika, salt, black pepper, tomatoes, broth, water, and fish.

Secure the lid and choose the "Manual" setting. Cook for 6 minutes at High pressure. Once cooking is complete, use a quick release; carefully remove the lid.

Ladle into individual bowls and serve garnished with fresh cilantro and well-chilled sour cream. Bon appétit!

Per serving: 310 Calories; 13.7g Fat; 14.4g Carbs; 32.3g Protein; 4.5g Sugars

462. Mahi-Mahi Fish with Cumin Guacamole

(Ready in about 30 minutes | Servings 4)

Ingredients

1 cup water
4 mahi-mahi fillets
2 tablespoons olive oil
Sea salt and ground black pepper, to taste
1/2 teaspoon red pepper flakes, crushed
1/2 cup shallots, sliced
2 tablespoons fresh lemon juice
1 teaspoon epazote
1/4 cup fresh coriander, chopped
1 teaspoon dried sage
For Cumin Guacamole:
2 medium tomatoes, chopped
1 large avocado, peeled, pitted and mashed
2 tablespoons salsa verde
1 clove garlic, minced
Fresh juice of 1 lime
Sea salt to taste

Directions

Pour 1 cup of water to the base of your Instant Pot.

Brush the mahi-mahi fillets with olive oil; then, sprinkle with salt, black pepper, and red pepper flakes.

Place the mahi-mahi fillets in the steaming basket; transfer it to the Instant Pot. Add the shallots on top; add the lemon juice, epazote, coriander, and sage.

Secure the lid. Choose "Manual" mode, Low pressure and 3 minutes. Once cooking is complete, use a quick release; carefully remove the lid.

Next, mix all ingredients for the cumin guacamole; place in your refrigerator for at least 20 minutes. Serve the mahi-mahi fillets with fresh cumin guacamole on the side. Bon appétit!

Per serving: 324 Calories; 18g Fat; 13.1g Carbs; 29.1g Protein; 4.6g Sugars

463. Halibut Steaks with Sautéed Tomatoes

(Ready in about 40 minutes | Servings 4)

Ingredients

2 tablespoons Worcestershire sauce
2 tablespoons oyster sauce
1/2 cup dry white wine
1 tablespoon Dijon mustard
1 (1-inch) piece fresh ginger, grated
4 halibut steaks
2 teaspoons olive oil
2 tomatoes, sliced
2 spring onions, sliced
2 garlic cloves, crushed
1 cup mixed salad greens, to serve

Directions

In a mixing bowl, whisk Worcestershire sauce, oyster sauce, white wine, mustard, and ginger. Add the fish steaks and let them marinate for 30 minutes in your refrigerator.

Meanwhile, press the "Sauté" button on your Instant Pot. Now, heat the olive oil and sauté the tomatoes with the spring onions and garlic until they are tender.

Add 2 cups of water to the base of your Instant Pot. Add the metal steamer insert to the Instant Pot.

Now, place the halibut steaks on top of the steamer insert. Secure the lid. Select the "Manual" mode. Cook for 5 minutes at Low pressure.

Once cooking is complete, use a quick release; remove the lid carefully. Serve the warm halibut steaks with the sautéed vegetables and mixed salad greens. Enjoy!

Per serving: 166 Calories; 3.8g Fat; 5g Carbs; 21.7g Protein; 1.5g Sugars

464. Creamy Shrimp Salad

(Ready in about 10 minutes | Servings 4)

Ingredients

1 pound shrimp, deveined and peeled
Fresh juice of 2 lemons
Salt and black pepper, to taste
1 red onion, chopped
1 stalk celery, chopped
1 tablespoon fresh dill, minced
1/2 cup mayonnaise
1 teaspoon Dijon mustard

Directions

Prepare your Instant Pot by adding 1 cup of water and steamer basket to the Instant Pot. Now, add the shrimp to the steamer basket.

Top with lemon slices.

Secure the lid. Choose the "Manual" mode and Low pressure; cook for 2 minutes. Once cooking is complete, use a quick pressure release; carefully remove the lid.

Add the remaining ingredients and toss to combine well. Serve well chilled and enjoy!

Per serving: 220 Calories; 10.5g Fat; 7.3g Carbs; 25.4g Protein; 2.9g Sugars

465. Risotto with Sea Bass and Leeks

(Ready in about 10 minutes | Servings 4)

Ingredients

2 tablespoons butter, melted
1/2 cup leeks, sliced
2 garlic cloves, minced
2 cups basmati rice
1 ½ pounds sea bass fillets, diced
2 cups vegetable broth
1 cup water
Salt, to taste
1/2 teaspoon ground black pepper
1 teaspoon fresh ginger, grated

Directions

Press the "Sauté" button to preheat your Instant Pot. Then, melt the butter and sweat the leeks for 2 to 3 minutes.

Stir in the garlic; continue to sauté an additional 40 seconds. Add the remaining ingredients.

Secure the lid. Choose the "Manual" mode and Low pressure; cook for 4 minutes. Once cooking is complete, use a quick pressure release; carefully remove the lid.

Serve warm in individual bowls and enjoy!

Per serving: 432 Calories; 22.2g Fat; 32.2g Carbs; 42g Protein; 1.1g Sugars

466. Simple Fish Mélange

(Ready in about 15 minutes | Servings 4)

Ingredients

1 tablespoon olive oil
2 shallots, diced
2 garlic cloves, smashed
2 carrots, diced
2 (6-ounce) cans crab, juice
reserved
1/2 pound cod, cut into bite-sized
chunks

Sea salt, to taste
1/2 teaspoon freshly ground black
pepper
2 bay leaves
1 tablespoon Creole seasoning
2 cups water
1 cup double cream
1 tablespoon lemon juice

Directions

Press the "Sauté" button to preheat your Instant Pot. Then, heat the oil and
sauté the shallots until tender.

Stir in the garlic and carrots; cook an additional minute or so. Add the canned
crab meat, cod, salt, black pepper, bay leaves, Creole seasoning, and water.

Secure the lid and choose the "Manual" setting. Cook for 6 minutes at
High pressure. Once cooking is complete, use a quick release; carefully
remove the lid.

Lastly, stir in the double cream and lemon juice. Press the "Sauté" button
one more time; let it simmer until heated through. Enjoy!

Per serving: 254 Calories; 15.4g Fat; 15.5g Carbs; 13.9g Protein; 7.9g Sugars

467. Easy Fish Burritos

(Ready in about 15 minutes | Servings 4)

Ingredients

2 tablespoons olive oil
4 catfish fillets
Sea salt to taste
1/3 teaspoon ground black pepper,
to taste
1/2 teaspoon cayenne pepper

1/2 teaspoon ground bay leaf
1 teaspoon dried thyme
4 burrito-sized tortillas
1 cup fresh salsa
1 large-sized tomato, sliced

Directions

Prepare your Instant Pot by adding 1 ½ cups of water and a metal rack to
its bottom.

Place the fish fillets in the center of a foil sheet. Drizzle olive oil over the
fish. Season with salt, black pepper, cayenne pepper, ground bay leaf and
dried thyme.

Wrap tightly and lower it onto the rack.

Secure the lid and choose "Manual" setting. Cook for 10 minutes at
High pressure. Once cooking is complete, use a natural release; carefully
remove the lid.

Divide the fish fillets among tortillas. Top it with the salsa and tomatoes.
Roll each tortilla into a burrito and serve immediately.

Per serving: 377 Calories; 14.2g Fat; 30.5g Carbs; 31.2g Protein; 5.3g Sugars

468. Easy Saucy Clams

(Ready in about 10 minutes | Servings 5)

Ingredients

1/2 cup bacon, smoked and cubed
2 onions, chopped
3 garlic cloves, minced
1 sprig thyme
3 (6.5-ounce) cans clams, chopped
1/3 cup tarty white wine
1/3 cup water

1/2 cup clam juice
A pinch of cayenne pepper
1 bay leaf
5 lime juice
2 tablespoons fresh chives,
roughly chopped

Directions

Press the "Sauté" button to preheat your Instant Pot. Add the cubed bacon.
Once your bacon releases its fat, add the onions, garlic, and thyme.

Cook for 3 minutes more or until the onion is transparent.

Add the clams, white wine, water, clam juice, cayenne pepper, and bay leaf.
Secure the lid. Select "Manual" mode and cook at Low pressure for 4 minutes.

Once cooking is complete, use a natural release; remove the lid carefully

Ladle into individual bowls and serve garnished with lime slices and fresh
chives. Bon appétit!

Per serving: 157 Calories; 4.6g Fat; 27.7g Carbs; 3.4g Protein; 8.3g Sugars

469. Sole Fillets with Pickle Mayo

(Ready in about 10 minutes | Servings 4)

Ingredients

1 ½ pounds sole fillets
Sea salt and ground black pepper,
to taste
1 teaspoon paprika

1/2 cup mayonnaise
1 tablespoon pickle juice
2 cloves garlic, smashed

Directions

Sprinkle the fillets with salt, black pepper, and paprika.

Add 1 ½ cups of water and a steamer basket to the Instant Pot. Place the
fish in the steamer basket.

Secure the lid and choose "Manual" setting. Cook for 3 minutes at Low
pressure. Once cooking is complete, use a quick release; carefully remove
the lid.

Then, make the sauce by mixing the mayonnaise with the pickle juice and
garlic. Serve the fish fillets with the well-chilled sauce on the side. Bon
appétit!

Per serving: 211 Calories; 12.0g Fat; 3.9g Carbs; 22.3g Protein; 1.1g Sugars

470. Fish Taco Bowl

(Ready in about 10 minutes | Servings 4)

Ingredients

1 pound halibut steaks
1/4 cup fresh cilantro leaves
chopped
2 garlic cloves, crushed
Sea salt and ground black pepper,
to taste

1 cup white cabbage, shredded
1 jalapeño, coarsely chopped
1 can black beans
1 cup Pico de gallo

Directions

Add 1 ½ cups of water and a steamer basket to the Instant Pot. Place the
fish in the steamer basket.

Top with cilantro and garlic. Season with salt and pepper.

Secure the lid and choose "Manual" setting. Cook for 4 minutes at High
pressure. Once cooking is complete, use a quick release; carefully remove
the lid.

Cut the cooked halibut into slices and transfer them to a serving bowl.
Garnish with cabbage, jalapeño, black beans, and Pico de gallo. Enjoy!

Per serving: 245 Calories; 15.7g Fat; 9.3g Carbs; 16.9g Protein; 5.4g Sugars

471. Vietnamese Fish Chowder in a Bread Bowl

(Ready in about 15 minutes | Servings 4)

Ingredients

2 ½ cups water
3 cod fillets
2 sweet potatoes, peeled and diced
1 parsnip, chopped
1 celery with leaves, chopped
2 shallots, chopped
1 green bell pepper, chopped
2 garlic cloves, minced
Salt, to taste
1/3 teaspoon ground black pepper

2 teaspoons capers, liquid
reserved
1 teaspoon sumac powder
1 teaspoon fennel seeds
1/2 teaspoon Vietnamese
cinnamon
1 ½ cups stock, preferably
homemade
2 tablespoons fish sauce
1 ½ cups double cream
4 (8-ounce) round bread loaves

Directions

Add the water, cod fillets, sweet potatoes, parsnip, celery, shallot, bell
pepper, garlic, salt, black pepper, capers, sumac powder, fennel seeds,
Vietnamese cinnamon, stock, and fish sauce to your Instant Pot.

Secure the lid and choose "Manual" mode. Cook for 8 minutes at Low pressure.

Once cooking is complete, use a natural release; remove the lid carefully.

Fold in the double cream, press the "Sauté" button and continue to cook
until it is thoroughly cooked.

Now, cut a slice off the top of each bread loaf. Now, gently pull the inner
bread from the round with a tablespoon, leaving a 1/4-inch thick shell.

Ladle the soup into bread loaves and serve hot.

Per serving: 419 Calories; 29.9g Fat; 17.6g Carbs; 21.2g Protein;
5.4g Sugars

472. Herbed Mackerel Fillets with Peppers

(Ready in about 15 minutes | Servings 5)

Ingredients

5 mackerel fillets, skin on
Sea salt, to taste
1/4 teaspoon ground black pepper, to taste
1/2 teaspoon cayenne pepper
1/2 teaspoon dried rosemary
1 teaspoon marjoram
1 tablespoon butter, melted
1 red bell pepper, deveined and sliced
1 green bell pepper, deveined and sliced

Directions

Prepare your Instant Pot by adding 1 ½ cups of water and steamer basket to its bottom.

Season the mackerel fillets with the salt, black pepper, cayenne pepper, rosemary, and marjoram.

Place the mackerel fillets in the steamer basket. Drizzle with melted butter. Top with sliced peppers.

Secure the lid and choose the "Manual" setting. Cook for 3 minutes at Low pressure. Once cooking is complete, use a quick release; carefully remove the lid. Serve immediately.

Per serving: 423 Calories; 7.9g Fat; 1.6g Carbs; 80g Protein; 0.9g Sugars

473. Seafood and Yellow Lentil Gumbo

(Ready in about 15 minutes | Servings 5)

Ingredients

2 tablespoons butter, at room temperature
2 garlic cloves, minced
1/2 (14-ounce) can diced tomatoes
1/3 cup Sauvignon Blanc
1 cup vegetable broth
1 ½ tablespoons apple cider vinegar
Sea salt and ground black pepper, to taste
1 cup French green lentils
1 ½ pounds shrimp, cleaned and deveined
5 ounces crabmeat

Directions

Press the "Sauté" button to preheat your Instant Pot. Melt the butter. Then, sauté the garlic until aromatic about 40 seconds.

Now, add the canned tomatoes, Sauvignon Blanc, broth, vinegar, salt, black pepper, and lentils to your Instant Pot.

Secure the lid and choose the "Manual" setting. Cook for 6 minutes at High pressure. Once cooking is complete, use a quick release; carefully remove the lid.

Press the "Sauté" button again. Stir in the shrimp and crabmeat; simmer until they become pink. Ladle into soup bowls. Bon appétit!

Per serving: 277 Calories; 9.2g Fat; 8.3g Carbs; 36.7g Protein; 3.1g Sugars

474. Fish Tikka Masala

(Ready in about 15 minutes | Servings 4)

Ingredients

2 tablespoons olive oil
1/2 cup scallions, chopped
2 garlic cloves, minced
1/4 cup tikka masala curry paste
1/3 teaspoon ground allspice
1 (14-ounce) can diced tomatoes
1 tablespoon brown sugar
1 teaspoon hot paprika
1 cup vegetable broth
1 ½ pounds haddock fillets, cut into bite-sized chunks
1 cup natural yogurt
1 lime, cut into wedges

Directions

Press the "Sauté" button to preheat your Instant Pot; heat the oil. Then, sauté the scallions until tender and translucent.

Now, add the garlic; continue to sauté for a further 30 seconds.

Stir the curry paste, allspice, tomatoes, sugar, paprika, broth, and haddock into the Instant Pot.

Secure the lid and choose the "Manual" setting. Cook for 5 minutes at Low pressure. Once cooking is complete, use a quick release; carefully remove the lid.

Then, fold in the natural yogurt and stir to combine well; seal the lid again and allow it to sit in the residual heat until warmed through.

Serve in individual bowls, garnished with lime wedges. Enjoy!

Per serving: 273 Calories; 9.3g Fat; 13.5g Carbs; 34.9g Protein; 6.6g Sugars

475. Shrimp and Ham Hock Soup

(Ready in about 45 minutes | Servings 6)

Ingredients

2 tablespoons olive oil
1/2 cup leeks, chopped
2 garlic cloves, minced
2 carrots, diced
1 parsnip, diced
2 tablespoons chickpea flour
2 tablespoons tomato paste
2 teaspoons chipotle in adobo sauce, chopped
1 ham hock
1 cup water
5 cups broth, preferably homemade
2 sprigs rosemary
1 teaspoon lemon thyme
Sea salt, to taste
1/2 teaspoon mixed peppercorns, freshly cracked
3/4 pound shrimp, peeled and deveined
1/2 cup double cream

Directions

Press the "Sauté" button and add the olive oil. Once hot, sauté the leeks together with the garlic, carrots, and parsnips; cook until the vegetables are just tender.

Add the chickpea flour and cook for a further 1 minute 30 seconds, stirring frequently.

Stir in the tomato paste, chipotle in adobo sauce, ham hock, water, and broth. Season with rosemary, lemon thyme, salt and mixed peppercorns. Secure the lid.

Choose the "Soup" function, High pressure and 35 minutes. Once cooking is complete, use a natural release; carefully remove the lid.

Place the ham hock on a cutting board; allow it to rest. Pull the meat from ham hock bone and shred. Add it back to the Instant Pot.

Stir in the shrimp and double cream. Close the Instant Pot and cook your shrimp in the residual heat for 8 minutes. Bon appétit!

Per serving: 298 Calories; 13.5g Fat; 10.5g Carbs; 34.1g Protein; 3.7g Sugars

476. Saucy and Spicy Halibut Steaks

(Ready in about 15 minutes | Servings 4)

Ingredients

2 tablespoons butter, melted
1 yellow onion, chopped
2 garlic cloves, pressed
2 bell peppers, chopped
1/4 cup Chardonnay
2 ripe tomatoes, puréed
1 pound halibut steaks
1 cup fish stock
1 dried red chili, coarsely chopped
1/2 teaspoon nigella seeds
2 bay leaves
1/2 teaspoon ground black pepper, to taste
Sea salt, to taste

Directions

Press the "Sauté" button to preheat your Instant Pot. Then, melt the butter and sauté the onion until tender and translucent.

Then, stir in the garlic and bell peppers; continue to cook an additional 2 minutes or until the peppers have softened.

Add a splash of wine to deglaze the bottom of the inner pot. Add the remaining ingredients and stir to combine.

Secure the lid and choose the "Manual" setting. Cook for 5 minutes at Low pressure. Once cooking is complete, use a quick release; carefully remove the lid.

Taste, adjust the seasonings and serve warm. Bon appétit!

Per serving: 174 Calories; 6.5g Fat; 27.7g Carbs; 6.2g Protein; 13.9g Sugars

477. Traditional Creole Jambalaya

(Ready in about 15 minutes | Servings 4)

Ingredients

6 ounces Andouille sausage, sliced
1 yellow onion, chopped
1 teaspoon garlic, minced
1 teaspoon fresh ginger, grated
1 ½ pounds shrimp, cleaned and deveined
2 sweet peppers, seeded and sliced
1 red chili pepper, seeded and minced

2 carrots, thinly sliced
Sea salt and ground black pepper, to taste
1 teaspoon Creole seasoning
2 ½ cups water
2 ripe tomatoes, puréed
2 chicken Bouillon cubes

Directions

Press the "Sauté" button to preheat your Instant Pot. Now, cook the sausage until delicately browned, about 3 minutes; add the onion, garlic, and ginger and continue to cook for a further 2 minutes, stirring periodically.

Throw the rest of the above ingredients into your Instant Pot.

Secure the lid. Choose the "Manual" mode and Low pressure; cook for 6 minutes. Once cooking is complete, use a quick pressure release; carefully remove the lid.

Ladle into individual bowls and serve garnished with fresh lemon slices if desired. Bon appétit!

Per serving: 366 Calories; 13g Fat; 18.3g Carbs; 45.1g Protein; 4.1g Sugars

478. Spanish Chorizo and Seafood Paella

(Ready in about 15 minutes | Servings 6)

Ingredients

3 teaspoons olive oil
1/2 ring of Chorizo sausage, sliced
1 onion, chopped
1 ½ cups basmati rice
2 cups water
1 cup tomato paste
1 red bell pepper, chopped
1 roasted yellow bell pepper, chopped

1 ½ pounds tiger shrimp, cleaned and divined
Sea salt, to taste
1/2 teaspoon ground black pepper
1/2 teaspoon sweet paprika
A pinch of saffron threads
1 bay leaf
1 cup frozen peas
1 cup frozen sweetcorn

Directions

Press the "Sauté" button to preheat your Instant Pot. Heat the olive oil; now, brown the sausage and onion for 2 to 3 minutes.

Add the rice and continue to cook an additional 3 minutes or until it starts to turn translucent.

Stir the remaining ingredients into your Instant Pot.

Secure the lid. Choose the "Manual" mode and High pressure; cook for 6 minutes. Once cooking is complete, use a quick pressure release; carefully remove the lid. Serve warm.

Per serving: 335 Calories; 11.8g Fat; 35.8g Carbs; 31.6g Protein; 12.6g Sugars

479. Scallops in Champagne-Butter Sauce

(Ready in about 10 minutes | Servings 3)

Ingredients

1 pound scallops
1 teaspoon ginger garlic paste
Sea salt and ground black pepper, to taste
1/2 teaspoon cayenne pepper

1/4 teaspoon pink peppercorns, crushed
1 cup vegetable broth
1/2 cup Champagne
2 tablespoons butter

Directions

Add all of the above ingredients to the Instant Pot.

Secure the lid. Choose the "Manual" mode and Low pressure; cook for 3 minutes. Once cooking is complete, use a quick pressure release; carefully remove the lid.

Then, press the "Sauté" button and cook the sauce, whisking constantly, until it has reduced by half. Bon appétit!

Per serving: 165 Calories; 7.6g Fat; 5.7g Carbs; 17.6g Protein; 0.3g Sugars

480. Home-Style Fish Burgers

(Ready in about 20 minutes | Servings 3)

Ingredients

1 cup water
1/2 pound tuna filets
1 onion, finely chopped
2 garlic cloves, chopped
1 sweet bell pepper, chopped
1 jalapeno pepper, chopped
1 egg
1 cup tortilla chips, crushed

1 teaspoon cayenne pepper
1/4 teaspoon dried dill weed
Salt and black pepper, to taste
3 teaspoons canola oil
3 tablespoons mayonnaise
2 teaspoon Dijon mustard
3 cornichons, diced
3 hamburger buns

Directions

Pour 1 cup of water into the base of your Instant Pot. Place the tuna fillets in the steaming basket; transfer it to the Instant Pot.

Secure the lid and choose the "Manual" mode, Low pressure and 4 minutes.

Once cooking is complete, use a quick release; remove the lid carefully. Now, flake the steamed fish with a fork.

Add the onion, garlic, pepper, egg, tortilla chips, cayenne pepper, dill, salt, and black pepper. Now, shape the fish mixture into patties.

Heat a frying pan over a moderately high heat. Now, heat the canola oil. Once hot, fry the fish patties until they're crispy and golden brown.

Pop the burger buns in the oven and lightly toast them.

Assemble the fish burgers, by spreading on a layer of mayo and mustard, followed by the cornichons, a fish patty, and then, the bun top. Bon appétit!

Per serving: 447 Calories; 17.6g Fat; 48.4g Carbs; 24.7g Protein; 11.9g Sugars

481. Greek-Style Seafood Dinner

(Ready in about 10 minutes | Servings 4)

Ingredients

1 tablespoon olive oil
1/2 cup scallions, chopped
2 garlic cloves, minced
Sea salt and ground black pepper, to taste
1/2 teaspoon cayenne pepper, or more taste
1 teaspoon dried oregano

2 ripe tomatoes, chopped
1 ½ pounds prawns, cleaned
6 ounces Halloumi cheese, sliced
1/2 cup Kalamata olives, pitted and sliced
2 tablespoons fresh cilantro, chopped

Directions

Press the "Sauté" button to preheat your Instant Pot. Then, heat the oil; sauté the scallions and garlic until tender and fragrant.

Add the salt, black pepper, cayenne pepper, oregano, tomatoes, and prawns.

Secure the lid. Choose the "Manual" mode and Low pressure; cook for 3 minutes. Once cooking is complete, use a quick pressure release; carefully remove the lid.

Ladle into serving bowls; top each serving with cheese, olives and fresh cilantro. Bon appétit!

Per serving: 351 Calories; 16.6g Fat; 11.9g Carbs; 37.8g Protein; 5.6g Sugars

482. Old Bay Fish with Gherkin Sauce

(Ready in about 15 minutes | Servings 3)

Ingredients

1/4 cup white wine
1 ½ teaspoons Old Bay seasoning
Sea salt, to taste
1/4 teaspoon ground black pepper, or more to taste
3/4 pound mackerel fillets
1 cup water
1 lime, sliced
For the Gherkin Sauce:

1/2 cup cream cheese
2 hard-boiled eggs
3 gherkins, chopped
1 tablespoon capers
A pinch of brown sugar
A pinch of cayenne pepper
2 tablespoons fresh cilantro leaves, chopped
Salt, to taste

Directions

In a mixing bowl, thoroughly combine the white wine, Old Bay seasoning, salt, and black pepper. Brush this mixture on both sides of mackerel fillets.

Add 1 cup of water to the base of your Instant Pot.

Place the mackerel fillets in the steaming basket; transfer it to the Instant Pot. Secure the lid and choose "Manual" mode, Low pressure and 5 minutes.

Once cooking is complete, use a quick release; remove the lid carefully.

In the meantime, mix all ingredients for the sauce; place in your refrigerator until ready to serve. Serve the steamed fish with the lime and Gherkin sauce on the side. Enjoy!

Per serving: 361 Calories; 20.6g Fat; 10g Carbs; 33.3g Protein; 7.1g Sugars

483. Paprika Seafood Boil

(Ready in about 10 minutes | Servings 4)

Ingredients

2 cups chicken stock
8 ounces smoked sausage, cut into bite-sized pieces
1 pound catfish
1 celery with leaves, chopped
1 carrot, chopped
1 leek, thinly sliced
2 garlic cloves, minced
Sea salt and ground black pepper, to taste
1 teaspoon smoked paprika
1 teaspoon hot paprika
1 teaspoon Old Bay seasoning
2 tomatoes, chopped

Directions

Add all of the above ingredients to your Instant Pot.

Secure the lid. Choose "Manual" mode and High pressure; cook for 4 minutes. Once cooking is complete, use a quick pressure release; carefully remove the lid.

Remove all ingredients from the Instant Pot using a slotted spoon; serve immediately.

Per serving: 301 Calories; 14.8g Fat; 10.1g Carbs; 31.4g Protein; 3.9g Sugars

484. Indian Meen Kulambu

(Ready in about 15 minutes | Servings 6)

Ingredients

1 tablespoon olive oil
1 cup scallions, chopped
1 teaspoon fresh garlic, smashed
2 pounds mackerel fillets, cut into bite-size chunks
1 ½ cups coconut milk
1 cup chicken bone broth, preferably homemade
2 dried red chilies, coarsely chopped
1 teaspoon curry powder
1 teaspoon ground coriander
1 teaspoon cayenne pepper
Sea salt and ground black pepper, to taste
2 tablespoons freshly squeezed lemon juice

Directions

Press the "Sauté" button to preheat your Instant Pot. Heat the oil until sizzling; once hot, sauté the scallions and garlic until tender and fragrant.

Add the remaining ingredients, except for the lemon juice, to the Instant Pot.

Secure the lid. Choose "Manual" mode and Low pressure; cook for 6 minutes. Once cooking is complete, use a quick pressure release; carefully remove the lid.

Divide among individual bowls. Drizzle lemon juice over each serving and enjoy!

Per serving: 335 Calories; 19.9g Fat; 6.2g Carbs; 33.4g Protein; 2.9g Sugars

485. Green Bean and Crab Casserole

(Ready in about 15 minutes | Servings 4)

Ingredients

2 tablespoons butter, melted
2 garlic cloves, minced
1/2 cup scallions, chopped
1/2 pound frozen green beans
1/2 cup dry white wine
1 ½ cups stock
1 ½ cups plain milk
1 pound crabmeat
Salt and ground pepper, to taste
1 can cream of mushroom soup
1 teaspoon cayenne pepper
1/2 teaspoon tarragon
1/2 teaspoon dried parsley flakes
1 cup seasoned breadcrumbs

Directions

Press the "Sauté" button to preheat your Instant Pot. Now, warm the butter and add the garlic, scallions, and green beans. Cook for 2 to 3 minutes.

Add a splash of wine to scrape up any browned bits from the bottom of the inner pot. Add the remaining wine, stock, milk, crabmeat, salt, pepper, and cream of mushroom soup.

Sprinkle with cayenne pepper, tarragon, and parsley flakes. Add the seasoned breadcrumbs to the top. Secure the lid.

Choose the "Manual' mode, Low pressure and 6 minutes. Once cooking is complete, use a quick release; remove the lid carefully.

Divide between individual serving plates and eat warm. Bon appétit!

Per serving: 435 Calories; 16.8g Fat; 33.1g Carbs; 32.1g Protein; 10.9g Sugars

486. Moroccan Fish Kebabs

(Ready in about 15 minutes | Servings 4)

Ingredients

1/2 pound yellow squash zucchini, cubed
1 red onion, cut into wedges
2 bell peppers, cut into strips
1 pound salmon, skinned, deboned and cut into bite-sized chunks
2 tablespoons toasted sesame oil
Sea salt and ground black pepper, to taste
1 teaspoon red pepper flakes
8 sticks fresh rosemary, lower leaves removed

Directions

Prepare your Instant Pot by adding 1½ cups of water and a metal rack to its bottom.

Thread vegetables and fish alternately onto rosemary sticks.

Drizzle with sesame oil; sprinkle with salt, black pepper, and red pepper flakes. Cover with a piece of foil.

Secure the lid. Choose "Manual" mode and Low pressure; cook for 6 minutes. Once cooking is complete, use a quick pressure release; carefully remove the lid. Serve immediately.

Per serving: 263 Calories; 15.1g Fat; 6.4g Carbs; 24.8g Protein; 3.7g Sugars

487. Tuna and Buckwheat Salad

(Ready in about 10 minutes + chilling time | Servings 4)

Ingredients

1 pound tuna, cut into bite-sized pieces
1 cup buckwheat
1/2 teaspoon dried or fresh dill
Salt and black pepper, to taste
2 cups water
1 white onion, thinly sliced
2 bell peppers, seeded and thinly sliced
1 carrot, grated
1 large-sized cucumber, thinly sliced
1/4 cup extra-virgin olive oil
2 tablespoons lemon juice, freshly squeezed

Directions

Throw the water, buckwheat, dill, salt, black pepper, and water into your Instant Pot

Secure the lid. Choose the "Manual" mode and Low pressure; cook for 3 minutes. Once cooking is complete, use a quick pressure release; carefully remove the lid.

Allow the fish and buckwheat to cool completely. Then, toss it with the remaining ingredients and serve well chilled. Bon appétit!

Per serving: 238 Calories; 6.8g Fat; 14.1g Carbs; 30.1g Protein; 3.3g Sugars

488. Polenta with Peppers and Fish

(Ready in about 20 minutes | Servings 4)

Ingredients

4 cups water
2 tablespoons butter
A pinch of salt
1 cup polenta
4 ounces bacon, diced
2 shallots, thinly sliced
2 garlic cloves, minced
2 bell peppers, chopped
2 tomatoes, puréed
1 cup fish stock, preferably homemade
1 sprig thyme
2 sprigs rosemary
1 ½ pounds cod fillets, chopped
Sea salt and ground black pepper, to taste

Directions

Press the "Sauté" button to preheat the Instant Pot. Then, add the water, butter, and salt; bring to a simmer. Whisk in the polenta.

Secure the lid. Choose the "Manual" mode and High pressure; cook for 7 minutes. Once cooking is complete, use a natural pressure release; carefully remove the lid.

Transfer the prepared polenta to a serving bowl. Wipe down the Instant Pot with a damp cloth.

Press the "Sauté" button to preheat the Instant Pot. Now, cook the bacon until crisp; reserve. Add the shallots and continue to cook for 2 to 3 minutes more or until tender.

Then, add the garlic and peppers. Continue sautéing for one minute longer. Add the remaining ingredients to the Instant Pot.

Secure the lid. Choose the "Manual" mode and Low pressure; cook for 3 minutes. Once cooking is complete, use a natural pressure release; carefully remove the lid.

Add the fish mixture to the serving bowl with polenta. Top with bacon and serve warm. Enjoy!

Per serving: 389 Calories; 18.1g Fat; 23.6g Carbs; 32.6g Protein; 6.2g Sugars

489. Steamed Oysters with Green Onion Sauce

(Ready in about 10 minutes | Servings 4)

Per serving: 443 Calories; 34.1g Fat; 13.4g Carbs; 15.1g Protein; 2.4g Sugars

Ingredients

2 tablespoons olive oil
1 ½ pounds fresh oysters, shucked
1/2 cup rose wine
1 ¼ cups chicken stock
1 teaspoon sweet paprika
Sea salt and ground black pepper, to taste
1/2 teaspoon fennel seeds
1 teaspoon marjoram
1 teaspoon ginger-garlic paste
Green Onion Sauce:
1/4 cup sour cream
1/2 cup mayonnaise
3 tablespoons fresh green onions, chopped
1 garlic clove, minced

Directions

Press the "Sauté" button to preheat your Instant Pot. Heat the oil until sizzling; once hot, sauté the oysters for 1 minute.

Add the wine, stock, paprika, salt, black pepper, fennel seeds, marjoram, and ginger-garlic paste.

Secure the lid. Choose "Manual" mode and Low pressure; cook for 6 minutes. Once cooking is complete, use a quick pressure release; carefully remove the lid.

Afterwards, make the sauce by mixing the sour cream, mayonnaise, green onions, and garlic. Serve the oysters with the sauce on the side. Bon appétit!

BEANS, PASTA & GRAINS

490. Risotto with Chorizo and Black Olives

(Ready in about 20 minutes | Servings 4)

Ingredients

2 tablespoons butter, melted
1 yellow onion, chopped
2 carrots, trimmed and chopped
1/2 pound Chorizo sausage, sliced
1 cup white long-grain rice
2 cups chicken stock

Sea salt and ground black pepper, to taste
1/4 cup lightly packed fresh coriander, roughly chopped
1 cup black olives, pitted and sliced

Directions

Press the "Sauté" button to preheat your Instant Pot. Now, melt the butter and cook the onion until aromatic.

Then, add the carrot and Chorizo; cook an additional 2 minutes. Add the remaining ingredients and stir to combine well.

Secure the lid. Choose the "Manual" mode and High pressure; cook for 3 minutes. Once cooking is complete, use a natural pressure release for 10 minutes; carefully remove the lid.

Ladle into individual bowls and serve warm. Bon appétit!

Per serving: 576 Calories; 34.7g Fat; 44.8g Carbs; 20.5g Protein; 2.3g Sugars

491. Corn on the Cob with Smoky Lime Butter

(Ready in about 15 minutes | Servings 3)

Ingredients

1 ¼ cups water
3 ears corn on the cob
1/2 stick butter, softened
A few drops of liquid smoke
1/2 lemon, juiced

1 tablespoon fresh cilantro, minced
A pinch of sugar
Sea salt and white pepper, to taste

Directions

Pour water into the base of your Instant Pot. Place three ears corn on the cob on a metal trivet. Secure the lid.

Choose the "Steam" mode and cook for 3 minutes under High pressure. Once cooking is complete, use a natural release; remove the lid carefully. Reserve the corn on the cob.

Press the "Sauté" button to heat up your Instant Pot. Melt the butter and remove from heat. Add the liquid smoke, lemon juice, cilantro, sugar, sea salt, and pepper; stir to combine.

Toss the corn on the cob with the smoky lemon butter. Bon appétit!

Per serving: 263 Calories; 16.2g Fat; 30.9g Carbs; 4.3g Protein; 1.1g Sugars

492. The Best Barley Salad Ever

(Ready in about 15 minutes | Servings 4)

Ingredients

1 ½ cups pearl barley
3 cups water
Sea salt and ground black pepper, to taste
1 leek, thinly sliced
2 cloves garlic, crushed
4 tablespoons extra-virgin olive oil

1/2 cup fresh parsley, chopped
2 tablespoons lime juice, freshly squeezed
1/2 cup canned chickpea, rinsed
1 cup pickles, diced
4 ounces feta cheese, crumbled

Directions

Add the barley and water to the Instant Pot.

Secure the lid. Choose the "Manual" mode and High pressure; cook for 9 minutes. Once cooking is complete, use a natural pressure release; carefully remove the lid.

Allow the barley to cool completely; then, transfer it to a salad bowl. Add the remaining ingredients and toss to combine well. Place in your refrigerator until ready to serve. Enjoy!

Per serving: 582 Calories; 22.1g Fat; 81g Carbs; 17.6g Protein; 6.4g Sugars

493. Bulgur Wheat with Pico de Gallo

(Ready in about 25 minutes | Servings 4)

Ingredients

2 tablespoons vegetable oil
1 yellow onion, chopped
2 garlic cloves, minced
1 ¼ cups bulgur wheat

3 cups roasted vegetable broth
Sea salt and white pepper, to taste
1 teaspoon smoked paprika
1/2 cup Pico de gallo

Directions

Press the "Sauté" button to preheat your Instant Pot. Now, sauté the onions with garlic for 1 minute or so.

Then, stir the bulgur wheat, broth, salt, pepper, and paprika into your Instant Pot.

Secure the lid. Choose the "Manual" mode and High pressure; cook for 12 minutes. Once cooking is complete, use a natural pressure release for 10 minutes; carefully remove the lid.

Serve topped with chilled Pico de gallo. Bon appétit!

Per serving: 184 Calories; 10.4g Fat; 17.8g Carbs; 6g Protein; 3.8g Sugars

494. Herby Pinto Beans with Rice

(Ready in about 30 minutes | Servings 6)

Ingredients

2 tablespoons olive oil
1 cup dry pinto beans
1 cup dry brown rice
2 tomatoes, puréed
3 cups water
3 bouillon cubes
1 tablespoon fresh parsley, chopped

1 tablespoon fresh rosemary, chopped
1 tablespoon fresh mint, chopped
1 ancho chili pepper, chopped
2 tablespoons fresh chives, roughly chopped

Directions

Add all ingredients, except for the chives, to your Instant Pot.

Secure the lid. Choose the "Bean/Chili" mode and High pressure; cook for 25 minutes. Once cooking is complete, use a natural pressure release; carefully remove the lid.

Garnish with the chopped chives and enjoy!

Per serving: 277 Calories; 5.9g Fat; 46.3g Carbs; 9.9g Protein; 2.4g Sugars

495. Chicken and Barley Soup

(Ready in about 40 minutes | Servings 6)

Ingredients

1 tablespoon butter, melted
1 ½ pounds chicken drumettes
1 onion, chopped
2 parsnips, trimmed and sliced
2 carrots, trimmed and sliced
1 celery stalk, chopped
2 cloves garlic, minced
1/2 teaspoon sea salt

1/3 teaspoon freshly ground black pepper
1/2 cup white wine
6 cups chicken broth, preferably homemade
2 bay leaves
1 1/3 cups barley, pearled

Directions

Press the "Sauté" button to heat up the Instant Pot. Now, melt the butter. Once hot, sear the chicken drumettes on all sides for 3 to 4 minutes. Discard the bones and reserve.

Then, sweat the onion until it is translucent.

Add the parsnips, carrots, and celery; cook an additional 3 minute or until the vegetables have softened. After that, stir in garlic and cook an additional 30 seconds.

Add the remaining ingredients and secure the lid. Choose "Soup" setting and cook at High pressure for 30 minutes.

Once cooking is complete, use a natural release; remove the lid carefully. Add the reserved chicken and stir to combine. Ladle into individual bowls and serve hot.

Per serving: 379 Calories; 5.9g Fat; 48.8g Carbs; 33.2g Protein; 5.3g Sugars

496. Decadent Baked Beans with Madeira Wine

(Ready in about 40 minutes | Servings 4)

Ingredients

2 red onions, thinly sliced
2 garlic cloves, smashed
1 pound dry Cannellini beans
2 cups tomatoes, puréed
2 tablespoons tomato ketchup

1 teaspoon whole grain mustard
2 bay leaves
2 canned chipotle chilies
1 lime, cut into wedges
1/2 cup Madeira wine

Directions

Add the red onions, garlic, beans, tomatoes, ketchup, mustard, bay leaves, and chilies to the Instant Pot.

Secure the lid. Choose the "Bean/Chili" mode and High pressure; cook for 30 minutes. Once cooking is complete, use a natural pressure release; carefully remove the lid.

Ladle into individual bowls; squeeze lime wedges into each serving; add the wine and stir to blend well. Serve warm.

Per serving: 226 Calories; 4.5g Fat; 29.3g Carbs; 12.9g Protein; 10.2g Sugars

497. Classic Navy Beans

(Ready in about 35 minutes | Servings 6)

Ingredients

1 ¼ pounds dry navy beans
6 cups water
2 tablespoons bouillon granules

2 bay leaves
1 teaspoon black peppercorns, to taste

Directions

Rinse off and drain the navy beans. Place the navy beans, water, bouillon granules, bay leaves, and black peppercorns in your Instant Pot.

Secure the lid. Choose the "Manual" mode and cook at High pressure for 20 minutes.

Once cooking is complete, use a natural release; remove the lid carefully. Bon appétit!

Per serving: 292 Calories; 1.6g Fat; 52.3g Carbs; 19g Protein; 3.6g Sugars

498. Coconut Buckwheat Porridge with Sultanas

(Ready in about 20 minutes | Servings 5)

Ingredients

2 teaspoons coconut butter
1 ½ cups buckwheat
1 ½ cups coconut milk
1 ½ cups water
1/2 teaspoon coconut extract

A pinch of salt
A pinch of grated nutmeg
1/2 teaspoon ground cinnamon
3/4 cup agave syrup
2/3 cup sultanas

Directions

Press the "Sauté" button to preheat your Instant Pot. Now, melt the butter and toast the buckwheat, stirring frequently, until it is aromatic or about 3 minutes.

Add the remaining ingredients and stir to combine well.

Secure the lid. Choose the "Manual" mode and High pressure; cook for 3 minutes. Once cooking is complete, use a natural pressure release for 10 minutes; carefully remove the lid. Serve right away.

Per serving: 371 Calories; 19.1g Fat; 53.6g Carbs; 3.3g Protein; 42.1g Sugars

499. Winter Oatmeal with Walnuts and Figs

(Ready in about 25 minutes | Servings 3)

Ingredients

1 cup steel cut oats
1 cup water
1/2 cup coconut milk
2 tablespoons coconut flakes
1/2 teaspoon star anise

2 tablespoons honey
3 fresh or dried figs, chopped
1/2 cup walnuts, chopped or ground

Directions

Add the steel cut oats, water, milk, coconut flakes, anise, and honey to your Instant Pot.

Secure the lid. Choose the "Manual" mode and High pressure; cook for 10 minutes. Once cooking is complete, use a natural pressure release for 12 minutes; carefully remove the lid.

Divide the oatmeal among 3 serving bowls; top each serving with chopped figs and walnuts. Bon appétit!

Per serving: 270 Calories; 13.3g Fat; 43g Carbs; 9.2g Protein; 19.6g Sugars

500. Red Bean Soup

(Ready in about 40 minutes | Servings 5)

Ingredients

2 tablespoons canola oil
1 cup red onions, chopped
1 parsnip, chopped
1 red bell pepper, seeded and chopped
1 carrot, chopped
3 garlic cloves, minced
1 pound dried red beans, soaked and rinsed

5 cups beef bone broth
1 teaspoon dried oregano
1 teaspoon dried sage
1 teaspoon dried rosemary
Kosher salt and freshly ground black pepper, to taste
2 bay leaves

Directions

Press the "Sauté" button to preheat your Instant Pot. Now, heat the oil and sweat the onions until they are translucent.

Then, add the parsnip, bell pepper, carrot, and garlic; cook an additional 3 minutes or until the vegetables are softened.

Stir in the remaining ingredients.

Secure the lid. Choose the "Bean/Chili" mode and High pressure; cook for 25 minutes. Once cooking is complete, use a natural pressure release for 10 minutes; carefully remove the lid.

Discard the bay leaves. You can purée the soup in your blender if you want to; serve in individual bowls. Bon appétit!

Per serving: 188 Calories; 9.6g Fat; 16.2g Carbs; 11.9g Protein; 4g Sugars

501. Oatmeal with Bananas and Walnuts

(Ready in about 25 minutes | Servings 4)

Ingredients

2 cups steel cut oats
5 ½ cups water
1/2 teaspoon ground cinnamon
1/4 teaspoon cardamom

1/4 teaspoon grated nutmeg
2 bananas
1/2 cup walnuts, chopped

Directions

Add the steel cut oats to your Instant Pot. Pour in the water. Add the cinnamon, cardamom, and nutmeg.

Secure the lid. Choose the "Manual" mode and cook for 10 minutes under High pressure.

Once cooking is complete, use a natural release for 10 minutes; remove the lid carefully. Ladle into serving bowls.

Top with bananas and walnuts. Bon appétit!

Per serving: 244 Calories; 10.1g Fat; 48.4g Carbs; 10.4g Protein; 9.2g Sugars

502. Cuban-Style Black Beans

(Ready in about 30 minutes | Servings 5)

Ingredients

2 tablespoons olive oil
2 red onions, diced
3 cloves garlic, smashed
1 bell pepper, chopped
1/2 teaspoon ancho chili pepper, minced
2 cups tomatoes, puréed
1 ¼ pounds dry black beans, rinsed and drained

2 cups vegetable broth
Morton kosher salt and ground black pepper, to taste
1 teaspoon cayenne pepper
2 bay leaves
2 tablespoons fresh cilantro leaves, roughly chopped

Directions

Press the "Sauté" button to preheat your Instant Pot. Now, heat the oil and sauté the onions until tender and aromatic.

Then, add the garlic and peppers; cook an additional 1 minute 30 seconds or until fragrant. After that, stir the puréed tomatoes, black beans, broth, salt, black pepper, cayenne pepper, and bay leaves into your Instant Pot.

Secure the lid. Choose the "Bean/Chili" mode and High pressure; cook for 25 minutes. Once cooking is complete, use a natural pressure release; carefully remove the lid.

Garnish with fresh cilantro leaves and serve.

Per serving: 276 Calories; 6.7g Fat; 43.1g Carbs; 13.3g Protein; 9.8g Sugars

503. Greek-Style Savory Polenta

(Ready in about 15 minutes | Servings 3)

Ingredients

2 tablespoons butter, at room temperature
1 cup scallions, chopped
2 garlic cloves, smashed
1 pound Crimini mushrooms, thinly sliced
1/2 teaspoon dried oregano
1/2 teaspoon dried basil
1/2 teaspoon dried dill weed
Sea salt and freshly ground black pepper, to taste
1 teaspoon cayenne pepper
2 cups water
2 cups vegetable broth
1 cup polenta
1 cup Kalamata olives, pitted and sliced
6 ounces feta cheese, crumbled

Directions

Press the "Sauté" button to preheat your Instant Pot. Now, melt the butter and cook the scallions until tender.

Stir in the garlic and mushrooms; cook an additional 40 seconds or until aromatic.

Then, add the herbs, salt, black pepper, and cayenne pepper. Add a splash of water to deglaze the pot; reserve the mushroom mixture. Press the "Cancel" button.

Add the water and broth. Press the "Sauté" button again. Slowly and gradually, pour the polenta into the liquid; make sure to whisk continuously.

Secure the lid. Choose the "Manual" mode and High pressure; cook for 5 minutes. Once cooking is complete, use a quick pressure release; carefully remove the lid.

Top the warm polenta with the mushroom mixture, olives, and feta cheese. Serve immediately.

Per serving: 420 Calories; 26.2g Fat; 32.1g Carbs; 17.8g Protein; 6.3g Sugars

504. Spaghetti with Arrabbiata Sauce

(Ready in about 40 minutes | Servings 4)

Ingredients

Arrabbiata Sauce:
2 tablespoons olive oil
1 (28-ounce) can tomatoes, with juice
4 garlic cloves, minced
1 tablespoon brown sugar
1 teaspoon dried oregano
1 teaspoon dried basil
Sea salt and ground black pepper, to your liking
1/2 teaspoon cayenne pepper
1/3 cup cooking wine
Pasta:
16 ounces spaghetti
2 cups vegetable stock
10 ounces cream cheese
6 ounces Parmesan cheese, grated

Directions

Put all ingredients for the sauce in the inner pot.

Secure the lid. Choose the "Manual" mode and cook for 10 minutes at High pressure. Once cooking is complete, use a natural pressure release for 10 minutes; carefully remove the lid.

Stir in the spaghetti and vegetable stock.

Secure the lid. Choose the "Manual" mode and cook for 5 minutes at High pressure. Once cooking is complete, use a natural pressure release for 10 minutes; carefully remove the lid.

Divide your pasta between four serving bowls. Top with cheese and serve. Bon appétit!

Per serving: 481 Calories; 29.2g Fat; 44.5g Carbs; 15.8g Protein; 11.5g Sugars

505. Italian Sausage Lasagna

(Ready in about 50 minutes | Servings 6)

Ingredients

1 tablespoon canola oil
3/4 pound Italian sausage, crumbled
1 small onion, chopped
2 garlic cloves, minced
1 fresh bell pepper, seeded and chopped
Sea salt and ground black pepper, to taste
1 teaspoon dried oregano
1 teaspoon dried basil
1/2 teaspoon dried rosemary
1 teaspoon red pepper flakes, crushed
14 ounces cream cheese
1 egg
1/4 cup Romano cheese, grated
2 ½ cups pasta sauce
8 lasagna sheets
1 cup Asiago cheese, shredded

Directions

Press the "Sauté" button and heat the oil. Once hot, cook the sausage for 3 to 4 minutes or until it starts to brown; crumble your sausage with a wooden spatula.

Now, stir in the onion, garlic, and bell pepper. Sauté for about 4 minutes or until the vegetables are fragrant. Season with salt, black pepper, oregano, basil, rosemary, and red pepper.

Add 1 ½ cups of water and a metal trivet in the inner pot of your Instant Pot. Spritz a casserole dish with cooking spray.

Then, thoroughly combine the cream cheese with an egg, and Romano cheese.

Place a thin layer of pasta sauce on the bottom of the prepared casserole dish.

Add 4 lasagna sheets and 1/2 the cheese mixture. Top with 1/2 of the meat/vegetable mixture.

Repeat the layers one more time, ending with the marinara sauce. Top with Asiago cheese. Cover with a sheet of aluminum foil.

Secure the lid. Choose the "Manual" mode and cook for 23 minutes at High pressure. Once cooking is complete, use a natural pressure release for 10 minutes; carefully remove the lid.

Let your lasagna rest for 5 to 6 minutes before slicing and serving. Bon appétit!

Per serving: 562 Calories; 25.1g Fat; 50.5g Carbs; 35.8g Protein; 11.1g Sugars

506. Homemade Spaghetti with Meat Sauce

(Ready in about 20 minutes | Servings 4)

Ingredients

2 teaspoons olive oil
1/2 pound ground pork
1/2 pound ground beef chuck
1/2 cup red wine
1 teaspoon cayenne pepper
Kosher salt and ground black pepper, to taste
1 teaspoon garlic powder
1/2 teaspoon shallot powder
1 cup marinara sauce
2 cups water
8 ounces dry spaghetti
1/2 cup Romano cheese, preferably freshly grated

Directions

Press the "Sauté" button and heat the oil. Once hot, brown the ground meat for about 5 minutes until no longer pink, stirring and breaking the meat into smaller chunks.

Scrape the bottom of the pot with red wine. Add the cayenne pepper, salt, black pepper, garlic powder, shallot powder, and marinara sauce; stir to combine.

Pour in the water and gently stir to combine. Add the dry spaghetti.

Secure the lid. Choose the "Manual" mode and cook for 8 minutes at High pressure. Once cooking is complete, use a quick pressure release; carefully remove the lid.

Serve warm with Romano cheese. Bon appétit!

Per serving: 539 Calories; 21.9g Fat; 49.9g Carbs; 35.1g Protein; 6.1g Sugars

507. Creamy Ziti Florentine

(Ready in about 20 minutes | Servings 4)

Ingredients

2 cups vegetable broth
1/2 cup double cream
2 garlic cloves, minced
Sea salt and ground black pepper, to taste
9 ounces dry ziti pasta
1 ½ cups tomato sauce
1 cup Mozzarella cheese, shredded

Directions

Add the broth, double cream, garlic, salt, black pepper, ziti pasta, and tomato sauce to the inner pot.

Secure the lid. Choose the "Manual" mode and cook for 8 minutes at High pressure. Once cooking is complete, use a quick pressure release; carefully remove the lid.

Stir in the Mozzarella cheese and seal the lid; let it sit in the residual heat until the cheese melts. The sauce will thicken as it cools. Bon appétit!

Per serving: 459 Calories; 8.2g Fat; 74.9g Carbs; 19.8g Protein; 13g Sugars

508. Spaghetti à la Philly

(Ready in about 20 minutes | Servings 4)

Ingredients

1 tablespoon olive oil
1/2 ground turkey
1/2 pound ground beef
1 onion, chopped
2 garlic cloves, minced
1 tablespoon fish sauce
2 tablespoons tomato paste
Kosher salt and cracked black pepper, to taste
1 bay leaf
2 cups vegetable broth
1/2 cup tomato sauce
8 ounces spaghetti
1 ½ cups Swiss cheese, shredded

Directions

Press the "Sauté" button and heat the oil. Once hot, brown the ground meat for about 5 minutes until no longer pink, stirring and breaking the meat into smaller chunks.

Add the onion and garlic and cook for a further 2 minutes or until they are fragrant.

Stir in the fish sauce, tomato paste, salt, black pepper, bay leaf, vegetable broth, tomato sauce and spaghetti; do not stir, but make sure the spaghetti is covered.

Secure the lid. Choose the "Manual" mode and cook for 8 minutes at High pressure. Once cooking is complete, use a quick pressure release; carefully remove the lid.

Top with Swiss cheese and gently stir to combine; serve immediately!

Per serving: 576 Calories; 29.3g Fat; 30.7g Carbs; 46.5g Protein; 7.7g Sugars

509. Mac 'n' Cheese Pot Pie

(Ready in about 20 minutes | Servings 4)

Ingredients

2 tablespoons olive oil
1 pound chicken drumsticks, boneless and cut into small cubes
1 shallot, chopped
2 garlic cloves, minced
1 bell pepper, seeded and chopped
1 habanero pepper, seeded and chopped
Kosher salt and ground black pepper, to taste
1 teaspoon cayenne pepper
2 cups chicken bone broth, preferably homemade
2 cups dried elbow pasta
1 cup cream cheese
1 tablespoon flaxseed meal

Directions

Press the "Sauté" button and heat the olive oil. Once hot, brown the chicken drumsticks for 3 to 4 minutes, stirring frequently to ensure even cooking.

Add the shallot, garlic, and peppers; continue to cook an additional 3 minute or until they have softened.

Add the salt, black pepper, cayenne pepper, broth, and pasta to the inner pot.

Secure the lid. Choose the "Manual" mode and cook for 6 minutes at High pressure. Once cooking is complete, use a quick pressure release; carefully remove the lid.

Add the cream cheese and flaxseed meal; stir to combine and press the "Sauté" button; let it cook for a few minutes longer or until your sauce has reduced slightly and the flavors have concentrated. Bon appétit!

Per serving: 608 Calories; 39.1g Fat; 32.3g Carbs; 31.2g Protein; 3.9g Sugars

510. Millet Porridge with Almonds and Raisins

(Ready in about 25 minutes | Servings 5)

Ingredients

1 ½ cups millet
3 cups water
1/2 cup golden raisins
1/4 cup almonds, roughly chopped
1 tablespoon orange juice
A pinch of sea salt

Directions

Place all ingredients in the inner pot of your Instant Pot and close the lid.

Secure the lid. Choose the "Manual" mode and cook for 12 minutes at High pressure. Once cooking is complete, use a natural pressure release for 10 minutes; carefully remove the lid.

Taste and adjust the seasonings. Bon appétit!

Per serving: 372 Calories; 10.1g Fat; 60.6g Carbs; 10.6g Protein; 10.7g Sugars

511. The Easiest Oatmeal Ever

(Ready in about 25 minutes | Servings 4)

Ingredients

1 ½ cups steel cut oats
4 ½ cups water
A pinch of kosher salt
A pinch of grated nutmeg

Directions

Place all ingredients in the inner pot.

Secure the lid. Choose the "Manual" mode and cook for 3 minutes at High pressure. Once cooking is complete, use a natural pressure release for 20 minutes; carefully remove the lid.

Serve warm with a splash of milk and fruits of choice. Enjoy!

Per serving: 228 Calories; 4.1g Fat; 60.6g Carbs; 9.6g Protein; 0g Sugars

512. Grandmother's Buttermilk Cornbread

(Ready in about 1 hour | Servings 8)

Ingredients

1 cup yellow cornmeal
1 cup all-purpose flour
1 tablespoon baking powder
1/2 cup granulated sugar
A pinch of salt
A pinch of grated nutmeg
1 cup buttermilk
1/4 cup safflower oil

Directions

Add 1 cup of water and metal rack to the inner pot. Spritz a baking pan with cooking oil.

Thoroughly combine the cornmeal, flour, baking powder, sugar, salt, and grated nutmeg. In another mixing bowl, whisk buttermilk with safflower oil.

Add the wet mixture to the cornmeal mixture. Scrape the mixture into the prepared baking pan. Cover with a sheet of greased aluminum foil.

Lower the pan onto the rack.

Secure the lid. Choose the "Manual" mode and cook for 55 minutes at High pressure. Once cooking is complete, use a quick pressure release; carefully remove the lid.

Place the cornbread on a cooling rack before slicing and serving. Bon appétit!

Per serving: 208 Calories; 7.8g Fat; 31.3g Carbs; 3.6g Protein; 7.7g Sugars

513. Easy Pearl Barley with Peppers

(Ready in about 30 minutes | Servings 3)

Ingredients

1 tablespoon sesame oil
1 yellow onion, chopped
2 garlic cloves, minced
2 bell peppers, seeded and chopped
1 jalapeno pepper, seeded and chopped
1 cups pearl barley, rinsed
2 ½ cups roasted vegetable broth
1/4 cup chives, chopped

Directions

Press the "Sauté" button and heat the oil. Once hot, cook the onion until just tender and fragrant or about 3 minutes.

Stir in the garlic and peppers; continue cooking for 2 minutes more or until they are aromatic. Add the barley and vegetable broth to the inner pot.

Secure the lid. Choose the "Multigrain" mode and cook for 20 minutes at High pressure. Once cooking is complete, use a quick pressure release; carefully remove the lid.

Fluff the barley with a fork; garnish with chopped chives and serve with your favorite main dish. Bon appétit!

Per serving: 339 Calories; 8.8g Fat; 60.3g Carbs; 7.6g Protein; 5.2g Sugars

514. Fast and Easy Quinoa Salad

(Ready in about 15 minutes + chilling time | Servings 3)

Ingredients

1 cup quinoa, rinsed
1 ½ cups water
1 cup boiled chickpeas
2 sweet peppers, seeded and chopped
1 serrano pepper, seeded and chopped
1 onion, thinly sliced
1/4 cup extra-virgin olive oil
2 tablespoons fresh lime juice
Sea salt and ground black pepper, to taste
1/4 teaspoon red pepper flakes

Directions

Spritz the inner pot with cooking oil and stir in the rinsed quinoa and water.

Secure the lid. Choose the "Manual" mode and cook for 1 minute at High pressure. Once cooking is complete, use a natural pressure release for 10 minutes; carefully remove the lid.

Fluff the quinoa with a fork and allow it to cool. Toss the cooled quinoa with the remaining ingredients; toss to combine well and serve. Bon appétit!

Per serving: 406 Calories; 12.8g Fat; 60.5g Carbs; 14.2g Protein; 3g Sugars

515. Creamy Moroccan Couscous with Vegetables

(Ready in about 15 minutes | Servings 4)

Ingredients

2 tablespoons butter, softened
1 small onion, chopped
1 teaspoon garlic, pressed
1 (1-inch) piece ginger, peeled and grated
2 carrots, trimmed and chopped
1 stalk celery, peeled and chopped
1 ½ cups couscous
3 cups water
1 tablespoon chicken bouillon granules
Sea salt and ground white pepper, to taste
1 teaspoon dried parsley flakes
1 teaspoon cayenne pepper
1/2 teaspoon ground cumin
1/4 teaspoon ground cinnamon
2 Peppadew peppers, chopped
1 cup tomato puree

Directions

Press the "Sauté" button and melt the butter. Once hot, cook the onion, garlic, ginger, carrots, and celery until tender or about 4 minutes.

Add the other ingredients; stir to combine well.

Secure the lid. Choose the "Manual" mode and cook for 3 minutes at High pressure. Once cooking is complete, use a quick pressure release; carefully remove the lid. Ladle into serving bowls and enjoy!

Per serving: 360 Calories; 6.8g Fat; 64.7g Carbs; 10.6g Protein; 6.6g Sugars

516. Best-Ever Beans with Turkey Sausage

(Ready in about 45 minutes | Servings 4)

Ingredients

2 tablespoons canola oil
6 ounces turkey sausage sliced
1 onion, chopped
2 cloves garlic, minced
1 bell pepper, sliced
1 ½ cups dry pinto beans
2 bay leaves
1 teaspoon dried sage
Sea salt and ground black pepper, to taste
1 teaspoon cayenne pepper
4 cups chicken broth
1 tomato, crushed

Directions

Press the "Sauté" button and heat the oil. Sauté the sausage until it becomes slightly crispy.

Now, add the onion, garlic, and pepper; continue to cook until they are tender. Add the remaining ingredients to the inner pot.

Secure the lid. Choose the "Bean/Chili" mode and cook for 30 minutes at High pressure. Once cooking is complete, use a natural pressure release for 10 minutes; carefully remove the lid.

Press the "Sauté" button and let it simmer until the cooking liquid has thickened. Serve with your favorite toppings. Bon appétit!

Per serving: 469 Calories; 13.6g Fat; 57.6g Carbs; 28.8g Protein; 4.9g Sugars

517. Rich Kidney Bean Soup

(Ready in about 25 minutes | Servings 4)

Ingredients

6 ounces bacon, cut into small pieces
1 leek, chopped
2 garlic cloves, sliced
1 parsnip, coarsely chopped
1 carrot, coarsely chopped
Sea salt and freshly cracked black pepper, to taste
2 canned chipotle chilis in adobo, chopped
1 teaspoon basil
1/2 teaspoon rosemary
2 cups dried red kidney beans, soaked and rinsed
4 cups chicken broth
A small handful cilantro leaves, roughly chopped

Directions

Press the "Sauté" button to preheat your Instant Pot. Now, cook the bacon until crisp; reserve.

Add the leek and garlic; continue to sauté an additional 3 minute or until they are fragrant.

Stir in the other ingredients, except for the fresh cilantro.

Secure the lid. Choose the "Manual" mode and cook for 8 minutes at High pressure. Once cooking is complete, use a natural pressure release for 10 minutes; carefully remove the lid.

Afterwards, purée your soup using a food processor or an immersion blender. Serve garnished with fresh cilantro and the reserved bacon. Bon appétit!

Per serving: 534 Calories; 15.2g Fat; 72.5g Carbs; 31.4g Protein; 5.9g Sugars

518. Easy Spicy Hummus

(Ready in about 1 hour | Servings 6)

Ingredients

1 ½ cups dry chickpeas, rinsed
1 ½ teaspoons sea salt
1 teaspoon baking soda
2 tablespoons fresh lemon juice
2 garlic cloves
1/4 cup olive oil
1 teaspoon cayenne pepper
4 dashes hot pepper sauce
2 tablespoons tahini (sesame butter)

Directions

Add the dry chickpeas to the inner pot; pour in 6 cups of water. Add the sea salt and baking soda.

Secure the lid. Choose the "Manual" mode and cook for 35 minutes at High pressure. Once cooking is complete, use a natural pressure release for 20 minutes; carefully remove the lid. Reserve the cooking liquid.

Transfer the warm, drained chickpeas to your food processor; add the remaining ingredients. While the food processor is running, pour in the cooking liquid to achieve the desired consistency.

To serve, drizzle olive oil on top of the hummus if desired. Bon appétit!

Per serving: 266 Calories; 12.2g Fat; 29.5g Carbs; 11.8g Protein; 1.2g Sugars

519. Du Puy Lentils with Brown Rice

(Ready in about 35 minutes | Servings 8)

Ingredients

1 ½ cups brown rice, rinsed
1 ½ cups du Puy lentils
2 cups cream of celery soup
1 cup water
1 cup shallots, chopped
1 teaspoon garlic, chopped

1 teaspoon cayenne pepper
1 teaspoon fennel seeds
Kosher salt and black pepper, to season
1 bay leaf
1 tablespoon balsamic vinegar

Directions

Place all ingredient, except for the vinegar, in the inner pot of your Instant Pot.

Secure the lid. Choose the "Manual" mode and cook for 15 minutes at High pressure. Once cooking is complete, use a natural pressure release for 15 minutes; carefully remove the lid.

Afterward, stir in the vinegar and serve immediately. Enjoy!

Per serving: 285 Calories; 2.9g Fat; 53.5g Carbs; 12.2g Protein; 1.9g Sugars

520. Black Eyed Peas with Pancetta

(Ready in about 50 minutes | Servings 6)

Ingredients

8 ounces pancetta
2 cups black eyed peas, rinsed
2 cups cream of celery soup
3 cups water

Sea salt and ground black pepper, to taste
1 teaspoon paprika
1 tablespoon fresh parsley, chopped

Directions

Press the "Sauté" button to preheat your Instant Pot; now, cook the pancetta until browned and reserve.

Add the black eyed peas, cream of celery soup, water, salt, pepper, and paprika to the inner pot.

Secure the lid. Choose the "Bean/Chili" mode and cook for 30 minutes at High pressure. Once cooking is complete, use a natural pressure release for 15 minutes; carefully remove the lid.

Ladle into serving bowls and garnish with fresh parsley and the reserved pancetta. Bon appétit!

Per serving: 308 Calories; 3.7g Fat; 46.3g Carbs; 24.1g Protein; 6.1g Sugars

521. Indian Masala Matar

(Ready in about 20 minutes | Servings 4)

Ingredients

1 tablespoon ghee, melted
1/2 teaspoon cumin seeds
1 yellow onion, chopped
2 cups green peas
2 tomatoes, pureed
1/2 teaspoon garam masala
1 tablespoon coriander

1/2 teaspoon chili powder
Sea salt and ground black pepper, to taste
4 curry leaves
3 cups vegetable broth
1 tablespoon chickpea flour
1 cup yogurt

Directions

Press the "Sauté" button and melt the ghee. Once hot, cook the cumin seeds for about 1 minute or until fragrant.

Add the onion and continue sautéing an additional 3 minutes.

Now, stir in the green peas, tomatoes, garam masala, coriander, chili powder, salt, black pepper, curry leaves, and broth.

Secure the lid. Choose the "Manual" mode and cook for 12 minutes at High pressure. Once cooking is complete, use a quick pressure release; carefully remove the lid.

Now, stir in the chickpea flour and let it simmer on the "Sauté" button until the cooking liquid has thickened. Serve in soup bowls with yogurt on the side. Bon appétit!

Per serving: 239 Calories; 9.1g Fat; 29.2g Carbs; 12.6g Protein; 14.9g Sugars

522. Classic Minestrone Soup

(Ready in about 35 minutes | Servings 4)

Ingredients

2 tablespoons olive oil
1 onion, chopped
1 teaspoon garlic, minced
2 carrots, sliced
2 celery stalks, diced
1 cup yellow squash, diced
1 cup dried Great Northern beans
4 medium-sized potatoes, peeled and diced

6 cups water
2 tomatoes, pureed
1 tablespoon Italian seasoning blend
Sea salt and ground black pepper, to taste
2 cups Swiss chard, torn into pieces

Directions

Press the "Sauté" button and heat the olive oil until sizzling. Then, sauté the onion and garlic until just tender and fragrant.

Now, add the remaining ingredients, except for the Swiss chard.

Secure the lid. Choose the "Bean/Chili" mode and cook for 30 minutes at High pressure. Once cooking is complete, use a quick pressure release; carefully remove the lid.

Stir in the Swiss chard. Seal the lid and let it sit in the residual heat until it wilts. Serve warm.

Per serving: 414 Calories; 7.6g Fat; 73.4g Carbs; 15.6g Protein; 5.7g Sugars

523. Favorite Refried Beans

(Ready in about 1 hour 5 minutes | Servings 4)

Ingredients

1 tablespoon olive oil
1 onion, chopped
2 cloves garlic, pressed
1 chili pepper, seeded and chopped
6 cups roasted vegetable broth

1 ½ cups white kidney beans, rinsed
2 bay leaves
Kosher salt and ground black pepper, to taste
1 teaspoon ground cumin
1 cup Colby cheese, shredded

Directions

Press the "Sauté" button and heat the olive oil until sizzling. Then, sauté the onion for about 3 minutes or until tender.

Now, stir in the garlic and chili pepper; continue to cook for 1 minute more or until fragrant. Add a splash of broth to deglaze the pan.

Add the remaining broth, beans, bay leaves, salt, black pepper, and cumin to the inner pot of your Instant Pot.

Secure the lid. Choose the "Bean/Chili" mode and cook for 40 minutes at High pressure. Once cooking is complete, use a natural pressure release for 20 minutes; carefully remove the lid. Reserve 1 cup of the cooking liquid.

Then, puree the beans with an immersion blender until they reach your desired consistency. Sprinkle with the shredded Colby cheese and serve warm.

Per serving: 472 Calories; 16.6g Fat; 49.1g Carbs; 32.3g Protein; 4.4g Sugars

524. Rainbow Lentil Salad

(Ready in about 30 minutes | Servings 4)

Ingredients

2 cups green lentils, rinsed
4 cups water
1/2 cup scallions, chopped
1 red bell pepper, seeded and sliced
1 green bell pepper, seeded and sliced
1 carrot, julienned

1 cucumber, sliced
1 cup grape tomatoes, halved
1/4 cup extra-virgin olive oil
1 fresh lemon, juiced
1/2 teaspoon red pepper flakes
Sea salt and ground white pepper, to taste

Directions

Add the lentils and water to the inner pot.

Secure the lid. Choose the "Manual" mode and cook for 8 minutes at High pressure. Once cooking is complete, use a natural pressure release for 15 minutes; carefully remove the lid.

In a salad bowl, combine the lentils with the remaining ingredients. Toss to combine well. Serve well chilled. Bon appétit!

Per serving: 492 Calories; 14.9g Fat; 68.6g Carbs; 25.6g Protein; 6.1g Sugars

525. Brown Lentil Curry

(Ready in about 30 minutes | Servings 3)

Ingredients

1 tablespoon sesame oil	1/2 teaspoon ground turmeric
1 onion, chopped	4 curry leaves
1 tablespoon fresh ginger, peeled and grated	1 cups brown lentils, rinsed
2 garlic cloves, minced	1 teaspoon cayenne pepper
1 teaspoon coconut sugar	12 ounces canned coconut milk
Sea salt and white pepper, to taste	2 tablespoons freshly squeezed lime juice

Directions

Press the "Sauté" button and heat the sesame oil. Once hot, cook the onion until tender and translucent.

Now, add the ginger and garlic and continue to sauté an additional minute or so.

Stir in the coconut sugar, salt, white pepper, ground turmeric, curry leaves, brown lentils, and cayenne pepper. Pour in 2 cups of water.

Secure the lid. Choose the "Manual" mode and cook for 14 minutes at High pressure. Once cooking is complete, use a natural pressure release for 10 minutes; carefully remove the lid.

Now, pour in the coconut milk and press the "Sauté" button. Let it simmer on the lowest setting until thoroughly warmed.

Taste and adjust the seasoning. Serve with a few drizzles of lime juice. Enjoy!

Per serving: 319 Calories; 5.6g Fat; 52.1g Carbs; 7.5g Protein; 6.1g Sugars

526. Indian Chote Rajma

(Ready in about 35 minutes | Servings 3)

Ingredients

1 tablespoon butter, at room temperature	2 ripe tomatoes, pureed
1 teaspoon cumin seeds	1 cup dried adzuki beans
1 onion, chopped	Kosher salt and ground black pepper, to taste
2 cloves garlic, pressed	1 teaspoon garam masala
1 ghost jolokia chili pepper, chopped	4 cups vegetable broth, preferably homemade
1 teaspoon red pepper flakes, crushed	1 bay leaf
1 teaspoon coriander	1-inch cinnamon stick
	1 green cardamom

Directions

Press the "Sauté" button and melt the butter. Once hot, cook the cumin seeds for 30 seconds to 1 minute or until the seeds begin to sizzle.

Now, stir in the onion, garlic, and chili pepper; continue to sauté an additional 3 minutes or until they have softened.

Stir in the remaining ingredients.

Secure the lid. Choose the "Bean/Chili" mode and cook for 25 minutes at High pressure. Once cooking is complete, use a quick pressure release; carefully remove the lid.

Serve with hot steamed rice if desired. Enjoy!

Per serving: 304 Calories; 5.6g Fat; 50.1g Carbs; 16.5g Protein; 4.6g Sugars

527. Chickpea Hot Pot

(Ready in about 55 minutes | Servings 4)

Ingredients

1 tablespoon olive oil	1 rosemary sprig
1 large yellow onion, chopped	1 thyme sprig
2 cups chickpeas	1 teaspoon mixed peppercorns
4 cups water	2 bay leaves
2 cups tomato sauce	1/2 whole capsicum, deseeded and chopped
1 teaspoon salt	Sea salt, to taste
1 teaspoon baking soda	

Directions

Press the "Sauté" button and heat the olive oil; now, sauté the onion until tender and translucent. Then, add the remaining ingredients and stir to combine.

Secure the lid. Choose the "Bean/Chili" mode and cook for 40 minutes at High pressure. Once cooking is complete, use a natural pressure release for 10 minutes; carefully remove the lid.

Ladle into serving bowls and garnish with fresh chives if desired. Bon appétit!

Per serving: 453 Calories; 11.9g Fat; 68.2g Carbs; 21.5g Protein; 14.1g Sugars

528. Sorakkai Sambar (Indian Lentil Stew)

(Ready in about 35 minutes | Servings 3)

Ingredients

1 cup Pigeon pea lentils	1 teaspoon Urad Dal
2 teaspoons sesame oil	1 tablespoon sambar powder
1 yellow onion, chopped	1 teaspoon turmeric powder
6 curry leaves	Sea salt and ground black pepper, to taste
1 Indian ghost jolokia chili pepper, chopped	1 teaspoon cayenne pepper
1 tablespoon tamarind	1 cup tomato sauce

Directions

Add the lentils and 4 cups of water to the inner pot.

Secure the lid. Choose the "Manual" mode and cook for 10 minutes at High pressure. Once cooking is complete, use a natural pressure release for 10 minutes; carefully remove the lid.

Meanwhile, heat a saucepan over medium-high heat. Cook the onion for about 3 minutes or until translucent. Now, add the curry leaves and chili pepper to the skillet. Let it cook for a further minute or until they are aromatic.

Add the other ingredients, cover, and reduce the heat to medium-low; let it simmer for about 13 minutes or until everything is thoroughly cooked.

Transfer the onion/tomato mixture to the inner pot of your Instant Pot. Stir to combine and serve immediately. Bon appétit!

Per serving: 248 Calories; 7.9g Fat; 36.8g Carbs; 6.9g Protein; 13.4g Sugars

529. Spicy Heirloom Beans

(Ready in about 45 minutes | Servings 3)

Ingredients

4 cups water	1 jalapeño pepper, seeded and chopped
1 pound heirloom beans	1 teaspoon liquid smoke
1 tablespoon Italian Seasoning blend	1 teaspoon onion powder
1 bell pepper, seeded and chopped	1 teaspoon granulated garlic

Directions

Add all ingredients to the inner pot of your Instant Pot.

Secure the lid. Choose the "Bean/Chili" mode and cook for 30 minutes at High pressure. Once cooking is complete, use a natural pressure release for 10 minutes; carefully remove the lid.

Ladle into serving bowls and garnish with fresh scallions if desired. Bon appétit!

Per serving: 525 Calories; 1.3g Fat; 95.2g Carbs; 36.3g Protein; 5.2g Sugars

530. Green Pea Soup with Herbs

(Ready in about 20 minutes | Servings 4)

Ingredients

2 teaspoons avocado oil
1 shallot, chopped
2 garlic cloves, minced
1 cups cream of mushroom soup
2 cup water
1 cup tomato sauce
1/2 teaspoon dried tarragon
1/2 teaspoon dried dill
Kosher salt and freshly ground black pepper, to taste
1 (10-oz) bag frozen green peas

Directions

Press the "Sauté" button and heat the oil. Once hot, cook the shallot until tender and translucent; add the garlic to the inner pot and continue sautéing an additional 30 seconds.

Now, stir in the remaining ingredients.

Secure the lid. Choose the "Manual" mode and cook for 12 minutes at High pressure. Once cooking is complete, use a quick pressure release; carefully remove the lid.

Ladle into soup bowls. Bon appétit!

Per serving: 178 Calories; 6g Fat; 24.6g Carbs; 4.9g Protein; 9.7g Sugars

531. Lima Bean Hot Pot with Bacon

(Ready in about 20 minutes | Servings 4)

Ingredients

8 ounces bacon
1 yellow onion, chopped
2 garlic cloves, pressed
1 pound dry lima beans
3 cups chicken broth
3 cups water
1 cup tomato sauce
1 bay leaf
1 sprig rosemary
1 sprig thyme

Directions

Press the "Sauté" button to preheat your Instant Pot. Cook the bacon until crisp; crumble with a fork and reserve.

Add the onion and garlic and continue to cook them in pan drippings until tender and fragrant.

Now, stir in the remaining ingredients.

Secure the lid. Choose the "Manual" mode and cook for 12 minutes at High pressure. Once cooking is complete, use a quick pressure release; carefully remove the lid.

Discard the bay leaf and garnish with the reserved bacon; serve warm. Bon appétit!

Per serving: 493 Calories; 27.7g Fat; 45.6g Carbs; 17.9g Protein; 11.7g Sugars

532. Japanese Black Soybeans (Kuromame)

(Ready in about 30 minutes | Servings 4)

Ingredients

1/2 pound black soybeans, rinsed
4 cups water
1 cup sugar
1 tablespoon soy sauce
A pinch of kosher salt
3-inch square of kombu

Directions

Add all ingredients to the inner pot of your Instant Pot.

Secure the lid. Choose the "Manual" mode and cook for 15 minutes at High pressure. Once cooking is complete, use a natural pressure release for 10 minutes; carefully remove the lid.

Let the beans soak in the sauce for 24 hours. The black soybeans should be soft and glossy. Cover and refrigerate. Enjoy!

Per serving: 302 Calories; 1.5g Fat; 61.2g Carbs; 12.5g Protein; 26.4g Sugars

533. Sugar Snap Peas with Chicken and Peanuts

(Ready in about 50 minutes | Servings 4)

Ingredients

1 pound chicken breast, cut into small chunks
2 tablespoons arrowroot powder
1 tablespoon teriyaki sauce
2 cloves garlic, minced
1/2 teaspoon cayenne pepper
2 teaspoons sesame oil, toasted
2 cups chicken broth
2 cups sugar snap peas
2 carrots, sliced
1 small onion, chopped
1/4 cup peanuts, dry-roasted and roughly chopped

Directions

Combine the chicken breasts, arrowroot powder, teriyaki sauce, garlic, and cayenne pepper in a mixing bowl.

Press the "Sauté" button. Preheat the oil and cook the seasoned chicken for 5 to 6 minutes or until no longer pink.

Pour in a splash of the broth, scraping the pot to loosen the browned bits. Stir in the remaining broth, sugar snap peas, carrots, and onions.

Secure the lid. Choose the "Slow Cook" button and "More" mode; cook for 30 minutes. When time is up, carefully remove the lid.

Garnish with the dry-roasted peanuts and serve warm. Enjoy!

Per serving: 387 Calories; 19.8g Fat; 18.7g Carbs; 33.3g Protein; 3.4g Sugars

534. Spicy Boiled Peanuts

(Ready in about 1 hour 5 minutes | Servings 10)

Ingredients

2 pounds raw peanuts in the shell
1/2 cup salt
2 tablespoons Creole seasoning
1 tablespoon garlic powder
1 tablespoon cayenne pepper
2 jalapenos, sliced

Directions

Add all ingredients to the inner pot of your Instant Pot. Pour in enough water to cover the peanuts.

Use a steamer to gently press down your peanuts.

Secure the lid. Choose the "Manual" mode and cook for 45 minutes at High pressure. Once cooking is complete, use a natural pressure release for 15 minutes; carefully remove the lid.

Place in a container with a bunch of the liquid; refrigerate for 3 hours. Bon appétit!

Per serving: 235 Calories; 18.8g Fat; 10.7g Carbs; 9.3g Protein; 2.7g Sugars

535. Mediterranean Spicy Bean Salad

(Ready in about 35 minutes | Servings 4)

Ingredients

1 pound cannellini beans, rinsed
1 cup fresh tomatoes, sliced
1 cucumber, sliced
1 onion, thinly sliced
1 teaspoon garlic, minced
1/2 cup Kalamata olives, pitted and halved
2 sweet peppers, seeded and diced
1 pepperoncini, seeded and diced
1/2 cup Halloumi cheese, crumbled
6 basil leaves, roughly chopped
1/4 cup extra virgin olive oil
3 tablespoons balsamic vinegar, or more to taste
Sea salt and freshly cracked black pepper, to taste

Directions

Add the cannellini beans to the inner pot of your Instant Pot. Pour in 8 cups of water.

Secure the lid. Choose the "Bean/Chili" mode and cook for 30 minutes at High pressure. Once cooking is complete, use a quick pressure release; carefully remove the lid.

Transfer your beans to a salad bowl. Add the remaining ingredients and toss to combine well.

Serve well chilled.

Per serving: 572 Calories; 19.8g Fat; 70.8g Carbs; 30.9g Protein; 4.7g Sugars

536. Green Bean and Lentil Stew

(Ready in about 20 minutes | Servings 3)

Ingredients

2 tablespoons peanut oil
1 cup scallions, chopped onion
2 cloves garlic, minced
2 bell peppers, chopped
2 carrots, chopped
1 celery rib, chopped
1 teaspoon oregano
1 teaspoon basil

1/2 teaspoon red pepper flakes, crushed
1 cup green lentils
3 cups vegetable broth
1 cup tomato sauce
1 cup green beans, trimmed
Sea salt and ground black pepper, to season

Directions

Press the "Sauté" button and heat the oil until sizzling; once hot, cook the scallions, garlic, bell peppers, carrots, and celery until they have softened.

Add the spices, lentils, broth, and tomato sauce; gently stir to combine.

Secure the lid. Choose the "Manual" mode and cook for 8 minutes at High pressure. Once cooking is complete, use a natural pressure release for 5 minutes; carefully remove the lid.

Afterwards, add the green beans, salt, and black pepper to the inner pot; gently stir to combine.

Secure the lid. Choose the "Manual" mode and cook for 3 minutes at High pressure. Once cooking is complete, use a quick pressure release; carefully remove the lid. Serve warm.

Per serving: 306 Calories; 11.5g Fat; 39.3g Carbs; 12.3g Protein; 15.7g Sugars

537. Winter Ham and Split Pea Soup

(Ready in about 35 minutes | Servings 3)

Ingredients

2 tablespoons butter
1 leek, diced
1 celery stalk, diced
1 carrot, diced
1 turnip, diced
1 jalapeno pepper, seeded and minced
4 ounces ham, diced

1 ½ cups split peas, rinsed
3 cups chicken stock, veggie stock, water, or a mixture
1/2 teaspoon dried thyme
1/2 teaspoon garlic powder
Kosher salt and ground black pepper, to taste

Directions

Press the "Sauté" button and melt the butter. Once hot, sauté the leek, celery, carrot, turnip, and jalapeno until they have softened.

Add the remaining ingredients to the inner pot.

Secure the lid. Choose the "Manual" mode and cook for 15 minutes at High pressure. Once cooking is complete, use a natural pressure release for 15 minutes; carefully remove the lid.

Taste and adjust seasonings. Serve warm.

Per serving: 403 Calories; 17.8g Fat; 26.7g Carbs; 36.7g Protein; 13g Sugars

538. Vegetarian Lebanese Mujadara

(Ready in about 35 minutes | Servings 4)

Ingredients

2 tablespoons grapeseed oil
1 large onion, thinly sliced
3 cloves garlic, rough chopped
1 teaspoon cumin
1 cinnamon stick
1 teaspoon turmeric powder
1/2 teaspoon ground ginger
Kosher salt and red pepper, to season

1/2 cup red cooking wine
1 cup brown lentils, sorted and rinsed
3 cups water
2 tablespoons fresh parsley
2 tablespoons fresh lemon juice
1 cup basmati rice, rinsed
4 cups mustard greens

Directions

Press the "Sauté" button and heat the oil until sizzling. Once hot, cook the onion and garlic until just tender and fragrant.

Stir in the remaining ingredients, except for the mustard greens. Give it a good stir.

Secure the lid. Choose the "Manual" mode and cook for 10 minutes at High pressure. Once cooking is complete, use a natural pressure release for 10 minutes; carefully remove the lid.

Add the mustard greens to the inner pot. Seal the lid and let it sit in the residual heat for 10 minutes. Serve warm.

Per serving: 403 Calories; 17.8g Fat; 26.7g Carbs; 36.7g Protein; 13g Sugars

539. Old-Fashioned Beans with Turkey Drumsticks

(Ready in about 40 minutes | Servings 4)

Ingredients

2 tablespoons grapeseed oil
1 onion, chopped
1 teaspoon garlic, minced
2 sweet peppers, seeded and chopped
1 poblano pepper, seeded and minced
12 ounces dry kidney bean, rinsed

1 smoked turkey drumsticks
2 bay leaves
1 teaspoon dried oregano
1 teaspoon dried basil
Sea salt and ground black pepper, to taste
4 cups chicken broth low sodium

Directions

Press the "Sauté" button and heat the oil until sizzling. Once hot, cook the onion for 3 to 4 minutes or until tender.

Now, stir in garlic and peppers; continue to cook until tender and aromatic. Str in the remaining ingredients.

Secure the lid. Choose the "Bean/Chili" mode and cook for 25 minutes at High pressure. Once cooking is complete, use a natural pressure release for 10 minutes; carefully remove the lid. Bon appétit!

Per serving: 422 Calories; 22.3g Fat; 16.3g Carbs; 39.7g Protein; 2.6g Sugars

540. Anasazi Beans with Smoked Bacon

(Ready in about 40 minutes | Servings 4)

Ingredients

6 ounces smoked bacon, chopped
16 ounces Anasazi beans, rinsed
4 cloves garlic, pressed
3 cups vegetable broth
1 cup tomato puree
1 cup water

2 bay leaves
1 teaspoon dried sage
1 teaspoon dried oregano
1 onion, chopped
Kosher salt and ground black pepper, to taste

Directions

Press the "Sauté" button to preheat the Instant Pot. Cook the bacon for 2 to 3 minutes or until it is crisp.

Place the other ingredients in the inner pot of your Instant Pot.

Secure the lid. Choose the "Bean/Chili" mode and cook for 25 minutes at High pressure. Once cooking is complete, use a natural pressure release for 10 minutes; carefully remove the lid.

Ladle into soup bowls and serve garnished with the reserved bacon. Serve with salsa if desired. Bon appétit!

Per serving: 477 Calories; 44.1g Fat; 15.1g Carbs; 6.5g Protein; 5.3g Sugars

541. Black Bean Tacos

(Ready in about 35 minutes | Servings 4)

Ingredients

2 tablespoons sesame oil
1 onion, chopped
1 teaspoon garlic, minced
1 sweet pepper, seeded and sliced
1 jalapeno pepper, seeded and minced
1 teaspoon ground cumin

1/2 teaspoon ground coriander
16 ounces black beans, rinsed
4 (8-inches), whole wheat tortillas, warmed
1 cup cherry tomatoes, halved
1/2 cup sour cream

Directions

Press the "Sauté" button and heat the oil. Now, cook the onion, garlic, and peppers until tender and fragrant.

Add the ground cumin, coriander, and beans to the inner pot.

Secure the lid. Choose the "Manual" mode and cook for 20 minutes at High pressure. Once cooking is complete, use a natural pressure release for 10 minutes; carefully remove the lid.

Serve the bean mixture in the tortillas; garnish with the cherry tomatoes and sour cream. Enjoy!

Per serving: 487 Calories; 11.5g Fat; 75.5g Carbs; 23.8g Protein; 8.1g Sugars

542. Tuscan Bean Soup with Parmigiano-Reggiano

(Ready in about 50 minutes | Servings 4)

Ingredients

2 tablespoons grapeseed oil
1 onion, chopped
2 garlic cloves, minced
1 carrot, chopped
1 celery rib, sliced
2 cups water
2 cups cream of mushroom soup
2 potatoes, peeled and grated
2 bay leaves

1/2 teaspoon marjoram
Sea salt and ground black pepper, to taste
10 ounces dry white kidney beans, rinsed
2 cups fresh spinach, torn into pieces
4 tablespoons Parmigiano Reggiano cheese, grated

Directions

Press the "Sauté" button and heat the oil. Now, cook the onion, garlic, carrot, and celery until they have softened.

Now, add the water, cream of mushrooms soup, potatoes, spices, and beans to the inner pot.

Secure the lid. Choose the "Bean/Chili" mode and cook for 30 minutes at High pressure. Once cooking is complete, use a natural pressure release for 15 minutes; carefully remove the lid.

Mash the soup with a potato masher or use an immersion blender. Add the spinach and press the "Sauté" button again. Let it simmer on the lowest setting until the leaves wilt.

Ladle the soup into four serving bowls. Top each serving with 1 tablespoon of the Parmigiano Reggiano cheese. Bon appétit!

Per serving: 453 Calories; 11.6g Fat; 65.3g Carbs; 24.5g Protein; 6.1g Sugars

543. Garbanzo Bean and Cream Cheese Dip

(Ready in about 55 minutes | Servings 10)

Ingredients

12 ounces garbanzo beans, rinsed
6 cups of water
1/2 cup cream cheese
1 teaspoon hot sauce
1/2 teaspoon dried thyme
1/2 teaspoon cumin

1 teaspoon garlic powder
1 teaspoon onion powder
2 tablespoons lime juice
2 tablespoons tahini (sesame butter)
2 tablespoons cilantro, chopped

Directions

Add the garbanzo beans and water to the inner pot.

Secure the lid. Choose the "Bean/Chili" mode and cook for 40 minutes at High pressure. Once cooking is complete, use a natural pressure release for 10 minutes; carefully remove the lid. Reserve the cooking liquid.

Transfer the boiled garbanzo beans to your blender or food processor; add the other ingredients and blend until smooth and creamy. Add the reserved liquid as needed for desired consistency.

Place in your refrigerator until ready to use. Enjoy!

Per serving: 206 Calories; 8.8g Fat; 22.7g Carbs; 10.3g Protein; 1.7g Sugars

544. Restaurant-Style Vegetarian Chili

(Ready in about 40 minutes | Servings 4)

Ingredients

2 tablespoons olive oil
1 onion, chopped
2 cloves garlic, minced
2 sweet peppers, chopped
1 red chili pepper, chopped
1 carrot, chopped
1 celery stalk, chopped
Sea salt and ground black pepper, to taste
1 teaspoon red pepper

1 teaspoon ground cumin
1 teaspoon Mexican oregano
1 (28-ounce) can tomatoes, diced with their juices
10 ounces dried navy beans
2 cups vegetable broth
1 bay leaf
1 thyme sprig
1/2 cup sour cream

Directions

Press the "Sauté" button and heat the oil. Now, cook the onion until it is softened. Stir in the garlic and peppers; continue sautéing an additional 2 minutes or until fragrant.

Add the carrot, celery, salt, black pepper, red pepper, cumin, oregano, tomatoes, beans, broth, bay leaf, and thyme sprig to the inner pot.

Secure the lid. Choose the "Bean/Chili" mode and cook for 25 minutes at High pressure. Once cooking is complete, use a natural pressure release for 10 minutes; carefully remove the lid.

Serve with a dollop of sour cream. Enjoy!

Per serving: 448 Calories; 12.5g Fat; 65.7g Carbs; 23g Protein; 11.4g Sugars

545. Fasolakia (Greek Green Beans)

(Ready in about 15 minutes | Servings 4)

Ingredients

2 tablespoons olive oil
4 garlic cloves, chopped
1 ½ pounds fresh green beans
2 vine-ripened tomatoes, pureed
Sea salt and freshly ground black pepper, to season

1 cup bone broth, preferably homemade
1 teaspoon paprika
1/2 teaspoon dried oregano
1/2 teaspoon dried basil
1/2 dried dill
6 ounces Feta cheese, crumbled

Directions

Press the "Sauté" button and heat the oil. Now, sauté the garlic until it is fragrant but not browned.

Add the other ingredients, except for the feta cheese, to the inner pot; and stir to combine.

Secure the lid. Choose the "Manual" mode and cook for 5 minutes at High pressure. Once cooking is complete, use a quick pressure release; carefully remove the lid.

Ladle into individual bowls and serve with Feta cheese on the side. Enjoy!

Per serving: 237 Calories; 17.5g Fat; 13.7g Carbs; 9.9g Protein; 4.9g Sugars

546. Refreshing Wax Bean Salad

(Ready in about 10 minutes + chilling time | Servings 4)

Ingredients

14 ounces yellow wax beans, trimmed and halved crosswise
1 red onion, sliced
2 bell peppers, deveined and sliced
1/4 cup extra-virgin olive oil
1 tablespoon fresh lemon juice
1 tablespoon balsamic vinegar

1 tablespoon peanut butter
1 teaspoon Dijon mustard
1/2 teaspoon garlic powder
Salt and white pepper, to taste
1/4 teaspoon red pepper flakes
2 tablespoons fresh Italian parsley, roughly chopped

Directions

Place 1 cup of water and a steamer basket in the inner pan of your Instant Pot. Place the wax beans in the steamer basket.

Secure the lid. Choose the "Manual" mode and cook for 3 minutes at High pressure. Once cooking is complete, use a quick pressure release; carefully remove the lid.

Toss the chilled wax beans with the other ingredients; toss to combine well. Serve well chilled.

Per serving: 196 Calories; 15.4g Fat; 13.5g Carbs; 3.8g Protein; 3.2g Sugars

547. Classic Lima Beans with Ham

(Ready in about 45 minutes | Servings 4)

Ingredients

1 pound dry baby lima beans, rinsed
8 ounces cooked ham, chopped
1 onion, chopped
2 cloves garlic, minced
4 cups beef bone broth

1 thyme sprig
1 rosemary sprig
1 teaspoon dried parsley flakes
Sea salt and freshly ground black pepper, to taste
2 bay leaves

Directions

Place all ingredients in the inner pot of your Instant Pot.

Secure the lid. Choose the "Bean/Chili" mode and cook for 25 minutes at High pressure. Once cooking is complete, use a natural pressure release for 10 minutes; carefully remove the lid.

Ladle into individual bowls and enjoy!

Per serving: 450 Calories; 3.1g Fat; 74.8g Carbs; 33.3g Protein; 10.6g Sugars

548. Herby Pea Dipping Sauce

(Ready in about 45 minutes | Servings 8)

Ingredients

14 ounces frozen peas
2 cups water
1/4 cup basil leaves, roughly chopped
2 tablespoons fresh parsley, chopped
1 tablespoon fresh cilantro, chopped

2 tablespoons fresh chives, chopped
1 fresh lemon, zested and juiced
1 teaspoon cayenne pepper
1/2 teaspoon hot sauce
Kosher salt and freshly ground black pepper, to taste

Directions

Add the frozen peas and water to the inner pot of your Instant Pot.

Secure the lid. Choose the "Manual" mode and cook for 10 minutes at High pressure. Once cooking is complete, use a natural pressure release for 15 minutes; carefully remove the lid.

Transfer the boiled green peas to a bowl of your food processor; add the remaining ingredients and process until creamy and smooth, gradually adding the cooking liquid.

Serve with pita bread, tortilla chips or bread sticks if desired. Bon appétit!

Per serving: 42 Calories; 0.1g Fat; 7.8g Carbs; 2.7g Protein; 2.9g Sugars

549. Grandma's Scarlet Runner with Smoked Turkey

(Ready in about 45 minutes | Servings 8)

Ingredients

2 tablespoons olive oil
1 onion, chopped
2 garlic cloves, minced
1 bell pepper, sliced
1 pound Scarlet Runner beans
10 ounces smoked turkey, boneless and shredded

2 tablespoons sherry wine
2 cups turkey broth
2 bay leaves
1 sprig thyme
1 sprig rosemary
Kosher salt and ground black pepper, to taste

Directions

Press the "Sauté" button and heat the oil. Now, sauté the onion until tender and translucent. Then, stir in the garlic and bell pepper and continue to sauté until they are aromatic but not browned.

Add the other ingredients to the inner pot; stir to combine well.

Secure the lid. Choose the "Bean/Chili" mode and cook for 25 minutes at High pressure. Once cooking is complete, use a natural pressure release for 10 minutes; carefully remove the lid.

Taste, adjust the seasonings and serve warm. Bon appétit!

Per serving: 42 Calories; 0.1g Fat; 7.8g Carbs; 2.7g Protein; 2.9g Sugars

550. Rustic Lahsooni Moong Dal

(Ready in about 20 minutes | Servings 4)

Ingredients

Moong Dal:
1 cup moong dal, soaked 2 hours and drained
4 cups water
1 teaspoon curry paste
Kosher salt and red pepper, to taste

1 teaspoon Garam masala
Tarka:
2 tablespoons butter
1/2 teaspoon cumin seeds
3 garlic cloves, pressed
1 white onion, chopped
1 bird eye chili, sliced

Directions

Add the moong dal, water, curry paste, salt, pepper, and Garam masala to the inner pot.

Secure the lid. Choose the "Manual" mode and cook for 2 minutes at High pressure. Once cooking is complete, use a natural pressure release for 10 minutes; carefully remove the lid.

Melt the butter in a nonstick skillet over medium-high heat. Then, sauté the cumin seeds for 30 seconds or until fragrant.

After that, sauté the garlic, onion, and chili pepper for 4 to 5 minutes or until they have softened. Stir the contents of the skillet into the warm dal.

Bon appétit!

Per serving: 235 Calories; 6.3g Fat; 33.8g Carbs; 12.3g Protein; 2.2g Sugars

551. Mom's Creamed Corn

(Ready in about 15 minutes | Servings 3)

Ingredients

2 cups corn kernels
2 tablespoons cold butter, cut into pieces
6 ounces Cottage cheese, at room temperature
1/2 cup double cream

1 cup water
Kosher salt and ground black pepper, to taste
1/2 teaspoon red pepper flakes
1/2 teaspoon dried parsley flakes

Directions

Put all ingredients into the inner pot of your Instant Pot; stir to combine.

Secure the lid. Choose the "Manual" mode and cook for 4 minutes at High pressure. Once cooking is complete, use a quick pressure release; carefully remove the lid.

Ladle into serving bowls and enjoy!

Per serving: 279 Calories; 19.3g Fat; 19.8g Carbs; 10g Protein; 5.6g Sugars

552. Kamut and Chicken Bake

(Ready in about 20 minutes | Servings 4)

Ingredients

1 cup kamut
1 cup vegetable broth
1 cup tomato puree
Sea salt and freshly ground black pepper, to taste
1 teaspoon basil
1 teaspoon thyme

1 pound chicken, boneless, skinless and chopped
1 shallot, chopped
1 teaspoon fresh garlic, pressed
1 sweet pepper, chopped
1 serrano pepper, chopped
2 tablespoons butter, melted
4 ounces Colby cheese, shredded

Directions

Add the kamut to the bottom of a lightly greased inner pot. Now, pour in the broth and tomato puree; add the spices.

Add the chicken, shallot, garlic, and peppers; drizzle melted butter over everything.

Secure the lid. Choose the "Manual" mode and cook for 12 minutes at High pressure. Once cooking is complete, use a quick pressure release; carefully remove the lid.

Top with shredded cheese and seal the lid again. Let it sit in the residual heat until the cheese melts, Enjoy!

Per serving: 495 Calories; 19.5g Fat; 43.1g Carbs; 39.4g Protein; 7.1g Sugars

553. Mediterranean-Style Wheat Berry Salad

(Ready in about 40 minutes + chilling time | Servings 4)

Ingredients

1 cup wheat berries	1/4 cup good olive oil
3 cups water	1/4 cup red wine vinegar
2 tomatoes, sliced	1/2 teaspoon oregano
1 cucumber, sliced	1 teaspoon basil
1 red onion, sliced	1/2 cup Kalamata olives

Directions

Add the wheat berries and water to the inner pot.

Secure the lid. Choose the "Manual" mode and cook for 35 minutes at High pressure. Once cooking is complete, use a quick pressure release; carefully remove the lid.

Now, toss the cooked wheat berries with the remaining ingredients. Cover and refrigerate; the longer your salad sits, the more intense the flavor becomes. Enjoy!

Per serving: 246 Calories; 16.5g Fat; 23.3g Carbs; 4.4g Protein; 0.4g Sugars

554. Autumn Sweet Amaranth Porridge

(Ready in about 15 minutes | Servings 4)

Ingredients

1 ½ cups amaranth	1/4 teaspoon ground cardamom
2 cups coconut milk	1/4 teaspoon ground cloves
2 cups water	1/2 teaspoon ground cinnamon
1 apple, cored and sliced	2 tablespoons honey
2 pears, cored and sliced	

Directions

Thoroughly combine all ingredients in the inner pot.

Secure the lid. Choose the "Manual" mode and cook for 4 minutes at High pressure. Once cooking is complete, use a quick pressure release; carefully remove the lid.

Ladle into individual bowls and enjoy!

Per serving: 425 Calories; 9.5g Fat; 74.8g Carbs; 14.4g Protein; 25g Sugars

555. Traditional Jowar Ki Kheer

(Ready in about 25 minutes | Servings 3)

Ingredients

1 cup dried sorghum	1/2 cup brown sugar
3 cups soy milk	1/2 cup cashews, roughly chopped
1 tablespoon ghee	

Directions

Place the dries sorghum, milk, ghee, and brown sugar in the inner pot.

Secure the lid. Choose the "Porridge" mode and cook for 20 minutes at High pressure. Once cooking is complete, use a quick pressure release; carefully remove the lid.

Serve in individual bowls garnished with chopped cashews. Enjoy!

Per serving: 485 Calories; 20.4g Fat; 64.2g Carbs; 14.1g Protein; 30.3g Sugars

556. Creamy Spanish Buckwheat

(Ready in about 15 minutes | Servings 3)

Ingredients

2 teaspoons olive oil	1 ½ cups buckwheat
1 shallot, chopped	2 cups chicken broth
1 teaspoon garlic, minced	1 cup water
2 bell peppers, chopped	1/2 cup Manchego curado, grated
2 Chiles de árbol, chopped	

Directions

Press the "Sauté" button and heat the oil until sizzling. Then, sauté the shallot until just tender or about 3 minutes.

Then, cook the garlic and peppers an additional 2 to 3 minutes or until they are fragrant.

Add the buckwheat, broth, and water to the inner pot.

Secure the lid. Choose the "Manual" mode and cook for 3 minutes at High pressure. Once cooking is complete, use a quick pressure release; carefully remove the lid.

Serve garnished with cheese. Enjoy!

Per serving: 235 Calories; 12g Fat; 21.4g Carbs; 12.1g Protein; 2.3g Sugars

557. Savory Za'atar Oatmeal with Eggs

(Ready in about 35 minutes | Servings 2)

Ingredients

1/2 cup steel cut oats	2 teaspoons olive oil
1 ½ cups vegetable broth	1 onion, chopped
1 tomato, pureed	2 bell peppers, seeded and sliced
Kosher salt and freshly ground black pepper, to taste	2 eggs, beaten

Directions

Place the steel cut oats, vegetable broth, tomato, salt, and black pepper in the inner pot.

Secure the lid. Choose the "Manual" mode and cook for 3 minutes at High pressure. Once cooking is complete, use a natural pressure release for 20 minutes; carefully remove the lid.

Meanwhile, heat the olive oil in a skillet over medium-high heat. Now, sauté the onion and peppers until they have softened or 3 to 4 minutes.

Then, add the beaten eggs and continue to cook until they are no longer liquid. Serve over the warm oatmeal.

Per serving: 381 Calories; 17g Fat; 40.9g Carbs; 17.6g Protein; 8.4g Sugars

558. Spelt Grains with Cremini Mushrooms

(Ready in about 35 minutes | Servings 3)

Ingredients

2 tablespoons olive oil	2 cups water
1 leek, chopped	Sea salt and white pepper, to taste
1 teaspoon garlic, minced	1 tablespoon oyster sauce
1 cup cremini mushrooms, sliced	1 cup spinach leaves
1 cup spelt grains	

Directions

Press the "Sauté" button and heat the oil until sizzling. Then, sauté the leek for 3 to 4 minutes or until tender.

Add the garlic and mushrooms and cook an additional 2 minutes or until they are fragrant. Reserve the sautéed mixture.

Add the spelt grains, water, salt, pepper, and oyster sauce to the inner pot.

Secure the lid. Choose the "Porridge" mode and cook for 30 minutes at High pressure. Once cooking is complete, use a quick pressure release; carefully remove the lid.

Afterwards, stir in the spinach leaves and seal the lid; let it sit until the leaves wilt. Serve topped with the sautéed mushroom mixture. Bon appétit!

Per serving: 307 Calories; 10.5g Fat; 47.7g Carbs; 9.6g Protein; 5.9g Sugars

559. Quinoa Pilau with Acorn Squash

(Ready in about 10 minutes | Servings 4)

Ingredients

1 pound acorn squash, peeled and sliced	3 ½ cups vegetable stock
1 tablespoon coconut oil, melted	1 ½ cups quinoa, rinsed
2 sweet onions, thinly sliced	6 prunes, chopped
1 teaspoon fresh ginger, chopped	2 tablespoons fresh mint leaves, roughly chopped

Directions

Add the acorn squash, coconut oil, sweet onions, ginger, and 1 cup of stock to the inner pot; stir to combine.

Secure the lid. Choose the "Manual" mode and cook for 3 minutes at High pressure. Once cooking is complete, use a quick pressure release; carefully remove the lid.

Add the remaining stock, quinoa, and prunes to the inner pot.

Secure the lid. Choose the "Manual" mode and cook for 1 minute at High pressure. Once cooking is complete, use a quick pressure release; carefully remove the lid.

Serve garnished with fresh mint leaves. Bon appétit!

Per serving: 418 Calories; 9g Fat; 72.5g Carbs; 15.4g Protein; 8.4g Sugars

560. Greek-Style Polenta

(Ready in about 15 minutes | Servings 4)

Ingredients

1 cup polenta	1/2 teaspoon dried parsley flakes
4 cups water	1/2 teaspoon oregano
A pinch of sea salt	1 teaspoon dried onion flakes
1/2 teaspoon red pepper flakes, crushed	4 tablespoons butter
	8 ounces Feta cheese, crumbled

Directions

Add the polenta, water, and salt to the inner pot of your Instant Pot. Press the "Sauté" button and bring the mixture to a simmer. Press the "Cancel" button.

Add the spices to your polenta. Secure the lid. Choose the "Manual" mode and cook for 8 minutes at High pressure. Once cooking is complete, use a quick pressure release; carefully remove the lid.

Stir the butter into the polenta, whisking until it has melted. Add more salt, if needed.

Top with Feta cheese and serve warm.

Per serving: 309 Calories; 23.9g Fat; 14.7g Carbs; 9.4g Protein; 2.7g Sugars

561. Authentic Hungarian Kukoricaprósza

(Ready in about 1 hour | Servings 5)

Ingredients

1 ½ cups yellow cornmeal	1 egg, beaten
1 ½ cups yogurt	1 teaspoon baking soda
1 ½ cups sour cream	1/4 teaspoon salt
1/4 cup water	10 tablespoons plum jam
1/4 cup safflower oil	

Directions

Add 1 cup of water and metal rack to the inner pot. Spritz a baking pan with cooking oil.

Thoroughly combine the cornmeal, yogurt, sour cream, water, oil, egg, baking soda, and salt.

Scrape the mixture into the prepared baking pan. Place the piles of plum jam all over the surface.

Cover with a sheet of greased aluminum foil. Lower the pan onto the rack.

Secure the lid. Choose the "Manual" mode and cook for 55 minutes at High pressure. Once cooking is complete, use a quick pressure release; carefully remove the lid.

Place the Kukoricaprósza on a cooling rack before slicing and serving. Bon appétit!

Per serving: 475 Calories; 23.9g Fat; 57g Carbs; 10.1g Protein; 24.7g Sugars

562. Swiss Cheese and Pancetta Pie

(Ready in about 35 minutes | Servings 5)

Ingredients

1 refrigerated pie crust	Sea salt and ground black pepper, to taste
5 eggs	
1/2 cup milk	4 ounces pancetta, chopped
1/2 cup sour cream	1 cup Swiss cheese, shredded
	4 tablespoons scallions, chopped

Directions

Press the pie crust into a baking pan, crimping the top edges. In a mixing bowl, combine the eggs, milk, sour cream, salt, and pepper.

Place the pancetta on the pie crust; pour the egg/milk mixture over the top. Top with Swiss cheese.

Add 1 cup of water and a metal trivet to the Instant Pot. Lower the baking pan onto the trivet; cover with a sheet of greased aluminum foil.

Secure the lid. Choose the "Manual" mode and cook for 25 minutes at High pressure. Once cooking is complete, use a quick pressure release; carefully remove the lid.

Garnish with scallions and serve warm.

Per serving: 489 Calories; 32.4g Fat; 22.5g Carbs; 25.8g Protein; 2.8g Sugars

563 Croissant Bread Pudding with Strawberries

(Ready in about 55 minutes | Servings 4)

Ingredients

4 cups croissants, cut into pieces	A pinch of salt
4 eggs	1/4 teaspoon ground cloves
10 ounces coconut milk	1 teaspoon ground cinnamon
5 ounces condensed milk	1 cup strawberries
1/4 cup sugar	2 tablespoon cold butter, cut into pieces.
1 teaspoon vanilla	

Directions

Add 1 cup of water and a metal trivet to the Instant Pot. Spritz a 7-inch springform pan with butter spray. Throw the croissant pieces into the pan.

In a mixing bowl, thoroughly combine the eggs, milk, sugar, vanilla, salt, cloves, and cinnamon. Pour 1/2 of the mixture over the croissants and let them soak approximately 15 minutes, until they no longer look dry.

Scatter the strawberries on top. Pour the leftover custard on top. Afterwards, top with the butter pieces and lower the pan onto the trivet.

Secure the lid. Choose the "Manual" mode and cook for 25 minutes at High pressure. Once cooking is complete, use a natural pressure release for 10 minutes; carefully remove the lid. Bon appétit!

Per serving: 430 Calories; 25.5g Fat; 34.7g Carbs; 14.8g Protein; 17.1g Sugars

564. Cream Cheese Grits

(Ready in about 25 minutes | Servings 3)

Ingredients

2 cups of water	1/2 teaspoon paprika
1 cup stone ground grits	1/4 teaspoon porcini powder
1/2 teaspoon sea salt	1/2 teaspoon garlic powder
1 cup cream cheese, room temperature	1/2 cup milk

Directions

Place the water, grits, and salt in the inner pot of your Instant Pot.

Secure the lid. Choose the "Manual" mode and cook for 10 minutes at High pressure. Once cooking is complete, use a natural pressure release for 10 minutes; carefully remove the lid.

Now, stir the cheese, paprika, porcini powder, garlic powder and milk into warm grits; stir to combine well and serve immediately.

Per serving: 412 Calories; 25.7g Fat; 36.7g Carbs; 10.4g Protein; 5.1g Sugars

565. Simple Bulgur Pilaf with Shallots

(Ready in about 25 minutes | Servings 2)

Ingredients

1 tablespoon butter
2 shallots, chopped
1 teaspoon fresh garlic, minced
1/2 cup bulgur wheat
1 cup vegetable broth
1/4 teaspoon ground black pepper
1/4 teaspoon fine sea salt

Directions

Press the "Sauté" button and melt the butter. Now, cook the shallots until just tender and fragrant.

Then, stir in the garlic and continue to sauté an additional minute or so. Add the remaining ingredients to the inner pot.

Secure the lid. Choose the "Manual" mode and cook for 10 minutes at High pressure. Once cooking is complete, use a natural pressure release for 10 minutes; carefully remove the lid.

Fluff the bulgur wheat with a fork and serve immediately. Bon appétit!

Per serving: 199 Calories; 6.9g Fat; 29.2g Carbs; 7.4g Protein; 1.1g Sugars

566. Old-Fashioned Chicken and Kamut Soup

(Ready in about 20 minutes | Servings 4)

Ingredients

1 tablespoon olive oil
1/2 cup chicken thighs, boneless
1 onion, chopped
1/2 cup kamut
1 celery stalk, chopped
1 parsnip, chopped
1 carrot, chopped
Sea salt and freshly ground black pepper, to taste
1 tablespoon Herbes de Provence
3 cups chicken broth
1 cup tomato puree

Directions

Press the "Sauté" button and heat the oil; now, cook chicken thighs for 3 to 4 minutes.

Add the onion and continue to sauté until tender and translucent. Add the remaining ingredients and stir to combine.

Secure the lid. Choose the "Manual" mode and cook for 12 minutes at High pressure. Once cooking is complete, use a quick pressure release; carefully remove the lid.

Ladle your soup into individual bowls. Bon appétit!

Per serving: 233 Calories; 9.1g Fat; 26.2g Carbs; 6.9g Protein; 1.1g Sugars

567. Farro with Mushrooms and Cheese

(Ready in about 35 minutes | Servings 3)

Ingredients

2 tablespoons olive oil
1 onion, chopped
1 cup mushrooms, sliced
2 sweet peppers, chopped
2 garlic cloves, minced
1/2 cup white wine
1 cup farro
2 ½ cups vegetable broth
Sea salt and ground black pepper, to taste
1/2 cup Swiss cheese, grated
1 heaping tablespoon fresh parsley, chopped

Directions

Press the "Sauté" button and heat the oil; now, cook the onion until tender or 3 to 4 minutes. Stir in the mushrooms and peppers and cook an additional 3 minutes.

Stir in the garlic and continue to sauté for a minute or so.

Add the white wine to deglaze the pan. Now, add the farro, vegetable broth, salt, and black pepper to the inner pot.

Secure the lid. Choose the "Manual" mode and cook for 11 minutes at High pressure. Once cooking is complete, use a natural pressure release for 10 minutes; carefully remove the lid.

Top each serving with cheese and fresh parsley. Bon appétit!

Per serving: 442 Calories; 16.7g Fat; 61.3g Carbs; 17.3g Protein; 9.6g Sugars

568. Corn on the Cob with Cilantro Butter

(Ready in about 15 minutes | Servings 6)

Ingredients

6 large ears corn, husked and halved
6 tablespoons butter, softened
2 heaping tablespoons cilantro, chopped
1 teaspoon paprika
Sea salt and ground black pepper, to taste

Directions

Place 1 cup of water and a metal trivet in your Instant Pot. Now, lower the corn onto the trivet.

Secure the lid. Choose the "Manual" mode and cook for 6 minutes at High pressure. Once cooking is complete, use a quick pressure release; carefully remove the lid.

Press the "Sauté" button and melt the butter; add the cilantro, paprika, salt, and black pepper to the melted butter.

Pour the cilantro butter over the steamed corn and enjoy!

Per serving: 225 Calories; 13.4g Fat; 26.7g Carbs; 4.8g Protein; 8.9g Sugars

569. Family Truffle Popcorn

(Ready in about 15 minutes | Servings 4)

Ingredients

1 stick butter
1 cup popcorn kernels
1 tablespoon truffle oil
1/4 cup parmesan cheese, grated
Sea salt, to taste

Directions

Press the "Sauté" button and melt the butter. Stir until it begins to simmer.

Stir in the popcorn kernels and cover. When the popping slows down, press the "Cancel" button.

Now, add the truffle oil, parmesan, and sea salt. Toss to combine and serve immediately.

Per serving: 365 Calories; 30.4g Fat; 18.8g Carbs; 5.1g Protein; 0.2g Sugars

570. Winter Couscous Chicken Soup

(Ready in about 20 minutes | Servings 4)

Ingredients

1 tablespoon chicken schmaltz
1/2 pound chicken breasts, cubed
1 onion, chopped
1 carrot, sliced
1 celery rib, sliced
1 parsnip, sliced
1 tablespoon lemongrass, minced
1 teaspoon garlic paste
1/2 teaspoon turmeric powder
1/4 teaspoon mustard powder
4 cups chicken bone broth
1 cup couscous
Sea salt and ground black pepper, to taste
1 tablespoon fresh parsley, chopped
1 tablespoon fresh chives, chopped

Directions

Press the "Sauté" button and melt the chicken schmaltz. Once hot, sauté the chicken until golden brown; reserve.

Cook the onion, carrot, celery, and parsnip in pan drippings until just tender and aromatic.

Add the reserved chicken, lemongrass, garlic paste, turmeric, mustard powder, and broth.

Secure the lid. Choose the "Manual" mode and cook for 11 minutes at High pressure. Once cooking is complete, use a quick pressure release; carefully remove the lid.

Now, stir in the couscous; season with salt and pepper.

Secure the lid. Choose the "Manual" mode and cook for 2 minutes at High pressure. Once cooking is complete, use a quick pressure release; carefully remove the lid.

Serve garnished with fresh parsley and chives. Bon appétit!

Per serving: 343 Calories; 7.2g Fat; 44.7g Carbs; 23.3g Protein; 3.6g Sugars

571. French Toast Casserole with Chocolate

(Ready in about 20 minutes | Servings 4)

Ingredients

8 slices of French bread, broken into pieces
2 eggs, whisked
1/2 cup milk
1/2 cup sour cream
4 tablespoons honey
1 teaspoon vanilla paste
1/4 teaspoon nutmeg, preferably freshly grated
1/2 teaspoon ground cardamom
1 teaspoon ground cinnamon
1 cup chocolate chips

Directions

Place 1 cup of water and metal rack in your Instant Pot. Now, spritz a round cake pan with cooking oil. Throw the bread pieces in the pan.

In a mixing bowl, thoroughly combine the eggs, milk, sour cream, honey, and spices. Pour the mixture over the bread pieces and press with a wide spatula.

Cover the pan with a sheet of aluminum foil. Lower the pan onto the rack.

Secure the lid. Choose the "Manual" mode and cook for 13 minutes at High pressure. Once cooking is complete, use a quick pressure release; carefully remove the lid.

Sprinkle with chocolate chips and serve. Bon appétit!

Per serving: 419 Calories; 18.3g Fat; 53.4g Carbs; 10.3g Protein; 25.4g Sugars

572. Teff Porridge with Kale and Goat Cheese

(Ready in about 20 minutes | Servings 4)

Ingredients

1 cup teff grains
4 cups water
1/2 teaspoon sea salt
2 tablespoons olive oil
2 cups kale, torn into pieces
1/2 cup goat cheese, crumbled
2 tomatoes, sliced

Directions

Place the teff grains, water, salt, and olive oil in the inner pot of your Instant Pot.

Secure the lid. Choose the "Manual" mode and cook for 3 minutes at High pressure. Once cooking is complete, use a quick pressure release; carefully remove the lid.

Add the kale and seal the lid again; let it sot for 5 to 10 minutes. Serve garnished with goat cheese and fresh tomatoes. Bon appétit!

Per serving: 419 Calories; 18.3g Fat; 53.4g Carbs; 10.3g Protein; 25.4g Sugars

573. Amaranth Pilau with Fried Eggs

(Ready in about 15 minutes | Servings 2)

Ingredients

3/4 cup amaranth
2 cups water
1/2 cup milk
Sea salt and freshly cracked black pepper, to taste
1 tablespoon olive oil
2 eggs
1/2 cup cheddar cheese, shredded
2 tablespoons fresh chives, roughly chopped

Directions

Place the amaranth, water, and milk in the inner pot of your Instant Pot.

Secure the lid. Choose the "Manual" mode and cook for 4 minutes at High pressure. Once cooking is complete, use a quick pressure release; carefully remove the lid. Season with salt and black pepper.

Meanwhile, heat the oil in a skillet over medium-high heat. Then, fry the egg until crispy on the edges.

Divide the cooked amaranth between serving bowls; top with the fried eggs and cheese. Garnish with fresh chives. Bon appétit!

Per serving: 536 Calories; 28.6g Fat; 46.5g Carbs; 24.5g Protein; 8.8g Sugars

574. Three-Grain Kedgeree

(Ready in about 30 minutes | Servings 5)

Ingredients

1 tablespoon olive oil
1 medium-sized leek, chopped
2 garlic cloves, pressed
1 sweet pepper, deveined and sliced
Sea salt and freshly ground black pepper, to taste
1/2 cup pearl barley
1/2 cup sorghum
1/2 cup congee
5 cups chicken bone broth

Directions

Press the "Sauté" button and heat the oil until sizzling. Once hot, sauté the leeks, garlic and peppers for 3 to 4 minutes or until just tender and fragrant.

Add a splash of broth to deglaze the pot. Next, stir in the remaining ingredients.

Secure the lid. Choose the "Multigrain" mode and cook for 20 minutes at High pressure. Once cooking is complete, use a quick pressure release; carefully remove the lid.

Ladle into individual bowls and serve immediately.

Per serving: 380 Calories; 8.6g Fat; 62.6g Carbs; 15.1g Protein; 2.2g Sugars

575. Indian Korma with Chicken and Bulgur

(Ready in about 30 minutes | Servings 4)

Ingredients

1 tablespoon sesame oil
1 pound chicken breasts, boneless and skinless, cut into bite-sized pieces
1 onion, chopped
1 teaspoon fresh garlic, minced
1 (2-inch) galangal piece, peeled and sliced
1 Bird's eye chili pepper, seeded and minced
1 teaspoon ground cumin
1 teaspoon turmeric powder
1 teaspoon garam masala
1 cup bulgur
1 cup coconut milk
2 cups chicken stock
Sea salt and ground black pepper, to taste
1 tablespoon fresh coriander, chopped

Directions

Press the "Sauté" button and heat the sesame oil. Now, brown the chicken breast for 3 to 4 minutes; reserve.

Then, add the onion and cook until just tender and fragrant. Stir in the garlic and continue to sauté an additional minute or so.

Stir in the galangal, chili pepper, cumin, turmeric powder, garam masala, bulgur, coconut milk, chicken stock, salt, and black pepper; add the reserved chicken to the inner pot.

Secure the lid. Choose the "Manual" mode and cook for 10 minutes at High pressure. Once cooking is complete, use a natural pressure release for 10 minutes; carefully remove the lid. Serve garnished with fresh coriander and enjoy!

Per serving: 425 Calories; 17.6g Fat; 35.1g Carbs; 33.4g Protein; 5.4g Sugars

576. Buckwheat Breakfast Bowl

(Ready in about 10 minutes | Servings 3)

Ingredients

1 cup buckwheat grouts
1 cup water
1 cup orange juice
1 cup coconut milk
2 tablespoons agave nectar
1 teaspoon carob powder
1/2 teaspoon ground cardamom
1/2 teaspoon ground cinnamon
A pinch of kosher salt
A pinch of grated nutmeg
1 cup fresh blueberries

Directions

Add the buckwheat, water, orange juice, coconut milk, agave nectar, carob powder, and spices to the inner pot.

Secure the lid. Choose the "Manual" mode and cook for 3 minutes at High pressure. Once cooking is complete, use a quick pressure release; carefully remove the lid.

Serve in individual bowls garnished with fresh blueberries. Bon appétit!

Per serving: 398 Calories; 5g Fat; 82.9g Carbs; 11.2g Protein; 36.8g Sugars

577. Cinnamon Almond Oatmeal

(Ready in about 15 minutes | Servings 4)

Ingredients

1 ½ cups regular oats
2 cups water
2 cups almond milk
1 teaspoon cinnamon, ground
2 tablespoons almond butter
1/2 cup chocolate chips

Directions

Simply throw the oats, water, milk, and cinnamon into the Instant Pot.

Secure the lid. Choose the "Manual" mode and High pressure; cook for 10 minutes. Once cooking is complete, use a quick pressure release; carefully remove the lid.

Divide the oatmeal between serving bowls; top with the almond butter and chocolate chips. Enjoy!

Per serving: 347 Calories; 12.1g Fat; 51.3g Carbs; 8.7g Protein; 25.1g Sugars

578. Refreshing Farro Salad

(Ready in about 15 minutes | Servings 4)

Ingredients

1 ¼ cups farro, semi-pearled and rinsed
3 cups water
1 Walla Walla onion, chopped
1 cup cherry tomatoes, halved
2 green garlic stalks, minced
Salt and ground black pepper, to taste
4 tablespoons extra-virgin olive oil
1 tablespoon fresh lime juice
2 tablespoons fresh parsley leaves, chopped

Directions

Add the rinsed farro and water to your Instant Pot.

Secure the lid. Choose the "Manual" mode and High pressure; cook for 10 minutes. Once cooking is complete, use a quick pressure release; carefully remove the lid.

Drain well; allow it to cool completely. Add the onion, tomatoes, garlic, salt, and pepper; toss to combine.

Toss with the olive oil, lime juice, and parsley leaves. Bon appétit!

Per serving: 329 Calories; 6.8g Fat; 61.3g Carbs; 7.6g Protein; 9.9g Sugars

579. Caribbean-Style Chili

(Ready in about 30 minutes | Servings 6)

Ingredients

2 tablespoons olive oil
1/2 pound ground pork
1/2 pound ground beef
1 cup leeks, chopped
2 garlic cloves, minced
1 tablespoon chili powder
1/2 teaspoon ground allspice
1/2 teaspoon ground bay leaf
1 teaspoon dried basil
1 tablespoon brown sugar
1/2 teaspoon celery salt
1/4 teaspoon black pepper, or more to taste
1 ½ cups stock, preferably homemade
2 ripe tomatoes, chopped
2 (15-ounce) cans black beans, rinsed and drained
2 tablespoons soy sauce
1 teaspoon cocoa powder, unsweetened
1/2 cup golden raisins
1/2 cup sour cream

Directions

Press the "Sauté" button to heat up your Instant Pot. Now, heat the olive oil until sizzling.

Cook the ground meat, crumbling it with a spatula, until it is no longer pink; reserve.

Now, stir in the leeks and garlic; cook until they have softened. Now, add the chili powder, ground allspice, ground bay leaf, basil, sugar, salt, and pepper. Continue to sauté for 4 minutes more.

Now, deglaze the bottom of the inner pot with the stock. Add the tomatoes, beans, soy sauce, and cocoa powder.

Then, choose the "Manual" button, High pressure and 8 minutes. Once cooking is complete, use a natural release; remove the lid carefully.

Add the raisins and cook in the residual heat for 5 to 6 minutes. Ladle into individual bowls and serve garnished with sour cream.

Per serving: 375 Calories; 20g Fat; 24.2g Carbs; 24.6g Protein; 13.3g Sugars

580. Herb and Tomato Bulgur Pilaf

(Ready in about 30 minutes | Servings 5)

Ingredients

2 tablespoons olive oil
1 red onion, chopped
1 teaspoon ginger-garlic paste
1 ½ cups bulgur wheat
4 ½ cups roasted vegetable broth
2 Roma tomatoes, seeded and diced
1/3 teaspoon ground turmeric
1/4 teaspoon ground cumin
1/4 cup lightly packed flat-leaf parsley, chopped
1/4 cup lightly packed fresh dill, chopped
Sea salt and freshly ground black pepper, to taste

Directions

Press the "Sauté" button to preheat the Instant Pot; heat the oil until sizzling.

Sauté the onion until fragrant or about 2 minutes. Stir the remaining ingredients into your Instant Pot.

Secure the lid. Choose the "Manual" mode and High pressure; cook for 12 minutes. Once cooking is complete, use a natural pressure release for 10 minutes; carefully remove the lid.

Ladle into serving bowls and garnish with some extra fresh herbs if desired. Serve immediately.

Per serving: 275 Calories; 7.6g Fat; 48.2g Carbs; 7.3g Protein; 5.3g Sugars

581. Pear and Almond Couscous

(Ready in about 15 minutes | Servings 4)

Ingredients

1 ½ cups couscous, well rinsed
3 cups water
A pinch of salt
1/3 cup honey
1/4 teaspoon ground cloves
1/3 teaspoon ground cinnamon
1/2 teaspoon freshly grated nutmeg
1 teaspoon pure vanilla extract
2 medium-sized pears, cored and diced
1/3 cup almonds, slivered

Directions

Place all of the above ingredients, except for the almonds, into your Instant Pot; stir to combine well.

Secure the lid. Choose the "Manual" mode and High pressure; cook for 8 minutes. Once cooking is complete, use a quick pressure release; carefully remove the lid.

Serve topped with slivered almonds. Bon appétit!

Per serving: 207 Calories; 0.3g Fat; 50g Carbs; 2.6g Protein; 31.8g Sugars

582. Spicy Millet with Peppers

(Ready in about 20 minutes | Servings 4)

Ingredients

1 tablespoon olive oil
1 red onion, chopped
1 red bell pepper, deveined and sliced
1 green bell pepper, deveined and sliced
1 ancho chili pepper, deveined and chopped
1/2 teaspoon granulated garlic
1 teaspoon salt
1/4 teaspoon ground black pepper
1/4 teaspoon cayenne pepper
1 ½ cups millet
3 cups water

Directions

Press the "Sauté" button to preheat your Instant Pot. Then, heat the oil until sizzling; sauté the onions until they are caramelized.

Stir in the peppers and continue to sauté an additional 2 minutes or until they are tender and fragrant.

Add the granulated garlic, salt, black pepper, cayenne pepper, millet, and water.

Secure the lid. Choose the "Manual" mode and High pressure; cook for 5 minutes. Once cooking is complete, use a natural pressure release for 10 minutes; carefully remove the lid.

Lastly, fluff the millet with a fork. Spoon into individual bowls and serve immediately. Bon appétit!

Per serving: 339 Calories; 6.6g Fat; 60.6g Carbs; 9.2g Protein; 2.9g Sugars

583. Pepper-Jack and Cilantro Cornbread

(Ready in about 35 minutes | Servings 8)

Ingredients

1 cup water
1 ½ cups cornmeal
1/2 cup all-purpose flour
1 teaspoon baking soda
1 teaspoon baking powder
1/2 teaspoon kosher salt
1/4 teaspoon black pepper, or more to taste
1/4 teaspoon cayenne pepper
1/2 teaspoon dried basil
1/4 teaspoon dried oregano
1/2 teaspoon ground allspice
1 cup Pepper-Jack cheese, grated
3/4 cup fresh corn kernels
2 tablespoons cilantro, roughly chopped
1 cup milk
1/2 teaspoon lime juice
1/2 stick butter, melted
2 tablespoons pure maple syrup
2 eggs

Directions

Add 1 cup of water and a metal trivet to the base of your Instant Pot. Lightly grease a baking pan that fits in your Instant Pot.

In a mixing bowl, thoroughly combine the cornmeal, flour, baking soda, baking powder, salt, black pepper, cayenne pepper, basil, oregano, and allspice.

Stir in the Pepper-Jack cheese, corn kernels, and cilantro. Mix to combine well.

In another mixing bowl, whisk the remaining ingredients; add this wet mixture to the dry mixture.

Pour the batter into the prepared baking pan. Cover with a paper towel; then, top with foil.

Lower the pan onto the trivet and secure the lid. Choose the "Manual" mode, High pressure, and 23 minutes. Once cooking is complete, use a natural release; remove the lid carefully.

Serve immediately and enjoy!

Per serving: 318 Calories; 14.3g Fat; 37.2g Carbs; 9.9g Protein; 5.6g Sugars

584. Favorite Cremini Mushroom Risotto

(Ready in about 15 minutes | Servings 5)

Ingredients

2 cups jasmine rice
2 cups water
1/4 teaspoon kosher salt
2 tablespoons butter
1 onion, chopped
2 garlic cloves, minced
1/2 pound Cremini mushrooms, thinly sliced

Directions

Rinse the rice under cold running water and transfer to the Instant Pot; add water and 1/4 teaspoon of salt.

Secure the lid and select the "Manual" mode. Cook at High pressure for 6 minutes. Once cooking is complete, use a natural release; remove the lid carefully.

Fluff the rice with the rice paddle or fork; reserve.

Press the "Sauté" button and melt the butter. Now, sauté the onion until tender and translucent. Add the garlic and cook an additional minute or until it is fragrant and lightly browned.

Add the Cremini mushrooms and continue to sauté until they are slightly browned. Add the reserved jasmine rice, stir and serve warm. Bon appétit!

Per serving: 335 Calories; 14.9g Fat; 60g Carbs; 11g Protein; 2.3g Sugars

585. Spicy Japanese Okayu

(Ready in about 15 minutes | Servings 6)

Ingredients

1 tablespoon sesame oil
1 cup white onions, chopped
1 teaspoon garlic, minced
1 thumb-size ginger, julienned
1 carrot, chopped
2 cups white short-grain rice, rinsed
1 cup water
2 cups dashi stock
Sea salt and ground black pepper, to taste
1 teaspoon gochujang
2 tablespoons Shoyu sauce

Directions

Press the "Sauté" button to preheat your Instant Pot. Then, heat the oil and sauté the onions until translucent.

Add the garlic and ginger; continue to sauté for 30 seconds more. Add the carrot, rice, water, stock, salt, black pepper, and gochujang.

Secure the lid. Choose the "Manual" mode and High pressure; cook for 8 minutes. Once cooking is complete, use a quick pressure release; carefully remove the lid.

After that, add the Shoyu sauce and stir to combine; divide the okayu among 6 serving bowls and serve immediately.

Per serving: 288 Calories; 3.3g Fat; 56.8g Carbs; 6.6g Protein; 1.9g Sugars

586. Romano Rice with Tomatoes and Cheese

(Ready in about 10 minutes | Servings 5)

Ingredients

1 tablespoon toasted sesame oil
1 yellow onion, chopped
2 cloves garlic, pressed
1 ½ cups Romano rice
Sea salt and ground black pepper, to taste
1/2 cup tomatoes, puréed
2 tablespoons tomato ketchup
3 cups water
1 teaspoon sweet paprika
2 ounces sun-dried tomatoes
1 cup Pecorino-Romano cheese, freshly grated

Directions

Press the "Sauté" button to preheat your Instant Pot. Then, heat the oil and sauté the onions until translucent.

Add the garlic and cook for a further 30 seconds. Add the Romano rice, salt, pepper, tomatoes, ketchup, water, and paprika.

Secure the lid. Choose the "Poultry" mode and High pressure; cook for 5 minutes. Once cooking is complete, use a natural pressure release; carefully remove the lid.

Ladle into individual bowls; garnish with sun-dried tomatoes and Pecorino-Romano cheese. Bon appétit!

Per serving: 354 Calories; 10.4g Fat; 52.7g Carbs; 11.1g Protein; 2.3g Sugars

587. Amaranth and Almond Porridge

(Ready in about 15 minutes | Servings 4)

Ingredients

1 ¼ cups amaranth
2 cups water
1 cup soy milk
1/3 teaspoon cinnamon, ground
1/2 teaspoon ground cloves
1/3 cup honey
1/2 cup almonds, slivered

Directions

Place the amaranth, water, milk, cinnamon, cloves and honey in your Instant Pot.

Secure the lid. Choose the "Manual" mode and High pressure; cook for 8 minutes. Once cooking is complete, use a natural pressure release; carefully remove the lid.

Ladle into individual bowls; top with slivered almonds and serve warm. Bon appétit!

Per serving: 347 Calories; 6.3g Fat; 65.5g Carbs; 10.2g Protein; 27.1g Sugars

588. Indian Upma with Mushrooms

(Ready in about 10 minutes | Servings 4)

Ingredients

1 tablespoon ghee
1 small-sized leek, finely diced
1 teaspoon garlic, minced
1/2 pound button mushrooms, chopped
1 red bell pepper, chopped
1 ¼ cups oat bran
2 cups water
2 cups cream of mushroom soup
1 sprig curry leaves
1/2 teaspoon chana dal
1/2 teaspoon urad dal
1/4 teaspoon ground turmeric
1/4 teaspoon dried dill
Sea salt and ground black pepper, to taste

Directions

Press the "Sauté" button to preheat your Instant Pot. Now, melt the ghee and cook the leek until tender and fragrant.

Then, stir in the garlic, mushrooms and pepper; cook an additional 2 minutes; reserve.

Wipe down the Instant Pot with a damp cloth. Stir the remaining ingredients into your Instant Pot.

Secure the lid. Choose the "Manual" mode and High pressure; cook for 2 minutes. Once cooking is complete, use a natural pressure release; carefully remove the lid.

Serve in individual bowls topped with the reserved mushroom mixture. Enjoy!

Per serving: 384 Calories; 12.3g Fat; 75.1g Carbs; 12.8g Protein; 3.6g Sugars

589. Quinoa with Scallions and Peppers

(Ready in about 10 minutes | Servings 4)

Ingredients

2 tablespoons butter, melted
2 tablespoons scallions, chopped
1 teaspoon garlic, minced
2 bell peppers, chopped
1 carrot, chopped
Salt and ground black pepper, to taste
1/2 teaspoon turmeric powder
1/2 teaspoon paprika
1/2 teaspoon dried rosemary
1 ½ cups water
1 cup quinoa

Directions

Press the "Sauté" button to preheat your Instant Pot. Melt the butter. Sauté the scallions, garlic, peppers, and carrot until tender.

Add the salt, black pepper, turmeric, paprika, and rosemary; cook an additional minute or until they are aromatic.

Wipe down the Instant Pot with a damp cloth. Then, stir in the water and quinoa.

Secure the lid. Choose the "Manual" mode and High pressure; cook for 1 minute. Once cooking is complete, use a natural pressure release; carefully remove the lid.

Ladle the prepared quinoa into individual bowls; top with the scallion mixture and serve immediately.

Per serving: 225 Calories; 8.4g Fat; 31.3g Carbs; 6.7g Protein; 1.9g Sugars

590. Creamy Polenta with Bacon

(Ready in about 15 minutes | Servings 4)

Ingredients

2 tablespoons butter, softened
2 cups vegetable broth
1 cup water
1 cup polenta
Ground black pepper, to taste
1/2 teaspoon sweet paprika
1/2 teaspoon smoked paprika
1/2 teaspoon dried basil
1/2 teaspoon dried oregano
1/2 teaspoon mustard powder
4 ounces Canadian bacon, chopped
1/4 cup scallions, chopped
1/4 cup fresh cilantro, chopped

Directions

Press the "Sauté" button to preheat your Instant Pot. Add the butter, broth, and water; bring to a rolling boil.

Gradually stir in the polenta, whisking continuously, for 2 minutes. Now, add the black pepper, paprika, basil, oregano, and mustard powder.

Secure the lid. Choose the "Manual" mode and High pressure; cook for 8 minutes. Once cooking is complete, use a natural pressure release; carefully remove the lid.

Ladle the polenta into four serving bowls; top each serving with Canadian bacon, scallions, and cilantro. Serve warm and enjoy!

Per serving: 165 Calories; 7.6g Fat; 14.3g Carbs; 9.6g Protein; 0.8g Sugars

591. Warming Brown Rice Risotto

(Ready in about 40 minutes | Servings 4)

Ingredients

1 tablespoon olive oil
1 shallot, chopped
2 garlic cloves, smashed
1 bell pepper, seeded and chopped
1 cup tomato, puréed
1 cup brown rice, well-rinsed
1/2 cup water
1 teaspoon oregano
1 teaspoon basil
1 teaspoon ancho chili powder
1/2 cup black olives, pitted and sliced

Directions

Press the "Sauté" button to preheat your Instant Pot. Heat the oil and sauté the onion, garlic, and pepper for 3 minutes.

Add the tomato purée, rice, water, oregano, basil, and chili powder.

Secure the lid. Choose the "Manual" mode and High pressure; cook for 22 minutes. Once cooking is complete, use a natural pressure release for 10 minutes; carefully remove the lid.

Serve topped with black olives. Bon appétit!

Per serving: 238 Calories; 6.7g Fat; 40.1g Carbs; 4.6g Protein; 2.2g Sugars

592. Grandma's Bean Medley

(Ready in about 40 minutes | Servings 4)

Ingredients

1 tablespoon olive oil
1 cup onions, chopped
4 garlic cloves, minced
1 bell pepper, thinly sliced
2 medium-sized carrots, thinly sliced
3/4 pound white kidney beans
6 cups water
Seasoned salt and ground black pepper, to taste
1 heaping teaspoon cayenne pepper
2 bay leaves

Directions

Press the "Sauté" button to preheat your Instant Pot. Heat the oil and sauté the onions and garlic for 2 minutes or until tender and fragrant.

Add the remaining ingredients. Stir to combine well.

Secure the lid. Choose the "Bean/Chili" mode and High pressure; cook for 30 minutes. Once cooking is complete, use a natural pressure release; carefully remove the lid.

Ladle into individual bowls and garnish with dried chili peppers if desired. Bon appétit!

Per serving: 238 Calories; 6.7g Fat; 40.1g Carbs; 4.6g Protein; 2.2g Sugars

593. Elegant Bean Purée

(Ready in about 30 minutes | Servings 4)

Ingredients

1 tablespoon canola oil
1/2 cup scallions, chopped
4 cloves garlic, smashed
1 ½ cups Adzuki beans
2 cups water
3 cups beef bone broth
Sea salt and freshly ground black pepper, to taste
1 teaspoon paprika

Directions

Press the "Sauté" button to preheat your Instant Pot. Then, heat the oil and cook the scallions and garlic until tender; reserve.

Wipe down the Instant Pot with a damp cloth. Add the Adzuki beans, water, broth, salt, pepper, and paprika.

Secure the lid. Choose the "Bean/Chili" mode and High pressure; cook for 20 minutes. Once cooking is complete, use a natural pressure release; carefully remove the lid.

Transfer to your food processor and add the reserved scallion/garlic mixture. Then, process the mixture, working in batches. Process until smooth and uniform. Serve warm and enjoy!

Per serving: 95 Calories; 4.9g Fat; 7.7g Carbs; 6.4g Protein; 0.4g Sugars

594. Aromatic Kamut with Sweet Onions

(Ready in about 15 minutes | Servings 4)

Ingredients

2 tablespoons olive oil
2 sweet onions, thinly sliced
1/2 teaspoon ground cinnamon
1/2 teaspoon cardamom
1 ½ cups kamut
4 ½ cups water
Sea salt and ground white pepper, to taste

Directions

Press the "Sauté" button and heat the olive oil. Add sweet onions, together with cinnamon and cardamom; sauté until sweet onions are caramelized.

Add the kamut, water, salt, and ground pepper. Now, secure the lid. Choose the "Manual" mode and cook at High pressure for 8 minutes.

Once cooking is complete, use a natural release; remove the lid carefully. Bon appétit!

Per serving: 349 Calories; 8.3g Fat; 62.1g Carbs; 11.5g Protein; 13.7g Sugars

595. Decadent Brioche Pudding with Sultanas

(Ready in about 40 minutes | Servings 6)

Ingredients

2 eggs, whisked
1/3 cup buttermilk
1/2 teaspoon ground cinnamon
1/4 teaspoon grated nutmeg
1 teaspoon vanilla paste
2 tablespoons coconut oil, melted
1 large brioche loaf, torn into pieces
1/4 cup white chocolate chips
1/4 cup Turbinado sugar
1/4 cup sultanas, soaked in rum
1 cup water

Directions

In a mixing dish, thoroughly combine the eggs, buttermilk, cinnamon, nutmeg, vanilla, and melted coconut oil.

Add the brioche and let it soak for 20 minutes; press the bread lightly with the back of a large spoon.

Stir in the chocolate chips, Turbinado sugar, and sultanas; stir gently to combine. Then, lightly grease a baking pan with a nonstick cooking spray.

Pour water into the base of your Instant Pot; add a metal trivet. Lower the baking pan onto the trivet. Secure the lid.

Choose the "Manual" mode, High pressure, and 15 minutes. Once cooking is complete, use a quick release; remove the lid carefully. Bon appétit!

Per serving: 337 Calories; 13g Fat; 42.4g Carbs; 12.1g Protein; 10.8g Sugars

596. Chili Con Carne

(Ready in about 35 minutes | Servings 8)

Ingredients

1 tablespoon lard
1 cup onion, chopped
3 garlic cloves, smashed
1/2 pound ground pork
1/2 pound ground beef
2 pounds red kidney beans, soaked overnight
2 cups tomato, puréed
1 cup onion, chopped
3 garlic cloves, smashed
2 bell peppers, deveined and chopped
1 cup water
1 cup chicken stock
Sea salt and freshly ground black pepper, to taste
1 teaspoon cayenne pepper
1 teaspoon red chili powder
1 teaspoon Mexican oregano
1 bay leaf
1 cup Pepper-Jack cheese, grated

Directions

Press the "Sauté" button to preheat your Instant Pot. Now, melt the lard and cook the onion until tender and translucent.

Add the garlic and ground meat; continue to cook until the meat is delicately browned.

Now, stir in the beans, tomato, onion, garlic, peppers, water, stock, salt, black pepper, cayenne pepper, chili powder, oregano and bay leaf.

Secure the lid. Choose the "Bean/Chili" mode and High pressure; cook for 30 minutes. Once cooking is complete, use a natural pressure release; carefully remove the lid.

Ladle into individual bowls; serve topped with grated cheese and enjoy!

Per serving: 300 Calories; 19.1g Fat; 9.7g Carbs; 22g Protein; 2.9g Sugars

597. Red Rice with Smoked Kielbasa

(Ready in about 40 minutes | Servings 4)

Ingredients

1 tablespoon canola oil
1/2 pound smoked Kielbasa, sliced
1 leek, chopped
1 cup red rice
1/4 cup tomato, puréed
1 cup vegetable broth
1 tablespoon ketchup
1/2 teaspoon mustard powder
1/2 teaspoon garlic powder
1/2 teaspoon dried marjoram

Directions

Press the "Sauté" button to preheat your Instant Pot. Now, heat the canola oil; cook the sausage and leek for 2 to 3 minutes.

Add the remaining ingredients; stir to combine well.

Secure the lid. Choose the "Porridge" mode and High pressure; cook for 25 minutes. Once cooking is complete, use a natural pressure release for 10 minutes; carefully remove the lid.

Ladle into serving bowls; serve with some extra mustard if desired and enjoy!

Per serving: 282 Calories; 20.1g Fat; 21.7g Carbs; 13.1g Protein; 2.3g Sugars

598. Carnaroli Rice Risotto with Ground Beef

(Ready in about 15 minutes | Servings 4)

Ingredients

2 tablespoons butter
1 cup shallots, diced
2 garlic cloves, minced
1/2 pound ground beef
2 bell peppers, seeded and chopped
1 red chili pepper, seeded and minced
2 cups Carnaroli rice, well-rinsed
4 cups beef stock
A pinch of saffron
Kosher salt and ground black pepper, to taste
1 teaspoon sweet paprika

Directions

Press the "Sauté" button to preheat your Instant Pot. Now, melt the butter; cook the shallots until they are softened.

Stir the garlic, ground beef, and peppers into your Instant Pot. Continue to cook an additional 2 minutes or until the beef is no longer pink and peppers are tender.

Add the rice, stock and seasonings to your Instant Pot; gently stir to combine.

Secure the lid. Choose the "Poultry" mode and High pressure; cook for 5 minutes. Once cooking is complete, use a quick pressure release; carefully remove the lid.

Serve in individual bowls. Bon appétit!

Per serving: 430 Calories; 26.3g Fat; 37.2g Carbs; 29.6g Protein; 4.2g Sugars

599. Savory Mediterranean Oatmeal

(Ready in about 15 minutes | Servings 3)

Ingredients

1 ½ cups oats, quick cooking
2 3/4 cups water
2 tablespoons flax seeds
1/3 teaspoon cayenne pepper
1 rosemary sprig, leaves picked and chopped

1/2 teaspoon sea salt
Ground black pepper, to your liking
1/2 cup feta cheese, crumbled
1/2 cup Kalamata olives, pitted and sliced

Directions

Add the quick cooking oats and water to your Instant Pot. Add the flax seeds, cayenne pepper, rosemary, salt, and black pepper. Secure the lid.

Choose the "Manual" button and cook for 6 minutes at High pressure. Once cooking is complete, use a natural release; remove the lid carefully.

Ladle the prepared oatmeal into individual bowls. Top with crumbled feta cheese and sliced olives and serve. Enjoy!

Per serving: 244 Calories; 14g Fat; 35.3g Carbs; 13.1g Protein; 1.8g Sugars

600. Tangy Wheat Berry Salad

(Ready in about 55 minutes | Servings 4)

Ingredients

1 ½ cups wheat berries
4 ½ cups water
1/4 teaspoon sea salt
1/4 teaspoon ground white pepper
1 large Fuji apple, unpeeled, diced
1 cucumber, sliced

1 carrot, julienned
1/3 cup almonds, toasted and chopped
2 tablespoons raspberry vinegar
1/4 cup extra-virgin olive oil

Directions

Add the wheat berries and water to the Instant Pot.

Secure the lid. Choose the "Multigrain" mode and High pressure; cook for 50 minutes. Once cooking is complete, use a natural pressure release; carefully remove the lid.

Allow the wheat berries to cool completely. Toss them with the remaining ingredients and serve well chilled.

Per serving: 371 Calories; 19.3g Fat; 44.9g Carbs; 8.1g Protein; 8.2g Sugars

601. Savory Millet with Sunflower Seeds

(Ready in about 20 minutes | Servings 4)

Ingredients

2 teaspoons pure sesame oil
1 cup carrots, chopped
A bunch of scallions, roughly chopped
1/2 teaspoon coarse salt
1/4 teaspoon ground white pepper
1/2 teaspoon cayenne pepper
1 teaspoon dried basil

1/2 teaspoon dried oregano
1 bay leaf
1/4 cup sunflower seeds
1 cup millet
1 2/3 cups water
3 tablespoons fresh chives, finely chopped

Directions

Press the "Sauté" button to preheat your Instant Pot. Now, heat the sesame oil until sizzling. After that, cook the carrots and scallions until they are just tender and fragrant, about 3 minutes.

Add the salt, white pepper, cayenne pepper, basil, oregano, bay leaf, sunflower seeds, and millet. Lastly, pour in the water and secure the lid.

Select the "Manual" function and cook for 10 minutes under High pressure. Once cooking is complete, use a quick release; remove the lid carefully.

Serve in individual bowls, garnished with fresh chives. Bon appétit!

Per serving: 275 Calories; 9.1g Fat; 41.5g Carbs; 7.8g Protein; 1.6g Sugars

602. Kamut Pilaf with Olives

(Ready in about 25 minutes | Servings 4)

Ingredients

1 tablespoon olive oil
2 shallots, chopped
2 cloves garlic minced
1 carrot, chopped
1 celery stalk, chopped
1 ½ cups kamut, soaked overnight
3 cups water

Salt and black pepper, to taste
1/2 teaspoon dried rosemary
1/4 cup fresh chives, chopped
1/4 cup fresh parsley, chopped
1/2 cup green olives, pitted and sliced

Directions

Press the "Sauté" button to preheat your Instant Pot. Now, heat the oil until sizzling; sauté the shallots for 2 minutes or until tender.

Next, stir in the garlic, carrots and celery; continue to sauté until they are tender. Add the kamut, water, salt, black pepper, and rosemary to the Instant Pot.

Secure the lid. Choose the "Porridge" mode and High pressure; cook for 20 minutes. Once cooking is complete, use a natural pressure release; carefully remove the lid.

Transfer to a serving bowl; garnish with chives, parsley and olives. Serve and enjoy!

Per serving: 285 Calories; 5g Fat; 53.6g Carbs; 10.8g Protein; 7.4g Sugars

603. Colombian Style Beans

(Ready in about 35 minutes | Servings 5)

Ingredients

1 tablespoon olive oil
1 purple onion, chopped
2 bell peppers, seeded and chopped
1 serrano pepper, seeded and minced
2 garlic cloves, minced
1/2 green plantain, cut into slices
1 ½ pounds dry Borlotti beans
4 cups roasted vegetable broth

2 ripe tomatoes, puréed
1/2 teaspoon cumin
1/2 teaspoon dried basil
1/2 teaspoon oregano
Salt and freshly ground black pepper, to taste
1 heaping tablespoon fresh parsley leaves, chopped
2 bay leaves

Directions

Press the "Sauté" button to preheat your Instant Pot. Now, heat the oil until sizzling; sauté the onion for 2 minutes or until tender.

Then, add the peppers, garlic, and plantain; continue to sauté an additional minute or until they are fragrant; reserve.

Add the remaining ingredients to your Instant Pot; stir to combine.

Secure the lid. Choose the "Bean/Chili" mode and High pressure; cook for 25 minutes. Once cooking is complete, use a natural pressure release; carefully remove the lid.

Add the reserved onion/pepper mixture. Seal the lid and let it sit for 5 minutes more or until everything is thoroughly warmed.

Discard the bay leaves. Taste for salt and serve warm.

Per serving: 553 Calories; 5.2g Fat; 93.3g Carbs; 37.2g Protein; 8.5g Sugars

604. Pot Barley with Vegetables

(Ready in about 45 minutes | Servings 4)

Ingredients

1 tablespoon olive oil
1 yellow onion, chopped
2 garlic cloves, minced
1 carrot, chopped
1 ½ cups button mushrooms, thinly sliced
1 cup pot barley

4 cups stock, preferably homemade
1/2 teaspoon salt
1/3 teaspoon freshly ground black pepper
1/4 teaspoon paprika
1/2 teaspoon ground bay leaf

Directions

Press the "Sauté" button and heat up your Instant Pot. Heat the olive oil until sizzling. Once hot, sweat the onion until tender.

Now, add the garlic, carrot, and mushrooms; cook until the mushrooms start to release their moisture and carrots are softened.

Rinse and drain the barley; transfer to the Instant Pot. Add the remaining ingredients; stir to combine.

Select the "Manual" mode and cook for 30 minutes under High pressure. Once cooking is complete, use a natural release for 10 minutes; remove the lid carefully. Bon appétit!

Per serving: 286 Calories; 8.3g Fat; 43.3g Carbs; 11.4g Protein; 2.6g Sugars

605. Buttermilk and Cottage Cheese Cornbread

(Ready in about 30 minutes | Servings 8)

Ingredients

1 ½ cups polenta	1/2 cup buttermilk
1 cup all-purpose flour	2/3 cup Cottage cheese, crumbled
2 tablespoons honey	1/2 teaspoon garlic powder
1 tablespoon baking powder	1/2 teaspoon onion powder
1/2 teaspoon baking soda	1/2 teaspoon oregano
1/2 teaspoon sea salt	1/2 teaspoon basil
1/3 cup olive oil	1 teaspoon rosemary
3 eggs	1 teaspoon thyme

Directions

Begin by adding 1 cup of water and a metal trivet to the bottom of your Instant Pot. Spritz the bottom and sides of a baking pan with a nonstick cooking pan.

Thoroughly combine the dry ingredients in a mixing bowl. In a separate mixing bowl, mix the wet ingredients.

Then, combine the wet mixture with the dry mixture; scrape the batter into the prepared baking pan. Place the baking pan on the trivet.

Secure the lid. Choose the "Porridge" mode and High pressure; cook for 20 minutes. Once cooking is complete, use a natural pressure release; carefully remove the lid.

Afterwards, transfer the cornbread to a cooling rack; allow it to sit for 5 to 6 minutes before slicing and serving. Enjoy!

Per serving: 266 Calories; 13.7g Fat; 27g Carbs; 8.2g Protein; 5.9g Sugars

606. Oatmeal and Purple Onion Soup

(Ready in about 30 minutes | Servings 4)

Ingredients

2 tablespoons ghee	Sea salt and ground black pepper, to taste
1 purple onion, chopped	
2 garlic cloves, minced	1/2 teaspoon cayenne pepper
2/3 cup oat groat	1/2 teaspoon turmeric powder
2 cups water	2 cups spinach leaves, roughly chopped
1 cup milk	
1 cup vegetable broth	

Directions

Press the "Sauté" button to preheat your Instant Pot. Then, melt the ghee and cook the onion and garlic until tender and fragrant.

Add the oat groat, water, milk, broth, salt, black pepper, cayenne pepper, and turmeric powder; stir to combine.

Secure the lid. Choose the "Manual" mode and High pressure; cook for 22 minutes. Once cooking is complete, use a natural pressure release; carefully remove the lid.

Add the spinach and seal the lid; let it sit until the spinach is wilted. Serve warm and enjoy!

Per serving: 160 Calories; 9.3g Fat; 18.6g Carbs; 7g Protein; 5.2g Sugars

607. Kamut with Cherries and Sour Cream

(Ready in about 45 minutes | Servings 4)

Ingredients

1 ½ cups kamut, well-rinsed	1/2 teaspoon ground cinnamon
4 ½ cups water	1 cup dried cherries
A pinch of salt	1 cup sour cream
2 tablespoons butter	1/3 cup honey
1/4 teaspoon grated nutmeg	

Directions

Add the kamut, water, and salt to your Instant Pot.

Secure the lid. Choose the "Multigrain" mode and High pressure; cook for 40 minutes. Once cooking is complete, use a natural pressure release; carefully remove the lid.

Now, add the butter, nutmeg, cinnamon and cherries to the Instant Pot; stir to combine and divide the porridge between four serving bowls.

Top each serving with sour cream; drizzle honey over the top and serve. Enjoy!

Per serving: 473 Calories; 13.4g Fat; 82.1g Carbs; 12.7g Protein; 33.2g Sugars

608. Easy Cheesy Polenta

(Ready in about 15 minutes | Servings 4)

Ingredients

6 cups roasted vegetable broth	1 cup Cheddar cheese, shredded
1/2 stick butter, softened	1/2 cup Ricotta cheese, at room temperature
1 ½ cups cornmeal	
Sea salt and ground black pepper, to taste	

Directions

Press the "Sauté" button to preheat the Instant Pot. Then, add the broth and butter; bring to a boil. Slowly and gradually, whisk in the cornmeal. Season with the salt and pepper.

Secure the lid. Choose the "Manual" mode and High pressure; cook for 8 minutes. Once cooking is complete, use a natural pressure release; carefully remove the lid.

Divide between individual bowls; serve topped with cheese. Bon appétit!

Per serving: 502 Calories; 22.1g Fat; 54.2g Carbs; 20.3g Protein; 4.6g Sugars

609. Italian-Style Baked Beans

(Ready in about 20 minutes | Servings 4)

Ingredients

1 pound pinto beans, soaked overnight	1 pound smoked Italian sausage, sliced
2 tablespoons brown sugar	1 yellow onion, chopped
1 bay leaf	2 cloves garlic, minced
2 tomatoes, puréed	1 carrot, sliced
1/2 teaspoon dried rosemary	1 parsnip, sliced
1 teaspoon dried marjoram	2 bell peppers, seeded and chopped
1/2 teaspoon freshly ground black pepper	1 Pepperoncini, seeded and minced
1/2 teaspoon cayenne pepper	1/2 cup sour cream
Sea salt, to taste	

Directions

Add the pinto beans to your Instant Pot; now, pour in enough water to cover the beans completely.

Next, stir in the sugar, bay leaf, tomatoes, rosemary, marjoram, black pepper, cayenne pepper, and salt; stir to combine well.

Secure the lid. Choose the "Bean/Chili" mode and High pressure; cook for 10 minutes. Once cooking is complete, use a natural pressure release; carefully remove the lid.

In the meantime, cook the sausage with the onion, garlic, carrot, parsnip, and peppers for 3 to 4 minutes; transfer the sausage mixture to the Instant Pot.

Top with well-chilled sour cream and serve. Bon appétit!

Per serving: 449 Calories; 26.8g Fat; 35.1g Carbs; 25g Protein; 10.2g Sugars

610. Hazelnut and Cranberry Buckwheat Porridge

(Ready in about 25 minutes | Servings 3)

Ingredients

3/4 cup raw buckwheat, rinsed
1 cup water
2 cups milk
1/3 cup dried cranberries
1/4 teaspoon cardamom
1/2 teaspoon ground cinnamon

1/2 teaspoon anise seed powder
1 teaspoon vanilla paste
1/2 teaspoon hazelnut extract
1/2 cup hazelnuts, chopped
1 tablespoon orange rind strips, for garnish

Directions

Add the buckwheat to the Instant Pot. Now, pour in the water and milk.

Stir in the dried cranberries, cardamom, cinnamon, anise seed powder, vanilla, and hazelnut extract. Secure the lid.

Choose the "Manual" button and cook for 7 minutes at High pressure. Once cooking is complete, use a natural release for 15 minutes; remove the lid carefully.

Divide the hot porridge among 3 serving bowls and top with hazelnuts; garnish with the orange rind strips and serve right now. Bon appétit!

Per serving: 301 Calories; 19.3g Fat; 24.4g Carbs; 10g Protein; 13g Sugars

611. Lime and Wild Rice Soup

(Ready in about 35 minutes | Servings 4)

Ingredients

2 tablespoons olive oil
1 onion, chopped
2 carrots, halved lengthwise and finely sliced
1 celery stalk, chopped
1 cup wild rice

6 cups water, bone broth, or a combination
1/2 teaspoon granulated garlic
2 tablespoons bouillon granules
1/4 cup freshly squeezed lime juice

Directions

Press the "Sauté" button to preheat the Instant Pot. Then, heat the oil; sauté the onions until tender and translucent.

Now, stir in the carrots and celery; continue to sauté until tender.

Add the rice, water, granulated garlic, and bouillon granules to the Instant Pot.

Secure the lid. Choose the "Soup" mode and High pressure; cook for 30 minutes. Once cooking is complete, use a natural pressure release; carefully remove the lid.

Ladle into soup bowls; drizzle each serving with fresh lime juice. Enjoy!

Per serving: 236 Calories; 7.7g Fat; 36.7g Carbs; 6.9g Protein; 3.2g Sugars

612. Barley and Beef Soup with Corn

(Ready in about 55 minutes | Servings 5)

Ingredients

1 tablespoon butter, softened
1 pound beef stew meat
1 shallot, chopped
Sea salt, to taste
1/4 teaspoon freshly ground black pepper, or more to taste
2 carrots, chopped
1 parsnip, chopped

2 celery stalks, chopped
1 teaspoon ginger-garlic paste
1/2 cup port wine
5 cups beef bone broth
1 cup barley, whole
5 ounces sweet corn kernels, frozen and thawed

Directions

Press the "Sauté" button to preheat the Instant Pot. Then, melt the butter; cook the meat and shallot until the meat is no longer pink.

Add the salt, pepper, carrots, parsnip, celery, ginger-garlic paste, wine, broth and barley.

Secure the lid. Choose the "Soup" mode and High pressure; cook for 40 minutes. Once cooking is complete, use a natural pressure release for 10 minutes; carefully remove the lid.

Add the corn and seal the lid. Allow it to seat until heated through. Ladle into individual bowls and serve right away!

Per serving: 366 Calories; 8.4g Fat; 44.1g Carbs; 30.2g Protein; 3.9g Sugars

LOW CARB

613. Homemade Blueberry Yogurt

(Ready in about 24 hours + chilling time | Servings 12)

Ingredients
3 quarts raw milk
15 grams probiotic yogurt starter
1 teaspoon stevia powder

1 cup blueberries, fresh or frozen (and thawed)

Directions
Add the milk to the Instant Pot.

Secure the lid. Choose "Yogurt" mode; now, press the "Adjust" button until you see the word "Boil". Turn off the Instant Pot.

Use a food thermometer to read temperature; 115 degrees is fine; stir in the starter.

Press the "Yogurt" button again and then, press the "Adjust" button to reach 24 hours.

Place in your refrigerator for a few hours to set up. Add the stevia and blueberries; serve well chilled. Bon appétit!

Per serving: 92 Calories; 0.6g Fat; 6.6g Carbs; 14.7g Protein; 5.4g Sugars

614. Breakfast Meatloaf Cups

(Ready in about 40 minutes | Servings 8)

Ingredients
1 pound ground pork
1 pound ground beef
1/2 cup onion, chopped
2 garlic cloves, minced
Salt and ground black pepper, to taste

1/3 cup Romano cheese, grated
1/4 cup pork rinds, crushed
4 eggs, whisked
2 ripe tomatoes, puréed
1/4 cup barbecue sauce, sugar-free

Directions
Start by adding 1 cup of water and a metal trivet to the bottom of your Instant Pot.

In a mixing bowl, thoroughly combine the ground meat, onion, garlic, salt, black pepper, cheese, pork rinds, and eggs.

Mix until everything is well incorporated. Divide the mixture among muffin cups.

In a small mixing bowl, whisk the puréed tomatoes with the barbecue sauce. Lastly, top your muffins with the tomato sauce.

Secure the lid. Choose "Manual" mode and High pressure; cook for 25 minutes. Once cooking is complete, use a quick pressure release; carefully remove the lid.

Allow them to cool for 10 minutes before removing from the muffin tin. Bon appétit!

Per serving: 375 Calories; 22.2g Fat; 6.5g Carbs; 35.4g Protein; 4.5g Sugars

615. Breakfast Casserole with Zucchini and Bacon

(Ready in about 25 minutes | Servings 8)

Ingredients
1/2 pound zucchini, grated and squeezed dry
1 white onion, chopped
1 clove garlic, minced
6 slices bacon, chopped
1 cup Colby cheese, shredded
1 cup Cottage cheese, room temperature

8 eggs, beaten
1/2 cup Greek yogurt, room temperature
Sea salt and ground black pepper, to taste
1/4 teaspoon dried marjoram
1/4 teaspoon dried rosemary
1 teaspoon dried parsley flakes

Directions
Start by adding 1 cup of water and a metal trivet to the bottom of your Instant Pot.

Mix the ingredients until everything is well incorporated. Spoon the mixture into a lightly greased casserole dish.

Lower the casserole dish onto the trivet.

Secure the lid. Choose "Manual" mode and High pressure; cook for 20 minutes. Once cooking is complete, use a quick pressure release; carefully remove the lid. Bon appétit!

Per serving: 320 Calories; 24.3g Fat; 5.3g Carbs; 19.7g Protein; 2.9g Sugars

616. Spicy and Cheesy Chard Quiche

(Ready in about 35 minutes | Servings 6)

Ingredients
10 large eggs
1/2 cup double cream
Seasoned salt and ground black pepper, to taste
1 teaspoon cayenne pepper
2 cups chard, roughly chopped

1 habanero pepper, seeded and chopped
1 tomato, chopped
1/2 cup red onion, thinly sliced
1/2 cup Pepper-Jack cheese, freshly grated

Directions
Start by adding 1 ½ cups of water and a metal trivet to the bottom of your Instant Pot. Now, lightly grease a baking dish with a nonstick cooking spray.

In a mixing bowl, thoroughly combine the eggs with the double cream, salt, black pepper, and cayenne pepper.

Now, stir in the chard, habanero pepper, tomato, and onion. Spoon the mixture into the prepared baking dish.

Cover with a piece of aluminum foil, making a foil sling.

Secure the lid. Choose "Manual" mode and High pressure; cook for 20 minutes. Once cooking is complete, use a quick pressure release; carefully remove the lid.

Top with the cheese and cover with the lid; allow it to sit in the residual heat for 10 minutes.

Serve immediately and enjoy!

Per serving: 183 Calories; 14.4g Fat; 5.6g Carbs; 8.1g Protein; 2.8g Sugars

617. Bacon Frittata Muffins

(Ready in about 15 minutes | Servings 6)

Ingredients
6 thin meaty bacon slices
1 large-sized zucchini, grated
1 red bell pepper, chopped
1 green bell pepper, chopped
4 teaspoons butter, melted
1/2 cup Colby cheese, shredded
3 egg, beaten

2 tablespoons cream cheese, room temperature
1 teaspoon shallot powder
1/2 teaspoon dried dill weed
1/2 teaspoon cayenne pepper
Salt and black pepper, to taste

Directions
Start by adding 1 ½ cups of water and a metal trivet to the bottom of your Instant Pot.

Place the bacon slices in 6 silicone cupcake liners. Add the zucchini and bell peppers.

Now, mix the butter, Colby cheese, eggs, cream cheese, shallot powder, dried dill weed, cayenne pepper, salt, and black pepper. Spoon this mixture into the liners.

Put the liners into an oven-safe bowl. Cover with a piece of foil. Lower the bowl onto the trivet.

Secure the lid. Choose "Manual" mode and High pressure; cook for 10 minutes. Once cooking is complete, use a natural pressure release; carefully remove the lid. Bon appétit!

Per serving: 226 Calories; 20.1g Fat; 2.3g Carbs; 9.3g Protein; 1.3g Sugars

618. Apple Pie Granola

(Ready in about 1 hour 35 minutes | Servings 4)

Ingredients
3 tablespoons coconut oil
1 teaspoon stevia powder
1 cup coconut, shredded
1/4 cup walnuts, chopped
1 ½ tablespoons sunflower seeds

1 ½ tablespoons pumpkin seeds
1 teaspoon apple pie spice mix
A pinch of salt
1 small apple, sliced

Directions
Place the coconut oil, stevia powder, coconut, walnuts, sunflower seeds, pumpkin seeds, apple pie spice mix, and salt in your Instant Pot.

Secure the lid. Choose "Slow Cook" mode and High pressure; cook for 1 hours 30 minutes. Once cooking is complete, use a quick pressure release; carefully remove the lid.

Spoon into individual bowls, garnish with apples and serve warm. Bon appétit!

Per serving: 234 Calories; 22.2g Fat; 5.5g Carbs; 2.5g Protein; 5.3g Sugars

619. Spinach and Cheese Muffins

(Ready in about 15 minutes | Servings 6)

Ingredients

6 eggs
1/3 cup double cream
1/4 cup cream cheese
Sea salt and freshly ground black pepper, to taste

1/2 teaspoon cayenne pepper
1 ½ cups spinach, chopped
1/4 cup green onions, chopped
1 ripe tomato, chopped
1/2 cup cheddar cheese, grated

Directions

Start by adding 1 cup of water and a metal rack to the Instant Pot. Now, spritz a muffin tin with a nonstick cooking spray.

In a mixing dish, thoroughly combine the eggs, double cream, cream cheese, salt, black pepper, and cayenne pepper.

Then, divide the spinach, green onions, tomato, and scallions among the cups. Pour the egg mixture over the vegetables. Top with the cheddar cheese.

Lower the cups onto the rack.

Secure the lid. Choose "Manual" mode and High pressure; cook for 10 minutes. Once cooking is complete, use a natural pressure release; carefully remove the lid. Serve immediately.

Per serving: 236 Calories; 18.8g Fat; 3.3g Carbs; 13.2g Protein; 2.2g Sugars

620. Shirred Eggs with Peppers and Scallions

(Ready in about 10 minutes | Servings 4)

Ingredients

4 tablespoons butter, melted
4 tablespoons double cream
4 eggs
4 scallions, chopped
2 red peppers, seeded and chopped

1/2 teaspoon granulated garlic
1/4 teaspoon dill weed
1/4 teaspoon sea salt
1/4 teaspoon freshly ground pepper

Directions

Start by adding 1 cup of water and a metal rack to the Instant Pot.

Grease the bottom and sides of each ramekin with melted butter. Divide the ingredients among the prepared four ramekins.

Lower the ramekins onto the metal rack.

Secure the lid. Choose "Manual" mode and High pressure; cook for 5 minutes. Once cooking is complete, use a natural pressure release; carefully remove the lid. Bon appétit!

Per serving: 208 Calories; 18.7g Fat; 3.9g Carbs; 6.7g Protein; 2.3g Sugars

621. Hungarian Hot Pot

(Ready in about 15 minutes | Servings 4)

Ingredients

1 tablespoon grapeseed oil
9 ounces Hungarian smoked sausage, casing removed and sliced
1 carrot, cut into thick slices
1 celery stalk, diced
2 bell peppers, cut into wedges
2 cups roasted vegetable broth

1/2 cup shallot, peeled and diced
Sea salt and ground black pepper, to taste
½ tablespoon hot pepper flakes
1 bay leaf
1/4 cup fresh cilantro leaves, roughly chopped

Directions

Press the "Sauté" button to heat up the Instant Pot. Now, heat the oil and brown the sausage for 2 to 3 minutes.

Stir in the other ingredients.

Secure the lid. Choose "Manual" mode and High pressure; cook for 10 minutes. Once cooking is complete, use a natural pressure release; carefully remove the lid. Bon appétit!

Per serving: 292 Calories; 21.6g Fat; 6.4g Carbs; 15.7g Protein; 3.5g Sugars

622. Spring Avocado Eggs

(Ready in about 25 minutes | Servings 5)

Ingredients

5 eggs
1 avocado, pitted, peeled and mashed
1 tablespoon fresh lemon juice
1 ripe tomato, chopped
1/2 teaspoon cayenne pepper

Kosher salt and white pepper, to taste
1/2 teaspoon chili powder
3 tablespoons spring onions, roughly chopped

Directions

Pour 1 cup of water into the Instant Pot; add a steamer basket to the bottom.

Arrange the eggs in the steamer basket.

Secure the lid. Choose "Manual" mode and High pressure; cook for 5 minutes. Once cooking is complete, use a natural pressure release; carefully remove the lid.

Allow the eggs to cool for 15 minutes. Peel the eggs, slice them into halves, and separate the egg whites from the yolks.

To make the filling, mix the avocado, lemon juice, tomato, cayenne pepper, salt, white pepper, and chili powder; stir in the reserved egg yolks. Now, stuff the egg whites with this mixture.

Garnish with green onions. Arrange on a nice serving platter and serve.

Per serving: 138 Calories; 10.2g Fat; 6.2g Carbs; 6.8g Protein; 1.7g Sugars

623. Dilled Cauliflower Purée with Au Jus Gravy

(Ready in about 20 minutes | Servings 4)

Ingredients

Cauliflower Purée:
1 head of fresh cauliflower, broken into florets
1/4 cup double cream
2 tablespoons butter
3 cloves garlic minced
4 tablespoons Romano cheese, grated

1 teaspoon dried dill weed
Kosher salt and ground black pepper, to taste
Gravy:
1 ½ cups beef stock
1/2 cup double cream
3 tablespoons butter

Directions

Add 1 cup of water and a steamer basket to the bottom of your Instant Pot.

Then, arrange the cauliflower in the steamer basket.

Secure the lid. Choose "Manual" mode and Low pressure; cook for 3 minutes. Once cooking is complete, use a quick pressure release; carefully remove the lid.

Now, puree the cauliflower with a potato masher. Add the remaining ingredients for the purée and stir well.

Press the "Sauté" button to heat up the Instant Pot. Now, combine the ingredients for the gravy and let it simmer for 10 minutes.

Stir until the gravy thickens down to a consistency of your liking. Serve the cauliflower purée with the gravy on the side. Bon appétit!

Per serving: 291 Calories; 26.6g Fat; 7.1g Carbs; 7.1g Protein; 4.5g Sugars

624. Aromatic Cheesy and Kale Bake

(Ready in about 30 minutes | Servings 6)

Ingredients

2 tablespoons olive oil
1/2 cup leeks, chopped
2 garlic cloves, minced
2 cups kale leaves, torn into pieces
7 eggs, whisked
2 cups cream cheese, shredded

1 cup Colby cheese, shredded
Sea salt and ground black pepper, to taste
1/4 teaspoon paprika
1/4 teaspoon dried rosemary
1/2 teaspoon dried thyme

Directions

Start by adding 1 cup of water and a metal trivet to the Instant Pot. Grease a baking pan with a nonstick cooking spray.

Simply mix all of the above ingredients until everything is well combined.

Spoon the batter into the prepared baking pan. Now, lower the baking pan onto the trivet.

Secure the lid. Choose "Meat/Stew" mode and High pressure; cook for 25 minutes. Once cooking is complete, use a quick pressure release; carefully remove the lid. Serve warm.

Per serving: 473 Calories; 43g Fat; 5.9g Carbs; 16.6g Protein; 3.2g Sugars

625. Coconut Porridge with Berries

(Ready in about 10 minutes | Servings 2)

Ingredients

4 tablespoons coconut flour
1 tablespoon sunflower seeds
3 tablespoons flax meal
1 ¼ cups water
1/4 teaspoon coarse salt
1/4 teaspoon grated nutmeg
1/2 teaspoon ground cardamom

2 eggs, beaten
2 tablespoons coconut oil, softened
2 tablespoons Swerve
1/2 cup mixed berries, fresh or frozen (thawed)

Directions

Add all ingredients, except for the mixed berries, to the Instant Pot.

Secure the lid. Choose "Manual" mode and High pressure; cook for 5 minutes. Once cooking is complete, use a quick pressure release; carefully remove the lid.

Divide between two bowls, top with berries, and serve hot. Bon appétit!

Per serving: 242 Calories; 20.7g Fat; 7.9g Carbs; 7.6g Protein; 2.8g Sugars

626. Cauliflower "Mac and Cheese"

(Ready in about 20 minutes | Servings 6)

Ingredients

1 medium head of cauliflower, broken into florets
2 tablespoons butter, melted
2/3 cup cream cheese
1/2 cup milk
1/2 teaspoon cumin powder

1/2 teaspoon mustard seeds
1/2 teaspoon fennel seeds
Salt and black pepper, to taste
2 cups Monterey-Jack cheese, shredded

Directions

Add 1 cup of water and a metal rack to the bottom of your Instant Pot.

Then, place the cauliflower in a casserole dish that is previously greased with melted butter.

In a mixing bowl, thoroughly combine the cream cheese, milk, cumin powder, mustard seeds, fennel seeds, salt, and black pepper.

Pour this mixture over the cauliflower.

Secure the lid. Choose "Manual" mode and High pressure; cook for 7 minutes. Once cooking is complete, use a quick pressure release; carefully remove the lid.

Top with shredded Monterey-Jack cheese. Return to the Instant Pot, cover with the lid, and let it sit in a residual heat for 10 minutes. Bon appétit!

Per serving: 306 Calories; 25.7g Fat; 5.4g Carbs; 14.4g Protein; 3.5g Sugars

627. Zucchini Sloppy Joe's

(Ready in about 10 minutes | Servings 2)

Ingredients

1 tablespoon olive oil
1/2 pound ground beef
Salt and ground black pepper, to taste

1 medium-sized zucchini, cut into 4 slices lengthwise
1 tomato, sliced
4 lettuce leaves
2 teaspoons mustard

Directions

Add the olive oil, ground beef, salt, and black pepper to your Instant Pot.

Secure the lid. Choose "Manual" mode and High pressure; cook for 5 minutes. Once cooking is complete, use a natural pressure release; carefully remove the lid.

Divide the ground meat mixture between 2 zucchini slices. Add the tomato slices, lettuce, and mustard. Top with the second slice of zucchini. Bon appétit!

Per serving: 159 Calories; 9.8g Fat; 1.5g Carbs; 15.5g Protein; 0.7g Sugars

628. Greek-Style Mushroom Muffins

(Ready in about 10 minutes | Servings 6)

Ingredients

6 eggs
1 red onion, chopped
2 cups button mushrooms, chopped

Sea salt and ground black pepper, to taste
1 ½ cups Feta cheese, shredded
1/2 cup Kalamata olives, pitted and sliced

Directions

Start by adding 1 ½ cups of water and a metal rack to the bottom of the Instant Pot. Spritz each muffin liner with a nonstick cooking spray.

In a mixing bowl, thoroughly combine the eggs, onions, mushrooms, salt, and black pepper. Now, pour this mixture into the muffin liners.

Secure the lid. Choose "Manual" mode and Low pressure; cook for 7 minutes. Once cooking is complete, use a quick pressure release; carefully remove the lid.

Sprinkle the cheese and olives on top of the cups; cover with the lid for a few minutes to allow it to melt. Enjoy!

Per serving: 259 Calories; 18.9g Fat; 6.7g Carbs; 15.7g Protein; 3.9g Sugars

629. Pancakes with Cottage Cheese Topping

(Ready in about 1 hour 15 minutes | Servings 4)

Ingredients

Pancakes:
2 tablespoons coconut oil
4 eggs
8 ounces cream cheese
1/4 teaspoon kosher salt
1 teaspoon granulated Swerve
1 teaspoon ground psyllium husk powder
Topping:

6 ounces Cottage cheese, room temperature
4 tablespoons low-carb mayonnaise, preferably homemade
1 small shallot, minced
Sea salt and ground black pepper, to taste

Directions

Thoroughly combine the ingredients for the pancakes.

Spritz the bottom and sides of your Instant Pot with a nonstick cooking spray. Add 1/2 of the pancake mixture and secure the lid.

Choose "Multigrain" mode and Low pressure; cook for 35 minutes. Cook until golden brown and crispy on the top.

Once cooking is complete, use a natural pressure release; carefully remove the lid.

Repeat with the remaining 1/2 of the pancake mixture.

In the meantime, thoroughly combine all ingredients for the topping. Spread the topping over your pancakes and serve warm. Bon appétit!

Per serving: 372 Calories; 31.7g Fat; 8g Carbs; 14.6g Protein; 4.8g Sugars

630. Sichuan-Style Duck Breast

(Ready in about 2 hours 15 minutes | Servings 4)

Ingredients

1 pound duck breast, boneless, skinless and cut into 4 pieces
1/2 teaspoon coarse sea salt
1/4 teaspoon Sichuan peppercorn powder
1/2 teaspoon cayenne pepper

2 garlic cloves, minced
2 tablespoons peanut oil
1/2 cup dry red wine
1 tablespoon sake
1/2 cup chicken broth

Directions

Place all ingredients, except for the broth, in a ceramic dish; place the dish in your refrigerator and let it marinate for 1 to 2 hours.

Then, transfer the meat along with its marinade to the Instant Pot. Pour in the chicken broth.

Secure the lid. Choose "Manual" mode and High pressure; cook for 10 minutes. Once cooking is complete, use a quick pressure release; carefully remove the lid.

Serve warm and enjoy!

Per serving: 256 Calories; 13.7g Fat; 1g Carbs; 29.1g Protein; 0g Sugars

631. Classic Chicken Gumbo

(Ready in about 20 minutes | Servings 6)

Ingredients

2 tablespoons grapeseed oil
2 pork sausages, smoked, sliced
3 chicken legs, boneless and skinless
1 cup onion, chopped
1 cup bell peppers, finely chopped
3 cloves garlic, finely minced
1/2 teaspoon salt
1/4 teaspoon black pepper

1 teaspoon cayenne pepper
1 teaspoon Cajun spice mix
1 teaspoon filé powder
5 cups chicken broth
2 tomatoes, pureed
1 ½ cups fresh or frozen (thawed) okra
1/4 cup fresh coriander leaves, chopped

Directions

Press the "Sauté" button to heat up the Instant Pot. Now, heat the oil and cook the sausage and chicken until browned; reserve.

Add the onion, bell peppers, and garlic and sauté in the pan drippings until they are softened.

Add the salt, black pepper, cayenne pepper, Cajun spice mix, filé powder, chicken broth and tomatoes.

Secure the lid. Choose "Manual" mode and High pressure; cook for 12 minutes. Once cooking is complete, use a natural pressure release; carefully remove the lid.

Stir the okra into the Instant Pot; press the "Sauté" button one more time and let it simmer until the okra is tender, for 5 to 8 minutes.

Serve in individual bowls, garnished with fresh coriander. Enjoy!

Per serving: 233 Calories; 13.8g Fat; 8.7g Carbs; 19.6g Protein; 4.3g Sugars

632. Chia and Blackberry Jam

(Ready in about 10 minutes | Servings 12)

Ingredients

10 ounces fresh blackberries, rinsed
1/2 cup Swerve, powdered

3 teaspoons chia seeds
1/2 cup water

Directions

Add the blackberries to your Instant Pot.

Sprinkle with the Swerve and chia seeds. Pour in 1/2 cup of water.

Secure the lid. Choose "Manual" mode and High pressure; cook for 2 minutes. Once cooking is complete, use a natural pressure release; carefully remove the lid.

Process the mixture with an immersion blender. Store your jam in a mason jar or serve immediately. Bon appétit!

Per serving: 38 Calories; 1.1g Fat; 5.2g Carbs; 1.2g Protein; 4.7g Sugars

633. Mushroom and Cream Cheese Pâté

(Ready in about 10 minutes | Servings 8)

Ingredients

3 tablespoons olive oil
1 pound brown mushrooms, chopped
1/2 yellow onion, chopped
2 garlic cloves, minced
2 tablespoons cognac

Sea salt, to taste
1/3 teaspoon black pepper
1/2 teaspoon cayenne pepper
1 cup cream cheese, at room temperature

Directions

Press the "Sauté" button to heat up the Instant Pot. Now, heat the oil and cook the mushrooms with the onions until softened and fragrant.

Stir in the garlic, cognac, salt, black pepper, and cayenne pepper.

Secure the lid. Choose "Manual" mode and High pressure; cook for 5 minutes. Once cooking is complete, use a quick pressure release; carefully remove the lid.

Transfer the mixture to a food processor. Add the cream cheese and continue to mix until everything is well incorporated. Serve with veggie sticks. Bon appétit!

Per serving: 162 Calories; 14.4g Fat; 3.6g Carbs; 3.9g Protein; 2.4g Sugars

634. Japanese-Style Savory Custard

(Ready in about 10 minutes | Servings 4)

Ingredients

4 eggs
3/4 cup dashi, cold
1/4 sour cream
2 teaspoons light soy sauce
1 tablespoon sesame oil

1 tablespoon mirin
1/2 yellow onion, minced
2 garlic cloves, minced
Salt and pepper, to taste
1/2 cup scallions, chopped

Directions

Prepare the Instant Pot by adding 1 ½ cups of water and a metal rack to its bottom.

Whisk the eggs, dashi, sour cream, soy sauce, sesame oil, and mirin in a mixing bowl. Now, strain this mixture over a fine mesh strainer into a baking dish.

Add the onions, garlic, salt, and pepper; stir to combine well. Lower the cooking dish onto the rack.

Secure the lid. Choose "Steam" mode and High pressure; cook for 6 minutes. Once cooking is complete, use a natural pressure release; carefully remove the lid.

Serve garnished with chopped scallions. Enjoy!

Per serving: 206 Calories; 15.3g Fat; 5.5g Carbs; 11.1g Protein; 2.2g Sugars

635. Zucchini Cardamom Bread

(Ready in about 35 minutes | Servings 8)

Ingredients

4 eggs
1/3 cup olive oil
1 cup almond flour
2 tablespoons coconut flour
1 teaspoon stevia, liquid

A pinch of salt
A pinch of grated nutmeg
1 teaspoon baking powder
1 teaspoon ground cardamom
1 cup zucchini, grated

Directions

Prepare the Instant Pot by adding 1 ½ cups of water and a metal rack to its bottom. Lightly grease a baking pan with a nonstick cooking spray.

In a mixing dish, thoroughly combine the dry ingredients. Then, in another bowl, thoroughly combine the wet ingredients.

Add the wet mixture to the dry mixture; continue to mix until uniform, creamy and smooth. Pour the batter into the prepared pan.

Lower the pan onto the trivet.

Secure the lid. Choose "Bean/Chili" mode and High pressure; cook for 25 minutes. Once cooking is complete, use a natural pressure release; carefully remove the lid.

Allow the zucchini bread to cool completely before cutting and serving. Bon appétit!

Per serving: 205 Calories; 19.1g Fat; 4.3g Carbs; 6.1g Protein; 0.9g Sugars

636. Creamy Breakfast "Cereals"

(Ready in about 15 minutes | Servings 4)

Ingredients

1/4 coconut flour	2 eggs, beaten
1/4 cup almond flour	1/4 stick butter
1 tablespoon flaxseed meal	4 tablespoons Swerve, granulated
1/4 teaspoon kosher salt	2 tablespoons double cream
1/2 cup milk	2 ounces raspberries
1/2 cup water	1 ounce blueberries

Directions

Add all ingredients to the Instant Pot.

Secure the lid. Choose "Manual" mode and High pressure; cook for 5 minutes. Once cooking is complete, use a quick pressure release; carefully remove the lid.

Serve garnished with some extra berries if desired. Enjoy!

637. Delicious Homemade Burgers

(Ready in about 35 minutes | Servings 4)

Per serving: 410 Calories; 30.1g Fat; 1.4g Carbs; 31.7g Protein; 0.5g Sugars

Ingredients

Keto Buns:	1/2 teaspoon granulated garlic
3 tablespoons butter, softened	1/2 teaspoon onion powder
3 eggs, whisked	Burgers:
1/2 teaspoon sea salt	1/3 pound ground pork
1/4 teaspoon cayenne pepper	1/2 pound ground beef
1/2 teaspoon freshly ground black pepper	Salt and ground black pepper, to taste
1 cup almond flour	2 garlic cloves, minced
1 teaspoon baking powder	1/2 teaspoon cumin powder

Directions

Start by preheating your oven to 420 degrees F.

Beat the butter and eggs until well combined. Add the remaining ingredients for the buns and continue to mix until the batter is smooth and uniform.

Divide the batter between muffin molds. Bake for 25 minutes and reserve.

Meanwhile, mix the ingredients for the burgers. Now, shape the mixture into four equal sized patties.

Add 1 cup of water and a steamer basket to the Instant Pot. Place the burgers in the steamer basket.

Secure the lid. Choose "Manual" mode and High pressure; cook for 6 minutes. Once cooking is complete, use a quick pressure release; carefully remove the lid.

Assemble your burgers with the prepared buns. Bon appétit!

Per serving: 185 Calories; 14.4g Fat; 6.2g Carbs; 5.9g Protein; 6.8g Sugars

638. Fluffy Berry Cupcakes

(Ready in about 30 minutes | Servings 6)

Ingredients

1/4 cup coconut oil, softened	A pinch of salt
3 ounces cream cheese, softened	1/3 cup Swerve, granulated
1/4 cup double cream	1 teaspoon baking powder
4 eggs	1/4 teaspoon cardamom powder
1/4 cup coconut flour	1/2 teaspoon star anise, ground
1/4 cup almond flour	1/2 cup fresh mixed berries

Directions

Start by adding 1 ½ cups of water and a metal rack to your Instant Pot.

Mix the coconut oil, cream cheese, and double cream in a bowl. Fold in the eggs, one at a time, and continue to mix until everything is well incorporated.

In another bowl, thoroughly combine the flour, salt, Swerve, baking powder, cardamom, and anise.

Add the cream/egg mixture to this dry mixture. Afterwards, fold in the fresh berries and gently stir to combine.

Divide the batter between silicone cupcake liners. Cover with a piece of foil. Place the cupcakes on the rack.

Secure the lid. Choose "Manual" mode and High pressure; cook for 25 minutes. Once cooking is complete, use a natural pressure release; carefully remove the lid. Enjoy!

Per serving: 238 Calories; 21.6g Fat; 4.1g Carbs; 7.5g Protein; 2.2g Sugars

639. Mediterranean-Style Savory Tart

(Ready in about 35 minutes | Servings 6)

Ingredients

10 ounces cream cheese	1/2 stick butter, melted
4 eggs, whisked	1 ½ cups zucchini, grated
1 cup almond flour	1 clove garlic, pressed
1 tablespoon flaxseed meal	1/4 teaspoon dried rosemary
1 teaspoon baking powder	1/4 teaspoon dried basil
Coarse sea salt and ground black pepper, to taste	1/2 cup Cheddar cheese, shredded

Directions

Begin by adding 1 cup of water and a metal rack to your Instant Pot. Then, spritz a heatproof bowl with a nonstick cooking spray and set aside.

In a mixing dish, thoroughly combine the cream and eggs. Gradually stir in the flour. Add the remaining ingredients, except for the Cheddar cheese.

Spoon the mixture into the prepared heatproof bowl; cover with a piece of aluminum foil, making a foil sling.

Secure the lid. Choose "Manual" mode and High pressure; cook for 25 minutes. Once cooking is complete, use a quick pressure release; carefully remove the lid.

Add the Cheddar cheese to the top of your tart and cover with the lid. Let it sit in a residual heat an additional 7 to 10 minutes. Bon appétit!

Per serving: 353 Calories; 32.1g Fat; 4g Carbs; 12.6g Protein; 2.5g Sugars

640. Salmon and Ricotta Fat Bombs

(Ready in about 15 minutes | Servings 6)

Ingredients

1/2 pound salmon fillets	4 ounces Ricotta cheese, room temperature
Salt and ground black pepper, to taste	1/4 cup green onions, chopped
1/4 teaspoon smoked paprika	1 garlic clove, finely chopped
1/4 teaspoon hot paprika	2 teaspoons fresh parsley, finely chopped
2 tablespoons butter, softened	

Directions

Start by adding 1 ½ cups of water and a metal rack to the bottom of your Instant Pot.

Place the salmon on the metal rack.

Secure the lid. Choose "Manual" mode and Low pressure; cook for 8 minutes. Once cooking is complete, use a quick pressure release; carefully remove the lid.

Chop the salmon. Add the salt, pepper, paprika, butter, cheese, onions, and garlic. Shape the mixture into balls and roll them in chopped parsley.

Arrange the fat bombs on a serving platter and enjoy!

Per serving: 130 Calories; 9.1g Fat; 1.7g Carbs; 10.2g Protein; 0.5g Sugars

641. Pork and Green Bean Casserole

(Ready in about 30 minutes | Servings 6)

Ingredients

1 pound ground pork
1 yellow onion, thinly sliced
2 garlic cloves, smashed
1 green bell pepper, thinly sliced
1 red bell pepper, thinly sliced
1 habanero chili pepper, thinly sliced
1 cup green beans

3 ripe tomatoes, chopped
1/2 teaspoon cumin, ground
Salt and ground black pepper, to taste
1/2 teaspoon cayenne pepper
1 cup Colby cheese, shredded
2 tablespoons fresh chives, chopped

Directions

Start by adding 1 ½ cups of water and a metal rack to the bottom of your Instant Pot.

Mix the pork, onion, garlic, pepper, green beans, tomatoes, cumin, salt, black pepper, and cayenne pepper until well combined.

Pour the mixture into a lightly greased casserole dish that will fit in your Instant Pot. Then, lower the dish onto the rack.

Secure the lid. Choose "Manual" mode and Low pressure; cook for 20 minutes. Once cooking is complete, use a quick pressure release; carefully remove the lid.

Top with the Colby cheese and cover with the lid. Let it sit in a residual heat an additional 7 to 10 minutes.

Serve garnished with fresh chives. Bon appétit!

Per serving: 348 Calories; 23.1g Fat; 8.6g Carbs; 26.3g Protein; 4.4g Sugars

642. Old-Fashioned Cherry Jam

(Ready in about 10 minutes | Servings 8)

Ingredients

2 cups cherries, pitted
1/2 cup Swerve, granulated
1 tablespoon vanilla extract
1 teaspoon rum extract

1/2 teaspoon ground cardamom
2 teaspoons arrowroot powder
1 cup water

Directions

Add the cherries to your Instant Pot.
Sprinkle with the Swerve, vanilla, rum extract, and cardamom. Now, add the arrowroot powder and water.

Secure the lid. Choose "Manual" mode and High pressure; cook for 2 minutes. Once cooking is complete, use a natural pressure release; carefully remove the lid.

Process the mixture with an immersion blender. Store in a mason jar or serve immediately. Bon appétit!

Per serving: 33 Calories; 0.1g Fat; 6.8g Carbs; 0.4g Protein; 3.6g Sugars

643. Spicy Mushroom Hot Pot

(Ready in about 10 minutes | Servings 4)

Ingredients

1 tablespoon olive oil
1 pound white mushrooms, thinly sliced
1/2 onion, chopped
1 cup water

Sea salt and ground black pepper, to taste
1 bay leaf
1 cup Colby cheese, shredded

Directions

Press the "Sauté" button to heat up the Instant Pot. Now, heat the oil and cook the mushrooms with the onions until softened and fragrant.

Add the water, salt, black pepper, and bay leaf.

Secure the lid. Choose "Manual" mode and High pressure; cook for 5 minutes. Once cooking is complete, use a quick pressure release; carefully remove the lid.

Add the cheese, cover with the lid and let it sit in the residual heat until the cheese is melted. Serve warm.

Per serving: 195 Calories; 14.3g Fat; 6.8g Carbs; 11.7g Protein; 3.5g Sugars

644. Egg Balls in Marinara Sauce

(Ready in about 15 minutes | Servings 6)

Ingredients

1 ½ cups low-carb marinara sauce
8 eggs, whisked
1 ½ cups Romano cheese, grated
1 cup pork rinds, crushed
2 cloves garlic, finely chopped

2 tablespoons fresh parsley, chopped
Sea salt and ground black pepper, to your liking
1 tablespoon olive oil

Directions

Press the "Sauté" button to heat up the Instant Pot. Add the marinara sauce and bring it to a boil.

Now, in a mixing bowl, thoroughly combine the remaining ingredients. Form the mixture into balls.

Then, drop the balls into the hot marinara sauce.

Secure the lid. Choose "Manual" mode and High pressure; cook for 8 minutes. Once cooking is complete, use a quick pressure release; carefully remove the lid. Bon appétit!

Per serving: 395 Calories; 26.2g Fat; 5.6g Carbs; 29.4g Protein; 5.1g Sugars

645. Lobster and Cheese Dip

(Ready in about 20 minutes | Servings 10)

Ingredients

2 tablespoons butter
1 onion, chopped
1 celery, chopped
2 garlic cloves, minced
2 tomatoes, puréed
1 cup chicken broth
1 teaspoon Old Bay seasoning

Salt and ground black pepper, to taste
1/2 teaspoon paprika
30 ounces frozen lobster
2 cups cream cheese
1 cup Cheddar cheese, shredded

Directions

Press the "Sauté" button to heat up the Instant Pot. Now, melt the butter and sauté the onion and celery until softened.

Then, add the garlic and continue to cook an additional minute or until aromatic.

Add the tomatoes, chicken broth, spices, lobster and cream cheese.

Secure the lid. Choose "Manual" mode and Low pressure; cook for 12 minutes. Once cooking is complete, use a quick pressure release; carefully remove the lid.

Using an immersion blender, puree the mixture to your desired consistency. Return the mixture to the Instant Pot.

Press the "Sauté" button and add Cheddar cheese. Let it simmer until everything is melted and incorporated. Bon appétit!

Per serving: 291 Calories; 20.7g Fat; 4.9g Carbs; 21.2g Protein; 3.2g Sugars

646. Party-Style Cheeseburger Dip

(Ready in about 10 minutes | Servings 10)

Ingredients

1 tablespoon olive oil
1 onion, chopped
1/3 pound ground pork
2/3 pound ground beef
2 ripe tomatoes, puréed

10 ounces Ricotta cheese
1/2 cup chicken broth
5 ounces Cheddar cheese, shredded

Directions

Press the "Sauté" button to heat up the Instant Pot. Then, heat the oil and sauté the onion until translucent and fragrant.

Now, add the ground meat, tomatoes, Ricotta cheese, and chicken broth.

Secure the lid. Choose "Manual" mode and High pressure; cook for 6 minutes. Once cooking is complete, use a quick pressure release; carefully remove the lid.

Top with the Cheddar cheese and serve warm.

Per serving: 224 Calories; 13.6g Fat; 4.4g Carbs; 19.9g Protein; 2.2g Sugars

647. Cauliflower Breakfast Cups

(Ready in about 15 minutes | Servings 6)

Ingredients

1/2 pound cauliflower, riced
Sea salt and ground black pepper, to taste
1/2 teaspoon cayenne pepper
1/2 teaspoon dried dill weed
1/2 teaspoon dried basil
1/4 teaspoon dried oregano
2 tablespoons olive oil
2 garlic cloves, minced
1/2 cup scallions, chopped
1 cup Romano cheese, preferably freshly grated
Salt and ground black pepper, to taste
7 eggs, beaten
1/2 cup Cotija cheese, grated

Directions

Start by adding 1 ½ cups of water and a metal rack to the bottom of the Instant Pot. Spritz each muffin cup with a nonstick cooking spray.

Mix the ingredients until everything is well incorporated.

Now, spoon the mixture into lightly greased muffin cups. Lower the cups onto the rack in the Instant Pot.

Secure the lid. Choose "Manual" mode and High pressure; cook for 10 minutes. Once cooking is complete, use a natural pressure release; carefully remove the lid. Bon appétit!

Per serving: 335 Calories; 25.9g Fat; 5.8g Carbs; 19.8g Protein; 2.6g Sugars

648. Mexican-Style Stuffed Peppers

(Ready in about 25 minutes | Servings 4)

Ingredients

1/2 pound ground beef
1/4 pound ground pork
4 eggs, whisked
2 garlic cloves, minced
1/2 cup onion, chopped
Salt and ground black pepper, to taste
1 (1-ounce) package taco seasoning mix
1 cup Cotija cheese, grated
4 bell peppers, remove seeds and cut the tops off
8 ounces canned tomato sauce

Directions

Start by adding 1 cup of water and a metal rack to the bottom of the Instant Pot. Spritz a casserole dish with a nonstick cooking spray.

In a mixing bowl, thoroughly combine the ground meat, eggs, garlic, onion, salt, pepper, taco seasoning mix, and Cotija cheese.

Fill the peppers with the cheese/meat mixture. Place the peppers on the rack in the Instant Pot. Pour the tomato sauce over the peppers.

Secure the lid. Choose "Manual" mode and High pressure; cook for 20 minutes. Once cooking is complete, use a natural pressure release; carefully remove the lid. Bon appétit!

Per serving: 407 Calories; 27g Fat; 6.3g Carbs; 32.4g Protein; 3.7g Sugars

649. Goat Cheese and Cauliflower Pancake

(Ready in about 35 minutes | Servings 4)

Ingredients

3/4 pound cauliflower, riced
4 eggs, beaten
1/2 cup goat cheese, crumbled
1/2 teaspoon onion powder
1 teaspoon garlic powder
Sea salt and white pepper, to taste
2 tablespoons butter, melted

Directions

Simply combine all ingredients in a mixing bowl.

Now, spritz the bottom and sides of your Instant Pot with a nonstick cooking spray. Pour the batter into the Instant Pot.

Secure the lid. Choose "Bean/Chili" mode and Low pressure; cook for 30 minutes. Once cooking is complete, use a natural pressure release; carefully remove the lid.

Serve with some extra butter or cream cheese if desired. Bon appétit!

Per serving: 198 Calories; 15.2g Fat; 4.9g Carbs; 11.2g Protein; 1.9g Sugars

650. Lasagna Cupcakes with Zucchini and Mozzarella

(Ready in about 20 minutes | Servings 6)

Ingredients

1 zucchini, thinly sliced
2 eggs, beaten
4 ounces cream cheese
10 ounces mozzarella cheese, grated
1/2 teaspoon dried dill weed
1 teaspoon cayenne pepper
1/2 cup pasta sauce

Directions

Add 1 ½ cups of water and a metal rack to the bottom of your Instant Pot. Spritz six cupcake molds with a nonstick cooking spray.

Line each cupcake mold with a zucchini slice.

In a mixing bowl, thoroughly combine eggs, cheese, dill, and cayenne pepper. Add 1/3 of this mixture to the cupcake molds; top with pasta sauce.

Repeat the layers of zucchini, cheese mixture, and sauce, creating 3 layers in all, ending with pasta sauce.

Lower the cupcake molds onto the rack.

Secure the lid. Choose "Manual" mode and High pressure; cook for 15 minutes. Once cooking is complete, use a quick pressure release; carefully remove the lid. Bon appétit!

Per serving: 173 Calories; 8.7g Fat; 4.3g Carbs; 19.7g Protein; 2.5g Sugars

651. Dad's Chorizo Dip

(Ready in about 15 minutes | Servings 12)

Ingredients

1 tablespoon olive oil
3/4 pound Chorizo, casings removed and crumbled
1 onion, peeled and chopped
15 ounces Ricotta cheese
1/2 teaspoon ground black pepper
2 tablespoons fresh parsley
2 tablespoons fresh chives, chopped

Directions

Press the "Sauté" button to heat up the Instant Pot. Now, heat the oil and brown the Chorizo sausage for 2 to 3 minutes.

Add the onion, cheese and black pepper to the Instant Pot.

Secure the lid. Choose "Manual" mode and High pressure; cook for 10 minutes. Once cooking is complete, use a quick pressure release; carefully remove the lid.

Garnish with fresh parsley and chives. Bon appétit!

Per serving: 210 Calories; 16.6g Fat; 3.8g Carbs; 11g Protein; 1.5g Sugars

652. Canapés with a Twist

(Ready in about 10 minutes | Servings 8)

Ingredients

1 pound tuna fillets
1/4 cup mayonnaise, preferably homemade
1/2 teaspoon dried dill
1/2 teaspoon sea salt
1/4 teaspoon ground black pepper, or more to taste
2 cucumbers, sliced

Directions

Prepare your Instant Pot by adding 1 ½ cups of water and steamer basket to the inner pot.

Place the tuna fillets in your steamer basket.

Secure the lid. Choose "Manual" mode and High pressure; cook for 4 minutes. Once cooking is complete, use a quick pressure release; carefully remove the lid. Flake the fish with a fork.

Add the mayonnaise, dill, salt, and black pepper. Divide the mixture among cucumber slices and place on a serving platter. Enjoy!

Per serving: 112 Calories; 5.8g Fat; 1.2g Carbs; 12.8g Protein; 0.7g Sugars

653. Egg Salad "Sandwich"

(Ready in about 25 minutes | Servings 4)

Ingredients

6 eggs
1/2 cup tablespoons mayonnaise
1 teaspoon Dijon mustard
1/2 cup cream cheese
1 cup baby spinach

Salt and ground black pepper, to taste
2 red bell peppers, sliced into halves
2 green bell pepper, sliced into halves

Directions

Place 1 cup of water and a steamer basket in your Instant Pot. Next, place the eggs in the steamer basket.

Secure the lid. Choose "Manual" mode and Low pressure; cook for 5 minutes. Once cooking is complete, use a quick pressure release; carefully remove the lid.

Allow the eggs to cool for 15 minutes. Chop the eggs and combine them with mayonnaise, Dijon mustard, cheese, and baby spinach.

Season with salt and pepper. Divide the mixture between four bell pepper "sandwiches". Serve well chilled and enjoy!

Per serving: 406 Calories; 37g Fat; 5.3g Carbs; 11.6g Protein; 4.2g Sugars

654. Mexican Beef Taco Lettuce Wraps

(Ready in about 15 minutes | Servings 4)

Ingredients

1 tablespoon olive oil
1/2 red onion, chopped
1 pound ground chuck
1 bell pepper, seeded and sliced

1 teaspoon taco seasoning
1 cup beef stock
Salt and ground black pepper, to taste

Directions

Press the "Sauté" button to heat up the Instant Pot. Now, heat the oil and sauté the onion until tender and translucent.

Then, add the ground chuck and cook an additional 2 minutes or until no longer pink.

Then, add the bell pepper, taco seasoning, stock, salt, and black pepper.

Secure the lid. Choose "Manual" mode and High pressure; cook for 5 minutes. Once cooking is complete, use a natural pressure release; carefully remove the lid.

To assemble the taco wraps, place a few lettuce leaves on each serving plate. Divide the meat mixture between lettuce leaves. Add toppings of choice and serve. Bon appétit!

Per serving: 219 Calories; 12.5g Fat; 2.7g Carbs; 24.1g Protein; 1.2g Sugars

655. Summer Picnic Fish Sandwiches

(Ready in about 30 minutes | Servings 3)

Ingredients

1/4 cup fresh lemon juice
1 cup water
3 cod fillets
2 tablespoons butter, softened
1/2 teaspoon salt
1/4 teaspoon ground black pepper
1/4 teaspoon paprika
1/4 teaspoon dried dill weed

1 teaspoon Dijon mustard
8 lettuce leaves
1 cucumber, thinly sliced
Oopsies:
2 eggs, separated yolks and whites
1/4 teaspoon sea salt
3 ounces cream cheese
1/4 teaspoon baking powder

Directions

Place 1/4 cup of fresh lemon juice and water in the bottom of your Instant Pot. Add a steamer basket.

Rub the cod fillets with softened butter. Season with salt, black pepper, paprika, and dill. Place the fillets in the steamer basket.

Secure the lid. Choose "Manual" mode and Low pressure; cook for 3 minutes. Once cooking is complete, use a quick pressure release; carefully remove the lid.

To make your oopsies, beat the egg whites together with salt until very firm peaks form.

In another bowl, thoroughly combine the egg yolks with cream cheese. Now, add the baking powder and stir well.

Next, fold the egg white mixture into the egg yolk mixture. Divide the mixture into 6 oopsies and transfer them to a silicon sheet.

Bake in the preheated oven at 290 degrees F for about 23 minutes. Serve the fish fillets between 2 oopsies, garnished with mustard, lettuce and cucumber. Enjoy!

Per serving: 280 Calories; 19.5g Fat; 4.1g Carbs; 22.3g Protein; 2.1g Sugars

656. Mexican-Style Muffins

(Ready in about 10 minutes | Servings 6)

Ingredients

6 eggs
1/4 cup almond milk, unsweetened
1/2 teaspoon salt
A pinch of ground allspice
1/2 teaspoon Mexican oregano

1/4 cup green onions, chopped
1 tomato, chopped
1 ½ cups bell peppers, chopped
1 jalapeño pepper, seeded and minced
1/2 cup Cotija cheese, crumbled

Directions

Prepare your Instant Pot by adding 1 ½ cups of water to the inner pot.

Spritz six ovenproof custard cups with a nonstick cooking spray.

In a mixing dish, thoroughly combine the eggs, milk, salt, allspice, and Mexican oregano; mix to combine well.

Add the green onions, tomato, bell peppers, and jalapeño pepper to the custard cups. Pour the egg mixture over them. Top with cheese.

Lower 3 custard cups onto a metal trivet; then, place the second trivet on top. Lower the remaining 3 cups onto it.

Secure the lid. Choose "Manual" mode and High pressure; cook for 7 minutes. Once cooking is complete, use a quick pressure release; carefully remove the lid. Serve at room temperature.

Per serving: 189 Calories; 13.4g Fat; 4.3g Carbs; 12.5g Protein; 2.8g Sugars

657. Easy Pizza Cups

(Ready in about 20 minutes | Servings 6)

Ingredients

12 turkey bacon slices
1 cup pizza sauce
2 cups mozzarella cheese
1 teaspoon dried oregano

1 teaspoon dried basil
1/2 cup Kalamata olives, pitted and sliced

Directions

Start by adding 1 cups of water and a metal rack to the bottom of the Instant Pot.

Place two slices of bacon crisscrossed in each muffin cup. Divide the remaining ingredients among the cups.

Lower the muffin pan onto the rack.

Secure the lid. Choose "Manual" mode and High pressure; cook for 10 minutes. Once cooking is complete, use a quick pressure release; carefully remove the lid.

Allow these pizza cups to stand for 5 minutes before removing from the muffin pan. Bon appétit!

Per serving: 301 Calories; 22.1g Fat; 6.2g Carbs; 19.5g Protein; 2.5g Sugars

658. Favorite Lettuce Wraps

(Ready in about 15 minutes | Servings 6)

Ingredients

2 chicken breasts
1 cup chicken stock
2 garlic cloves, minced
1/2 teaspoon black pepper
1 cup green onions, chopped
1 bell pepper, seeded and chopped
1 red chili pepper, seeded and chopped
1 cup cream cheese
1/2 cup mayonnaise
1 teaspoon yellow mustard
Sea salt, to taste
1 head of lettuce

Directions

Add the chicken breasts, stock, garlic, and black pepper to your Instant Pot.

Secure the lid. Choose "Poultry" mode and High pressure; cook for 10 minutes. Once cooking is complete, use a quick pressure release; carefully remove the lid.

Then, shred the chicken and divide it between lettuce leaves. Divide the remaining ingredients between the lettuce leaves and serve immediately. Bon appétit!

Per serving: 301 Calories; 22.1g Fat; 6.2g Carbs; 19.5g Protein; 2.5g Sugars

659. Classic Turkey Sandwiches

(Ready in about 25 minutes | Servings 6)

Ingredients

Keto Buns:
2/3 almond flour
1/2 teaspoon baking soda
1 teaspoon baking powder
A pinch of salt
A pinch of grated nutmeg
4 tablespoons butter
2 eggs, whisked
Filling:
1 pound turkey breast, chopped
1 cup turkey stock
2 garlic cloves, smashed
1/2 teaspoon seasoned salt
1/4 teaspoon ground black pepper

Directions

Mix the dry ingredient for the buns. In another bowl, thoroughly combine the wet ingredients for the buns. Add the wet mixture to the dry mixture.

Pour the mixture into a lightly greased muffin pan.

Secure the lid. Choose "Manual" mode and High pressure; cook for 10 minutes. Once cooking is complete, use a quick pressure release; carefully remove the lid.

Wipe down the Instant Pot with a damp cloth. Add the remaining ingredients and stir to combine.

Secure the lid. Choose "Manual" mode and High pressure; cook for 10 minutes. Once cooking is complete, use a quick pressure release; carefully remove the lid.

Assemble your sandwiches and serve warm.

Per serving: 299 Calories; 21.8g Fat; 2.9g Carbs; 22.8g Protein; 0.6g Sugars

660. Tacos with Pulled Pork and Pico de Gallo

(Ready in about 55 minutes | Servings 4)

Ingredients

1 tablespoon lard, at room temperature
1 pound pork shoulder
1 cup broth, preferably homemade
Salt and black pepper, to taste
1/2 teaspoon cayenne pepper
1/2 pound sharp Cheddar cheese, shredded
1 cup Pico de Gallo

Directions

Press the "Sauté" button to heat up the Instant Pot. Melt the lard and sear the pork for 5 minutes, turning occasionally.

Use the broth to deglaze the pan. Season with salt, black pepper, and cayenne pepper.

Secure the lid. Choose the "Manual" setting and cook for 50 minutes at High pressure. Once cooking is complete, use a natural pressure release; carefully remove the lid.

Shred the prepared pork and reserve.

Place the cheese in a large pile in a preheated pan. When the cheese is bubbling, top it with the meat. Add Pico de Gallo.

Afterward, fold over and place on a serving plate. Enjoy!

Per serving: 429 Calories; 26.7g Fat; 4.4g Carbs; 41g Protein; 2.3g Sugars

661. Savory Cheese Biscuits with Bacon

(Ready in about 20 minutes | Servings 6)

Ingredients

1 cup almond flour
1 teaspoon baking powder
1/2 teaspoon salt
1/4 teaspoon dried oregano
1/2 teaspoon dried basil
3 teaspoons butter, melted
3 eggs, whisked
1/2 cup double cream
6 ounces Colby cheese, grated
4 slices bacon, chopped

Directions

Start by adding 1 ½ cups of water and a metal rack to the Instant Pot. Line a cake pan with a piece of parchment paper.

Mix the almond flour, baking powder, salt, oregano and basil until well combined.

Mix in the melted butter, eggs, and double cream; fold in the cheese and bacon; mix until everything is well incorporated.

Now, grab your dough, smoothen a little bit and roll it to 1/2-inch thickness. Then, cut down the cookies with a cookie cutter.

Arrange the cookies on the prepared cake pan and lower it onto the rack in your Instant Pot.

Secure the lid. Choose "Manual" mode and Low pressure; cook for 15 minutes. Once cooking is complete, use a natural pressure release; carefully remove the lid. Bon appétit!

Per serving: 271 Calories; 23.8g Fat; 1.8g Carbs; 12.2g Protein; 1.2g Sugars

662. Chicken Liver Mousse

(Ready in about 10 minutes | Servings 8)

Ingredients

1 pound chicken livers
1 Spanish onion, chopped
1/2 cup chicken stock
1/2 cup white wine
1 tablespoon olive oil
1 cup heavy cream
1/2 teaspoon dried basil
1/2 teaspoon dried oregano
1 sprig rosemary
1/4 teaspoon ground black pepper
A pinch of salt
A pinch of ground cloves

Directions

Simply mix all ingredients in your Instant Pot

Secure the lid. Choose "Manual" mode and High pressure; cook for 3 minutes. Once cooking is complete, use a quick pressure release; carefully remove the lid.

Afterwards, purée the mixture with an immersion blender until smooth and uniform. Serve with veggie sticks. Bon appétit!

Per serving: 143 Calories; 10.1g Fat; 2.2g Carbs; 10.4g Protein; 1.2g Sugars

VEGAN

663. Pumpkin Porridge with Dried Cherries

(Ready in about 25 minutes | Servings 4)

Ingredients

2 ½ pounds pumpkin, cleaned and seeds removed
1/2 cup rolled oats
4 tablespoons honey
1/2 teaspoon ground cinnamon
A pinch of salt
A pinch of grated nutmeg
4 tablespoons dried berries
1 cup water

Directions

Add 1 ½ cups of water and a metal trivet to the Instant Pot. Now, place the pumpkin on the trivet.

Secure the lid. Choose the "Manual" mode and cook for 12 minutes under High pressure. Once cooking is complete, use a natural release; carefully remove the lid.

Then, purée the pumpkin in the food processor.

Wipe down the Instant Pot with a damp cloth. Add the remaining ingredients to the Instant Pot, including pumpkin purée.

Secure the lid. Choose the "Manual" mode and cook for 10 minutes under High pressure. Once cooking is complete, use a natural release; carefully remove the lid.

Per serving: 201 Calories; 1.1g Fat; 51.8g Carbs; 5g Protein; 31.9g Sugars

664. Easy Vegan Risotto

(Ready in about 15 minutes | Servings 2)

Ingredients

1 tablespoon olive oil
2 garlic cloves, minced
1 white onion, finely chopped
1 cup Arborio rice
1 cup water
1 cup vegetable stock
1/2 teaspoon dried basil
1/2 teaspoon dried oregano
Sea salt and ground black pepper, to taste
1 teaspoon smoked paprika

Directions

Press the "Sauté" button to preheat your Instant Pot. Heat the oil and sauté the garlic and onion until tender and fragrant or about 3 minutes.

Add the remaining ingredients; stir to combine well.

Secure the lid. Choose the "Manual" mode and cook for 5 minutes under High pressure. Once cooking is complete, use a quick release; carefully remove the lid.

Ladle into individual bowls and serve warm. Enjoy!

Per serving: 291 Calories; 20g Fat; 35.4g Carbs; 11.3g Protein; 2.8g Sugars

665. Refreshing Bean Salad

(Ready in about 35 minutes + chilling time | Servings 4)

Ingredients

1 cup Great Northern beans
6 cups water
1 cucumber, peeled and sliced
1 red bell pepper, seeded and chopped
1 green bell pepper, seeded and chopped
1 teaspoon ground sumac
3 tablespoons extra-virgin olive oil
1 tablespoon fresh lime juice
1/4 cup fresh parsley leaves, roughly chopped
1/4 teaspoon freshly ground black pepper
1/2 teaspoon red pepper flakes
Salt, to taste

Directions

Place the beans and water in your Instant Pot.

Secure the lid. Choose the "Bean/Chili" mode and cook for 30 minutes under High pressure. Once cooking is complete, use a natural release; carefully remove the lid.

Allow the prepared beans to cool completely. Now, add the remaining ingredients to the Instant Pot.

Toss to combine and serve well chilled. Enjoy!

Per serving: 207 Calories; 5.1g Fat; 31.2g Carbs; 10.6g Protein; 2.3g Sugars

666. Root Vegetable and Noodle Soup

(Ready in about 20 minutes | Servings 6)

Ingredients

2 tablespoons olive oil
2 shallots, peeled and chopped
1 carrot, chopped
1 parsnip, chopped
1 turnip, chopped
3 garlic cloves, smashed
1 teaspoon cumin powder
1/2 teaspoon dried rosemary
1/2 teaspoon dried thyme
6 cups vegetable stock, preferably homemade
9 ounces vegan noodles
1 cup corn kernels
Salt and freshly ground black pepper, to taste

Directions

Press the "Sauté" button to heat up your Instant Pot. Now, heat the oil and sauté the shallots with the carrot, parsnip, and turnip until they have softened.

Stir in the garlic and cook an additional 40 seconds. Add the cumin powder, rosemary, thyme, stock, and noodles.

Now, secure the lid and choose the "Soup" setting.

Cook for 7 minutes at High pressure. Once cooking is complete, use a quick release; remove the lid carefully.

Add the corn kernels, cover with the lid, and cook in the residual heat for 5 to 6 minutes more. Season with salt and pepper. Taste adjust the seasoning and serve warm. Bon appétit!

Per serving: 194 Calories; 5.4g Fat; 29.9g Carbs; 8g Protein; 5.1g Sugars

667. Green Pea Medley

(Ready in about 25 minutes | Servings 6)

Ingredients

2 tablespoons canola oil
1 teaspoon cumin seeds
2 ½ cups green peas, whole
2 ripe Roma tomatoes, seeded and crushed
3 cups roasted vegetable stock
1 shallot, diced
2 cloves garlic, minced
2 carrots, chopped
2 parsnips, chopped
1 red bell pepper, seeded and chopped
2 bay leaves
Sea salt and ground black pepper, to taste
1 teaspoon cayenne pepper
1/2 teaspoon dried dill

Directions

Press the "Sauté" button to preheat the Instant Pot. Once hot, add the oil. Then, sauté the cumin seeds for 30 seconds.

Add the shallot, garlic, carrots, parsnip and pepper; continue to sauté for 3 to 4 minutes more or until vegetables are tender.

Now, stir in the remaining ingredients.

Secure the lid. Choose the "Manual" mode and cook for 18 minutes under High pressure. Once cooking is complete, use a natural release; carefully remove the lid.

Serve with cream cheese if desired. Bon appétit!

Per serving: 173 Calories; 6.6g Fat; 22.7g Carbs; 7.7g Protein; 7.9g Sugars

668. Spicy Veggie and Adzuki Bean Soup

(Ready in about 30 minutes | Servings 4)

Ingredients

2 tablespoons olive oil
2 onions, chopped
2 carrots chopped
2 parsnips, chopped
1 celery with leaves, chopped
2 Yukon gold potatoes, peeled and diced
2 ripe tomatoes, pureed
12 ounces Adzuki brans, soaked overnight
1 teaspoon cayenne pepper
1 teaspoon dried basil
1/2 teaspoon marjoram
1 teaspoon black garlic powder
1 teaspoon dried chive flakes
A few drops Sriracha
Kosher salt and ground black pepper, to taste
4 cups boiling water

Directions

Press the "Sauté" button to heat up the Instant Pot. Now, heat the olive oil and sweat the onions until just tender.

Add the other ingredients; stir to combine well. Secure the lid and choose the "Manual" mode. Cook for 10 minutes at High Pressure.

Once cooking is complete, use a natural release for 15 minutes; remove the lid carefully.

Ladle into individual serving bowls and eat warm. Bon appétit!

Per serving: 474 Calories; 7.6g Fat; 84g Carbs; 20.5g Protein; 7.8g Sugars

669. Italian-Style Asparagus Salad

(Ready in about 10 minutes | Servings 4)

Ingredients

1 pound asparagus, trimmed
2 tomatoes, diced
4 tablespoons olive oil
1 shallot, chopped
1 teaspoon garlic, minced

Sea salt and ground black pepper, to taste
2 tablespoons lemon juice
1 tablespoon Dijon mustard
1/2 cup Romano cheese, grated
1 handful Italian parsley

Directions

Add 1 cup of water and metal trivet to the Instant Pot. Place the asparagus on the trivet.

Secure the lid. Choose the "Manual" mode and cook for 1 minute under High pressure. Once cooking is complete, use a quick release; carefully remove the lid.

Toss the prepared asparagus with the remaining ingredients; toss to combine well. Place in your refrigerator until ready to serve. Enjoy!

Per serving: 230 Calories; 19.1g Fat; 10.1g Carbs; 7.9g Protein; 4.9g Sugars

670. Quinoa Pilaf with Cremini Mushrooms

(Ready in about 15 minutes | Servings 4)

Ingredients

2 cups dry quinoa
3 cups water
2 tablespoons olive oil
1 onion, chopped
1 bell pepper, chopped
2 garlic cloves, chopped
2 cups Cremini mushrooms, thinly sliced

1/2 teaspoon sea salt
1/3 teaspoon ground black pepper, or more to taste
1 teaspoon cayenne pepper
1/2 teaspoon dried dill
1/4 teaspoon ground bay leaf

Directions

Add the quinoa and water to your Instant Pot.

Secure the lid. Choose the "Manual" mode and cook for 1 minute under High pressure. Once cooking is complete, use a natural release; carefully remove the lid.

Drain the quinoa and set it aside.

Press the "Sauté" button to preheat your Instant Pot. Once hot, heat the oil. Then, sauté the onion until tender and translucent.

Add the bell pepper, garlic, and mushrooms and continue to sauté for 1 to 2 minutes more or until they are fragrant. Stir the remaining ingredients into your Instant Pot.

Add the reserved quinoa and stir to combine well. Serve warm. Bon appétit!

Per serving: 401 Calories; 12.1g Fat; 60.2g Carbs; 14.1g Protein; 2.7g Sugars

671. Traditional Russian Borscht

(Ready in about 15 minutes | Servings 4)

Ingredients

1 ½ tablespoons olive oil
1/2 cup onions, chopped
2 garlic cloves, pressed
Kosher salt and ground black pepper, to taste
1/2 pound potatoes, peeled and diced
2 carrots, chopped

1/2 pound beets, peeled and coarsely shredded
2 tablespoons red-wine vinegar
1 tomato, chopped
4 cups vegetable stock
1/2 teaspoon caraway seeds
1/4 cup fresh dill, roughly chopped

Directions

Press the "Sauté" button to preheat your Instant Pot. Heat the oil and cook the onions and garlic until tender and fragrant.

Add the remaining ingredients, except for the fresh dill.

Secure the lid. Choose the "Manual" mode and cook for 10 minutes under High pressure. Once cooking is complete, use a natural release; carefully remove the lid.

Serve the soup with chopped fresh dill. Enjoy!

Per serving: 183 Calories; 7.3g Fat; 22.5g Carbs; 8.4g Protein; 7.7g Sugars

672. Winter Curry Cabbage

(Ready in about 20 minutes | Servings 4)

Ingredients

2 tablespoons olive oil
1 medium-sized leek, chopped
2 cloves garlic, smashed
1 ½ pounds white cabbage, shredded
1 cup vegetable broth
1 cup tomatoes, puréed
1 parsnip, chopped
2 carrots, chopped
2 stalks celery, chopped

1 turnip, chopped
1/2 tablespoon fresh lime juice
1 teaspoon dried basil
1/2 teaspoon dried dill
1 teaspoon ground coriander
1 teaspoon ground turmeric
1 bay leaf
Kosher salt and ground black pepper, to taste
1 (14-ounce) can coconut milk

Directions

Press the "Sauté" button to preheat your Instant Pot. Now, heat the oil and cook the leeks and garlic until tender and fragrant.

After that, add the remaining ingredients; stir to combine well.

Secure the lid. Choose the "Manual" mode and cook for 12 minutes under High pressure. Once cooking is complete, use a natural release; carefully remove the lid.

Ladle into soup bowls and serve immediately.

Per serving: 223 Calories; 8.2g Fat; 33.8g Carbs; 7.6g Protein; 15.1g Sugars

673. The Easiest Hummus Ever

(Ready in about 35 minutes | Servings 8)

Ingredients

10 cups water
3/4 pound dried chickpeas, soaked
2 tablespoons tahini
1/2 lemon, juiced
1 teaspoon granulated garlic

Salt and black pepper, to taste
1/3 teaspoon ground cumin
1/2 teaspoon cayenne pepper
1/2 teaspoon dried basil
3 tablespoon olive oil

Directions

Add water and chickpeas to the Instant Pot. Secure the lid.

Choose the "Manual" mode and cook for 25 minutes under High pressure. Once cooking is complete, use a natural release; carefully remove the lid.

Now, drain your chickpeas, reserving the liquid. Transfer the chickpeas to a food processor. Add the tahini, lemon juice, and seasonings.

Puree until it is creamy; gradually pour in the reserved liquid and olive oil until the mixture is smooth and uniform. Serve with a few sprinkles of cayenne pepper. Bon appétit!

Per serving: 186 Calories; 7.7g Fat; 22.8g Carbs; 7.6g Protein; 4g Sugars

674. Green Beans with Shiitake Mushrooms

(Ready in about 25 minutes | Servings 4)

Ingredients

2 cups water
6 dried shiitake mushrooms
2 tablespoons sesame oil
2 cloves garlic, minced
1/2 cup scallions, chopped
1 ½ pounds green beans, fresh or frozen (and thawed)

1/4 teaspoon ground black pepper
1/2 teaspoon red pepper flakes, crushed
1 bay leaf
Sea salt, to taste

Directions

Press the "Sauté" button and bring the water to a rapid boil; remove from the heat; add the dried shiitake mushrooms.

Allow the mushrooms to sit for 15 minutes to rehydrate. Then cut the mushrooms into slices; reserve the mushroom stock.

Wipe down the Instant Pot with a kitchen cloth. Press the "Sauté" button to preheat your Instant Pot. Once hot, heat the sesame oil.

Then, sauté the garlic and scallions until tender and aromatic. Add the green beans, black pepper, red pepper, bay leaf, salt, reserved mushrooms and stock; stir to combine well.

Secure the lid. Choose the "Manual" mode and cook for 4 minutes under High pressure. Once cooking is complete, use a quick release; carefully remove the lid. Serve warm.

Per serving: 119 Calories; 7.6g Fat; 12.6g Carbs; 2.6g Protein; 2.6g Sugars

675. Collard Greens with Vegan Sauce

(Ready in about 15 minutes | Servings 4)

Ingredients

1 cup silken tofu, cut into cubes
Salt and black pepper, to taste
1/2 teaspoon mustard powder
1/2 teaspoon cumin powder
1/2 teaspoon red pepper flakes, crushed
1/4 teaspoon curry powder

1 tablespoon balsamic vinegar
2 tablespoons toasted sesame oil
1 teaspoon garlic, minced
1 cup button mushrooms, sliced
1 pound collard greens, torn into pieces

Directions

In your food processor, blend the tofu, salt, black pepper, mustard powder, cumin powder, red pepper, curry powder, and balsamic vinegar.

Pour the sauce into a pan and cook over low heat for 2 to 3 minutes; reserve.

Press the "Sauté" button to preheat your Instant Pot. Now, heat the sesame oil and cook the garlic and mushrooms until tender and fragrant.

Add the collard greens to the Instant Pot. Secure the lid. Choose the "Manual" mode and cook for 4 minutes under High pressure. Once cooking is complete, use a quick release; carefully remove the lid.

Serve with a dollop of the reserved vegan sauce. Enjoy!

Per serving: 199 Calories; 13.1g Fat; 11.1g Carbs; 13.7g Protein; 1.9g Sugars

676. Butternut Squash and Barley Bowl

(Ready in about 45 minutes | Servings 4)

Ingredients

2 tablespoons olive oil divided
2 cloves garlic, minced
1/2 cup scallions, chopped
2 cups butternut squash, peeled and cubed

1/2 teaspoon turmeric powder
2 cups barley, whole
4 ½ cups water
Sea salt and ground black pepper, to taste

Directions

Press the "Sauté" button to preheat your Instant Pot. Once hot, heat the oil. Now, cook the garlic and scallions until tender.

Add the remaining ingredients and stir to combine.

Secure the lid. Choose the "Multigrain" mode and cook for 40 minutes under High pressure. Once cooking is complete, use a natural release; carefully remove the lid.

Ladle into individual bowls and serve warm.

Per serving: 360 Calories; 6.4g Fat; 70g Carbs; 8.7g Protein; 2.2g Sugars

677. Colorful Veggie and Coconut Soup

(Ready in about 25 minutes | Servings 5)

Ingredients

1 tablespoon olive oil
1/2 cup white onions, chopped
1 teaspoon garlic, minced
2 carrots, chopped
1 parsnip, chopped
1 celery, chopped
1 head cauliflower, cut into small florets

1 zucchini, diced
5 cups vegetable stock
Sea salt and ground black pepper, to taste
1/2 cup coconut cream
2 tablespoons fresh cilantro, chopped

Directions

Press the "Sauté" button to preheat your Instant Pot. Now, heat the oil until sizzling.

Sauté the onion and garlic until tender. Add the carrots, parsnip, celery, cauliflower, zucchini, stock, salt, and black pepper, and stir to combine.

Secure the lid. Choose the "Soup" mode and cook for 20 minutes under High pressure. Once cooking is complete, use a quick release; carefully remove the lid.

Add the coconut cream and seal the lid; let it sit until heated through. Ladle into soup bowls and serve garnished with fresh cilantro. Bon appétit!

Per serving: 176 Calories; 13.1g Fat; 9.3g Carbs; 7.9g Protein; 3.4g Sugars

678. Broccoli and Carrots with Peanut Sauce

(Ready in about 10 minutes | Servings 4)

Ingredients

1 ¼ cups water
1 pound broccoli florets
1 carrot, diced
1/2 teaspoon sea salt
1/2 teaspoon cayenne pepper
1/4 teaspoon ground white pepper

For the Sauce:
4 tablespoons silky peanut butter
3 tablespoons water
1 tablespoon champagne vinegar
1 tablespoons poppy seeds

Directions

Add 1 ¼ cups of water to the base of your Instant Pot. Arrange the broccoli and carrots in a steaming basket and transfer them to the Instant Pot.

Secure the lid, choose the "Manual" mode, and cook for 3 minutes at High pressure. Once cooking is complete, use a quick release; carefully remove the lid.

Season your vegetables with salt, cayenne pepper, and ground white pepper.

Meanwhile, in a mixing bowl, thoroughly combine the peanut butter, water, vinegar, and poppy seeds.

Serve the steamed broccoli and carrots with the peanut sauce on the side. Bon appétit!

Per serving: 90 Calories; 4.3g Fat; 9.3g Carbs; 5.2g Protein; 4.3g Sugars

679. Delicious Old-Fashioned Chili

(Ready in about 15 minutes | Servings 6)

Ingredients

2 tablespoons olive oil
1 red onion, chopped
3 cloves garlic minced or pressed
1 red bell pepper, diced
1 green bell pepper, diced
1 red chili pepper, minced
Sea salt and ground black pepper, to taste
1 teaspoon cayenne pepper

1/2 teaspoon ground cumin
2 cups vegetable stock
2 ripe tomatoes, chopped
2 (15-ounce) cans beans, drained and rinsed
1 handful fresh cilantro leaves, chopped
1/2 cup tortilla chips

Directions

Press the "Sauté" button to preheat your Instant Pot. Now, heat the oil until sizzling.

Sauté the onion tender and translucent. Add the garlic, peppers, salt, and pepper; continue to sauté until they are tender.

Now, stir in the cayenne pepper, cumin, stock, tomatoes, and beans.

Secure the lid. Choose the "Manual" mode and cook for 10 minutes under High pressure. Once cooking is complete, use a quick release; carefully remove the lid.

Divide the chili between six serving bowls; top with fresh cilantro and tortilla chips. Enjoy!

Per serving: 204 Calories; 6.5g Fat; 27.9g Carbs; 10.4g Protein; 6.9g Sugars

680. Saucy Brussels Sprouts with Cashews

(Ready in about 15 minutes | Servings 4)

Ingredients

1 pound Brussels sprouts, cut into halves
1/2 cup water
1/2 cup tomato purée
Salt and ground black pepper, to taste

1/2 teaspoon cayenne pepper or more to taste
2 tablespoons soy sauce
1 fresh lime juice
1/4 cup cashew nuts, chopped
1/4 cup fresh cilantro leaves, chopped

Directions

Add the Brussels sprouts, water, tomato purée, salt, black pepper, and cayenne pepper to the Instant Pot.

Secure the lid. Choose the "Manual" mode and cook for 4 minutes under High pressure. Once cooking is complete, use a quick release; carefully remove the lid.

Drizzle soy sauce and lime juice over the top. Add the cashew nuts and fresh cilantro leaves. Serve immediately.

Per serving: 132 Calories; 5.7g Fat; 17.8g Carbs; 6.3g Protein; 5.9g Sugars

681. Aromatic Risotto with Tomatoes

(Ready in about 25 minutes | Servings 4)

Ingredients

1 tablespoon sesame oil
1 yellow onion, peeled and chopped
2 cloves garlic, minced
1 cup tomatoes, pureed
1 carrot, chopped
1 tablespoon tomato powder
1 teaspoon curry powder

1 teaspoon citrus & ginger spice blend
1/2 teaspoon paprika
Sea salt and freshly ground black pepper, to taste
1 cup white rice, soaked for 30 minutes
2 ½ cups water

Directions

Press the "Sauté" button to heat up the Instant Pot. Heat the sesame oil until sizzling.

Sweat the onion for 2 to 3 minutes. Add the garlic and cook an additional 30 to 40 seconds.

Add the tomatoes and carrot; cook for a further 10 minutes, stirring periodically. Add the seasonings, rice, and water to the Instant Pot. Secure the lid.

Select the "Manual" mode and cook for 8 minutes at High pressure. Once cooking is complete, use a natural release; remove the lid carefully.

Taste, adjust the seasonings and serve warm. Bon appétit!

Per serving: 251 Calories; 6.2g Fat; 44.1g Carbs; 4.2g Protein; 3g Sugars

682. Vegan Lentil and Tomato Bowl

(Ready in about 20 minutes | Servings 4)

Ingredients

1 tablespoon olive oil
2 cups red lentils
1/2 cup scallions, finely chopped
1 teaspoon garlic, minced
1 teaspoon turmeric powder
Sea salt and ground black pepper, to taste

1 teaspoon sweet paprika
1 (15-ounce) can tomatoes, crushed
1 bay leaf
1 handful fresh cilantro leaves, chopped

Directions

Add the olive oil, lentils, scallions, garlic, turmeric, salt, black pepper, paprika, tomatoes, and bay leaf to your Instant Pot.

Secure the lid. Choose the "Manual" mode and cook for 12 minutes under High pressure. Once cooking is complete, use a natural release; carefully remove the lid.

Discard the bay leaf and spoon the lentil into serving bowls. Serve topped with fresh cilantro. Enjoy!

Per serving: 405 Calories; 5.9g Fat; 67.5g Carbs; 24.5g Protein; 3.8g Sugars

683. Minty Split Pea Dip

(Ready in about 15 minutes | Servings 8)

Ingredients

1 pound dried split peas, rinsed
6 cups vegetable stock
1 tablespoon fresh lemon juice
4 tablespoons extra-virgin olive oil
1 teaspoon fresh mint, chopped

1 tablespoon fresh parsley, chopped
1/2 teaspoon paprika
Sea salt and freshly ground black pepper, to taste

Directions

Add the split peas and vegetable stock to your Instant Pot.

Secure the lid. Choose the "Manual" mode and cook for 5 minutes under High pressure. Once cooking is complete, use a natural release; carefully remove the lid.

Transfer the split peas to your food processor; add the remaining ingredients. Process until everything is creamy and well combined. Serve well chilled. Bon appétit!

Per serving: 79 Calories; 4.5g Fat; 4.4g Carbs; 5.6g Protein; 2.3g Sugars

684. Classic Tomato Soup with Pepitas

(Ready in about 15 minutes | Servings 4)

Ingredients

2 tablespoons olive oil
1/2 cup green onions, chopped
2 cloves garlic, crushed
2 carrots, roughly chopped
1 red chili pepper, seeded and chopped
1 pound ripe tomatoes, puréed
1 zucchini, chopped
1 teaspoon dried rosemary

1/2 teaspoon dried basil
1/2 teaspoon dried marjoram
1 teaspoon sweet paprika
Sea salt and ground black pepper, to taste
1 cup vegetable stock
2 tablespoons fresh chives, chopped
2 tablespoons pepitas

Directions

Press the "Sauté" button to preheat your Instant Pot. Then, heat the oil until sizzling.

Now, cook the green onions and garlic until tender and fragrant. Add the carrots, chili pepper, tomatoes, zucchini, seasonings, and stock.

Secure the lid. Choose the "Manual" mode and cook for 6 minutes under High pressure. Once cooking is complete, use a quick release; carefully remove the lid.

Then, purée the mixture with an immersion blender until the desired thickness is reached.

Ladle into soup bowls; serve garnished with fresh chives and pepitas. Enjoy!

Per serving: 125 Calories; 9.4g Fat; 8.1g Carbs; 4.2g Protein; 1.8g Sugars

685. Mushroom Soup with Rice Noodles

(Ready in about 25 minutes | Servings 6)

Ingredients

6 cups vegan cream of mushroom soup
1/2 teaspoon dried basil
1 teaspoon dried oregano
1 teaspoon dried parsley flakes
1 teaspoon fennel seeds
2 carrots, thinly sliced
1 celery stalk, chopped
1 parsnip, chopped
1 red onion, chopped

2 cloves garlic, minced
1 cup brown mushrooms, chopped
2 cups rice noodles
1/2 tablespoon miso paste
1/2 teaspoon freshly ground black pepper
1/4 teaspoon red pepper flakes, crushed
Salt, to taste

Directions

Place the cream of mushroom soup, basil, oregano, parsley, fennel seeds, carrots, celery, parsnip, onion, garlic, mushrooms in your Instant Pot.

Secure the lid. Choose the "Soup" mode and cook for 8 minutes under High pressure. Once cooking is complete, use a natural release; carefully remove the lid.

Add the rice noodles, miso paste, black pepper, red pepper, and salt to the Instant Pot.

Press the "Sauté" button and cook an additional 7 to 10 minutes. Ladle into individual bowls and serve right away!

Per serving: 292 Calories; 13.7g Fat; 37.7g Carbs; 5.5g Protein; 3.1g Sugars

686. Purple Cabbage with Basmati Rice

(Ready in about 25 minutes | Servings 4)

Ingredients

2 tablespoons olive oil
2 shallots, diced
1 garlic clove, minced
1 head purple cabbage, cut into wedges
2 ripe tomatoes, pureed
2 tablespoons tomato ketchup
1 cup basmati rice
1 ½ cups water
1 bay leaf
1/4 teaspoon marjoram
1/2 teaspoon cayenne pepper
Salt and freshly ground black pepper, to taste
1/4 cup fresh chives, chopped

Directions

Press the "Sauté" button to preheat the Instant Pot. Heat the olive oil and sauté the shallots until they are just tender.

Now, stir in the minced garlic and cook until it is lightly browned and aromatic.

Stir in the cabbage, tomatoes, ketchup, rice, water, bay leaf, marjoram, cayenne pepper, salt, and black pepper.

Secure the lid. Select the "Manual" mode and cook for 6 minutes under High pressure. Once cooking is complete, use a natural release for 15 minutes; remove the lid carefully. Serve warm garnished with fresh chopped chives. Bon appétit!

Per serving: 242 Calories; 13.3g Fat; 35.2g Carbs; 7.8g Protein; 10g Sugars

687. Summer Zucchini Bowl

(Ready in about 15 minutes | Servings 4)

Ingredients

2 tablespoons garlic-infused olive oil
1 garlic clove, minced
1/2 cup scallions, chopped
1 pound zucchini, sliced
1/2 cup tomato paste
1/2 cup vegetable broth
Salt, to taste
1/2 teaspoon ground black pepper
1/2 teaspoon dried oregano
1/2 teaspoon dried basil
1 teaspoon paprika
1/2 cup Kalamata olives, pitted and sliced

Directions

Press the "Sauté" button to preheat the Instant Pot. Now, heat the oil; sauté the garlic and scallions for 2 minutes or until they are tender and fragrant.

Add the zucchini, tomato paste, broth, salt, black pepper, oregano, basil, and paprika.

Secure the lid. Choose the "Manual" mode and Low pressure; cook for 4 minutes. Once cooking is complete, use a quick pressure release; carefully remove the lid.

Serve garnished with Kalamata olives. Bon appétit!

Per serving: 143 Calories; 9.4g Fat; 12.7g Carbs; 5.6g Protein; 4.4g Sugars

688. Jasmine Rice with Curried Sauce

(Ready in about 20 minutes | Servings 3)

Ingredients

1/4 cup water
2 cups vegetable broth
1 tablespoon olive oil
1 cup jasmine rice
1 tablespoon vegan margarine
1 yellow onion, chopped
1 teaspoon curry powder
Fresh juice of 1/2 lemon
Zest of 1/2 lemon
Sea salt and ground black pepper, to taste

Directions

Place the water, 1 cup of vegetable broth, olive oil, and rice in your Instant Pot.

Secure the lid. Choose the "Manual" mode and High pressure; cook for 2 minutes. Once cooking is complete, use a natural pressure release for 10 minutes; carefully remove the lid.

Fluff the rice with a fork and reserve.

Wipe down the Instant Pot with a kitchen cloth. Press the "Sauté" button and melt the margarine. Then, sauté the onion until tender and translucent.

Add the remaining cup of vegetable broth, curry powder, lemon, salt, and black pepper. Press the "Sauté" button and stir until everything is incorporated.

Spoon the sauce over the hot rice. Bon appétit!

Per serving: 353 Calories; 9.6g Fat; 56.8g Carbs; 8g Protein; 1.7g Sugars

689. Penne with Leek-Tomato Sauce

(Ready in about 15 minutes | Servings 4)

Ingredients

1 tablespoon canola oil
1 small-sized leek, chopped
1 teaspoon garlic, smashed
1 ¼ pounds penne pasta
4 ripe tomatoes, pureed
2 cups roasted vegetable stock, preferably homemade
1 teaspoon dried rosemary
1/2 teaspoon dried oregano
1/2 teaspoon daikon radish seeds
A pinch of sugar
Sea salt and freshly ground black pepper, to your liking
1 teaspoon cayenne pepper
1/3 cup dry sherry

Directions

Press the "Sauté" button to heat up your Instant Pot. When hot, add the canola oil and sauté the leeks and garlic until aromatic.

Stir in the penne, tomatoes, and roasted vegetable stock. Now, add the other ingredients and secure the lid. Choose the "Manual" function and cook for 6 minutes under High pressure.

Once cooking is complete, use a natural release; remove the lid carefully.

Divide among four serving bowls and serve garnished with vegan parmesan. Bon appétit!

Per serving: 281 Calories; 5g Fat; 54g Carbs; 7.6g Protein; 8.8g Sugars

690. Red Kidney Bean Delight

(Ready in about 30 minutes | Servings 4)

Ingredients

1 pound dried red kidney beans
1/2 cup shallots, chopped
2 cloves garlic, chopped
2 roasted peppers, cut into strips
1 teaspoon ground cumin
1/2 teaspoon mustard powder
1 teaspoon celery seeds
Sea salt and ground black pepper, to taste
2 cups roasted vegetable broth

Directions

Add all of the above ingredients to your Instant Pot.

Secure the lid. Choose the "Bean/Chili" mode and cook for 25 minutes under High pressure. Once cooking is complete, use a natural release; carefully remove the lid.

You can thicken the cooking liquid on "Sauté" function if desired. Serve warm.

Per serving: 418 Calories; 2.1g Fat; 72.9g Carbs; 30.1g Protein; 4.5g Sugars

691. Chinese Soup with Zha Cai

(Ready in about 35 minutes | Servings 4)

Ingredients

1 tablespoon toasted sesame oil
1 yellow onion, peeled and chopped
2 garlic cloves, minced
1 teaspoon fresh ginger, peeled and grated
1 jalapeño pepper, minced
1 celery stalk, chopped
2 carrots, chopped
1 teaspoon Five-spice powder
Sea salt, to taste
1/2 teaspoon ground black pepper, to taste
1/2 teaspoon red pepper flakes
1 teaspoon dried parsley flakes
4 cups vegetable broth
2 ripe tomatoes, finely chopped
1 tablespoon soy sauce
1 cup sweet corn kernels, frozen and thawed
1 cup zha cai

Directions

Press the "Sauté" button to preheat your Instant Pot. Once hot, add the oil. Sauté the onion, garlic, ginger and jalapeño pepper for 2 to 3 minutes, stirring occasionally.

Add the remaining ingredients, except for corn and zha cai; stir to combine well.

Secure the lid. Choose the "Bean/Chili" mode and cook for 25 minutes under High pressure. Once cooking is complete, use a natural release; carefully remove the lid.

After that, add the corn and seal the lid again. Let it sit until heated through. Serve in individual bowls with zha cai on the side. Enjoy!

Per serving: 177 Calories; 8.8g Fat; 18.5g Carbs; 7.8g Protein; 7.1g Sugars

692. Quinoa and Chickpea Bowl

(Ready in about 10 minutes | Servings 4)

Ingredients

2 teaspoons sesame oil
1 shallot, thinly sliced
2 bell peppers, thinly sliced
1 jalapeño pepper, seeded and sliced
1 teaspoon garlic, minced
Sea salt and ground black pepper, to taste
1/2 teaspoon mustard powder

1 teaspoon fennel seeds
1/2 teaspoon ground cumin
1 ½ cups quinoa, rinsed
1 ½ cups water
1 cup tomato purée
1 (15-ounce) can chickpeas, drained and rinsed
1 lime, cut into wedges

Directions

Press the "Sauté" button to preheat your Instant Pot. Heat the sesame oil. Then, sweat the shallot and peppers until they are tender and fragrant.

Now, add the garlic, salt, black pepper, mustard powder, fennel seeds, cumin, quinoa, water, tomato purée, and chickpeas.

Secure the lid. Choose the "Manual" mode and High pressure; cook for 1 minute. Once cooking is complete, use a natural pressure release; carefully remove the lid.

Serve with fresh lime wedges. Bon appétit!

Per serving: 392 Calories; 8.1g Fat; 66.9g Carbs; 15.5g Protein; 7.9g Sugars

693. Spaghetti Squash with Pesto Sauce

(Ready in about 15 minutes | Servings 4)

Ingredients

1 cup water
1 pound spaghetti squash, cut into halves
For the Pesto:
1/2 cup raw walnut halves
1 ½ tablespoons nutritional yeast
Salt, to taste

1/4 teaspoon ground black
1/4 teaspoon cayenne pepper
1 ½ cups fresh basil
1 tablespoon fresh lemon juice
2 cloves garlic, minced
3 tablespoons olive oil

Directions

Grab your spaghetti squash and scoop out the seeds and most of the stringy parts with an ice cream.

Pour water into the base of your Instant Pot. Add the squash to your Instant Pot and secure the lid.

Select the "Manual" mode and cook for 7 minutes under High pressure. Once cooking is complete, use a quick release; remove the lid carefully.

Next, place the walnuts, nutritional yeast, salt, black pepper, and cayenne pepper in your food processor; pulse until it is the consistency of fine meal.

Add the remaining ingredients for the pesto and pulse again until evenly combined. Serve the spaghetti squash with pesto sauce. Bon appétit!

Per serving: 218 Calories; 16.9g Fat; 15.6g Carbs; 4.4g Protein; 0.5g Sugars

694. Beluga Lentil Stew with Kale

(Ready in about 15 minutes | Servings 4)

Ingredients

2 teaspoons toasted sesame oil
1 yellow onion, chopped
2 cloves garlic, pressed
1 teaspoon fresh ginger, grated
1 bell pepper, chopped
1 serrano pepper, chopped
1/2 teaspoon ground allspice
1/2 teaspoon ground cumin
1/2 teaspoon dried basil

1 teaspoon dried parsley flakes
Sea salt and black pepper, to taste
1 ½ cups tomato purée
2 cups vegetable stock
1 cup beluga lentils
2 cups kale leaves, torn into pieces
1 teaspoon fresh lemon juice
1/2 cup cashew cream

Directions

Press the "Sauté" button to preheat your Instant Pot. Now, heat the oil; sauté the onion until tender and translucent.

Then, add the garlic, ginger, and peppers; continue to sauté until they have softened.

Add the seasonings, tomato purée, stock and lentils.

Secure the lid. Choose the "Manual" mode and High pressure; cook for 8 minutes. Once cooking is complete, use a natural pressure release; carefully remove the lid.

Add the kale and lemon juice; seal the lid again and let it sit until thoroughly warmed. Serve dolloped with cashew cream. Enjoy!

Per serving: 311 Calories; 22.9g Fat; 21.8g Carbs; 9.9g Protein; 6.7g Sugars

695. Jamaican-Style Chili

(Ready in about 25 minutes | Servings 4)

Ingredients

2 tablespoons sesame oil
1/2 cup red onion, sliced
2 cloves garlic crushed
1 roasted bell pepper, cut into strips
1 teaspoon habanero pepper, minced
1 pound sweet potatoes, peeled and cut into bite-sized chunks
1 cup vegetable broth
1 cup water
Sea salt, to taste

1 teaspoon black peppercorns, crushed
1/4 teaspoon allspice
1/8 teaspoon ground clove
1 teaspoon sweet paprika
1/2 teaspoon smoked paprika
1 pound red kidney beans, soaked overnight and well-rinsed
1/2 (15-ounce) can tomatoes, diced
1/4 cup rum
1 (7-ounce) can salsa verde

Directions

Press the "Sauté" button to preheat your Instant Pot. Now, heat the oil; sauté the onion until tender and translucent or about 2 minutes.

Then, stir in the garlic and peppers; continue to sauté for a further 2 minutes. Now, add the sweet potatoes, broth, water, spices, beans, and tomatoes.

Secure the lid. Choose the "Bean/Chili" mode and High pressure; cook for 15 minutes. Once cooking is complete, use a natural pressure release; carefully remove the lid.

Add the rum and salsa verde. Press the "Sauté" button and continue to cook until everything is thoroughly heated. Enjoy!

Per serving: 300 Calories; 11.4g Fat; 36.1g Carbs; 8.3g Protein; 7.9g Sugars

696. Thai Rice with Green Peas

(Ready in about 20 minutes | Servings 3)

Ingredients

1 cup basmati rice, rinsed
1 ¼ cups water
Kosher salt and white pepper, to taste
2 tablespoons fresh coriander
4 ounces fresh green peas

2 fresh green chilies, chopped
1 garlic clove, pressed
1/2 cup candy onions, chopped
4 whole cloves
1/2 cup creamed coconut
1 tablespoon fresh lime juice

Directions

Combine all of the above ingredients, except for the lime juice, in your Instant Pot.

Secure the lid. Choose the "Manual" mode and High pressure; cook for 2 minutes. Once cooking is complete, use a natural pressure release for 10 minutes; carefully remove the lid.

Serve in individual bowls, drizzled with fresh lime juice. Bon appétit!

Per serving: 306 Calories; 16.7g Fat; 42.7g Carbs; 9.1g Protein; 18.2g Sugars

697. Mom's Peppery Beans

(Ready in about 50 minutes | Servings 6)

Ingredients

2 tablespoons olive oil
1 yellow onion, chopped
2 garlic cloves, roughly chopped
2 medium-sized bell peppers, deveined and thinly sliced
1 teaspoon habanero pepper, minced
1 teaspoon dried rosemary
1/2 teaspoon ground cumin
Salt and ground black pepper, to taste
1 ½ pounds dried Cannellini beans
2 bay leaves
6 cups water

Directions

Press the "Sauté" button. Heat the olive oil and cook the onion until tender and fragrant.

Now, add the garlic and peppers; cook until they have softened, about 4 minutes. Add the remaining ingredients.

Secure the lid. Select the "Bean/Chili" mode and cook for 25 minutes under High pressure.

Once cooking is complete, use a natural release for 20 minutes; remove the lid carefully. Serve warm and enjoy!

Per serving: 159 Calories; 10.1g Fat; 13.5g Carbs; 8.4g Protein; 3.2g Sugars

698. Italian Lasagna Bowl

(Ready in about 25 minutes | Servings 4)

Ingredients

2 teaspoons canola oil
1 red onion, chopped
2 cloves garlic, minced
2 carrots chopped
2 bell peppers, chopped
1/2 cup French green lentils, well-rinsed
2 ripe tomatoes, puréed
1 tablespoon Italian seasoning
Sea salt and ground black pepper, to taste
1 teaspoon red pepper flakes, crushed
1 cup water
1 cup vegetable stock
6 ounces lasagna sheets, broken into small pieces
1/2 cup vegan mozzarella, to serve

Directions

Press the "Sauté" button to preheat your Instant Pot. Now, heat the oil and cook the onion until tender and translucent.

Now, add the garlic and continue to sauté it for 30 seconds more.

Add the carrots, peppers, lentils, tomatoes, seasonings, water vegetable stock, and lasagna sheets.

Secure the lid. Choose the "Manual" mode and High pressure; cook for 10 minutes. Once cooking is complete, use a natural pressure release for 10 minutes; carefully remove the lid.

Serve with vegan mozzarella. Bon appétit!

Per serving: 269 Calories; 3.9g Fat; 49.2g Carbs; 11.8g Protein; 6.4g Sugars

699. Curried Cumin Baby Potatoes

(Ready in about 15 minutes | Servings 6)

Ingredients

1 tablespoon canola oil
1/2 cup scallions, chopped
2 cloves garlic, minced
1 teaspoon red chili pepper, minced
2 pounds baby potatoes, diced
1 tablespoon curry paste
1 cup water
1 cup vegetable broth
1 cup full-fat coconut milk
Salt, to taste
1/2 teaspoon ground black pepper
1 teaspoon cayenne pepper
1 teaspoon cumin

Directions

Press the "Sauté" button to preheat your Instant Pot. Now, heat the canola oil until sizzling; sauté the scallions until just tender.

Add the garlic and chili pepper; allow it to cook an additional 30 seconds, stirring continuously. Add the remaining ingredients.

Secure the lid. Choose the "Manual" mode and High pressure; cook for 5 minutes. Once cooking is complete, use a quick pressure release; carefully remove the lid. Serve hot.

Per serving: 246 Calories; 12.4g Fat; 31.1g Carbs; 5.3g Protein; 3.1g Sugars

700. Russet Potato and Chanterelle Stew

(Ready in about 25 minutes | Servings 4)

Ingredients

1 pound russet potatoes, peeled and diced
3/4 pound chanterelle mushrooms, sliced
1 tablespoon olive oil
1 carrot, chopped
1 parsnip, chopped
1 yellow onion, chopped
2 cloves garlic, peeled and minced
2 sprigs fresh rosemary
2 sprigs fresh thyme
1 teaspoon red chili flakes
2 tablespoons fresh parsley, chopped
2 cups vegetable stock
1/3 cup port wine
1 ripe Roma tomato, chopped
Sea salt and ground black pepper, to taste
1 tablespoon paprika
1 tablespoon flax seeds meal

Directions

Throw all ingredients, except for the flax seeds meal, in your Instant Pot.

Secure the lid. Choose the "Soup" mode and High pressure; cook for 20 minutes. Once cooking is complete, use a natural pressure release; carefully remove the lid.

Stir the flax seeds into your Instant Pot. Press the "Sauté" button and let it simmer until cooking the liquid has thickened and reduced. Serve hot. Bon appétit!

Per serving: 456 Calories; 5.7g Fat; 99g Carbs; 15.4g Protein; 7.9g Sugars

701. Garden Vegetable and Wild Rice Soup

(Ready in about 35 minutes | Servings 4)

Ingredients

2 tablespoons olive oil
1/2 cup leeks, roughly chopped
2 garlic cloves, minced
1 bell pepper, chopped
1 serrano pepper, chopped
2 carrots, chopped
1 fennel, diced
3/4 cup wild rice
1 cup tomato purée
2 cups water
2 cups vegetable broth
2 tablespoons fresh coriander, chopped
1 teaspoon fresh or dried rosemary
Salt, to taste
1/2 teaspoon ground black pepper

Directions

Press the "Sauté" button to preheat your Instant Pot. Once hot, heat the oil.

Then, sauté the leeks, garlic, and pepper for 2 to 4 minutes, stirring periodically; add a splash of broth if needed.

Stir the remaining ingredients into your Instant Pot; stir to combine well.

Secure the lid. Choose the "Soup" mode and High pressure; cook for 30 minutes. Once cooking is complete, use a natural pressure release; carefully remove the lid.

Taste and adjust the seasonings; ladle into soup bowls and serve hot. Enjoy!

Per serving: 235 Calories; 8.1g Fat; 34.2g Carbs; 8.6g Protein; 6.3g Sugars

702. Hearty Mushroom Goulash with Chickpeas

(Ready in about 15 minutes | Servings 4)

Ingredients

2 tablespoons peanut oil
1 cup scallions, chopped
1 ½ pounds Cremini mushrooms, thinly sliced
2 garlic cloves, smashed
1/4 cup white wine
Sea salt and freshly ground black pepper, to taste
1/2 teaspoon cayenne pepper
1/4 teaspoon dried dill weed
1/2 teaspoon dried rosemary
1 can chickpeas, drained well
1/4 cup fresh parsley, roughly chopped

Directions

Press the "Sauté" button and heat the peanut oil. Now, cook the scallions until they are tender.

Add the mushrooms and garlic; cook for 3 to 4 minutes, stirring periodically. Add a splash of white wine to deglaze the pot.

Season with salt, black pepper, cayenne pepper, dill, and rosemary.

Secure the lid. Choose the "Manual" mode and High pressure; cook for 10 minutes. Once cooking is complete, use a quick pressure release; carefully remove the lid.

Add the chickpeas and stir. Divide among serving plates and serve garnished with fresh chopped parsley. Bon appétit!

Per serving: 198 Calories; 9.1g Fat; 22.9g Carbs; 10.5g Protein; 6.7g Sugars

703. Great Northern Beans on Toast

(Ready in about 35 minutes | Servings 6)

Ingredients

2 cups Great Northern beans
1 red onion, peeled and chopped
1 cup water
2 cups vegetable broth
1/2 cup ketchup
Garlic salt, to taste
1 teaspoon chili powder

1/2 teaspoon mixed peppercorns, crushed
1/4 cup dark brown sugar
2 cloves garlic, minced
2 sprigs fresh sage, roughly chopped
2 tablespoons canola oil
6 slices sourdough bread, toasted

Directions

Add the beans, onion, water, and broth to the Instant Pot.

Secure the lid. Choose the "Soup" mode and High pressure; cook for 25 minutes. Once cooking is complete, use a natural pressure release; carefully remove the lid.

Add the ketchup, salt, chili powder, mixed peppercorns, sugar, garlic, sage, and oil. Press the "Sauté" button.

Let it simmer an additional 5 to 7 minutes or until everything is heated through. Spoon the hot beans over the toasted bread and serve immediately.

Per serving: 393 Calories; 6.5g Fat; 67.4g Carbs; 18.4g Protein; 16.8g Sugars

704. Classic Lentil Gumbo

(Ready in about 15 minutes | Servings 4)

Ingredients

2 tablespoons sesame oil
1 shallot, chopped
3 cloves garlic, minced
1 teaspoon jalapeño pepper, minced
1 celery stalk, chopped
1 carrot, chopped
1 parsnip, chopped
1/2 teaspoon dried basil
1 teaspoon dried parsley flakes

1 teaspoon red pepper flakes, crushed
1 1/3 cups lentils, regular
4 cups vegetable broth
1 ½ cups fresh or frozen chopped okra
2 ripe tomatoes, chopped
Salt, to taste
1/2 teaspoon ground black pepper
1 teaspoon light brown sugar

Directions

Press the "Sauté" button to preheat the Instant Pot. Heat the oil, then sauté the shallot until tender and fragrant.

After that, stir in the garlic; cook an additional 30 seconds or until aromatic. Then, stir in the remaining ingredients.

Secure the lid. Choose the "Manual" mode and High pressure; cook for 12 minutes. Once cooking is complete, use a natural pressure release; carefully remove the lid.

Taste, adjust the seasonings and serve warm. Bon appétit!

Per serving: 196 Calories; 8.8g Fat; 22.7g Carbs; 9.6g Protein; 7.7g Sugars

705. Mediterranean-Style Wheat Berry Salad

(Ready in about 45 minutes + chilling time | Servings 6)

Ingredients

2 cups wheat berries, soaked overnight and rinsed well
6 cups water
Salt and pepper, to taste
1 cup baby tomatoes, halved
1 red onion, thinly sliced

1/3 cup Kalamata olives, halved
1/4 cup extra-virgin olive oil
1/4 cup red wine vinegar
1 tablespoon tahini
1 teaspoon yellow mustard
3 cloves garlic, minced

Directions

Add the soaked wheat berries and water to the Instant Pot.

Secure the lid. Choose the "Multigrain" mode and High pressure; cook for 40 minutes. Once cooking is complete, use a natural pressure release; carefully remove the lid.

Place in a salad bowl. Add the salt, pepper, tomatoes, onion and Kalamata olives.

In a small-sized mixing bowl, whisk the remaining ingredients for the dressing. Dress your salad and serve well-chilled.

Per serving: 207 Calories; 7.1g Fat; 32.2g Carbs; 6.2g Protein; 1.5g Sugars

706. Easy Breakfast Coconut Oatmeal

(Ready in about 15 minutes | Servings 2)

Ingredients

4 cups water
1 ½ cups steel cut oats
1 tablespoon coconut oil
1/2 teaspoon cardamom
1/4 teaspoon grated nutmeg

1/2 teaspoon ground cinnamon
1/2 teaspoon vanilla essence
1/2 teaspoon ground star anise
1/2 cup coconut, flaked

Directions

Add the water and oats to your Instant Pot.

Secure the lid and choose the "Manual" mode. Cook for 10 minutes at High pressure.

Once cooking is complete, use a quick release; remove the lid carefully. Add the coconut oil and seasonings to the warm oatmeal and stir to combine well.

Divide among individual bowls and serve topped with flaked coconut. Bon appétit!

Per serving: 243 Calories; 11.8g Fat; 48g Carbs; 12.6g Protein; 2.5g Sugars

707. The Best Mac and Cheese Ever

(Ready in about 15 minutes | Servings 4)

Ingredients

1 (8-ounce) box elbow macaroni
3 Yukon gold potatoes, peeled and diced
1 yellow onion, chopped
1 garlic clove, minced
2 cups water

3 tablespoons nutritional yeast flakes
Seasoned salt and ground black pepper, to taste
1/2 teaspoon red pepper flakes
1/2 cup cashews
1/3 cup almond milk

Directions

Place the macaroni, potatoes, onion, garlic, and water in your Instant Pot.

Secure the lid. Choose the "Soup" mode and High pressure; cook for 4 minutes. Once cooking is complete, use a quick pressure release; carefully remove the lid.

Then, remove the potatoes from the cooking liquid using a slotted spoon; transfer them to your blender. Add the nutritional yeast flakes, salt, black pepper, red pepper, cashews, and almond milk; blend until everything is creamy, uniform and smooth.

Add the "cheese" mixture to the Instant Pot; stir with the warm pasta and serve immediately.

Per serving: 415 Calories; 11.5g Fat; 66g Carbs; 14.4g Protein; 6.7g Sugars

708. Old-Time Mashed Potatoes

(Ready in about 15 minutes | Servings 6)

Ingredients

2 pounds potatoes, peeled and diced
3 garlic cloves, peeled
1 cup vegetable stock
Salt, to taste
1/3 teaspoon ground black pepper
A pinch of grated nutmeg
4 tablespoons vegan butter, softened
2 tablespoons soy milk
1 teaspoon paprika powder

Directions

Add the potatoes, garlic, stock, salt, pepper, nutmeg and butter to your Instant Pot.

Secure the lid. Choose the "Manual" mode and High pressure; cook for 5 minutes. Once cooking is complete, use a quick pressure release; carefully remove the lid.

Then, purée the mixture with a potato masher; add soy milk and continue to mash until your desired texture is reached.

Sprinkle paprika over the top and serve warm. Bon appétit!

Per serving: 196 Calories; 8.3g Fat; 27.2g Carbs; 4.2g Protein; 1.4g Sugars

709. Creamy Chowder with Peppers

(Ready in about 15 minutes | Servings 4)

Ingredients

3 teaspoons sesame oil
1/2 cup leeks, chopped
1 garlic clove, minced
1 celery with leaves, chopped
1 carrot, trimmed and chopped
1 red bell pepper, thinly sliced
1 green bell pepper, thinly sliced
1 serrano pepper, deveined and thinly sliced
4 ½ cups water
Salt and ground black pepper, to taste
1 tablespoon soy sauce
1/2 cup raw cashews, soaked for 3 hours
1/2 cup almond milk, unsweetened

Directions

Press the "Sauté" button on your Instant Pot. Heat the sesame oil and sauté the leeks until they are just tender.

Add the garlic, celery, carrot, and peppers; continue sautéing until they have softened, about 3 minutes.

Add the water, salt, and pepper. Choose the "Manual" mode and cook for 4 minutes at High pressure.

Once cooking is complete, use a quick release; remove the lid carefully.

Next, puree the soy sauce, raw cashews, and almond milk in your food processor or blender; process until creamy and uniform.

Stir this cream base into the soup; cook in the residual heat until everything is well incorporated.

Divide the warm chowder among individual serving bowls. Side with crackers and enjoy!

Per serving: 282 Calories; 22.2g Fat; 18.4g Carbs; 6.1g Protein; 7.9g Sugars

710. Lentil Gazpacho Salad

(Ready in about 15 minutes + chilling time | Servings 4)

Ingredients

1 ½ cups yellow lentils
3 cups water
2 bay leaves, dry or fresh
1 sprig thyme
1 sprig rosemary
2 garlic cloves, halved
1 red bell pepper, sliced
1 green bell pepper, sliced
1 cucumber, sliced
2 cups baby spinach leaves
1/2 cup red onion, thinly sliced
1/2 cup black olives, pitted and sliced
1 jalapeño, minced
A large handful fresh parsley, finely chopped
2 ripe tomatoes, chopped
1/4 cup extra-virgin olive oil
1 tablespoon peanut butter
1 tablespoon lime juice

Directions

Add the lentils, water, bay leaves, thyme, rosemary, and garlic to your Instant Pot.

Secure the lid. Choose the "Manual" mode and High pressure; cook for 2 minutes. Once cooking is complete, use a natural pressure release; carefully remove the lid.

Allow the lentils to cool to room temperature. Then, add the remaining ingredients; toss to combine well.

Serve well chilled and enjoy!

Per serving: 375 Calories; 9.4g Fat; 55.7g Carbs; 20.3g Protein; 5.9g Sugars

711. Tempeh and Sweet Potato Curry

(Ready in about 15 minutes | Servings 4)

Ingredients

1 tablespoon toasted sesame oil
1 onion, thinly sliced
2 garlic cloves, minced
1 red chili pepper, chopped
1/2 pound tempeh, steamed
1 cup vegetable broth
1 teaspoon curry paste
1/2 teaspoon cumin
Sea salt and ground black pepper, to taste
1 pound sweet potatoes, peeled and diced
1 tablespoon peanut butter
4 ounces coconut milk
2 cups spinach leaves

Directions

Press the "Sauté" button to preheat your Instant Pot. Now, heat the oil; sauté the onion until tender and translucent.

Add the garlic and chili pepper; continue to sauté an additional 40 seconds.

Add the tempeh, broth, curry paste, cumin, salt, black pepper, sweet potatoes, peanut butter and coconut milk.

Secure the lid. Choose the "Manual" mode and High pressure; cook for 8 minutes. Once cooking is complete, use a natural pressure release; carefully remove the lid.

Add the spinach leaves; seal the lid again and let it sit until wilted completely. Serve in individual bowls and enjoy!

Per serving: 272 Calories; 11.1g Fat; 31.2g Carbs; 15.6g Protein; 3.8g Sugars

712. Spring Green Lentil Salad

(Ready in about 25 minutes | Servings 4)

Ingredients

3 cups water
1 ½ cups dried French green lentils, rinsed
2 bay leaves
A bunch of spring onions, roughly chopped
2 garlic cloves, minced
2 carrots, shredded
1 green bell pepper, thinly sliced
1 red bell pepper, thinly sliced
1/2 cup radishes, thinly sliced
1 cucumber, thinly sliced
1/4 cup extra-virgin olive oil
2 tablespoons balsamic vinegar
1/4 cup fresh basil, snipped
1 teaspoon mixed peppercorns, freshly cracked
Sea salt, to taste

Directions

Place the water, lentils, and bay leaves in your Instant Pot. Secure the lid.

Choose "Soup" function and cook for 20 minutes under High pressure. Once cooking is complete, use a quick release; carefully remove the lid.

Drain the green lentils and discard bay leaves; transfer to a large salad bowl.

Add the spring onions, garlic, carrots, bell peppers, radishes, cucumber, olive oil, vinegar, and basil. Season with crushed peppercorns and sea salt.

Toss to combine and place in your refrigerator until ready to serve. Bon appétit!

Per serving: 183 Calories; 13.8g Fat; 13.7g Carbs; 3.5g Protein; 4g Sugars

VEGETABLES & SIDE DISHES

713. French-Style Onion Soup

(Ready in about 35 minutes | Servings 6)

Ingredients

3 tablespoons ghee
6 sweet onions, sliced
2 garlic cloves
Kosher salt and ground black pepper, to taste
1/2 teaspoon cayenne pepper
1 tablespoon granulated sugar
1/3 cup sherry wine
1/2 cup water
5 cups chicken stock, preferably homemade
2 fresh rosemary sprigs
1 loaf French bread, cut into slices and toasted
1 ½ cups Munster cheese, shaved

Directions

Press the "Sauté" button to heat up the Instant Pot. Then, melt the ghee; sauté the onions until translucent, about 5 minutes.

Add the garlic and sauté it for 1 to 2 minutes more. Reduce the heat to low; add the salt, black pepper, cayenne pepper, and white sugar. Continue to cook, stirring frequently, until sweet onions are slightly browned.

Pour in the sherry wine, and scrape off any brown bits from the bottom of your Instant Pot. Now, pour in the water and chicken stock; add the rosemary and stir to combine.

Secure the lid. Select the "Manual" setting; cook for 8 minutes under High pressure. Once cooking is complete, use a quick pressure release; carefully remove the lid.

Then, preheat your oven to broil.

Divide the soup among ovenproof bowls; top with toasted bread and shaved Munster cheese; place your soup under the broiler for 5 to 6 minutes, or until the cheese is bubbly. Serve warm and enjoy!

Per serving: 353 Calories; 15.4g Fat; 40.5g Carbs; 15.4g Protein; 20.2g Sugars

714. Mashed Potatoes with Spring Garlic and Sour Cream

(Ready in about 15 minutes | Servings 4)

Ingredients

1 cup water
1 pound Yukon Gold potatoes, peeled and cubed
1/2 stick butter, softened
2 tablespoons spring garlic, minced
1/4 cup milk
1/3 cup sour cream
1/2 teaspoon dried oregano
1/2 teaspoon dried rosemary
1/2 teaspoon paprika
Salt and ground black pepper, to taste

Directions

Add 1 cup of water and steamer basket to the base of your Instant Pot.

Place the cubed potatoes in the steamer basket; transfer it to the Instant Pot. Secure the lid. Select the "Manual" mode; cook for 4 minutes under High pressure.

Once cooking is complete, use a quick release; carefully remove the lid.

Meanwhile, heat a pan over a moderate heat. Melt the butter and cook the spring garlic until it is tender and aromatic.

Add the milk and scrape up any browned bits with a spatula. Allow it to cool slightly.

In a mixing bowl, mash the cooked potatoes. Add the butter/garlic mixture along with the other ingredients.

Taste, adjust the seasonings and serve warm. Bon appétit!

Per serving: 230 Calories; 14g Fat; 23.3g Carbs; 3.8g Protein; 1.7g Sugars

715. Bok Choy with Black Sesame and Olives

(Ready in about 10 minutes | Servings 4)

Ingredients

1 pound Bok choy, leaves separated
2 teaspoons canola oil
3 tablespoons black sesame seeds
2 tablespoons soy sauce
1/2 teaspoon smoked paprika
Salt and ground black pepper, to taste
1/2 cup Kalamata olives, pitted and sliced

Directions

Prepare the Instant Pot by adding 1 ½ cups of water and a steamer basket to the bottom. Place the Bok choy in the steamer basket.

Secure the lid. Select the "Manual" mode and cook for 4 minutes under High pressure. Once cooking is complete, use a quick pressure release; carefully remove the lid.

Transfer the Bok choy to a bowl and toss with the remaining ingredients. Bon appétit!

Per serving: 178 Calories; 10.8g Fat; 14.3g Carbs; 12.8g Protein; 2.1g Sugars

716. Buttery Steamed Sweet Potatoes

(Ready in about 35 minutes | Servings 4)

Ingredients

1 pound whole small sweet potatoes, cleaned
1/4 teaspoon salt
1/4 teaspoon freshly grated nutmeg
2 tablespoons light butter

Directions

Add 1 cup of water and a steamer basket to the Instant Pot. Arrange the sweet potatoes in the steamer basket.

Secure the lid and choose the "Steam" mode. Cook for 10 minutes under High pressure. Once cooking is complete, use a natural release for 20 minutes; carefully remove the lid.

Toss the steamed sweet potatoes with salt, nutmeg and butter. Eat warm. Bon appétit!

Per serving: 154 Calories; 5.9g Fat; 23.5g Carbs; 2.3g Protein; 7.3g Sugars

717. Artichokes with Avocado Feta Dip

(Ready in about 20 minutes | Servings 3)

Ingredients

1 cup water
3 globe artichokes
1/2 lemon
For the Sauce:
1 avocado, peeled, pitted and diced
3 ounces feta cheese
1/2 lemon, juiced
1/2 yellow onion, chopped
2 tablespoons fresh parsley leaves, chopped
1/2 teaspoon sea salt
1/3 teaspoon black pepper

Directions

Add 1 cup of water and a steamer basket to the base of your Instant Pot. Now, discard the damaged leaves of the artichokes.

Cut the bottoms to be flat. Cut off the excess stem and remove the tough ends of the leaves; rub with a lemon half.

Arrange the artichokes in the steamer basket.

Secure the lid. Choose the "Manual" mode, High pressure and 11 minutes. Once cooking is complete, use a natural release; carefully remove the lid.

In a mixing bowl, combine all the sauce ingredients. Serve the artichokes with the sauce on the side. Bon appétit!

Per serving: 282 Calories; 17.7g Fat; 26.3g Carbs; 10.9g Protein; 4.2g Sugars

718. Moong Dal and Green Bean Soup

(Ready in about 45 minutes | Servings 6)

Ingredients

1 ½ tablespoons olive oil
2 shallots, chopped
2 garlic cloves, minced
1 teaspoon cilantro, ground
1/2 teaspoon ground allspice
1/2 teaspoon smoked paprika
1 teaspoon celery seeds
1/2 teaspoon fennel seeds
1/2 teaspoon ground cumin
1 ½ cups moong dal
7 cups water
Sea salt and ground black pepper, to your liking
2 cups green beans, fresh

Directions

Press the "Sauté" button to heat up your Instant Pot. Then, heat the olive oil and cook the shallots until just tender.

Now, add the garlic and cook 30 to 40 seconds more or until it is aromatic and slightly browned. Stir in all seasonings; cook until aromatic or 2 minutes more, stirring continuously.

Add the moong dal and water. Secure the lid. Select the "Manual" mode and cook for 17 minutes under High pressure.

Once cooking is complete, use a natural pressure release for 20 minutes; carefully remove the lid.

Season with sea salt and black pepper; add the green beans and secure the lid again. Select the "Manual" mode one more time and cook for 2 minutes under High pressure.

Once cooking is complete, use a quick pressure release; carefully remove the lid. Serve immediately with garlic croutons. Bon appétit!

Per serving: 221 Calories; 4.3g Fat; 34.7g Carbs; 12.8g Protein; 2.1g Sugars

719. Russet Potato Bites

(Ready in about 15 minutes | Servings 6)

Ingredients

2 pounds russet potatoes, peeled and diced
1/2 stick butter, melted
2 garlic cloves, pressed
1/2 teaspoon mustard powder
1/2 teaspoon sea salt
1/4 teaspoon ground black pepper
1/2 teaspoon cayenne pepper
1 teaspoon thyme
2 tablespoons mayonnaise
2 tablespoons balsamic vinegar

Directions

Add a metal rack and 1 cup of water to your Instant Pot. Place the potatoes on the rack.

Secure the lid. Select the "Steam" mode and cook for 10 minutes under High pressure. Once cooking is complete, use a quick pressure release; carefully remove the lid.

Cut your potatoes into wedges and toss them with the remaining ingredients. Serve at room temperature. Bon appétit!

Per serving: 221 Calories; 11.2g Fat; 27.9g Carbs; 3.4g Protein; 1g Sugars

720. Creamy Couscous Florentine

(Ready in about 10 minutes | Servings 4)

Ingredients

1 tablespoon olive oil
2 bell peppers, diced
1 pound couscous
2 cups vegetable broth
1 cucumber, diced
2 tomatoes, sliced
2 tablespoons fresh mint, roughly chopped
A bunch of scallions, sliced
1/4 cup yogurt
2 tablespoons sesame butter (tahini)
1 tablespoon honey

Directions

Press the "Sauté" button and heat the oil; then, sauté the peppers until tender and aromatic. Stir in the couscous and vegetable broth.

Secure the lid. Choose the "Manual" mode and cook for 2 minutes at High pressure. Once cooking is complete, use a quick pressure release; carefully remove the lid.

Then, stir in the remaining ingredients; stir to combine well and enjoy!

Per serving: 563 Calories; 9.2g Fat; 98g Carbs; 19.6g Protein; 7.3g Sugars

721. Eggplant with Mediterranean Dressing

(Ready in about 10 minutes | Servings 4)

Ingredients

1 pound eggplant, sliced
1 tablespoon sea salt
2 tablespoons olive oil
1/4 cup Greek yogurt
1/4 cup mayonnaise
1 teaspoon balsamic vinegar
1 garlic clove, minced
2 tablespoons olives, pitted and minced
1 tablespoon fresh coriander, chopped

Directions

Toss the eggplant with sea salt in a colander. Let it sit for 30 minutes; then squeeze out the excess liquid.

Press the "Sauté" button and heat the olive oil. Now, cook the eggplant until lightly charred. Add 1 cup of water to the inner pot.

Secure the lid. Choose the "Manual" mode and cook for 2 minutes at High pressure. Once cooking is complete, use a quick pressure release; carefully remove the lid.

Meanwhile, whisk the remaining ingredients until well combined. Drizzle this dressing over the eggplant and serve at once. Bon appétit!

Per serving: 198 Calories; 18.2g Fat; 8.2g Carbs; 1.6g Protein; 5g Sugars

722. Potatoes Au Gratin

(Ready in about 20 minutes | Servings 4)

Ingredients

6 medium potatoes, peeled and thinly sliced
1 cup vegetable broth
1 shallot, chopped
2 garlic cloves, sliced
1/2 teaspoon dried basil
Sea salt and ground black pepper, to taste
1/2 teaspoon paprika
1/2 cup heavy cream
1 cup Romano cheese, preferably freshly grated

Directions

Arrange the sliced potatoes on the bottom of a lightly greased inner pot. Add the vegetable broth, shallot, garlic, basil, salt, black pepper and paprika to the inner pot.

Secure the lid. Choose the "Manual" mode and cook for 4 minutes at High pressure. Once cooking is complete, use a quick pressure release; carefully remove the lid.

Preheat your oven to broil. Transfer the potatoes to an oven-safe dish. Top with the heavy cream and Romano cheese.

Broil until the cheese is bubbling and golden brown. Let it sit on a cooling rack for 5 minutes before slicing and serving. Enjoy!

Per serving: 440 Calories; 16.2g Fat; 58g Carbs; 16.5g Protein; 3.9g Sugars

723. Broccoli with Italian-Style Mayonnaise

(Ready in about 10 minutes | Servings 4)

Ingredients

1 pound broccoli florets
3 garlic cloves, smashed
Kosher salt and ground black pepper, to taste
1/2 cup mayonnaise
1 tablespoon Italian seasoning mix

Directions

Add 1 cup of water and steamer basket to the inner pot. Place the broccoli florets in the steamer basket.

Secure the lid. Choose the "Manual" mode and cook for 1 minute at High pressure. Once cooking is complete, use a quick pressure release; carefully remove the lid.

Sprinkle the garlic, salt, and black pepper over the cooked broccoli florets.

Mix the mayonnaise with the Italian seasoning mix; serve your broccoli with the Italian mayo on the side. Bon appétit!

Per serving: 227 Calories; 21.2g Fat; 6.4g Carbs; 4.5g Protein; 1.4g Sugars

724. Black Eyed Peas with Bacon

(Ready in about 40 minutes | Servings 3)

Ingredients

3 strips bacon, cut into 1/2-inch pieces
1/2 pound dry black eyed peas
3 cups chicken stock
1/2 teaspoon cayenne pepper
1/4 teaspoon dried dill
1/4 teaspoon dried oregano
1/4 teaspoon dried sage
Kosher salt and freshly ground black pepper, to taste
2 cups spinach, torn into pieces

Directions

Press the "Sauté" button to preheat your Instant Pot. Now, cook the bacon until it is crisp; reserve.

Add the black eyed peas, chicken stock, and all the slices to the inner pot.

Secure the lid. Choose the "Manual" mode and cook for 18 minutes at High pressure. Once cooking is complete, use a natural pressure release for 10 minutes; carefully remove the lid.

Lastly, stir in the spinach leaves; seal the lid and let it sit in the residual heat for 5 to 10 minutes.

Ladle into serving bowls and garnish with the reserved bacon. Bon appétit!

Per serving: 416 Calories; 13.1g Fat; 49.5g Carbs; 27.2g Protein; 6.4g Sugars

725. Vegan Baked Beans

(Ready in about 1 hour 10 minutes | Servings 6)

Ingredients

1 ½ pounds pinto beans, rinsed and drained
8 cups water
2 tablespoons olive oil
2 onions, chopped
5 cloves garlic, minced
1 cup molasses
1 cup ketchup
1 teaspoon salt
2 tablespoons soy sauce
1 tablespoon Cholula hot sauce

Directions

Place the beans and water in your Instant Pot.

Secure the lid. Choose the "Bean/Chili" mode and cook for 40 minutes at High pressure. Once cooking is complete, use a natural pressure release for 10 minutes; carefully remove the lid. Set aside.

Press the "Sauté" button and heat the oil until sizzling. Now, cook the onion and garlic until tender and fragrant. Add the reserved beans back to the inner pot. Stir in the remaining ingredients.

Secure the lid. Choose the "Manual" mode and cook for 10 minutes at High pressure. Once cooking is complete, use a quick pressure release. Bon appétit!

Per serving: 594 Calories; 5.6g Fat; 114g Carbs; 26.2g Protein; 51.4g Sugars

726. Kale with Garlic and Lemon

(Ready in about 10 minutes | Servings 4)

Ingredients

1 tablespoon olive oil
3 cloves garlic, slivered
1 pound kale, cleaned and trimmed
1 cup water
Kosher salt and ground black pepper, to taste
1/4 teaspoon cayenne pepper
Fresh juice squeezed from 1/2 a lemon

Directions

Press the "Sauté" button and heat the oil until sizzling. Now, cook the garlic until just tender and aromatic.

Add the chopped kale and water to the inner pot. Sprinkle with salt, black pepper, and cayenne pepper.

Secure the lid. Choose the "Manual" mode and cook for 4 minutes at High pressure. Once cooking is complete, use a quick pressure release.

Scoop the kale out of the inner pot with a slotted spoon, leaving as much cooking liquid behind as possible. Drizzle fresh lemon juice over the kale and serve. Bon appétit!

Per serving: 89 Calories; 4.4g Fat; 10.4g Carbs; 5g Protein; 2.5g Sugars

727. Warm Cabbage Slaw

(Ready in about 10 minutes | Servings 4)

Ingredients

2 tablespoons olive oil
3 cloves garlic, minced
1/2 cup green onions, sliced
1 pound purple cabbage, shredded
2 carrots, cut into sticks
Kosher salt and ground black pepper, to taste
2 tablespoons soy sauce

Directions

Press the "Sauté" button and add the oil. Once hot, cook the garlic and green onions until softened.

Add the cabbage, carrots, salt, and black pepper.

Secure the lid. Choose the "Manual" mode and cook for 4 minutes at High pressure. Once cooking is complete, use a quick pressure release.

Lastly, add the soy sauce to the cabbage mixture and stir to combine well. Place in a serving bowl and serve immediately.

Per serving: 136 Calories; 8.4g Fat; 14.5g Carbs; 2.8g Protein; 7.6g Sugars

728. Boiled Potatoes with Ranch Dressing

(Ready in about 20 minutes | Servings 4)

Ingredients

4 large Yukon gold potatoes
1/2 cup sour cream
4 tablespoons reduced-fat mayonnaise
1 teaspoon fresh parsley, chopped
1 teaspoon fresh chives, chopped
1 garlic clove, minced
Sea salt and ground black pepper, to taste

Directions

Add 1 ½ cups of water and a steamer basket to the inner pot. Now, place the potatoes in the steamer basket.

Secure the lid. Choose the "Steam" mode and cook for 10 minutes at High pressure. Once cooking is complete, use a quick pressure release; carefully remove the lid.

Meanwhile, in a mixing bowl, whisk together the sour cream and mayonnaise. Stir in the fresh herbs, garlic, salt, and black pepper.

Drain your potatoes, peel and slice them; toss your potatoes with ranch dressing. Bon appétit!

Per serving: 379 Calories; 9.4g Fat; 66.7g Carbs; 8.5g Protein; 2.9g Sugars

729. Italian Bucatini Puttanesca

(Ready in about 25 minutes | Servings 4)

Ingredients

1 tablespoon olive oil
2 garlic cloves, pressed
1/2 cup black olives, pitted, and thinly sliced
2 tablespoons capers, soaked and rinsed
2 vine-ripened tomatoes, pureed
1 tablespoon Italian seasoning blend
Coarse salt, to taste
3/4 pound bucatini pasta
1 cup water

Directions

Press the "Sauté" button and add the oil. Once hot, cook the garlic until aromatic. Add the black olives, capers, tomatoes, Italian seasoning blend, and salt.

Bring to a boil and turn the Instant Pot to the lowest setting; let the sauce simmer for 10 to 13 minutes. Stir in the bucatini pasta and water.

Secure the lid. Choose the "Manual" mode and cook for 8 minutes at High pressure. Once cooking is complete, use a quick pressure release.

Serve warm and enjoy!

Per serving: 374 Calories; 7.1g Fat; 72.7g Carbs; 7.3g Protein; 1.8g Sugars

730. Quick Chili Rice

(Ready in about 45 minutes | Servings 4)

Ingredients

2 tablespoons canola oil
2 shallots, finely chopped
1 red chili pepper, seeded and minced
1 sweet pepper, seeded and finely chopped
2 tablespoons garlic, minced
1 cup tomato puree

1 cup brown rice
10 ounces black beans
2 ½ cups chicken stock
Sea salt and ground black pepper, to taste
2 tablespoons fresh chives, chopped

Directions

Press the "Sauté" button and heat the oil until sizzling. Now, cook the shallots, peppers, and garlic until tender and fragrant.

Add the tomato puree, rice, beans, stock, salt, and black pepper to the inner pot.

Secure the lid. Choose the "Manual" mode and cook for 25 minutes at High pressure. Once cooking is complete, use a natural pressure release for 15 minutes; carefully remove the lid.

Ladle into individual bowls and serve with fresh chives. Enjoy!

Per serving: 358 Calories; 10.7g Fat; 57g Carbs; 10.6g Protein; 7.8g Sugars

731. Authentic Tex-Mex Rice

(Ready in about 30 minutes | Servings 5)

Ingredients

2 tablespoons canola oil
2 garlic cloves, minced
1 medium-sized leek, chopped
1 bell pepper, seeded and finely chopped
2 fresh serrano peppers, seeded and finely chopped
4 cups vegetable stock

2 tablespoons fresh parsley leaves, chopped
1/2 tablespoon cumin seeds
1 teaspoon mustard seeds
1 ½ cups white rice
1 teaspoon salt
1/2 teaspoon cayenne pepper
1/2 teaspoon freshly ground black pepper

Directions

Press the "Sauté" button and heat the oil. Once hot, cook the garlic, leek, and peppers until tender and aromatic.

Add the remaining ingredients and stir to combine.

Secure the lid. Choose the "Rice" mode and cook for 10 minutes. Once cooking is complete, use a natural pressure release for 15 minutes; carefully remove the lid.

Serve in individual bowls and enjoy!

Per serving: 316 Calories; 7.7g Fat; 51g Carbs; 8.9g Protein; 1.3g Sugars

732. Colorful Kamut Bowl

(Ready in about 20 minutes | Servings 5)

Ingredients

1 ½ cups dried kamut
3 cups water
2 cups baby spinach
1 large carrot, cut into sticks
1 celery rib, sliced

1 shallot, finely chopped
4 tablespoons olive oil
Salt and freshly ground black pepper, to taste
2 tablespoons fresh lime juice

Directions

Add the kamut and water to the inner pot.

Secure the lid. Choose the "Manual" mode and cook for 9 minutes at High pressure. Once cooking is complete, use a quick pressure release.

Add the vegetables, olive oil, salt, and black pepper.

Secure the lid. Choose the "Manual" mode and cook for 3 minutes at High pressure. Once cooking is complete, use a quick pressure release.

Drizzle fresh lime juice over each serving and enjoy!

Per serving: 295 Calories; 12g Fat; 42g Carbs; 8.6g Protein; 5.3g Sugars

733. Buttery Cauliflower Rice

(Ready in about 10 minutes | Servings 3)

Ingredients

1 ½ pounds cauliflower
Sea salt, to taste
1/2 teaspoon white pepper

2 tablespoons butter
2 tablespoons fresh parsley, roughly chopped

Directions

Add the cauliflower florets and 1 cup of water to the inner pot.

Secure the lid. Choose the "Manual" mode and cook for 2 minutes at High pressure. Once cooking is complete, use a quick pressure release.

Stir the salt, pepper, and butter into warm cauliflower rice.

Serve garnished with fresh parsley and enjoy!

Per serving: 127 Calories; 8.3g Fat; 11.7g Carbs; 4.5g Protein; 4.4g Sugars

734. French Balsamic Peppers

(Ready in about 10 minutes | Servings 2)

Ingredients

2 tablespoons olive oil
4 bell peppers, seeded and sliced
Sea salt and ground black pepper, to taste

1/2 cup court bouillon
1/2 cup water
2 tablespoons balsamic vinegar

Directions

Press the "Sauté" button and heat the oil. Once hot, cook the peppers until just tender and fragrant.

Add the salt and black pepper. Pour in the bouillon and water.

Secure the lid. Choose the "Manual" mode and cook for 3 minutes at High pressure. Once cooking is complete, use a quick pressure release.

Drizzle balsamic vinegar over your peppers and serve immediately.

Per serving: 178 Calories; 13.7g Fat; 13.7g Carbs; 2.3g Protein; 8.4g Sugars

735. Tamatar Wangun (Indian Kashmiri Eggplant)

(Ready in about 40 minutes | Servings 4)

Ingredients

1 pound eggplant, sliced
1 tablespoon sea salt
1 tablespoon sesame oil
1 teaspoon cumin seeds
2 shallots, chopped

1 tablespoon butter
1 cup water
1 Kashmiri chili pepper, chopped
2 tomatoes, pureed
4 curry leaves

Directions

Toss the eggplant with sea salt in a colander. Let it sit for 30 minutes; then squeeze out the excess liquid.

Press the "Sauté" button and heat the sesame oil; now sauté the cumin seeds for 30 seconds or until aromatic. Then, cook the shallots for 2 to 3 minutes more or until they have softened.

Then, melt the butter. Now, cook the eggplant until lightly charred. Add the water, chili pepper, tomatoes, and curry leaves to the inner pot.

Secure the lid. Choose the "Manual" mode and cook for 2 minutes at High pressure. Once cooking is complete, use a quick pressure release; carefully remove the lid.

Serve in individual bowls and enjoy!

Per serving: 105 Calories; 6.7g Fat; 11.2g Carbs; 2.1g Protein; 6.6g Sugars

736. Thayir Saadam (Indian Yogurt Rice)

(Ready in about 25 minutes | Servings 5)

Ingredients

4 tablespoons grapeseed oil
1 teaspoon fennel seeds
8 curry leaves
1 ½ cups basmati rice, rinsed
1 chili pepper, minced
1 teaspoon fresh ginger, peeled and grated

1 cinnamon stick
Himalayan salt and ground black pepper, to taste
1 cup full-fat yogurt
2 tablespoons fresh dhania (coriander), chopped

Directions

Press the "Sauté" button and heat the oil; now sauté the fennel seeds and curry leaves for 30 seconds or until aromatic.

Now, stir in the basmati rice, chili pepper, ginger, cinnamon, salt, and black pepper. Pour in 2 cups of water.

Secure the lid. Choose the "Manual" mode and cook for 4 minutes at High pressure. Once cooking is complete, use a natural pressure release for 15 minutes; carefully remove the lid.

Fluff your rice with a fork and stir in the yogurt. Stir until everything is well combined. Serve garnished with fresh dhania and enjoy!

Per serving: 323 Calories; 11.7g Fat; 49.2g Carbs; 4.5g Protein; 1.2g Sugars

737. Easy Parmesan Fettuccine

(Ready in about 20 minutes | Servings 6)

Ingredients

1 pound fettuccine
4 cups water
4 tablespoons butter, cubed

Sea salt and ground black pepper, to season
4 tablespoons Parmesan cheese, grated

Directions

Place the fettuccine and water in the inner pot of your Instant Pot.

Secure the lid. Choose the "Manual" mode and cook for 4 minutes at High pressure. Once cooking is complete, use a natural pressure release for 10 minutes; carefully remove the lid.

Toss the boiled fettuccine with the butter, salt, black pepper, and parmesan cheese; serve immediately. Bon appétit!

Per serving: 348 Calories; 9.6g Fat; 57.2g Carbs; 12.5g Protein; 0.3g Sugars

738. Garlicky Green Beans

(Ready in about 10 minutes | Servings 4)

Ingredients

2 tablespoons olive oil
2 garlic cloves, minced
1 ½ pounds green beans, trimmed
Salt and freshly ground black pepper, to taste

1 teaspoon cayenne pepper
2 tablespoons fresh chives, chopped

Directions

Press the "Sauté" button and heat the oil until sizzling. Now, sauté the garlic until tender but not browned.

Add the green beans, salt, black pepper, and cayenne pepper to the inner pot. Pour in 1 cup of water.

Secure the lid. Choose the "Manual" mode and cook for 3 minutes at High pressure. Once cooking is complete, use a quick pressure release; carefully remove the lid.

Garnish with fresh chives and serve warm.

Per serving: 117 Calories; 7.2g Fat; 12.6g Carbs; 3.3g Protein; 5.6g Sugars

739. Punjabi Bean Curry

(Ready in about 35 minutes | Servings 5)

Ingredients

1 pound red kidney beans
8 cups water
2 tablespoons canola oil
1 onion, finely sliced
1 teaspoon ginger garlic paste
1/4 teaspoon red curry paste
2 small-sized potatoes, peeled and diced

1 green chili pepper, finely chopped
Sea salt and freshly ground black pepper, to taste
1/2 teaspoon turmeric powder
1/2 teaspoon avocado powder
2 tomatoes, pureed
1 tablespoon fenugreek, chopped

Directions

Add the red kidney beans and water to the inner pot of your Instant Pot.

Secure the lid. Choose the "Bean/Chili" mode and cook for 25 minutes at High pressure. Once cooking is complete, use a quick pressure release; carefully remove the lid. Drain and reserve.

Press the "Sauté" button and heat the oil until sizzling. Now, sauté the onion until tender and translucent.

Add the remaining ingredients. Gently stir to combine.

Secure the lid. Choose the "Manual" mode and cook for 4 minutes at High pressure. Once cooking is complete, use a quick pressure release; carefully remove the lid.

Stir the reserved beans into the potato mixture and serve warm. Bon appétit!

Per serving: 406 Calories; 6.2g Fat; 66g Carbs; 24.5g Protein; 1.1g Sugars

740. Masala Sweet Corn

(Ready in about 10 minutes | Servings 4)

Ingredients

2 cups sweet corn kernels, frozen
2 tablespoons ghee
1/2 teaspoon turmeric powder

Himalayan salt and ground black pepper, to taste
1/2 teaspoon red chili powder
1/2 teaspoon chaat masala powder

Directions

Place all ingredients in the inner pot of your Instant Pot.

Secure the lid. Choose the "Manual" mode and cook for 4 minutes at High pressure. Once cooking is complete, use a quick pressure release; carefully remove the lid.

Serve immediately.

Per serving: 124 Calories; 6.7g Fat; 16.1g Carbs; 2.8g Protein; 3.1g Sugars

741. Okra in Tomato Sauce

(Ready in about 25 minutes | Servings 5)

Ingredients

1 tablespoon olive oil
2 shallots, chopped
1 cup tomato puree
4 tablespoons tomato ketchup
2 pounds okra
1 cup chicken stock

1 teaspoon garlic powder
1 teaspoon turmeric powder
1 teaspoon porcini powder
1 teaspoon fish sauce
Sea salt and ground black pepper, to taste

Directions

Press the "Sauté" button and heat the oil until sizzling. Now, sauté the shallot until tender and fragrant.

Add in the remaining ingredients and gently stir to combine well.

Secure the lid. Choose the "Manual" mode and cook for 5 minutes at High pressure. Once cooking is complete, use a natural pressure release for 15 minutes; carefully remove the lid.

Divide between serving bowls and serve warm. Bon appétit!

Per serving: 162 Calories; 4.5g Fat; 27.8g Carbs; 7.8g Protein; 8.7g Sugars

742. Authentic Cauliflower Kurma

(Ready in about 30 minutes | Servings 4)

Ingredients

2 cups cauliflower florets
2 tablespoons grapeseed oil
1 teaspoon cumin seeds
1 teaspoon fennel seeds
1 dried red chili pepper, minced
1 onion, chopped
1 cup tomato puree
Kosher salt and ground black pepper, to taste
1 teaspoon turmeric powder
1 cup fresh coconut, shredded
2 cups water
Tempering:
1 tablespoon peanut oil
1 teaspoon cumin seeds
4 curry leaves

Directions

Add 1 cup of water and a steamer basket to the inner pot of your Instant Pot. Place the cauliflower florets in the steamer basket.

Secure the lid. Choose the "Steam" mode and cook for 3 minutes at High pressure. Once cooking is complete, use a quick pressure release; carefully remove the lid. Drain and reserve.

Press the "Sauté" button and heat the grapeseed oil until sizzling. Now, sauté the cumin seeds and fennel seeds for 30 seconds.

Stir in the chili pepper and onion and continue to sauté an additional 2 to 3 minutes. Add the tomato puree and let it cook on the lowest setting for 3 minutes longer.

Add the salt, black pepper, turmeric, coconut, and water.

Secure the lid. Choose the "Manual" mode and cook for 5 minutes at High pressure. Once cooking is complete, use a natural pressure release for 10 minutes; carefully remove the lid. Stir in the steamed cauliflower florets.

Meanwhile, heat the peanut oil in a cast-iron skillet over medium heat. Cook the cumin seeds and curry leaves until they are fragrant. Stir the tempering into the cauliflower mixture and serve warm.

Per serving: 216 Calories; 11.2g Fat; 28.1g Carbs; 6g Protein; 14.3g Sugars

743. Roasted Herbed Baby Potatoes

(Ready in about 15 minutes | Servings 4)

Ingredients

1 ½ pounds baby potatoes, scrubbed
2 garlic cloves, smashed
1/2 cup roasted vegetable broth
1/2 cup water
2 tablespoons olive oil
1/2 teaspoon paprika
1 teaspoon oregano
1 teaspoon basil
1 teaspoon rosemary
1/2 teaspoon sage
Sea salt and ground black pepper, to taste

Directions

Pierce the baby potatoes with a fork; place them in the inner pot along with the garlic, broth, and water.

Secure the lid. Choose the "Manual" mode and cook for 10 minutes at High pressure. Once cooking is complete, use a quick pressure release; carefully remove the lid. Drain and reserve.

Press the "Sauté" button and heat the olive oil until sizzling. Now, sauté the seasonings for 30 seconds, stirring frequently. Throw the reserved potatoes into the inner pot.

Cook until they are browned and crisp on all sides. Serve warm.

Per serving: 198 Calories; 7.1g Fat; 30.3g Carbs; 4.1g Protein; 1.3g Sugars

744. Italian Caponata with Butternut Squash

(Ready in about 15 minutes | Servings 4)

Ingredients

4 tablespoons olive oil
1 onion, diced
2 garlic cloves, minced
Sea salt and ground black pepper
1 cup butternut squash, cut into 1/2-inch chunks
4 bell peppers, cut into 1/2-inch chunks
1 cup vine-ripened tomatoes, pureed
1 tablespoon Italian seasoning mix
4 tablespoons Parmigiano-Reggiano cheese, grated

Directions

Press the "Sauté" button and heat the olive oil until sizzling. Now, sauté the onion until tender and translucent.

Stir in the garlic and continue to sauté an additional 30 seconds, stirring frequently.

Stir in the salt, black pepper, butternut squash, peppers, tomatoes, and Italian seasoning mix.

Secure the lid. Choose the "Manual" mode and cook for 4 minutes at High pressure. Once cooking is complete, use a quick pressure release; carefully remove the lid.

Afterwards, scatter the grated cheese over the caponata and serve warm. Bon appétit!

Per serving: 194 Calories; 15.1g Fat; 13.5g Carbs; 3.4g Protein; 5.3g Sugars

745. Spicy Red Lentils

(Ready in about 10 minutes | Servings 4)

Ingredients

1 cup red lentils
2 cups water
1 sweet pepper, seeded and chopped
1 habanero pepper, seeded and chopped
1 medium-sized leek, sliced
1 teaspoon garlic, pressed
Kosher salt and ground black pepper, to taste
1/4 cup fresh cilantro, roughly chopped

Directions

Add all ingredients, except for the fresh cilantro, to the inner pot of your Instant Pot.

Secure the lid. Choose the "Manual" mode and cook for 2 minutes at High pressure. Once cooking is complete, use a quick pressure release; carefully remove the lid.

Spoon the lentil mixture into a nice serving bowl. Serve garnished with fresh cilantro and enjoy!

Per serving: 242 Calories; 1g Fat; 47.5g Carbs; 15.1g Protein; 9.3g Sugars

746. Maple-Orange Glazed Root Vegetables

(Ready in about 20 minutes | Servings 5)

Ingredients

1 pound carrots
1/2 pound yellow beets
1/2 pound red beets
2 tablespoons cold butter
2 tablespoons orange juice
1 teaspoon orange peel, finely shredded
1 tablespoon maple syrup
Kosher salt and ground black pepper, to taste

Directions

Place 1 cup of water and a steamer basket in your Instant Pot. Place the carrots and beets in the steamer basket.

Secure the lid. Choose the "Steam" mode and cook for 10 minutes at High pressure. Once cooking is complete, use a quick pressure release; carefully remove the lid.

Peel the carrots and beets and reserve; slice them into bite-sized pieces.

Press the "Sauté" button and choose the lowest setting. Cut in butter and add the remaining ingredients.

Drain the carrots and beets and add them back to the inner pot; let them cook until your vegetables are nicely coated with the glaze or about 5 minutes. Bon appétit!

Per serving: 131 Calories; 4.9g Fat; 20.8g Carbs; 2.4g Protein; 13.4g Sugars

747. Roasted Cauliflower with Tahini Sauce

(Ready in about 15 minutes | Servings 4)

Ingredients

1 pound cauliflower florets
1 tablespoon olive oil
1/3 cup tahini
2 tablespoons freshly squeezed lemon juice
2 cloves garlic, grated
1 teaspoon agave syrup
Kosher salt and freshly ground black pepper, to taste
2 tablespoons fresh parsley, chopped

Directions

Place 1 cup of water and a steamer basket in your Instant Pot. Place the cauliflower florets in the steamer basket.

Secure the lid. Choose the "Steam" mode and cook for 3 minutes at High pressure. Once cooking is complete, use a quick pressure release; carefully remove the lid.

Press the "Sauté" button and heat the oil. Roast the cauliflower florets for 2 to 3 minutes, stirring periodically to ensure even cooking.

Whisk the tahini, lemon juice, garlic agave syrup, salt, and black pepper until everything is well incorporated. Drizzle the tahini sauce over the roasted cauliflower and garnish with fresh parsley. Enjoy!

Per serving: 185 Calories; 14.2g Fat; 12.8g Carbs; 5.4g Protein; 3.7g Sugars

748. The Best Sweet Potatoes Ever

(Ready in about 30 minutes | Servings 5)

Ingredients

5 medium sweet potatoes, scrubbed
1 cup water
1/2 stick butter

Directions

Place 1 cup of water and a steamer basket in your Instant Pot. Place the sweet potatoes in the steamer basket.

Secure the lid. Choose the "Manual" mode and cook for 15 minutes at High pressure. Once cooking is complete, use a natural pressure release for 10 minutes; carefully remove the lid.

Garnish with butter and serve. Bon appétit!

Per serving: 196 Calories; 9.3g Fat; 26.7g Carbs; 2.1g Protein; 8.7g Sugars

749. Easy and Healthy Vegetable Mash

(Ready in about 10 minutes | Servings 4)

Ingredients

1/2 pound carrots, quartered
1/2 pound parsnip, quartered
1/2 pound pumpkin, cut into small pieces
2 tablespoons butter
2 cloves garlic, crushed
1/2 teaspoon basil
1/2 teaspoon thyme
1/2 teaspoon rosemary

Directions

Add the carrots, parsnips, and pumpkin to the inner pot of your Instant Pot. Pour in 1 cup of water.

Secure the lid. Choose the "Manual" mode and cook for 6 minutes at High pressure. Once cooking is complete, use a quick pressure release; carefully remove the lid.

Drain your vegetables and mash them with a potato masher.

Press the "Sauté" button and melt the butter; the, sauté the aromatics for 1 minute or so. Add the vegetable mash and stir to combine well.

Transfer to a nice serving bowls and garnish with some extra herbs if desired. Bon appétit!

Per serving: 134 Calories; 6.3g Fat; 19.8g Carbs; 2g Protein; 6.9g Sugars

750. Smoked Sausage Stuffed Mushrooms

(Ready in about 15 minutes | Servings 5)

Ingredients

20 button mushrooms, stems removed
1/2 pound smoked pork sausage, crumbled
1 shallot, finely chopped
2 cloves garlic, minced
4 ounces cream cheese, softened
1/2 cup seasoned breadcrumbs
1/2 cup cheddar cheese, shredded
1/2 cup vegetable broth
2 tablespoons fresh parsley leaves, roughly chopped

Directions

Clean your mushrooms and set them aside.

Press the "Sauté" button to preheat your Instant Pot. Then, brown the sausage until it is fully cooked.

Stir in the shallot and garlic; cook for a further 4 minutes, or until they have softened. Scoop this mixture out of the inner pot into a mixing bowl. Stir in the cream cheese, breadcrumbs, and cheddar cheese.

Now, add a splash of the vegetable broth to deglaze the pan. Press the "Cancel" button.

Next, fill the mushroom caps with the stuffing mixture. Arrange the mushrooms in the bottom of the inner pot.

Secure the lid. Choose the "Manual" mode and cook for 5 minutes at High pressure. Once cooking is complete, use a quick pressure release; carefully remove the lid.

Sprinkle fresh parsley leaves on top before serving and enjoy!

Per serving: 254 Calories; 20.3g Fat; 7.2g Carbs; 11.5g Protein; 2.7g Sugars

751. Millet with Roasted Tomatoes

(Ready in about 45 minutes | Servings 6)

Ingredients

1 pound small-sized tomatoes, halved
1 tablespoon olive oil
Sea salt and ground black pepper, to taste
1 cup millet
2 cups water

Directions

Preheat your oven to 350 degrees F. Place your tomatoes in a roasting pan. Drizzle olive oil over them; season with salt and pepper. Roast for about 35 minutes or until the tomatoes are soft.

Meanwhile, combine the millet with water in the inner pot of your Instant Pot.

Secure the lid. Choose the "Manual" mode and cook for 9 minutes at High pressure. Once cooking is complete, use a natural pressure release for 10 minutes; carefully remove the lid.

Add the roasted tomatoes to the warm millet and serve immediately.

Per serving: 162 Calories; 3.8g Fat; 27.2g Carbs; 4.5g Protein; 2.7g Sugars

752. Chickpea and Avocado Bowl

(Ready in about 1 hour | Servings 6)

Ingredients

1 cup chickpeas, rinsed
1 teaspoon sea salt
1 teaspoon baking soda
1 avocado, peeled, pitted, and sliced
1/2 cup scallions, sliced
1 cup cherry tomatoes, halved
1 bell pepper, sliced
1/4 cup olive oil
2 tablespoons fresh lemon juice
1/4 teaspoon curry powder
Sea salt and ground black pepper, to taste

Directions

Add the dry chickpeas to the inner pot; pour in 6 cups of water. Add the sea salt and baking soda.

Secure the lid. Choose the "Manual" mode and cook for 35 minutes at High pressure. Once cooking is complete, use a natural pressure release for 20 minutes; carefully remove the lid.

Drain and transfer to a nice serving bowl. Toss the cooked chickpeas with the other ingredients; toss to combine well. Bon appétit!

Per serving: 190 Calories; 7g Fat; 26.2g Carbs; 8g Protein; 5.1g Sugars

753. Parmesan Brussels Sprouts

(Ready in about 15 minutes | Servings 6)

Ingredients

1 ½ pounds Brussels sprouts, trimmed and halved
1 stick butter
1/2 teaspoon basil
1 teaspoon rosemary
1 teaspoon garlic, minced
1 teaspoon shallot powder
Sea salt and red pepper, to taste

Directions

Place 1 cup of water and a steamer basket in the inner pot of your Instant Pot. Place the Brussels sprouts in the steamer basket.

Secure the lid. Choose the "Steam" mode and cook for 3 minutes at High pressure. Once cooking is complete, use a quick pressure release; carefully remove the lid.

Press the "Sauté" button and melt the butter; once hot, cook the basil, rosemary, and garlic for 40 seconds or until aromatic.

Add in the Brussels sprouts, shallot powder, salt, and pepper. Press the "Cancel" button. Scatter the grated parmesan cheese over the Brussels sprouts and serve immediately. Bon appétit!

Per serving: 184 Calories; 15.8g Fat; 10.1g Carbs; 3.9g Protein; 2.5g Sugars

754. Steamed Root Veggies with Spicy Horseradish Mayo

(Ready in about 10 minutes | Servings 4)

Ingredients

1 1/3 cups water
1 celery with leaves, chopped
1 turnip, sliced
1 carrot, sliced
1 red onion, sliced
1/4 teaspoon dried dill weed
1 teaspoon garlic powder
1/2 teaspoon sea salt
1/2 teaspoon ground pepper
2 tablespoons fresh parsley
For the Horseradish Mayo:
1 tablespoon horseradish, well drained
1/2 cup mayonnaise
2 teaspoons Dijon mustard

Directions

Add 1 1/3 cups of water and a steamer basket to the Instant Pot.

Arrange the celery, turnip, carrot, and onion in the steamer basket. Season the vegetables with dried dill weed, garlic powder, sea salt, and ground pepper.

Secure the lid and choose the "Manual" mode, High pressure and 3 minutes. Once cooking is complete, use a quick release; remove the lid carefully.

In a mixing bowl, combine the horseradish, mayonnaise, and Dijon mustard. Garnish the steamed vegetables with fresh parsley; serve with the horseradish mayo on the side. Bon appétit!

Per serving: 116 Calories; 9.7g Fat; 5.2g Carbs; 2.4g Protein; 2.6g Sugars

755. Steamed Broccoli with Seeds

(Ready in about 10 minutes | Servings 4)

Ingredients

1 head (1 ½-pound) broccoli, broken into florets
2 tablespoons extra-virgin olive oil
2 garlic cloves, pressed
2 tablespoons mayonnaise
2 tablespoons balsamic vinegar
1 teaspoon Dijon mustard
Salt and black pepper, to taste
1/2 teaspoon dried basil
1/2 teaspoon dried oregano
1 teaspoon dried parsley flakes
2 tablespoons pepitas
2 tablespoons sunflower seeds
2 tablespoons sesame seeds

Directions

Add 1 cup of water and a steamer basket to the bottom of your Instant Pot. Place the broccoli florets in the steamer basket.

Secure the lid and choose the "Steam" mode; cook for 6 minutes under High pressure. Once cooking is complete, use a quick release; carefully remove the lid.

While the broccoli is still hot, add the remaining ingredients. Toss to combine and serve at room temperature.

Per serving: 199 Calories; 15.6g Fat; 9.9g Carbs; 8.7g Protein; 2.9g Sugars

756. Buttery Wax Beans with Sunflower Kernels

(Ready in about 10 minutes | Servings 6)

Ingredients

2 pounds wax beans
1 red onion, finely chopped
1 teaspoon garlic, smashed
1 ½ cups chicken stock
Black pepper, to taste
1/2 teaspoon cayenne pepper
2 tablespoons butter, melted
1 tablespoon fresh Italian parsley, roughly chopped
2 tablespoons toasted sunflower kernels

Directions

Add the wax beans, onion, garlic, stock, black pepper, cayenne pepper, and butter to the Instant Pot.

Secure the lid and choose the "Steam" mode; cook for 3 minutes under High pressure. Once cooking is complete, use a quick release; carefully remove the lid.

Transfer the cooked beans to a serving bowl; garnish with parsley and sunflower kernels and serve right now. Bon appétit!

Per serving: 115 Calories; 6.8g Fat; 11.2g Carbs; 4.2g Protein; 3.1g Sugars

757. Broccoli with Two-Cheese and Chili Dip

(Ready in about 15 minutes | Servings 6)

Ingredients

1 cup water
1 ½ pounds broccoli, broken into florets
For the Sauce:
1 (15-ounces) can of chili
1 cup Ricotta cheese, crumbled
1 ¼ cups Gruyère cheese shredded
1/4 cup salsa

Directions

Add water to the base of your Instant Pot.

Put the broccoli florets into the steaming basket. Transfer the steaming basket to the Instant Pot.

Secure the lid. Choose the "Manual" mode and High pressure; cook for 3 minutes. Once cooking is complete, use a quick pressure release; carefully remove the lid.

Now, cook all the sauce ingredients in a sauté pan that is preheated over medium-low flame. Cook for 7 minutes or until everything is incorporated.

Serve the steamed broccoli with the sauce on the side. Bon appétit!

Per serving: 246 Calories; 14.5g Fat; 13.6g Carbs; 17.1g Protein; 2.8g Sugars

758. Winter Root Vegetable Soup

(Ready in about 45 minutes | Servings 8)

Ingredients

2 stalks celery, chopped
2 parsnips, chopped
2 carrots, chopped
1 pound potatoes, cubed
1/2 pound turnip, chopped
1 onion, chopped
2 garlic cloves, minced
4 cups water, or as needed
3 cups chicken stock
1/2 stick butter, at room temperature
1/2 teaspoon mustard seeds
2 bay leaves
1 teaspoon paprika
1/2 teaspoon ground black pepper
Salt, to taste

Directions

Place the celery, parsnip, carrots, potatoes, turnip, onion and garlic in the Instant Pot; now, pour in the water and stock.

Secure the lid. Select the "Soup" setting; cook for 25 minutes at High pressure. Once cooking is complete, use a quick pressure release; carefully remove the lid.

Stir in the butter and seasonings; press the "Sauté" button and continue to cook the soup for 14 to 16 minutes more or until everything is heated through. Discard the bay leaves and serve hot.

Per serving: 150 Calories; 6.7g Fat; 18.9g Carbs; 4.7g Protein; 3.3g Sugars

759. Acorn Squash and Candy Onion Soup

(Ready in about 25 minutes | Servings 6)

Ingredients

2 tablespoons ghee, melted
1 cup candy onions, chopped
1 garlic clove, minced
2 bell peppers, deveined and chopped
1 ½ pounds acorn squash, shredded
1 carrot, chopped
1 celery, chopped
6 ounces cream cheese
1 bay leaf
2 cups water
4 cups vegetable stock

Directions

Press the "Sauté" button to heat up the Instant Pot; melt the ghee and sauté the candy onions, garlic and peppers until they are softened.

Add the remaining ingredients.

Secure the lid. Select the "Soup" setting; cook for 20 minutes at High pressure. Once cooking is complete, use a quick pressure release; carefully remove the lid.

Afterwards, purée the soup with an immersion blender and serve hot. Enjoy!

Per serving: 365 Calories; 23.3g Fat; 32.1g Carbs; 8.8g Protein; 16.8g Sugars

760. Aromatic Snow Peas

(Ready in about 10 minutes | Servings 4)

Ingredients

1 ½ tablespoons coconut oil
1 pound snow peas, frozen
2 carrots, sliced
1 parsnip, sliced
Seasoned salt, to taste
1 cup water
1/2 teaspoon ground black pepper
1/2 teaspoon red pepper flakes, crushed
1 tablespoon white sugar

Directions

Add all of the above ingredients to your Instant Pot.

Secure the lid. Select the "Steam" setting; cook for 4 minutes at High pressure. Once cooking is complete, use a quick pressure release; carefully remove the lid.

Transfer everything to a serving dish. Enjoy!

Per serving: 126 Calories; 5.4g Fat; 16.9g Carbs; 3.6g Protein; 8.1g Sugars

761. Easy and Delicious Petite Potatoes

(Ready in about 30 minutes | Servings 4)

Ingredients

3 tablespoons butter, melted
2 garlic cloves, minced
2 tablespoons parsley, finely chopped
1 ½ pounds baby potatoes
2 sprigs rosemary, leaves only
1/2 teaspoon ginger powder
1/2 teaspoon lime zest, grated
1 cup chicken stock
1/2 teaspoon turmeric powder
Coarse sea salt and ground black pepper, to taste

Directions

Press the "Sauté" button to heat up the Instant Pot. Warm the butter and the add garlic, parsley, potatoes, rosemary, ginger, and lime zest.

Sauté the potatoes, turning them periodically, about 8 minutes. Add the stock, turmeric powder, salt, and black pepper.

Secure the lid. Select the "Manual" setting; cook for 12 minutes at High pressure. Once cooking is complete, use a quick pressure release; carefully remove the lid.

Serve warm and enjoy!

Per serving: 220 Calories; 9.2g Fat; 30.4g Carbs; 5g Protein; 1.3g Sugars

762. Creamed Cabbage with Ham

(Ready in about 20 minutes | Servings 4)

Ingredients

1 ½ tablespoons olive oil
1 leek, chopped
1 celery rib, chopped
2 garlic cloves, chopped
1 pound cabbage, shredded
3 ½ cups broth, preferably homemade
Sea salt, to taste
1/2 teaspoon black peppercorns
2 bay leaves
1 cup fully cooked ham, cubed
1 cup double cream
1/4 cup fresh chives, chopped

Directions

Press the "Sauté" button on your Instant Pot; add the olive oil. Once hot, cook the leeks for 3 minutes or until they are softened.

Stir in the celery and cook for 3 minutes more. Add a splash of broth if needed. Now, add the garlic and cook for 30 seconds more or until it is fragrant.

Add the cabbage, broth, salt, black peppercorns, and bay leaves. Secure the lid.

Choose the "Manual" mode and cook for 3 minutes at High pressure. Once cooking is complete, use a quick release; carefully remove the lid.

Fold in the ham and double cream and continue to cook in the residual heat for 5 minutes longer.

Taste, adjust the seasonings and serve in individual bowls, garnished with fresh chopped chives. Enjoy!

Per serving: 292 Calories; 19.5g Fat; 16.6g Carbs; 14.6g Protein; 7.9g Sugars

763. Chinese-Style Glazed Baby Carrots

(Ready in about 20 minutes | Servings 4)

Ingredients

3 tablespoons ghee
1/4 cup champagne vinegar
2 teaspoons honey
3/4 cup water
2 tablespoons soy sauce
1/2 teaspoon kosher salt
1/2 teaspoon ground white pepper
1/2 teaspoon paprika
1 ½ pounds baby carrots
2 tablespoons sesame seeds, toasted

Directions

Press the "Sauté" button on your Instant Pot. Place all of the above ingredients, except for the carrots and sesame seeds, in your Instant Pot.

Cook this mixture for 1 minute, stirring frequently. Stir in baby carrots.

Secure the lid. Select the "Steam" setting; cook for 10 minutes at High pressure. Once cooking is complete, use a quick pressure release; carefully remove the lid.

Press the "Sauté" button one more time. Let it simmer until the sauce has reduced and thickened. Sprinkle with sesame seeds and serve at room temperature. Enjoy!

Per serving: 175 Calories; 10.3g Fat; 19.4g Carbs; 1.8g Protein; 12.6g Sugars

764. Broccoli and Celery Chowder

(Ready in about 35 minutes | Servings 6)

Ingredients

1/2 cup leeks, chopped
1 pound broccoli, broken into small florets
1/2 pound celery, chopped
1 carrot, sliced
2 potatoes, peeled and diced
3 cups water
2 cups roasted-vegetable stock
Kosher salt, to taste
1/4 teaspoon ground black pepper
1/4 teaspoon red pepper flakes, crushed
1 cup sour cream

Directions

Simply place all of the above ingredients, except for the sour cream, in your Instant Pot.

Secure the lid. Select the "Soup" setting; cook for 30 minutes at High pressure. Once cooking is complete, use a quick pressure release; carefully remove the lid.

Then, puree the soup with an immersion blender. Serve in individual bowls, garnished with a dollop of sour cream. Bon appétit!

Per serving: 193 Calories; 5.5g Fat; 28.6g Carbs; 9.2g Protein; 2.1g Sugars

765. Golden Potato and Cauliflower Soup

(Ready in about 35 minutes | Servings 6)

Ingredients

1 pound cauliflower, broken into florets
1/2 pound yellow potatoes, diced
1 carrot, sliced
1 celery, chopped
2 garlic cloves, pressed
1/2 cup yellow onion, chopped
4 cups vegetable broth
1 cup water
1/2 teaspoon turmeric powder
1/4 teaspoon ground black pepper
1/2 teaspoon sea salt
1/2 teaspoon mustard seeds
1 cup yellow Swiss cheese, shredded

Directions

Throw all of the above ingredients, except for the Swiss cheese, into the Instant Pot.

Secure the lid. Select the "Soup" setting; cook for 30 minutes at High pressure. Once cooking is complete, use a quick pressure release; carefully remove the lid.

After that, puree the soup with an immersion blender. Divide the soup among six soup bowls; top each serving with shredded Swiss cheese. Bon appétit!

Per serving: 175 Calories; 8.2g Fat; 13.9g Carbs; 11.7g Protein; 2.7g Sugars

766. Chinese-Style Vegetable Soup

(Ready in about 15 minutes | Servings 4)

Ingredients

2 tablespoons sesame oil, softened
2 shallots, chopped
2 cloves garlic, smashed
1/2 pound mushroom, sliced
2 carrots, trimmed and chopped
Sea salt and freshly ground pepper, to taste
1/2 teaspoon dried dill
1 teaspoon smoked paprika
2 tablespoons mijiu (rice wine)
3 cups water
1/2 cup milk
1 tablespoon light soy sauce
2 tablespoons fresh parsley, roughly chopped

Directions

Press the "Sauté" button and heat the oil. Once hot, sweat the shallots and garlic until tender and translucent.

Add the mushrooms and carrots. Season with salt, ground pepper, dill, and paprika. Sauté for 3 more minutes more or until the carrots have softened. Add rice wine to deglaze the pan.

Add the water, milk, and light soy sauce. Secure the lid. Choose the "Manual" function, High pressure and 5 minutes.

Once cooking is complete, use a quick release; carefully remove the lid. Taste, adjust the seasonings and serve in individual bowls, garnished with fresh parsley. Bon appétit!

Per serving: 117 Calories; 8.7g Fat; 7.6g Carbs; 3.4g Protein; 4.6g Sugars

767. Vegetarian Mushroom Stroganoff

(Ready in about 45 minutes | Servings 8)

Ingredients

2 tablespoons olive oil
1 cup shallots, chopped
2 garlic cloves, minced
2 russet potatoes, chopped
1 celery with leaves, chopped
1 bell pepper, seeded and thinly sliced
1 habanero pepper, minced
14 ounces brown mushrooms, thinly sliced
1 cup water
1 cup vegetable stock
Sea salt and ground black pepper, to taste
1/2 teaspoon Hungarian paprika
1/2 teaspoon cayenne pepper
2 bay leaves
1 ripe tomato, seeded and chopped
2 tablespoons corn flour, plus 3 tablespoons of water

Directions

Press the "Sauté" button to heat up the Instant Pot. Then, heat the olive oil and sauté the shallot, garlic, potatoes, and celery until they are softened; add a splash of vegetable stock, if needed.

Stir in the mushrooms, water, stock, paprika, cayenne pepper, bay leaves, and tomatoes.

Secure the lid. Select the "Meat/Stew" setting; cook for 35 minutes at High pressure. Once cooking is complete, use a quick pressure release; carefully remove the lid.

Make the slurry by whisking the corn flour with 3 tablespoons of water. Add the slurry back to the Instant Pot and press the "Sauté" button one more time.

Allow it to cook until the liquid has thickened. Discard the bay leaves and serve warm.

Per serving: 137 Calories; 3.9g Fat; 23g Carbs; 4.5g Protein; 2.8g Sugars

768. Springtime Broccoli Salad

(Ready in about 10 minutes | Servings 4)

Ingredients

1 large (1 ½-pound) head broccoli, cut into small florets
1 teaspoon Dijon seeds
1/4 cup extra-virgin olive oil
1 tablespoon tahini paste
2 tablespoons lemon juice
2 spring garlic stalks, smashed
2 green onions, chopped
1 cup radishes, sliced
2 tablespoons parsley leaves, roughly chopped
Salt and ground black pepper, to taste
1 ½ cups feta cheese, crumbled

Directions

Prepare your Instant Pot by adding 1 cup of water and a steamer basket to its bottom.

Place the broccoli in the steamer basket.

Secure the lid. Choose the "Manual" mode and High pressure; cook for 5 minutes. Once cooking is complete, use a quick pressure release; carefully remove the lid.

Afterwards, toss your broccoli with the remaining ingredients. Serve at room temperature with garlic croutons if desired. Enjoy!

Per serving: 302 Calories; 21.1g Fat; 18.2g Carbs; 14.2g Protein; 7.4g Sugars

769. Classic Green Artichoke Dip

(Ready in about 20 minutes | Servings 10)

Ingredients

1 can (14-ounce) artichoke hearts, drained and roughly chopped
1/2 pound kale leaves, fresh or frozen torn into pieces
1 cup cream cheese
1 cup Colby cheese, shredded
1 cup mayonnaise
1 teaspoon yellow mustard
2 garlic cloves, minced
1 teaspoon shallot powder
1 teaspoon fennel seeds
Sea salt and ground black pepper, to taste

Directions

Place 1 cup of water and a metal rack in your Instant Pot.

Then, thoroughly combine all ingredients in a casserole dish that is previously greased with a nonstick cooking spray; cover the casserole dish with a piece of aluminum foil, making a foil sling if needed.

Lower the casserole dish onto the rack.

Secure the lid. Select the "Steam" setting; cook for 10 minutes at High pressure. Once cooking is complete, use a quick pressure release; carefully remove the lid.

Serve with chips or pita wedges. Enjoy!

Per serving: 219 Calories; 19g Fat; 5.5g Carbs; 7.6g Protein; 1.7g Sugars

770. Cheesy Sweet Potatoes with Spring Onions

(Ready in about 15 minutes | Servings 4)

Ingredients

1 cup water
1 ½ pounds sweet potatoes, cubed
1/2 cup spring onions, roughly chopped
2 tablespoons extra-virgin olive oil
1/2 cup Romano cheese, freshly grated
1/2 teaspoon cayenne pepper
Kosher salt and freshly ground black pepper, to taste

Directions

Pour 1 cup of water into the base of your Instant Pot. Put the sweet potatoes into the steaming basket. Transfer the steaming basket to the Instant Pot.

Secure the lid and choose the "Manual" button, High pressure and 9 minutes. Once cooking is complete, use a natural release; carefully remove the lid.

Toss the warm potatoes with the spring onions, olive oil, Romano cheese, cayenne pepper, salt, and black pepper. Serve immediately and enjoy!

Per serving: 109 Calories; 5.9g Fat; 10g Carbs; 5.6g Protein; 0.2g Sugars

771. Classic Belgian Endive

(Ready in about 6 minutes | Servings 2)

Ingredients

2 tablespoons sesame oil
2 garlic cloves, minced
1/2 cup scallions, chopped
1 pound Belgian endive, halved lengthwise
1/4 cup champagne vinegar
1 teaspoon lime juice
1 teaspoon Dijon mustard
1 tablespoon soy sauce
1 cup water
1/2 teaspoon crushed red pepper flakes
Sea salt and ground black pepper, to taste
1 bay leaf

Directions

Press the "Sauté" button to heat up the Instant Pot; heat the sesame oil. Once hot, cook the garlic and scallions for 40 seconds to a minute or until aromatic.

Add the Belgian endive, vinegar, lime juice, mustard, soy sauce water, red pepper, salt, black pepper, and bay leaf.

Secure the lid. Choose the "Manual" mode and Low pressure; cook for 2 minutes or until tender when pierced with the tip of a knife.

Once cooking is complete, use a quick pressure release; carefully remove the lid. Serve immediately.

Per serving: 203 Calories; 15.6g Fat; 13g Carbs; 4.1g Protein; 2.9g Sugars

772. Italian-Style Potatoes

(Ready in about 20 minutes | Servings 6)

Ingredients

6 white potatoes, cut into cubes
1/2 teaspoon shallot powder
1 teaspoon garlic powder
1 teaspoon oregano, dried
2 sprigs rosemary, leaves picked
Coarse salt, to taste
1/2 teaspoon freshly ground black pepper
1/4 cup extra-virgin olive oil
3/4 cup beef broth
1/4 cup brown ale
1 cup Pecorino Romano cheese, grated
1/4 cup Italian flat-leaf parsley, chopped

Directions

Toss the potato cubes with shallot powder, garlic powder, oregano, rosemary, salt, and black pepper.

Press the "Sauté" button and heat the oil. Now, cook the potatoes for 5 minutes, stirring periodically.

Add the broth and brown ale; secure the lid. Choose the "Manual" mode and cook for 9 minutes at High pressure.

Once cooking is complete, use a quick release; carefully remove the lid. Toss the warm potatoes with the Pecorino Romano and serve garnished with Italian parsley. Enjoy!

Per serving: 270 Calories; 9g Fat; 38.8g Carbs; 9.2g Protein; 1.6g Sugars

773. Green Beans with Pancetta

(Ready in about 10 minutes | Servings 4)

Ingredients

2 tablespoons sesame oil
2 garlic cloves, pressed
1 yellow onion, chopped
5 ounces pancetta, diced
1 ½ pounds green beans, cut in half
Kosher salt, to taste
1/4 teaspoon ground black pepper
1/2 teaspoon cayenne pepper
1/2 teaspoon dried oregano
1/2 teaspoon dried dill
1 cup water

Directions

Press the "Sauté" button to heat up your Instant Pot. Now, heat the sesame oil and sauté the garlic and onion until softened and fragrant; set it aside.

After that, stir in the pancetta and continue to cook for a further 4 minutes; crumble with a fork and set it aside.

Add the remaining ingredients; stir to combine.

Secure the lid. Choose the "Manual" mode and Low pressure; cook for 3 minutes. Once cooking is complete, use a quick pressure release; carefully remove the lid.

Serve warm, garnished with the reserved onion/garlic mixture and pancetta. Bon appétit!

Per serving: 177 Calories; 12.1g Fat; 9.9g Carbs; 8.8g Protein; 2.3g Sugars

774. Kid-Friendly Stuffed Peppers

(Ready in about 10 minutes | Servings 4)

Ingredients

8 baby bell peppers, seeded and sliced lengthwise
1 tablespoon peanut oil
6 ounces Cheddar cheese, grated
2 ounces sour cream
2 garlic cloves, smashed
1/2 white onion, finely chopped
Sea salt and ground black pepper, to taste
1/2 teaspoon paprika
1/2 teaspoon dill, fresh or dried

Directions

Start by adding 1 cup of water and a steamer basket to the Instant Pot.

Then, thoroughly combine all ingredients, except for the peppers. Then, stuff the peppers with this mixture.

Arrange the peppers in the steamer basket.

Secure the lid. Choose the "Manual" mode and High pressure; cook for 5 minutes. Once cooking is complete, use a quick pressure release; carefully remove the lid.

Serve immediately and enjoy!

Per serving: 168 Calories; 8.8g Fat; 15.8g Carbs; 8.2g Protein; 8.2g Sugars

775. Greek-Style Veggie Souvlaki

(Ready in about 10 minutes | Servings 4)

Ingredients

1 head broccoli, broken into florets and blanched
2 bell peppers, seeded and diced
2 medium zucchinis, cut into 1-inch slices
8 ounces button mushrooms, whole
2 cups cherry tomatoes
4 tablespoons olive oil
Fresh juice of 1/2 lemon
Sea salt and ground black pepper, to taste
1 teaspoon dried oregano
1 teaspoon dried rosemary
1/4 teaspoon ground bay leaves
1/2 teaspoon crushed red pepper

Directions

Prepare your Instant Pot by adding 1 cup of water and a metal rack to its bottom.

Thread the vegetables onto bamboo or wooden skewers.

Drizzle them with olive oil and fresh lemon juice; add the seasonings.

Secure the lid. Choose the "Manual" mode and High pressure; cook for 3 minutes. Once cooking is complete, use a quick pressure release; carefully remove the lid. Bon appétit!

Per serving: 224 Calories; 14.3g Fat; 22.5g Carbs; 6.4g Protein; 13.4g Sugars

776. Ranch Cauliflower Dipping Sauce

(Ready in about 10 minutes | Servings 8)

Ingredients

1 head cauliflower, cut into florets
1 cup tomato puree
1/2 cup red onion, chopped
1 teaspoon fresh garlic, pressed
1 tablespoon fresh cilantro, chopped
1/2 tablespoon fresh rosemary, chopped
Sea salt, to taste
1/4 teaspoon ground black pepper, or more to taste
1 teaspoon crushed red pepper
1 teaspoon Ranch seasoning mix
1 cup mayonnaise
1 cup Ricotta cheese, at room temperature

Directions

Prepare your Instant Pot by adding 1 cup of water and a steamer basket to its bottom.

Arrange the cauliflower florets in the steamer basket.

Secure the lid. Choose the "Manual" mode and Low pressure; cook for 5 minutes. Once cooking is complete, use a quick pressure release; carefully remove the lid.

Add the cauliflower to your food processor; add the remaining ingredients. Process until everything is well incorporated.

Place in your refrigerator until ready to use. Bon appétit!

Per serving: 176 Calories; 13.7g Fat; 7.4g Carbs; 6.5g Protein; 2.8g Sugars

777. Cheesy Brussels Sprouts

(Ready in about 15 minutes | Servings 4)

Ingredients

1 ½ pounds Brussels sprouts, trimmed
3 tablespoons ghee
2 garlic cloves, minced
1/2 cup scallions, finely chopped
Salt, to taste
1/2 teaspoon freshly ground black pepper
1/2 teaspoon red pepper flakes
1 cup Romano cheese, grated

Directions

Place 1 cup of water and a steamer basket on the bottom of your Instant Pot. Place the Brussels sprouts in the steamer basket.

Secure the lid. Choose the "Steam" mode and High pressure; cook for 5 minutes. Once cooking is complete, use a quick pressure release; carefully remove the lid.

While the Brussels sprouts are still hot, add the ghee, garlic, scallions, salt, black pepper, red pepper, and Romano cheese; toss to coat well and serve.

Per serving: 261 Calories; 16.2g Fat; 20.1g Carbs; 13.2g Protein; 4.1g Sugars

778. Red Beet Salad with Goat Cheese

(Ready in about 30 minutes | Servings 6)

Ingredients

1 ½ pounds red beets
1/4 cup apple cider vinegar
1 teaspoon yellow mustard
1 teaspoon honey
Kosher salt and ground black pepper, to taste
1 teaspoon cumin seeds
1/4 cup extra-virgin olive oil
1 cup goat cheese, crumbled

Directions

Add 1 ½ cups of water and beets to your Instant Pot.

Secure the lid. Choose "Manual" mode and High pressure; cook for 25 minutes. Once cooking is complete, use a quick pressure release; carefully remove the lid.

After that, rub off the skins; cut the beets into wedges. Transfer them to a serving bowl.

Thoroughly combine the vinegar, mustard, honey, salt, black pepper, cumin seeds, and olive oil. Dress the salad, top with goat cheese and serve well chilled.

Per serving: 222 Calories; 16.1g Fat; 12.9g Carbs; 7.5g Protein; 9.1g Sugars

779. Holiday Mashed Carrots

(Ready in about 10 minutes | Servings 6)

Ingredients

1 cup water
2 pounds carrots, chopped
2 tablespoons butter, room temperature
1 teaspoon paprika
1 teaspoon coriander
Kosher salt, to taste
1/2 teaspoon ground black
1/4 cup heavy cream

Directions

Add water to the base of your Instant Pot.

Put the carrots into the steaming basket. Transfer the steaming basket to the Instant Pot.

Secure the lid and choose the "Manual" button, High pressure and 3 minutes. Once cooking is complete, use a natural release; remove the lid carefully.

Mash the carrots with a fork or potato masher. Add the butter, paprika, coriander, salt, ground black, and heavy cream.

Taste, adjust the seasonings and serve immediately. Bon appétit!

Per serving: 113 Calories; 6g Fat; 14.6g Carbs; 1.5g Protein; 7.3g Sugars

780. Spicy Chanterelles with Purple Cabbage

(Ready in about 15 minutes | Servings 4)

Ingredients

3 teaspoons olive oil
1/2 pound Chanterelle mushrooms, thinly sliced
1 pound purple cabbage, cut into wedges
2 red onions, cut into wedges
2 garlic cloves, smashed
1/3 cup Worcestershire sauce
2 tablespoons champagne vinegar
1 teaspoon cayenne pepper
Salt, to taste
1/2 teaspoon ground bay leaf
1/3 teaspoon white pepper
1/2 teaspoon adobo seasoning

Directions

Press the "Sauté" button to heat up the Instant Pot; heat the oil. Once hot, add the mushrooms; cook until they are lightly browned, about 4 minutes.

Add the other ingredients in the order listed above. Gently stir to combine and secure the lid.

Now, choose the "Manual" setting, High pressure and 4 minutes.

Once cooking is complete, use a quick release; remove the lid carefully. Bon appétit!

Per serving: 121 Calories; 3.8g Fat; 20.3g Carbs; 4g Protein; 10.1g Sugars

781. Greek-Style Vegetables with Halloumi Cheese

(Ready in about 10 minutes | Servings 4)

Ingredients

1 tablespoon olive oil
1 tablespoon butter
2 garlic cloves, minced
1/2 cup shallots, chopped
12 ounces button mushrooms, thinly sliced
1 pepperoncini pepper, minced
1/2 pound eggplant, sliced
1/2 pound zucchini, sliced
1 teaspoon dried basil
2 rosemary sprigs, leaves picked
1 thyme sprig, leaves picked
2 tomatoes, chopped
1/3 cup water
1/2 cup dry Greek wine
8 ounces Halloumi cheese, cubed
1/2 cup Kalamata olives, pitted and halved

Directions

Press the "Sauté" button to heat up your Instant Pot; heat the olive oil and butter. Cook the garlic and shallots for 1 to 2 minutes, stirring occasionally.

Stir in the mushrooms, pepper, eggplant, and zucchini and continue to sauté an additional 2 to 3 minutes.

After that, add the basil, rosemary, thyme, tomatoes, water, and wine.

Secure the lid. Choose the "Manual" mode and Low pressure; cook for 3 minutes. Once cooking is complete, use a quick pressure release; carefully remove the lid.

Garnish each serving with the Halloumi cheese and olives; serve warm or at room temperature.

Per serving: 305 Calories; 20.8g Fat; 18.4g Carbs; 15.2g Protein; 10.4g Sugars

782. Herbed Zucchini Appetizer

(Ready in about 10 minutes | Servings 4)

Ingredients

1 ½ tablespoons olive oil
2 garlic cloves, minced
1 ½ pounds zucchini, cut into thick slices
1/2 cup water
1/2 cup vegetable broth
1/2 teaspoon dried oregano
1 teaspoon basil, fresh or dried
1 teaspoon rosemary, fresh or dried
1/3 teaspoon smoked paprika
1/3 teaspoon ground black pepper
Coarse sea salt, to taste

Directions

Press the "Sauté" button to heat up your Instant Pot; heat the olive oil. Once hot, cook the garlic for 1 minute.

Add the remaining ingredients.

Secure the lid. Choose the "Manual" mode and Low pressure; cook for 3 minutes. Once cooking is complete, use a quick pressure release; carefully remove the lid. Bon appétit!

Per serving: 88 Calories; 5.9g Fat; 5.9g Carbs; 5.3g Protein; 0g Sugars

783. Farmhouse Vegetable Stew

(Ready in about 35 minutes | Servings 4)

Ingredients

2 tablespoons butter, at room temperature
1 leek, chopped
2 carrots, trimmed and chopped
2 cups white mushrooms, thinly sliced
1 teaspoon garlic, minced
2 sprigs rosemary, leaves picked
2 sprigs thyme, leaves picked
2 ½ cups stock, preferably homemade
3 ripe tomatoes, pureed
1 jalapeno pepper, deveined and chopped
1/2 pound white potatoes, peeled and diced
Sea salt, to taste
1/2 teaspoon ground black pepper
1 ½ tablespoons cornstarch

Directions

Pres the "Sauté" button and melt the butter. Now, sauté the leek and carrots until they are tender, about 3 minutes.

Add the mushrooms, garlic, rosemary, and thyme; cook an additional 3 minutes or until they are aromatic and tender.

Add a splash of homemade stock to deglaze the pan. Add the remaining stock, pureed tomatoes, jalapeno pepper, potatoes, salt, and black pepper.

Secure the lid and choose "Soup" mode. Cook for 20 minutes at High pressure. Once cooking is complete, use a quick release; carefully remove the lid.

Meanwhile, make the cornstarch slurry by whisking 1 ½ tablespoons of cornstarch with 2 tablespoons of water. Add the slurry to the Instant Pot.

Cook the cooking liquid in the residual heat for 5 minutes longer or until it has thickened. Ladle into individual bowls and serve warm. Enjoy!

Per serving: 181 Calories; 7.3g Fat; 24.1g Carbs; 6.1g Protein; 5.1g Sugars

784. Saucy and Sticky Portobellos

(Ready in about 10 minutes | Servings 4)

Ingredients

1 ½ pounds portobello mushrooms
1 cup vegetable stock
2 ripe tomatoes, chopped
2/3 teaspoon porcini powder
Sea salt and ground black pepper, to taste
2 garlic cloves, minced
1/2 teaspoon mustard seeds
1 teaspoon celery seeds
1 tablespoon apple cider vinegar
1 tablespoon dark soy sauce
1 tablespoon brown sugar
1/2 teaspoon liquid smoke

Directions

Add all of the above ingredients to your Instant Pot; stir to combine well.

Secure the lid. Choose the "Manual" mode and High pressure; cook for 4 minutes. Once cooking is complete, use a natural pressure release; carefully remove the lid. Serve warm and enjoy!

Per serving: 89 Calories; 2.1g Fat; 14.2g Carbs; 6.2g Protein; 9.2g Sugars

785. Spicy Cauliflower with Yogurt Sauce

(Ready in about 10 minutes | Servings 4)

Ingredients

1 tablespoon peanut oil
1 yellow onion, chopped
1 clove garlic, pressed
1 teaspoon curry powder
1 habanero pepper, minced
1 tablespoon fresh cilantro, chopped
1 tablespoon fresh parsley, chopped
1/2 teaspoon ground black pepper
1/2 teaspoon red pepper flakes
Sea salt, to taste
2 tomatoes, puréed
1 ½ pounds cauliflower, broken into florets
1/2 cup vegetable stock, preferably homemade
1/2 cup Greek-style yogurt

Directions

Press the "Sauté" button to heat up your Instant Pot. Now, heat the oil and sauté the onion for 1 to 2 minutes.

Add the garlic and continue to cook until fragrant.

Stir in the remaining ingredients, except the yogurt; stir to combine well.

Secure the lid. Choose the "Manual" mode and High pressure; cook for 3 minutes. Once cooking is complete, use a quick pressure release; carefully remove the lid.

Pour in the yogurt, stir well, and serve immediately.

Per serving: 121 Calories; 6.6g Fat; 13.4g Carbs; 4.8g Protein; 5.8g Sugars

786. Old-Fashioned Italian Pepperonata

(Ready in about 15 minutes | Servings 4)

Ingredients

1 tablespoon olive oil
1 red onion, chopped
1 pepperoncini, seeded and minced
1 red bell pepper, seeded and chopped
1 yellow bell pepper, seeded and chopped
1 green bell peppers, seeded and chopped
2 ripe Roma tomatoes, pureed
1 teaspoon ginger-garlic paste
1 teaspoon dried rosemary
1 teaspoon dried oregano
1 teaspoon dried sage
1 cup vegetable broth
1/4 cup Italian dry white wine
1/2 teaspoon ground black pepper
1/2 teaspoon red pepper flakes, crushed
Sea salt, to taste

Directions

Press the "Sauté" button to heat up your Instant Pot. Heat the olive oil and sauté the onion until it is softened.

Add the remaining ingredients to your Instant Pot.

Secure the lid. Choose the "Manual" mode and High pressure; cook for 3 minutes. Once cooking is complete, use a quick pressure release; carefully remove the lid.

Press the "Sauté" button one more time and thicken the liquid about 4 minutes, stirring periodically.

Serve warm in individual bowls. Bon appétit!

Per serving: 97 Calories; 4.1g Fat; 10g Carbs; 3.1g Protein; 4.1g Sugars

787. Classic Cream of Celery Soup

(Ready in about 10 minutes | Servings 4)

Ingredients

1 tablespoon sesame oil
1 teaspoon garlic, minced
1/2 cup leeks, chopped
1 pound celery with leaves, chopped
1 (2-inch) piece young galangal, peeled and chopped
1/2 teaspoon ground bay leaves

1 fresh jalapeño peppers, seeded and finely chopped
4 cups roasted vegetable stock, preferably homemade
Sea salt and freshly ground black pepper, to taste
1/4 teaspoon grated nutmeg
1/2 cup coconut cream, unsweetened

Directions

Press the "Sauté" button to heat up your Instant Pot. Heat the sesame oil and sauté the garlic and leeks until tender about 1 minute 30 seconds.

Stir in the celery and galangal; continue to cook for a further 2 minutes.

Next, add the ground bay leaves, jalapeño peppers, stock, salt, black pepper and nutmeg.

Secure the lid. Choose the "Manual" mode and High pressure; cook for 3 minutes. Once cooking is complete, use a quick pressure release; carefully remove the lid.

Then, purée the soup with an immersion blender until smooth and creamy. Return the pureed soup to the Instant Pot; fold in the coconut cream.

Afterwards, press the "Sauté" button. Allow your soup to simmer until thoroughly warmed. Ladle into soup bowls and serve hot. Bon appétit!

Per serving: 200 Calories; 15.9g Fat; 9.5g Carbs; 7.7g Protein; 3.7g Sugars

788. Dad's Gourmet Beet Salad

(Ready in about 15 minutes + chilling time | Servings 6)

Ingredients

2 cups water
1 ½ pounds red beets, washed, stems and leaves removed
2 tablespoons gourmet mustard
2 tablespoons honey
1/4 cup balsamic vinegar

1/4 cup olive oil
2 cups baby spinach
2 garlic cloves, pressed
2 tablespoons pecan halves, toasted

Directions

Add the water to the base of the Instant Pot. Put the beets into the steaming basket. Transfer the steaming basket to the Instant Pot.

Secure the lid and choose "Manual" button, High pressure and 8 minutes. Once cooking is complete, use a natural release; remove the lid carefully.

Let the beets cool enough to handle. Peel the cooked beets and cut them into thin slices.

Meanwhile, whisk the mustard, honey, vinegar, and olive oil. Toss the beets with this vinaigrette and add the baby spinach and garlic; stir to combine.

Garnish with toasted pecan halves and serve well-chilled. Bon appétit!

Per serving: 182 Calories; 11.1g Fat; 19.7g Carbs; 2.6g Protein; 15.1g Sugars

789. Indian-Style Vegetables with Naan

(Ready in about 20 minutes | Servings 6)

Ingredients

1 tablespoon sesame oil
2 bell pepper, seeded and sliced
1 red chili pepper, seeded and sliced
1 teaspoon garlic paste
1/2 teaspoon fresh ginger, grated
1 tablespoon garam masala
1/2 teaspoon dhania
1/2 teaspoon haldi
1/2 teaspoon ground black pepper

Sea salt, to taste
Naan:
1 tablespoon dry active yeast
1 teaspoon sugar
2/3 cup warm water
2 ½ cups all-purpose flour
1/2 teaspoon salt
1/4 cup vegetable oil
1 egg

Directions

Press the "Sauté" button to heat up your Instant Pot. Heat the oil until sizzling. Once hot, sauté the peppers, garlic, ginger, and spices.

Secure the lid. Choose the "Manual" mode and Low pressure; cook for 4 minutes. Once cooking is complete, use a quick pressure release; carefully remove the lid.

Meanwhile, make the naan by mixing the yeast, sugar and 2 tablespoons of warm water; allow it sit for 5 to 6 minutes.

Add the remaining ingredients for the naans; let it rest for about 1 hour at room temperature.

Now, divide the dough into six balls; flatten the balls on a working surface.

Heat up a large-sized pan over moderate heat. Cook the naans until they are golden on both sides. Serve these naans with the reserved vegetables and enjoy!

Per serving: 319 Calories; 12.7g Fat; 43.5g Carbs; 7.6g Protein; 1.7g Sugars

790. Swiss Chard with Caciocavallo

(Ready in about 15 minutes | Servings 4)

Ingredients

1/2 pound Canadian bacon, chopped
12 ounces Swiss chard, torn into pieces
1/2 cup vegetable broth
1/4 cup water
1/4 cup rose wine

1 teaspoon paprika
1/2 teaspoon dried basil
1/2 teaspoon dried marjoram
Sea salt and ground black pepper, to taste
1 cup Caciocavallo cheese, shredded

Directions

Press the "Sauté" button to heat up your Instant Pot. Once hot, cook the Canadian bacon until crisp; crumble with a fork and set it aside.

Stir in the remaining ingredients, except for the Caciocavallo cheese.

Secure the lid. Choose the "Manual" mode and Low pressure; cook for 4 minutes. Once cooking is complete, use a quick pressure release; carefully remove the lid.

Add the Caciocavallo cheese, cover with the lid and allow it to sit for a further 4 minutes or until your cheese is melted. Top each serving with the reserved bacon and serve warm.

Per serving: 214 Calories; 12.1g Fat; 5.8g Carbs; 22.1g Protein; 2.4g Sugars

791. Root Vegetable Sticks

(Ready in about 10 minutes | Servings 6)

Ingredients

2 tablespoons sesame oil
2 parsnips, peeled and halved lengthwise
2 carrots, cut into sticks
1 turnip, cut into sticks
1/2 teaspoon baking soda

1 tablespoon agave nectar
1/2 teaspoon kosher salt
1/2 teaspoon white pepper, ground
1/2 teaspoon fresh ginger, grated
1 teaspoon grated orange peel
1 cup water

Directions

Press the "Sauté" button to heat up your Instant Pot; heat the oil.

Sauté the vegetables until aromatic and tender. Now, add the remaining ingredients and gently stir to combine.

Secure the lid. Choose the "Manual" mode and High pressure; cook for 4 minutes. Once cooking is complete, use a quick pressure release; carefully remove the lid.

Serve warm or at room temperature.

Per serving: 99 Calories; 4.7g Fat; 14.4g Carbs; 1g Protein; 6.7g Sugars

RICE

792. Late Summer Rice Salad

(Ready in about 30 minutes | Servings 4)

Ingredients

1 ½ cups long-grain white rice, rinsed
1 3/4 cups water
1/2 teaspoon table salt
4 tablespoons extra-virgin olive oil
1 tablespoon orange zest
1/4 cup orange juice, freshly squeezed
1 cup grapes, cut in half
1/4 cup dried cranberries
1/2 cup pecans
2 tablespoons pomegranate arils

Directions

Place the rice, water, and salt in the inner pot of your Instant Pot; stir to combine.

Secure the lid. Choose the "Rice" mode and cook for 10 minutes. Once cooking is complete, use a natural pressure release for 15 minutes; carefully remove the lid.

Fluff the rice with a fork and allow it to cool to room temperature.

Add the remaining ingredients to a nice salad bowl; add the chilled rice. Toss to combine and serve chilled or at room temperature. Bon appétit!

Per serving: 544 Calories; 23.6g Fat; 77.9g Carbs; 6.5g Protein; 14.1g Sugars

793. Chicken Soup with Brown Basmati Rice

(Ready in about 45 minutes | Servings 4)

Ingredients

2 tablespoons olive oil
1/2 pound chicken breast, boneless and cut into small chunks
1 onion, chopped
2 cloves garlic, minced
2 carrots, peeled and diced
1 rib celery, diced
1 parsnip, peeled and diced
1/2 teaspoon dried basil
1/2 teaspoon dried thyme
5 cups chicken broth
1 cup brown basmati rice
Kosher salt and ground black pepper, to taste
1/2 cup coconut milk

Directions

Press the "Sauté" button and heat the oil until sizzling. Then, cook the chicken breast for 3 to 4 minutes or until no longer pink; reserve.

Now, add the onion and garlic and continue sautéing in pan drippings for 2 to 3 minutes more or until they are tender and fragrant.

Add the carrots, celery, parsnip, basil, thyme, broth, rice, salt, and black pepper. Add the chicken breasts back to the inner pot.

Secure the lid. Choose the "Soup/Broth" mode and cook for 20 minutes at High pressure. Once cooking is complete, use a natural pressure release for 15 minutes; carefully remove the lid.

Pour in the coconut milk; seal the lid and let it sit in the residual heat until heated through. Serve in soup bowls and enjoy!

Per serving: 435 Calories; 13.1g Fat; 51.9g Carbs; 27.8g Protein; 6.6g Sugars

794. Chicken Fillets Rice Bowl

(Ready in about 40 minutes | Servings 4)

Ingredients

2 tablespoons olive oil
1 pound chicken fillets, cut into strips
1 onion, chopped
1 teaspoon garlic, minced
1 teaspoon sea salt
1/2 teaspoon black pepper, divided
1/2 teaspoon ground coriander
1/4 teaspoon paprika
1 cup white rice
1 cup water
2 red chili peppers, seeded and chopped
1 cup green peas, thawed
1/2 cup salsa

Directions

Press the "Sauté" button and heat 1 tablespoon of olive oil until sizzling. Then, cook the chicken until no longer pink or about 4 minutes.

Then, heat another tablespoon of olive oil and add the onion and garlic. Cook for 2 to 3 minutes or until fragrant. Now, sauté the garlic until it is aromatic but not browned.

Add the spices, rice, water, and peppers. Add the reserved chicken back to the inner pot.

Secure the lid. Choose the "Rice" mode and cook for 10 minutes. Once cooking is complete, use a natural pressure release for 15 minutes; carefully remove the lid.

Add the green peas and press the "Sauté" button; cook on Less setting until thoroughly heated. Serve with salsa and enjoy!

Per serving: 418 Calories; 10.5g Fat; 50.1g Carbs; 29.5g Protein; 4.9g Sugars

795. Risotto ai Funghi

(Ready in about 30 minutes | Servings 4)

Ingredients

2 tablespoons olive oil
1 onion, chopped
1 teaspoon garlic, minced
2 cups Cremini mushrooms, chopped
1/2 teaspoon basil
1 teaspoon thyme
Sea salt and ground black pepper, to taste
1/3 cup Sauvignon Blanc
1 cup Arborio rice
4 cups vegetable broth
1/2 cup Romano cheese, grated

Directions

Press the "Sauté" button and heat the olive oil until sizzling. Then, cook the onion until tender and translucent.

Now, stir in the garlic and mushrooms; cook until they are just tender or about 3 minutes.

Add the basil, thyme, salt, black pepper, Sauvignon Blanc, rice, and vegetable broth.

Secure the lid. Choose the "Manual" mode and cook for 4 minutes at High pressure. Once cooking is complete, use a natural pressure release for 15 minutes; carefully remove the lid.

Divide between individual bowls and serve garnished with Romano cheese. Bon appétit!

Per serving: 296 Calories; 19.5g Fat; 21.6g Carbs; 14.9g Protein; 3.3g Sugars

796. Wild Rice with Shrimp

(Ready in about 50 minutes | Servings 4)

Ingredients

2 tablespoons olive oil
1 leek, chopped
1 teaspoon garlic, minced
2 bell peppers, chopped
1 cup wild rice
1 cup chicken broth
1 rosemary sprig
1 thyme sprig
1 teaspoon kosher salt
1/2 teaspoon ground black pepper
1/2 teaspoon cayenne pepper
1 pound shrimp, deveined
2 tablespoons fresh chives

Directions

Press the "Sauté" button and heat the olive oil. Once hot, sauté the leek until just tender or about 3 minutes.

Then, stir in the garlic and peppers. Continue to cook for 3 minutes more or until they are tender and fragrant.

Add the wild rice, broth, and seasonings to the inner pot.

Secure the lid. Choose the "Manual" mode and cook for 30 minutes at High pressure. Once cooking is complete, use a natural pressure release for 10 minutes; carefully remove the lid.

Add the shrimp to the inner pot.

Choose the "Manual" mode and cook for 3 minutes at High pressure. Once cooking is complete, use a quick pressure release; carefully remove the lid.

Serve garnished with fresh chives and enjoy!

Per serving: 334 Calories; 8.5g Fat; 36.1g Carbs; 30.9g Protein; 3.1g Sugars

797. Famous Seafood Jambalaya

(Ready in about 15 minutes | Servings 4)

Ingredients

2 tablespoons olive oil
1/2 pound Andouille sausage, sliced
1/2 pound chicken cutlets, cut into 1-inch cubes
1 onion, chopped
2 bell peppers, seeded and chopped
2 stalks celery, chopped
3 cloves garlic, minced
1 tablespoon pimentón de la Vera
2 tablespoons Cajun seasoning
Sea salt and ground black pepper, to taste
1 teaspoon cayenne pepper
2 ripe tomatoes, pureed
1 tablespoon fish sauce
1 cup white rice
2 cups chicken broth
1 pound shrimp, deveined
1 small handful fresh parsley, chopped

Directions

Press the "Sauté" button and heat the olive oil. Once hot, sauté the Andouille sausage and chicken cutlets for 4 to 5 minutes until they are brown; reserve.

Now, cook the onion in pan drippings; cook until it is tender and translucent.

Add the remaining ingredients, except for the fresh parsley, to the inner pot.

Secure the lid. Choose the "Manual" mode and cook for 4 minutes at High pressure. Once cooking is complete, use a quick pressure release; carefully remove the lid.

Serve garnished with fresh parsley. Enjoy!

Per serving: 551 Calories; 14.5g Fat; 54.9g Carbs; 49.2g Protein; 7.2g Sugars

798. Arborio Rice and Broccoli Pottage

(Ready in about 15 minutes | Servings 4)

Ingredients

2 tablespoons butter
1 onion, chopped
2 cloves garlic, minced
1 celery stalk, chopped
1 carrot, chopped
1 pound broccoli, broken into florets
1 cup cream of mushroom soup
1 cup plain milk
1 cup Arborio rice

Directions

Press the "Sauté" button and melt the butter. Once hot, cook the onion and garlic for 3 to 4 minutes or until just tender and fragrant.

Add the remaining ingredients and gently stir to combine.

Secure the lid. Choose the "Manual" mode and cook for 4 minutes at High pressure. Once cooking is complete, use a quick pressure release; carefully remove the lid.

Serve warm.

Per serving: 356 Calories; 11.9g Fat; 53.2g Carbs; 10.1g Protein; 5.2g Sugars

799. Mexican-Style Salsa Rice

(Ready in about 35 minutes | Servings 4)

Ingredients

1 cup brown rice
1 cup chicken broth
1 cup chunky salsa
1 cup Cotija cheese, shredded

Directions

Add the brown rice, chicken broth, salsa, oregano, salt, and black pepper to the inner pot.

Secure the lid. Choose the "Manual" mode and cook for 22 minutes at High pressure. Once cooking is complete, use a natural pressure release for 10 minutes; carefully remove the lid.

Divide between serving bowls and serve with shredded cheese. Enjoy!

Per serving: 408 Calories; 15.6g Fat; 40.7g Carbs; 25.7g Protein; 3.2g Sugars

800. Arroz Con Leche (Spanish Rice Pudding)

(Ready in about 25 minutes | Servings 4)

Ingredients

1 cup white rice
2 cups milk
4 tablespoons honey
1 teaspoon vanilla paste
1/2 teaspoon ground cinnamon
4 (2-inch) strips lemon zest

Directions

Place all ingredients in the inner pot.

Secure the lid. Choose the "Manual" mode and cook for 4 minutes at High pressure. Once cooking is complete, use a natural pressure release for 15 minutes; carefully remove the lid.

Fluff the rice with a fork and serve immediately.

Per serving: 324 Calories; 4.4g Fat; 64.6g Carbs; 7.7g Protein; 24.7g Sugars

801. Wild Rice Chowder

(Ready in about 35 minutes | Servings 4)

Ingredients

1 cup wild rice
4 cups chicken bone broth
1 onion, chopped
2 cloves garlic, pressed
1 carrot, chopped
1 parsnip, chopped
2 bay leaves
1 tablespoon Cajun seasoning
Sea salt and cracked black pepper, to taste
2 tablespoons olive oil
2 tablespoons cornstarch
1 egg, whisked
1 handful fresh cilantro, chopped

Directions

Add the wild rice, broth, vegetables, spices, and olive oil to the inner pot of your Instant Pot.

Secure the lid. Choose the "Soup/Broth" mode and cook for 30 minutes at High pressure. Once cooking is complete, use a quick pressure release; carefully remove the lid.

Mix the cornstarch with 4 tablespoons of water and the whisked egg. Stir the mixture into the cooking liquid.

Press the "Sauté" button and let it simmer for 3 to 4 minutes or until heated through.

Ladle into individual bowls. Top each serving with fresh cilantro and serve warm. Bon appétit!

Per serving: 320 Calories; 11.1g Fat; 41.6g Carbs; 13.8g Protein; 4.1g Sugars

802. Japanese-Style Rice Stew

(Ready in about 45 minutes | Servings 4)

Ingredients

1 ½ cups brown rice
3 cups water
1 pound potatoes, peeled and diced
2 tomatoes, pureed
1 teaspoon sweet paprika
Kosher salt and ground black pepper, to your liking
1/3 cup rice wine
1 tablespoon Tonkatsu sauce
2 bay leaves
2 tablespoons soy sauce

Directions

Add all ingredients, except for the soy sauce, to the inner pot.

Secure the lid. Choose the "Manual" mode and cook for 24 minutes at High pressure. Once cooking is complete, use a natural pressure release for 15 minutes; carefully remove the lid.

Ladle into individual bowls; drizzle soy sauce over each serving and enjoy!

Per serving: 354 Calories; 2.1g Fat; 76.2g Carbs; 7.8g Protein; 2.7g Sugars

803. Ground Meat and Rice Bowl

(Ready in about 45 minutes | Servings 4)

Ingredients

1 tablespoon lard, melted
1/2 pound ground turkey
1/2 pound ground beef
2 garlic cloves, minced
2 tablespoons brown sugar
2 tablespoons Worcestershire sauce
1/2 teaspoon crushed red pepper flakes
Sea salt and ground black pepper, to taste
1 cup brown rice

Directions

Press the "Sauté" button and melt the lard. Once hot, cook the ground meat until no longer pink or about 3 to 4 minutes.

Then, stir in the garlic and let it cook an additional minute or until it is aromatic.

Add the remaining ingredients; stir to combine.

Secure the lid. Choose the "Manual" mode and cook for 22 minutes at High pressure. Once cooking is complete, use a natural pressure release for 10 minutes; carefully remove the lid.

Per serving: 435 Calories; 15.1g Fat; 43.4g Carbs; 30.1g Protein; 5.7g Sugars

804. Red Rice and Shrimp Risotto

(Ready in about 45 minutes | Servings 4)

Ingredients

2 tablespoons butter, melted
1 onion, chopped
2 cloves garlic, minced
1/2 cup rice wine
1 ½ cups red rice
2 tablespoons Shoyu sauce
4 cups shellfish stock
1/2 pound shrimp, deveined
Sea salt and ground black pepper, to taste
4 tablespoons goat cheese, crumbled

Directions

Press the "Sauté" button and melt the butter. Once hot, cook the onion and garlic for 2 to 3 minutes or until they are just tender.

Add a splash of rice wine; deglaze the bottom of the inner pot with a wooden spoon. Now, stir in the red rice, wine, Shoyu sauce, and shellfish stock to the inner pot.

Secure the lid. Choose the "Multigrain" mode and cook for 20 minutes at High pressure. Once cooking is complete, use a natural pressure release for 10 minutes; carefully remove the lid.

Next, stir in the shrimp, salt, and black pepper.

Secure the lid. Choose the "Manual" mode and cook for 4 minutes at High pressure. Once cooking is complete, use a quick pressure release; carefully remove the lid. Serve garnished with goat cheese and enjoy!

Per serving: 352 Calories; 18.5g Fat; 22.2g Carbs; 25.4g Protein; 4.3g Sugars

805. Authentic Paella Valenciana

(Ready in about 25 minutes | Servings 4)

Ingredients

2 tablespoons ghee, at room temperature
2 cloves garlic, pressed
1 red bell pepper, cut in strips
1 cup basmati rice
1 pound tiger prawns, deveined
Sea salt and ground black pepper, to taste
1 bay leaf
1 teaspoon paprika
1/4 teaspoon saffron threads
1 tablespoon capers, drained
2 cups chicken broth
1 cup green peas, thawed

Directions

Press the "Sauté" button and melt the ghee. Once hot, cook the garlic and pepper for about 2 minutes or until just tender and fragrant.

Add the basmati rice, tiger prawns, salt, black pepper, bay leaf, paprika, saffron, capers, and chicken broth to the inner pot.

Secure the lid. Choose the "Manual" mode and cook for 4 minutes at High pressure. Once cooking is complete, use a natural pressure release for 10 minutes; carefully remove the lid.

Add the green peas to the inner pot; press the "Sauté" button one more time and let it simmer until heated through. Enjoy!

Per serving: 389 Calories; 7.8g Fat; 48.1g Carbs; 31.2g Protein; 2.7g Sugars

806. Spicy Jasmine Rice with Peppers

(Ready in about 25 minutes | Servings 4)

Ingredients

2 teaspoons olive oil
1 onion, chopped
2 cups sweet peppers, chopped
1 jalapeno pepper, minced
1 teaspoon garlic powder
1/2 teaspoon ground bay leaf
1/2 teaspoon dried sage, crushed
1 ½ cups jasmine rice, rinsed
1 ½ cups water
1/2 teaspoon sea salt

Directions

Press the "Sauté" button and heat the olive oil. Once hot, cook the onion and peppers until just tender and fragrant.

Now, add the remaining ingredients and stir to combine well.

Secure the lid. Choose the "Manual" mode and cook for 4 minutes at High pressure. Once cooking is complete, use a natural pressure release for 15 minutes; carefully remove the lid.

Serve in individual bowls and enjoy!

Per serving: 309 Calories; 4.5g Fat; 59.8g Carbs; 6.4g Protein; 3.8g Sugars

807. Asian Congee with Pao Cai

(Ready in about 35 minutes | Servings 3)

Ingredients

1 cup sushi rice, rinsed
6 cups roasted vegetable broth
1 teaspoon fresh ginger, grated
Kosher salt and ground black pepper, to taste
2 tablespoons soy sauce
2 tablespoons chili oil
1 cup pao cai

Directions

Place the rice, vegetable broth, ginger, and salt in the inner pot of the Instant Pot.

Secure the lid. Choose the "Multigrain" mode and cook for 20 minutes at High pressure. Once cooking is complete, use a natural pressure release for 10 minutes; carefully remove the lid.

Your congee will thicken as it cools. Stir in the black pepper, soy sauce, and chili oil. Serve garnished with pao cai and enjoy!

Per serving: 326 Calories; 22.5g Fat; 26.8g Carbs; 16.4g Protein; 4.1g Sugars

808. Rice, Yellow Lentil and Kale Porridge

(Ready in about 50 minutes | Servings 3)

Ingredients

1 cup brown jasmine rice
9 cups water
1 teaspoon sea salt
2 cups kale, torn into pieces
1/2 cup yellow lentils
Salt and ground black pepper, to taste
2 tablespoons pepitas, toasted

Directions

Place the rice, water, and salt in the inner pot.

Secure the lid. Choose the "Manual" mode and cook for 25 minutes at High pressure. Once cooking is complete, use a natural pressure release for 20 minutes; carefully remove the lid.

Add the kale, lentils, salt, and black pepper to the inner pot.

Secure the lid. Choose the "Manual" mode and cook for 2 minutes at High pressure. Once cooking is complete, use a quick pressure release; carefully remove the lid.

Serve in individual bowls garnished with toasted pepitas.

Per serving: 380 Calories; 4.7g Fat; 70.8g Carbs; 15.4g Protein; 2.2g Sugars

809. Traditional Greek Rizogalo

(Ready in about 30 minutes | Servings 4)

Ingredients

2 tablespoons butter
1 ½ cups white rice
4 cups milk
2 ounces sugar

1 (3-inch strip) of lemon rind
1 teaspoon vanilla extract
1 teaspoon ground cinnamon
4 tablespoons honey

Directions

Place the butter, rice, milk, sugar, lemon rind, and vanilla extract in the inner pot.

Secure the lid. Choose the "Rice" mode and cook for 10 minutes at Low pressure. Once cooking is complete, use a natural pressure release for 15 minutes; carefully remove the lid.

Ladle your rizogalo into four serving bowls; top with cinnamon and honey and serve at room temperature.

Per serving: 550 Calories; 14.7g Fat; 91.6g Carbs; 12.6g Protein; 31.5g Sugars

810. Pulao Rice Pakistani Style

(Ready in about 30 minutes | Servings 4)

Ingredients

2 tablespoons ghee
1 shallot, chopped
2 garlic cloves, minced
1 ½ cups basmati rice, rinsed
2 cups vegetable broth
Sea salt and white pepper, to taste

1 teaspoon coriander seeds
2 black cardamoms
2 green cardamoms
2 tez patta (bay leaf)
1 teaspoon turmeric powder
1 cup sweet corn kernels, thawed

Directions

Press the "Sauté" button and melt the ghee. Once hot, cook the shallot for 4 minutes or until just tender and fragrant. Stir in the garlic and cook an additional minute or until aromatic.

Now, add the basmati rice, broth, and spices.

Secure the lid. Choose the "Manual" mode and cook for 4 minutes at High pressure. Once cooking is complete, use a natural pressure release for 15 minutes; carefully remove the lid.

Add the sweet corn kernels and seal the lid again. Let it sit in the residual heat until thoroughly heated. Enjoy!

Per serving: 392 Calories; 7.3g Fat; 72.2g Carbs; 9.2g Protein; 0.9g Sugars

811. Kinoko Gohan (Japanese Mushroom Rice)

(Ready in about 30 minutes | Servings 4)

Ingredients

4 tablespoons shoyu
2 cups maitake mushrooms, sliced
2 cups shiitake mushrooms, sliced
1/4 cup mirin
1/4 cup sake
2 cups water
1 piece dried kombu

4 tablespoons sesame oil
1 shallot, chopped
1 teaspoon garlic, minced
1 ½ cups Kokuho Rose rice
2 cups chicken stock
Kosher salt and ground black pepper, to taste

Directions

Press the "Sauté" button to preheat your Instant Pot. Put the shoyu, mushrooms, mirin, sake, water, and dried kombu.

Bring to a simmer on the lowest setting; allow it to cook for 5 to 6 minutes. Discard the kombu and save for another use.

Add the other ingredients to the inner pot.

Secure the lid. Choose the "Manual" mode and cook for 6 minutes at High pressure. Once cooking is complete, use a natural pressure release for 15 minutes; carefully remove the lid. Serve in individual bowls and enjoy!

Per serving: 463 Calories; 15.3g Fat; 63.5g Carbs; 9.8g Protein; 1.5g Sugars

812. Chicken, Broccoli and Rice Casserole

(Ready in about 30 minutes | Servings 4)

Ingredients

3 tablespoons butter, melted
1 chicken breast, skinless
1 shallot, sliced
1 teaspoon garlic, minced
1 pound broccoli florets
1 cup white rice
1 cup tomato puree

2 cups chicken broth
1 teaspoon paprika
1 teaspoon Italian seasoning blend
Kosher salt and freshly ground pepper, to taste
5 ounces cheddar cheese, shredded

Directions

Press the "Sauté" button and melt 1 tablespoon of butter. Once hot, cook the chicken breast until it is golden brown on both sides.

Shred the chicken with two forks. Add it back to the inner pot. Add the shallots, garlic, broccoli, rice, tomato puree, and chicken broth; stir in the remaining butter.

Season with the paprika, Italian seasonings, salt, and black pepper.

Secure the lid. Choose the "Rice" mode and cook for 10 minutes at Low pressure. Once cooking is complete, use a natural pressure release for 10 minutes; carefully remove the lid.

Top with cheese. Seal the lid again and let it sit in the residual heat until the cheese melts. Serve immediately.

Per serving: 563 Calories; 21.2g Fat; 56.5g Carbs; 36.5g Protein; 6.7g Sugars

813. Vegan Rice and Beans

(Ready in about 40 minutes | Servings 4)

Ingredients

1 cup brown rice
1 cup kidney beans
1 cup marinara sauce
2 tablespoons fresh parsley, chopped

2 tablespoons fresh scallions, chopped
1 tablespoon fresh basil, chopped
2 green garlic stalks, chopped
2 ½ cups vegetable broth

Directions

Add all ingredients to the inner pot of your Instant Pot.

Secure the lid. Choose the "Manual" mode and cook for 25 minutes at High pressure. Once cooking is complete, use a natural pressure release for 15 minutes; carefully remove the lid.

Ladle into individual bowls and serve warm. Enjoy!

Per serving: 354 Calories; 1.9g Fat; 70.5g Carbs; 15.1g Protein; 5.2g Sugars

814. Two-Cheese Risotto with Vegetables

(Ready in about 25 minutes | Servings 4)

Ingredients

1 cup white rice, rinsed
1 onion, chopped
1 cup carrots, chopped
1 cup celery ribs, chopped
Sea salt and ground black pepper, to taste

1/2 teaspoon dried dill weed
2 cups roasted vegetable broth
1/2 cup Swiss cheese, shredded
1/2 cup Manchego cheese, shredded

Directions

Add the rice, onion, carrots, celery, salt, black pepper, dill, and vegetable broth to the inner pot.

Secure the lid. Choose the "Manual" mode and cook for 5 minutes at High pressure. Once cooking is complete, use a natural pressure release for 15 minutes; carefully remove the lid.

After that, stir in the cheese; stir well to combine and seal the lid. Let it sit in the residual heat until the cheese melts. Bon appétit!

Per serving: 444 Calories; 14.3g Fat; 48.7g Carbs; 27.2g Protein; 4.3g Sugars

815. Authentic Indian Jeera Rice

(Ready in about 30 minutes | Servings 4)

Ingredients

1 ½ cups rice basmati rice, rinsed
1 cup water
1 cup cream of celery soup
1 green chili deveined and chopped
Sea salt and ground black pepper, to taste
1 bay leaf
1 teaspoon Jeera (cumin seeds)
2 tablespoons sesame oil

Directions

Place all ingredients in the inner pot. Stir until everything is well combined.

Secure the lid. Choose the "Rice" mode and cook for 10 minutes at Low pressure. Once cooking is complete, use a natural pressure release for 15 minutes; carefully remove the lid.

Serve with Indian main dishes of choice. Enjoy!

Per serving: 346 Calories; 10.3g Fat; 57.1g Carbs; 6.2g Protein; 1.2g Sugars

816. One Pot Enchilada Rice

(Ready in about 35 minutes | Servings 4)

Ingredients

1 tablespoon canola oil
1 onion, chopped
2 garlic cloves, minced
1 sweet pepper, seeded and chopped
1 habanero pepper, seeded and minced
1 cup vegetable broth
1 cup long grain rice, rinsed
1 cup pinto beans, boiled
1 cup sweet corn, frozen and thawed
1/2 teaspoon cumin powder
1/3 teaspoon Mexican oregano
Sea salt and ground black pepper, to taste
1 cup enchilada sauce
1 cup Mexican blend cheese, shredded
A small handful of cilantro, roughly chopped

Directions

Press the "Sauté" button to preheat your Instant Pot and add the oil. Once hot, cook the onion, garlic, and peppers until they are just tender and fragrant.

Next, add the vegetable broth followed by rice, beans, corn, cumin powder, oregano, salt, black pepper, and enchilada sauce; do not stir.

Secure the lid. Choose the "Manual" mode and cook for 5 minutes at High pressure. Once cooking is complete, use a natural pressure release for 15 minutes; carefully remove the lid.

After that, stir in Mexican blend cheese and seal the lid again. Let it sit in the residual heat for 5 to 10 minutes until the cheese melts.

Serve with fresh cilantro and enjoy!

Per serving: 559 Calories; 15.3g Fat; 83.4g Carbs; 24.1g Protein; 6.5g Sugars

817. Exotic Peanut Rice

(Ready in about 30 minutes | Servings 4)

Ingredients

1 cup white rice
2 tablespoons peanut oil
1 Vidalia onion, chopped
2 cloves garlic, minced
1 teaspoon cayenne pepper
Sea salt and ground black pepper, to taste
1 tomato, pureed
1 ½ cups vegetable broth
1 bay leaf
1/2 cup frozen petite peas, thawed
1/2 cup peanuts, dry roasted and roughly chopped

Directions

Add the white rice, peanut oil, Vidalia onion, garlic, cayenne pepper, salt, black pepper, tomato, vegetable broth, and bay leaf to the inner pot.

Secure the lid. Choose the "Manual" mode and cook for 5 minutes at High pressure. Once cooking is complete, use a natural pressure release for 20 minutes; carefully remove the lid.

Now, stir in the thawed petite peas and seal the lid. Let it sit in the residual heat until everything is heated through.

Serve with roasted peanuts and enjoy!

Per serving: 473 Calories; 19.5g Fat; 63g Carbs; 14.6g Protein; 8.9g Sugars

818. Hot and Spicy Pork Pilaf

(Ready in about 30 minutes | Servings 4)

Ingredients

1/2 pound pork sausage, sliced
1/2 pound ground beef
1 medium-sized leek, chopped
2 garlic cloves, minced
1 celery stalk, chopped
2 carrots, chopped
1 parsnip, chopped
2 sweet peppers, chopped
1 poblano pepper, chopped
1 tablespoon Old Bay seasoning
1 teaspoon dried parsley
1 tablespoon fish sauce
1 ½ cups Arborio rice, rinsed
1 ½ cup beef broth

Directions

Press the "Sauté" button to preheat your Instant Pot. Once hot, cook the pork sausage and ground beef until they have browned.

Add the leek, garlic, celery, carrots, parsnip, peppers, seasoning, and fish sauce to the inner pot. Continue to cook until the vegetables have softened.

Stir in the rice and beef broth; stir to combine well.

Secure the lid. Choose the "Rice" mode and cook for 10 minutes at Low pressure. Once cooking is complete, use a natural pressure release for 15 minutes; carefully remove the lid. Fluff your rice with a fork before serving. Bon appétit!

Per serving: 425 Calories; 19.1g Fat; 44.7g Carbs; 33.3g Protein; 4.3g Sugars

819. Southwestern Rice with Chicken and Beans

(Ready in about 40 minutes | Servings 4)

Ingredients

1 cup brown rice
1 cup navy beans, drained and rinsed
1 cup chicken stock
1/2 cup salsa
2 garlic cloves, minced
1 sweet pepper, chopped
1/2 teaspoon cumin
1/2 teaspoon salt
1/2 teaspoon black peppercorns
2 bay leaves
1 pound chicken cutlets

Directions

Place all ingredients in the inner pot. Stir until everything is well combined.

Secure the lid. Choose the "Bean/Chili" mode and cook for 25 minutes at High pressure. Once cooking is complete, use a natural pressure release for 10 minutes; carefully remove the lid.

Ladle into individual bowls and serve warm. Enjoy!

Per serving: 388 Calories; 4.9g Fat; 53.6g Carbs; 31.6g Protein; 1.8g Sugars

820. Easy Afghani Pulao

(Ready in about 50 minutes | Servings 3)

Ingredients

1 tablespoon coconut oil
2 carrots, grated
1/2 cup raisins, soaked
4 tablespoons granulated sugar
1 cup wild rice
1 ½ cups water
A pinch of salt
A pinch of saffron
1/4 teaspoon cardamom powder

Directions

Press the "Sauté" button to preheat your Instant Pot. Once hot, melt the coconut oil. Now, cook the grated carrots for 2 to 3 minutes or until they are tender.

Add the other ingredients to the inner pot.

Secure the lid. Choose the "Manual" mode and cook for 30 minutes at High pressure. Once cooking is complete, use a natural pressure release for 15 minutes; carefully remove the lid. Serve warm.

Per serving: 291 Calories; 5.9g Fat; 55.2g Carbs; 8.3g Protein; 14.1g Sugars

821. Spanish Arroz Rojo

(Ready in about 45 minutes | Servings 4)

Ingredients

1 tablespoon olive oil
1 onion, chopped
1 teaspoon garlic paste
1 teaspoon ginger, grated
2 sweet peppers, deveined and sliced
1 red chili pepper, minced

1 ½ cups red rice
1 ½ cups water
1 cube tomato-chicken bouillon
1/2 cup tomato sauce
1 tablespoon taco seasoning
Sea salt, to taste

Directions

Press the "Sauté" button and heat the oil until sizzling. Now, sauté the onion until just tender or about 3 minutes.

Add the remaining ingredients and stir to combine.

Secure the lid. Choose the "Manual" mode and cook for 30 minutes at High pressure. Once cooking is complete, use a natural pressure release for 10 minutes; carefully remove the lid.

Taste, adjust the seasonings and serve with salsa on the side. Enjoy!

Per serving: 375 Calories; 5.8g Fat; 72.3g Carbs; 8.3g Protein; 6.1g Sugars

822. Authentic Indian Khichri

(Ready in about 30 minutes | Servings 3)

Ingredients

2 tablespoons butter
1 teaspoon cumin seeds
2 bay leaves
1 shallot, sliced
1 cup basmati rice

1 cup moong dal lentils
1/2 teaspoon ground turmeric
Sea salt and ground black pepper, to taste

Directions

Press the "Sauté" button and melt the butter. Once hot, sauté the cumin seeds and bay leaf until they are fragrant.

Now, add the shallot and continue to sauté an additional 3 minute or until it is just tender.

Add the remaining ingredients; stir to combine.

Secure the lid. Choose the "Manual" mode and cook for 4 minutes at High pressure. Once cooking is complete, use a natural pressure release for 15 minutes; carefully remove the lid. Serve warm.

Per serving: 530 Calories; 8.8g Fat; 92.3g Carbs; 20.2g Protein; 1.3g Sugars

823. Wild Rice and Chicken Casserole

(Ready in about 50 minutes | Servings 4)

Ingredients

2 tablespoons butter
2 cups chicken breasts, cut into chunks
1 onion, chopped
2 celery ribs, chopped
1 teaspoon garlic, minced
1 cup wild rice

1 cup cream of celery soup
1 cup tomato sauce
Sea salt and ground black pepper, to taste
1 cup sour cream
2 cup goat cheese, crumbled

Directions

Press the "Sauté" button and melt the butter. Once hot, cook the chicken until it is no longer pink; reserve.

Now, sauté the onion in the pan drippings until tender. Then, add the celery and garlic; continue to sauté an additional minute or so.

Add the wild rice, cream of celery soup, tomato sauce, salt, and black pepper to the inner pot. Stir in the reserved chicken.

Secure the lid. Choose the "Manual" mode and cook for 30 minutes at High pressure. Once cooking is complete, use a natural pressure release for 15 minutes; carefully remove the lid.

Mix the sour cream with goat cheese; place the cheese mixture over your casserole. Let it sit, covered, for 10 minutes before serving. Bon appétit!

Per serving: 489 Calories; 20.1g Fat; 42.5g Carbs; 36.3g Protein; 5.2g Sugars

824. Easy Vegan Tomato Pilau

(Ready in about 30 minutes | Servings 4)

Ingredients

1 tablespoon olive oil
1 onion, chopped
1 teaspoon garlic, chopped
1 ½ cups long grain white rice
2 cups water
2 carrots, thinly sliced
1 green zucchini, cut into thick sliced

2 (12-ounce) cans tomato paste
1 teaspoon Italian seasoning blend
Sea salt and ground black pepper, to your liking
1 bay leaf
4 cups spinach
2 teaspoons fresh lime juice

Directions

Press the "Sauté" button and heat the oil. Once hot, cook the onion and garlic for 2 to 3 minutes or until just tender and aromatic.

Stir in the rice, water, carrots, zucchini, tomato paste, Italian seasoning blend, salt, black pepper, and bay leaf.

Secure the lid. Choose the "Rice" mode and cook for 10 minutes at Low pressure. Once cooking is complete, use a natural pressure release for 15 minutes; carefully remove the lid.

Add the spinach and press the "Sauté" button. Let it simmer on the lowest setting until wilts. Drizzle lime juice over each portion and serve. Bon appétit!

Per serving: 473 Calories; 4.9g Fat; 98.5g Carbs; 15.1g Protein; 26.2g Sugars

825. Perfect Sushi Rice

(Ready in about 30 minutes | Servings 4)

Ingredients

1 ½ cups sushi rice, rinsed
1 ½ cups water
1/4 cup rice vinegar

1 tablespoon brown sugar
1/2 teaspoon salt
2 tablespoons soy sauce

Directions

Place the sushi rice and water in the inner pot of your Instant Pot.

Secure the lid. Choose the "Rice" mode and cook for 10 minutes at Low pressure. Once cooking is complete, use a natural pressure release for 15 minutes; carefully remove the lid.

Meanwhile, whisk the rice vinegar, sugar, salt and soy sauce in a mixing dish; microwave the sauce for 1 minute.

Pour the sauce over the sushi rice; stir to combine. Assemble your sushi rolls and enjoy!

Per serving: 291 Calories; 1.9g Fat; 60.7g Carbs; 5.1g Protein; 3.5g Sugars

826. Beef and Rice Stew

(Ready in about 30 minutes | Servings 4)

Ingredients

2 tablespoons lard, at room temperature
1 pound beef stew meat, cut into bite-sized chunks
4 cups beef bone broth
1 onion, chopped
2 garlic cloves, minced
2 sweet peppers, deveined and chopped
1 red chili pepper, chopped

1 teaspoon dried basil
1 teaspoon dried oregano
1 teaspoon dried rosemary
Sea salt and ground black pepper, to taste
1 bay leaf
2 tablespoons cornstarch, dissolved in 1/4 cup cold water
1 cup brown rice

Directions

Press the "Sauté" button and melt the lard. When the lard starts to sizzle, add the beef stew meat and cook until browned on all sides; reserve.

Add a splash of beef broth to the inner pot; use a spoon to scrape the brown bits from the bottom of the pan.

Then, sauté the onion, garlic, and peppers for about 3 minutes or until they are just tender.

Add the other ingredients and stir to combine.

Secure the lid. Choose the "Soup/Broth" mode and cook for 20 minutes at High pressure. Once cooking is complete, use a quick pressure release; carefully remove the lid.

Mix the cornstarch with cold water in a small bowl; stir the slurry into the stew and cook on the "Sauté" function until the cooking liquid has thickened.

Serve warm and enjoy!

Per serving: 291 Calories; 1.9g Fat; 60.7g Carbs; 5.1g Protein; 3.5g Sugars

827. Risotto with Smoked Salmon

(Ready in about 20 minutes | Servings 4)

Ingredients

1 tablespoon butter
1 onion, chopped
2 cloves garlic, minced
1 cup white rice
1 cup vegetable broth
1/2 cup milk
1 pound smoked salmon steak
4 ounces green beans
Sea salt and ground black pepper, to season

Directions

Press the "Sauté" button and melt the butter. When the butter starts to sizzle, add the onion; sauté the onion until just tender and fragrant.

Now, stir in the garlic and continue to sauté an additional minute or until fragrant.

Add the rice, broth, milk, salmon, and green beans; season with salt and black pepper.

Secure the lid. Choose the "Manual" mode and cook for 4 minutes at High pressure. Once cooking is complete, use a natural pressure release for 10 minutes; carefully remove the lid. Bon appétit!

Per serving: 340 Calories; 18.6g Fat; 20.6g Carbs; 30.2g Protein; 3.3g Sugars

EGGS & DAIRY

828. Easiest Hard-Boiled Eggs Ever

(Ready in about 15 minutes | Servings 3)

Ingredients

5 eggs
1/2 teaspoon salt
1/4 teaspoon red pepper flakes, crushed

2 tablespoons fresh chives, chopped

Directions

Place 1 cup of water and a steamer rack in the inner pot. Arrange the eggs on the rack.

Secure the lid. Choose the "Manual" mode and cook for 5 minutes at High pressure. Once cooking is complete, use a quick pressure release; carefully remove the lid.

Transfer the eggs to icy-cold water. Now, let them sit in the water bath a few minutes until cool.

Peel your eggs and season with salt and red pepper. Serve garnished with freshly chopped chives. Enjoy!

Per serving: 106 Calories; 6.9g Fat; 0.6g Carbs; 9.2g Protein; 0.3g Sugars

829. Cheesy Hash Brown Egg Bake

(Ready in about 30 minutes | Servings 3)

Ingredients

3 ounces bacon, chopped
1 onion, chopped
1 cup frozen hash browns
5 eggs
1/4 cup milk

1/3 cup Swiss cheese, shredded
1 teaspoon garlic powder
1/4 teaspoon turmeric powder
Kosher salt and ground black pepper, to taste

Directions

Place 1 cup of water and a metal trivet in the inner pot.

Press the "Sauté" button and cook the bacon until it is crisp and browned. Add in the onions and cook for 3 to 4 minutes, stirring occasionally.

Stir in the frozen hash browns and cook until slightly thawed. Grease an oven-proof dish with cooking oil.

In a mixing bowl, whisk the eggs, milk, shredded cheese, garlic powder, turmeric powder, salt and black pepper; now add the bacon/onion mixture to the egg mixture.

Spoon the egg mixture into the prepared dish. Lower the dish onto the trivet.

Secure the lid. Choose the "Manual" mode and cook for 20 minutes at High pressure. Once cooking is complete, use a quick pressure release; carefully remove the lid. Bon appétit!

Per serving: 475 Calories; 38g Fat; 17.6g Carbs; 13.6g Protein; 2.9g Sugars

830. Mini Egg Frittatas with Cheese

(Ready in about 10 minutes | Servings 3)

Ingredients

6 eggs
1/4 cup milk
1/2 teaspoon cayenne pepper

Sea salt and ground black pepper, to taste
1/2 cup cream cheese

Directions

Place 1 cup of water and a metal trivet in the inner pot.

Mix all ingredients until everything is well incorporated. Pour the egg mixture into silicone molds.

Lower the molds onto the prepared trivet.

Secure the lid. Choose the "Manual" mode and cook for 5 minutes at High pressure. Once cooking is complete, use a quick pressure release; carefully remove the lid. Bon appétit!

Per serving: 277 Calories; 22.3g Fat; 4.7g Carbs; 14.6g Protein; 3.4g Sugars

831. Cocktail Party Deviled Eggs

(Ready in about 10 minutes | Servings 6)

Ingredients

6 eggs
1/4 cup Cottage cheese, crumbled
1 tablespoon butter, softened
2 tablespoons fresh parsley, minced

1 teaspoon paprika
Sea salt and ground black pepper, to taste

Directions

Place 1 cup of water and a steamer rack in the inner pot. Arrange the eggs on the rack.

Secure the lid. Choose the "Manual" mode and cook for 5 minutes at High pressure. Once cooking is complete, use a quick pressure release; carefully remove the lid.

Peel the eggs and slice them into halves.

In a mixing bowl, thoroughly combine the Cottage cheese, butter, parsley, paprika, sea salt, and black pepper. Stir in the egg yolks. Stir to combine well.

Use a piping bag to fill the egg white halves. Place on a nice serving platter and enjoy!

Per serving: 93 Calories; 6.5g Fat; 1.6g Carbs; 6.7g Protein; 0.8g Sugars

832. Dilled Stuffed Eggs

(Ready in about 10 minutes | Servings 5)

Ingredients

10 eggs
1/2 teaspoon coarse sea salt
1/4 teaspoon black pepper, to taste
1/2 teaspoon turmeric powder

2 teaspoons balsamic vinegar
2 tablespoons Greek-style yogurt
4 tablespoons mayonnaise
1 teaspoon fresh dill, chopped

Directions

Place 1 cup of water and a steamer rack in the inner pot. Arrange the eggs on the rack.

Secure the lid. Choose the "Manual" mode and cook for 5 minutes at High pressure. Once cooking is complete, use a quick pressure release; carefully remove the lid.

Peel the eggs and slice them into halves.

In a mixing bowl, thoroughly combine the sea salt, black pepper, turmeric powder, vinegar, yogurt, and mayonnaise. Stir in the egg yolks.

Use a piping bag to fill the egg white halves. Garnish with fresh dill. Bon appétit!

Per serving: 209 Calories; 16.6g Fat; 1.6g Carbs; 12g Protein; 0.9g Sugars

833. Easy Homemade Yogurt

(Ready in about 9 hours | Servings 12)

Ingredients

2 quarts milk
2 tablespoons prepared yogurt with cultures

A pinch of salt

Directions

Pour the milk into the inner pot. Press the "Yogurt" button; adjust the temperature until the screen reads "Boil".

Let it sit for 5 minutes and then remove the inner pot. Allow the milk to cool to about 115 degrees F. Whisk in the prepared yogurt with the cultures; add a pinch of salt.

Add the inner pot back to the Instant Pot.

Secure the lid. Choose the "Yogurt" mode and adjust until the screen reads 8:00. Once the cycle is complete, remove the lid.

Transfer the prepared yogurt to your refrigerator until ready to use. Bon appétit!

Per serving: 99 Calories; 5.6g Fat; 7.7g Carbs; 5.2g Protein; 8.2g Sugars

834. Mexican-Style Omelet with Chanterelles

(Ready in about 30 minutes | Servings 4)

Ingredients

1 tablespoon olive oil
1 medium onion, chopped
2 cloves garlic, minced
1 cup Mexica cheese blend, crumbled
1 cup Chanterelle mushrooms, chopped

1 bell pepper, sliced
1 Poblano pepper, seeded and minced
5 eggs
4 ounces cream cheese
Sea salt and ground black pepper, to taste

Directions

Add 1 cup of water and a metal rack to the inner pot of your Instant Pot. Spray a souffle dish and set aside.

Mix all ingredients until well combined. Scrape the mixture into the prepared dish. Lower the souffle dish onto the rack.

Secure the lid. Choose the "Manual" mode and cook for 11 minutes at High pressure. Once cooking is complete, use a natural pressure release for 15 minutes; carefully remove the lid.

Serve with salsa if desired. Enjoy!

Per serving: 333 Calories; 26.6g Fat; 8.6g Carbs; 16.2g Protein; 3.9g Sugars

835. Authentic Spanish Tortilla

(Ready in about 30 minutes | Servings 4)

Ingredients

8 eggs
8 ounces hash browns
1 ½ tablespoons olive oil
1 onion, sliced
Sea salt and ground black pepper, or to taste

1 teaspoon taco seasoning mix
1 teaspoon fresh garlic, minced
1/3 cup milk
4 ounces Manchego cheese, grated

Directions

Add 1 cup of water and a metal rack to the inner pot of your Instant Pot. Spritz a souffle dish with nonstick cooking oil.

In a mixing bowl, thoroughly combine all ingredients, except for the Manchego cheese; mix until everything is well incorporated.

Scrape the mixture into the prepared souffle dish.

Secure the lid. Choose the "Manual" mode and cook for 17 minutes at High pressure. Once cooking is complete, use a natural pressure release for 10 minutes; carefully remove the lid.

Top with Manchego cheese and seal the lid again. Let it sit in the residual heat until the cheese melts. Enjoy!

Per serving: 398 Calories; 26.7g Fat; 22.6g Carbs; 18.2g Protein; 4.3g Sugars

836. Mini Pancakes with Raisins

(Ready in about 25 minutes | Servings 4)

Ingredients

1 cup all-purpose flour
2 teaspoons baking powder
1 teaspoon salt
1/4 cup milk

2 eggs, whisked
2 tablespoons maple syrup
1/2 cup raisins
2 tablespoons almonds, chopped

Directions

Add 1 cup of water and a metal trivet to the inner pot.

Mix all ingredients until everything is well combined. Pour the batter into a muffin tin that is previously greased with cooking spray. Lower the muffin tin onto the trivet.

Secure the lid. Choose the "Manual" mode and cook for 8 minutes at High pressure. Once cooking is complete, use a natural pressure release for 10 minutes; carefully remove the lid. Bon appétit!

Per serving: 276 Calories; 6.7g Fat; 47.3g Carbs; 8.5g Protein; 18g Sugars

837. Egg Muffins with Ham and Cheese

(Ready in about 15 minutes | Servings 4)

Per serving: 369 Calories; 23.7g Fat; 6.5g Carbs; 31.3g Protein; 1.5g Sugars

Ingredients

8 eggs
1/4 teaspoon ground black pepper, or more to taste
1 teaspoon paprika
Sea salt, to taste
1 cup green peppers, seeded and chopped

8 ounces ham, chopped
1/2 cup sour cream
1/2 cup Swiss cheese, shredded
2 tablespoons parsley, chopped
2 tablespoons cilantro, chopped
2 tablespoons scallions, chopped

Directions

Mix all ingredients until everything is well combined.

Add 1 cup of water and a metal rack to the inner pot of your Instant Pot.

Spoon the prepared mixture into silicone molds. Lower the molds onto the prepared trivet.

Secure the lid. Choose the "Manual" mode and cook for 6 minutes at High pressure. Once cooking is complete, use a quick pressure release; carefully remove the lid. Bon appétit!

838. Home-Style Fresh Cream Cheese

(Ready in about 20 minutes + chilling time | Servings 10)

Ingredients

3 ½ cups whole milk
1 cup double cream

1 teaspoon kosher salt
2 tablespoons lemon juice

Directions

Place the milk, double cream, and salt in the inner pot of your Instant Pot and stir to combine well.

Secure the lid. Choose the "Manual" mode and cook for 5 minutes at Low pressure. Once cooking is complete, use a natural pressure release for 10 minutes; carefully remove the lid.

Add the lemon juice and stir the mixture one more time.

Line a strainer with cheesecloth and pour the mixture into the cheesecloth. Allow the curds to continue to drain in the strainer for about 1 hour. Discard the whey.

Pat your cheese into a ball and remove from the cheesecloth. This cheese will last about a week in your refrigerator. Bon appétit!

Per serving: 124 Calories; 7.2g Fat; 12.1g Carbs; 3.3g Protein; 11.9g Sugars

839. Delicious Mac and Cheese

(Ready in about 15 minutes | Servings 6)

Ingredients

12 ounces elbow macaroni
2 tablespoons butter
1/2 teaspoon celery seeds
Kosher salt, to taste
3 cups water

4 ounces milk
2 ½ cups cheddar cheese, shredded
1 cup Parmesan cheese, shredded

Directions

Throw the elbow macaroni, butter, celery seeds, salt, and water into the inner pot.

Secure the lid. Choose the "Manual" mode and cook for 5 minutes at High pressure. Once cooking is complete, use a quick pressure release; carefully remove the lid.

Next, stir in the milk and half of the cheeses. Stir until the cheeses has melted; add the second half of the cheeses and stir to combine well.

The sauce will thicken as it cools. Bon appétit!

Per serving: 518 Calories; 25.9g Fat; 46.2g Carbs; 24.3g Protein; 2.6g Sugars

840. Mom's Cheese Dip

(Ready in about 15 minutes | Servings 10)

Ingredients

1/2 stick butter
1/2 teaspoon onion powder
1/2 teaspoon garlic powder
1/4 teaspoon dried dill weed

Sea salt and ground black pepper,
to taste
2 tablespoons tapioca starch
1 ½ cups whole milk
1 ½ cups Swiss cheese, grated

Directions

Press the "Sauté" button and melt the butter. Now, add the onion powder, garlic powder, dill, salt, and black pepper. Stir in the tapioca starch and stir to combine well.

Gradually pour in the milk, stirring continuously to avoid clumps. Bring to a boil and press the "Cancel" button.

Add in the Swiss cheese and stir until the cheese has melted. Serve warm with breadsticks or veggie sticks. Bon appétit!

Per serving: 148 Calories; 11.3g Fat; 5.2g Carbs; 6.7g Protein; 2.4g Sugars

841. Italian Frittata with Mushrooms and Spinach

(Ready in about 15 minutes | Servings 4)

Ingredients

6 eggs
1/4 cup double cream
1 cup Asiago cheese, shredded
Sea salt and freshly ground black pepper, to taste
1 teaspoon cayenne pepper
2 tablespoons olive oil

1 yellow onion, finely chopped
2 cloves garlic, minced
6 ounces Italian brown mushrooms, sliced
4 cups spinach, torn into pieces
1 tablespoon Italian seasoning mix

Directions

In a mixing bowl, thoroughly combine the eggs, double cream, Asiago cheese, salt, black pepper, and cayenne pepper.

Grease a baking dish with olive oil. Add the remaining ingredients; stir in the egg mixture. Spoon the mixture into the prepared baking dish.

Place 1 cup of water and a metal trivet in the inner pot. Lower the baking dish onto the prepared trivet.

Secure the lid. Choose the "Manual" mode and cook for 5 minutes at High pressure. Once cooking is complete, use a quick pressure release; carefully remove the lid. Bon appétit!

Per serving: 335 Calories; 26.5g Fat; 6.5g Carbs; 18.7g Protein; 2.6g Sugars

842. Keto Cauliflower Mac n' Cheese

(Ready in about 15 minutes | Servings 4)

Ingredients

1 pound cauliflower florets
1 cup heavy cream
4 ounces Ricotta cheese
1 ½ cups Cheddar cheese, shredded
Sea salt and ground white pepper, to taste

1/2 teaspoon garlic powder
1/2 teaspoon shallot powder
1/2 teaspoon celery seeds
1/2 teaspoon red pepper flakes
1/4 cup Parmesan cheese

Directions

Place 1 cup of water and a steamer basket in the inner pot of your Instant Pot. Throw the cauliflower florets into the steamer basket.

Secure the lid. Choose the "Manual" mode and cook for 2 minutes at High pressure. Once cooking is complete, use a quick pressure release; carefully remove the lid. Drain and reserve.

Press the "Sauté" button and use the lowest setting. Now, cook the heavy cream, Ricotta cheese, Cheddar cheese, and spices; let it simmer until the cheeses has melted.

Add in the cauliflower and gently stir to combine. Scatter the Parmesan cheese over the cauliflower and cheese and serve warm. Bon appétit!

Per serving: 387 Calories; 31.2g Fat; 10.2g Carbs; 18.2g Protein; 3.8g Sugars

843. Spanish Dip de Queso

(Ready in about 10 minutes | Servings 10)

Ingredients

3 tablespoons butter
3 tablespoons all-purpose flour
1 cup whole milk

8 ounces Monterey Jack, shredded
Kosher salt, to taste
1/2 teaspoon hot sauce

Directions

Press the "Sauté" button and melt the butter. Now, add the flour and stir to combine well.

Gradually pour in the milk, stirring continuously to avoid clumps. Bring to a boil and press the "Cancel" button.

Add in the Monterey Jack cheese and stir until cheese has melted; add the salt and hot sauce. Serve warm with tortilla chips if desired. Bon appétit!

Per serving: 146 Calories; 11.2g Fat; 5.1g Carbs; 6.6g Protein; 3.3g Sugars

SNACKS & APPETIZERS

844. Honey-Glazed Baby Carrots

(Ready in about 15 minutes | Servings 6)

Ingredients

1 ½ cups water
2 ½ pounds baby carrots, trimmed
1 teaspoon thyme
1 teaspoon dill
Salt and white pepper, to taste
2 tablespoons coconut oil
1/4 cup honey

Directions

Add 1½ cups of water to the base of your Instant Pot.

Now, arrange the baby carrots in the steaming basket. Transfer the steaming basket to the Instant Pot.

Secure the lid and choose the "Manual" function; cook for 3 minutes at High pressure. Once cooking is complete, use a quick release; carefully remove the lid.

Strain the baby carrots and reserve.

Then, add the other ingredients to the Instant Pot. Press the "Sauté" button and cook until everything is heated through.

Add the reserved baby carrots and gently stir. Bon appétit!

Per serving: 151 Calories; 4.8g Fat; 28g Carbs; 1.3g Protein; 21.1g Sugars

845. Party Dilled Deviled Eggs

(Ready in about 15 minutes + chilling time | Servings 6)

Ingredients

10 eggs
1/4 cup extra-virgin olive oil
2 tablespoons mayonnaise
1 teaspoon yellow mustard
1 tablespoon dill pickle juice
1/2 teaspoon Sriracha sauce
Maldon salt and freshly ground black pepper, to taste
1 tablespoon fresh parsley, chopped
2 tablespoons dill pickle, chopped

Directions

Begin by adding 1 cup of water and a steamer basket to your Instant Pot. Place the eggs in the steamer basket.

Secure the lid and choose the "Manual" function; cook for 5 minutes at High pressure. Once cooking is complete, use a natural release; carefully remove the lid.

Slice each egg in half lengthwise.

Transfer the egg yolks to your food processor. Now, add the remaining ingredients; process until creamy and smooth.

Then, pipe the chilled filling mixture into the egg whites, overstuffing each. Serve on a nice serving platter and enjoy!

Per serving: 277 Calories; 21.9g Fat; 3.7g Carbs; 15.8g Protein; 1.4g Sugars

846. Classic Hummus Dip

(Ready in about 45 minutes | Servings 8)

Ingredients

1 tablespoon olive oil
1 yellow onion, chopped
2 garlic cloves, minced
1 ½ cups dried chickpeas
4 cups water
3 tablespoons tahini paste
2 tablespoons fresh lemon juice

Directions

Press the "Sauté" button to preheat your Instant Pot. Once hot, heat the olive oil until sizzling. Then, cook the onion and garlic until tender and fragrant; reserve.

Wipe down the Instant Pot with a damp cloth. Then, add the chickpeas and water to the Instant Pot.

Secure the lid and choose the "Bean/Chili" function; cook for 40 minutes at High pressure. Once cooking is complete, use a natural release; carefully remove the lid.

Drain the chickpeas, reserving cooking liquid. Now, transfer chickpeas to your blender. Add the tahini, lemon juice, and reserved onion/garlic mixture.

Process until everything is creamy, uniform, and smooth, adding a splash of cooking liquid. Serve with pita bread and vegetable sticks.

Per serving: 206 Calories; 8.1g Fat; 26.1g Carbs; 8.8g Protein; 4.6g Sugars

847. Ranch-Style Popcorn

(Ready in about 10 minutes | Servings 6)

Ingredients

2 tablespoons olive oil
3/4 cup corn kernels
4 tablespoons butter
1-ounce packet ranch seasoning mix
Sea salt, to taste

Directions

Press the "Sauté" button to preheat your Instant Pot.

Now, heat the olive oil; add corn kernels. Sauté until the corn kernels are well coated with oil.

Secure the lid and choose the "Manual" function; cook for 5 minutes at High pressure. Once cooking is complete, use a quick release; carefully remove the lid.

In a saucepan, melt the butter with ranch seasoning mix. Lastly, toss the ranch butter with popcorn; season with salt. Enjoy!

Per serving: 177 Calories; 13.9g Fat; 11.1g Carbs; 2.4g Protein; 3.5g Sugars

848. Cheesy Artichoke and Kale Dip

(Ready in about 15 minutes | Servings 8)

Ingredients

12 ounces canned artichoke hearts, chopped
2 cups kale, chopped
1 cup Ricotta cheese
1 ¼ cups Romano cheese, grated
1/2 cup mayonnaise
1 teaspoon gourmet mustard
Salt and ground black pepper, to taste
1 teaspoon garlic powder
1/2 teaspoon shallot powder
1/2 teaspoon cumin powder

Directions

Lightly grease a baking pan that fits inside your Instant Pot. Add all of the above ingredients and stir to combine well.

Add a metal rack to the Instant Pot.

Then, create a foil sling and place it on a rack; lower the baking pan onto the foil strip.

Secure the lid and choose "Manual" function; cook for 9 minutes at High pressure. Once cooking is complete, use a quick release; remove the lid carefully.

Serve with breadsticks on the side. Bon appétit!

Per serving: 190 Calories; 13.2g Fat; 8.3g Carbs; 10.3g Protein; 1g Sugars

849. Whiskey Glazed Ribs

(Ready in about 25 minutes | Servings 6)

Ingredients

1 ½ pounds baby back ribs
1 teaspoon salt
1/2 teaspoon ground black pepper
1 teaspoon smoked paprika
1/2 teaspoon ancho chili powder
1/2 teaspoon granulated garlic
1 teaspoon shallot powder
1/2 teaspoon mustard seeds
1 teaspoon celery seeds
1/2 cup whiskey
1 cup ketchup
1/3 cup dark brown sugar
1/4 cup rice vinegar
1 teaspoon fish sauce
1 teaspoon Worcestershire sauce

Directions

Season the ribs with salt, black pepper, paprika, chili powder, garlic, shallot powder, mustard seeds, and celery seeds.

Add the seasoned ribs to the Instant Pot.

In a mixing bowl, thoroughly combine the whiskey, ketchup, sugar, vinegar, fish sauce, and Worcestershire sauce.

Then, pour the sauce into the Instant Pot.

Secure the lid and choose the "Meat/Stew" function; cook for 20 minutes at High pressure. Once cooking is complete, use a natural release; carefully remove the lid. Reserve the ribs.

Press the "Sauté" button to preheat your Instant Pot. Simmer the sauce until it has reduced to your desired thickness. Pour the glaze over the ribs and serve. Bon appétit!

Per serving: 359 Calories; 17.9g Fat; 28g Carbs; 22.8g Protein; 25.1g Sugars

850. Chicken Wings with Barbecue Sauce

(Ready in about 20 minutes | Servings 3)

Ingredients

1 cup water
6 chicken wings
For the Barbecue Sauce:
1/3 cup water
1/3 cup ketchup
2 tablespoons brown sugar
2 tablespoons blackstrap molasses
1 tablespoon mustard

1 tablespoon cider vinegar
1 tablespoon olive oil
1 teaspoon garlic, minced
1 teaspoon chipotle powder
1/4 teaspoon sea salt
1/4 teaspoon freshly ground black pepper
1/4 teaspoon ground allspice

Directions

Pour 1 cup of water into the base of your Instant Pot.

Now, arrange the wings in the steaming basket. Transfer the steaming basket to the Instant Pot.

Secure the lid and choose the "Poultry" function; cook for 15 minutes at High pressure. Once cooking is complete, use a natural release; carefully remove the lid.

In a pan, combine all of the ingredients for the sauce and bring to a boil. Remove from the heat and stir well. Add the chicken wings and serve. Bon appétit!

Per serving: 204 Calories; 6.7g Fat; 23.1g Carbs; 13.2g Protein; 20.1g Sugars

851. Hoisin-Glazed White Mushrooms

(Ready in about 10 minutes | Servings 5)

Ingredients

20 ounces fresh white mushrooms
1/3 cup water
1 tablespoon apple cider vinegar
3 tablespoons soy sauce
1 tablespoon peanut butter
1 tablespoon molasses

2 garlic cloves, minced
2 tablespoons olive oil
1/2 teaspoon hot sauce
Sea salt and ground black pepper, to taste
1 teaspoon paprika

Directions

Add all ingredients to your Instant Pot.

Secure the lid. Choose the "Manual" mode and High pressure; cook for 5 minutes. Once cooking is complete, use a quick pressure release; carefully remove the lid; remove the mushrooms from the cooking liquid.

Then, press the "Sauté" button and continue to simmer until the sauce has reduced and thickened.

Place the reserved mushrooms in a serving bowl, add the sauce and serve.

Per serving: 124 Calories; 8.1g Fat; 10.2g Carbs; 4.4g Protein; 7.7g Sugars

852. Easy Brussels Sprout Appetizer

(Ready in about 10 minutes | Servings 4)

Ingredients

2 tablespoons butter
1/2 cup shallots, chopped
1/4 cup dry white wine
1 ½ pounds Brussels sprouts, trimmed and halved

1 cup water
Salt, to taste
1/4 teaspoon ground black pepper, or more to taste

Directions

Press the "Sauté" button to preheat your Instant Pot. Once hot, melt the butter and sauté the shallots until tender.

Add a splash of wine to deglaze the bottom of the Instant Pot. Add the remaining ingredients to the Instant Pot.

Secure the lid. Choose the "Manual" mode and High pressure; cook for 4 minutes. Once cooking is complete, use a quick pressure release; carefully remove the lid. Bon appétit!

Per serving: 145 Calories; 7.7g Fat; 15.5g Carbs; 7.3g Protein; 3.8g Sugars

853. Appetizer Meatballs with Barbecue Sauce

(Ready in about 15 minutes | Servings 12)

Ingredients

For the Meatballs:
1 pound ground chuck
1/2 pound ground pork
Seasoned salt and ground black pepper, to taste
1 onion, chopped
2 garlic cloves, minced
1 egg, well-beaten
1/2 cup Romano cheese, preferably freshly grated

2/3 cup tortilla chips, crushed
For the Sauce:
1 cup water
1 cup ketchup
1/4 cup apple cider vinegar
6 tablespoons light brown sugar
1/2 teaspoon onion powder
1 teaspoon ground mustard

Directions

Mix all ingredients for the meatballs. Spritz a sauté pan with a nonstick cooking spray.

Heat the sauté pan over a medium-high heat. Then, brown the meatballs until they are delicately browned on all sides.

In another mixing dish, thoroughly combine all ingredients for the sauce. Add the sauce to the Instant Pot.

Drop the meatballs into the sauce.

Secure the lid and choose the "Poultry" function; cook for 5 minutes at High pressure. Once cooking is complete, use a natural release; carefully remove the lid.

Serve on a nice platter with toothpicks. Enjoy!

Per serving: 178 Calories; 9.4g Fat; 8.3g Carbs; 15g Protein; 5.1g Sugars

854. Sticky Chinese-Style Cocktail Sausages

(Ready in about 15 minutes | Servings 8)

Ingredients

2 teaspoons toasted sesame oil
10 hot dogs, chopped into thirds
1/2 cup ketchup
1/3 cup chicken stock
2 tablespoons tamari sauce
1 tablespoon rice vinegar
1 teaspoon chili powder

Salt, to taste
1/2 teaspoon Szechuan pepper
1 teaspoon cayenne pepper
1 teaspoon Dijon mustard
1/2 teaspoon fresh ginger, peeled and grated

Directions

Add all of the above ingredients to the Instant Pot.

Secure the lid. Choose "Manual" mode and High pressure; cook for 5 minutes. Once cooking is complete, use a quick pressure release; carefully remove the lid.

Serve with cocktail sticks; garnish with sesame seeds if desired. Enjoy!

Per serving: 270 Calories; 20g Fat; 5.4g Carbs; 16.4g Protein; 3.5g Sugars

855. Herby and Garlicky Fingerling Potatoes

(Ready in about 25 minutes | Servings 6)

Ingredients

4 tablespoons butter, melted
1 ½ pounds fingerling potatoes
2 sprigs thyme
2 sprigs rosemary
1 teaspoon garlic paste
3/4 cup vegetable broth

Sea salt, to taste
1/2 teaspoon ground black pepper
1/2 teaspoon cayenne pepper
1/2 teaspoon shallot powder
1/2 teaspoon porcini powder

Directions

Press the "Sauté" button to preheat your Instant Pot; now, melt the butter.

Sauté the potatoes, rolling them around for about 9 minutes. Now, pierce the middle of each potato with a knife.

Secure the lid. Choose the "Manual" mode and High pressure; cook for 10 minutes. Once cooking is complete, use a quick pressure release; carefully remove the lid.

Serve with toothpicks and enjoy!

Per serving: 391 Calories; 35.1g Fat; 19.9g Carbs; 2.4g Protein; 0.8g Sugars

856. Kid-Friendly Pizza Dip

(Ready in about 25 minutes | Servings 10)

Ingredients

10 ounces cream cheese
1 cup tomato sauce
1/2 cup mozzarella cheese, shredded
1/2 cup green olives, pitted and sliced

1/2 teaspoon oregano
1/2 teaspoon basil
1/2 teaspoon garlic salt
1/2 cup Romano cheese, shredded

Directions

Add 1 ½ cups of water and metal trivet to the inner pot. Spritz a souffle dish with cooking spray.

Place the cream cheese on the bottom of the souffle dish. Add the tomato sauce and mozzarella cheese. Scatter sliced olives over the top.

Add the oregano, basil, and garlic salt. Top with Romano cheese. Lower the dish onto the prepared trivet.

Secure the lid. Choose the "Manual" mode and cook for 18 minutes at High pressure. Once cooking is complete, use a quick pressure release; carefully remove the lid.

Serve with chips or breadsticks if desired. Enjoy!

Per serving: 158 Calories; 11.8g Fat; 6.9g Carbs; 5.7g Protein; 3.9g Sugars

857. Spicy Beer Little Smokies

(Ready in about 10 minutes | Servings 12)

Ingredients

16 ounces little smokies
1/2 cup roasted vegetable broth
1/2 cup light beer
14 ounces grape jelly

2 tablespoons white vinegar
1/3 cup chili sauce
1/3 brown sugar
1 jalapeno, minced

Directions

Place all ingredients in the inner pot of your Instant Pot.

Secure the lid. Choose the "Manual" mode and cook for 2 minutes at High pressure. Once cooking is complete, use a quick pressure release; carefully remove the lid.

Serve hot or keep on warm in your Instant Pot until ready to serve.

Per serving: 209 Calories; 16.1g Fat; 11.5g Carbs; 7g Protein; 6.2g Sugars

858. Nacho Bean Dip

(Ready in about 35 minutes | Servings 10)

Ingredients

1 tablespoon olive oil
1 onion, chopped
2 cloves garlic, minced
1 red chili pepper, finely chopped
1 cup pinto beans, rinsed
1/2 cup chunky salsa
2 cups vegetable broth
1 teaspoon ground cumin

Kosher salt and ground black pepper, to taste
1 ounce package taco seasoning mix
1 cup Cheddar cheese, shredded
1 cup queso fresco cheese, crumbled
2 tablespoons fresh cilantro, chopped

Directions

Press the "Sauté" button and heat the olive oil until sizzling. Once hot, cook the onion for 3 to 4 minutes or until tender and fragrant.

After that, stir in the garlic and chili pepper; continue sautéing an additional 30 to 40 seconds.

Stir in the beans, salsa, broth, cumin, salt, black pepper, and taco seasoning mix.

Secure the lid. Choose the "Bean/Chili" mode and cook for 25 minutes at High pressure. Once cooking is complete, use a quick pressure release; carefully remove the lid.

Then, mash your beans with a potato masher or use your blender. Return to the Instant Pot and press the "Sauté" button; stir in the cheese and let it melt on the lowest setting. Serve garnished with cilantro and enjoy!

Per serving: 146 Calories; 4.8g Fat; 17.3g Carbs; 8.1g Protein; 2.5g Sugars

859. Zingy Cilantro Lime Wings

(Ready in about 30 minutes | Servings 4)

Ingredients

2 teaspoons butter
8 chicken wings
3 cloves garlic, minced
1 teaspoon cayenne pepper
1/2 teaspoon smoked paprika

Sea salt and ground black pepper, to taste
1/2 cup chicken broth
1 lime, freshly squeezed
1/4 cup fresh cilantro, chopped

Directions

Press the "Sauté" button and heat the olive oil until sizzling. Once hot, brown the chicken wings for 2 to 3 minutes per side.

Add in the remaining ingredients and toss to coat well.

Secure the lid. Choose the "Manual" mode and cook for 10 minutes at High pressure. Once cooking is complete, use a natural pressure release for 10 minutes; carefully remove the lid.

Broil the chicken wings for about 5 minutes or until they are golden brown. Bon appétit!

Per serving: 108 Calories; 4.3g Fat; 3.3g Carbs; 13.9g Protein; 0.9g Sugars

860. Easy Cocktail Meatballs

(Ready in about 20 minutes | Servings 8)

Ingredients

1/2 pound ground chicken
1/2 pound ground turkey
1 egg
1 cup tortilla chips, crumbled
1 onion, finely chopped
2 garlic cloves, minced

1/2 teaspoon basil
Sea salt and ground black pepper, to taste
1 tablespoon olive oil
16 ounces grape jelly

Directions

In a mixing bowl, thoroughly combine all ingredients, except for the olive oil and grape jelly. Shape the mixture into 24 meatballs.

Press the "Sauté" button and heat the olive oil. Once hot, brown meatballs for 3 to 4 minutes.

Add the grape jelly to the inner pot.

Secure the lid. Choose the "Manual" mode and cook for 6 minutes at High pressure. Once cooking is complete, use a natural pressure release for 5 minutes; carefully remove the lid.

Serve with cocktail sticks and enjoy!

Per serving: 199 Calories; 9.1g Fat; 17.2g Carbs; 12.9g Protein; 11.4g Sugars

861. Sinfully Delicious Cinnamon Popcorn

(Ready in about 10 minutes | Servings 4)

Ingredients

2 tablespoons coconut oil
1/2 cup popcorn kernels

1/4 cup icing sugar
1/2 tablespoon ground cinnamon

Directions

Press the "Sauté" button and melt the coconut oil. Stir until it begins to simmer.

Stir in the popcorn kernels and cover. When the popping slows down, press the "Cancel" button.

Toss the freshly popped corn with icing sugar and cinnamon. Toss to evenly coat the popcorn and serve immediately.

Per serving: 295 Calories; 11.5g Fat; 42.2g Carbs; 6.3g Protein; 6.6g Sugars

862. Old-Fashioned Short Ribs

(Ready in about 1 hour 45 minutes | Servings 8)

Ingredients
1 tablespoon lard
3 pounds short ribs
Sea salt and ground black pepper, to season
1/2 cup port wine
1 teaspoon cayenne pepper
2 tablespoons molasses
2 tablespoons rice vinegar
4 cloves of garlic
2 rosemary sprigs
2 thyme sprigs
1 cup beef bone broth

Directions
Press the "Sauté" button and melt the lard. Once hot, cook the short ribs for 4 to 5 minutes, turning them periodically to ensure even cooking.

Add the other ingredients.

Secure the lid. Choose the "Manual" mode and cook for 90 minutes at High pressure. Once cooking is complete, use a natural pressure release; carefully remove the lid.

Afterwards, place the short ribs under the broiler until the outside is crisp or about 10 minutes. Transfer the ribs to a platter and serve immediately.

Per serving: 372 Calories; 27.6g Fat; 4.9g Carbs; 25.7g Protein; 3.4g Sugars

863. Chinese Sticky Baby Carrots

(Ready in about 10 minutes | Servings 6)

Ingredients
2 pounds baby carrots, trimmed and scrubbed
1/2 cup orange juice
1/2 cup water
2 tablespoons raisins
2 tablespoons soy sauce
2 tablespoons Shaoxing wine
1 teaspoon garlic powder
1/2 teaspoon shallot powder
1 teaspoon mustard powder
1/4 teaspoon cumin seeds
2 teaspoons butter, at room temperature
2 tablespoons sesame seeds, toasted

Directions
Place all ingredients, except for the sesame seeds, in the inner pot of your Instant Pot.

Secure the lid. Choose the "Manual" mode and cook for 2 minutes at High pressure. Once cooking is complete, use a quick pressure release; carefully remove the lid.

Serve in a nice bowl, sprinkle the sesame seeds over the top and enjoy!

Per serving: 110 Calories; 4.5g Fat; 17.2g Carbs; 2.3g Protein; 8.1g Sugars

864. Artichokes with Greek Dipping Sauce

(Ready in about 20 minutes | Servings 4)

Ingredients
4 artichokes
4 tablespoons mayonnaise
2 tablespoons Greek yogurt
1 tablespoon Dijon mustard
1/2 teaspoon tzatziki spice mix

Directions
Place 1 cup of water and a steamer basket in the inner pot of your Instant Pot.

Place the artichokes in the steamer basket.

Secure the lid. Choose the "Manual" mode and cook for 11 minutes at High pressure. Once cooking is complete, use a quick pressure release; carefully remove the lid.

Meanwhile, whisk the remaining ingredients to prepare the sauce. Serve the artichokes with the Greek sauce on the side. Bon appétit!

Per serving: 177 Calories; 10.9g Fat; 17.6g Carbs; 5.8g Protein; 2.1g Sugars

865. Herbed Butter Mushrooms

(Ready in about 10 minutes | Servings 5)

Ingredients
20 ounces button mushrooms, brushed clean
2 cloves garlic, minced
1 teaspoon onion powder
1 teaspoon dried basil
1/2 teaspoon dried oregano
1/2 teaspoon dried rosemary
1 teaspoon smoked paprika
Coarse sea salt and ground black pepper, to taste
1 cup vegetable broth
2 tablespoons butter
2 tablespoons tomato paste

Directions
Place the mushrooms, garlic, spices, and broth in the inner pot.

Secure the lid. Choose the "Manual" mode and cook for 4 minutes at High pressure. Once cooking is complete, use a quick pressure release; carefully remove the lid.

Now, stir in the butter and tomato paste. Serve with cocktail sticks or toothpicks. Enjoy!

Per serving: 88 Calories; 5.5g Fat; 7.6g Carbs; 5.2g Protein; 3.6g Sugars

866. Candied Nuts with Sultanas

(Ready in about 25 minutes | Servings 12)

Ingredients
1 cup pecans halves
1 cup almonds
1 cup canned chickpeas
2 tablespoons sunflower seeds
2 tablespoons pumpkin seeds
2 tablespoons butter
1/2 cup maple syrup
1/4 teaspoon grated nutmeg
1/4 teaspoon ground ginger
1/4 teaspoon kosher salt
1 cup Sultanas

Directions
Place all ingredients, except for the Sultanas, in the inner pot of your Instant Pot. Stir to combine well.

Press the "Sauté" button and cook until the butter has melted and the nuts are well coated.

Secure the lid. Choose the "Manual" mode and cook for 10 minutes at High pressure. Once cooking is complete, use a quick pressure release; carefully remove the lid.

Bake on a roasting pan at 370 degrees F for about 8 minutes. Add the Sultanas and stir to combine. Bon appétit!

Per serving: 149 Calories; 9.5g Fat; 14.6g Carbs; 2.8g Protein; 9.1g Sugars

867. Authentic Greek Fava Dip

(Ready in about 50 minutes | Servings 10)

Ingredients
1 tablespoon olive oil
1 red onion, finely chopped
1 teaspoon garlic, minced
Sea salt and ground black pepper, to taste
1 pound fava beans, rinsed
1 teaspoon basil
1 teaspoon oregano
Juice of 1/2 lemon
1/2 cup Kalamata olives, pitted
1 tablespoon fresh mint leaves, roughly chopped

Directions
Press the "Sauté" button and heat the oil. Once hot, cook the onion until tender and translucent.

Now, stir in the garlic and let it cook for 30 seconds more, stirring frequently. Then, add the salt, pepper, fava beans, basil, and oregano. Add enough water to fully submerge the beans.

Secure the lid. Choose the "Bean/Chili" mode and cook for 40 minutes at High pressure. Once cooking is complete, use a natural pressure release for 5 minutes; carefully remove the lid.

Add the lemon juice and puree the mixture with an immersion blender, Transfer to a nice serving bowl and serve garnished with Kalamata olives and mint leaves. Enjoy!

Per serving: 178 Calories; 2.5g Fat; 29.4g Carbs; 11g Protein; 1.7g Sugars

868. Buffalo Chicken Dip

(Ready in about 25 minutes | Servings 12)

Ingredients

1 pound chicken breasts, chopped
10 ounces hot sauce
4 tablespoons butter
1 cup cream cheese, softened
Salt to taste
2 cups cheddar cheese, shredded
2 tablespoons fresh parsley, chopped
2 tablespoons fresh chives, chopped

Directions

Add the chicken breasts to the inner pot of your Instant Pot; add in the hot sauce and butter.

Secure the lid. Choose the "Manual" mode and cook for 8 minutes at High pressure. Once cooking is complete, use a quick pressure release; carefully remove the lid.

Stir in the cream cheese and salt. Spoon chicken dip into a baking dish; top with the cheddar cheese and bake at 395 degrees F for about 8 minutes or until cheese is bubbling.

Scatter fresh parsley and chives over the top and serve warm.

Per serving: 219 Calories; 17g Fat; 2.6g Carbs; 14g Protein; 1.7g Sugars

869. Garlic Butter Shrimp

(Ready in about 10 minutes | Servings 8)

Ingredients

1 ½ pounds shrimp, deveined
1/2 stick butter
1/4 cup soy sauce
2 garlic cloves, minced
Sea salt and ground black pepper, to taste
2 tablespoons fresh scallions, chopped

Directions

Throw all ingredients, except for the scallions, into the inner pot of your Instant Pot.

Secure the lid. Choose the "Manual" mode and cook for 4 minutes at High pressure. Once cooking is complete, use a quick pressure release; carefully remove the lid.

Transfer your shrimp to a nice serving bowl. The sauce will thicken as it cools. Garnish with fresh scallions and serve with toothpicks.

Per serving: 142 Calories; 6.2g Fat; 4.5g Carbs; 17.4g Protein; 3.3g Sugars

870. Asian-Style Lettuce Wraps

(Ready in about 20 minutes | Servings 4)

Ingredients

1/2 pound chicken breasts
2 teaspoons sesame oil
1 small onion, finely diced
2 garlic cloves, minced
1 teaspoon ginger, minced
Kosher salt and ground black pepper, to taste
2 tablespoons hoisin sauce
2 tablespoons soy sauce
2 tablespoons rice vinegar
1 small head butter lettuce, leaves separated

Directions

Add the chicken breasts and 1 cup of water to the inner pot of your Instant Pot.

Secure the lid. Choose the "Manual" mode and cook for 8 minutes at High pressure. Once cooking is complete, use a quick pressure release; carefully remove the lid. Shred your chicken with two forks.

Press the "Sauté" button and heat the oil. Once hot, cook the onion and garlic for 3 to 4 minutes or until they are softened.

Now, add the chicken and cook for 2 to 3 minutes more. Add the ginger, salt, black pepper, hoisin sauce, soy sauce, and rice vinegar; let it cook for a few minutes more.

Spoon the chicken mixture into the lettuce leaves, wrap them and serve immediately. Bon appétit!

Per serving: 179 Calories; 9.3g Fat; 9.7g Carbs; 13.7g Protein; 5.4g Sugars

871. Taco Mini Stuffed Peppers

(Ready in about 20 minutes | Servings 5)

Ingredients

4 ounces bacon, chopped
1 small onion, chopped
1 garlic clove, minced
6 ounces Mexican cheese blend, crumbled
1 teaspoon Worcestershire sauce
1 teaspoon Taco seasoning mix
10 mini sweet bell peppers, seeds and membranes removed
2 tablespoons fresh cilantro, finely chopped

Directions

Press the "Sauté" button to preheat your Instant Pot. Now, cook the bacon until it is crisp; crumble with a spatula and reserve.

Now, cook the onion and garlic in pan drippings until just tender and fragrant. Add the cheese, Worcestershire sauce, and Taco seasoning mix. Stir in the reserved bacon.

Evenly divide the bacon/cheese mixture among the peppers.

Place a metal trivet and 1 cup of water in your Instant Pot. Arrange the stuffed peppers onto the trivet.

Secure the lid. Choose the "Manual" mode and cook for 5 minutes at High pressure. Once cooking is complete, use a natural pressure release for 5 minutes; carefully remove the lid.

Serve on a platter garnished with fresh cilantro. Enjoy!

Per serving: 234 Calories; 15.7g Fat; 11.9g Carbs; 13.3g Protein; 5.7g Sugars

872. Polenta Bites with Cheese and Herbs

(Ready in about 20 minutes | Servings 8)

Ingredients

1 cup cornmeal
3 cups water
1 cup milk
1 teaspoon kosher salt
1 tablespoon butter
1/2 cup cream cheese
2 tablespoons cilantro, finely chopped
2 tablespoons chives, finely chopped
1 tablespoon thyme
1 teaspoon rosemary
1 teaspoon basil
1/2 cup bread crumbs
2 tablespoons olive oil

Directions

Add the polenta, water, milk. and salt to the inner pot of your Instant Pot. Press the "Sauté" button and bring the mixture to a simmer. Press the "Cancel" button.

Secure the lid. Choose the "Manual" mode and cook for 8 minutes at High pressure. Once cooking is complete, use a quick pressure release; carefully remove the lid.

Grease a baking pan with butter. Add the cream cheese and herbs to your polenta.

Scoop the hot polenta into the prepared baking pan and refrigerate until firm. Cut into small squares. Spread the breadcrumbs on a large plate; coat each side of the polenta squares with breadcrumbs.

Heat the olive oil in a nonstick pan over medium heat; cook the polenta squares approximately 3 minutes per side or until golden brown. Bon appétit!

Per serving: 181 Calories; 8.2g Fat; 22.6g Carbs; 4.1g Protein; 2.7g Sugars

873. Vegetable and Turkey Cocktail Meatballs

(Ready in about 15 minutes | Servings 8)

Ingredients

2 shallots, peeled and finely chopped
2 garlic cloves, minced
1 parsnip, grated
2 carrots, grated
1 cup button mushrooms, chopped
1/2 cup all-purpose flour
Sea salt and ground black pepper, to taste

2 pounds turkey, ground
2 tablespoons olive oil
3 ripe tomatoes, pureed
1 teaspoon dried oregano
2 sprigs rosemary, leaves picked
2 sprigs thyme, leaves picked
3/4 cup broth, preferably homemade

Directions

In a mixing bowl, combine the shallots, garlic, parsnip, carrots, mushrooms, flour, salt, pepper, and ground turkey.

Shape the mixture into small cocktail meatballs.

Press the "Sauté" button and heat the olive oil. Once hot, sear the meatballs on all sides until they are browned.

Thoroughly combine the pureed tomatoes, oregano, rosemary, and thyme. Pour in the tomato mixture and broth. Secure the lid.

Now, choose the "Manual" function; cook for 9 minutes at High pressure. Once cooking is complete, use a natural release; remove the lid carefully.

Serve with cocktail sticks or toothpicks. Bon appétit!

Per serving: 319 Calories; 21.9g Fat; 12.6g Carbs; 17.5g Protein; 3g Sugars

874. Buttery Carrot Sticks

(Ready in about 10 minutes | Servings 4)

Ingredients

1 pound carrots, cut into sticks
1/2 cup dry white wine
1/4 cup water
Sea salt and white pepper, to taste
1/2 stick butter, softened

2 tablespoons agave nectar
1 teaspoon ground allspice
1/2 teaspoon caraway seeds
1 tablespoon fresh lime juice

Directions

Add all of the above ingredients to your Instant Pot.

Secure the lid. Choose the "Manual" mode and High pressure; cook for 2 minutes. Once cooking is complete, use a quick pressure release; carefully remove the lid.

Transfer to a nice serving bowl and enjoy!

Per serving: 199 Calories; 14.9g Fat; 13.7g Carbs; 4.5g Protein; 6.2g Sugars

875. Beet Appetizer Salad with Cherry Vinaigrette

(Ready in about 15 minutes + chilling time | Servings 4)

Ingredients

1 pound red beets
1 cup baby spinach leaves
1/2 cup cream cheese
2 tablespoons dried cherries
1/2 teaspoon ground cumin

2 tablespoons sherry vinegar
1/4 cup extra-virgin olive oil
Sea salt and freshly cracked black pepper

Directions

Add 1 ½ cups of water and steamer basket to your Instant Pot. Place the whole and unpeeled beets in the steamer basket.

Secure the lid. Choose the "Steam" mode and High pressure; cook for 10 minutes. Once cooking is complete, use a quick pressure release; carefully remove the lid.

Allow the red beets to cool completely. Then, rub the skin off the beets and cut them into very thin slices.

Transfer the beets to a salad bowl; add baby spinach, and cream cheese.

In a food processor, purée the dried cherries, cumin, vinegar, olive oil, salt, and black pepper. Add this vinaigrette to the salad; toss to combine and serve.

Per serving: 197 Calories; 14.6g Fat; 13.1g Carbs; 4.3g Protein; 9.3g Sugars

876. Crispy Chicken Drumettes

(Ready in about 30 minutes | Servings 6)

Ingredients

1 ½ pounds chicken drumettes
Kosher salt, to taste
1/2 teaspoon mixed peppercorns, crushed
1/2 teaspoon cayenne pepper
1 teaspoon shallot powder

1 teaspoon garlic powder
1/2 stick butter, melted
2 tablespoons hot sauce
1 tablespoon fish sauce
1/3 cup ketchup

Directions

Prepare your Instant Pot by adding 1 cup of water and metal trivet to its bottom. Place the chicken drumettes on the trivet.

Secure the lid. Choose the "Manual" mode and High pressure; cook for 6 minutes. Once cooking is complete, use a natural pressure release; carefully remove the lid.

Toss the chicken wings with the remaining ingredients.

Arrange the chicken wings, top side down, on a broiler pan. Place rack on top. Broil for 10 minutes; flip over and broil for 10 minutes more.

Top with the remaining sauce and serve immediately.

Per serving: 212 Calories; 10.7g Fat; 4.6g Carbs; 23.6g Protein; 3.2g Sugars

877. Spicy Boiled Peanuts

(Ready in about 1 hour 25 minutes | Servings 8)

Ingredients

1 ½ pounds raw peanuts in the shell, rinsed an cleaned
1/2 cup salt
Water
3 jalapenos, sliced

2 tablespoons red pepper flakes
2 tablespoons Creole seasoning
1 teaspoon garlic powder
1 teaspoon lemon pepper

Directions

Place the peanuts and salt in your Instant Pot; cover with water. Add all seasonings and stir to combine.

Place a trivet on top to hold down the peanuts.

Secure the lid and choose the "Manual" mode. Cook for 1 hour 20 minutes at High pressure.

Once cooking is complete, use a natural release; remove the lid carefully. Enjoy!

Per serving: 340 Calories; 28.1g Fat; 13.6g Carbs; 14.1g Protein; 3.6g Sugars

878. Party Cauliflower Balls

(Ready in about 25 minutes | Servings 6)

Ingredients

1 pound cauliflower, broken into small florets
2 tablespoons butter
2 cloves garlic, minced
1/2 cup Parmesan cheese, grated
2 eggs, beaten

1 cup Swiss cheese, shredded
2 tablespoons fresh parsley, minced
1 teaspoon cayenne pepper
Sea salt and ground black pepper, to taste

Directions

Prepare your Instant Pot by adding 1 cup of water and a steamer basket to its bottom.

Place the cauliflower florets in the steamer basket.

Secure the lid. Choose the "Steam" mode and High pressure; cook for 3 minutes. Once cooking is complete, use a quick pressure release; carefully remove the lid.

Transfer the cauliflower florets to your blender. Add the remaining ingredients; process until everything is well incorporated.

Roll the cauliflower mixture into bite-sized balls. Bake in the preheated oven at 400 degrees F for 16 minutes. Bon appétit!

Per serving: 194 Calories; 13.8g Fat; 6.5g Carbs; 11.6g Protein; 1.8g Sugars

879. Double Cheese Burger Dip

(Ready in about 15 minutes | Servings 10)

Ingredients

1 tablespoon canola oil
1 pound ground turkey
1 onion, chopped
1 clove garlic, chopped
2 cups ripe tomato purée

1/4 cup vegetable broth
1 tablespoon Worcestershire sauce
10 ounces Ricotta cheese, crumbled
10 ounces Colby cheese, shredded

Directions

Press the "Sauté" button to preheat your Instant Pot. Once hot, heat the oil.

Then, cook the ground turkey, onion and garlic for 2 to 3 minutes or until the meat is no longer pink. Add the tomato purée, broth, and Worcestershire sauce.

Secure the lid. Choose the "Manual" mode and High pressure; cook for 5 minutes. Once cooking is complete, use a quick pressure release; carefully remove the lid.

Now, stir in the cheese. Stir until everything is well incorporated; serve immediately.

Per serving: 253 Calories; 17.7g Fat; 4.2g Carbs; 19.3g Protein; 1.6g Sugars

880. Minty Party Meatballs

(Ready in about 15 minutes | Servings 8)

Ingredients

1 pound ground chuck
1/2 pound ground pork
1 cup scallions, chopped
1/2 cup tortilla chips, crushed
2/3 cup Parmesan cheese, grated
1 egg, beaten
3 tablespoons full-fat milk

1 teaspoon garlic, minced
Sea salt and ground black pepper, to taste
1 teaspoon dried oregano
1 teaspoon dried basil
2 cups tomato sauce
1/4 cup fresh mint, plus minced

Directions

In a mixing bowl, thoroughly combine the ground meat, scallions, tortilla chips, Parmesan cheese, egg, milk, garlic, salt, black pepper, oregano, and basil.

Shape the mixture into balls using an ice cream scoop.

Spritz the bottom and sides of the Instant Pot with a nonstick cooking spray; add the meatballs; pour in the sauce.

Secure the lid. Choose the "Manual" setting and cook for 9 minutes under High pressure. Once cooking is complete, use a quick pressure release; carefully remove the lid.

Sprinkle minced mint leaves over the meatballs and serve. Bon appétit!

Per serving: 241 Calories; 10.9g Fat; 14.5g Carbs; 19.2g Protein; 6.5g Sugars

881. Mini Pork Tacos

(Ready in about 1 hour | Servings 10)

Ingredients

2 tablespoons olive oil
2 pounds pork shoulder
2 tablespoons honey
Kosher salt, to taste
1/4 teaspoon freshly ground black pepper
1 teaspoon cayenne pepper

1/2 teaspoon celery seeds
1 teaspoon ground cumin
1/3 cup rice wine
1 tablespoon rice vinegar
1 cup beer
1/2 cup ketchup
2 cups coleslaw, for serving

Directions

Press the "Sauté" button to preheat your Instant Pot. Then, heat the oil until sizzling.

Once hot, cook the pork until well browned on all sides. Add the honey, salt, black pepper, cayenne pepper, celery seeds, cumin, wine, vinegar, and beer to your Instant Pot.

Secure the lid. Choose the "Manual" mode and High pressure; cook for 50 minutes. Once cooking is complete, use a natural pressure release; carefully remove the lid.

Then, shred the meat with two forks. Return it to the Instant Pot. Add ketchup and seal the lid one more time.

Press the "Sauté" button and let it simmer for 2 to 3 minutes more or until heated through. Serve in 6-inch corn tortillas, garnished with coleslaw.

Per serving: 388 Calories; 25.9g Fat; 13.1g Carbs; 25.1g Protein; 9.4g Sugars

882. Harissa Meat and Tomato Dip

(Ready in about 20 minutes | Servings 10)

Ingredients

2 tablespoons canola oil
1 pound ground pork
1/2 pound ground beef
1/2 cup leeks, finely chopped
1 garlic clove, minced
1 ½ teaspoons Cajun seasonings

1 teaspoon harissa spice blend
1/2 teaspoon cayenne pepper
1 teaspoon sea salt
1/2 teaspoon ground black pepper, to taste
2 ripe tomatoes, chopped

Directions

Press the "Sauté" button and heat the oil. Once hot, cook the ground meat, stirring with a Silicone spatula so that it gets broken up as it cooks.

Stir in the leeks and garlic; cook until they are tender and fragrant. Stir in the Cajun seasonings, harissa spice blend, cayenne pepper, sea salt, and ground black pepper.

Add the pureed tomatoes and secure the lid. Now, choose the "Manual" mode and cook for 13 minutes at High pressure.

Once cooking is complete, use a natural release; remove the lid carefully. Serve with fresh veggie sticks. Bon appétit!

Per serving: 226 Calories; 15.4g Fat; 2.2g Carbs; 18.6g Protein; 0.8g Sugars

883. Cheese and Pepper Stuffed Mushrooms

(Ready in about 10 minutes | Servings 4)

Ingredients

2 tablespoons butter, at room temperature
1/2 cup scallions, chopped
2 cloves garlic, minced
1 cup cream cheese, at room temperature
1 cup cheddar cheese, grated

1 bell pepper, seeded and chopped
1 chili pepper, seeded and minced
1 teaspoon dried oregano
1 teaspoon dried parsley flakes
1 teaspoon dried rosemary
16 medium-sized button mushrooms, stems removed

Directions

Press the "Sauté" button to preheat your Instant Pot. Now, melt the butter and sauté the scallions until tender and fragrant.

Stir in the garlic; continue to sauté an additional 30 seconds or until fragrant. Add the cheese, peppers, oregano, parsley, and rosemary.

After that, fill the mushroom caps with the pepper/cheese mixture.

Place 1 cup of water and a steamer basket in the Instant Pot. Arrange the stuffed mushrooms in the steamer basket.

Secure the lid. Choose the "Manual" mode and High pressure; cook for 5 minutes. Once cooking is complete, use a quick pressure release; carefully remove the lid. Bon appétit!

Per serving: 304 Calories; 25.4g Fat; 10.9g Carbs; 10.7g Protein; 6.7g Sugars

884. Pinto Bean Dip with Sour Cream

(Ready in about 30 minutes | Servings 12)

Ingredients

2 cups dried pinto beans, soaked overnight
2 cloves garlic, minced
1/2 cup shallots, chopped
1 red chili pepper, minced
2 (14.5-ounce) cans tomatoes
1 cup beef bone broth
Sea salt and ground black pepper, to taste
1 teaspoon sweet paprika
1 teaspoon mustard powder
1 teaspoon marjoram, dried
1/4 teaspoon ground bay leaves
1 cup sour cream
2 heaping tablespoons fresh chives, roughly chopped

Directions

Add the beans, garlic, shallots, chili pepper, tomatoes, broth, salt, black pepper, paprika, mustard powder, marjoram, and ground bay leaves to your Instant Pot.

Secure the lid. Choose "Bean/Chili" mode and High pressure; cook for 25 minutes. Once cooking is complete, use a natural pressure release; carefully remove the lid.

Transfer the bean mixture to your food processor; mix until everything is creamy and smooth. Serve topped with sour cream and fresh chives. Enjoy!

Per serving: 154 Calories; 2.6g Fat; 25.1g Carbs; 8.3g Protein; 3.1g Sugars

885. Party Deviled Eggs

(Ready in about 20 minutes | Servings 8)

Ingredients

1 ½ cups water
8 eggs
3 teaspoons mayonnaise
1 tablespoon sour cream
1 teaspoon gourmet mustard
1/2 teaspoon hot sauce
1/3 teaspoon ground black pepper
Crunchy sea salt, to taste
3 tablespoons fresh chives, thinly sliced

Directions

Pour the water into the base of your Instant Pot.

Now, arrange the eggs in the steaming basket. Transfer the steaming basket to the Instant Pot.

Secure the lid and choose the "Manual" function; cook for 13 minutes at Low pressure. Once cooking is complete, use a quick release; remove the lid carefully.

Peel the eggs under running water. Remove the yolks and smash them with a fork; reserve.

Now, mix the mayonnaise, sour cream, gourmet mustard, hot sauce, black pepper, and salt; add reserved yolks and mash everything.

Fill the whites with this mixture, heaping it lightly. Garnish with fresh chives and place in the refrigerator until ready to serve. Bon appétit!

Per serving: 138 Calories; 10.4g Fat; 1.2g Carbs; 9.1g Protein; 0.7g Sugars

886. Salad Snack on a Stick

(Ready in about 10 minutes | Servings 6)

Ingredients

1 ½ pounds shrimp, peeled and deveined
2 tablespoon apple cider vinegar
1 tablespoon lime juice
1 cup water
1 red onion, cut into wedges
1 red bell pepper, sliced
1 green bell pepper, sliced
1 orange bell pepper, sliced
1/2 cup black olives, pitted
1 ½ cups cherry tomatoes
2 tablespoons olive oil
1/2 cup ground black pepper
Sea salt, to taste
1 teaspoon paprika
1 teaspoon oregano

Directions

Place the shrimp, vinegar, lime juice, and water in your Instant Pot.

Secure the lid. Choose the "Manual" mode and High pressure; cook for 1 minute. Once cooking is complete, use a quick pressure release; carefully remove the lid.

Thread the cooked shrimp, onion, peppers, olives and cherry tomatoes onto cocktail sticks.

Drizzle olive oil over them; sprinkle with black pepper, salt, paprika, and oregano. Bon appétit!

Per serving: 185 Calories; 7.3g Fat; 5.1g Carbs; 23.9g Protein; 2.3g Sugars

887. Traditional Eggplant Dip

(Ready in about 10 minutes | Servings 10)

Ingredients

1 cup water
3/4 pound eggplant
3 tablespoons olive oil
1/2 cup yellow onion, chopped
1 garlic cloves, roasted and 1 raw, crushed
Sea salt, to taste
1 teaspoon fresh oregano, chopped
1/3 teaspoon cayenne pepper
1/4 teaspoon ground black pepper, or more to taste
1 tablespoon fresh lime juice
¼ cup tahini, plus more as needed
¼ cup brine-cured black olives, brine-cured

Directions

Add water to the base of your Instant Pot. Now, choose "Manual" and cook the eggplant in the steaming basket for 4 minutes at High Pressure.

Once cooking is complete, use a quick release; remove the lid carefully.

Drain the excess water out of the eggplant. Then, peel and slice the eggplant.

Press the "Sauté" button and add the oil. Once hot, cook the eggplant with the onions and garlic until they have softened.

Season with salt, oregano, cayenne pepper, and ground black pepper. Transfer the mixture to your blender or food processor.

Add the lime juice, tahini, and olives. Blend until everything is well incorporated. Serve well chilled and enjoy!

Per serving: 209 Calories; 18.9g Fat; 8.5g Carbs; 4.6g Protein; 1.5g Sugars

888. Lager and Cheese Dip

(Ready in about 10 minutes | Servings 12)

Ingredients

1/2 cup sour cream
1/2 cup cheddar cheese, grated
12 ounces cream cheese, softened
1/2 teaspoon garlic powder
1 teaspoon shallot power
1 teaspoon porcini powder
1/4 teaspoon cumin powder
1/2 teaspoon dried basil
1/2 teaspoon dried oregano
1/2 cup lager
1/2 pound ham, cooked and chopped
2 heaping tablespoons fresh chives, chopped
2 heaping tablespoons fresh cilantro, chopped

Directions

Spritz the bottom and sides of your Instant Pot with a nonstick cooking spray.

Then, add the sour cream, cheese, spices, lager, and ham.

Secure the lid. Choose the "Manual" mode and High pressure; cook for 4 minutes. Once cooking is complete, use a quick pressure release; carefully remove the lid.

Top with fresh chives and cilantro. Serve with your favorite dippers. Bon appétit!

Per serving: 131 Calories; 10.2g Fat; 3.1g Carbs; 6.3g Protein; 1.4g Sugars

889. Hearty Nacho Dip

(Ready in about 15 minutes | Servings 16)

Ingredients

1 pound chicken breasts, boneless and skinless
20 ounces tomato, puréed
2 bell peppers, chopped
1 tablespoon jalapeño, seeded and minced
1 cup beef stock
1 cup Mexican cheese blend, grated
1/2 cup avocado, chopped
10 ounces tortilla chips, baked

Directions

Place the chicken, tomato, peppers, and stock in your Instant Pot.

Secure the lid. Choose the "Manual" mode and High pressure; cook for 7 minutes. Once cooking is complete, use a natural pressure release; carefully remove the lid.

Add the Mexican cheese blend to the Instant Pot. Seal the lid and let it sit until warmed through.

Shred the chicken with two forks; top with chopped avocado and serve with tortilla chips. Enjoy!

Per serving: 145 Calories; 6.5g Fat; 11.6g Carbs; 9.8g Protein; 1.9g Sugars

890. Classic Chicken Collard Wraps

(Ready in about 25 minutes | Servings 8)

Ingredients

2 chicken breasts, boneless and skinless
1 yellow onion, chopped
2 cloves garlic, minced
1 ½ cups roasted vegetable broth
1 cup tomato, puréed
2 tablespoons hoisin sauce
1 head butter lettuce
2 carrots, grated
1 cucumber, grated
2 tablespoons mayonnaise
2 tablespoons olives, pitted and chopped
1 teaspoon Dijon mustard

Directions

Place the chicken, onion, garlic, broth, and puréed tomatoes in the Instant Pot.

Secure the lid. Choose the "Poultry" mode and High pressure; cook for 15 minutes. Once cooking is complete, use a natural pressure release; carefully remove the lid.

Remove the chicken from the Instant Pot; now, shred the chicken with two forks and return to the Instant Pot.

Add the hoisin sauce. Press the "Sauté" button and let it simmer until the cooking liquid has reduced by half.

To serve, place a generous spoonful of the chicken mixture in the middle of a lettuce leaf; top with carrots, cucumber, mayo, olives, and mustard. Bon appétit!

Per serving: 179 Calories; 9.5g Fat; 6.4g Carbs; 16.1g Protein; 3.5g Sugars

891. Super Bowl Italian Dip

(Ready in about 10 minutes | Servings 10)

Ingredients

8 ounces Asiago cheese, grated
9 ounces Mozzarella cheese, crumbled
2 ripe Roma tomatoes, puréed
8 ounces pancetta, chopped
1/2 cup green olives, pitted and halved
1 bell pepper, chopped
1 teaspoon garlic powder
1 teaspoon shallot powder
1 teaspoon porcini powder
1 teaspoon dried oregano
1 teaspoon dried basil
1 teaspoon dried marjoram
2/3 cup beef bone broth
6 ounces Parmigiano-Reggiano cheese, grated

Directions

Combine all ingredients, except for the Parmigiano-Reggiano cheese, in your Instant Pot.

Secure the lid. Choose the "Manual" mode and High pressure; cook for 5 minutes. Once cooking is complete, use a quick pressure release; carefully remove the lid.

Top with the Parmigiano-Reggiano cheese; cover and allow it to sit in the residual heat until the cheese is melted. Bon appétit!

Per serving: 209 Calories; 11.4g Fat; 5.3g Carbs; 21.1g Protein; 3.3g Sugars

892. Bacon Wrapped Lil Smokies

(Ready in about 10 minutes | Servings 12)

Ingredients

2 pounds Little Smokies sausage
1 pound bacon slices
1 (12-ounce) bottle chili sauce
1 cup grape jelly

Directions

Wrap each sausage in a piece of bacon; secure with toothpicks; place in your Instant Pot.

Add the chili sauce and grape jelly.

Secure the lid. Choose the "Manual" mode and High pressure; cook for 5 minutes. Once cooking is complete, use a quick pressure release; carefully remove the lid. Bon appétit!

Per serving: 317 Calories; 21.5g Fat; 12.8g Carbs; 17.1g Protein; 8.2g Sugars

893. Barbecue Chicken Dip

(Ready in about 10 minutes | Servings 12)

Ingredients

1 pound chicken white meat, boneless
1 cup barbecue sauce
1/3 cup water
6 ounces Ricotta cheese
3 ounces blue cheese dressing
1 parsnip, chopped
1/2 teaspoon dried rosemary
1/2 teaspoon cayenne pepper
1/4 teaspoon ground black pepper, or more to taste
Sea salt, to taste

Directions

Place all of the above ingredients in your Instant Pot.

Secure the lid. Choose the "Manual" mode and High pressure; cook for 6 minutes. Once cooking is complete, use a natural pressure release; carefully remove the lid.

Transfer to a nice serving bowl and serve warm or at room temperature. Bon appétit!

Per serving: 179 Calories; 7.5g Fat; 14.3g Carbs; 12.9g Protein; 10.3g Sugars

894. Aunt's Traditional Queso

(Ready in about 15 minutes | Servings 10)

Ingredients

1 pound hot breakfast sausage, ground
2 shallots, chopped
2 cloves garlic, minced
2 cups tomatoes, pureed
2 cans green chiles, chopped
1 cup broth
1 pound block processed cheese

Directions

Press the "Sauté" button to heat up your Instant Pot. Now, cook the ground sausage with shallots.

Stir in the garlic and cook 30 seconds more, stirring frequently. Add the tomatoes, green chiles, and broth.

Secure the lid and choose "Manual" function; cook for 6 minutes at Low pressure. Once cooking is complete, use a quick release; remove the lid carefully.

Add the block processed cheese and stir until it has melted. Bon appétit!

Per serving: 295 Calories; 24.2g Fat; 10.1g Carbs; 13g Protein; 2.4g Sugars

895. Creamy Ricotta Hummus

(Ready in about 45 minutes | Servings 10)

Ingredients

1 ½ cups dried garbanzo beans, soaked overnight
4 cups water
1/4 cup extra-virgin olive oil
2 tablespoons light tahini
2 tablespoons fresh lemon juice
1 teaspoon garlic, minced
1 teaspoon onion powder
1/2 teaspoon dried dill weed
1/2 teaspoon dried oregano
1/2 teaspoon cumin powder
1 teaspoon spicy brown mustard
1 teaspoon kosher salt
1/3 cup ricotta cheese
1/2 teaspoon red chili pepper

Directions

Add the soaked garbanzo beans with 4 cups of water to your Instant Pot.

Secure the lid and choose the "Bean/Chili" function; cook for 40 minutes at High pressure. Once cooking is complete, use a natural release; carefully remove the lid.

Drain the garbanzo beans, reserving cooking liquid. Transfer chickpeas to your food processor. Add the olive oil, tahini, lemon juice, garlic, onion powder, dill weed, oregano, cumin powder, mustard, and salt.

Add the ricotta cheese and about 1 cup of cooking liquid; process until everything is creamy and smooth. Sprinkle red chili pepper over the top. Bon appétit!

Per serving: 153 Calories; 5.7g Fat; 19.8g Carbs; 6.7g Protein; 3.3g Sugars

896. Crispy and Cheesy Broccoli Tots

(Ready in about 30 minutes | Servings 8)

Ingredients

1 head of broccoli, broken into florets
1 ½ cups water
1 white onion, minced
1 garlic clove, minced
2 eggs, beaten
1 cup Colby cheese, grated
1 tablespoon fresh parsley, chopped
1 tablespoon fresh coriander, chopped
Sea salt and ground black pepper, to taste

Directions

Add 1 cup of water and a steamer basket to the bottom of your Instant Pot. Place the broccoli florets in the steamer basket.

Secure the lid and choose the "Steam" mode; cook for 6 minutes under High pressure. Once cooking is complete, use a quick release; carefully remove the lid.

Allow the broccoli florets to cool completely; then, add the remaining ingredients.

Mash the mixture and shape into tots with oiled hands.

Place the broccoli tots on a lightly greased baking sheet. Bake in the preheated oven at 390 degrees F approximately 18 to 20 minutes, flipping them once. Bon appétit!

Per serving: 142 Calories; 8.1g Fat; 9.6g Carbs; 9.5g Protein; 2.7g Sugars

897. Vegetable and Tahini Dipping Sauce

(Ready in about 10 minutes | Servings 8)

Ingredients

1 ½ cups water
1 head cauliflower, cut into florets
1 cup broccoli, cut into florets
1 celery, sliced
1 carrot, sliced
1/3 cup tahini
2 tomatoes, pureed
1 serrano pepper, chopped
2 bell pepper, chopped
2 garlic cloves, chopped
Salt and ground black pepper, to taste
1 teaspoon onion powder
1/2 teaspoon cayenne pepper
1/2 teaspoon cumin powder

Directions

Add the water, cauliflower, broccoli, celery, and carrot to your Instant Pot.

Choose the "Manual" function and cook at High pressure for 3 minutes. Once cooking is complete, use a quick release; carefully remove the lid.

Then, drain the excess water out of vegetables. Transfer to a food processor and add the other ingredients.

Blend until everything is well incorporated. Serve with pita bread and enjoy!

Per serving: 77 Calories; 5.5g Fat; 5.9g Carbs; 2.9g Protein; 1.7g Sugars

898. Garlicky Petite Potatoes

(Ready in about 15 minutes | Servings 6)

Ingredients

1 tablespoon butter, melted
2 pounds baby potatoes
3 garlic cloves, with outer skin
Sea salt and ground black pepper, to taste
1/2 teaspoon cayenne pepper
1 sprig thyme, leaves only
1 sprig rosemary, leaves only
1 tablespoon olive oil
1 cup vegetable broth
1/4 cup fresh Italian parsley, chopped

Directions

Press the "Sauté" button to preheat your Instant Pot. Once hot, warm the butter; now, cook potatoes with garlic for 5 to 6 minutes.

Add the salt, black pepper, cayenne pepper, thyme, rosemary, olive oil, and broth.

Secure the lid. Choose the "Manual" mode and High pressure; cook for 5 minutes. Once cooking is complete, use a quick pressure release; carefully remove the lid.

Scatter chopped parsley over the potatoes and serve warm.

Per serving: 166 Calories; 4.6g Fat; 28.1g Carbs; 4.2g Protein; 1.6g Sugars

899. Sesame Turnip Greens

(Ready in about 10 minutes | Servings 6)

Ingredients

1 tablespoon sesame oil
1 shallot, chopped
2 garlic cloves, minced
1 pound turnip greens, leaves separated
1 cup vegetable broth
Sea salt, to taste
1/2 teaspoon ground black pepper
1 teaspoon red pepper flakes
2 teaspoons Worcestershire sauce
2 tablespoons sesame seeds, toasted

Directions

Press the "Sauté" button to preheat your Instant Pot. Once hot, heat the sesame oil.

Then, cook the shallot and garlic until they are fragrant and tender. Add the turnip greens, broth, salt, black pepper, red pepper flakes, and Worcestershire sauce.

Secure the lid. Choose the "Manual" mode and High pressure; cook for 3 minutes. Once cooking is complete, use a quick pressure release; carefully remove the lid.

Sprinkle sesame seeds over the top and serve right away!

Per serving: 73 Calories; 4.3g Fat; 7.1g Carbs; 2.6g Protein; 1.2g Sugars

900. Kalbi (Korean Short Ribs)

(Ready in about 1 hour 5 minutes | Servings 6)

Ingredients

2 pounds Korean-style beef short ribs
1 Asian pear, peeled and grated
2 tablespoons brown sugar
1/2 teaspoon salt
1/3 teaspoon ground black pepper
1 teaspoon granulated garlic
1/2 cup water
1/2 cup soy sauce
1/4 cup mirin
1 teaspoon liquid smoke

Directions

Add all of the above ingredients to your Instant Pot.

Secure the lid. Choose the "Manual" mode and High pressure; cook for 60 minutes. Once cooking is complete, use a natural pressure release; carefully remove the lid.

Cut the ribs, slicing between the bones. Serve with barbecue sauce, if desired. Enjoy!

901. Perfect Cocktail Wieners

(Ready in about 10 minutes | Servings 12)

Per serving: 333 Calories; 23.4g Fat; 19.6g Carbs; 10g Protein; 13.2g Sugars

Ingredients

2 (16-ounce) packages little wieners
1/2 (18-ounce) bottle barbeque sauce
1/2 cup ketchup
3 tablespoons honey
1/2 yellow onion, chopped
2 jalapenos, sliced
1 teaspoon garlic powder
1 teaspoon cumin powder
1/2 teaspoon mustard powder

Directions

Add the little wieners, barbecue sauce, ketchup, honey, onion, jalapenos, garlic powder, cumin, and mustard powder to the Instant Pot. Stir to combine well.

Choose "Manual" setting and cook at Low pressure for 2 minutes.

Once cooking is complete, use a natural release; carefully remove the lid. You can thicken the sauce to your desired thickness on the "Sauté" function.

Serve warm with toothpicks. Bon appétit!

Per serving: 250 Calories; 13.1g Fat; 7.9g Carbs; 24.1g Protein; 6.2g Sugars

902. Movie Night Almond Popcorn

(Ready in about 10 minutes | Servings 4)

Ingredients

3 tablespoons butter, at room temperature
1/4 cup popcorn kernels
A pinch of sugar
Sea salt, to taste
2 tablespoons Habanero BBQ almonds

Directions

Press the "Sauté" button to heat up the Instant Pot. Melt the butter until sizzling.

Stir in the popcorn kernels; stir until they are covered with melted butter.

Once the popcorn starts popping, cover with the lid. Shake for a few seconds.

Now, turn off the Instant Pot when 2/3 of kernels have popped. Allow all kernels to pop.

Add salt and Habanero BBQ almonds; toss and serve immediately. Enjoy!

Per serving: 119 Calories; 9.5g Fat; 7.3g Carbs; 1.3g Protein; 0.1g Sugars

903. Sticky Chicken Nuggets

(Ready in about 20 minutes | Servings 6)

Ingredients

1 ½ pounds chicken breast, cut into 1-inch chunks
1/4 cup soy sauce
1/4 cup tomato, puréed
1/2 cup chicken stock
Sea salt and ground black pepper, to taste
1/2 stick butter
2 tablespoons hoisin sauce
1 teaspoon fresh ginger root, peeled and grated
1 tablespoon Sriracha
2 green onions, thinly sliced

Directions

Add the chicken, soy sauce, puréed tomatoes, stock, salt, pepper, butter, hoisin sauce, ginger, and Sriracha to the Instant Pot.

Secure the lid. Choose the "Manual" mode and cook for 6 minutes under High pressure. Once cooking is complete, use a quick release; carefully remove the lid.

Transfer the ingredients to a baking dish. Bake in the preheated oven at 390 degrees F for 10 minutes.

Serve topped with green onions. Bon appétit!

Per serving: 313 Calories; 20.4g Fat; 6.1g Carbs; 25.3g Protein; 4.1g Sugars

904. Artichokes with Hollandaise Sauce

(Ready in about 15 minutes | Servings 3)

Ingredients

3 small-sized artichokes
1 teaspoon lemon zest
The Sauce:
1/2 stick butter, at room temperature
2 egg yolks
1/2 tablespoon lemon juice
1/2 teaspoon salt
1/4 teaspoon ground black pepper
1/4 teaspoon cayenne

Directions

Add 1 ½ cups of water and lemon zest to the Instant Pot. Now, place a metal rack on the top.

Lower the artichokes onto the rack.

Secure the lid. Choose the "Manual" mode and cook for 7 minutes under High pressure. Once cooking is complete, use a quick release; carefully remove the lid.

To make the sauce, melt the butter in a pan. When the butter has melted, remove the pan from the heat.

Then, in a blender, mix the egg yolks with lemon juice, salt, black pepper, and cayenne pepper.

Transfer the egg mixture to a heatproof bowl; place it over the pan of simmering water over a low heat.

Then, keep whisking the mixture, adding the melted butter slowly and gradually; whisk until everything is well incorporated.

Serve the prepared artichokes with the Hollandaise on the side. Bon appétit!

905. The Best Party Mix Ever

(Ready in about 25 minutes | Servings 10)

Ingredients

2 tablespoons butter
2 cups puffed-rice cereal
1 cup raw walnuts, halved
2 cups raw almonds
1/3 cup raw pumpkin seeds
1/3 cup raw sunflower seeds
1 cup roasted peas
2 tablespoons light brown sugar
1/2 teaspoon cayenne pepper
1/2 teaspoon garlic powder
1/2 teaspoon dried oregano
Salt and black pepper, to taste
1/2 teaspoon Tabasco sauce

Directions

Press the "Sauté" button to heat up the Instant Pot. Now, melt the butter.

Add the other ingredients and stir until they are coated with butter; add water as needed. Secure the lid.

Select the "Manual" mode and cook for 11 minutes at High pressure. Once cooking is complete, use a natural release; carefully remove the lid.

Transfer the mixture to a parchment-lined cookie sheet.

Next, preheat your oven to 365 degrees F. Bake the party mix for 8 minutes, turning halfway through cooking time. Store in an airtight container. Bon appétit!

Per serving: 208 Calories; 16.8g Fat; 16.9g Carbs; 6.5g Protein; 3.1g Sugars

906. Chunky Cream Cheese and Sausage Dip

(Ready in about 20 minutes | Servings 12)

Ingredients

1 tablespoon canola oil
1 pound turkey smoked sausage
1 (28-ounce) can tomatoes, crushed
1/2 cup water
2 red chili peppers, minced
1 teaspoon yellow mustard
1 teaspoon basil
1 teaspoon oregano
1 (8-oz) package cream cheese, at room temperature
1/2 cup sour cream

Directions

Press the "Sauté" button to preheat your Instant Pot. Once hot, heat the oil. Then, cook the sausage until it is delicately browned, crumbling it with a fork.

Then, add the canned tomatoes, water, peppers, mustard, basil, and oregano.

Secure the lid. Choose the "Manual" mode and cook for 6 minutes under High pressure. Once cooking is complete, use a natural release; carefully remove the lid.

Add the cream cheese and sour cream; seal the lid. Allow it to sit for at least 5 minutes or until heated through. Serve with tortilla chips or pretzel bun bites. Enjoy!

Per serving: 157 Calories; 11.4g Fat; 6.3g Carbs; 8.1g Protein; 4.1g Sugars

907. Blue Cheese and Sweet Potato Balls

(Ready in about 1 hour 5 minutes | Servings 10)

Ingredients

2 pounds sweet potatoes, peeled and diced
1 onion, chopped
1 garlic clove, minced
Sea salt and ground black pepper, to taste
1 teaspoon dried marjoram
1 teaspoon basil
1/2 teaspoon ground allspice
1/2 stick butter, softened
1 cup blue cheese, crumbled
2 eggs, whisked
2/3 cup breadcrumbs

Directions

Prepare your Instant Pot by adding 1½ cups of water and a metal trivet to its bottom. Lower the sweet potatoes onto the trivet.

Secure the lid. Choose the "Manual" mode and cook for 15 minutes under High pressure. Once cooking is complete, use a natural release; carefully remove the lid.

Peel and mash the prepared sweet potatoes with the onion, garlic, and all of the seasonings. Now, stir in softened butter, cheese, and eggs.

Place this mixture in your refrigerator for 30 minutes; then, shape into bite-sized balls.

Coat each ball with breadcrumbs. Now, sprits the balls with a nonstick cooking spray. Bake the balls in the preheated oven at 425 degrees F approximately 15 minutes. Bon appétit!

Per serving: 200 Calories; 10.6g Fat; 19.7g Carbs; 7.1g Protein; 1.8g Sugars

908. Barbecue Corn with Potato Chips

(Ready in about 10 minutes | Servings 4)

Ingredients

4 ears corn on the cob, husks removed

1/3 cup barbecue sauce

1/2 cup potato chips, crushed

Directions

Add water and a metal trivet to the base of your Instant Pot. Place the ears corn on the cob on the metal trivet.

Secure the lid. Choose the "Steam" mode and cook for 2 minutes under High pressure. Once cooking is complete, use a quick release; carefully remove the lid.

Brush each corn on the cob with barbecue sauce; sprinkle with crushed chips. Bon appétit!

Per serving: 260 Calories; 5.2g Fat; 52.5g Carbs; 5.7g Protein; 7.8g Sugars

909. Fish and Cucumber Bites

(Ready in about 10 minutes + chilling time | Servings 5)

Ingredients

1/2 pound fish fillets

4 medium-sized tomatoes, chopped

1/3 cup Kalamata olives, pitted and chopped

1/2 cup feta cheese, crumbled

1 tablespoon fresh lemon juice

2 cloves garlic, minced

2 tablespoons olive oil

1/2 teaspoon oregano

1/2 teaspoon dried rosemary

Sea salt and freshly ground black pepper, to taste

5 cucumbers

Directions

Add 1 cup of water and a steamer basket to your Instant Pot. Then, place the fish fillets in the steamer basket.

Secure the lid. Choose the "Steam" mode and cook for 3 minutes under Low pressure. Once cooking is complete, use a quick release; carefully remove the lid.

Flake the fish with a fork. Now, add the tomatoes, olives, cheese, lemon juice, garlic, olive oil, oregano, rosemary, salt, and black pepper; mix until everything is well combined.

Cut the cucumbers into pieces. Then, make a well in each cucumber using a spoon. Spoon the prepared fish mixture into cucumber pieces. Serve well-chilled and enjoy!

Per serving: 217 Calories; 14.3g Fat; 10g Carbs; 12.7g Protein; 6.1g Sugars

910. Mediterranean Calamari Bites

(Ready in about 15 minutes | Servings 6)

Ingredients

2 teaspoons olive oil

1 pound squid, cleaned and sliced into rings

4 garlic cloves, whole

1 cup dry white wine

1 teaspoon dried basil

1 teaspoon dried rosemary

1 teaspoon dried marjoram

1 cup tomatoes, puréed

1 cup chicken stock

Sea salt and ground black pepper, to taste

1/2 teaspoon red pepper flakes

1 heaping tablespoon fresh cilantro leaves, chopped

1 fresh lemon, cut into wedges

Directions

Press the "Sauté" button to preheat your Instant Pot. Once hot, heat the olive oil. Then, sauté the squid with garlic for 3 to 4 minutes or so.

Add a splash of wine to deglaze the bottom of the Instant Pot.

Now, add the basil, rosemary, marjoram, puréed tomatoes, chicken stock, salt, black pepper, and red pepper flakes.

Secure the lid. Choose the "Manual" mode and cook for 4 minutes under High pressure. Once cooking is complete, use a natural release; carefully remove the lid.

Serve garnished with fresh cilantro leaves and lemon wedges. Enjoy!

Per serving: 155 Calories; 6.9g Fat; 5.7g Carbs; 17.1g Protein; 1.3g Sugars

DESSERTS

911. Chocolate and Cranberry Oatmeal Bars

(Ready in about 20 minutes | Servings 8)

Ingredients

3 eggs, whisked
1/2 cup sour cream
1/4 cup honey
2 teaspoons coconut oil, melted
1/2 teaspoon rum extract
1/2 teaspoon vanilla extract
3/4 cup quick oats, pudding-y
1/3 cup all-purpose flour
1 teaspoon baking soda
1 teaspoon baking powder
1/2 teaspoon cardamom
1/2 teaspoon cinnamon
1 cup dark chocolate chips
A pinch of kosher salt
3/4 cup cranberries

Directions

Add 1 cup of water and a metal trivet to the Instant Pot. Now, spritz a baking pan with a nonstick cooking spray.

In a mixing bowl, whisk the eggs, sour cream, honey, coconut oil, rum extract, and vanilla extract.

Add the oats, flour, baking soda, baking powder, cardamom, cinnamon, salt, and chocolate chips; stir until everything is well incorporated. After that, fold in the cranberries.

Scrape the batter into the baking pan.

Secure the lid. Choose the "Manual" mode and High pressure; cook for 12 minutes. Once cooking is complete, use a natural pressure release; carefully remove the lid.

Serve chilled and enjoy!

Per serving: 201 Calories; 7.3g Fat; 27.2g Carbs; 6.9g Protein; 11.8g Sugars

912. Coconut and Avocado Delight

(Ready in about 20 minutes | Servings 8)

Ingredients

1/3 cup avocado, mashed
2 plantains
1 ½ tablespoons butter, softened
1/4 cup agave syrup
4 tablespoons cocoa powder
1/2 cup coconut flakes
1 teaspoon baking soda
1/2 teaspoon vanilla paste
1 teaspoon star anise, ground
1/8 teaspoon cream of tartar

Directions

Prepare your Instant Pot by adding 1 cup of water and a metal rack to its bottom. Grease the sides and bottom of a baking pan with melted butter.

Then, mix all of the above ingredients in your blender or food processor. Next, pour the batter into the prepared baking pan.

Secure the lid. Choose the "Porridge" mode and High pressure; cook for 15 minutes. Once cooking is complete, use a quick pressure release; carefully remove the lid.

Garnish with some fresh or dried fruit if desired. Bon appétit!

Per serving: 144 Calories; 5.1g Fat; 27.3g Carbs; 1.3g Protein; 16.9g Sugars

913. Coconut and Chocolate Cheesecake

(Ready in about 1 hour + freezing time | Servings 10)

Ingredients

1 ½ cups vanilla sugar cookies, crumbled
1/2 stick butter, melted
For the Filling:
22 ounces cream cheese, room temperature
3/4 cup granulated sugar
1 ½ tablespoons cornstarch
2 eggs, room temperature
1/3 cup sour cream
1/2 teaspoon coconut extract
1/2 teaspoon pure anise extract
1/4 teaspoon freshly grated nutmeg
6 ounces semisweet chocolate chips
3 ounces sweetened shredded coconut

Directions

Lightly oil a baking pan that fits in your Instant Pot. Cover the bottom with a baking paper.

Thoroughly combine the crumbled cookies with the melted butter; now, press the crust into the baking pan and transfer to your freezer.

Next, beat the cream cheese with a mixer on low speed. Stir in the sugar and cornstarch and continue mixing on low speed until everything is uniform and smooth.

Fold in the eggs, one at a time, and continue to beat with the mixer. Now, stir in the sour cream, coconut extract, anise extract, and nutmeg; mix again.

Then, microwave the chocolate chips about 1 minute, stirring once or twice. Add the melted chocolate to the cheesecake batter; add the shredded coconut and stir to combine.

Pour the chocolate mixture into the baking pan on top of the crust.

Add 1 cup of water and trivet to the Instant Pot. Lower the prepared pan onto the trivet and secure the lid. Select the "Manual" mode. Bake at High pressure for 40 minutes.

Once cooking is complete, use a natural release for 15 minutes; remove the lid carefully.

Allow your cheesecake to cool completely before slicing and serving. Enjoy!

Per serving: 487 Calories; 33.5g Fat; 39.1g Carbs; 8.7g Protein; 28.2g Sugars

914. Double-Chocolate and Peanut Fudge

(Ready in about 15 minutes | Servings 6)

Ingredients

8 ounces semisweet chocolate, chopped
2 ounces milk chocolate, chopped
1/3 cup applesauce
1 egg, beaten
1/2 teaspoon vanilla extract
1/2 teaspoon almond extract
1/4 teaspoon ground cinnamon
1/3 cup peanut butter
A pinch of coarse salt
1/4 cup arrowroot powder

Directions

Add 1½ cups of water and a metal trivet to the Instant Pot. Press the "Sauté" button and add the chocolate to a heatproof bowl; melt the chocolate over the simmering water. Press the "Cancel" button.

In a mixing dish, thoroughly combine the applesauce, egg, and vanilla, almond extract, cinnamon, peanut butter and salt.

Then, add the arrowroot powder and mix well to combine. Afterwards, fold in the melted chocolate; mix again.

Spritz six heat-safe ramekins with a nonstick cooking spray. Pour in the batter and cover with foil.

Secure the lid. Choose the "Manual" mode and High pressure; cook for 5 minutes. Once cooking is complete, use a quick pressure release; carefully remove the lid.

Let your dessert cool on a wire rack before serving. Bon appétit!

Per serving: 347 Calories; 22.3g Fat; 30.7g Carbs; 5.6g Protein; 21.4g Sugars

915. Festive Rum Cheesecake

(Ready in about 25 minutes + chilling time | Servings 6)

Ingredients

14 ounces full-fat cream cheese
3 eggs, whisked
1/2 teaspoon vanilla extract
1 teaspoon rum extract
1/2 cup agave syrup
1/4 teaspoon cardamom
1/4 teaspoon ground cinnamon

Butter-Rum Sauce:
1/2 cup granulated sugar
1/2 stick butter
1/2 cup whipping cream
1 tablespoon dark rum
1/3 teaspoon nutmeg

Directions

Add the cream cheese, eggs, vanilla, rum extract, agave syrup, cardamom, and cinnamon to your blender or food processor; blend until everything is well combined.

Transfer the batter to a baking pan; cover with a sheet of foil.

Add 1 ½ cups of water and a metal trivet to the Instant Pot. Lower the pan onto the trivet.

Secure the lid. Choose the "Soup" mode and High pressure; cook for 20 minutes. Once cooking is complete, use a natural pressure release; carefully remove the lid.

In a sauté pan, melt the sugar with butter over a moderate heat. Add the whipping cream, rum, and nutmeg.

Drizzle the warm sauce over the cooled cheesecake. Serve and enjoy!

Per serving: 399 Calories; 23.7g Fat; 36.7g Carbs; 9.9g Protein; 34.6g Sugars

916. Cherry and Almond Crisp Pie

(Ready in about 15 minutes | Servings 4)

Ingredients

1 pound sweet cherries, pitted
1 teaspoon ground cinnamon
1/3 teaspoon ground cardamom
1 teaspoon pure vanilla extract
1/3 cup water
1/3 cup honey

1/2 stick butter, at room temperature
1 cup rolled oats
2 tablespoons all-purpose flour
1/4 cup almonds, slivered
A pinch of salt
A pinch of grated nutmeg

Directions

Arrange the cherries on the bottom of the Instant Pot. Sprinkle cinnamon, cardamom, and vanilla over the top. Add water and honey.

In a separate mixing bowl, thoroughly combine the butter, oats, and flour. Spread topping mixture evenly over cherry mixture.

Secure the lid. Choose the "Manual" mode and High pressure; cook for 10 minutes. Once cooking is complete, use a natural pressure release; carefully remove the lid.

Serve at room temperature. Bon appétit!

Per serving: 335 Calories; 13.4g Fat; 60.5g Carbs; 5.9g Protein; 38.1g Sugars

917. Chocolate and Mango Mug Cakes

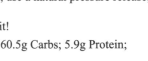

(Ready in about 15 minutes | Servings 2)

Ingredients

1/2 cup coconut flour
2 eggs
2 tablespoons honey
1 teaspoon vanilla

1/4 teaspoon grated nutmeg
1 tablespoon cocoa powder
1 medium-sized mango, peeled and diced

Directions

Combine the coconut flour, eggs, honey, vanilla, nutmeg and cocoa powder in two lightly greased mugs.

Then, add 1 cup of water and a metal trivet to the Instant Pot. Lower the uncovered mugs onto the trivet.

Secure the lid. Choose the "Manual" mode and High pressure; cook for 10 minutes. Once cooking is complete, use a quick pressure release; carefully remove the lid.

Top with diced mango and serve chilled. Enjoy!

Per serving: 268 Calories; 10.5g Fat; 34.8g Carbs; 10.6g Protein; 31.1g Sugars

918. Carrot Pudding with Almonds and Figs

(Ready in about 30 minutes | Servings 4)

Ingredients

1 ½ cups jasmine rice
1 ½ cups milk
1/2 cup water
2 large-sized carrots, shredded
1/4 cup kosher salt
1/3 cup granulated sugar
2 eggs, beaten

1/3 cup almonds, ground
1/4 cup dried figs, chopped
1/2 teaspoon pure almond extract
1/2 teaspoon vanilla extract
1/3 teaspoon ground cardamom
1/2 teaspoon ground star anise

Directions

Place the jasmine rice, milk, water, carrots, and salt in your Instant Pot.

Stir to combine and secure the lid. Choose "Manual" and cook at High pressure for 10 minutes. Once cooking is complete, use a natural release for 15 minutes; carefully remove the lid.

Now, press the "Sauté" button and add the sugar, eggs, and almonds; stir to combine well. Bring to a boil; press the "Keep Warm/Cancel" button.

Add the remaining ingredients and stir; the pudding will thicken as it sits. Bon appétit!

Per serving: 331 Calories; 17.2g Fat; 44.5g Carbs; 13.9g Protein; 19.5g Sugars

919. Italian Bread Pudding with Dried Apricots

(Ready in about 20 minutes | Servings 6)

Ingredients

4 cups Italian bread, cubed
1/2 cup granulated sugar
2 tablespoons molasses
1/2 cup dried apricots, soaked and chopped
2 tablespoons coconut oil
1 teaspoon vanilla paste

A pinch of grated nutmeg
A pinch of salt
1 teaspoon cinnamon, ground
1/2 teaspoon star anise, ground
2 cups milk
4 eggs, whisked
1 1/3 cups heavy cream

Directions

Add 1 ½ cups of water and a metal rack to the Instant Pot.

Grease a baking dish with a nonstick cooking spray. Throw the bread cubes into the prepared baking dish.

In a mixing bowl, thoroughly combine the remaining ingredients. Pour the mixture over the bread cubes. Cover with a piece of foil, making a foil sling.

Secure the lid. Choose the "Porridge" mode and High pressure; cook for 15 minutes. Once cooking is complete, use a quick pressure release; carefully remove the lid. Enjoy!

Per serving: 410 Calories; 24.3g Fat; 37.4g Carbs; 11.5g Protein; 25.6g Sugars

920. Indian Rice Pudding (Kheer)

(Ready in about 10 minutes | Servings 4)

Ingredients

1 ½ cups basmati rice
3 cups coconut milk
1 teaspoon rosewater
A pinch of coarse salt
1/4 teaspoon saffron, crushed

4 tablespoons unsalted pistachios, minced
1/2 cup jaggery
1/2 cup raisins

Directions

Add all of the above ingredients, except for the raisins, to your Instant Pot; stir to combine well.

Secure the lid. Choose the "Soup" mode and High pressure; cook for 3 minutes. Once cooking is complete, use a natural pressure release; carefully remove the lid.

Serve topped with raisins and enjoy!

Per serving: 408 Calories; 18.7g Fat; 62.4g Carbs; 13.8g Protein; 35.6g Sugars

921. Chocolate-Glazed Little Pumpkin Puddings

(Ready in about 30 minutes + chilling time | Servings 4)

Ingredients

1/2 cup half-and-half
1 cup pumpkin puree
1/3 cup Turbinado sugar
1 egg plus 1 egg yolk, beaten
1/3 teaspoon crystallized ginger
1/2 teaspoon ground cinnamon

1/4 teaspoon ground nutmeg
A pinch of table salt
For the Chocolate Ganache:
1/2 cup chocolate chips
1/4 cup double cream

Directions

Prepare your Instant Pot by adding the water and a steam rack to the pot. Butter four ramekins and set them aside.

In a mixing bowl, thoroughly combine the half-and-half with the pumpkin puree and sugar; now, gently fold in the eggs and mix to combine well.

Then, scrape the mixture into the prepared ramekins, dividing evenly, and place side by side on the steam rack.

Secure the lid. Choose the "Manual" setting and cook at High pressure for 25 minutes. Once cooking is complete, use a quick release; carefully remove the lid.

Let the pudding cool about 2 hours before serving.

Meanwhile, make the chocolate ganache by melting the chocolate in the microwave for 30 seconds; stir and microwave for a further 15 seconds.

Add the double cream and stir to combine well.

Lastly, pour this chocolate ganache over the pumpkin puddings, letting it run over sides; spread gently with a table knife. Let them set in your refrigerator. Enjoy!

Per serving: 366 Calories; 19.3g Fat; 40.1g Carbs; 11.4g Protein; 29g Sugars

922. Chocolate Pots de Crème

(Ready in about 15 minutes | Servings 4)

Ingredients

1/2 cup granulated sugar
1/3 cup cocoa powder
2 tablespoons carob powder
2/3 cup whipping cream
1 cup coconut milk
1 teaspoon vanilla

1/2 teaspoon hazelnut extract
5 eggs, well-beaten
1/4 teaspoon nutmeg, preferably freshly grated
A pinch of coarse salt

Directions

In a sauté pan, melt the sugar, cocoa powder, carob powder, cream, milk, vanilla, and hazelnut extract over medium-low heat; whisk until everything is well incorporated and melted.

Fold in the eggs; whisk to combine well. Add the nutmeg and salt. Divide the mixture among jars.

Place 1 cup of water and a metal trivet in the Instant Pot.

Secure the lid. Choose the "Manual" and cook at High pressure for 7 minutes. Once cooking is complete, use a quick pressure release; carefully remove the lid.

Place in your refrigerate for about 4 hours and serve chilled. Enjoy!

Per serving: 299 Calories; 17.2g Fat; 24.8g Carbs; 14.8g Protein; 18.6g Sugars

923. Cranberry-Maple Rice Pudding

(Ready in about 20 minutes | Servings 4)

Ingredients

1 cup white rice
1 ½ cups water
A pinch of salt
2 cups milk
1/3 cup maple syrup

2 eggs, beaten
1 teaspoon vanilla extract
1/4 teaspoon cardamom
A pinch of grated nutmeg
1/2 cup dried cranberries

Directions

Place the rice, water, and salt in the inner pot of your Instant Pot.

Secure the lid. Choose the "Manual" mode and cook for 3 minutes at High pressure. Once cooking is complete, use a natural pressure release for 10 minutes; carefully remove the lid.

Add in the milk, maple syrup, eggs, vanilla extract, cardamom, and nutmeg; stir to combine well.

Press the "Sauté" button and cook, stirring frequently, until your pudding starts to boil. Press the "Cancel" button. Stir in the dried cranberries.

Pudding will thicken as it cools. Bon appétit!

Per serving: 403 Calories; 6.6g Fat; 75.6g Carbs; 9.8g Protein; 31.9g Sugars

924. Vegan Coconut Mini Cheesecakes

(Ready in about 45 minutes | Servings 4)

Ingredients

1/2 cup almonds
1/2 cup sunflower kernels
6 dates, chopped

16 ounces coconut milk
3/4 cup coconut yogurt

Directions

Spritz four ramekins with nonstick cooking spray.

Process the almonds, sunflower kernels, and dates in your blender until it turns into a sticky mixture.

Press the crust mixture into the prepared ramekins.

Thoroughly combine the coconut milk and yogurt in a mixing bowl. Pour this mixture into the ramekins and cover them with a piece of foil.

Place a metal trivet and 1 cup of water in your Instant Pot. Lower the ramekins onto the trivet.

Secure the lid. Choose the "Manual" mode and cook for 25 minutes at High pressure. Once cooking is complete, use a natural pressure release for 15 minutes; carefully remove the lid. Bon appétit!

Per serving: 439 Calories; 39.2g Fat; 18.1g Carbs; 11.2g Protein; 8.5g Sugars

925. Old-Fashioned Apple Cake

(Ready in about 1 hour 25 minutes | Servings 8)

Ingredients

4 apples, peeled, cored and chopped
1/2 teaspoon ground cloves
1/2 teaspoon ground cardamom
1 teaspoon ground cinnamon
3 tablespoons sugar
1 1/3 cups flour

1 teaspoon baking powder
A pinch of salt
1 stick butter, melted
1/2 cup honey
2 tablespoons orange juice
1/2 teaspoon vanilla paste

Directions

Grease and flour a cake pan and set it aside. Toss the apples with the ground cloves, cardamom. cinnamon and sugar.

In a mixing bowl, thoroughly combine the flour, baking powder and salt.

In another mixing bowl, mix the butter, honey, orange juice, and vanilla paste. Stir the wet ingredients into the dry ones; spoon 1/2 of the batter into the prepared cake pan.

Spread half of the apples on top of the batter. Pour in the remaining batter covering the apple chunks. Spread the remaining apples on top.

Cover the cake pan with a paper towel.

Add 1 cup of water and a metal rack to your Instant Pot. Lower the cake pan onto the rack.

Secure the lid. Choose the "Manual" mode and cook for 55 minutes at High pressure. Once cooking is complete, use a natural pressure release for 10 minutes; carefully remove the lid.

Transfer the cake to a cooling rack and allow it to sit for about 15 minutes before slicing and serving.

Per serving: 304 Calories; 11.8g Fat; 49.7g Carbs; 2.6g Protein; 30.2g Sugars

926. Country-Style Apples

(Ready in about 10 minutes | Servings 4)

Ingredients

4 apples
1 teaspoon ground cinnamon
1/2 teaspoon ground cloves
2 tablespoons honey

Directions

Add all ingredients to the inner pot. Now, pour in 1/3 cup of water.

Secure the lid. Choose the "Manual" mode and cook for 2 minutes at High pressure. Once cooking is complete, use a quick pressure release; carefully remove the lid.

Serve in individual bowls. Bon appétit!

Per serving: 128 Calories; 0.3g Fat; 34.3g Carbs; 0.5g Protein; 27.5g Sugars

927. Peach and Raisin Crisp

(Ready in about 25 minutes | Servings 6)

Ingredients

6 peaches, pitted and chopped
1/2 teaspoon ground cardamom
1 teaspoon ground cinnamon
1 teaspoon vanilla extract
1/3 cup orange juice
2 tablespoons honey
4 tablespoons raisins
4 tablespoons butter
1 cup rolled oats
4 tablespoons all-purpose flour
1/3 cup brown sugar
A pinch of grated nutmeg
A pinch of salt

Directions

Place the peaches on the bottom of the inner pot. Sprinkle with cardamom, cinnamon and vanilla. Top with the orange juice, honey, and raisins.

In a mixing bowl, whisk together the butter, oats, flour, brown sugar, nutmeg, and salt. Drop by a spoonful on top of the peaches.

Secure the lid. Choose the "Manual" mode and cook for 8 minutes at High pressure. Once cooking is complete, use a natural pressure release for 10 minutes; carefully remove the lid. Bon appétit!

Per serving: 329 Calories; 10g Fat; 56g Carbs; 6.9g Protein; 31g Sugars

928. Mixed Berry Jam

(Ready in about 25 minutes | Servings 10)

Ingredients

2 ½ pounds fresh mixed berries
1 ¼ cups granulated sugar
2 tablespoons fresh lemon juice
3 tablespoons cornstarch

Directions

Add the fresh mixed berries, sugar, and lemon juice to the inner pot.

Secure the lid. Choose the "Manual" mode and cook for 2 minutes at High pressure. Once cooking is complete, use a natural pressure release for 15 minutes; carefully remove the lid.

Whisk the cornstarch with 3 tablespoons of water until well combined. Stir in the cornstarch slurry.

Press the "Sauté" button and bring the mixture to a rolling boil. Let it boil for about 5 minutes, stirring continuously, until your jam has thickened. Bon appétit!

Per serving: 143 Calories; 0.3g Fat; 36.1g Carbs; 0.7g Protein; 30.5g Sugars

929. Delicious Dulce de Leche

(Ready in about 35 minutes | Servings 2)

Ingredients

1 can (14-ounce) sweetened
condensed milk

Directions

Place a trivet and steamer basket in the inner pot. Place the can of milk in the steamer basket.

Add water until the can is covered.

Secure the lid. Choose the "Manual" mode and cook for 20 minutes at High pressure. Once cooking is complete, use a natural pressure release for 10 minutes; carefully remove the lid.

Don't open the can until it is completely cooled. Bon appétit!

Per serving: 360 Calories; 8.4g Fat; 66.1g Carbs; 7g Protein; 57g Sugars

930. Light Carrot Souffle

(Ready in about 1 hour | Servings 6)

Ingredients

1 ½ pounds carrots, trimmed and cut into chunks
3/4 cup sugar
1 teaspoon baking powder
1 teaspoon vanilla paste
1/4 teaspoon ground cardamom
1/2 teaspoon ground cinnamon
3 tablespoons flour
3 eggs
1/3 cup cream cheese room temperature
1 stick butter, softened

Directions

Place 1 cup of water and a steamer basket in the bottom of your Instant Pot. Place the carrots in the steamer basket.

Secure the lid. Choose the "Steam" mode and cook for 10 minutes at High pressure. Once cooking is complete, use a quick pressure release; carefully remove the lid.

Process the mashed carrots, sugar, baking powder, vanilla, cardamom, cinnamon, and flour in your food processor until creamy, uniform, and smooth.

Add the eggs one at a time and mix to combine well. Stir in the cream cheese and butter; mix to combine well.

Spritz a baking pan with cooking spray; spoon the carrot mixture into the baking dish.

Add 1 cup of water and metal trivet to the bottom of the inner pot; cover with a paper towel.

Secure the lid. Choose the "Manual" mode and cook for 35 minutes at High pressure. Once cooking is complete, use a natural pressure release for 10 minutes; carefully remove the lid. Bon appétit!

Per serving: 344 Calories; 24.1g Fat; 26.1g Carbs; 6.8g Protein; 17.1g Sugars

931. Sunday Banana Bread

(Ready in about 50 minutes | Servings 8)

Ingredients

1 stick butter, melted
2 eggs
1 teaspoon vanilla extract
3/4 cup sugar
1 teaspoon baking soda
2 bananas, mashed
1 ½ cups all-purpose flour
1/2 cup coconut flaked

Directions

Mix all ingredients in a bowl until everything is well incorporated.

Add 1 cup of water and metal trivet to the bottom of the inner pot. Spritz a baking pan with nonstick cooking oil.

Scrape the batter into the prepared pan. Lower the pan onto the trivet.

Secure the lid. Choose the "Manual" mode and cook for 45 minutes at High pressure. Once cooking is complete, use a quick pressure release; carefully remove the lid.

Allow the banana bread to cool slightly before slicing and serving. Enjoy!

Per serving: 320 Calories; 17.1g Fat; 37.1g Carbs; 5.4g Protein; 13.1g Sugars

932. Easy Cheesecake with Almonds

(Ready in about 45 minutes | Servings 8)

Ingredients

1 cup cookies, crushed
3 tablespoons coconut oil, melted
18 ounces cream cheese
1 cup granulated sugar
2 eggs
1/3 cup sour cream
1/4 teaspoon grated nutmeg
1/2 teaspoon pure vanilla extract
1/2 cup almonds, slivered

Directions

Place a metal trivet and 1 cup of water in your Instant Pot. Spritz a baking pan with nonstick cooking spray.

Next, mix the cookies and coconut oil into a sticky crust. Press the crust into the prepared baking pan.

Thoroughly combine the cream cheese, sugar, eggs, sour cream, nutmeg, and vanilla extract in a mixing bowl. Pour this mixture over the crust and cover it with a piece of foil.

Lower the baking pan onto the trivet.

Secure the lid. Choose the "Manual" mode and cook for 25 minutes at High pressure. Once cooking is complete, use a natural pressure release for 15 minutes; carefully remove the lid.

Top with slivered almonds and serve well chilled. Bon appétit!

Per serving: 388 Calories; 28.8g Fat; 25.9g Carbs; 8.4g Protein; 19.9g Sugars

933. Fresh Blueberry Butter

(Ready in about 25 minutes | Servings 10)

Ingredients

2 pounds fresh blueberries
1 pound granulated sugar
1/2 teaspoon vanilla extract
1 tablespoon freshly grated lemon zest
1/4 cup fresh lemon juice

Directions

Place the blueberries, sugar, and vanilla in the inner pot of your Instant Pot.

Secure the lid. Choose the "Manual" mode and cook for 2 minutes at High pressure. Once cooking is complete, use a natural pressure release for 15 minutes; carefully remove the lid.

Stir in the lemon zest and juice. Puree in a food processor; then, strain and push the mixture through a sieve before storing. Enjoy!

Per serving: 230 Calories; 0.3g Fat; 59g Carbs; 0.7g Protein; 53.6g Sugars

934. Valentine's Day Pots de Crème

(Ready in about 25 minutes | Servings 6)

Ingredients

2 cups double cream
1/2 cup whole milk
4 egg yolks
1/3 cup sugar
1 teaspoon instant coffee
A pinch of pink salt
9 ounces chocolate chips

Directions

Place a metal trivet and 1 cup of water in your Instant Pot.

In a saucepan, bring the cream and milk to a simmer.

Then, thoroughly combine the egg yolks, sugar, instant coffee, and salt. Slowly and gradually whisk in the hot cream mixture.

Whisk in the chocolate chips and blend again. Pour the mixture into mason jars. Lower the jars onto the trivet.

Secure the lid. Choose the "Manual" mode and cook for 6 minutes at High pressure. Once cooking is complete, use a natural pressure release for 10 minutes; carefully remove the lid.

Serve well chilled and enjoy!

Per serving: 351 Calories; 19.3g Fat; 39.3g Carbs; 5.5g Protein; 32.1g Sugars

935. Lemon Butter Cake

(Ready in about 35 minutes | Servings 6)

Ingredients

1 cup butter cookies, crumbled
3 tablespoons butter, melted
1 egg
2 egg yolks
1/2 cup lemon juice
1 (14-ounce) can sweetened condensed milk
3 tablespoons honey
1/2 cup heavy cream
1/4 cup sugar

Directions

Place a metal trivet and 1 cup of water in your Instant Pot. Spritz a baking pan with nonstick cooking spray.

Next, mix the cookies and butter until well combined. Press the crust into the prepared baking pan.

Then, thoroughly combine the eggs, lemon juice, condensed milk, and honey with a hand mixer.

Pour this mixture on top of the prepared crust. Lower the baking pan onto the trivet and cover with a piece of foil.

Secure the lid. Choose the "Manual" mode and cook for 15 minutes at High pressure. Once cooking is complete, use a natural pressure release for 15 minutes; carefully remove the lid.

Afterwards, whip the heavy cream with sugar until the cream becomes stiff. Frost your cake and serve well chilled. Bon appétit!

Per serving: 369 Calories; 21.1g Fat; 40g Carbs; 7.3g Protein; 28.9g Sugars

936. Spring Berry Compote

(Ready in about 30 minutes | Servings 4)

Ingredients

1 pound blueberries
1/2 pound blackberries
1/2 pound strawberries
1/2 cup brown sugar
1 tablespoon orange juice
1/4 teaspoon ground cloves
1 vanilla bean

Directions

Place your berries in the inner pot. Add the sugar and let sit for 15 minutes. Add in the orange juice, ground cloves, and vanilla bean.

Secure the lid. Choose the "Manual" mode and cook for 2 minutes at High pressure. Once cooking is complete, use a natural pressure release for 10 minutes; carefully remove the lid.

As your compote cools, it will thicken. Bon appétit!

Per serving: 224 Calories; 0.8g Fat; 56.3g Carbs; 2.1g Protein; 46.5g Sugars

937. Home-Style Mexican Horchata

(Ready in about 20 minutes | Servings 8)

Ingredients

20 ounces rice milk, unsweetened
8 ounces almond milk, unsweetened
5 tablespoons agave syrup
1 cinnamon stick
1 vanilla bean

Directions

Combine all ingredients in the inner pot of your Instant Pot.

Secure the lid. Choose the "Manual" mode and cook for 5 minutes at High pressure. Once cooking is complete, use a natural pressure release for 10 minutes; carefully remove the lid.

Serve garnished with a few sprinkles of ground cinnamon if desired. Enjoy!

Per serving: 107 Calories; 2.4g Fat; 17.5g Carbs; 4.6g Protein; 17.7g Sugars

938. Authentic Agua de Jamaica

(Ready in about 20 minutes | Servings 4)

Ingredients

4 cups water
1/2 cup dried hibiscus flowers
1/2 cup brown sugar
1/2 teaspoon fresh ginger, peeled and minced
2 tablespoons lime juice

Directions

Combine all ingredients, except for the lime juice, in the inner pot of your Instant Pot.

Secure the lid. Choose the "Manual" mode and cook for 5 minutes at High pressure. Once cooking is complete, use a natural pressure release for 10 minutes; carefully remove the lid.

Stir in the lime juice and serve well chilled.

Per serving: 118 Calories; 0.2g Fat; 29.8g Carbs; 0.2g Protein; 28.5g Sugars

939. Molten Chocolate Cakes

(Ready in about 30 minutes | Servings 4)

Ingredients

1/2 stick butter
1 cup sugar
2 eggs
3 tablespoons coconut milk
1 teaspoon vanilla

1 ½ cups self-rising flour
2 tablespoons cocoa powder
1 tablespoon carob powder
4 ounces bittersweet chocolate
4 ounces semisweet chocolate

Directions

Place a metal trivet and 1 cup of water in your Instant Pot. Butter custard cups and set aside.

Then, beat the butter and sugar until creamy. Fold in the eggs, one at a time, and mix until everything is well combined.

Add the milk and vanilla and mix again. Then, stir in the flour, cocoa powder, and carob powder. Fold in the chocolate and stir to combine. Divide the mixture between the prepared custard cups.

Lower the cups onto the trivet.

Secure the lid. Choose the "Steam" mode and cook for 15 minutes at High pressure. Once cooking is complete, use a natural pressure release for 10 minutes; carefully remove the lid. Enjoy!

Per serving: 671 Calories; 27.4g Fat; 95g Carbs; 10.6g Protein; 53.5g Sugars

940. Spanish Arroz Con Leche

(Ready in about 25 minutes | Servings 4)

Ingredients

1 cup white pearl rice
1 cup water
A pinch of salt
2 ¼ cups milk
1/2 cup sugar

1/4 teaspoon grated nutmeg
1 teaspoon vanilla extract
1 teaspoon cinnamon
Peel of 1/2 lemon

Directions

Place the rice, water, and salt in the inner pot of your Instant Pot.

Secure the lid. Choose the "Rice" mode and cook for 10 minutes at Low pressure. Once cooking is complete, use a natural pressure release for 10 minutes; carefully remove the lid.

Add in the milk, sugar, nutmeg, vanilla, cinnamon, and lemon peel; stir to combine well.

Press the "Sauté" button and cook, stirring continuously, until your pudding starts to boil. Press the "Cancel" button. Enjoy!

Per serving: 370 Calories; 4.4g Fat; 72.4g Carbs; 7.6g Protein; 32.2g Sugars

941. Granny's Monkey Bread with Walnuts

(Ready in about 40 minutes | Servings 6)

Ingredients

12 frozen egg dinner rolls, thawed
1/4 cup brown sugar
1 teaspoon ground cinnamon
1/4 cup walnuts, ground

1/4 cup coconut oil, melted
1/3 cup powdered sugar
1 tablespoon coconut milk

Directions

Place 1 cup of water and a metal trivet in the inner pot of your Instant Pot. Spray a Bundt pan with cooking spray and set aside.

Cut each dinner roll in half.

In a mixing bowl, thoroughly combine the brown sugar, cinnamon, and walnuts. In another bowl, place the melted coconut oil. Dip the rolls halves in the coconut oil and roll them in the brown sugar mixture.

Arrange the rolls in the prepared Bundt pan. Cover the pan with a piece of aluminum foil; allow it to rise overnight at room temperature.

On the next day, lower the pan onto the trivet.

Secure the lid. Choose the "Manual" mode and cook for 25 minutes at High pressure. Once cooking is complete, use a natural pressure release for 10 minutes; carefully remove the lid.

After that, invert the bread onto a serving plate.

In a mixing bowl, whisk the powdered sugar and coconut milk until smooth. Drizzle the glaze over the top and sides of your cake. Bon appétit!

Per serving: 355 Calories; 15.8g Fat; 46.9g Carbs; 7.2g Protein; 12.7g Sugars

942. Cinnamon Pull-Apart Coffee Cake

(Ready in about 40 minutes | Servings 10)

Ingredients

2 (16.3-ounce) cans refrigerated biscuits
3/4 cup granulated sugar
1 tablespoon ground cinnamon

1/4 teaspoon nutmeg, preferably freshly grated
1/2 cup raisins, if desired
3/4 cup butter, melted
1/2 cup firmly packed brown sugar

Directions

Place 1 cup of water and a metal trivet in the inner pot of your Instant Pot. Lightly grease 12-cup fluted tube pan with cooking spray.

In a food bag, mix the granulated sugar, cinnamon, and nutmeg.

Separate the dough into biscuits and cut each into quarters. Place them in the food bag and shake to coat on all sides. Place them in the prepared pan, adding raisins among the biscuit pieces.

In a small mixing bowl, whisk the melted butter with brown sugar; pour the butter mixture over the biscuit pieces.

Secure the lid. Choose the "Manual" mode and cook for 25 minutes at High pressure. Bake until no longer doughy in the center.

Once cooking is complete, use a natural pressure release for 10 minutes; carefully remove the lid.

Turn upside down onto serving plate and serve warm. Bon appétit!

Per serving: 512 Calories; 24.1g Fat; 69.4g Carbs; 5.9g Protein; 21.3g Sugars

943. Autumn Compote with Honeyed Greek Yogurt

(Ready in about 20 minutes | Servings 4)

Ingredients

1 cup rhubarb
1 cup plums
1 cup apples
1 cup pears
1 teaspoon ground ginger

1 vanilla bean
1 cinnamon stick
1/2 cup caster sugar
1 cup Greek yoghurt
4 tablespoons honey

Directions

Place the fruits, ginger, vanilla, cinnamon, and caster sugar in the inner pot of your Instant Pot.

Secure the lid. Choose the "Manual" mode and cook for 2 minutes at High pressure. Once cooking is complete, use a natural pressure release for 10 minutes; carefully remove the lid.

Meanwhile, whisk the yogurt with honey.

Serve your compote in individual bowls with a dollop of honeyed Greek yogurt. Enjoy!

Per serving: 304 Calories; 0.3g Fat; 75.4g Carbs; 5.1g Protein; 69.2g Sugars

944. Polynesian Hazelnut Pinch Me Cake

(Ready in about 35 minutes | Servings 8)

Ingredients

1 cup granulated sugar
4 tablespoons hazelnuts, ground
10 refrigerated biscuits
1 stick butter, melted

4 ounces cream cheese, at room temperature
1/4 cup powdered sugar
2 tablespoons apple juice
1 teaspoon vanilla extract

Directions

Place 1 cup of water and a metal trivet in the inner pot of your Instant Pot. Lightly grease 10-inch fluted tube pan with cooking spray.

In a shallow bowl, mix the 1 cup of granulated sugar and ground hazelnuts.

Cut each biscuit in half. Dip your biscuits into the melted butter; then, roll them in the hazelnut/sugar mixture.

Arrange them in the fluted tube pan.

Secure the lid. Choose the "Manual" mode and cook for 25 minutes at High pressure. Once cooking is complete, use a natural pressure release for 5 minutes; carefully remove the lid.

In the meantime, whip the cream cheese with the powdered sugar, apple juice, and vanilla extract. Drizzle over the hot cake and serve.

Per serving: 444 Calories; 28.9g Fat; 42.4g Carbs; 5.9g Protein; 18.3g Sugars

945. Chocolate Pudding Cake with Apricots

(Ready in about 55 minutes | Servings 10)

Ingredients

4 ounces instant pudding mix
3 cups milk
1 package vanilla cake mix
1/2 cup peanut butter
1 ½ cups chocolate chips
1/2 cup dried apricots, chopped

Directions

In a mixing bowl, thoroughly combine the pudding mix and milk. Por the mixture into a lightly greased inner pot.

Prepare the cake mix according to the manufacturer's instructions, gradually adding in the peanut butter. Pour the batter over the pudding.

Secure the lid. Choose the "Manual" mode and cook for 30 minutes at High pressure. Once cooking is complete, use a natural pressure release for 10 minutes; carefully remove the lid.

Sprinkle the chocolate chips and dried apricots on top. Seal the lid and let it stand for 10 to 15 minutes until the chocolate melts. Enjoy!

Per serving: 408 Calories; 13.9g Fat; 64.2g Carbs; 8.2g Protein; 39.7g Sugars

946. Decadent Caramel Croissant Pudding

(Ready in about 40 minutes | Servings 6)

Ingredients

6 stale croissants, cut into chunks
1 cup granulated sugar
4 tablespoons water
1 cup milk
1 cup heavy cream
3 tablespoons rum
1/4 teaspoon ground cinnamon
3 eggs, whisked

Directions

Place 1 cup of water and a metal trivet in the inner pot of your Instant Pot. Place the croissants in the lightly greased casserole dish.

Press the "Sauté" button and use the lowest setting. Then, place the granulated sugar and water and let it cook until the mixture turns a deep amber color.

Now, add the milk and heavy cream, and cook until heated through. Stir in the rum, cinnamon, and eggs; stir to combine.

Secure the lid. Choose the "Manual" mode and cook for 25 minutes at High pressure. Once cooking is complete, use a natural pressure release for 10 minutes; carefully remove the lid. Bon appétit!

Per serving: 414 Calories; 22.3g Fat; 39.4g Carbs; 10.2g Protein; 24.1g Sugars

947. Chai Spiced White Hot Chocolate

(Ready in about 10 minutes | Servings 5)

Ingredients

4 cups whole milk
1/3 cup almond butter
4 tablespoons honey
2 tablespoons Masala Chai Syrup
1 teaspoon vanilla extract
A pinch of sea salt
A pinch of grated nutmeg
2 tablespoons gelatin

Directions

Add the milk, almond butter, honey, Masala Chai Syrup, vanilla extract, sea salt, and grated nutmeg to the inner to of your Instant Pot.

Secure the lid. Choose the "Manual" mode and cook for 6 minutes at Low pressure. Once cooking is complete, use a quick pressure release; carefully remove the lid.

Add the gelatin and mix with an immersion blender until your hot chocolate is frothy and smooth. Enjoy!

Per serving: 278 Calories; 15.5g Fat; 27.3g Carbs; 9.7g Protein; 25.7g Sugars

948. Greek Stewed Dried Fruits (Hosafi)

(Ready in about 20 minutes | Servings 8)

Ingredients

1/2 cup dried figs
1 cup dried apricots
1/2 cup sultana raisins
1 cup prunes, pitted
1 cup almonds
1 cup sugar
1 cinnamon stick
1 vanilla bean
1/2 teaspoon whole cloves
1/2 teaspoon whole star anise
2 cups water
2 tablespoons Greek honey

Directions

Place all ingredients in the inner pot of your Instant Pot.

Secure the lid. Choose the "Manual" mode and cook for 2 minutes at High pressure. Once cooking is complete, use a natural pressure release for 10 minutes; carefully remove the lid.

Serve with Greek yogurt or ice cream, if desired.

Per serving: 215 Calories; 0.4g Fat; 55.4g Carbs; 1.8g Protein; 35.8g Sugars

949. Hot Spiced Apple Cider

(Ready in about 55 minutes | Servings 6)

Ingredients

6 apples, cored and diced
3/4 cup brown sugar
2 cinnamon sticks
1 vanilla bean
1 teaspoon whole cloves
1 small naval orange
4 tablespoons rum
4 cups water

Directions

Place the ingredients in the inner pot of your Instant Pot.

Secure the lid. Choose the "Manual" mode and cook for 50 minutes at High pressure. Once cooking is complete, use a quick pressure release; carefully remove the lid.

Mash the apples with a fork or a potato masher. Pour the mixture over a mesh strainer and serve hot. Bon appétit!

Per serving: 173 Calories; 0.4g Fat; 39.5g Carbs; 0.6g Protein; 32.6g Sugars

950. Hungarian Aranygaluska Cake

(Ready in about 35 minutes | Servings 8)

Ingredients

1 cup granulated sugar
4 ounces walnuts, ground
1 tablespoon grated lemon peel
4 tablespoons butter, at room temperature
1 tablespoon fresh lemon juice
16 ounces refrigerated buttermilk biscuits
2 tablespoons cream cheese, at room temperature
1/2 cup powdered sugar
1 teaspoon vanilla extract

Directions

Place 1 cup of water and a metal trivet in the inner pot of your Instant Pot. Lightly grease a loaf pan with shortening of choice.

In a shallow bowl mix the granulated sugar, walnuts, and lemon peel. Mix the melted butter and lemon juice in another shallow bowl.

Cut each biscuit in half. Dip your biscuits into the butter mixture; then, roll them in the walnut/sugar mixture.

Arrange them in the loaf pan.

Secure the lid. Choose the "Manual" mode and cook for 25 minutes at High pressure. Once cooking is complete, use a natural pressure release for 5 minutes; carefully remove the lid.

In the meantime, whip the cream cheese with the powdered sugar, and vanilla extract. Drizzle over the hot cake and serve.

Per serving: 485 Calories; 23.4g Fat; 64.9g Carbs; 6.8g Protein; 36.9g Sugars

951. Perfect Holiday Cupcakes

(Ready in about 40 minutes | Servings 4)

Ingredients

1 cup cake flour
1 ½ teaspoons baking powder
A pinch of salt
1/4 teaspoon ground cardamom
1/4 teaspoon ground cinnamon
1 teaspoon vanilla extract
1 egg
1/2 cup honey
1/4 almond milk
4 ounces cream cheese
1/3 cup powdered sugar
1 cup heavy cream, cold

Directions

In a mixing bowl, thoroughly combine the flour, baking powder, salt, cardamom, cinnamon, and vanilla.

Then, gradually add in the egg, honey, and milk. Mix to combine well. Now, spoon the batter into silicone cupcake liners and cover them with foil.

Place 1 cup of water and a metal trivet in your Instant Pot. Lower your cupcakes onto the trivet.

Secure the lid. Choose the "Manual" mode and cook for 25 minutes at High pressure. Once cooking is complete, use a natural pressure release for 10 minutes; carefully remove the lid.

While the cupcakes are cooking, prepare the frosting by mixing the remaining ingredients. Frost your cupcakes and enjoy!

Per serving: 497 Calories; 17.8g Fat; 77g Carbs; 9.8g Protein; 48.5g Sugars

952. Giant German Pancake

(Ready in about 40 minutes | Servings 4)

Ingredients

4 tablespoons butter, melted
5 eggs
1 ¼ cups milk
1 cup all-purpose flour
1/4 teaspoon kosher salt
1/2 teaspoon cinnamon powder
1/2 teaspoon vanilla extract
1 cup canned blueberries with syrup

Directions

Place 1 cup of water and a metal trivet in your Instant Pot. Line the bottom of a springform pan with parchment paper; grease the bottom and sides of the pan with melted butter.

Mix the eggs, milk, flour, salt, cinnamon, and vanilla until everything is well combined. Now, spoon the batter into the prepared pan. Lower the pan onto the trivet.

Secure the lid. Choose the "Manual" mode and cook for 30 minutes at High pressure. Once cooking is complete, use a quick pressure release; carefully remove the lid.

Serve garnished with fresh blueberries and enjoy!

Per serving: 399 Calories; 19.8g Fat; 42.3g Carbs; 13.1g Protein; 17.5g Sugars

953. Hot Mulled Apple Cider

(Ready in about 1 hour 35 minutes | Servings 8)

Ingredients

8 cups apple cider
1 (1-inch piece) fresh ginger, peeled and sliced
2 cinnamon sticks
2 vanilla beans
1 teaspoon whole cloves
1 teaspoon allspice berries
1 orange, sliced into thin rounds
1/2 cups brandy

Directions

Place all ingredients, except for the brandy, in the inner pot of your Instant Pot.

Secure the lid. Choose the "Slow Cook" mode and cook for 1 hour 30 minutes at the lowest temperature.

Strain the cider mixture and stir in the brandy. Serve immediately.

Per serving: 124 Calories; 0.8g Fat; 28.7g Carbs; 0.3g Protein; 24.1g Sugars

954. Vegan Butternut Squash Pudding

(Ready in about 20 minutes | Servings 6)

Ingredients

2 pounds butternut squash, peeled, seeded, and diced
1 cup coconut cream
1/2 cup maple syrup
A pinch of kosher salt
1 teaspoon pumpkin pie spice mix
6 tablespoons almond milk

Directions

Add 1 cup of water and a metal rack to the bottom of the inner pot. Place your squash in a steamer basket; lower the basket onto the rack.

Secure the lid. Choose the "Steam" mode and cook for 10 minutes at High pressure. Once cooking is complete, use a quick pressure release; carefully remove the lid.

Stir the remaining ingredients into the cooked squash; combine all ingredients with a potato masher.

Let it cook on the "Sauté" function until everything is thoroughly heated or about 4 minutes. Serve immediately.

Per serving: 315 Calories; 8.8g Fat; 60.5g Carbs; 2.3g Protein; 42.1g Sugars

955. Dutch Cinnamon Pear Pie

(Ready in about 35 minutes | Servings 8)

Ingredients

2 cans (12-ounce) refrigerated cinnamon rolls
1/4 cup all-purpose flour
1/4 cup packed brown sugar
1/2 teaspoon cinnamon
2 tablespoons butter
1/3 cup pecans, chopped
5 pears, cored and sliced

Directions

Separate the dough into 8 rolls. Press and flatten the rolls into a lightly greased pie plate. Make sure there are no holes between the flattened rolls.

In a mixing bowl, mix the flour, brown sugar, cinnamon, butter, and pecans. Place the slices of pears on the prepared cinnamon roll crust. Spoon the streusel onto the pear slices.

Add 1 cup of water and a metal rack to the bottom of the inner pot. Lower the pie plate onto the rack.

Secure the lid. Choose the "Manual" mode and cook for 25 minutes at High pressure. Once cooking is complete, use a natural pressure release for 5 minutes; carefully remove the lid. Bon appétit!

Per serving: 497 Calories; 28.6g Fat; 56.5g Carbs; 4.9g Protein; 30.4g Sugars

956. Old-Fashioned Stuffed Apples

(Ready in about 25 minutes | Servings 4)

Ingredients

4 baking apples
1/3 cup granulated sugar
1/2 teaspoon cardamom
1/2 teaspoon cinnamon
1/3 cup walnuts, chopped
4 tablespoons currants
2 tablespoons coconut oil

Directions

Add 1 ½ cups of water and a metal rack to the bottom of the inner pot.

Core the apples and use a melon baller to scoop out a bit of the flesh. Mix the remaining ingredients. Divide the filling between your apples.

Secure the lid. Choose the "Steam" mode and cook for 15 minutes at High pressure. Once cooking is complete, use a quick pressure release; carefully remove the lid.

Serve with ice cream, if desired. Bon appétit!

Per serving: 266 Calories; 11.5g Fat; 43.9g Carbs; 1.6g Protein; 36g Sugars

957. Chocolate Mini Crepes

(Ready in about 40 minutes | Servings 6)

Ingredients

1/2 cup all-purpose flour
1/2 cup rice flour
1 ½ teaspoons baking powder
1 teaspoon vanilla paste
1/4 teaspoon ground cinnamon
A pinch of salt
2 tablespoons granulated sugar
2 eggs, whisked
1 cup milk
1/4 cup coconut oil
1 cup chocolate syrup

Directions

Add 1 cup of water and a metal rack to the bottom of the inner pot. Lightly grease a mini muffin tin with shortening of choice.

Mix the flour, baking powder, vanilla, cinnamon, salt, sugar, eggs, milk, and coconut oil until thoroughly combined and smooth.

Pour the batter into the muffin tin and lower it onto the rack.

Secure the lid. Choose the "Manual" mode and cook for 25 minutes at High pressure. Once cooking is complete, use a natural pressure release for 10 minutes; carefully remove the lid.

Serve with chocolate syrup and enjoy!

Per serving: 364 Calories; 12.5g Fat; 56.5g Carbs; 6.1g Protein; 29.6g Sugars

958. Puerto Rican Pudding (Budin)

(Ready in about 1 hour | Servings 8)

Ingredients

1 pound Puerto Rican sweet bread, torn into pieces
1 cup water
1 teaspoon cinnamon powder
1/2 teaspoon ground cloves
1 teaspoon vanilla essence
1 cup brown sugar
4 cups coconut milk
2 tablespoons rum
4 eggs, beaten
A pinch of salt
1/2 stick butter, melted

Directions

Place 1 cup of water and a metal trivet in the inner pot of your Instant Pot. Place the pieces of sweet bread in a lightly greased casserole dish.

Now, mix the remaining ingredients; stir to combine well and pour the mixture over the pieces of sweet bread. Let it stand for 20 minutes, pressing down with a wide spatula until the bread is covered.

Secure the lid. Choose the "Manual" mode and cook for 25 minutes at High pressure. Once cooking is complete, use a natural pressure release for 10 minutes; carefully remove the lid. Bon appétit!

Per serving: 377 Calories; 18.4g Fat; 41.7g Carbs; 10.1g Protein; 24.5g Sugars

959. Orange Cranberry Spritzer

(Ready in about 25 minutes | Servings 8)

Ingredients

12 ounces fresh cranberries
1/2 cup granulated sugar
2 cups pulp-free orange juice
1 cup water

Directions

Place all ingredients in the inner pot.

Secure the lid. Choose the "Manual" mode and cook for 5 minutes at High pressure. Once cooking is complete, use a natural pressure release for 15 minutes; carefully remove the lid.

Divide between eight glasses and fill with club soda. Enjoy!

Per serving: 103 Calories; 0g Fat; 25.6g Carbs; 0.8g Protein; 24.7g Sugars

960. Famous New York-Style Cheesecake

(Ready in about 45 minutes | Servings 10)

Ingredients

4 tablespoons granulated sugar
4 tablespoons butter
10 large graham crackers, crumbled
3 tablespoons almonds, ground
1/3 teaspoon cinnamon
12 ounces Philadelphia cheese
1 teaspoon vanilla extract
1 tablespoon lemon zest
1 tablespoon arrowroot powder
1/2 cup golden caster sugar
3 eggs
1 cup creme fraiche
2 tablespoons golden caster sugar

Directions

Place a metal trivet and 1 cup of water in your Instant Pot. Spritz a baking pan with nonstick cooking spray.

Next, mix 4 tablespoons of granulated sugar, butter, crackers, almonds, and cinnamon into a sticky crust. Press the crust into the prepared baking pan.

In a mixing bowl, combine the Philadelphia cheese, vanilla extract, lemon zest, arrowroot powder, 1/2 cup of golden caster sugar, and eggs. Pour the filling mixture over the crust and cover it with a piece of foil.

Lower the baking pan onto the trivet.

Secure the lid. Choose the "Manual" mode and cook for 25 minutes at High pressure. Once cooking is complete, use a natural pressure release for 15 minutes; carefully remove the lid.

Lastly, beat the creme fraiche with 2 tablespoons of golden caster sugar. Spread this topping over the cheesecake right to the edges. Cover loosely with foil and refrigerate overnight. Bon appétit!

Per serving: 340 Calories; 20.1g Fat; 29.7g Carbs; 10.7g Protein; 18.1g Sugars

961. Classic Chewy Brownies

(Ready in about 40 minutes | Servings 12)

Ingredients

1/2 cup walnut butter
1/2 cup sunflower seed butter
1 cup coconut sugar
1/2 cup cocoa powder
2 eggs
A pinch of grated nutmeg
A pinch of salt
1/2 cardamom powder
1/2 teaspoon cinnamon powder
1/2 teaspoon baking soda
1 teaspoon vanilla extract
1/2 cup dark chocolate, cut into chunks

Directions

Place a metal trivet and 1 cup of water in your Instant Pot. Spritz a baking pan with nonstick cooking spray.

In a mixing bowl, combine all ingredients, except for the chocolate; stir well to create a thick batter.

Spoon the batter into the prepared pan. Sprinkle the chocolate chunks over the top; gently press the chocolate chunks into the batter.

Lower the baking pan onto the trivet.

Secure the lid. Choose the "Manual" mode and cook for 20 minutes at High pressure. Once cooking is complete, use a natural pressure release for 10 minutes; carefully remove the lid.

Place your brownies on a cooling rack before slicing and serving. Bon appétit!

Per serving: 264 Calories; 18.1g Fat; 24.2g Carbs; 4.5g Protein; 19.3g Sugars

962. Old-Fashioned Chocolate Fudge

(Ready in about 15 minutes + chilling time | Servings 12)

Ingredients

16 ounce canned condensed milk
2 tablespoons peanut butter
1/2 teaspoon ground cardamom
1/2 teaspoon ground cinnamon
1 teaspoon vanilla extract
8 ounces bittersweet chocolate chips
8 ounces semisweet chocolate chips

Directions

Line the bottom of a baking sheet with a piece of foil.

Add the milk, peanut butter, cardamom, cinnamon, and vanilla to the inner pot of your Instant Pot; stir until everything is well incorporated.

Next, press the "Sauté" button and use the lowest setting to cook the mixture until thoroughly warmed. Now, fold in the chocolate chips and stir again to combine well.

Lastly, pour the mixture into the prepared baking sheet and transfer to your refrigerator; let it sit until solid.

Cut into squares and serve. Bon appétit!

Per serving: 223 Calories; 11g Fat; 27.7g Carbs; 3.2g Protein; 18.3g Sugars

963. Blood Orange Upside-Down Cake

(Ready in about 45 minutes | Servings 8)

Ingredients

Nonstick cooking spray
3 teaspoons granulated sugar
3 blood oranges, peeled and cut into slices
1 egg plus 1 egg yolk, beaten
1 cup sugar
1 stick butter, at room temperature
1/3 cup plain 2% yogurt
1/2 teaspoon ground cloves
1/4 teaspoon ground cardamom
1/4 teaspoon ginger flavoring
2 tablespoons fresh orange juice
1 1/3 cups cake flour
1 ½ teaspoons baking powder
A pinch of table salt

Directions

Spritz a baking pan with a nonstick cooking spray. Now, arrange the orange slices in the bottom your pan.

In a mixing bowl, whisk the eggs until they are frothy. Now, add the sugar and mix well. Stir in the butter and mix again.

After that, add the yogurt, cloves, cardamom, ginger flavoring, and fresh orange juice. In another mixing bowl, thoroughly combine the flour with the baking powder and salt.

Slowly and gradually, stir the flour mixture into the wet egg mixture; pour the batter on top of the orange slices.

Add 1 cup of water and a metal trivet to the bottom of your Instant Pot. Lower the baking pan onto the trivet.

Secure the lid. Choose the "Soup" mode and cook for 40 minutes at High pressure. Once cooking is complete, use a quick release; remove the lid carefully.

Place a platter on the cake and invert the baking pan, lifting it to reveal the oranges on top. Bon appétit!

Per serving: 354 Calories; 13.1g Fat; 55.4g Carbs; 4.3g Protein; 37.1g Sugars

964. Decadent Bourbon Bread Pudding

(Ready in about 2 hours 45 minutes | Servings 8)

Ingredients

1 loaf Brioche bread, cubed
2 ½ cups milk
4 eggs, beaten
1 teaspoon vanilla extract
1/2 teaspoon coconut extract
1/4 cup coconut oil, melted
4 tablespoons agave syrup
1/4 cup bourbon whiskey

Directions

Place the bread in a baking dish that is previously greased with a nonstick cooking spray.

Then, in another bowl, thoroughly combine the milk, eggs, vanilla, coconut extract, coconut oil, agave syrup, and bourbon whiskey.

Pour the milk/bourbon mixture over the bread; press with a wide spatula to soak and place in the refrigerator for 1 to 2 hours.

Add 1 ½ cups of water and a metal trivet to your Instant Pot. Lower the baking dish onto the trivet.

Secure the lid. Choose the "Soup" mode and cook for 40 minutes at High pressure. Once cooking is complete, use a quick release; remove the lid carefully. Serve warm or at room temperature.

Per serving: 352 Calories; 13.2g Fat; 43.9g Carbs; 14.2g Protein; 10.1g Sugars

965. Country-Style Fruit Compote

(Ready in about 15 minutes | Servings 5)

Ingredients

1/2 pound peaches, pitted and halved
1/2 pound pears, cored and quartered
1 cup prunes, pitted
1/4 cup granulated sugar
1 tablespoon fresh apple juice
1 tablespoon fresh lemon juice
1/2 teaspoon apple pie spice mix
1 cinnamon stick
1 teaspoon whole cloves
1 large vanilla bean pod, split open lengthwise

Directions

Add all of the above ingredients to your Instant Pot. Secure the lid.

Choose the "Manual" mode and cook under High Pressure for 3 minutes. Once cooking is complete, use a natural release for 10 minutes; remove the lid carefully.

Serve warm or at room temperature. Enjoy!

Per serving: 164 Calories; 0.3g Fat; 42.9g Carbs; 1.4g Protein; 16.9g Sugars

966. Peanut Butter and Cheese Fudge

(Ready in about 10 minutes + chilling time | Servings 8)

Ingredients

8 ounces cream cheese, at room temperature
4 ounces coconut cream, at room temperature
1/2 cup coconut oil
1/2 cup cocoa butter
1/2 cup peanut butter
1 teaspoon pure vanilla extract
1 teaspoon pure almond extract
2/3 cup almond flour
1/2 cup agave syrup

Directions

Press the "Sauté" button to preheat your Instant Pot. Add the cheese, sour cream, coconut oil, cocoa butter, and peanut butter to your Instant Pot.

Let it simmer until it is melted and warmed through.

Add the vanilla, almond extract, almond flour, and agave syrup; continue to stir until everything is well combined.

Then, spoon the mixture into a cookie sheet lined with a piece of foil. Place in your refrigerator; refrigerate at least for 2 hours.

Cut into squares and serve.

Per serving: 415 Calories; 36.3g Fat; 21.9g Carbs; 3.4g Protein; 20.8g Sugars

967. Hazelnut Millet Pudding

(Ready in about 15 minutes | Servings 4)

Ingredients

1 ½ cups millet
1 ½ cups water
1 (14-ounce) can coconut milk
1/2 cup Medjool dates, finely chopped
1/2 teaspoon ground cardamom
1/2 teaspoon ground cinnamon

Directions

Add all of the above ingredients to your Instant Pot; stir to combine well.

Secure the lid. Choose the "Manual" mode and cook for 1 minute at High pressure. Once cooking is complete, use a natural pressure release for 10 minutes; carefully remove the lid.

Serve warm or at room temperature.

Per serving: 320 Calories; 3.3g Fat; 63.1g Carbs; 9.3g Protein; 6.7g Sugars

968. Apples with Wine-Cranberry Sauce

(Ready in about 20 minutes | Servings 4)

Ingredients

1 pound Bramley apples cored
1/3 cup cranberries, dried
1/2 cup red wine
1/2 cup orange juice
1 teaspoon grated orange peel
1/2 cup granulated sugar
1/3 teaspoon ground star anise
1/3 teaspoon cinnamon

Directions

Place the cored apples in your Instant Pot. Now, add the remaining ingredients.

Secure the lid. Choose the "Manual" mode and cook for 3 minutes under High pressure. Once cooking is complete, use a natural pressure release for 10 minutes; carefully remove the lid.

Serve with whipped cream if desired. Bon appétit!

Per serving: 184 Calories; 0.2g Fat; 47.5g Carbs; 0.6g Protein; 42.2g Sugars

969. Blackberry Pudding Cake

(Ready in about 45 minutes | Servings 8)

Ingredients

Nonstick cooking spray
3/4 cup all-purpose flour
1/2 teaspoon baking soda
1 teaspoon baking powder
A pinch of grated nutmeg
A pinch of salt
1 stick butter, cold
1/4 cup vanilla cookies, crumbled
1/3 cup brown sugar
2 eggs, whisked
1/2 cup almond milk
2 cups blackberries
4 dollops of vanilla ice cream, to serve

Directions

Spritz a baking pan with a nonstick cooking spray.

In a mixing bowl, thoroughly combine the flour, baking soda, baking powder, nutmeg, and salt.

Cut in the butter using two knives; now, add the crumbled cookies and sugar; mix until everything is combined well. Add the eggs and almond milk; fold in the blackberries.

Finally, scrape the mixture into the prepared baking pan. Cover with a sheet of foil; make sure that foil fits tightly around sides and under the bottom of your baking pan.

Add water and a metal trivet to the Instant Pot. Lower the baking pan onto the trivet and secure the lid.

Select the "Manual" mode. Bake for 30 minutes at High pressure.

Once cooking is complete, use a quick release; remove the lid carefully. Remove the baking pan from the Instant Pot using rack handles. Remove the foil and allow the cake to cool approximately 10 minutes.

Serve on individual plates, garnished with a dollop of vanilla ice cream.

Per serving: 164 Calories; 0.3g Fat; 42.9g Carbs; 1.4g Protein; 16.9g Sugars

970. Country Berry Compote

(Ready in about 10 minutes | Servings 4)

Ingredients

1 pound mixed berries, fresh
1 cup mixed berries, dried
3/4 cup sugar
1/2 cup rose wine

2 tablespoons fresh orange juice
1 teaspoon cloves
1 vanilla bean, split in half
1 cinnamon stick

Directions

Simply throw all of the above ingredients into your Instant Pot.

Secure the lid. Choose the "Manual" and cook at High pressure for 6 minutes. Once cooking is complete, use a natural release; carefully remove the lid.

Serve over vanilla ice cream if desired and enjoy!

Per serving: 236 Calories; 0.8g Fat; 61.3g Carbs; 1.1g Protein; 50.2g Sugars

971. Mini Molten Butterscotch Cakes

(Ready in about 20 minutes | Servings 6)

Ingredients

1 stick butter
6 ounces butterscotch morsels
3/4 cup powdered sugar
3 eggs, whisked

1/2 teaspoon vanilla extract
7 tablespoons all-purpose flour
A pinch of coarse salt

Directions

Add 1 ½ cups of water and a metal rack to the Instant Pot. Line a standard-size muffin tin with muffin papers.

In a microwave-safe bowl, microwave the butter and butterscotch morsels for about 40 seconds. Stir in the powdered sugar.

Add the remaining ingredients. Spoon the batter into the prepared muffin tin.

Secure the lid. Choose the "Manual" and cook at High pressure for 10 minutes. Once cooking is complete, use a quick release; carefully remove the lid.

To remove, let it cool for 5 to 6 minutes. Run a small knife around the sides of each cake and serve. Enjoy!

Per serving: 393 Calories; 21.1g Fat; 45.6g Carbs; 5.6g Protein; 35.4g Sugars

972. Mini Coconut Cream Cakes

(Ready in about 15 minutes | Servings 4)

Ingredients

12 ounces cream cheese
2 ounces sour cream
1/3 cup coconut sugar
1/2 teaspoon vanilla extract
1/2 teaspoon coconut extract

1 teaspoon orange zest
1/2 cup coconut flakes
2 eggs
4 tablespoons orange curd

Directions

Start by adding 1 ½ cups of water and a metal trivet to the bottom of the Instant Pot.

In a mixing bowl, combine the cream cheese, sour cream, coconut sugar, vanilla, coconut extract, and orange zest.

Now, add the coconut flakes and eggs; whisk until everything is well combined.

Divide the batter between four jars. Top with orange curd. Lower the jars onto the trivet. Now, cover your jars with foil.

Secure the lid. Choose the "Manual" and cook at High pressure for 9 minutes. Once cooking is complete, use a natural pressure release; carefully remove the lid.

Garnish with fruits if desired. Bon appétit!

Per serving: 425 Calories; 33.6g Fat; 20.2g Carbs; 11.4g Protein; 16.7g Sugars

973. Vanilla and Wine Poached Peaches

(Ready in about 15 minutes | Servings 4)

Ingredients

8 firm peaches, cut into halves
1/2 orange, cut into rounds
1/2 lemon, cut into rounds
1/2 cup water
1/2 cup apple juice
1 bottle white wine

1 ½ cups sugar
2 cinnamon sticks
2 whole cloves
1 large vanilla bean pod, split open lengthwise
1 tablespoon crystallized ginger

Directions

Arrange the peaches in the bottom of your Instant Pot.

Mix the remaining ingredients until they are thoroughly combined. Add this poaching liquid to the Instant Pot.

Secure the lid. Choose the "Manual" mode and cook at Low pressure for 3 minutes. Once cooking is complete, use a quick pressure release; carefully remove the lid.

Remove the peaches from the Instant pot and set them aside. Press the "Sauté" button and simmer the poaching liquid until reduced by half, about 10 minutes.

Serve the peaches in individual bowls drizzled with the sauce. Bon appétit!

Per serving: 405 Calories; 0.8g Fat; 75.1g Carbs; 3g Protein; 67.8g Sugars

974. Mom's Orange Flan

(Ready in about 25 minutes | Servings 4)

Ingredients

2/3 cup muscovado sugar
3 tablespoons water
5 eggs, whisked
15 ounces condensed milk, sweetened

10 ounces evaporated milk
1/4 cup orange juice
1/2 teaspoon pure vanilla extract

Directions

Place the sugar and water in a microwave-safe dish; microwave approximately 3 minutes.

Now, pour the caramel into four ramekins.

Then, whisk the eggs with milk, orange juice, and vanilla. Pour the egg mixture into the ramekins.

Add 1 ½ cups of water and a metal rack to the Instant Pot. Now, lower your ramekins onto the rack.

Secure the lid. Choose the "Manual" and cook at High pressure for 9 minutes. Once cooking is complete, use a natural pressure release for 10 minutes; carefully remove the lid. Refrigerate overnight and enjoy!

Per serving: 343 Calories; 17.8g Fat; 28.2g Carbs; 16.9g Protein; 27.4g Sugars

975. Bundt Cake with Sour Cream Glaze

(Ready in about 35 minutes | Servings 10)

Ingredients

Nonstick cooking spray
4 eggs, beaten
1/3 cup sugar
1 tablespoon coconut oil, softened
1/2 cup full-fat cream cheese
1 cup sour cream
1 teaspoon vanilla extract
1/2 teaspoon cardamom

3/4 cup whole wheat flour
A pinch of coarse salt
1 teaspoon baking soda
1 teaspoon baking powder
Sour Cream Glaze:
1/2 cup sour cream
1/2 cup powdered sugar
1 teaspoon vanilla extract

Directions

Prepare your Instant Pot by adding 1 cup of water and a metal rack to its bottom. Spritz a bundt pan with a nonstick cooking spray.

Then, whisk the eggs and sugar until creamy and pale. Add the coconut oil, cheese, sour cream, vanilla, and cardamom; beat until everything is well incorporated.

In another mixing bowl, thoroughly combine the flour with salt, baking soda, and baking powder. Add the flour mixture to the egg mixture. Spoon the batter into the prepared pan. Lower the pan onto the rack.

Secure the lid. Choose the "Bean/Chili" and cook at High pressure for 25 minutes. Once cooking is complete, use a natural pressure release; carefully remove the lid.

Meanwhile, make the glaze by whisking sour cream, powdered sugar, and vanilla. Brush the cake with glaze and place in your refrigerator until ready to serve.

Per serving: 200 Calories; 10.9g Fat; 18.7g Carbs; 6.9g Protein; 9.2g Sugars

976. Irish Crème Brûlée

(Ready in about 15 minutes + chilling time | Servings 4)

Ingredients

1 ½ cups double cream
4 egg yolks
1/3 cup Irish cream liqueur
1 teaspoon pure vanilla extract
8 tablespoons golden caster sugar
1/8 teaspoon kosher salt
1/8 teaspoon grated nutmeg

Directions

Start by adding 1 cup of water and a metal rack to your Instant Pot.

Then, microwave the double cream until thoroughly warmed.

In a mixing bowl, whisk the egg yolks, Irish cream liqueur, vanilla extract, 4 tablespoons caster sugar, salt, and nutmeg.

Gradually add the warm cream, stirring continuously. Spoon the mixture into four ramekins; cover with foil; lower onto the rack.

Secure the lid. Choose the "Manual" mode and cook for 6 minutes under High pressure. Once cooking is complete, use a natural pressure release; carefully remove the lid.

Place in your refrigerator for 4 to 5 hours to set. To serve, top each cup with a tablespoon of sugar; use a kitchen torch to melt the sugar and form a caramelized topping. Serve right away.

Per serving: 334 Calories; 25.7g Fat; 20.7g Carbs; 5.6g Protein; 19.9g Sugars

977. Delicious Stewed Fruit

(Ready in about 15 minutes | Servings 6)

Ingredients

1/2 pound blueberries
1/2 pound blackberries
1/2 pound mango, pitted and diced
1 cup Muscovado sugar
1 cinnamon stick
1 vanilla pod
1 teaspoon whole cloves
2 tablespoons orange juice
1 teaspoon orange zest

Directions

Add all of the above ingredients to your Instant Pot.

Secure the lid. Choose the "Manual" mode and cook for 7 minutes under High pressure. Once cooking is complete, use a natural pressure release; carefully remove the lid.

Transfer to a nice serving bowl; serve with frozen yogurt or shortcake. Bon appétit!

Per serving: 193 Calories; 0.4g Fat; 48.8g Carbs; 1.1g Protein; 44.5g Sugars

978. Pumpkin Cake with Cream Cheese Frosting

(Ready in about 25 minutes + chilling time | Servings 10)

Ingredients

Batter:
2 cups pumpkin purée
3/4 cup applesauce
1 cup granulated sugar
1 tablespoon molasses
1/2 teaspoon crystallized ginger
1/8 teaspoon salt
1/8 teaspoon grated nutmeg
1/4 teaspoon cardamom, ground
1/2 teaspoon cinnamon, ground
1 teaspoon vanilla extract
1 ½ cups all-purpose flour
1 teaspoon baking powder
Cream Cheese Frosting:
7 ounces cream cheese, at room temperature
1 stick butter, at room temperature
2 cups powdered sugar

Directions

In a mixing bowl, combine all dry ingredients for the batter. Then, in a separate mixing bowl, thoroughly combine all wet ingredients.

Then, add the wet mixture to the dry mixture; pour the batter into a cake pan that is previously greased with melted butter.

Add 1 ½ cups of water and a metal trivet to the Instant Pot. Lower the cake pan onto the trivet.

Secure the lid. Choose the "Porridge" mode and cook for 20 minutes under High pressure. Once cooking is complete, use a natural pressure release; carefully remove the lid.

Meanwhile, make the frosting. Beat the cream cheese and butter with an electric mixer on high speed. Add the powdered sugar.

Continue to beat until the frosting has thickened. Spread the frosting on the cooled cake. Refrigerate until ready to serve. Bon appétit!

Per serving: 357 Calories; 15.2g Fat; 52.6g Carbs; 4.1g Protein; 34.9g Sugars

979. Pear and Plum Crumble Delight

(Ready in about 25 minutes | Servings 6)

Ingredients

2 pears, cored, peeled and sliced
10 plums, pitted and halved
3/4 cup rolled oats
3 tablespoons flour
1/4 cup sugar
2 tablespoons maple syrup
2 tablespoons caramel syrup, plus more for topping
2 tablespoons fresh orange juice
1 teaspoon ground cinnamon
A pinch of salt
3 tablespoons coconut oil

Directions

Arrange the pears and plums on the bottom of a lightly buttered baking pan.

In a mixing bowl, thoroughly combine the rolled oats, flour, sugar, maple syrup, caramel syrup, orange juice, cinnamon, salt and coconut oil.

Top the prepared pears and plums with the oat layer. Now, distribute the oat layer evenly using a spatula.

Add 1 cup of water and a metal trivet to your Instant Pot. Lower the baking pan onto the trivet. Cover with a sheet of foil.

Secure the lid. Select the "Manual" mode and cook at High pressure for 10 minutes. Once cooking is complete, use a natural release for 10 minutes; carefully remove the lid.

Remove the foil and let your crumble cool to room temperature before serving. Bon appétit!

Per serving: 227 Calories; 8.1g Fat; 42.8g Carbs; 3.4g Protein; 28.1g Sugars

980. Banana Bread in a Jar

(Ready in about 1 hour 5 minutes| Servings 8)

Ingredients

1 stick butter, at room temperature
3/4 cup granulated sugar
3 eggs, whisked
1/2 pound overripe bananas, mashed
1/4 cup sour cream
2 ½ cups all-purpose flour
1 teaspoon baking soda
A pinch of salt
A pinch of nutmeg, preferably freshly grated
1/2 teaspoon pumpkin pie spice
1/2 cup semi-sweet chocolate chips

Directions

Start by adding 1 ½ cups of water and a metal trivet to the base of your Instant Pot.

In a mixing bowl, thoroughly combine the butter, sugar, eggs, banana, and sour cream. Then, in another mixing bowl, combine the flour, baking soda, salt, nutmeg, and pumpkin pie spice.

Then, add the butter mixture to the flour mixture; mix to combine well. Fold in the chocolate chips. Divide the batter between mason jars. Lower the jars onto the trivet.

Secure the lid. Choose the "Multigrain" mode and cook for 55 minutes under High pressure. Once cooking is complete, use a natural pressure release; carefully remove the lid.

Let it sit for 5 to 10 minutes before serving. Bon appétit!

Per serving: 453 Calories; 17.1g Fat; 69.4g Carbs; 7.9g Protein; 26.3g Sugars

981. Easy Cherry Cobbler

(Ready in about 20 minutes | Servings 6)

Ingredients

30 ounces cherry pie filling
1 box yellow cake mix
1/2 cup coconut butter, melted
1/2 teaspoon ground cinnamon
1/2 teaspoon ground cardamom
1/4 teaspoon grated nutmeg

Directions

Add 1 cup of water and metal rack to the Instant Pot. Place the cherry pie filling in a pan.

Mix the remaining ingredients; spread the batter over the cherry pie filling evenly.

Secure the lid. Choose the "Manual" mode and cook for 10 minutes under High pressure. Once cooking is complete, use a natural pressure release; carefully remove the lid.

Serve with whipped topping. Enjoy!

Per serving: 499 Calories; 16.2g Fat; 82g Carbs; 4.5g Protein; 24.3g Sugars

982. Summer Pineapple Cake

(Ready in about 30 minutes | Servings 8)

Ingredients

1 pound pineapple, sliced	1/4 teaspoon salt
1 tablespoon orange juice	1/2 cup margarine, melted
1/2 cup cassava flour	1/2 cup honey
1/2 cup almond flour	1/2 teaspoon vanilla extract
1 teaspoon baking powder	1/2 teaspoon coconut extract
1/2 teaspoon baking soda	1 tablespoon gelatin powder

Directions

Add 1 ½ cups of water and a metal rack to the Instant Pot. Cover the bottom of your cake pan with a parchment paper.

Then, spread the pineapple slices evenly in the bottom of the cake pan; drizzle with orange juice.

In a mixing bowl, thoroughly combine the flour, baking powder, baking soda, and salt.

In another bowl, combine the margarine, honey, vanilla, and coconut extract; add gelatin powder and whisk until well mixed.

Add the honey mixture to the flour mixture; mix until you've formed a ball of dough. Flatten your dough; place on the pineapple layer.

Cover the pan with foil, creating a foil sling.

Secure the lid. Choose the "Bean/Chili" mode and cook for 25 minutes under High pressure. Once cooking is complete, use a natural pressure release; carefully remove the lid.

Lastly, turn the pan upside down and unmold it on a serving platter. Enjoy!

Per serving: 258 Calories; 14.4g Fat; 33.2g Carbs; 1.8g Protein; 26.5g Sugars

983. Tropical Bread Pudding

(Ready in about 25 minutes | Servings 8)

Ingredients

Nonstick cooking spray	1 tablespoon finely grated orange zest
3 eggs, beaten	
3/4 cup almond milk	A pinch of salt
1/4 cup honey	1 loaf day-old challah bread, cubed into 1-inch pieces
1 teaspoon pure vanilla extract	
1/2 teaspoon pure coconut extract	1/2 cup sweetened shredded coconut
1/2 teaspoon ground cinnamon	
1/4 teaspoon grated nutmeg	4 tablespoons crushed pineapple, drained
1/2 teaspoon ground cardamom	

Directions

Spritz the sides and bottom of a baking pan with a nonstick cooking spray.

In a mixing bowl, whisk the eggs with the almond milk, honey, vanilla, coconut extract, cinnamon, cardamom, orange zest, and salt.

Stir in the bread pieces along with the shredded coconut and crushed pineapple; press down into pan slightly.

Cover the baking pan with a sheet of foil and make a foil sling. Add 1 cup of water and the metal trivet to the Instant Pot.

Lower the baking pan onto the trivet. Secure the lid. Choose the "Manual" mode, High pressure, and 20 minutes. Once cooking is complete, use a quick release; carefully remove the lid.

Serve at room temperature. Bon appétit!

Per serving: 333 Calories; 7.2g Fat; 53.7g Carbs; 13.4g Protein; 16.5g Sugars

984. Almond Chocolate Brownie

(Ready in about 25 minutes | Servings 8)

Ingredients

3 ounces chocolate, chopped into small chunks	2/3 cup all-purpose flour
	1 teaspoon baking powder
1/3 cup coconut oil	A pinch of salt
1/2 cup brown sugar	3 tablespoons cocoa powder
3 eggs, well beaten	1 tablespoon carob powder
1/2 teaspoon almond extract	1/2 cup almonds, chopped
1 teaspoon vanilla extract	

Directions

Microwave the chocolate and coconut oil until they melt.

In a bowl, thoroughly combine the sugar, eggs, almond, vanilla extract, and melted chocolate mixture.

Add the flour, baking powder, salt, cocoa powder, and carob powder; mix well to combine. Afterwards, fold in the almonds. Transfer the mixture to a lightly greased baking pan.

Add 1 cup of water and a metal rack to the Instant Pot. Lower the baking pan onto the rack.

Secure the lid. Choose the "Manual" mode and cook for 18 minutes under High pressure. Once cooking is complete, use a quick pressure release; carefully remove the lid. Serve well chilled and enjoy!

Per serving: 265 Calories; 16.4g Fat; 24.9g Carbs; 6.5g Protein; 12.4g Sugars

985. Lava Dulce de Leche Cake

(Ready in about 20 minutes | Servings 6)

Ingredients

A nonstick cooking spray	1/4 teaspoon star anise, ground
1 tablespoon granulated sugar	1/4 teaspoon ground cinnamon
1/4 cup butter, melted	1/3 cup powdered sugar
3 eggs, beaten	3/4 cup canned dulce de leche
1 teaspoon vanilla extract	4 tablespoons all-purpose flour
1/2 teaspoon pure almond extract	1/8 teaspoon kosher salt

Directions

Spritz a cake pan with a nonstick cooking spray. Then, sprinkle the bottom of your pan with granulated sugar.

Beat the butter with eggs, vanilla, almond extract, star anise, and ground cinnamon. Add the powdered sugar, canned dulce de leche, flour, and salt. Mix until a thick batter is achieved.

Scrape the batter into the prepared cake pan.

Place 1 cup of water and a metal trivet in the Instant Pot. Place the cake pan on the trivet.

Secure the lid. Choose the "Manual" mode and cook for 10 minutes under High pressure. Once cooking is complete, use a quick pressure release; carefully remove the lid. Serve hot with ice cream.

Per serving: 301 Calories; 15.4g Fat; 32.5g Carbs; 7.7g Protein; 26.1g Sugars

986. Crumble-Stuffed Nectarines

(Ready in about 15 minutes | Servings 4)

Ingredients

1/4 cup tapioca starch	1/8 teaspoon salt
5 tablespoons honey	2 gingersnaps, crushed
3 tablespoons coconut oil	1/2 teaspoon pure vanilla extract
1 teaspoon ground cinnamon	1/2 teaspoon pure coconut extract
1/2 teaspoon ground cardamom	4 large-sized nectarines, halved and pitted
1/8 teaspoon nutmeg, preferably freshly grated	
	1/2 cup low-fat vanilla yogurt

Directions

Start by adding 1 cup of water and a metal trivet to the bottom of your Instant Pot.

Mix the tapioca, honey, coconut oil, cinnamon, cardamom, nutmeg, salt, gingersnaps, vanilla, and coconut extract in a bowl.

Divide this mixture among nectarine halves. Place the nectarines on the metal trivet.

Secure the lid. Choose the "Manual" mode and cook for 4 minutes under High pressure. Once cooking is complete, use a natural pressure release; carefully remove the lid.

Serve topped with vanilla yogurt. Enjoy!

Per serving: 463 Calories; 12.8g Fat; 87.1g Carbs; 4.3g Protein; 40.6g Sugars

987. Lemon Curd Mousse

(Ready in about 35 minutes | Servings 4)

Ingredients

1 stick butter, softened
1 ¼ cups sugar
3 eggs
1 large egg yolks
1/2 cup fresh lemon juice
1 tablespoon lemon zest, finely grated

A pinch of salt
2 teaspoons cornstarch
1/4 cup heavy whipping cream
6 tablespoons blueberries
Mint leaves, for garnish

Directions

Beat the butter and sugar with an electric mixer. Gradually, add the eggs and yolks; mix until pale and smooth.

Add the lemon juice and lemon zest; add salt and cornstarch; mix to combine well. Pour the mixture into four jars; cover your jars with the lids.

Add 1 cup of water and a trivet to the Instant Pot. Lower the jars onto the trivet; secure the lid. Select "Manual" mode, High pressure and 15 minutes.

Once cooking is complete, use a natural release for 15 minutes; carefully remove the lid. Serve well-chilled, garnished with heavy whipping cream, blueberries, and mint leaves. Bon appétit!

Per serving: 445 Calories; 30.1g Fat; 40.6g Carbs; 5.4g Protein; 36.7g Sugars

988. Favorite Almond Cheesecake

(Ready in about 45 minutes | Servings 8)

Ingredients

24 ounces Neufchâtel cheese
1 cup sour cream
5 eggs
1/4 cup flour
1/2 teaspoon pure vanilla extract

1/2 teaspoon pure almond extract
1 ½ cups graham cracker crumbs
1/2 cup almonds, roughly chopped
1/2 stick butter, melted

Directions

In a mixing bowl, beat the Neufchâtel cheese with the sour cream. Now, fold in the eggs, one at a time.

Stir in the flour, vanilla extract, and almond extract; mix to combine well.

In a separate mixing bowl, thoroughly combine the graham cracker crumbs, almonds, and butter. Press this crust mixture into a baking pan.

Pour the egg/cheese mixture into the pan. Cover with a sheet of foil; make sure that the foil fits tightly around the sides and under the bottom of your baking pan.

Add 1 cup of water and a metal trivet to your Instant Pot. Secure the lid. Choose the "Bean/Chili" mode and bake for 40 minutes at High pressure.

Once cooking is complete, use a quick release; carefully remove the lid. Allow your cheesecake to cool completely before serving. Bon appétit!

Per serving: 445 Calories; 33.2g Fat; 15.3g Carbs; 21.2g Protein; 7.4g Sugars

989. Fancy Buckwheat Pudding with Figs

(Ready in about 15 minutes | Servings 4)

Ingredients

1 ½ cups buckwheat
3 ½ cups milk
1/2 cup dried figs, chopped
1/3 cup honey

1/2 teaspoon ground cinnamon
1 teaspoon pure vanilla extract
1/2 teaspoon pure almond extract

Directions

Add all of the above ingredients to your Instant Pot.

Secure the lid. Choose the "Multigrain" mode and cook for 10 minutes under High pressure. Once cooking is complete, use a natural pressure release; carefully remove the lid.

Serve topped with fresh fruits, nuts or whipped topping. Bon appétit!

Per serving: 320 Calories; 7.5g Fat; 57.7g Carbs; 9.5g Protein; 43.2g Sugars

990. Cardamom and Banana Tapioca Pudding

(Ready in about 20 minutes | Servings 4)

Ingredients

1 cup small pearl tapioca, soaked and well-rinsed
1 teaspoon cardamom
4 cups coconut milk

1 teaspoon vanilla extract
1/2 cup coconut sugar
2 bananas, peeled and sliced
4 peaches, diced

Directions

Start by adding 1½ cups of water and a metal trivet to the base of your Instant Pot.

Mix the tapioca, cardamom, coconut milk, vanilla, and sugar in a baking dish. Lower the dish onto the trivet.

Secure the lid. Choose the "Multigrain" mode and cook for 10 minutes under High pressure. Once cooking is complete, use a quick pressure release; carefully remove the lid.

Add the banana and peaches; gently stir to combine and serve.

Per serving: 449 Calories; 8.5g Fat; 86.1g Carbs; 9.8g Protein; 45.7g Sugars

991. Chocolate, Raisin and Coconut Cake

(Ready in about 45 minutes | Servings 8)

Ingredients

10 ounces cream cheese
7 ounces sour cheese
1 cup granulated sugar
3 eggs
2 tablespoons cornstarch
1 teaspoon vanilla extract
14 ounces chocolate cookies, crumbled

1/3 cup raisins, soaked for 15 minutes
3 teaspoons coconut oil
Topping:
4 ounces dark chocolate, melted
1 cup sweetened coconut milk
1/2 cup coconut, shredded

Directions

In a mixing bowl, thoroughly combine the cream cheese, sour cream, and sugar. Add the eggs and mix again; add the cornstarch and vanilla.

In another bowl, thoroughly combine the cookies, raisins, and coconut oil. Press the crust into the bottom of a cake pan.

Spread the cheesecake mixture over the crust.

Add 1 ½ cups of water and metal trivet to the Instant Pot. Lower the pan onto the trivet. Cover with foil, making a foil sling.

Secure the lid. Choose "Multigrain" mode and cook for 40 minutes under High pressure. Once cooking is complete, use a quick pressure release; carefully remove the lid.

Meanwhile, make the topping by vigorously whisking all ingredients. Spread the topping over the cake.

Place in your refrigerator to cool completely. Enjoy!

Per serving: 575 Calories; 35.6g Fat; 54.1g Carbs; 11.1g Protein; 33.1g Sugars

992. Apricot and Almond Cupcakes

(Ready in about 30 minutes | Servings 6)

Ingredients

Cupcakes:
1 cup apricots, pitted and chopped
3/4 cup almond flour
1 teaspoon baking powder
A pinch of coarse salt
2 eggs, beaten
1/2 teaspoon vanilla paste

1/2 cup honey
1/4 almond milk
Frosting:
1/3 cup almond butter
1 teaspoon cocoa powder
3 tablespoons honey

Directions

Thoroughly combine all ingredients for the cupcakes. Spoon the batter into cupcake liners; cover with foil.

Add 1 cup of water and a metal trivet to the bottom of your Instant Pot. Now, place the cupcake liners on the trivet.

Secure the lid. Choose the "Bean/Chili" mode and cook for 25 minutes under High pressure. Once cooking is complete, use a natural pressure release; carefully remove the lid.

Meanwhile, prepare the frosting by mixing all ingredients. Transfer to a plastic bag for piping the frosting on your cupcakes. Bon appétit!

Per serving: 311 Calories; 13.9g Fat; 46.5g Carbs; 4.3g Protein; 44.2g Sugars

993. Key Lime Mini Cakes

(Ready in about 35 minutes | Servings 6)

Ingredients

Cakes:
3 eggs, beaten
3 tablespoons butter, melted
3 tablespoons coconut milk
1 teaspoon vanilla extract
1/2 cup coconut flour
1 teaspoon baking powder

1/2 cup agave syrup
1/4 cup fresh key lime juice
Frosting:
3 ounces cream cheese
3 tablespoons butter, softened
2 tablespoons agave syrup

Directions

Spritz the bottom and sides of four ramekins with a nonstick cooking spray.

In a mixing bowl, whisk the eggs with the melted butter, coconut milk, vanilla, coconut flour, baking powder, agave syrup, and key lime juice.

Spoon the batter into greased ramekins and cover them loosely with foil.

Add 1 cup of water and a metal rack to the bottom of your Instant Pot. Now, lower the ramekins onto the rack.

Secure the lid. Choose the "Bean/Chili" mode and cook for 25 minutes under High pressure. Once cooking is complete, use a natural pressure release; carefully remove the lid.

Meanwhile, prepare the frosting by mixing the cream cheese and butter with an electric mixer. Add the agave syrup and continue mixing until everything is well incorporated.

Transfer the mixture to a plastic bag for piping the frosting on your cupcakes. Bon appétit!

Per serving: 320 Calories; 20.7g Fat; 29.6g Carbs; 5.9g Protein; 29.2g Sugars

994. Luscious Butterscotch Pudding

(Ready in about 20 minutes | Servings 4)

Ingredients

1 stick butter, melted
1/4 cup milk
2 eggs, well-beaten
1/2 teaspoon vanilla essence
1/3 cup sugar
1 cup cake flour
1/2 teaspoon baking powder

1/4 cup freshly squeezed orange juice
4 caramels
Sauce:
1 cup boiling water
2 teaspoons corn flour
1/2 cup golden syrup

Directions

Melt the butter and milk in the microwave. Whisk in the eggs, vanilla, and sugar. After that, stir in the flour, baking powder, and orange juice.

Lastly, add the caramels and stir until everything is well combined and melted.

Divide between the four jars. Add 1 ½ cups of water and a metal trivet to the bottom of the Instant Pot. Lower the jars onto the trivet.

To make the sauce, whisk the boiling water, corn flour, and golden syrup until everything is well combined. Pour the sauce into each jar.

Secure the lid. Choose the "Steam" mode and cook for 15 minutes under High pressure. Once cooking is complete, use a natural pressure release; carefully remove the lid. Enjoy!

Per serving: 565 Calories; 25.9g Fat; 79.6g Carbs; 6.4g Protein; 51.5g Sugars

995. Grandma's Walnut Cake

(Ready in about 55 minutes | Servings 6)

Ingredients

1 ¼ cups coconut flour
1/4 cup walnuts, ground
1 ½ teaspoons baking powder
1 cup sugar
1 teaspoon ground cinnamon
1/2 teaspoon grated nutmeg

1 teaspoon orange zest, finely grated
1/4 teaspoon ground star anise
2 eggs plus 1 egg yolk, whisked
1/2 stick butter, at room temperature
3/4 cup double cream

Directions

Add 1 ½ cups of water and a steamer rack to your Instant Pot. Spritz the inside of a baking pan with a nonstick cooking spray.

Thoroughly combine the dry ingredients. Then, mix the the wet ingredients. Add the wet mixture to the dry flour mixture and mix until everything is well incorporated.

Scrape the batter mixture into the prepared baking pan. Now, cover the baking pan with a piece of foil, making a foil sling.

Place the baking pan on the steamer rack and secure the lid.

Select "Manual" mode. Bake for 35 minutes at High pressure. Once cooking is complete, use a natural release for 15 minutes; carefully remove the lid.

Just before serving, dust the top of the cake with icing sugar. Lastly cut the cake into wedges and serve. Bon appétit!

Per serving: 244 Calories; 17.3g Fat; 21.3g Carbs; 2.7g Protein; 18.8g Sugars

996. Old-Fashioned Sponge Pudding

(Ready in about 25 minutes | Servings 6)

Ingredients

Nonstick cooking spray
3 tablespoons crumbled butter cookies
1 stick butter, at room temperature
1 cup sugar

1/2 teaspoon pure vanilla extract
1/2 teaspoon pure coconut extract
3 eggs, beaten
1 ¼ cups cake flour
1/4 cup coconut milk

Directions

Spritz the bottom and sides of a steam bowl with a nonstick cooking spray. Add the crumbled butter cookies to the bottom.

Then, beat the butter, sugar, vanilla, and coconut extract until very creamy; now, add the eggs, one at a time and continue to mix.

Stir in the flour and milk; mix to combine well. Scrape the batter into the prepared steam bowl.

Secure the lid. Choose the "Steam" mode and cook for 20 minutes under High pressure. Once cooking is complete, use a natural pressure release; carefully remove the lid. Bon appétit!

Per serving: 426 Calories; 26.4g Fat; 39.9g Carbs; 7.3g Protein; 17.3g Sugars

997. Rum and Raisin Custard

(Ready in about 15 minutes | Servings 4)

Ingredients

2 cups milk
3 eggs, beaten
1/2 cup superfine sugar
2 tablespoons molasses

1/2 teaspoon vanilla paste
1/4 cup dark rum
1/4 cup raisins

Directions

Add the milk to a sauté pan that is preheated over a moderate flame; bring to a boil.

Let it cool to room temperature.

In a mixing bowl, whisk the eggs, sugar, molasses, and vanilla paste until sugar dissolves.

Then, slowly and gradually pour the milk into the egg mixture, stirring continuously. Mix until smooth and uniform. Finally, add the rum and raisins.

Spoon the mixture into four ramekins. Cover with foil.

Add 1 ½ cups of water and metal trivet to your Instant Pot. Then, lower the ramekins onto the trivet.

Secure the lid. Choose the "Manual" mode and cook for 9 minutes under High pressure. Once cooking is complete, use a quick pressure release; carefully remove the lid.

The custard will still wobble slightly but will firm up as it cools. Bon appétit!

Per serving: 324 Calories; 19.1g Fat; 21.9g Carbs; 9.7g Protein; 20.4g Sugars

998. Almond and Chocolate Delight

(Ready in about 15 minutes | Servings 3)

Ingredients

3 eggs
2 tablespoons butter
3 tablespoons whole milk
3 tablespoons honey
1 teaspoon pure vanilla extract

1/4 teaspoon freshly grated nutmeg
1/4 teaspoon ground cardamom
A pinch of salt
1 cup almond flour
3 chocolate cookies, chunks

Directions

In a mixing bowl, beat the eggs with butter. Now, add the milk and continue mixing until well combined.

Add the remaining ingredients in the order listed above. Divide the batter among 3 ramekins.

Add 1 cup of water and a metal trivet to the Instant Pot. Cover the ramekins with foil and lower them onto the trivet.

Secure the lid and select "Manual" mode. Cook at High pressure for 12 minutes. Once cooking is complete, use a quick release; carefully remove the lid.

Transfer the ramekins to a wire rack and allow them to cool slightly before serving. Enjoy!

Per serving: 304 Calories; 18.9g Fat; 23.8g Carbs; 10g Protein; 21.1g Sugars

999. Rich Brownie Fudge

(Ready in about 25 minutes | Servings 6)

Ingredients

1/2 stick butter, at room temperature
1 egg, beaten
2 tablespoons Greek yogurt
1/2 cup cake flour
1/2 teaspoon baking soda
1/4 cup cocoa powder

1/8 teaspoon salt
1/8 teaspoon nutmeg, freshly grated
1/2 teaspoon ground cinnamon
1 teaspoon vanilla extract
1/4 cup honey
1/4 cup chocolate, cut into chunks

Directions

Begin by adding 1 ½ cups of water and a metal trivet to the bottom of your Instant Pot.

Thoroughly combine the butter, egg, Greek yogurt, flour, baking soda, cocoa powder, salt, nutmeg, cinnamon, vanilla, and honey.

Fold in the chocolate chunks; stir to combine well.

Scrape the batter into a cake pan and cover with a piece of foil. Place the pan on top of the trivet.

Secure the lid. Choose "Porridge" mode and cook for 20 minutes under High pressure. Once cooking is complete, use a quick pressure release; carefully remove the lid. Enjoy!

Per serving: 270 Calories; 12.5g Fat; 41.1g Carbs; 6g Protein; 14.2g Sugars

1000. Winter Date Pudding

(Ready in about 15 minutes | Servings 3)

Per serving: 270 Calories; 12.5g Fat; 41.1g Carbs; 6g Protein; 14.2g Sugars

Ingredients

2 teaspoons coconut oil, softened
1 ½ cups jasmine rice, rinsed
1 ½ cups water
10 dates, pitted, soaked and chopped

2 eggs, beaten
1 teaspoon pure vanilla extract
1/8 teaspoon pumpkin pie spice

Directions

Press the "Sauté" button to preheat your Instant Pot. Now, add the coconut oil and rice; stir until it is well coated.

Add the remaining ingredients and stir again.

Secure the lid. Choose the "Manual" mode and cook for 2 minutes under High pressure. Once cooking is complete, use a natural pressure release for 10 minutes; carefully remove the lid.

Divide between three dessert bowls and serve with double cream. Enjoy!